THE
PHOTOGRAPH
COLLECTOR'S
GUIDE

Some of the many photographic items that appeal to collectors are displayed here — daguerreotypes, stereographs, modern silver prints, books, albums, and portfolios. The photographs on the wall, clockwise from upper left, are by Jerry Uelsmann, Ansel Adams, Bill Brandt, Imogen Cunningham, Arnold Newman (photograph © by Arnold Newman), and Berenice Abbott. (Photo by Scott Hyde)

THE PHOTOGRAPH COLLECTOR'S GUIDE

Lee D. Witkin

Barbara London

Foreword by Alan Shestack

Boston
NEW YORK GRAPHIC SOCIETY

TO NANNETTE
Lee D. Witkin

TO JOHN
Barbara London

First Edition

LIBRARY OF CONGRESS CATALOGING IN PUBLICATION DATA
Witkin, Lee D
    The photograph collector's guide.

    Bibliography: p.
    Includes index.
    1. Photographs—Collectors and collecting.
I. London, Barbara, 1936-   II. Title.
TR6.5.W57   770'.75   79-17019
ISBN 0-8212-0681-8

New York Graphic Society books are published by Little, Brown and Company.

Published simultaneously in Canada by Little, Brown and Company (Canada) Limited.

PRINTED IN THE UNITED STATES OF AMERICA.

Contents

Eight color plates follow page 310

Foreword

Alan Shestack

Almost a century and a half after its invention, photography seems to have come of age. Few critics today would deny that in gifted, sensitive hands, the camera can produce compelling images of enduring aesthetic or social value. Although the heated debate over the status of photography as an art form seems to be on the wane, there are, in fact, some who harbor lingering doubts as to the aesthetic legitimacy of photography. The speed and apparent ease with which photographic images can be produced as well as the mechanical nature of the process contribute to these critics' misgivings. The notion that photography, outside its obvious commercial, journalistic, and documentary uses, is more a hobby than an art form is reinforced by the fact that so many people own cameras and that virtually millions of pictures are taken on any given day. It is also true, however, that painting and etching are practiced by amateurs — yet no one would seriously urge that these media be rejected as inartistic simply because unskilled and untutored people paint or make prints. In any medium, the work of art must speak for itself and be judged on its individual merits. Obviously not everyone who picks up an Instamatic or Polaroid camera is capable of making profound visual statements or even well-composed pictures of the family on a picnic. Even the best photographers do not produce masterpieces every time they click the shutter; they edit their own work mercilessly, discarding the unsuccessful negatives or selecting particularly effective details for enlargement. This process of selection gives shape and meaning to the photographer's work every bit as much as does the initial camera work. In other words, for the photographer, editing is an expression of aesthetic judgment.

Everyone would agree that an immense number of undistinguished snapshots is made every day. But the widespread interest in photography responsible for this output also means that there is an enormous audience for serious photography. People who have tried their hand at picture-making can understand the visual and technical problems that confront the photographer trying to capture a particular mood or image and can thus begin to perceive the differences between amateur photographs and professional ones, between clichés and creative statements.

Learning to look at photographs and comprehend them as works of art is a slow process. Most people have certain expectations about "art" (in all media) and at first respond most positively to those works that appear to be painstakingly executed ("It must have taken a long time to do that!"). Conversely, the response to works of abstract art or tribal art is often negative precisely because these objects sometimes appear to have been made quickly, sloppily, and without skill ("Any child could do that!"). Aesthetic appreciation of photographs suffers from these same prejudices. For a person with an untrained eye, a Walker Evans or a Robert Frank is much harder to admire than is a Jerry Uelsmann, since in Uelsmann's prints there is tangible evidence of technical adroitness. In photography, as in all other art forms, understanding comes only when technical virtuosity is not confused with quality of expression. This, of course, is a crucial question in all areas of connoisseurship.

The current surge of interest in photography as a fine art and the burgeoning of public photographic collections have led to a brand-new phenomenon: private individuals, many of whom previously collected modern paintings or graphic art, are increasingly collecting photographic works. There are now, in New York City alone, more than a dozen photography dealers; moreover, the major art auction houses have entered the field. As with old-master prints, some photographs have attained "stardom" and are considered most desirable from the collector's point of view — Julia Margaret Cameron's portraits of Sir John Herschel, Frederick H. Evans's *Sea of Steps*, Alfred Stieglitz's *The Steerage*, and Edward Weston's nudes, to name a few. These prints have a kind of elevated status of their own, quite apart from their artistic merit, and they are commanding increasingly higher prices at every turn. Some photographic images are so frequently reproduced, however, that they are in danger of becoming overly familiar and tiresome, "old chestnuts" that, like the *Mona Lisa*, might lose their power to grip our attention or imagination.

The explosion of interest in photography has come as a surprise to many in the museum profession who, with notable exceptions, have been slow to concede that photography is a significant artistic medium. Some curators deny the validity of the photograph as collectible art or are stymied by its sudden popularity. One question often asked about photographs (but almost never about Rembrandt etchings or Daumier lithographs) is how they can be valuable, since the negative can, theoretically at least, yield an infinite number of prints. Especial concern is expressed about contemporary photo-

graphs that are printed to order, making the edition virtually limitless. Uniqueness is somehow seen to be a virtue and is equated — erroneously — with quality. Those of us who have specialized in the history of printmaking have found it easier to develop a sympathy for works of art that exist as multiple originals. Indeed, what I have learned about printmaking has strengthened my conviction that the photographic print is a creative means of expression. I can also testify that photography has taught me new ways of seeing and has expanded my visual and spiritual consciousness. Because of my familiarity with the work of Diane Arbus, I now see each face and the life it reflects through her perspective. Likewise, Aaron Siskind has opened my eyes to the abstract beauty of the most unglamorous surfaces. Berenice Abbott has reshaped my experience of the city, and Brassaï has made me sensitive to the romantic aspects of Paris. Photography, like other art forms, is capable of giving life new dimensions. The idea that art helps us to experience nature is no less true of photography than of painting or poetry.

Until very recently only a few American museums collected photographs for their artistic merit rather than for their documentary interest. Hence, some of the questions that concern collectors are only now attracting attention. Guidance was clearly necessary to help define the questions and provide reasonable answers. Thus, *The Photograph Collector's Guide* is an extremely timely and welcome addition to the literature on photography. It provides at once concise biographies of the most important figures in photographic history, lucid discussions of the major questions about collecting, conservation, and value, and explanations of the many historical photographic processes. It is a source book long overdue.

Acknowledgments

John D. Upton was originally a part of this undertaking, and he made many contributions until the press of other projects forced him to withdraw from this one.

In the early stages of the book, many people made valuable suggestions, including Tom Barrow, Van Deren Coke, Barbara Michaels, Beaumont Newhall, and Leland Rice.

Special thanks to all the photographers, collectors, galleries, and museums who so generously made their work available for reproduction.

Without the help and support of many members of The Witkin Gallery staff this project would have been impossible. Jain Kelly assisted in its initial preparation. The major work of compiling and checking appendixes A and B was performed by Bruce Cratsley. Appendix C was handled by Bruce Cratsley and Courtia Worth. Much research and expertise by Carol Fruchter went into making the bibliographies throughout the book as complete and accurate as possible. The illustrations, permissions, and captions were coordinated by Karen Skove. The mailing of questionnaires and followup processing was done over a long period of time by many members of the gallery staff, including Evelyne Daitz, Rixon Reed, Hilarie Friedlander, and Joel Herschman.

Alice Swan, John Witter, and Robert Lyons made many suggestions that greatly improved the chapter on care and restoration (any errors of fact or procedure are entirely the responsibility of the authors).

Thanks also to Ronald A. Parham and Julie Rutgers, who assisted with the chronology; to Jim Stone, who answered many questions regarding the processes listed in the glossary; to Tina Lent, who did research for many of the biographies; and to Stuart Bennett, for permission to quote from his address to a collectors' symposium.

Almost every biography in chapter 5 was reviewed by one or more persons who had special knowledge about the life of the particular photographer or the period in which he or she lived. Our heartfelt thanks to the following readers, who responded with great generosity to our requests for assistance: Tom Barrow, Dan Berley, Peter C. Bunnell, Sean Callahan, Carl Chiarenza, Caldecot Chubb, Ellen Fritz Clattenburg, Van Deren Coke, Philip L. Condax, John Coplans, Howard C. Daitz, Sue Davies, Jacob Deschin, Robert J. Doherty, Robert M. Doty, James L. Enyeart, Gisèle Freund, Carol Fruchter, Constance W. Glenn, Jonathan Green, David Haberstich, Betty Hahn, Gordon Hendricks (Eakins and Muybridge entries), Therese Heyman, William Innes Homer, Graham Howe, Walter Johnson, William Justema, Barry Lane, Anna McCauley, Jerald C. Maddox, Bernard Marbot, Anita Ventura Mozley, Joan Murray, Weston J. Naef, Hank O'Neal, Marcuse Pfeifer, Allan Porter, Naomi Rosenblum, Walter Rosenblum, Marina Schinz Rubin, Naomi Savage, Robert Sobieszek, Ruth Spencer, Rick Steadry, Peter Hunt Thompson, George A. Tice, Anne Tucker, Andrea Turnage, William H. Webb, Adam D. Weinberg, Robert A. Weinstein, and Stephen White.

At New York Graphic Society and Little, Brown, very special thanks are due to Robin Bledsoe, editor, and Michael Brandon, copyeditor. Robin provided invaluable help in coordinating numerous sources of information, contributors, and readers; Mike was untiring in vigilantly tracking down discrepancies in various parts of the book. Both focused their considerable intelligence and expertise on the organization, content, style, and accuracy of the book. Thanks also to Don Ackland, who originally contracted for the book; to Tim Hill, who for much of the production was editor in chief at New York Graphic Society; and to Janis Capone for her artful design.

We are grateful to Scott Hyde, Keith Knight, and William F. Robinson, photographers; to Lista Duren, illustrator for chapter 4; to Nan Jernigan (of Little, Brown) and Martha Johnson, production assistants; to Lee Carr, proofreader; to Nancy Donovan, indexer; and to Barbara Kolins, typist.

Though facts, data, and other material were extensively reviewed, checked, and updated, there are undoubtedly oversights and errors which even the most diligent rechecking failed to bring to light. The authors would appreciate receiving corrections, in care of New York Graphic Society, 41 Mt. Vernon Street, Boston, Massachusetts 02106.

LEE D. WITKIN
BARBARA LONDON

THE
PHOTOGRAPH
COLLECTOR'S
GUIDE

Ansel Adams. *Moonrise, Hernandez, New Mexico,* ca. 1941. Silver print. The best-selling print of all time? In all likelihood, yes. Adams has made around nine hundred prints of this image for museums and collectors. (Courtesy the artist)

1

The Art of Collecting Photographs

Lee D. Witkin

Something exciting is happening in photography. This is one reason why you are looking at this book. You have seen photographs on the walls of major museums and in friends' homes. You have read art gallery advertisements for photography shows and have heard about auctions where prices for photographic prints have made dramatic increases.

Well, it is true: the photographic print is at long last being granted its rightful place as a work of art. The names of nineteenth-century masters like Julia Margaret Cameron, Hill and Adamson, Timothy H. O'Sullivan, and Nadar are becoming familiar to more than just the few collectors who were active in earlier years. Major attention in North America and abroad is being paid to twentieth-century photographers such as Berenice Abbott, W. Eugene Smith, Bill Brandt, Edward Weston, Harry Callahan, and Jerry N. Uelsmann.

The explosion of interest in photography during the 1970s is a truly remarkable phenomenon in light of the century and a quarter of neglect the medium and those practicing it suffered. In years past the idea of the photograph as a collectible art object was certainly suspect, if not inconceivable. A few die-hards exist even today. Because the photograph involves in some part the use of a machine, some believe it should not be considered art. The question "Is photography art?" echoes dully down the corridors of the nineteenth and twentieth centuries. The answer, of course, is that photography is an art *form*. It remains for the photographer alone to create art. The camera is the photographer's means, just as brush and paint are the painter's.

I remember only eleven years ago when I began charting the course for opening The Witkin Gallery. For a few years I had been collecting paintings and etchings, using whatever I could save from my salary as a writer-editor for an engineering magazine. Going to art galleries was one of my great pleasures. I dreamed of someday having one of my own. It did not seem too likely, though, because of the huge investment necessary to procure first-quality material. But I had an inspiration! After finding myself tremendously attracted to the photographs I saw at a few museum shows, I discovered that no one was offering such prints for sale in a gallery setting. With the $6,000 I had saved, I set out to remedy this by opening a photograph gallery.

The reactions from people in the field whom I approached for advice were all negative. I got praise for my intentions and a pat on the back. Sure, photographers "needed" someone to believe in them, but there was little hope of a gallery making it. I was warned that six months, one year at most, was as long as I could expect to last — because no one collected photographs.

This pessimism was not without foundation. The past, if not exactly filled with glorious but doomed attempts to establish ongoing photo galleries, was intermittently dotted with them. Early in this century there was Alfred Stieglitz's Little Galleries of the Photo-Secession (or "291"). Stieglitz began by showing photographs of the Photo-Secession group but ended up featuring works by Picasso, Rodin, Marin, and other painters and sculptors. He tried again from 1930 to 1946 with An American Place, where photographs were only occasionally shown. The Julien Levy Gallery (1931 to 1949) featured photographs along with other surrealist work. In 1954, Helen Gee opened her Limelight Gallery/Cafe in Greenwich Village, and with the income from cake and coffee, survived for seven years. There were other attempts in the late 1950s and early 1960s, notably by Roy DeCarava and by David Kelly, but few of them lasted very long.

So, in 1968, when I rented my first gallery space at 237 East Sixtieth Street (less than five hundred square feet for $200 a month), my hopes were slight and the prospect of my finally reading all of Proust during the slow hours large. At the time, the only other photographic ventures in New York were The Underground Gallery on East Tenth Street, run by Norbert Kleber in conjunction with his camera-equipment business, and The Photographers' Gallery on East Seventy-eighth Street, where entrepreneur Joyce Schwartz hung images on the walls of a furniture showroom. The hours of both were erratic. I had no reason at all to expect success.

What I did have, however, along with the instincts of a professional, were the passions of a collector. Collecting (and every collector knows the symptoms) means seeking, desiring, wanting, yearning for, coveting, having to have . . . and — as soon as possible — acquiring, possessing, hugging to the bosom, and savoring with all the joys and prides of ownership.

It is impossible to explain to someone who is not consumed by such passions why the purchase of a special painting, book, or photograph takes priority over a trip to Europe, a new pair of shoes, or a gold inlay. We all know collecting art is not a pursuit basic for survival. However, it is an exquisite involvement with aesthetic achievements — a kind of mingling with the gods. Though we may not live by bread alone, collecting is one of the few pursuits in which we can have our cake and eat it, too.

The opportunity to collect well without investing large amounts of money is present today in photography as in none of the other arts. Photography is still relatively untapped. Many masterworks and gentler minor works have yet to be discovered and appreciated. A solid base for collecting and for future interest has been established not only by the serious activity of major museums and individuals, but also by educational programs. Universities are graduating future historians and curators and collectors

Unidentified photographer. Shoe still life, ca. 1900. Albumen print. Proving that not all good photographs have to be expensive, I found this charming little print for only $15 in an antique shop in southern California. I consider it an important addition to my collection. (Courtesy Lee D. Witkin)

who have had the chance to study intensively, in newly developed courses, the history and art of photography. These young people will shape the future. By all reliable indications, photography as a collected art is here to stay.

Many beginning collectors ask, "What should I collect?" My advice always has been and always will be: Collect what you like and trust your instincts. The good fortune of a young woman who years ago bought on instinct what is now a highly valued Imogen Cunningham print illustrates what I mean. She tells me whenever we meet, "I love my Cunningham — every day!"

Here are a few wise words from Dan Berley, one of my gallery's first customers, who over the years has assembled a creative and distinctly personal collection: "I have always used two criteria in my collecting: first, the image must produce a strong emotional feeling in me; and, second, there must be a high quality to the photographic print itself. Because I never collect 'names,' per se, I buy the work of unknown or forgotten photographers as well as famous ones.''

Determining the category or focus of your collection is something you should do early on. Will you concentrate on the images of one or more photographers who work in a certain style, like Edward Weston or Paul Caponigro? Or perhaps nature studies in color by Eliot Porter? Remember that the work of a famous photographer is usually much more expensive than that of a young one still struggling to establish his or her name. If you have limited funds, or even if you have a lot of money and wish to be adventuresome, you might well consider buying the photographs of newly rediscovered or budding talents. Here are the real opportunities to collect before prices go high. (In addition, it is a challenge and a pleasure for the concerned dealer to serve such interests.)

If you intend to collect nineteenth-century prints by such photographers as P. H. Emerson, Frederick H. Evans, Roger Fenton, Gustave Le Gray, Alfred Stieglitz, and their like, you must be prepared to pay hundreds, even thousands, of dollars for a single print. Prints by these photographers are rare because they were not produced in large numbers. Major images by them are even rarer. Consider, too, the high mortality rate of this material over the years.

Collecting daguerreotypes can be expensive or inexpensive, depending on their subject, size, and condition. Outdoor scenes, portraits of famous people, occupational portraits, nudes, death portraits, and anything *unusual* are the most sought after and bring the highest prices. Anonymous portraits, on the other hand, are commonplace and can be found for $5 and up. With a selective eye and patience, however, you can build an interesting collection even of the latter. A friend of mine who has been buying daguerreotype images and cases for many years, paying no more than $25 each, has assembled an admirable group.

Other categories you may want to consider collecting are: stereographs; illustrated books; images with special historical content; movements such as surrealism; mixed media; or themes such as regional and travel views, street photography, portraiture, theater, nudes, trees, architecture, and so on. One man I know collects only images featuring hands; another prefers daguerreotypes and ambrotypes showing people with eye irregularities. The fact that

Wallace Nutting. *The Daguerreotype,* ca. 1910. Hand-tinted platinum print. Items such as this parlor scene can be found readily in antique shops across America at modest cost. (Courtesy Howard C. Daitz)

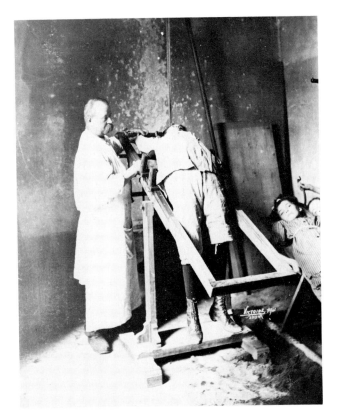

Victoire. *Patients in a Children's Hospital, France,* ca. 1880s–1890s. Albumen or toned silver print. Little is known about this photographer, identified on the print as Victoire, of Lyon, yet he was skilled and compassionate. It remains for someone to be fortunate enough to discover more of his photographs and reestablish his reputation. (Courtesy The Witkin Gallery)

A. J. Russell. *Rebel Caisson Destroyed by Federal Shells, at Fredericksburgh, May 3, 1863. Eight Horses Killed.* Albumen print. Civil War photographs are rare but can be found in unlikely places. I bought this "anonymous" image as part of a collection in 1970, only to have the photographer identified years later, increasing its value considerably. (Courtesy Lee D. Witkin)

the former is a hand surgeon and the latter an optometrist explains their specialized interests; anyway, you see how it is possible to shape a collection to individual taste.

To collect photographs well, you are required to do some homework. *The Photograph Collector's Guide* deals with many areas you need to know about. These include a chronology of key dates, a glossary of photographic terms, currently recommended techniques for caring for your collection, descriptions of limited-edition portfolios, and a survey of recent exhibitions of contemporary photographers. The core of the book is chapter 5, which, in addition to discussing major photographic themes, organizations, and so forth, focuses on over two hundred photographers, providing for each a

biographical career summary, a rundown of their work (including subject matter, media, availability and price, and collections), facsimile signature (if available), and a selected bibliography. And there's more: in case you come across an unfamiliar name on a daguerreotype or print you discover in an attic or junk shop, the supplemental lists of over eight thousand photographers may provide you with a bit of information you can find nowhere else. Finally, there are address lists of suppliers of care-and-restoration materials and of collections and dealers in the United States and throughout the world, plus an extensive bibliography that will guide you to other sources of information.

Because the field of photograph collecting is relatively new, it is important for you to learn as much as you can on your own. One of the ways to acquire expertise is to frequent galleries and exhibitions. Here you can view prints firsthand, learn something about the various printing papers and techniques, and come to discern the qualities so important in determining value. One collector I know describes the pursuit as "a gut-level feeling — but you have to have as informed a gut as possible."

Safeguards against misrepresentation, unintentional or otherwise, must also be learned, such as how different photographers mounted or signed their prints and how to identify the various processes they used. A wisely selected dealer will help you by supplying tips about quality, authenticity, good buys, bad buys, and so forth. A gallery is also a place where you can ask questions, exchange ideas and information, and meet other collectors. In addition, you can examine photographs closely and discover that original prints have unique qualities of tone, luminosity, and "presence" that no book or magazine reproduction can duplicate. From the first day I opened the doors of my gallery, I have repeatedly heard the remark: "I'd only seen the image in books — I had no idea it was so beautiful!"

Even if you don't have access to museums and galleries, you can learn a lot through reading. In the last few years the number of books on photography has multiplied greatly. You have a wide choice of histories, biographies, anthologies, autobiographies, exhibition catalogues, collected images (some of coffee-table size and price), and critical studies.

You are probably asking, "How are prices set?" Both dealers in their galleries and bidders (private and professional) at auction help set prices. But the value of a photograph comes basically from the reputation of the photographer responsible for it. The vintage of a print is also an important factor. Imogen Cunningham, who died in 1976 at the age of ninety-three, made prints from 1901 until shortly before her death. The old prints she made, done in platinum and warm-toned silver, are more appealing to most collectors and exist in fewer numbers; so one of her platinum prints can bring as much as $3,000, while a silver print she made in 1970 from the same negative is worth approximately $750.

Most living photographers try to standardize the price of their work, and galleries usually cooperate. I recall a conversation I had in 1970 with Imogen Cunningham. Her prints were then selling for $35 each. I telephoned her in San Francisco to ask if she

Imogen Cunningham. *Two Callas,* ca. 1929. Silver print. For years, the negative of this, one of her most beautiful images, was misplaced. Cunningham discovered it again in 1973 and was able to make several prints of it before her death in 1976. (Courtesy The Imogen Cunningham Trust)

would agree to an increase to $50 for her forthcoming show. "But if I ask fifty dollars in New York, I'll have to ask fifty dollars here," she exclaimed. I agreed. "But no one will buy them here for fifty dollars," she lamented. There was a long silence. Suddenly she said, "Well, they don't buy them here *anyway,* so go ahead and charge fifty dollars." Today, how incredibly low that $50 seems.

Prices of photographs by deceased photographers are generally determined by the estate, if one exists, or by the galleries who handle the prints. Winning bids at auction have a definite effect, too, on the market. In his address to a collectors' symposium in Arles, France, in July 1977, Stuart Bennett, representing Christie's, made several valuable points about the auction scene:

Photography at auction is not a new event. At least as early as 1854, Puttick and Simpson, the London auctioneers, were selling documentary and topographical photographs by James Robertson and Roger Fenton [although] it is probably fair to refer to all this early auctioneering activity as little more than estate clearing. . . . It seems to me that the first stage in the development of the modern collector's market in photography came . . . with two booksellers' catalogues in 1939, then considered to be the centenary of photography. . . . For collectors and dealers the centenary was also a reminder that these early images were now artifacts in their own right, and that the passage of time had ensured that they were no longer capable of being produced in the way they were then. . . .

The most dramatic development in photographic collecting in the early 1970s, seen from the auctioneer's viewpoint, was the rapid increase in price of the work of the English nineteenth-century photographers, . . . and a continuing supply of fine examples of this work found its way to the auction rooms from English attics. The London auction houses Christie's and Sotheby's were well placed to receive this new material. Both houses had been in business over two hundred years, and since nineteenth-century photography was largely a pastime (both collecting and practising) of the aristocracy, their long-standing connections with English families meant that as country-houses were cleared, photographs and albums found their way to auction. . . .

Very few active photography dealers have stock older than a very few years, and the relatively few auctions per year — six in England, perhaps eight in New York — means that determined collectors can compete in the salesrooms themselves, and dealers must compete at retail levels in order to buy stock. . . . What this means is that the auction market in photography is not "firm" in the traditional sense: it is an individual collector's market. Prices can be low if current collectors have what is offered, then rise again [when] new collectors come into the market. It is also becoming much more discriminating, and this of course is an encouraging sign.

The condition of a print also plays a part in the price asked for it. Nicks and abrasions as well as fading or foxing lower the value. You should examine a photograph very carefully if you are considering buying it to be sure it has no defects, or, at least, to be aware of them. Sometimes an old, rare print is in poor shape, but your choice is often that print or no print at all.

"Even in a market increasingly and properly dominated by concern with condition, even less-than-perfect rarities sell well," Bennett points out.

Ideally auctioneers should try to provide prospective buyers with all the information they need — attractive and unattractive — but I [know of] too many collectors who have received photographs which have been chewed, torn, covered with bird droppings, faded, or otherwise decayed to accept this as always the case. Likewise, auctioneers' estimates can be wrong — more often too low than too high — but the collector still must decide values for himself, no easy matter in the heat of bidding.

As you view more and more original prints, you eventually will be able to see the differences in print quality quickly. Aside from physical considerations, there are aesthetic differences. One print may be a little darker or have more contrast than another. The camera used and the size of the negative also affect print quality. Large view-camera negatives (usually 4×5 or 8×10 inches) produce rich, sharp prints. Smaller negatives when enlarged in printing usually lose some sharpness and show some grain. The photographer chooses the camera and printing technique best suited for the subject. Landscape offers a rich range of tones and detail and is best served by a view camera. Action and "decisive moments" are best captured with smaller, faster cameras.

Printing is a demanding craft. You will find it interesting to learn how different photographers

Thomas Eakins. *Three Female Nudes, Pennsylvania Academy of the Fine Arts,* ca. 1883. Albumen print. At a 10 November 1977 auction of twenty-one photographs by the American painter Thomas Eakins, this 4⅞×3⅝-inch print brought the highest price: $11,000. The others sold for from $1,300 to $9,000. (Courtesy Sotheby Parke Bernet Inc., New York City)

have handled it. To many photographers the making of rich prints with as few imperfections as possible is equal in importance to exposing the original negative. They explore tonal qualities to the fullest. Other photographers are concerned more with the image and not so much with the print. The success of a photograph is based on many ingredients, not solely on excellent craftsmanship. As a collector, you must be the judge.

You will also have to decide how important it is to you whether the print you are considering buying has been made by the photographer who exposed the negative. Some collectors hesitate to purchase a print that was not made and signed by the photographer. But that rules out many fine images. Jacques Henri Lartigue does not make his own prints, nor does André Kertész — and what about Cole Weston's fine prints from his father Edward's negatives? You must consider the circumstances. Opinions differ greatly.

"Intensification of my effects is often done in the process of printing," wrote Bill Brandt in his book *Camera in London.*

Each subject must determine its own treatment. I consider it essential that the photographer should do his own printing and enlarging. The final effect of the finished print depends so much on these operations. And only the photographer himself knows the effect he wants. He should know by instinct, grounded in experience, what subjects are enhanced by hard or soft, light or dark treatment.

André Kertész. *Martinique, January 1, 1972.* Silver print. Kertész's work ranges from World War I to the present. He is one of the masters, yet, owing to allergies, he cannot make his own prints. He personally approves the printing and signs the back of each print. (Courtesy the artist. Copyright © 1972 by André Kertész)

In contrast to Bill Brandt's position is that of Edward Weston. Unable to print in the last years of his life due to crippling Parkinson's disease, he trained his son Cole to make his prints. Codes were developed to achieve the definitive printing of the negatives. It was Edward's wish to have his son continue to make prints after his death. Cole's fine prints allow collectors of modest means to own an Edward Weston photograph. These prints by Cole have increased in price from $50 in 1969, when I first exhibited them, to $300 in 1979, and will no doubt continue to grow in value. Cole projects a time soon when he will stop printing these negatives. The price of the prints then seems likely to escalate quickly, in much the same way Berenice Abbott's prints from Eugène Atget's negatives did.

Berenice Abbott, an important photographer in her own right, struggled for years on Atget's behalf to secure him major recognition. From the 1930s into the 1960s, she printed from his glass-plate negatives. The prints sold for as little as $10. In May 1969, I hung a show of these prints in my new little gallery; they were $50 each then and became my first "success." Today Abbott cannot make any more of these prints because she sold the plates to the Museum of Modern Art. The prints now sell for from $200 to $600.

As a collector you will ask about the number of prints made from a particular negative. Is it limited in the same way as an etching or a lithograph? The answer to this is not a simple yes or no. Again, to understand requires a little familiarity with the unique medium of photography. Making a photographic print is not like setting up a printing press to run off an entire edition from an etched plate or litho stone; often in that process much of the setup work is done at one time, and after the press run the plate is defaced and retired. In photographic printing, each print requires the same time and individual attention as the print before it; the negative may be saved and new prints made sporadically over a period of years. Photographers who are demanding about their craft are lucky to produce more than a handful of prints as an entire day's work. In a more practical economic vein, the market could not absorb large numbers of prints at one time; therefore, photographers usually print "to order," leaving the edition "open," and almost never produce a standard quantity comparable to other graphic editions. Ed-

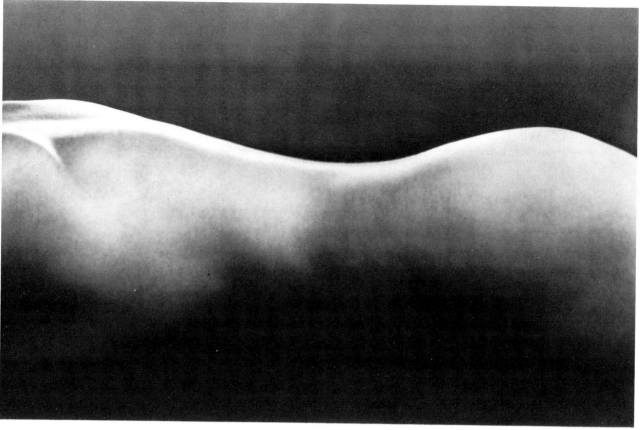

Edward Weston. Untitled nude, ca. 1930. Silver print. To the best of my knowledge, this Weston nude has never before been published and no negative exists, so it is impossible for Weston's son Cole to make modern prints. I bought it for $300 in 1969 from the collection of Rockwell Kent. It was given to him at Christmas, 1930, by Merle Armitage. Because of its beauty and rarity it would be difficult to assign a value of less than $5,000 to it. (Courtesy The Gilman Paper Company Collection)

ward Weston's best-selling print during his lifetime is said to be *Pepper No. 30* (page 271). His records show that he sold, in all, twelve.

The complaint most heard from photographers concerns having to go into the darkroom and make prints. For the most part, they are keen to make new images, not spend their time reprinting old ones. "There is nothing in photography I hate more than printing," W. Eugene Smith once told me.

The care I give the prints and the agony I go through in making them makes it a most unpleasant — but necessary — task. Because of the time it consumes, I could never "flood" the market with my prints. I make my own prints because no language or communication allows me, or anyone else, to tell another person the very subtle balances of print quality only I can register. Anyone else's print of my negative is a rough approximation, even with the best of printmakers. I struggled all my life to come back from assignments and make my own prints.

"The photographer is not a puppet," says Jerry N. Uelsmann, whose own prints require complicated use of up to seven enlargers. "Printing raises human issues. Time and enjoyment enter into consideration. Beyond enjoyment, [at] what point do I stop being an artist and become my own manager-workshop? I'm too full of new ideas for darkroom play." In order to discourage collectors from ordering prints from his old negatives, Uelsmann is asking a higher price for them than for his new work.

Because the negative is durable, in years to come a photographer can interpret its image differently; the freedom to do so is one of the special qualities of photography. George Tice reinterpreted his 1973 *Strand Theater* negative after many months (see illustrations). By printing it darker and using various darkroom controls, he was able to suggest a more mysterious quality of oncoming dusk; the theater lights burn more brightly, the shadows are deeper. Ansel Adams has put it most succinctly: "The negative is the score; the print is the performance."

To ask a photographer to retire a negative — to

George A. Tice. *Strand Theater, New Jersey,* 1973. These two silver prints from the same negative illustrate how the photographer's reinterpretation (BOTTOM) of an image and his modification of printing technique can dramatically alter the final print. (Courtesy The Witkin Gallery)

stop printing it after a few years in the hope of making it more valuable — is unreasonable. If a collector wishes to place a higher premium on an earlier printing of a negative than on a later one (and many do), that is his or her prerogative. But today's print is tomorrow's vintage print. The later *Strand Theater* print by Tice may, in years to come, appear the more interesting of his interpretations and bring a higher price.

So, part of the answer to the question about limitations on the number of prints is no — most photographers up to now have *not* set specific limits on the number they will eventually make from a negative. And part of the answer is yes — due to the work required and the lack of a big enough market to justify great numbers of prints, the output has been very limited. All this may change as the sale of photographs becomes more syndicated and publishers use financing and distribution clout to commission large editions and demand that negatives be retired. But at the moment the photographer is in the driver's seat, and it is important to remember that he or she, even more than the collector, wishes to protect and increase the value of the work. Many older photographers have already seen to it that their negatives will go to reputable archives upon their death so that no unauthorized posthumous prints can be made. The Center for Creative Photography at the University of Arizona in Tucson has already been promised the negatives of Paul Strand, Ansel Adams, Aaron Siskind, Harry Callahan, and Wynn Bullock.

The price of photographs is not solely related to scarcity, though, as many photographers who have produced small limited editions with high hopes but disappointing sales have discovered. Nor will abundant supply necessarily limit demand. Ansel Adams has made perhaps nine hundred prints of his great image *Moonrise, Hernandez, New Mexico* (page 2), which may be the best-selling fine photograph of all time. Yet, far from the quantity of existing prints discouraging collectors from purchasing it, *Moonrise* is the most requested Ansel Adams print and keeps bringing the highest price of any of his many images — $7,500 to date for the standard 16×20 print.

The success of *Moonrise* points out a recurrent situation in collecting. Adams, along with many other well-known photographers, has a large body of work, yet we keep seeing many of the same images over and over again in books and shows. Many of these masters' lesser-known photographs are exceptionally fine; you may wish to consider seeking out some of them as a means of expressing your individual taste and creativity. Overlooked gems are to be found this way. Intriguing collections are put together by people who have looked around and learned to trust their own taste and judgment. Give yourself time to acquire this self-assurance.

A few last words. While the concepts of collecting for pleasure and collecting as a speculative financial investment are not necessarily in conflict, I believe strongly the former is *first* in importance. Aesthetics usually leads the way to monetary value. Collecting photographs solely for profit takes the true joy out of it, and besides, there are too many intangibles, too many unpredictable turns of events to assure anyone success along this line. An increase in appraised print value is a solid and flattering tribute to a collector's taste and foresight, but most collectors would never consider selling their collections for cash value — and those who do may be disappointed. You should remember that works of art are not as liquid as stocks or bonds, and value *increases* are usually long-term affairs. You cannot expect automatically to sell a print back to a dealer for its full market value for the simple reason that a dealer has to buy at a discount and sell at a profit in order to cover overhead. Full retail value for a print is usually realized only by selling to another collector or at auction, and even here the auction house takes a commission (usually 20 percent).

When you collect, collect for pleasure and life-enrichment, *and trust your instincts*. The photograph collector who acquires a work of art not only gains the fruit of the artist's life and labor, but personally shares in a very special level of human achievement and appreciation. Whether your prints are framed and on your walls for all to see or kept in a special case to be viewed with close friends, your collection reflects your tastes and acumen, and you can rightly take pride in it.

Framed photographs fit comfortably in attractive groupings with
a variety of other art objects to create a handsome interior. (Photo
by Scott Hyde)

Joseph Nicéphore Niepce. View from his window at Le Gras, 1826 ("the world's first photograph"). Heliograph. (Courtesy Gernsheim Collection, Humanities Research Center, The University of Texas at Austin)

A Collector's Chronology

Photography has been on view a relatively short time — less than 150 years. Within that short span, styles and movements have flowered and died away; some photographers have spent their lives at their art, others have made a few images and stopped working; inventions have changed the way pictures were taken, while aesthetic styles have affected subject matter and presentation. This chronology follows the flow of events in photography and pinpoints certain key events within that flow. It is a brief overview of some of the items of interest to collectors of photography — a combination of objective history plus the authors' personal choices of events.

4th c. B.C.– Numerous writers mention the basic optical
16th c. A.D. principle of photography: a pinhole (later a lens) forms an image. The camera obscura, a device for forming a pinhole image, is used to observe solar eclipses, later as an aid in drawing.

1725 Discovery of basic photochemical principle of photography: German physicist Johann Heinrich Schulze notices sensitivity of silver nitrate to light.

1802 In England, publication of Thomas Wedgwood's photographic experiments with silhouettes of leaves and other objects placed on paper or leather sensitized with silver nitrate. He is unable to find a way to fix the prints permanently.

1826 In France, Joseph Nicéphore Niepce's experiments since 1814 culminate in the earliest surviving photograph from a camera-obscura image: Niepce's courtyard as viewed from his workshop window. His process, heliography, involves the light sensitivity of bitumen of Judea, which he uses to coat a polished pewter plate.

1829 Louis Jacques Mandé Daguerre and Niepce enter into partnership for the advancement of photography.

1833 Death of Niepce. Daguerre continues his own experiments.

In England, William Henry Fox Talbot grows frustrated by his attempts to sketch using a prismatic drawing aid, the camera lucida; he muses about the possibility of fixing the image of the camera obscura.

1834 Talbot experiments with photographic processes. He inserts paper sensitized with silver chloride into the camera obscura.

1835 Talbot develops his photogenic-drawing process and produces silhouettes of objects laid on sensitized paper. Then, using a tiny "mouse-trap" camera, he exposes *Latticed Window, Lacock Abbey,* the earliest surviving negative.

1837 Daguerre perfects the first practical photographic process: the daguerreotype. The image is formed by a mercury compound on a silver-

1837
(cont.) coated metal plate; each image is unique and nonreplicable. (His earliest surviving daguerreotype is a still life, *The Artist's Studio.*)

1839 Daguerre's invention announced to the French Academy of Sciences by François Arago. (7 January)

Talbot hears of Daguerre's announcement and presents his own claim of being the inventor of photography.

Hippolyte Bayard produces direct images on paper, later is persuaded by Arago to withhold publication of his method, thereby leaving the limelight to Daguerre.

Sir John Herschel, applying to photography his 1819 discovery that hypo (thiosulfite of soda) dissolves silver salts, finds that hypo will permanently fix an image. Herschel later invents a number of other photographic techniques, including cyanotype (1840). He is one of the first to use the term *photography* and initiates the usage of *positive* and *negative.*

Bayard mounts the first public exhibition of photography. (June)

First printed account of daguerreotype process reaches America. (September)

Hercules Florence, a Frenchman living in Brazil, writes a letter to a newspaper claiming to have experimented with *photographie* since 1832. His is one of the first published uses of this term. (October)

The French painter Paul Delaroche, upon seeing a daguerreotype for the first time, delivers his now much-quoted declaration: "From today, painting is dead!"

Within months of Daguerre's announcement, photographers travel to Egypt, Russia, and other areas remote from Europe to satisfy the growing public demand for pictures. Written reports and manuals on the photographic process proliferate throughout the world.

1840 Talbot improves his photographic process, calling it calotype, later talbotype.

1840–44 N.-M. P. Lerebours, a French publisher, issues *Excursions Daguérriennes,* a series of travel views comprised of aquatint engravings and other prints made from daguerreotypes.

1843 Albert S. Southworth and Josiah J. Hawes enter into partnership in Boston, producing fine daguerreotype portraits.

Talbot opens the first establishment to mass-produce photographic prints.

In Scotland, David O. Hill and Robert Adamson, using calotype, team up to begin series of fine portraits.

1844 Talbot publishes initial installment of the first major book illustrated with photographs, *The Pencil of Nature.*

1845 Mathew Brady makes daguerreotype of Andrew Jackson, first of his many portraits of U.S. presidents.

1847 In America, Edward Anthony imports daguerreotype materials, soon afterward becomes a manufacturer and distributor.

1849 Sir David Brewster perfects a stereoscopic viewer.

1849–51 Maxime Du Camp and Gustave Flaubert make a photographic tour of the Middle East. Pop-

Auguste Salzmann. *Sainte-Sépulcre, Jerusalem,* 1852. Calotype made by L.-D. Blanquart-Evrard. (Courtesy The Witkin Gallery)

ularity of views of the Holy Land prompts many such expeditions in following decades.

1850s Viewing stereographs becomes a popular pastime. "Instantaneous" photographs that stop motion (for example, of people walking) become possible with the short exposures of the stereo cameras.

1850 First number of *Daguerreian Journal*, the first photographic periodical, is published in New York City. (November)

Jenny Lind, the Swedish Nightingale, on her first American tour, has her daguerreotype portrait "struck" by Brady, starting a vogue among other celebrities for "Brady of Broadway."

Louis-Désiré Blanquart-Evrard introduces albumen paper, which becomes the standard paper used in nineteenth-century photographic printing.

1851 Frederick Scott Archer invents collodion wet-plate process. Its image is replicable, unlike the daguerreotype, and sharper than the calotype; thus it quickly replaces both processes.

First photographic organization, Société Héliographique, founded in France.

Many photographs shown at the Great Exhibition, Crystal Palace, London.

1851–52 Comité des Monuments Historiques, France, commissions documentation of historic monuments with photographs by Bayard, Edouard-Denis Baldus, Gustave Le Gray, Henri Le Secq, O. Mestral, and others.

1853 Photographic Society of Great Britain (now Royal Photographic Society) established — earliest such society that is still active.

Daguerreotypist Eliphalet Brown, Jr., accompanies Commodore Perry expedition to Japan. Japanese woodcut prints show photographers at work.

Nadar (G.-F. Tournachon) photographs in Paris, later gains reputation for portraits of celebrities such as Sarah Bernhardt.

1854 Earliest surviving photograph from a war zone — Varna (Black Sea supply port for Crimean War) — taken by Richard Nicklin. (8 September)

BRADY'S GALLERY
OF
DAGUERREOTYPE
PORTRAIT AND FAMILY GROUPS,

Nos. 205 and 207 Broadway, 3d Door South of St. Paul's Church, 2d, 3d, and 4th Stories.

ADMISSION FREE.
PRICES FOR PICTURES
Regulated by their Size and Character, and the Style and Richness of the Case or Frame.

Mr. Brady has been awarded the First Premium, by the American Institute, for the best plain and colored Daguerreotype Likenesses, for three successive years.

The pictures taken at this establishment, are pronounced by artists and scientific men, unrivalled for depth of tone, and softness of light and shade. While they display all the artistic arrangements of the highest efforts of the painter.

Citizens or strangers visiting this gallery, can have their Miniatures or Portraits taken in the most perfect manner, and neatly set in Morocco Cases. Gold Lockets, Breast-pins, &c., in a few minutes.

Family Portraits, Miniatures, &c.,
COPIED WITH GREAT FIDELITY.

His new and superior arrangements for light, (acquired by the addition of another story to the building) under his facilities in that important respect, inferior to no establishment in the Union.

Mr. B. will give his personal attention to obtain the most grateful, easy, and natural position of individuals or groups.

The best hours for children is from 10 A. M. to 2 P. M., all others from 8 A. M. to 6 P. M.

Advertisement for Brady's Gallery at 205 and 207 Broadway, New York City, ca. 1850s. (Courtesy The Witkin Gallery)

Richard Nicklin. Varna (Black Sea supply port for Crimean War), 8 September 1854. (Courtesy Bensusan Museum of Photography, Johannesburg, South Africa)

mid-1850s Ambrotypes (direct positive pictures on glass) become a popular, cheaper replacement for daguerreotype portraits.

1855 Roger Fenton photographs scenes of Crimean War — the first surviving extensive photographic coverage of any war.

Bisson *frères* photograph the Alps.

1856 Francis Frith makes his first trip to Egypt to photograph antiquities.

Lewis Carroll first photographs Alice Liddell, his inspiration for *Alice's Adventures in Wonderland.*

1857 O. G. Rejlander produces *Two Ways of Life,* an allegorical composite photograph combining thirty negatives.

1858 Henry Peach Robinson makes *Fading Away,* a story-telling genre print combining five negatives. He becomes very influential in establishing rules for photographic "art."

Nadar makes the first successful aerial photograph, from a balloon. Honoré Daumier caricatures him in a popular lithograph.

1859 Cartes de visite become immensely popular; for the first time images of famous people such as Napoleon III are readily available to the public.

1861 Carleton E. Watkins first photographs in Yosemite Valley.

Photographer's studio. Illustration in *Les Merveilles de la science* by Louis Figuier (Paris: Furne, Jouvet, ca. 1868). (Courtesy The Witkin Gallery)

Brady conceives of plan to document Civil War. Travels to battlegrounds himself and equips teams of photographers to record war scenes.

1861–65 Wood engravings drawn from photographs of Civil War scenes appear in illustrated journals such as *Harper's Weekly* and *Frank Leslie's Illustrated Newspaper.* No way yet exists for newspapers to print photographs directly.

Tintypes, cheap and sturdy direct positives on metal, grow popular. Many Civil War soldiers carry tintype portraits of their families and send home tintypes of themselves.

1863 Timothy H. O'Sullivan photographs scenes of carnage after the Battle of Gettysburg.

Samuel Bourne makes his first expedition to photograph in the Himalayas.

1864 In England, Julia Margaret Cameron begins to photograph notables of her time, including Tennyson, Herschel, Longfellow; her powerful portrait heads are not as much appreciated by her contemporaries as her sentimental tableaux.

1865 Alexander Gardner makes last photographs to be taken of Lincoln. (9 April)

John Thomson leaves England to photograph China and other parts of the Far East.

Views of foreign life continue to be popular in Europe, particularly England, for their entertainment and educational value.

George N. Barnard accompanies General Sherman's army, records its devastating march through Georgia.

mid-1860s Cabinet-size prints (on paper) become popular for portraits.

1865–66 Gardner publishes his *Photographic Sketch Book of the War,* including photographs by himself, O'Sullivan, Barnard, and others.

1867 Major photographic documentation of western U.S. is underway: Eadweard Muybridge in Yosemite; O'Sullivan with Clarence King's geological exploration of the fortieth parallel; Gardner along Union Pacific Railroad route in Kansas. Such images influence Congress to create national parks.

1869 Transcontinental railroad joined at Promontory Point, Utah, and photographed by Andrew Joseph Russell, Charles R. Savage, and Alfred A. Hart.

Louis Ducos du Hauron and Charles Cros independently announce discovery of principles of color subtractive photography, the basis of modern color materials.

Napoleon Sarony, well known as a photographer of theatrical personalities, photographs Joseph Jefferson as Rip Van Winkle.

1870s William Notman uses authentic props to re-create in his studio outdoor scenes of Canadian hunters, trappers, etc.

Introduction of the more convenient gelatin dry plate rapidly makes collodion wet-plate process obsolete.

1870 William Henry Jackson photographs with Hayden Survey in the Rocky Mountains, exposes collodion wet-plates to 20×24 inches in size.

1872 Muybridge employed by Leland Stanford to photograph a horse in motion — first of many Muybridge photographic studies of animal and human locomotion.

Platinotype process patented in England.

1876-1885 *Galerie Contemporaine*, Paris, publishes woodburytypes of portraits by Nadar, Antoine Samuel Adam-Salomon, Etienne Carjat, and others.

1877-78 Thomson publishes *Street Life in London*, illustrated with woodburytypes — the first major work on social problems to be illustrated with photographs.

1879 First photogravures made.

1880 First reproduction of a photographic halftone in a daily newspaper, the New York *Daily Graphic*. (4 March)

1885 P. H. Emerson begins his attack on "high art" artificiality of Henry Peach Robinson and his followers. Emerson's naturalistic photographs and extensive writings create an aesthetic of photography as an independent art form that does not have to imitate painting.

Antoine Samuel Adam-Salomon. *Alphonse Karr*, ca. 1880. From the *Galerie Contemporaine* series. Carbon print. (Courtesy The Witkin Gallery)

1886 First photographic interview: Nadar discussing "the art of living 100 years" with centenarian Michel-Eugène Chevreul, the French scientist.

1887 Alfred Stieglitz receives his first photographic award, given to him by P. H. Emerson for his image *A Good Joke*.

1888 Jacob A. Riis photographs slums of New York to illustrate his crusading newspaper stories, often using the newly invented *Blitzlichtpulver* (flash light powder). His *How the Other Half Lives* (1890) is the first book to contain a number of photographs reproduced directly as halftones.

1890s Pictorialism spreads. Clubs actively promote photography as an art form, including Vienna Camera Club; The Linked Ring, London; Photo-Club de Paris.

Stieglitz active in New York City photographing, writing, editing, lecturing, organizing shows to promote photography as a fine art.

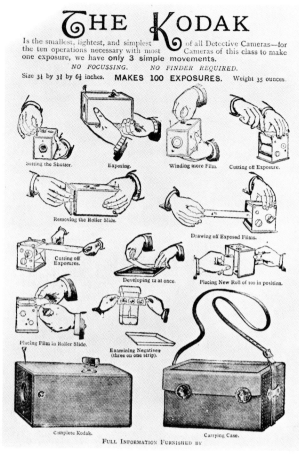

Advertisement for the Kodak camera, 1888. (From *The Illustrated History of the Camera* by Michel Auer, Boston: New York Graphic Society, 1975)

1890s (cont.) Hand cameras and gelatin films begin to make photography practical for amateurs. Improvements and simplifications continue in such cameras as the Kodak, first introduced in 1888 by George Eastman.

1895 Adam Clark Vroman, among others, sees the importance of documenting American Indian life, and begins photographing in the American Southwest.

1896–1906 Arnold Genthe uses a concealed camera to photograph in Old Chinatown, San Francisco.

1897 Gertrude Käsebier opens photographic studio in New York City and is successful in one of the few professions open to women.

1898 F. Holland Day photographs himself in chief role of the Passion of Christ, including the crucifixion.

Frederick H. Evans retires from his bookstore at age forty-five to devote himself to photographic study of English and French architecture and landscapes.

1899 Jacques Henri Lartigue receives his first camera at age five.

Thomas Eakins paints *The Wrestlers* directly from a photograph he made as a sketch for the work.

late 1890s Eugène Atget conceives project to make a grand collection of images of Paris and its surroundings and devotes the rest of his life, almost thirty years, to its fulfillment.

1899–1900 Frances Benjamin Johnston, prominent as a photojournalist in Washington, D.C., photographs black students of Hampton (Va.) Institute.

1900s Pictorialists explore "fine" photographic processes such as platinum, gum bichromate, carbon, for exhibition prints.

Alfred Stieglitz. *The Steerage,* 1907. From *Camera Work,* no. 36, 1911. Gravure. (Courtesy The Witkin Gallery)

ca. 1901 Imogen Cunningham makes her first photograph, remains active in photography until her death in 1976.

1902 Edward Weston makes his first photograph, using a Bulls-Eye No. 2 camera.

Photo-Secession is formed by Stieglitz to promote pictorial photography.

1903 Stieglitz publishes first issue of *Camera Work* for the Photo-Secessionists; Edward Steichen influential in its design and content.

1905 Lewis W. Hine begins his first documentary series, immigrants on Ellis Island; later photographs child-labor conditions.

Little Galleries of the Photo-Secession opens in New York City.

1907 First volume of Edward S. Curtis's study and re-creation of North American Indian life appears. His twenty-volume project is financed by J. P. Morgan.

1912 André Kertész buys his first camera, begins photographing vignettes of life in Austria-Hungary.

Francis Bruguière begins experimenting with photographic abstractions.

1914 The Clarence H. White School of Photography opens in New York City. Margaret Bourke-White, Laura Gilpin, Dorothea Lange, Paul Outerbridge, Doris Ulmann, and many others study there.

1916 James Van Der Zee opens photographic studio in Harlem, N.Y.

1917 Paul Strand's nonpictorial, "modern" photographs appear in last issues of *Camera Work.*

1918 August Sander begins documentation of social types in Germany.

1920s Albert Renger-Patzsch, Cunningham, Strand, Weston, and others photograph common objects closeup — plants, machine parts, etc.

Alvin Langdon Coburn. *Self-Portrait with Copper-Plate Printing Press,* 1908. Gravure. (Courtesy IMP/GEH)

1909 Alvin Langdon Coburn issues *London,* the first of his major books illustrated with his own gravures.

1910 Pictorial movement peaks. Photo-Secession arranges international exhibition at Albright Art Gallery, Buffalo, N.Y.

Paul Strand. *Wire Wheel, New York,* 1918. Silver print. (Courtesy Philadelphia Museum of Art; purchased with funds given by Mr. and Mrs. Robert A. Hauslohrer)

1920 Edward Weston begins to turn from soft-focus pictorial work to sharp, "straight" photographs. He meets Stieglitz, who shows no particular enthusiasm for his work.

1922 László Moholy-Nagy and Lucia Moholy collaborate on series of photograms. Man Ray makes photograms he calls rayographs.

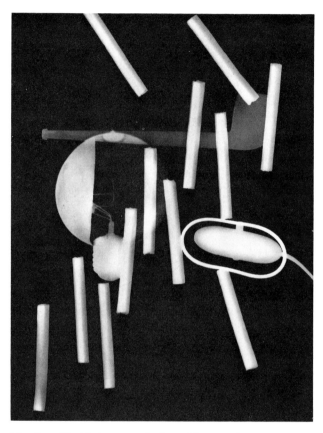

Man Ray. Untitled rayograph. From *Photographies, 1920-1934, Paris,* 1934. Gravure. (Courtesy Lee D. Witkin)

1923 Steichen becomes chief photographer for Condé Nast publications *Vanity Fair* and *Vogue.*

1924 Museum of Fine Arts, Boston, receives photographs by Stieglitz, the first by any artist to enter a U.S. museum.

ca. 1925 Ulmann begins photographing people in Appalachia and the rural South.

1926 Metropolitan Museum of Art, New York City, accepts its first collection of photographs, Stieglitz's personal one.

1927 Atget, his photographic work almost unknown, dies; Berenice Abbott rescues many of his negatives.

1929 Abbott returns from Paris, photographs changing New York City's old buildings and new skyscrapers.

Film und Foto exhibit in Stuttgart features work of U.S. photographers selected by Steichen and Weston.

late 1920s Age of modern photojournalism begins. Newspapers and periodicals crave on-the-spot coverage. Erich Salomon, Alfred Eisenstaedt, Tim Gidal, and others use small cameras and available light to record political events in Europe.

1931 The Julien Levy Gallery opens in New York City with a retrospective of American photography. Specializing in surrealism, the gallery continues until 1949.

1932 Willard Van Dyke, Ansel Adams, Cunningham, Weston, and others informally organize Group *f*/64 to promote "straight" photography.

Anton Bruehl contracts with Condé Nast to do color editorial work and advertising — one of the early uses of creative color photography in this field.

1933 Brassaï publishes *Paris de Nuit,* his photographs of cafés, street scenes, etc.

John Heartfield has to flee Germany because of his photomontages directed against the Nazis.

Roman Vishniac begins documentation of Eastern European Jews, sensing the coming destruction of Jewish life by Hitler.

Ansel Adams meets Stieglitz, who praises his work and reinforces Adams's commitment to a career in photography.

1935 Roy Stryker begins, for the Resettlement Administration (later the Farm Security Administration), massive photographic survey of American life during the Depression. Arthur Rothstein is the first photographer to be hired, followed by Lange, Walker Evans, Ben Shahn, others.

Weegee (A. H. Fellig) becomes a free-lance news photographer based at Manhattan police headquarters.

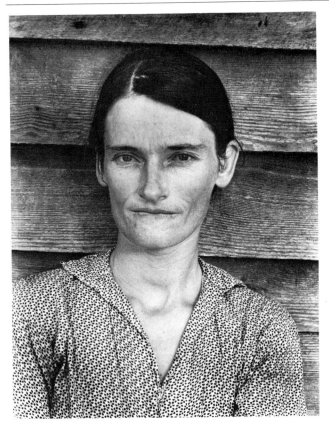

Walker Evans. *Allie Mae Burroughs, Wife of a Cotton Share-cropper, Hale County, Alabama, Summer 1936.* Modern silver print from the original negative. (Courtesy Library of Congress)

Kodachrome, color transparency film, first marketed.

1935-36 Walker Evans and James Agee collaborate on project about southern sharecroppers, published in 1941 as *Let Us Now Praise Famous Men.*

1936 The Photo League, New York City, organizes shows, classes, lectures with emphasis on documentary photography — "a true image of the world as it is today."

First issue of *Life* magazine bears Bourke-White's cover photograph of Fort Peck (Mont.) Dam. (23 November)

1937 Museum of Modern Art, New York City, offers first survey exhibition of photography; catalogue, *Photography 1839–1937*, by Beaumont Newhall.

Weston receives first Guggenheim Fellowship awarded to a photographer, uses the grant to produce *California and the West* with Charis Wilson.

Bourke-White and Erskine Caldwell publish *You Have Seen Their Faces*, a pioneer work that influences future documentary photographers.

1940 Department of photography opens at Museum of Modern Art in New York City; Beaumont Newhall is appointed curator.

early 1940s Aaron Siskind turns from documentary photography to abstract work.

1942 Outerbridge's carbro prints are first color prints to be acquired by Museum of Modern Art.

William Henry Jackson, the last surviving nineteenth-century expeditionary photographer, dies at ninety-nine.

1945 First retrospective exhibition of Strand's photographs is organized by Nancy Newhall at New York City's Museum of Modern Art. The following year she organizes the first Weston retrospective.

William Garnett, traveling with GI troop transport, sits with pilot on flight across U.S. and realizes expressive potential of aerial photography.

1946 Minor White meets Stieglitz, continues Stieglitz's idea of photograph as metaphor or equivalent.

W. Eugene Smith, recovering from war injuries, makes *The Walk to Paradise Garden*, an image "of a gentle moment of spiritual purity" (illustrated on next page).

The Inhabitants is published, pairing prose and photographs by Wright Morris.

1947 Edwin H. Land introduces Polaroid instant pictures.

Photo League labeled "subversive" by U.S. Department of Justice.

1949 The International Museum of Photography at George Eastman House established at the former residence of the late founder of Eastman Kodak Company, Rochester, N.Y.

1950 Introduction of Kodacolor, color negative film.

Installation view of The Family of Man exhibition, 1955. (Courtesy The Museum of Modern Art, New York City. Photo © 1955 by Ezra Stoller/ESTO)

W. Eugene Smith. *The Walk to Paradise Garden,* 1946. Silver print. (Courtesy the artist and The Witkin Gallery)

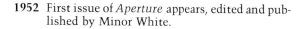

Steichen, director of the photography department at the Museum of Modern Art, New York City, since 1947, organizes The Family of Man exhibition. It is seen by more visitors than any other photographic show.

1952 First issue of *Aperture* appears, edited and published by Minor White.

The Decisive Moment by Henri Cartier-Bresson is published, influencing many photographers to use the camera as an instant extension of the eye.

George Eastman House accepts Lewis W. Hine Collection from Photo League after Museum of Modern Art turns it down.

1954 Limelight Gallery/Cafe opened by Helen Gee. The only photographic gallery in New York City at the time, it becomes a popular meeting place for photographers before closing in 1961.

1955 Helmut and Alison Gernsheim publish their influential book *The History of Photography.*

The Sweet Flypaper of Life is published — a study of life in Harlem, N.Y., with photos by Roy DeCarava and text by Langston Hughes.

Major collector Georges Sirot donates five truckloads of photographs and related material to Bibliothèque Nationale, Paris, forming the basis of its collection.

1957 Nathan Lyons begins association with George Eastman House, where he is responsible for many influential shows and books.

1958 Robert Frank publishes *Les Américains,* a book that shapes a new style of personal social documentation.

1959 Jerry N. Uelsmann begins work with multiple imagery.

1960s Growing attention to photography in colleges, universities, and art schools: many general-interest courses offered, as well as advanced degrees in photography as an art form and in the history of photography.

1961 Robert Heinecken experiments with combined graphic and photographic techniques.

1962 Eliot Porter publishes *"In Wildness Is the Preservation of the World,"* first of several popular books for Sierra Club.

Polaroid instant-picture color film introduced.

Society for Photographic Education founded; Lyons is first chairman.

John Szarkowski succeeds Steichen as director of photography at the Museum of Modern Art.

1963 Eikoh Hosoe photographs Yukio Mishima, Japanese literary and political figure, in *Killed by Roses.*

1964 University of Texas, Austin, acquires Gernsheim Collection, one of the largest private collections of photographic material.

Van Deren Coke publishes *The Painter and the Photograph,* an exploration of the relationship between painting and photography.

1967 The Exchange National Bank of Chicago commissions the collecting of photographs for display in its corporate headquarters — Beaumont Newhall and Nancy Newhall, cocurators.

1968 Museum of Modern Art purchases Atget Collection from Berenice Abbott and Julien Levy.

1969 Lee D. Witkin opens New York City gallery exclusively devoted to photography.

Eikoh Hosoe. Untitled. From the series "Kamaitachi," 1969. Silver print. (Courtesy Light Gallery. Copyright © by Eikoh Hosoe)

Lyons founds Visual Studies Workshop, Rochester, N.Y.

1970s Many new books appear, significantly influencing photographic style and subject matter — for example:

Bruce Davidson, *East 100th Street,* 1970. Residents of one Harlem street.
Lee Friedlander, *Self Portrait,* 1970. The photographer in the social landscape.
Ralph Gibson, *The Somnambulist,* 1970. First book in a trilogy interpreting surrealism.
Duane Michals, *Sequences,* 1970. Serial imagery.
Larry Clark, *Tulsa,* 1971. His friends and the drug scene.
Danny Lyon, *Conversations with the Dead,* 1971. Biographies and autobiographies of men in prison.
Lucas Samaras, *Samaras Album,* 1971. Manipulated SX-70 color Polaroid images.
Les Krims, *Making Chicken Soup,* 1972. His mother and his mother's recipe.
Bill Owens, *Suburbia,* 1973. Life in middle-class heaven.
Lewis Baltz, *The New Industrial Parks near Irvine, California,* 1974. More formal documents.
W. Eugene Smith and Aileen Smith, *Minamata,* 1975. The poisoning of a Japanese town.
Joel Meyerowitz, *Cape Light,* 1978. View-camera color images of Provincetown, Mass.

Interest surges in photography as a collectible art:

Magazines and newspapers give critical attention to photography and collecting.
Photographic auctions in U.S. and Europe attract many collectors; 1977 sees ten major auctions in New York City alone.
Prominent art galleries, which hitherto had excluded photographic work, begin to feature it.
New galleries specializing in photography open in many European and U.S. cities.

Major museum exhibitions reflect growing acceptance of photography as an art — for example:

Strand retrospective, Philadelphia Museum of Art, 1971.
Metropolitan Museum of Art's first exhibition of work by a living photographer: Stephen Shore, 1971.
From Today Painting Is Dead: The Beginnings of Photography; Victoria and Albert Museum, 1972.
Permanent exhibit on history of photography opens at Smithsonian Institution, 1975.

**1970s
(cont.)** Women of Photography, San Francisco Museum of Art, 1975.

The Land: Twentieth-Century Landscape Photographs (selected by Bill Brandt); Victoria and Albert Museum, 1975–76.

Harry Callahan retrospective, Museum of Modern Art, 1977.

Dialogue between Painting and Photography opens at the Kunsthaus Zürich, 1977; 900 items on view spanning 136 years.

First photographer's show at the Hirshhorn Museum and Sculpture Garden, Washington, D.C.: Leland Rice, 1977.

New museums and university departments devoted to photography proliferate and actively acquire collections — for example:

First endowed history-of-photography professorship in the U.S. is established at Princeton University through a gift by David H. McAlpin, 1972; Peter C. Bunnell is first appointee.

International Center of Photography, New York City, 1974; Cornell Capa, director.

Center for Creative Photography at University of Arizona, Tucson, 1975; Harold Jones the first director, followed in 1977 by James L. Enyeart.

View of gallery and study area, Center for Creative Photography, University of Arizona, Tucson. (Courtesy Center for Creative Photography)

Victoria and Albert Museum creates position of keeper of photographs, 1977; Mark Haworth-Booth appointed.

Museum Ludwig (Cologne) acquires L. Fritz Gruber Collection, 1977.

International Museum of Photography at George Eastman House acquires the 3M/Sipley Collection, 1977.

Both nationally and regionally in the United States, Great Britain, and elsewhere, grants become increasingly available for photographers, museums, researchers, etc., as institutional acceptance of photography as an art increases.

Photography workshops grow in popularity and become an important source of contact among photographers, students, and collectors.

1970 Cunningham, at age eighty-seven, is granted a Guggenheim Fellowship to print her past work. Six years earlier she had been denied the fellowship to photograph the "grandes dames" of England.

Lucien Clergue directs first international photographic festival at Arles, France.

Sonia Sheridan teaches course at the School of the Art Institute of Chicago, exploring the use of office-copy and other machines in generative-systems imagery.

Ellen Land-Weber. Untitled, 1978. Black-and-white print from 3M VQC office copy machine. (Courtesy the artist)

1970–72 The Life Library of Photography — seventeen volumes (plus yearbooks thereafter) dealing with technique, history, and aesthetics — is widely distributed.

1971 George A. Tice, after extensive testing, begins printing in platinum and teaching the process.

1972 Last weekly issue of *Life* magazine. (29 December)

Diane Arbus, one year after her death, is first U.S. photographer to have works exhibited at Venice Biennale.

1973 Publication of *Looking at Photographs* by John Szarkowski — analysis of 100 photographs in the Museum of Modern Art.

1976 Interest grows in color photography. William Eggleston exhibition opens at Museum of Modern Art.

1977 Sotheby's, Belgravia (London), purchases Cecil Beaton archive for a reputed £500,000.

1978–79 Major auctions of photographic prints and books multiply — key cities: New York City, Los Angeles, London, Paris.

Increasing value of collectible photographs and growing interest in them spurs research in the proper care and storage of photographic materials; stability of color prints becomes a major concern for collectors.

Harry Bowers. *Going My Way*, 1978. Dye coupler print, 30×40 inches. (Courtesy Hansen Fuller Gallery)

The parts of a dismantled daguerreotype, in order of assembly (clockwise, from lower right): the image plate, brass mat, cover glass, preserver frame, case with decorative velvet pad for protection. Unidentified photographer. Untitled, ca. 1850. Quarter plate. See entries in this chapter: *cases,* page 32; *daguerreotype,* page 35.

A Collector's Glossary

What is the difference between a daguerreotype and an ambrotype? How do you tell a platinum print from a silver print? What is a cyanotype or an albumen print? These matters are of prime concern to many collectors of photography. The best way to become familiar with different media is to learn the facts, then examine and compare specimens. This glossary provides considerable background information about various objects and processes — both common and rarer ones — as well as help in distinguishing them.

albertype. *See* collotype.

album. A popular means of storing photographs in book form, especially in the nineteenth century, when albums were used to collect prints of family members, friends, famous people, and scenic travel views. Prints were pasted in, or inserted in slits or pockets. Bindings ranged from simple paper or leather to elaborately decorated and inlaid covers with ornate clasps and sometimes a music box, clock, or other insert. The term also refers to a published book containing photographic prints.

albumen on glass. The first practical photographic process on glass. Invented in the late 1840s by Claude Félix Abel Niepce de Saint-Victor (French), a cousin of Joseph Nicéphore Niepce, the albumen-on-glass process was soon replaced in the 1850s by the faster collodion process.

Albumen (from egg white) was one of the few substances suitable as a medium for a light-sensitive emulsion found to adhere to glass. Glass-based negatives eliminated the visible texture and loss of detail caused by printing through paper-based negatives. The albumen-on-glass negative produced very fine detail but required a long exposure (five to fifteen minutes). The glass negative was printed onto paper to make a positive or again onto glass for lantern slides.

Surviving albumen-on-glass plates are extremely rare. The process was used for architectural and landscape views, but not for portraits because of the long exposure. Frederick and William Langenheim of Philadelphia used the process around 1849 for glass lantern slides and stereoscopic glass positives. About 1850, John A. Whipple made paper prints that he called crystalotypes from albumen-on-glass (and also from collodion wet-plate) negatives. A. and C.-M. Ferrier made glass stereos of the Alps and other scenic views using the albumen-on-glass process about 1851. Hippolyte Bayard and a few others also tried it, but collodion wet plates soon made the process obsolete.

albumen print. The most common kind of print in the nineteenth century, the albumen print was introduced by Louis-Désiré Blanquart-Evrard (French) in 1850 and was supplanted by the silver print around 1890. Collodion wet-plate negatives were ordinarily printed onto albumen papers.

Paper coated with albumen and salt solution was purchased and then light-sensitized by the photographer with silver nitrate; by 1872 presensitized paper was being sold. The paper, which was too slow for use in enlarging, was printed out (exposed to sunlight through a negative until the image became visible). The albumen gave the paper a smooth surface that reproduced more details than the salted paper used previously. The rather unattractive image color, variously described as yellow, cheesy, or bronze, was usually toned after exposure to sepia (a rich brown) in a gold-chloride solution that also helped prevent fading. Prints were often burnished to a glossy surface by being rubbed with a smooth-surfaced object or run through a pressure roller device.

Most albumen prints were mounted, because the paper was thin and unmounted prints curled, cracked, and tore easily. Surviving albumen prints that were stored in albums are frequently lighter around the edges, while those that were unprotected from light are often faded overall. The glossy surface of most albumen prints makes them distinguishable from salt prints, which have a smooth but sheenless surface. Distinguishing albumen prints from the silver prints that followed is sometimes more difficult. The image tone of albumen is brown, compared to the more neutral black of most silver prints; however, some silver prints were toned sepia and some early silver printing-out papers resemble albumen very much. The only sure tests are to clip off part of the print for an enzyme test (to determine the presence of albumen) or to use an instrument that gives a spectral analysis of the material; most collectors and museums are content with simply giving an educated guess.

ambrotype. A collodion wet-plate negative mounted in front of a dark surface so as to produce a positive image. Sometimes called a wet collodion positive on glass. Developed by Frederick Scott Archer and Peter Wickens Fry (English), details were first published in 1851. Popular until about the mid-1860s as a less expensive substitute for a daguerreotype.

The positive image of an ambrotype is brought about by positioning a black sheet behind the glass, as shown here, or by painting the reverse side of the glass black. Unidentified photographer. Untitled, ca. 1850s, quarter plate. (Courtesy Lee D. Witkin)

Unidentified photographer. *Chess Players*, ca. 1850s. Ambrotype, quarter plate. (Courtesy The Witkin Gallery)

After development the collodion negative was backed with black velvet, paper, metal, or varnish; sometimes the ambrotype was made directly on dark glass. It was then mounted in a case in the same way as a daguerreotype. Each image was one of a kind, since the negative actually became the positive.

At first glance, an ambrotype and a daguerreotype may appear similar — each is mounted in a small case with the image behind glass. However, unlike daguerreotypes, ambrotypes do not have a mirrorlike surface, nor will they appear to change from a positive to a negative image when held at different angles. Like daguerreotypes, most specimens are unidentified portraits, though outdoor scenes and other subjects can be found. *See also* cases.
ILLUSTRATED   This page.

aristotype. A printing-out paper used in the late nineteenth and early twentieth centuries, or a print made on such paper, in which the light-sensitive part of the emulsion was silver chloride. The emulsion base may be gelatin, albumen, or collodion; without destructive testing it is difficult to identify which base was used. Eugène Atget's vintage prints are sometimes called aristotypes.

artotype. *See* collotype.

autochrome. A type of positive color transparency patented in 1904 by Auguste and Louis Lumière (French). The autochrome became commercially available in 1907 and was the first color process to gain relative popularity.

Starch grains dyed to primary colors (red, green, and blue-violet) were sifted onto a sticky glass plate. The spaces between the grains were covered with a sifting of carbon and the plate was coated with a panchromatic emulsion. The screen of colored grains faced the lens and thus selectively exposed the emulsion. The plate was processed to produce a positive image of tiny specks of color. The plates are rather dark, and viewed through a magnifying glass the grains form an irregular mosaic pattern. For viewing some plates were fitted into a small folding frame called a diascope.

Alfred Stieglitz, Edward Steichen, Frank Eugene, and other members of the Photo-Secession group experimented with this process, and *Camera Work* (no. 22) reproduced several autochromes as four-color halftones. The Library of Congress has a large collection of autochromes by Arnold Genthe.
ILLUSTRATED   Stieglitz, color plate 1.

autotype. *See* carbon print.

blueprint. *See* cyanotype.

boudoir photograph. A size of print popular in the late 1870s for almost any subject. It measures 8¼ × 5 inches mounted.

bromoil print. Bromoil prints resembled oil prints, but unlike them were not limited to contact prints and could be used for enlargements. Developed by E. J. Wall and C. Welbourne Piper (English) in 1907, bromoil prints could be made in any one of a number of colors. They were popular with the Photo-Secessionists and other pictorial photographers.

A gelatin-bromide print was treated with a bichromate solution that both bleached out the dark silver image and chemically changed the gelatin so that it selectively absorbed oil pigment in proportion to the amount of silver in the original image. Thus the image could be produced in any color the photographer desired. In a bromoil transfer, a modification of the process, the inked image was transferred under pressure to another surface. Transferring the image several times in register increased the tonal control of the print. *See also* oil print; pigment printing.

cabinet photograph. A size of photograph popular from the mid-1860s to about 1900. Introduced by G. W. Wilson (Scottish) in 1862 for scenic views, it was suggested for portraits in 1867 by F. R. Window, a London photographer who found it better than the small carte-de-visite size for group shots and for picturing the billowing crinoline dresses then in fashion.

A 4×5½-inch paper print was mounted on a 4¼×6½-inch heavy card (sizes vary slightly). The photographer's name was often imprinted or embossed on the photograph or card mount, with an elaborate design advertising the studio gracing the back of the mount.

Surviving cabinet photographs are almost always portraits. Pictures of family, friends, and public figures were collected in albums just as cartes de visite had been collected in the 1850s–1860s. Photographs of stage performers were especially popular.

Among the makers of cabinet prints who photographed famous personalities in the nineteenth century were those that follow (*italicized* photographers have entries in chapter 5).
CANADA: *William Notman.* FRANCE: *Etienne Carjat, Nadar.* GREAT BRITAIN: William Barraud, Alexander Bassano, W. and D. Downey, Elliott and Fry, Hills and Saunders, A. and G. Taylor. UNITED STATES: *Mathew B. Brady,* Frederick Gutekunst, William Kurtz, José Maria Mora, *Napoleon Sarony.*
ILLUSTRATED This page; Ponti, page 256; Sarony, page 230.

Benjamin J. Falk. *The Little Mascot,* © 1890. Albumen cabinet card. (Courtesy The Witkin Gallery)

Byrne & Co. (imprint). *Their Majesties The Queen and Empress Frederick of Germany,* ca. 1898. Albumen cabinet card. (Courtesy Lee D. Witkin)

Advertising logo of Frederick Argall, mid-1890s. Typical cabinet-card back. (Courtesy The Witkin Gallery)

calotype. The first practical photographic process to produce a negative from which identical positives could be printed was patented by William Henry Fox Talbot (English) in 1840. Also known as the talbotype. The process was never as popular as the daguerreotype, but was used until both were supplanted in 1851 by the collodion wet-plate process.

An improvement upon Talbot's photogenic-drawing process, the calotype considerably shortened exposure of the negative. Sensitized paper was exposed only long enough to produce a latent (still invisible) image that was made visible by chemical development. The negative thus obtained was printed onto another sheet of sensitized paper to produce a positive image (a salt print).

Calotypes do not show as much detail as albumen or silver prints since paper fibers present in the negative as well as on the print surface break down the resolution of fine detail. Print color is usually brown, sometimes with red or purple overtones. Paper stock is thin, with a smooth but dull surface. Some calotype negatives were waxed before printing, thus they may be more or less translucent.

A list of some of the better-known nineteenth-century calotypists follows (*italicized* photographers have entries in chapter 5).
FRANCE: *Edouard-Denis Baldus, Hippolyte Bayard, Louis-Désiré Blanquart-Evrard, Maxime Du Camp, Gustave Le Gray, Henri Le Secq, Charles Marville, Charles Nègre,* Henri-Victor Regnault. GERMANY: Hermann Biow, Franz Hanfstaengl, Aloïs Löcherer, August Jakob Lorent, A. F. Oppenheim, Auguste Salzmann. GREAT BRITAIN: Philip Henry Delamotte, *Roger Fenton,* Peter Wickens Fry, *D. O. Hill and Robert Adamson,* Thomas Keith, John Shaw Smith, *William Henry Fox Talbot.* ITALY: F. Flachéron. UNITED STATES: Josiah Parsons Cooke, *Frederick and William Langenheim,* Victor Prevost.

See also waxed-paper negative.
ILLUSTRATED Marville, page 188; Salzmann, page 16.

carbon print. The first fully practical method for printing an image in a permanent pigment. Patented by Alphonse Poitevin (French) in 1855 and perfected by Joseph Wilson Swan (English) in 1866, carbon prints are also known as autotypes.

Carbon tissue (paper coated with gelatin and carbon or other pigments) was sensitized with potassium bichromate. Exposure under a negative selectively hardened the gelatin in proportion to the amount of light that reached it. A double transfer system was then used to transfer the image on the tissue to paper, since with only one transfer the image was reversed. Commercially made carbon tissue was available in many colors. Carbon prints generally are printed on smooth, heavy paper and show a slight relief in the image. They have a rich tonal range and are capable of showing fine detail. A deep brownish black is the most common color.

The tonal range, choice of colors (more than fifty), and permanence made the carbon process popular in the late nineteenth and early twentieth centuries for exhibition prints, especially among pictorial photographers. It was also used for facsimiles of drawings and other art works. *See also* pigment printing.

carbro print. A carbon print made from a silver print. The process was introduced by Thomas Manly (English) in 1905, first as the ozobrome, then with improvements as the carbro process. A silver print was pressed in contact with a specially treated carbon tissue. The gelatin of the carbon tissue hardened on contact with the silver and was then processed like an ordinary carbon print. Carbros had permanence and considerable choice of color as do carbon prints, though they are not quite as sharp. Enlarging was easy since the print was made from an ordinary silver print. The carbro process was popular with some pictorial photographers. Paul Outerbridge made full-color prints with this process; silver prints made from three color separation negatives were contacted to color carbon tissues in the three primary colors, and the carbon images were then transferred in register. *See also* carbon print; pigment printing.

carte de visite. A small-size print very popular in the 1860s, about as big as a visiting card or wallet-size portrait. It was popularized by Adolphe-Eugène Disdéri (French), who also invented a method of taking eight to ten carte photographs on one plate and then cutting apart the prints individually. The carte was immensely popular until about 1867, when the cabinet print gradually replaced it. Cartes continued to be made into the 1900s.

A 2¼ × 3½ -inch paper print was mounted on a 2½ × 4-inch card (sizes varied slightly). Most are albumen prints, although collotypes, woodburytypes, and other photomechanical printing processes were also used. The back of the carte often bears the photographer's name and address in an ornate design. American cartes may carry a tax stamp on the back (photographs sent through the U.S. mail between 1864 and 1866 were taxed as a source of Civil War revenue).

Cartes de visite were the first mass-produced photographs of famous people; pictures of rulers such as Napoleon III and Queen Victoria, entertainers, and other public figures were issued in large quantities and were collected in home albums along with portraits of family and friends. Most cartes are unidentified single portraits, but other subjects, such as celebrities, groups, travel views, and comic scenes, can be found.
ILLUSTRATED Facing page; Silvy, page 234.

cases. The cases into which daguerreotypes and ambrotypes were fitted are collectible items in their own right, and many collectors primarily seek cases, irrespective of the image, if any, inside.

The most common kind of daguerreotype case consisted of two thin pieces of wood covered with embossed leather and hinged together to open like a book. The image is typically overlaid with a thin gilt mat, covered with glass, and sealed with paper around the edges and back (this segment is often found today with the paper seal broken open or missing). A thin gilt frame called a protector or preserver was often placed on top, with flaps that bent behind the daguerreotype. The whole assemblage was fitted into the right side of the case, which was padded with a narrow strip of velvet plush around the edges. The left side was padded and covered with silk, satin, or velvet. Ambrotype cases were similar, though often less elaborate. Some cases or liners were stamped or embossed with the photogra-

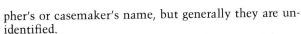

MILLIE CHRISTINE.

PERMANENT PHOTOGRAPH.   BROWN, BARNES & BELL.

pher's or casemaker's name, but generally they are unidentified.

After 1854, a new type of case was introduced that is a prime collector's item today. Thermoplastic "union" cases were made of shellac, finely ground wood fiber, and brown or black coloring. This mixture was heated until soft, then pressed into elaborate molds. Thermoplastic cases are today sometimes misidentified as gutta percha, a hard rubberlike substance which they resemble, but the thermoplastic is more brittle than gutta percha and can chip if mishandled. The designs appearing in relief molding on the union cases are commonly nature scenes: birds, flowers, fruits, et cetera. Designs less often found include Washington crossing the Delaware, Columbus landing in America, and other patriotic or religious motifs. Also relatively uncommon are papier-mâché cases inlaid with mother-of-pearl, tortoiseshell, or handpainted scenes. Generally, the earlier the case, the simpler it and its gilt protector are. ILLUSTRATED   Pages 28, 34.

Unidentified casemaker. Birds and flower-basket design, ca. 1853. Embossed leather case, sixth plate. See *cases* entry, page 32. (Courtesy Lee D. Witkin)

Critchlow & Co., casemaker. *The Tryst (The Appointment),* ca. 1857. Thermoplastic union case, 4×5 inches. See *cases* entry, page 32. (Courtesy Lee D. Witkin)

chromoscope. *See* Ives color process.

cliché-verre. An image drawn or painted on glass or film, then printed onto photographic paper.

collage. *See* combination print.

collodio-albumen. A variation of the collodion wet-plate process in which the collodion was coated with a layer of iodized albumen. The plates required more exposure than collodion wet-plates, but could be used dry. The process was invented by J. M. Taupenot (French) in 1855. *See also* collodion wet plate.

collodion dry plate. Any of several variations of the collodion wet-plate process in which the exposure could be made after the plate had dried. *See also* collodio-albumen; collodion wet plate.

collodion wet plate. A process in which the negative consisted of a collodion-based, light-sensitive emulsion coated on a sheet of glass. Also known as wet plate or wet-collodion process, from the time of its invention by Frederick Scott Archer (English) in 1851, it was the standard method of producing a negative until it was supplanted by the gelatin dry plate in the 1870s. Wet-plate negatives were usually printed on albumen paper.

The process was truly "wet" since immediately before the exposure the photographer had to coat the glass with collodion (nitrocellulose dissolved in ether and alcohol), sensitize it with potassium iodide and silver nitrate, then expose and develop it before the emulsion dried. Although it was necessary to transport virtually an entire darkroom to wherever a wet-plate photograph was to be made, the process quickly supplanted both the calotype, which did not produce as sharp a negative, and the daguerreotype, which did not produce a negative at all. It had the additional advantage of needing less exposure than either of the other two processes.

Collodion wet-plate negatives that survive generally have a thicker glass than the gelatin dry plates that followed. The emulsion coating is often uneven and in a raking light shows swirls, thick or thin areas, or minute bumps. The surface may be dull but will be shiny if varnish was applied as a protective coating. Emulsion color is gray or slightly yellow. By comparison, gelatin dry plates have thin glass with sharp edges and a blackish emulsion.

Collodion emulsion was overly sensitive to blue light; therefore skies in landscapes were overexposed and almost white. Some photographers, such as George N. Barnard, added clouds from a second (underexposed) negative during the printing process. *See also* ambrotype; collodio-albumen; tintype.
ILLUSTRATED   Le Gray, page 182.

collotype. A photomechanical printing process with an extremely fine grain; the basic technique was patented in 1855 by Alphonse Poitevin (French) and perfected by Josef Albert (German) in 1868. Similar processes include phototype, artotype, albertype, *Lichtdruck,* and heliotype.

A coating of bichromated gelatin on glass is first dried to produce a finely reticulated (wrinkled) surface. This replaces the halftone dot pattern that most other photomechanical processes employ to reproduce a photograph. The image is exposed on the gelatin, which hardens in proportion to the amount of light each area receives. Less exposed, less hardened areas absorb relatively more water and thus repel a greasy ink. The inked image is then transferred to paper. Some collotypes are of such high quality that they may be difficult to distinguish from original photographs; under magnification they show a fine, meshlike pattern, unlike the dots of a halftone.

O. G. Rejlander's illustrations for Charles Darwin's *The Expression of the Emotions in Man and Animals* (1872) was illustrated in heliotype, Eadweard Muybridge's *Animal Locomotion* (1887) in collotype. The process is still used for high-quality, relatively short printing runs.

color processes. A number of experiments were made in the last half of the nineteenth century to produce an image in full color. The Ives color process was one early attempt, but the autochrome process was the first to be relatively popular.

Most modern color materials, such as Type C prints and color transparencies, consist of three layers of emulsion, each sensitive to a different third of the color spectrum. During processing, compounds coupled to each layer of emulsion produce dyes that form the color image. *See also* autochrome; dye coupler print; dye transfer; instant photography; Ives color process; Type C print; *color plates following page 310.*

combination print. A print in which two or more separate images have been combined by multiple exposures, sandwiching negatives, collaging, or other means. A combination, or composite, print usually refers to multiple images printed onto the same sheet of paper, while a photomontage often, but not always, refers to two or more pieces of paper assembled in a collage.
ILLUSTRATED   Heartfield, page 159; Hyde, page 168; Moholy-Nagy, page 195; Robinson, page 223; Singley, page 44; Uelsmann, page 259.

composite print. *See* combination print.

contact print. A print that is made by placing a sheet of sensitized material in contact with a negative, then passing light through the negative to expose the material. A contact print is the same size as the negative. *See also* enlargement.

copy print. A duplicate print made by photographing an original photograph.

corona-discharge photograph. *See* Kirlian photograph.

crystallotype. *See* albumen on glass.

Curt-tone. *See* orotone.

cyanotype. A printing process based on the light sensitivity of iron salts. Also known as the blueprint or ferroprussiate process, cyanotype was first demonstrated successfully in 1840 by Sir John Herschel (English).

The light-sensitive emulsion consists of a mixture of ferric ammonium citrate and potassium ferricyanide, which darkens on exposure to light. The emulsion is coated on paper or cloth, and after exposure it is processed simply by washing in water to remove unexposed emulsion. The resulting print is quite stable and long lasting. It is possible to tone the brilliant blue image to black or other colors, but this is seldom done. The particular hue of a cyanotype would be called Prussian blue by a painter.

For many years the cyanotype's chief commercial use has been to reproduce drawings for engineers or architects. It was occasionally used by various photographers, including Thomas Anschutz, Edward S. Curtis, Thomas Eakins, Henri Le Secq, Charles F. Lummis, and others, and in the late nineteenth century was popular with amateurs. Robert Rauschenberg and Susan Weil used large-size commercial blueprint paper in the 1950s to make photographic images. Since the emulsion can be coated on any size of paper or cloth, it is popular among photographers who want to make oversize prints or three-dimensional objects or who want to combine it with other techniques such as gum-bichromate printing, hand art, collage, et cetera. Among contemporary photographers, Bobbi Carrey, Darryl J. Curran, Robert W. Fichter, Betty Hahn, Catherine Jansen, and others interested in expanded imagery have used the process.
ILLUSTRATED   Hahn, page 156.

daguerreotype. The first practical photographic process was invented by L. J. M. Daguerre (French) and announced on 7 January 1839. The daguerreotype is a direct positive image (without an intermediate negative) and was the principal photographic medium until the collodion wet-plate process supplanted it in the 1850s.

A copper sheet was coated with a light-sensitive silver halide. After exposure in a camera the silver was fumed with mercury vapor, which formed a frostlike coating on the exposed areas of silver. The lightest areas of the resulting image have heavy deposits of mercury, middle tones have less concentrated deposits, and the darkest areas are the plate itself. Hand tinting was sometimes added. Daguerreotypes were usually fitted into special cases; some were framed to be hung on a wall or mounted in lockets or other jewelry.

Daguerreotype images are reversed, just as a mirror image is reversed. A few are not reversed, since the photographer could attach a prism or mirror to the camera to correct the image, but this increased the required exposure time, so it was seldom done. Each image is one of a kind: a daguerreotype could not be duplicated unless it was copied onto another daguerreotype.

Daguerreotype sizes vary considerably, but are approximately (in inches):

double whole		quarter plate	$3\frac{1}{4} \times 4\frac{1}{4}$
plate	$8\frac{1}{2} \times 13$	sixth plate	$2\frac{3}{4} \times 3\frac{1}{4}$
whole plate	$6\frac{1}{2} \times 8\frac{1}{2}$	eighth plate	$2\frac{1}{8} \times 3\frac{1}{4}$
half plate	$4\frac{1}{4} \times 6\frac{1}{2}$	sixteenth plate	$1\frac{5}{8} \times 2\frac{1}{8}$

The sixth plate is the size most often found.

The silver coating of the daguerreotype base gives it a mirrorlike surface and readily distinguishes it from an ambrotype, with which it can be confused. The positive image is visible only from certain angles, and tilting the daguerreotype slightly will show a negative image on a highly reflective surface. An ambrotype will not do this.

The daguerreotypes most often found are portraits of unknown persons made by regional daguerreotypists who are only occasionally identified by name on the case. These range in quality from poorly executed (tonally flat, out of focus, unimaginative) to excellent (rich in tone and tinting, sharp and detailed, sensitive in posing and lighting). The most sought-after examples are any variation from the single portrait: outdoor scenes, funerary portraits, nudes, famous people,

Unidentified photographer. Brother and sister, ca. 1850s. Daguerreotype, larger than sixth plate. Light tinting throughout the plate. Folding leather case with satin liner; "Austria" stamped in gold on the inside of the case. (Courtesy Lee D. Witkin)

Unidentified photographer. Young boy, ca. 1850s. Daguerreotype, sixth plate, in passe-partout mount (one that has its central portion cut out to receive a picture, thus serving as a mat or border for it). Delicate coloring throughout the plate. A typical advertising label pasted on the back lists the studio location and two medals of honor awarded the photographer (who, however, is not named). A separate label further credits the piece with having once been part of the collection of A. Gilles, a well-known collector. (Courtesy The Witkin Gallery)

Albert Sands Southworth and Josiah Johnson Hawes; or Platt D. Babbitt. Niagara Falls, mid-nineteenth century. Daguerreotype, whole plate. (Courtesy IMP/GEH)

Death portrait, ca. 1850s. Daguerreotype, sixth plate. Soft tinting on the face and hands. Velvet pad bears: "By [S. L.?] Walker, Poughkeepsie, N.Y." (Courtesy Lee D. Witkin)

groups, soldiers, tradespeople with tools, and so forth. *See also* ambrotype; cases; etched daguerreotype; appendix A (list of daguerreotypists).
ILLUSTRATED   Facing page; pages 28, 42.

dallastype. *See* photogalvanography.

developing-out paper. Photographic printing paper that, in order to produce a visible image, must be chemically treated after exposure to light. Also called DOP. *See also* printing-out paper.

diascope. *See* autochrome.

DOP. *See* developing-out paper.

dry plate. *See* gelatin dry plate.

duotone. *See* halftone.

dye coupler print. A technical term for certain types of modern color prints. Generically, a Type C print (see entry).

dye transfer. A method of making color prints or transparencies that gives the maximum control of color balance and contrast. Dye transfer prints are longer lasting than Type C prints, though like all color images they are subject to fading in strong light.
  The original color image is divided into its primary colors by making separation negatives (three black-and-white negatives individually exposed through red, green, and blue filters). The negatives are used to make separation positives, or matrices, which are gelatin relief images that soak up dyes in proportion to the thickness of the gelatin. The dye-soaked images are transferred in exact alignment onto another sheet to reproduce the original color image.
  Dye transfer prints are made on thicker paper than Type C prints and have a smooth but not "plastic-coated" surface. *See also* Type C print.

enlargement. A print that is larger than its negative. Made by projecting a magnified image of the negative onto sensitized material. *See also* contact print.

etched daguerreotype. An early photomechanical process in which the printing plate was made out of a daguerreotype directly. Acid etched the exposed silver to produce a plate from which paper prints could be made. In 1841 Hippolyte Fizeau (French) improved the process by electrotyping the plate so that it gave more impressions. Volume two of *Excursions Daguérriennes,* published in 1842 by N.-M. P. Lerebours, included two prints from etched daguerreotypes. The process was not fully satisfactory, and a more common way of reproducing a daguerreotype was to redraw the image for an engraving.

ferroprussiate process. *See* cyanotype.

ferrotype. *See* tintype.

film. A flexible, transparent support coated with a light-sensitive emulsion. The combination in the late 1880s of gelatin emulsion and roll film led to the development of small, hand-held cameras, the widespread use of photography by amateurs, and the growth of the modern photoprocessing industry. Early films known as nitrate films used a highly flammable nitrocellulose base and are a safety hazard if collected (see Film Negatives, page 51). Modern films have a safe base of either cellulose acetate or polyester.

gelatin dry plate. A process for making negatives in which a sheet of glass was coated with an emulsion consisting of light-sensitive silver halides suspended in a layer of gelatin. In 1871 Richard Leach Maddox (English) suggested that gelatin might replace collodion as the medium for photographic emulsions. Unlike the collodion wet plate, gelatin emulsions were usable when dry and, in addition, needed much less exposure to light. By 1873, gelatin-coated dry plates were commercially available, and by the early 1880s they had almost completely replaced collodion wet plates for negatives. *See also* collodion wet plate (for information on distinguishing the two processes).

gelatin-silver print. *See* silver print.

generative systems. Image-making that involves the use of office-copy machines, teleprinters, video scanners, computer printouts, or other instant-feedback devices. In the U.S., Sonia Sheridan has innovated and experimented extensively with generative systems, as have Tom Barrow, Ellen Land-Weber, William Larson, Keith Smith, Arthur Taussig, Peter Hunt Thompson, and others.
ILLUSTRATED   Land-Weber, page 26.

glass-collodion positive. *See* ambrotype.

glass-plate negative. *See* collodion wet plate; gelatin dry plate.

goldtone. *See* orotone.

gravure. *See* photogravure.

gum-bichromate print. A print in which the image is formed of pigment, such as watercolor dyes, suspended in gum arabic sensitized with potassium bichromate. Paper is coated with the emulsion, dried, then contact printed (exposed to light passed through a negative in direct contact with the paper). The emulsion hardens where it is exposed to light and is made permanent simply by washing away the unexposed and thus still unhardened areas. The emulsion is spread on with a brush, so brush strokes or other irregularities may be visible. Image sharpness ranges from very slightly unsharp to quite fuzzy. Such a print can be made in any single color or in a combination of colors by recoating and reexposing the print. Gum printing was popular with pictorial photographers such as Robert Demachy and has been used by contemporary photographers such as Robert W. Fichter, Betty Hahn, and Scott Hyde. *See also* pigment printing.

halftone. The development of this photomechanical printing process led to widespread dissemination of photographic images because it enabled them to be printed on the same press as ordinary raised type. Several people experimented with the process, but the technique patented by Frederick Eugene Ives (U.S.) in 1878 is generally considered to be the first commercially successful method.

First the image is rephotographed through a screen of fine crosslines that converts the continuous tones of the original picture into a pattern of tiny dots that are larger and closer together in dark areas, smaller and farther apart in light areas. The dot-pattern image is then chemically etched onto a printing plate, which is then inked to transfer the image to paper.

Under magnification, the distinct dot pattern is visible in a halftone reproduction (as in the photographs in this book, which are reproduced as halftones). In duotone printing, the halftone image receives two press runs, with the second inking sometimes a different color from the first. The first published halftone appeared in the New York *Daily Graphic,* 4 March 1880.

heliography. The process by which the first permanent photographic images, heliographs, were produced by Joseph Nicéphore Niepce (French) in the 1820s. A polished metal or glass plate was coated with an asphalt (bitumen of Judea), then exposed to light under an engraving or in a camera obscura. The asphalt hardened where it was struck by light so that washing the plate in a solvent of lavender oil and light petroleum removed the unexposed and still-soft coating and permanently fixed the image.

Niepce's earliest heliograph was a contact print on glass of an engraving, 1822. His earliest surviving camera image was on pewter, 1826. He also experimented with the photomechanical printing applications of his process.
ILLUSTRATED   Niepce, page 14.

heliogravure. *See* photogravure.

heliotype. *See* collotype.

hyalotype. A term used by Frederick and William Langenheim for their prints made on glass or paper from albumen-on-glass or collodion wet-plate negatives, 1849 and after.

imperial photograph. A size of print made in the late nineteenth century, 7×10 inches mounted.

instant photography. Instant pictures were first demonstrated to the public in 1947 by Edwin H. Land (U.S.), the inventor, as the Polaroid Land process. Full development of the image takes place within seconds after exposure; negative, positive, and developing chemicals are squeezed together in a packet, usually by rollers in the camera. Kodak entered the market in the mid-1970s with its own brand of instant-picture cameras and film.

A number of photographers have adapted instant-picture materials to their individual needs. Ansel Adams has done considerable research and work with them. Marie Cosindas's portraits and still lifes are made with Polaroid color film. Les Krims, Norman Locks, Lucio Pozzi, and Lucas Samaras manipulate the surface of Polaroid SX-70 film to produce extensive form and color changes.
ILLUSTRATED   Samaras, color plate 7.

Ives color process. An early color process developed by Frederick Eugene Ives (U.S.) in 1891. Negatives were made through three different-colored filters. Positive transparencies made from the negatives were then projected or viewed, also through filters, to re-create the image in color. The devices for taking and for viewing the images were called chromoscopes or *krömsköps.*

ivorytype. A process in which a photographic image was transferred to imitation ivory or to glass backed with ivory-colored paper. Popular in the late nineteenth century, the ivorytype was intended to resemble a painting on ivory.

kallitype. A printing process invented by W. J. Nichol in 1889 that produced prints so like platinum prints that fine kallitypes were sometimes said to be indistinguishable from them. Kallitypes have a reddish brown to brown color; platinum prints are usually warm black, but are occasionally brown in tone. The kallitype was favored for its simplicity of preparation and for its modest expense. Paper coated with a mixture of ferric salt and silver nitrate was exposed to light passed through a negative; upon chemical development an image in silver was precipitated. *See also* platinum print.

Kirlian photography. A method of visually recording the aura that surrounds electrically conductive entities (such as coins, plants, and human beings) in a high-voltage, high-frequency electric field. Named after Semyon and Valentina Kirlian, who experimented with the effect in Russia as early as 1939, the process is also known as radiation-field or corona-discharge photography. Kirlian photography has gained attention from medical, parapsychological, and other investigators. A few photographers, such as Walter Chappell, have experimented with Kirlian photography as an expressive medium.

Kwik-Print. A commercial photographic process originally designed to produce proofs for printers. The Kwik-Print emulsion contains pigments (ready-mixed or added by the artist) and can be coated on paper or cloth. It produces an effect similar to a gum-bichromate print or, if used with color-separation negatives, a full-color print can be made. Eileen Cowin, Scott Hyde, Bea Nettles, and Charles Swedlund, among others, have used the process as a creative medium. Formerly called Kwik-Proof.
ILLUSTRATED   Nettles, color plate 6.

lantern slide. An image on glass, used for projecting photographs to audiences larger than could easily view prints. Standard sizes in the nineteenth century were 3½×4 inches in America and most of Europe, 3¼ inches square in Great Britain. Today, largely replaced by the slide (see entry).

Lichtdruck. *See* collotype.

magic lantern. *See* projector.

mammoth plate. A size of glass-plate negative (and print) used in the nineteenth century; dimensions varied — 18×22 inches was typical.

melainotype. *See* tintype.

microphotograph. A photograph greatly reduced in size (for example, microfilm). *See also* photomicrograph.

monoprint. A one-of-a-kind print that cannot be duplicated exactly because of complex darkroom manipulations or handwork on the print.

montage. *See* combination print.

multiple imagery. Two or more images exposed on the same piece of film or paper. *See also* combination print. Illustrated   Teske, page 251.

negative. An image in which the tones are the reverse of those in the original scene — that is, dark areas are light, light areas are dark. Also, the film, plate, or paper that was in the camera during exposure and that was subsequently processed to form a negative image. *See also* positive.

nitrate film. Film on a nitrocellulose base (note caution, Film Negatives, page 51). *See also* film.

oil print. A print in which the image consists of pigment suspended in gelatin. The process was popular with pictorial photographers at the turn of the century. Like other pigment processes, oil prints depended on the hardening of bichromated gelatin upon exposure to light. After exposure, the print was soaked in water, which penetrated the print in proportion to the softness of the gelatin. An oily pigment (of any color) was then brushed or rolled on, penetrating in inverse proportion to the amount of water the gelatin had absorbed to produce the final image. As in the bromoil process, the image could also be transferred. The pigment was usually daubed on with the bristle ends of a brush, so the image is often granular and may be uneven in tone. *See also* bromoil print; pigment printing.

orotone. An image printed on glass, then backed in gold. Also called goldtone or Curt-tone, it is often found in an ornate molded and gilded frame. Edward S. Curtis's photographs of Indians may be found as orotones. Illustrated   This page.

ozobrome. *See* carbro print.

Edward S. Curtis. *The Vanishing Race,* 1904. Orotone. (Courtesy Lee D. Witkin)

ozotype. An early pigment-print process, developed by Thomas Manly (English) in 1899, but soon replaced by his ozobrome process. *See also* carbro print; pigment printing.

palladiotype. *See* palladium print.

palladium print. A print similar to a platinum print that uses palladium salts instead of platinum. The process was popular for a while after World War I when the price of platinum was high, but the eventual scarcity of palladium made it obsolete. Also called palladiotype. *See also* platinum print.

panel photograph. A print-and-mount format popular in the late nineteenth century. Sizes varied, but a 4×8-inch print on a 7½×13-inch mount was common.

parmelian print. A term coined to describe silver prints in a 1927 Ansel Adams portfolio.

photoaquatint. *See* photogravure.

photoengraving. A photomechanical printing process in which the inked parts of the image are on the surface of the printing plate, while the uninked parts lie below the surface of the plate. Photoengravings can be printed simultaneously with ordinary raised metal type. Photoengraving is sometimes called photoetching, since the process involves etching with acid, but strictly speaking the terms are not interchangeable. *See also* photoetching.

photoetching. A photomechanical printing process in which the inked parts of the image lie below the surface of the printing plate. Photoetchings are sometimes loosely referred to as photoengravings.

Also, in recent usage, a work of metal with an etched-on image (for example, some works by Naomi Savage). *See also* photoengraving.
ILLUSTRATED N. Savage, page 231; K. Smith, page 237.

photogalvanography. An early photomechanical printing process, somewhat like photogravure, patented by Paul Pretsch (Austrian) in 1854. Dallastype is a variation of the process. Pretsch's *Photographic Art Treasures, or Nature and Art Illustrated by Art and Nature* (1856–1857) contained photogalvanographic illustrations by Roger Fenton, O. G. Rejlander, William Lake Price, and others.

photogenic drawing. The first photographic process to yield a negative from which positives could be printed; invented by William Henry Fox Talbot (English) in 1835, but not announced by him until 1839.

Talbot sensitized writing paper with silver chloride, exposed it to light until an image was visible, then fixed the resulting negative in a strong salt solution. His first images were photograms, negatives produced by exposing the sensitized paper beneath objects such as lace or botanical specimens. He also produced negatives in the camera obscura with exposures of thirty minutes to one hour. Sometime between 1835 and 1839 he began to make positive prints by exposing another piece of sensitized paper to light transmitted through the fixed negatives. Most of the surviving images by this process have badly faded; image color may be lilac, pink, or yellow.

photogenics. Lotte Jacobi's term for her darkroom-made abstractions.
ILLUSTRATED Jacobi, page 169.

photoglyphy. A photomechanical printing process that was the forerunner of modern photogravure processes. The process was patented in 1852 and 1858 by William Henry Fox Talbot (English). Talbot used an adaptation of the aquatint process in which a coating of powdered resin on the printing plate forms a grain that breaks up the image into tiny dots of ink. Examples of photoglyphy were included with the *Photographic News* (London) of 12 November 1858 and in September 1859. Distinct from the French term *photoglyptie* (*see* woodburytype).

photogram. A photographic image made without a camera by placing translucent or opaque objects on a sheet of film or sensitized paper, then exposing the sheet to light. Man Ray called his photograms rayographs; Christian Schad referred to his as schadographs. William Henry Fox Talbot's first photogenic-drawing images were photograms.
ILLUSTRATED Man Ray, page 22.

photogravure. A photomechanical printing process that gives prints (gravures or photogravures) of high quality; invented by Karl Klíč (Czech) in 1879. In earlier days, especially in Europe, the method was known as heliogravure; photoaquatint was an early modification of the process.

A copper plate is chemically etched to different depths in proportion to the darkness of the image in the original print. The darkest tones are etched the deepest, thus hold the most ink. Under magnification, the black areas in a gravure show a meshlike pattern or a solid inking instead of the distinct dot pattern of a halftone reproduction. Most of the reproductions in Stieglitz's magazine *Camera Work* were gravures and the process is still occasionally used for fine printing.

photolithography. A photomechanical printing process based on the mutual repulsion of water and oil (in the form of a greasy ink). The parts of an image exposed on a plate's light-sensitive coating attract or repel ink depending on the amount of light exposure each has received. Alphonse Poitevin (French) in 1855 developed the first practical process for reproducing photographs by lithography. A rare early example is John Pouncy's *Dorsetshire Photographically Illustrated* (1857). Photozincography is a similar early process. Modern photolithography employs a number of variations on the basic process.

photomechanical printing. Any process in which plates are prepared for a printing press with the aid of a camera. In an intaglio process, inked areas lie below the surface of the plate and clear areas rise above them. In a relief process, the inked areas are raised above the clear areas and can be printed on the same press as ordinary raised letterpress type. In a planographic process, both the inked and clear areas are on the surface of the plate, chemically separated.

Photomechanical processes include the following:
Intaglio: etched daguerreotype, heliography, photoetching, photogalvanography, photoglyphy, photogravure, woodburytype. *Relief:* halftone, photoengraving. *Planographic:* collotype, photolithography.
See also individual processes.

photomezzotint. *See* woodburytype.

photomicrograph. A photograph taken through a compound microscope, thus greatly enlarged. *See also* microphotograph.

photomontage. *See* combination print.

phototype. *See* collotype.

photozincography. *See* photolithography.

pigment printing. A general term that encompasses several processes. Photographers first sought a permanent-pigment image because calotypes and albumen prints tended to fade. In pigment processes the image consists of relatively stable pigment, such as a watercolor dye, suspended in a colloid, such as gelatin or gum arabic. The processes are based on the discovery by William Henry Fox Talbot (English) in 1852 that gelatin sensitized with potassium bichromate hardens on exposure to light and becomes insoluble in water. When a pigment is added to the gelatin, unexposed areas can be washed away, leaving an image formed by the pigment in the hardened gelatin.

Interest in pigment processes was revived in the late nineteenth century by pictorial photographers who liked the surface manipulations possible with many of these processes, as well as the prints' resemblance to other art media, such as charcoal drawings or etchings.

Pigment processes include: bromoil, carbon, carbro, gum bichromate, oil, ozobrome, ozotype.

See also individual processes.

platinotype. *See* platinum print.

platinum print. A print in which the final image is formed in platinum. The procedure was patented by William Willis (English) in 1873, and commercially coated papers were available until 1937, when the increased cost of platinum made the process impractical and the Platinotype Company, which had manufactured the paper, ceased to do so. Also called platinotype.

The process employs light-sensitive iron salts that during development cause platinum precipitate to form the image. Platinum prints were favored for their very long tonal scale — that is, for their numerous tones of gray, particularly in the midtone range between shadows and highlights. They are also more permanent than silver prints.

Platinum prints are distinguishable from most silver prints in several ways. Platinum lies on the paper surface; silver lies in the gelatin or albumen emulsion that coats the paper (salt prints are an exception). This causes a platinum image to appear embedded in the paper fibers and to be absolutely matte, while a silver image appears more glossy and seems to sit on top of the paper. It also causes platinum prints to remain flat, while silver prints often curl toward the emulsion side of the paper. Platinum prints may appear to have a flaky buildup in dark values, and they will not show the metallic discoloration sometimes found in old silver prints. Platinum prints generally appear to have less tonal contrast than silver prints and to have more delicate grays. The image color is usually warm black, but ranges from reddish brown to neutral black.

The process was popular for fine prints from the late nineteenth century until the process went out of use in the early twentieth century. The process today is restricted to a few photographers such as George Tice and Irving Penn who hand-sensitize their own printing paper. *See also* kallitype; palladium print.

Polaroid Land process. *See* instant photography.

POP. *See* printing-out paper.

portfolio. Usually, a number of loose or individually mounted prints presented as a unit in a box or other container. *See chapter 6.*

positive. An image in which the tones correspond to those in the original scene — that is, light areas are light in tone, dark areas are dark. *See also* negative.

postcard. The familiar picture postcard was introduced in the late nineteenth century and is a readily available and relatively inexpensive source of picture material. A postcard can be an actual photographic print or a gravure or halftone. Cards are collectible by period, region, subject matter, or just for the uniqueness of imagery. The photographer or photographic firm is usually unidentified, though there are exceptions (for example,

Francis Frith, F. Jay Haynes, and William Henry Jackson).

ILLUSTRATED   This page.

print. *See* silver print.

printing-out paper. Photographic printing paper that produces a visible image upon exposure to light, without any chemical development. Also called POP. A print on such paper is sometimes called a solio print. *See also* developing-out paper.

projector. A device for projecting and enlarging a photographic image for viewing. Today called a slide projector; earlier variations known as a magic lantern or stereopticon.

promenade photograph. A size of print made in the late nineteenth century, about $3\frac{3}{4} \times 7\frac{1}{2}$ inches.

radiation-field photography. *See* Kirlian photography.

rayograph. *See* photogram.

RC paper. *See* resin-coated paper.

resin-coated paper. A photographic printing paper, abbreviated RC, with a water-resistant resin coating that absorbs less moisture than conventional, uncoated papers during processing, thus shortening processing times. The surface of resin-coated papers has a characteristic "plastic" look when compared to uncoated papers. Type C color prints use resin-coated papers, and some manufacturers are preparing to resin-coat all their black-and-white printing papers.

Sabattier effect. A partial reversal of tones caused by re-exposure to light during development of film or paper. Named for Armand Sabattier (French) who in 1862 described the effect. Often termed solarization, though, strictly speaking, the two are different. *See also* solarization.

ILLUSTRATED   Walker, page 264.

Brück & Sohn, Meissen (imprint). *Karlsbad. Das Kurhaus,* ca. 1900. Gravure postcard. (Courtesy The Witkin Gallery)

salt print. The most common type of print until the invention of the albumen print in the 1850s. Similar to William Henry Fox Talbot's photogenic-drawing process, the salt-print process used an emulsion of common table salt (sodium chloride) plus silver nitrate, making light-sensitive silver chloride. Salt prints were often toned in gold or platinum to a brown or sepia color. The fixer that was used to remove unexposed silver and make the prints permanent was hypo rather than a salt solution as in Talbot's method. As in a platinum print, the image in a salt print appears to be embedded in the paper fibers, rather than in a surface coating of albumen or gelatin emulsion.

schadograph. *See* photogram.

silver print. The standard contemporary black-and-white print, consisting of paper coated with gelatin containing light-sensitive silver halides. Also called gelatin-silver print, or often, simply, print. In most sources, if no other designation is given, a "print" or "photograph" can be assumed to be a black-and-white print on gelatin-silver paper. Printing papers coated with gelatin were introduced in 1882 and had replaced albumen papers by about 1895. *See also* albumen print; platinum print (for information on distinguishing from silver prints).

slide. An image, usually on film, mounted in a frame of cardboard or other material so it can be readily inserted into a projector or viewer. Most slides are 35mm (1×1½-inch) positives in color. *See also* lantern slide.

solarization. A reversal of tones caused by massive overexposure of photographic materials. A common, though inaccurate, term for the Sabattier effect. *See also* Sabattier effect.

solio print. *See* printing-out paper.

stabilized print. A print that is processed by chemically converting the unexposed light-sensitive silver halide to a relatively stable, colorless compound instead of removing it from the print by fixing and washing. Stabilization processing provides usable prints in a matter of seconds, so it is used by newspapers, for example, if a print is needed in a hurry. However, the prints remain laden with chemicals and will contaminate other photographic materials if they are stored together. Stabilized prints can later be fixed and washed by ordinary methods to make them safe; if this is not done the image will begin to fade within a month to a year or so, depending on storage conditions. Freshly made stabilized prints have an ammonia-like odor, and they can also be identified by testing for residual silver (see page 59).

stannotype. *See* woodburytype.

stereo; stereograph. *See* stereoscopic photography.

stereopticon. *See* projector. (Unrelated to stereoscopic photography.)

stereoscope. *See* stereoscopic photography.

stereoscopic photography. The production of a pair of images (a stereograph or stereo) that gives the illusion of depth when seen through a special viewer (a stereoscope) that presents one of the pair to each eye. The effect depends on normal human binocular vision, in which the brain fuses the slightly different images seen by each eye into a single image that appears to have three dimensions.

In 1832, before the invention of photography, Charles Wheatstone (English) demonstrated the effect by making pairs of drawings from slightly different viewpoints. Later, stereoscopic photographs were taken either with a camera with two lenses side by side — separated by about 2½ inches, the approximate distance between the pupils of a human's eyes — or with a single-lensed camera that first took one picture, then was moved slightly to one side for a second exposure.

An early craze for collecting and viewing stereos as home entertainment peaked in the 1860s, and the London Stereoscopic Company, E. and H. T. Anthony and Company, the American Stereoscopic Company, Kilburn Brothers, George Stacey, D. Appleton and Company, and others produced millions of landscapes, celebrity portraits, comic cards, still lifes, and other stereo views. Another peak of popularity came in the 1890s; Underwood and Underwood, the Keystone View Company, H. C. White and Company, Griffith and Griffith, and others again distributed huge quantities of views. Until the development of photomechanical printing processes, stereographs were the main means for the dissemination of photographic images. Daguerreotype, glass, or tissue stereos are uncommon. More often found are card stereos, a pair of prints mounted side by side on a single card about 3½×7 inches or slightly larger. ILLUSTRATED This page, facing page, page 44.

William Edward Kilburn. Portrait, ca. 1850s. Stereo daguerreotype. Folding stereo viewing case registered in England by Kilburn in January 1853. (Courtesy Lee D. Witkin)

Printed information of some sort frequently appears on the back of a stereo card. One might find: a numbered listing of a series offered by the publisher; a label identifying the view; the photographer's studio location, credentials, and services offered; various testimonials; or even an advertisement for tobacco. (Courtesy Lee D. Witkin)

Unidentified photographer. *Howard University, Washington, D.C.*, ca. 1870s. Albumen stereograph. (Courtesy Lee D. Witkin)

A. D. Bonney, Portland, Maine (imprint). Interior of a shoe factory, ca. 1880s. Albumen stereograph. (Courtesy Lee D. Witkin)

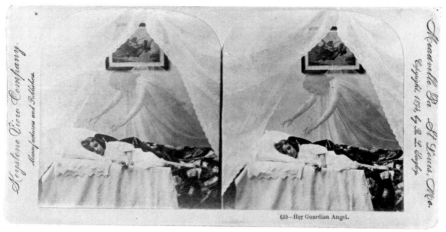

B. L. Singley. *Her Guardian Angel*, ©
1894. Silver stereograph combination
print. Published by Keystone View
Company. (Courtesy Lee D. Witkin)

Léon and J. Lévy. *Séracs avant la jonc-
tion*, ca. 1870s. Positive collodion stereograph on glass. (Courtesy Lee D.
Witkin)

talbotype. *See* calotype.

tintype. A variation of the collodion wet-plate process in
which the emulsion was coated on a sheet of black
japanned iron to produce a direct positive image. Also
called ferrotype or melainotype. Patented by Hamilton
Smith (U.S.) in 1856, the tintype was cheap, sturdy, and
quick to produce, though usually of poorer image quality than the ambrotype.

Tintypes were popular with street and itinerant photographers, particularly during the Civil War, when soldiers sent home pictures of themselves in uniform and
carried with them portraits of loved ones. Tintypes are
often about 2½ × 3½ inches or smaller, down to the tiny
gem size of ½-inch square or less. They were collected
in albums, sometimes mounted in jewelry, album covers, fans, or other objects. Tintypes were made by street
photographers well into the twentieth century, and they
are still sometimes made as a nostalgia item.

An unmounted tintype is immediately identifiable by
the thin metal plate on which the emulsion was coated.
Some tintypes are mounted in daguerreotype cases, but
they can be readily distinguished from daguerreotypes
by their nonreflective surface. It is more difficult to
distinguish a cased tintype under glass from a cased
ambrotype: a tintype usually has a duller, less contrasty
image; sometimes creases or ripples in the metal of the

tintype are visible. Unless a tintype is of an identifiable
scene or person or of unusual subject matter or mounting, it is generally worth considerably less than an ambrotype. *See also* collodion wet plate.

toning. A chemical process that alters the appearance of
a print by converting the image to, or coating it with,
another compound. Sometimes toning is done primarily
to intensify the print contrast and the image color
changes very slightly. Other toners produce a distinctly
brown, blue, or other hue. Selenium or gold toners are
often used in archival processing since they give chemical protection against image deterioration.

transparency. Any image on a transparent base such as
film or glass that can be viewed by transmitted light.
See also slide.

Type C print. A term for a color print made from a color
negative or color transparency. Color-sensitive layers in
the paper, each responsive to a different segment of the
color spectrum, respond proportionately to colors in the
negative or transparency. Development produces layers
of superimposed color which appear as a full-color image. The name derives from Kodak Ektacolor Paper
Type C, which dominated the color-print market for
many years. Kodak prints are currently made on Ekta-

color RC paper, and several processes by other companies — Cibachrome, for example — have become popular, but *Type C* is still often used as a generic term. *See also* dye transfer (for information on distinguishing the two processes).

uranium print. Les Krims's term for a print treated with a uranium-nitrate toner. Also, a print from a now obsolete nineteenth-century process.

vandyke process. An early-twentieth-century process that uses an emulsion containing light-sensitive iron and silver salts to produce a brown image.

vortograph. A term used by Alvin Langdon Coburn to describe his abstract images made with a kaleidoscope device.

waxed-paper negative. A calotype improvement introduced by Gustave Le Gray (French) in 1850 and used until supplanted by the collodion wet plate. The paper was waxed before sensitizing and gave greater detail than an ordinary calotype, but the process required considerably more exposure and thus was used primarily for architecture or landscape views.

wet collodion positive. *See* ambrotype.

wet plate. *See* collodion wet plate.

woodburygravure. *See* woodburytype.

woodburytype. A photomechanical printing process that produced very fine prints. Developed in 1865 by Walter Bentley Woodbury (English), it was used for book illustrations and other relatively large-quantity printings from about 1875 to the end of the century. Known in French as *photoglyptie*; stannotype and photomezzotint are similar processes.

A mold of an image was prepared in which the deepest parts of the mold were to be the darkest in the print. Pigmented gelatin was poured into the mold, a sheet of paper was laid on top, and the gelatin was pressed against the paper. The thickest areas of the colored gelatin were the darkest in the print. Prints were then generally trimmed flush and mounted onto another page. An exception is the woodburygravure process (1891 and after) in which the print was pressed face down against another page and the backing paper peeled off so that the image appeared to be printed directly on the page.

Dark red-brown is the most common color, although theoretically the woodburytype could be made in any single color. A black image is uncommon. The prints are practically grainless and may be almost impossible to distinguish from photographs because no screen or dot pattern is visible. Occasional dark specks that look like tiny splashes of pigment can be seen in the light areas of most woodburytypes. Their surfaces are generally shiny and may show uneven surface reflectivity caused by buildup of pigment in dark areas. John Thomson's *Street Life in London* (1877–1878) was illustrated with woodburytypes.

ILLUSTRATED   This page; Carjat, page 108; Thomson, page 252.

Nadar. *Lina Munte.* From *Paris-Portrait*, May 1879. Woodburytype illustration printed by Lemercier et Cie, mounted within printed borders. (Courtesy The Witkin Gallery)

Proper matting and framing not only enhance the appearance of works of art but also help to preserve them while on display. Appropriate mats and frames are especially important in pro-tecting the surface of photographs, which are particularly vul-nerable to fingerprints, scratches, and similar damage. (Photo by Scott Hyde)

4

The Care and Restoration of Photographs

With every newly purchased photograph a collector has to make some important decisions. How should the image be framed and where should it be hung? If it is not going on display, how should it be wrapped and stored? Perhaps it is a rare but deteriorated item: a tarnished daguerreotype landscape or an unusual but yellowed early movie still. Can it be cleaned? Should it be treated? Is it best to leave it as is?

These decisions are important, because with improper care photographs can fade, stain, discolor, abrade, or otherwise deteriorate in ways that are sometimes irreversible. The collector who is aware of methods of *conservation* will be able to maintain a photograph in its current condition. Knowledge of basic *restoration* techniques is useful when the condition might be improved.

The field of photographic care is a relatively new one. Photography itself is less than 150 years old, and during much of that period photographs were not always treated with the respect that they command today. Glass plates bearing historically important negatives such as portraits of Lincoln were "salvaged" around the turn of the century by scraping off the emulsion, then selling the glass. A monumental collection of Mathew Brady's Civil War negatives was so badly stored by the U.S. War Department during the late nineteenth century that many of the images were permanently lost. Many other photographic horror stories tell of images that would be treasured today being damaged or destroyed through carelessness or neglect.

Even though important photographs are less likely to be deliberately destroyed today, relatively little accurate and up-to-date information on their care and restoration exists. Many different photographic processes have been used at various times and each has particular characteristics and problems. The currently standard gelatin-silver print on paper is a multilayered combination of complex and interacting materials with characteristics that are still not fully understood. And a conservation procedure that is suitable for a freshly made object may be damaging when that object is fifty or a hundred years old. There are few qualified photographic conservators, even in museums. Only a few places, such as the Smithsonian Institution in Washington, D.C., and the International Museum of Photography at the George Eastman House in Rochester, New York, are doing research or disseminating current conservation information.

Fortunately, the growing interest in collecting has led to increased activity in institutions, and curators, photographers, and collectors themselves are investigating the best means of caring for photographs. The collector needs to be aware that recommended practices may change as new information is established. For example, the once common practice of storing items in glassine envelopes is now not recommended, because most glassine deteriorates and emits damaging compounds. Other practices are tentatively recommended — for example, storing paper prints with paper that is high in alkalinity (discussed later).

This chapter describes conditions that can seriously damage photographs, as well as the current options of care and restoration that are available to collectors. Different levels of care exist. The museum ideal of total atmospheric control and steel-cabinet storage may be impossible for an individual collector, but reasonable protection from sunlight and damaging substances is within the reach of anyone. Suppliers for the special products described here are listed on page 61.

How Damage Occurs and How to Prevent It

A number of very common situations are potentially dangerous to photographs. Collectors who are aware of the factors that *could* cause damage can at least minimize the exposure of their collections to them and so reduce the chances that irreparable changes will take place. Photographs can be damaged by careless handling, excessive exposure to light, extremes of heat and humidity, pollutants, residual chemicals, insects, and destructive attempts at restoration.

Handling

Careful handling is the simplest and one of the most important conservation techniques. Museum practice is to handle photographs as little as possible, to wash hands before touching prints, and sometimes to wear clean cotton gloves as well. Photographs should be picked up by their edges, using both hands, with the fingers supporting the print from underneath and thumbs or palms steadying the print at its edges. Avoid touching the mount surface and especially the image surface to prevent depositing body oils or chemicals, which can easily cause smudges or stains and may react with print compounds to cause permanent damage. One of the most frequent handling mistakes is to pick up a print by one corner; doing so can cause the weight of the print to bend or crease it, and there is a good chance of leaving a fingerprint on the corner. Avoid sliding one print against another, since this can cause abrasions. Dropping a print or putting things on top of it can also cause serious damage. Once a print has been physically damaged, there is often little that can be done to repair it.

Light

Light is energy. Upon exposure to light, molecules in papers and photographic emulsions absorb some of this energy, increasing the possibility of chemical changes. This is readily seen with newsprint, which quickly yellows if left in the sun. Light causes colors to fade, causes some substances to discolor, and makes paper brittle by breaking down fiber compounds. Short wavelengths, those toward the blue and ultraviolet end of the light spectrum, are the most damaging. Daylight is rich in blue and ultraviolet light, as are many fluorescent lamps, while incandescent tungsten lamps (ordinary household bulbs, for example) are relatively low in such rays. Never hang prints in direct sunlight, and avoid strong, indirect daylight, especially for long periods of time. Frequently change prints that must hang in strong window light or, better yet, hang a plant there instead. Filters are available for fluorescent fixtures to remove most of the ultraviolet radiation. Some conservators recommend ultraviolet-shielding Plexiglas instead of ordinary glass for framed photographs. (See the information on framing, page 56.)

Heat and Humidity

Controlling temperature and humidity is important because lowering them decreases unwanted chemical activity. Although excessively low humidity is sometimes the cause of brittleness and cracking, high humidity is much more often the problem. Microorganisms in the atmosphere (such as the molds that can stain or yellow prints) need only moisture and nutrients to commence growth. High humidity supplies moisture; the nutrients are at hand in the gelatin in emulsions and in the starch in paper or adhesives. Foxing, a mold growth that causes rust-colored spots, is a common result of high humidity. Fading due to oxidation of silver is also related to high humidity. The safest and most effective way to prevent these problems is to keep the humidity low. Good circulation of air also helps.

A typical museum goal for photographs is a constant atmosphere of 18° Celsius (65° Fahrenheit) temperature and 40% relative humidity. This is difficult to achieve but a private collector can at least avoid extremes of heat and humidity (for example, near a fireplace, on top of a radiator, in a damp cellar) and try for a temperature no higher than 21°C. (70°F.) and a relative humidity kept below 60%. Avoiding extreme fluctuations in heat and humidity is also desirable, since this can cause repeated — and damaging — swelling and contracting of the emulsion or, in extreme cases, condensation of moisture. Air conditioners, heaters, dehumidifiers, and humidifiers are useful for large areas; bags of silica gel will remove moisture from closed containers.

In areas such as the tropics, where the relative humidity frequently rises above 65%, fungus attack can be so damaging as to destroy the image entirely. A fungus-preventing print bath (marketed as Rohm and Haas Hyamine 1622) is available, but this is intended for amateur or commercial prints and should not be used on a collectible photograph. Thymol fumigation arrests mold, and although it is safe for paper, its long-term effect on photographic emulsion is as yet untested. Keeping the relative humidity low as a precaution is much safer. (For information on fresh-air treatment for a moldy print, see page 60.)

Pollutants

Two types of exterior pollutants can cause image deterioration — general atmospheric pollutants and those introduced by storage with or near improper materials. The most widespread atmospheric pollutant, sulfur dioxide, combines with oxygen and moisture to produce sulfuric acid, a corrosive substance that discolors prints and makes them brittle. Ammonia, ozone, and nitrogen oxides in smog, as well as fumes from fresh paint, solvents, motor exhausts, burning tobacco or wood, certain adhesives, and rubber-based products (including rubber bands) can also damage the image if exposure to them is excessive. Airborne dust particles can be destructive: they may be chemically active, can serve as nutrients for microorganisms, and can abrade a print if it slides across another surface. Airborne salt in sea air attracts moisture, which can activate damaging chemical reactions.

The best control for atmospheric pollutants is filtering (again, this is the museum optimum). Air is first passed through particulate filters to remove airborne solids, then through activated-charcoal filters to remove most harmful vapors. The private collector can at least try to maintain as clean an atmosphere as possible.

Residual Chemicals

Since the fibrous base of photographic paper absorbs chemicals, prints must be carefully processed. Chemicals remaining due to poor original processing are extremely damaging. Residual fixer (hypo) left by improper fixing or incomplete washing eventually yellows and fades the image, showing first in lighter tones. Complex silver compounds left by inadequate fixing will yellow, then darken the lighter print tones. Not only will the chemical-laden print be damaged but the chemicals can transfer to properly processed materials if the two are brought into contact. Damage may not be visible for years or may appear so gradually that it is hard to notice.

Insects

Insects eat emulsion gelatin, paper, and certain glues such as wheat-flour paste and can also be attracted by the microorganisms that grow on prints in high humidity. In addition to direct physical damage, insect secretions can stain a print. Prints that are removed and viewed from time to time are in less danger than those that are stored away for months on end. If insects are a problem, place bait outside storage containers, but not near prints.

Restoration Dangers

While restoration techniques are useful and sometimes necessary, it is wise not to be eager to improve an image. All procedures, without exception, carry some risks and can produce effects that are much worse than the condition the restoration was trying to improve; considerable damage has been caused while trying to fix minor problems. Private collectors can easily follow museum practice here: spend time and money on proper display and storage — that is, on conservation — before attempting restoration. If an image has deteriorated only moderately in a hundred years, proper display and storage will be much better than trying to return the image to a pristine condition. These cautions do not mean that restoration is always too dangerous to attempt, but are simply meant to remind collectors that any photograph that is worth the trouble of restoring is also important enough to be protected from unnecessary risks. In fact, the more important the photograph is, probably the less should be done to it from a restoration standpoint. The following section, which offers specific information about individual processes and collectible objects, describes some of the tradeoffs between possible improvement and possible damage. (See the bibliography on page 61 for other sources of information on care and restoration.)

Readers of care-and-restoration literature should remember that much basic research is just now being done and that some of the practices described in even recent publications are outmoded. Also, a more conservative attitude seems to be surfacing toward many restoration techniques — which are much less freely recommended than they once were. The pros and cons of any type of treatment should always be considered carefully beforehand.

Care and Restoration of Specific Items

Chapter 3 contains more-detailed descriptions of most of the media mentioned here.

Daguerreotypes

The daguerreotype image is an extremely thin layer of mercury on a silver-coated metal plate, which is protected by a piece of glass. Daguerreotypes are often discolored by purplish or orange-brownish tarnish, especially around the edges of the plate. This is the same tarnish that discolors silverware, and it can be removed with a cleaning solution of thiourea and phosphoric acid (for formula and procedure, see page 58). Some collectors use commercial tarnish-removing baths such as Dip-It, but such products' formulas vary without notice, so they are not recommended. It is safer to mix a solution from known ingredients. For reasons that will become obvious, polishing pastes are never used.

Some publications seem to recommend cleaning as almost a standard procedure, to be done with any daguerreotype, but, in fact, there are a number of risks involved. The surface of a daguerreotype is extremely fragile, and anything that rubs across the plate, such as a fingertip or the covering glass, will scratch the image irreparably. The chemical formula generally works well, but not always: surface contaminants, residual thiourea, or careless drying may leave surface spots; if the silver coating of the plate is too thin, there is danger of it being removed along with the tarnish. Due to the risks, some conservators do not recommend cleaning unless the tarnish is so bad that the image is almost totally obscured. Sometimes the image can be greatly improved simply by cleaning the protective glass. Color may be lost by cleaning a hand-tinted daguerreotype.

An original daguerreotype mounting generally includes a strip of paper tape holding together the edges of the image plate, its brass overmat, and the cover glass on top of the mat. To some collectors the value of the original tape can outweigh the importance of cleaning, and they will not clean a well-taped daguerreotype unless it is in extremely poor condition. If the photographer's name is on the brass mat, breaking the paper-tape seal calls this valuable identification into question, since any image can be placed under the mat once the tape is removed.

Ambrotypes

The ambrotype is a glass-plate image backed with a black surface such as paper, cloth, or varnish. Like the daguerreotype, the image surface is protected with a covering piece of glass. If the image looks damaged, it may simply be deterioration of the black backing. Carefully disassemble the parts and replace the backing with good-quality black paper — ideally, fully blackened, archivally processed photographic paper or film. Clean the image surface only if absolutely necessary (for procedure, see page 58). Color may be lost by cleaning a hand-tinted ambrotype.

Tintypes

These small photographs on metal look sturdy but they can be bent or damaged relatively easily. The emulsion may be so dried out as to be powdery and quite fragile. Rust is another problem, one which is more likely to occur on the back than the front of the image. If it is absolutely necessary to remove excessive surface dirt, see the cleaning procedure on page 59.

Glass-plate Negatives

The image-carrying emulsion of a glass-plate negative may be either gelatin or collodion (albumen plates also exist, but they are very rare). The most vulnerable part of a glass plate, besides its breakability, is the bond between emulsion and glass. The deterioration of this bond can be accelerated by wetting the plate, for example, to clean it. This is particularly true with gelatin since it swells as it absorbs moisture, and this swelling may also embed dirt permanently in the emulsion. (See chapter 3, *collodion wet plate*, for information on how to distinguish it from a gelatin plate.) The safest treatment for a glass-plate negative is to leave it as is, but if it is absolutely necessary to remove excessive surface dirt, see the procedure on page 59.

Glass plates are easily scratched. Handle them carefully, store them in individual envelopes, and avoid sliding them across other surfaces. Store glass plates on edge instead of in stacks.

Film Negatives

Film washes clear of residual chemicals relatively easily and so is likely to have been properly processed originally. However, it sometimes becomes contaminated when stored with poorly processed materials. If the film is no more than a few years old and is known to have been contaminated or improperly processed, it can be refixed and rewashed (see page 60). However, if the film is old, storing it carefully but otherwise leaving it alone is probably safer than attempting reprocessing. Store film that is suspected of contamination away from other photographic materials.

Flexible film with a nitrocellulose base (also called nitrate film) should not be stored with other photographic materials since it decomposes readily and, in the process, emits corrosive acids. It is highly flammable, even explosive, and temperatures as low as 49°C. (120°F.) can cause it to ignite. Problems are most likely to occur when large quantities of film are stored in small, unventilated spaces. Since nitrate films break down unpredictably and in ways that cannot be restored, they should be copied, stored in a cool place where they can be checked from time to time, then discarded when they begin to deteriorate.

Nitrocellulose films were manufactured between 1888 until as late as 1951, though acetate "safety" films began to replace them about 1930. To test for nitrocellulose, immerse a small piece of film in trichlorethylene. (*Caution*: Use in a well-ventilated area and store as directed.) Nitrate film sinks, safety film floats.

Paper Prints

Theoretically a print that is suspected of chemical contamination can be tested for residual hypo or silver and can be refixed or rewashed if necessary. But it is difficult to make blanket recommendations about paper prints since the age of the print, the original processing, the conditions under which it was stored, and other factors all affect a print's response to reprocessing. Even testing procedures such as Kodak's Formula HT-2 test for residual hypo or its Formula ST-1 test for residual silver can leave a permanent spot on the print, an effect worse than simply leaving the print as is. And there are a number of other reasons why reprocessing is of questionable value. It is difficult to rewash a fragile print effectively. Hand-tinting or inscriptions on the print may bleed through or run and stain the print. If the print is mounted on another sheet of paper, removing the print to reprocess it may cause more damage than leaving it as it is. Certainly prints that are suspect should at least be isolated to avoid contaminating other prints. And, given a clear need, refixing and rewashing can be done (for procedures, see pages 59–60).

Stabilized prints (see chapter 3 entry) are one case in which reprocessing is a clear need. These prints (not to be confused with instant photographs such as Polaroid prints) are processed in special rapid-access machines when photographs are needed right away but long-term permanence is not required. Processing chemicals are not removed, but are merely stabilized for a short period. Unless prints are refixed and rewashed they will fade within several days to a few years, depending on storage conditions. Until they are reprocessed, they stay loaded with contaminating chemicals and should not be stored with other photographic materials. Stabilized prints fade somewhat with reprocessing, but will fade much more without it. A test for residual silver (see page 59) identifies them.

The long-range life of resin-coated (RC) papers (see chapter 3 entry) is not known, since the stability of the resin coating has not yet been established. Stored under optimum conditions, they may have the same stability as ordinary silver prints that are not resin-coated. However, under storage conditions that are less than perfect, RC prints will deteriorate faster than conventional papers. They are particularly vulnerable to ultraviolet light.

Photographs may show specks, small spots, or

other local imperfections. If they can be ignored, let them be. No collector would take pencil to a Dürer print to "improve" it, and a valuable photograph should not be treated casually either. However, if it is impossible to resist trying to darken white or light specks (a procedure called spotting), many museum curators recommend using a high-quality artist's pigment watercolor instead of a liquid photographic dye such as Spotone, since Spotone may fade more slowly than the print. Even more important, Spotone mistakes are more difficult to correct, while a professional conservator can treat a watercolor error more easily. On the other hand, since Spotone sinks into the emulsion, the surface reflectivity of the treated area may match the rest of the print (particularly a glossy-surfaced one) better than it will with watercolors; also, a specific tone is usually easier to match with Spotone. Practice first before using either method, and also remember that the more valuable the print is, the less you should touch it.

Color Photographs

Color prints and film are generally less stable than black-and-white materials, with the exception of pigment processes such as carbro prints. Colors will fade and color balance will change faster than black-and-white materials deteriorate when stored under similar conditions. Light and heat are the prime destructive factors. For maximum protection store color materials away from light altogether, use ultraviolet-filtering Plexiglas for their short-term display, do not leave them on permanent display, and do not expose them to strong light at any time. Store in a cool, dry area: temperature below 21°C. (70°F.), relative humidity about 40%, if possible. Store as much as possible away from atmospheric or other contaminants.

Other Photographic Processes

In recent years many new processes have been combined with photography — for example, vacuum-formed plastic — and many old processes, such as gum-bichromate printing, have been revived and adapted. Good photographic storage is probably safe for them, but if a work in an unusual process is acquired, ask the artist, dealer, or other specialist if there are any special handling or storage procedures to follow.

Books

As the collectibility of photographs has increased in recent years, so has the demand for photographically illustrated books. In general, the same storage conditions suitable for photographs are also desirable for books, with a few extra precautions. Insects may be even more of a problem with books than with prints since the spine and inside covers offer excellent hiding places for them. Opening a book flat may weaken or break the spine, particularly with older, somewhat brittle, bindings, so it is a good idea to support the front or back cover so the book opens to a bit less than a 180° angle. An original dust jacket in good condition adds to the value of a book, and it is worthwhile to invest in transparent protective book covers, which are made to fit most book sizes. The most valuable books can be kept inside closed cases, or at least in individual protective envelopes. Store books upright, snugly, but not tightly, on the shelf. Books too large to fit upright on the shelf can be stored flat, if not in too high a stack; storing a book with its spine facing up or down may put excessive pressure on the binding. Photographs mounted face to face should be interleaved with a soft, museum-quality tissue paper.

Matting

If a paper print is acquired unmatted (that is, if it is loose and not attached to a backing), it is necessary to decide whether to leave it as is or to mat it before framing or storing it. One reason for matting a print is aesthetic: it helps present the image in the way the photographer or collector wants it shown. Most mats provide a border of blank area around the print in order to set it off from other objects and focus attention on the print itself. Edward Weston trimmed his prints to the edge of the image, then dry mounted each on a fairly stiff white board, leaving a wide border around the print. Diane Arbus left a margin of white photographic paper around her images and said she liked the ripply border of a large unmounted print. Other photographers may bleed mount a print (trim the image to the edges of the mount) or they may print a black border around the image.

Another purpose for matting a print is so that it can be safely handled and displayed. One type of protective mat is illustrated here. It consists of a *backing board* attached with a *hinge* of gummed linen tape to an *overmat* with a *window* cut in it through which the *print* is viewed. There must be some means of attaching the print to the backing, such as *photo corners*. A lightweight, loose *cover sheet*, or interleaver, separates the overmat from the print. The cover sheet prevents abrasion of the print surface when prints are stacked. It is more convenient but less protective of the photograph to put the cover sheet on top of the overmat rather than underneath it.

Unmatted photographs can be hinged or slipped into corner holders or dry mounted directly to the backing board. Photographs that are already attached to a backing can simply be overmatted. If the original mounting is itself valuable (for example, for its signature) or if it is fragile, the entire print and original mount can be attached to a new backing board and overmat. A print that is on a damaged mount can similarly be enclosed in a new mount assembly. Very badly damaged mounts can be trimmed, attached to new mount board with jumbo photo corners reinforced with linen tape, then over-

A BASIC PROTECTIVE MAT

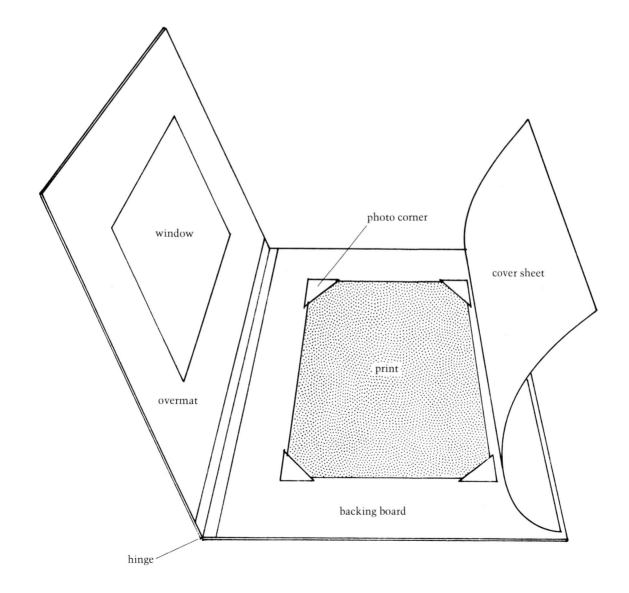

matted. This is generally better than submitting the print to possible damage by trying to remove it from the mount if it is glued or dry mounted.

Matting Materials

Photographic paper, gelatin, silver, and so forth can interact readily with other materials with which they come in contact, so it is essential that all matting, framing, and storage materials be of a suitable composition — that is, photographically inert. The first choice for mounts is an acid-free, heavyweight paper called museum board. It is expensive, but worth the price if long-term preservation is desired.

Museum-quality materials for matting contain a large percentage of alpha cellulose, a long-lasting, highly purified fibrous substance. They are free of plant materials that produce destructive peroxides as they deteriorate, and are also free of copper, iron, and other metallic impurities. They are processed to be free of the potentially damaging acids usually present in paper and are either pH neutral or slightly alkaline. (The pH scale measures relative acidity and alkalinity: a reading of 7 is neutral; numbers below 7 indicate acidity, above 7 alkalinity. Devices for testing pH are available from chemical suppliers.) Photographic printing paper is somewhat acidic, with a pH of about 5.5. Papers for matting should be at least 6.2 to 6.5; papers on the alkaline side are even more desirable. Though research is not complete, most conservators feel that storage in a slightly alkaline environment helps neutralize airborne acid pollutants. In addition, archival-quality papers are buffered with an acid-neutralizing chemical such as calcium carbonate, which maintains the effectiveness of the paper over a long period of time. (*Caution:* Under certain conditions a cyanotype may be adversely affected by alkalinity, so storage of this medium with buffered papers is unwise.)

Museum boards are generally available in white or cream in three thicknesses: 2-ply ($^1/_{32}''$); 4-ply ($^1/_{16}''$), the most often used; and heavy-duty 8-ply ($^1/_8''$), which is sometimes desirable for large prints. The boards are sold in large sheets (32×40 inches, for example) and are then cut to the desired mat size.

A few other materials are generally considered safe. For cover sheets, acid-free papers are best. Japanese rice paper (actually made of mulberry bark) is usually acceptable. Also chemically suitable are some transparent plastics: cellulose triacetate, such as Kodacel; uncoated polyester, such as Mylar-D; and polyethylene. These are made in sheets and bags of various thicknesses and sizes. Plastic should be used with caution. If it is wrapped tight around a print, moisture can accumulate inside and even condense. If the plastic contacts the image surface under pressure, it can adhere or cause glossy spots (ferrotyping). Even if loosely wrapped, plastic should not be used where humidity is a problem.

Some materials are undesirable and should not be used. Ordinary brown wrapping paper, brown kraft envelopes, manila folders, cardboard, most cheap papers, most glassine, and polyvinyl-chloride plastic all produce destructive byproducts.

Attaching a Print to a Backing Board

The three main means of attaching a print to the backing board are dry mounting, cornering, and hinging. Regardless of the method used, care should be exercised when choosing adhesives.

DRY MOUNTING Dry-mount tissue is a sheet of thin paper coated on both sides with a waxy adhesive. When placed between a print and a backing and heated, usually in a special dry-mount press, the adhesive becomes sticky and forms a tight bond between print and backing. For many years dry mounting has been a popular means of attaching a print to a board. It is neat, holds the print flat, and provides a strong reinforcement that protects the print even if it is dropped.

Museums readily buy dry-mounted prints, but if a loose print is purchased, the museum probably will not dry mount it. Conservators do not themselves like to do anything that is not easily reversible, so they use less-permanent attachments, such as corners or hinges. In case a print has to be removed from its mount for chemical treatment or in the event the mount becomes damaged or contaminated, it is theoretically possible to work solvents between a print and its mount board to gradually free a dry-mounted print, but obviously it is simpler to remove a print from a photo corner.

CORNERING Photo corners, similar to the ones used to mount pictures in snapshot albums, are a convenient and safe means of attachment. The corners are easy to apply and are hidden by the overmat. Making your own corners out of all-rag paper is simple, as shown here. Ordinary white photo cor-

MAKING A PHOTO CORNER

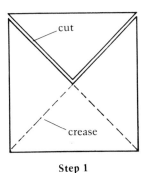

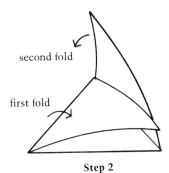

Step 1   **Step 2**

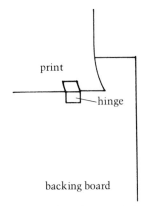

A folded hinge is hidden when the print is in place.

ners are acceptable, but instead of the glue that is coated on the corner, use a drop of polyvinyl acetate (PVA) glue to adhere the corner to the board (see ADHESIVES, below). Reinforce corners with a strip of archival gummed tape, since glue alone may not be strong enough to hold the print in place. Hard-plastic corners or flanges are not recommended; they may not be chemically neutral and some have sharp edges that can scratch or emboss the print.

HINGING   Hinging holds the print in place with two strips attached to the upper back edge of the print and to the backing board (see illustration). The hinge is contacted directly to the print, so good-quality materials must be used. Archival gummed paper or linen tape will support a small, lightweight print, but they may not hold a heavy print; and they are too thick for prints on a thin base, such as un-mounted albumen prints. A rice-paper hinge attached with starch paste will be better for such prints.

ADHESIVES   It is easier to say what should not be used to attach a print to a board than to give unqualified recommendations about what should be used. Definitely not recommended are: rubber cement; pressure-sensitive tapes, such as masking tape or cellophane tape; most gummed paper tapes, especially standard brown packaging tape; animal glues; spray adhesives, including those advertised for photo mounting; and synthetic adhesives, except for polyvinyl acetate (PVA) glue such as Jade 403.

   In the safe category, in addition to PVA glue, are gummed linen or paper tape of museum quality, such as Holland tape. A reliable archival starch paste can be prepared at home, but it is easier for the private collector to order it from a supplier such as TALAS. Dry-mount tissue is also safe.

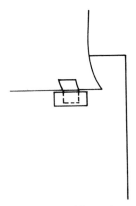

A folded hinge can be reinforced by a piece of tape.

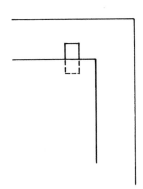

A pendant hinge is hidden if an overmat is used.

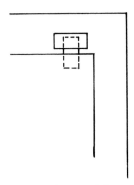

Reinforcing helps support a heavy print.

Cutting a Mat

Cutting a mat and overmat is not difficult but will be easier with practice and the proper tools. A metal straightedge and a heavy-duty mat knife with a sharp blade are essential. Mat cutters of various kinds are sold to help guide the knife. In some cities, do-it-yourself picture-framing shops can be found that supply assistance, good tools, and a work space in exchange for the purchase of a frame or other materials. Or professional picture framers will do matting and framing. For details on cutting mats and on framing, consult *Frame It* by Lista Duren (see bibliography on page 61).

Standardized mat sizes are convenient, though they cannot be used with all prints. Standardization also makes framing and replacing framed items easier, and it makes it possible to order some items in quantity, which generally saves money. Some standard mat and frame sizes, in inches, are: 11×14, 12×16, 14×17 (or 18), 16×20, 18×22 (or 24), 20×24, and 22×28.

The window may be centered on the overmat, but is more often cut so that the side and top margins between the window and the outside edges of the overmat are equal, with the bottom margin slightly larger.

Depending on the print, the overmat window can be cut larger than, the same size as, or smaller than the image area. A window that is larger than the image is suitable for a print that is dry mounted onto a backing or that is printed with a border of photographic paper around the image. An oversize window can also display a title or signature that is visible near the image.

If the image is printed with a border of photographic paper around it, the window also can be cut exactly even with the image. This is not recommended if the photographic paper has been trimmed to the edge of the image, since opening and shutting the overmat can rub or catch the edge of the print and damage it.

The window can also be cut to overlap the edges of the image slightly. This loses a bit of the image area but protects the edges of a borderless print, and it may be needed to hold a thin paper print flat. Store photographs matted in this way with interleaving tissue between the overmat and the image and avoid excessive pressure on them to prevent embossing of the window outline on the print.

After cutting a window, smooth the sharp edges of the cuts by rubbing with fine sandpaper or by lightly running a rounded object like a knife handle along them. This prevents surface damage to the print when print and overmat are brought together. The position of the overmat window is usually penciled in on the inside surface as a guide before cutting; any such marks remaining after cutting should be erased to prevent their possible transfer to the print or mat underneath.

Framing

A number of different frames are available, either completely assembled or sold in sections that screw together. Metal frames are best; avoid wooden ones unless they are finished with a permanent wood sealer. Plexiglas has some advantages over glass for framing. It is lightweight and unbreakable, and may be legally required as a safety precaution in public institutions such as schools. Ultraviolet-blocking Plexiglas is available that helps protect prints from strong light; Rohm and Haas UF-1 Plexiglas reduces damaging ultraviolet rays by 90%, UF-3 by 95%. But there are disadvantages. Plexiglas attracts dust and scratches easily. The UV-blocking kind has a yellow-orange cast. Most seriously, it may give off damaging fumes from undissolved esters, so it is definitely not recommended for long-term use. Most conservators do recommend UV-blocking Plexiglas for short-term use to protect a print that must be hung in bright light.

To fit the print tightly into the frame, pieces of lightweight Fome-Cor board placed behind the print are much preferable to cardboard. Some conservators recommend covering the back of the frame with alkaline paper to act as a barrier to air pollutants — without, however, sealing the frame airtight.

The print surface should not touch the glass, and an overmat makes the ideal separator. If a print is not overmatted, narrow strips of matting board between the print and the inside edges of the glass will separate them. Some frames have channeling around the inside edges to keep the print away from the glass. Prints that appear to be in contact with the glass, either all over or in part, should be removed very carefully from the frame. The emulsion may be solidly stuck to the glass and pulling it away

even gently may leave most of the image on the glass. It may be best simply to clean the exterior surface of the glass and leave the print as is.

Storage

Eugene Ostroff, Curator of Photography at the Smithsonian Institution, described somewhat facetiously the ideal in photographic storage: an inert atmosphere maintained at a constant 50° Fahrenheit and 50% relative humidity in a sterilized, stainless-steel container, welded shut. Some of the more practical do's and don'ts of storage were discussed earlier in this chapter. Storage containers are described here.

Envelopes

Acetate or polyester envelopes are available in a variety of sizes and weights. Acid-free paper envelopes are desirable, and a few types are commercially available. They can be improvised out of archival paper, or, for short-term storage, good-quality commercial envelopes can be used. Filing envelopes ideally should have narrow side seams rather than a thick central seam, in order to prevent embossing and to minimize contact with seam adhesives. Never use an envelope with a metal clasp: embossing is almost guaranteed.

Boxes

Solander boxes are the most popular storage box, especially where frequent access to prints is impor-

tant. They are hinged to open to a flat tray shape for viewing prints. Some conservators question their chemical safety since they are made of wood, even though it is well seasoned. Nevertheless, they are still widely used by museums and collectors. If they are not already lined with acid-free paper, the collector can minimize possible danger to prints by doing so. Two-piece boxes are less convenient and less sturdy than solander boxes but are available made of acid-free mount board, thus providing a better environment. In order to minimize the risk of surface abrasions caused by movement of prints within a box, choose a box into which the prints fit somewhat snugly.

Cabinets and Files

First choice is a steel cabinet with a baked-on finish. Wood cabinets may be more attractive, but are flammable and, if well constructed, are costly. Avoid unseasoned wood, particle board, and pressboard; they emit damaging acids. A cabinet with several shallow drawers such as those used for filing blueprints is better than one with deep drawers into which all items must be stacked, then removed for viewing. Ideally, cabinets for materials such as collodion should be vented to disperse gases that may be produced by deterioration.

Restoration Procedures and Formulas

The following procedures are given with some cautions. The long-term effects of many restoration procedures are not clearly understood, and all procedures involve risks of leaving the image in a worse condition than when you found it. Ideally, anyone attempting to treat a photograph should have both a theoretical understanding of the chemical principles involved as well as skill and experience in handling prints. Do not attempt restoration procedures without practicing first on similar, expendable items — although this is not a guarantee of success

since two photographs may look alike but react differently.

Concepts of preservation (or the lack of them) in the past often turned on the perception of a photograph as a cheap, reproducible, mass-produced item. As the awareness of photographs as irreplaceable and rare objects has heightened, attitudes about how to treat them have become much stricter. Collectors have a responsibility to preserve unique images for future generations, in addition to protecting their own acquisitions. Consult a professional conservator if there is any question about safety with historically important images.

There are relatively few experienced photographic conservators and even fewer who do free-lance work. Recently, as photograph collecting has risen in popularity, more people are going into conservatorial training. A museum with a large photographic collection would be likely to know where the private collector could turn for qualified help.

Museums ordinarily copy images before treating them if there is any risk involved. An unaltered copy photograph may be made to give information to conservators, for example about the condition of a stain before treatment. But to preserve the best possible record of the image itself, especially when deterioration is irreversible, another copy photograph may be made in which the image is enhanced by using copy techniques, such as filters on the camera lens, to eliminate stains and surface imperfections as much as possible from the copy print.

The formulas and procedures that follow will be understandable by anyone with photographic darkroom experience. If you do not know how to measure chemicals or if the procedures are puzzling in any other way, consult a basic photography textbook or someone familiar with photographic processing. All solutions described should be at room temperature, unless otherwise specified. Use chemically neutral utensils and containers for solutions — glass, stainless steel, or plastics intended for darkroom use. For more information on care and restoration, consult the sources listed at the end of this chapter.

Cleaning a Daguerreotype

See the cautions about daguerreotypes on page 50. Practice on a less valuable daguerreotype before attempting to clean a good one. The image is extremely fragile and can literally be wiped off at the touch of a finger, so hold the plate by the edges and do not touch the image surface with anything except as described in the cleaning procedure.

Gently remove the image plate from its case or frame. To remove surface dirt, immerse the plate face up in a tray containing a weak solution of distilled water and soap (not detergent). Gently agitate (move) the solution back and forth over the plate by rocking the tray or carefully moving the plate. Rub the back of the plate clean. Rinse in distilled water. Drain.

Place plate face up in a solution of:

500 cc	distilled water
70 g	thiourea
15 cc	phosphoric acid (85%)
2cc	wetting agent, such as Photo-Flo
plus:	distilled water to make 1,000 cc

Gently agitate until discoloration is removed. This usually takes a minute or less, 3–4 minutes at the most.

Rinse well by immersing in a series of 4 or 5 distilled-water baths. Immerse in 95% grain alcohol to help prevent water spots. The alcohol must be absolutely clean; use a fresh tray for each daguerreotype. Dry in a gentle stream of warm air, as from a hair dryer. Hold the plate almost vertical, tilted slightly back. Hold the dryer about one foot away and move the stream of air back and forth across the plate from top to bottom.

Wash the cover glass in soap and distilled water. Rinse in distilled water and dry with a lint-free cloth. Gently brush clean the framing parts and reassemble the daguerreotype. The thin gilt mat between the image surface and cover glass serves to keep them apart and prevent abrasions. In some cases this mat has become flattened and no longer keeps the glass far enough above the plate. It can be raised slightly by inserting underneath the mat a narrow frame of 1-ply museum-quality board. Seal all around the edges of the plate, mat, and cover glass with a strip of archival-quality tape and polyvinyl acetate glue.

Cleaning an Ambrotype

See the information about ambrotypes on page 50.

Carefully remove the image plate from its case or frame. Wash the protective cover glass in soap and distilled water. Rinse in distilled water and dry with a lint-free cloth. Gently brush clean the framing parts.

The emulsion side of the image plate may be extremely fragile and should not be touched or abraded in any way. It can usually be identified by slight irregularities in the emulsion surface, whereas the backing side will be quite smooth. Clean the backing side of the image plate with a clean cloth slightly dampened with distilled water, but do this only if you are sure which side is which.

If the black backing has deteriorated, replace with a piece of black paper as described under Ambrotypes. Reassemble the parts and seal around the edges as for a daguerreotype (see page 58).

Cleaning a Tintype

See the information about tintypes on page 50. Tintypes appear sturdy but the emulsion may not be so. Do not wet a rusted tintype.

First blow away loose dust with a blower designed for dusting negatives. Then dust gently with a very soft brush. Evaluate the image; it may be sufficiently clean. Proceed beyond this point only if absolutely necessary. If surface grime is still excessive, there are two possible procedures.

Some conservators recommend the following: If the plate is not rusted, immerse it in a weak soap solution (21°C./70°F.) for 1 minute. Agitate gently but do not rub the image surface. Rinse in distilled water. To prevent water spotting, rinse again in distilled water containing a few drops of wetting solution (Photo-Flo). Stand on edge to dry.

Other conservators do not recommend immersing the entire plate, since this may weaken the bond between the emulsion and the backing and cause them to separate. They suggest the following: Dampen a cotton swab slightly with distilled water and *very* gently stroke a small area along the edge of the plate. (One conservator tells of dabbing gently at a tintype portrait and finding the emulsion had come off on the cotton swab she was using; unfortunately, she had dabbed first at the nose.) Don't dig at the emulsion, rub hard, or wet a rusted area. Continue cleaning a small area at a time, working along the edges first and evaluating the condition of the plate as you go. This procedure may work better than immersion, especially if only a small area needs to be cleaned, but it is dangerous if you have a heavy hand.

Cleaning a Glass-plate Negative

First, it is essential to distinguish whether the emulsion on the plate is collodion or gelatin. See chapter 3 (*collodion wet plate*) for information on how to tell the two apart. See also Glass-plate Negatives, page 50.

If the emulsion is gelatin, wetting the emulsion surface is not recommended. The gelatin will swell as it absorbs moisture and may peel off the glass backing immediately or at some later time. The swelling may also permanently embed dirt in the emulsion. Remove loose dust with a negative blower or a very soft brush. If necessary, clean the back of the plate (the shiny side) with a soft cloth dampened with distilled water. Dry carefully.

Conservators differ in what they recommend for a collodion emulsion. The safest course is to do nothing except remove loose dust with a negative blower or a very soft brush. Some conservators will do nothing beyond this. Others will experiment very gingerly with a cotton swab and distilled water, and a few are willing to immerse the plate in water (see instructions for tintypes, this page). The backing side (if you are sure which it is) can be cleaned with a dampened cloth. The varnish that was used on many collodion negatives may make the emulsion side as shiny as the backing side, but the emulsion will have surface irregularities, whereas the backing will be evenly smooth.

Testing for Residual Silver (Kodak Formula ST-1) to Identify a Stabilized Print

See Paper Prints, page 51. Prepare the stock solution:

    100 cc   distilled water
      2 g   sodium sulfide (anhydrous)

Store the stock solution no longer than three months and working solution no longer than a week.

To make working solution, dilute 1 part stock solution with 9 parts water. Place a drop on a clear margin area of the print that is being tested and let stand 2 minutes. Blot off the excess. A dark stain identifies a stabilized print. Since this procedure may cause a visible stain, test in a peripheral area.

Reprocessing Black-and-white Paper Prints

See Paper Prints, page 51, and instructions on next page for stabilized prints and resin-coated (RC) papers. Reprocessing involves the following steps.

    fixing
    washing, including treatment with a hypo-
        neutralizing wash accelerator such as Kodak
        Hypo Clearing Agent or HEICO Perma-Wash
    optional hypo eliminator treatment (this will
        totally remove hypo but may cause softening
        of the emulsion or frilling at the edges of the
        print; not recommended for old prints)
    drying

Mix fresh fixer (hypo) according to directions on package. One or two prints can be refixed in one tray of fixer; for more than a few prints, prepare two trays of fixer. Fixer with hardener helps prevent softening of emulsion when tap water temperatures are high, but it may retard thorough washing; use it only in the first tray of two-tray fixing. Do not use rapid fixer.

Soak the print for a few minutes in water to wet it completely. Drain briefly and immerse in fixing solution. Agitate gently and constantly for 6 minutes; if using two trays of fixer, agitate for 3 minutes in each tray. When fixing several prints at a time, rotate prints individually from the bottom of the tray to the top.

Promptly remove print from fixer, drain briefly, and immerse in a tray of water. Wash in running water for 5 minutes, agitating and dumping the water several times to remove hypo residue, which accumulates at the bottom of the tray.

Dilute the wash accelerator as recommended by manufacturer; agitate prints in solution for 3 minutes.

Wash again for 60 minutes agitating frequently and completely changing water every 5 minutes. Water at 24°C. (75°F.) is recommended; higher temperatures cause softening of the emulsion, lower ones are less efficient.

For total removal of hypo, agitate 6 minutes in Kodak HE-1 hypo eliminator (formula follows) and wash an additional 20 minutes. Mix the formula just before use. Keep in an open container, since the solution generates gases that can crack a closed bottle.

    500 cc water
    125 cc hydrogen peroxide (3% solution)
    100 cc dilute ammonia solution (1 part
                 28% ammonia mixed with 9 parts
                 water)
  plus: water to make 1,000 cc

Stabilized prints should not be presoaked. Put them directly in fixer (without hardener) to minimize fading.

Resin-coated (RC) papers require less fixing time (2 minutes) and less washing time (4 minutes); do not exceed these times. Wash at 20°C. (68°F.); do not use wash accelerator or hypo eliminator.

Dry carefully to avoid contaminating the print. Drying face down on a clean fiberglass screen is recommended. Or use brand-new photo drying blotters, laid flat and not rolled.

Reprocessing Black-and-white Film

Observe extra care when dealing with negatives; they are subject to spotting, damage to softened emulsion, scratching, et cetera. See Film Negatives, page 51.

Agitate in fresh fixer for the minimum time recommended by the manufacturer. Rinse for 2 minutes in running water at 20°C. (68°F.). Treat with a wash accelerator for the minimum recommended time. Wash again for 20 minutes.

Rinse for 1 minute in distilled water containing a few drops of Photo-Flo. Hang in a dust-free place to dry.

Treating a Moldy Print

Gelatin emulsions can be so attacked by mold that they develop fuzzy or powdery mold growth similar to that which occurs on food. One simple treatment is to expose the affected print to several hours of sunlight and fresh air outdoors on a dry day. Brush the surface of the print gently with a soft brush to remove visible mold. Do this outdoors so as not to bring mold spores in contact with other prints. Then store the print in a drier environment than the one that caused the problem. This treatment will kill spores on top of the gelatin, though probably not those under the surface, so watch for a recurrence of the mold. Killing the spores this way may cause discoloration, so professional treatment is better for a valuable print. However, the sunlight treatment is better than no treatment at all. (For more about mold and fungus, see Heat and Humidity, page 48.)

Care-and-Restoration Sources

Since information on the proper care of photographs is growing and changing as additional basic research is being done, some older and even not-so-old printed sources may recommend procedures that are outmoded. Also, some experts freely recommend procedures, such as cleaning daguerreotypes, that other experts do not. Be cautious about doing anything to your collection beyond storing it away from bright light in a clean, cool, dry, acid-free environment.

In addition to the published sources listed here, information about photographic care and restoration is available from:

American National Standards Institute
1430 Broadway
New York, N.Y. 10018

Eastman Kodak Company
Rochester, N.Y. 14650

International Museum of Photography at George Eastman House
Center for the Conservation of Photographic Materials
900 East Ave.
Rochester, N.Y. 14607

Bibliography

Barth, Miles. "Notes on Conservation and Restoration of Photographs." *Print Collector's Newsletter* 7 (May/June 1976): 48–51.

Bry, Doris. *An Approach to the Care of Photographs.* New York: Sotheby Parke Bernet, 1976. Single copies of this pamphlet may be obtained by sending a stamped, self-addressed envelope to Sotheby Park Bernet, Dept. AH, 980 Madison Ave., New York, N.Y. 10021.

Doloff, Francis W., and Perkinson, Roy L. *How to Care for Works of Art on Paper.* Boston: Museum of Fine Arts, 1971.

Duren, Lista. *Frame It: A Complete Do-It-Yourself Guide to Picture Framing.* Boston: Houghton Mifflin, 1976.

Life Library of Photography. *Caring for Photographs.* New York: Time-Life Books, 1972.

Orraca, Jose. "The Preservation and Restoration of Glass Plate Negatives." *Image* 60 (June 1973): 8–9.

Ostroff, Eugene. "Conserving and Restoring Photographic Collections." *Museum News* (in four parts), May, Sept., Nov., Dec. 1974. Revised reprint available for $1.25 from American Association of Museums, 1055 Thomas Jefferson St. N.W., Washington, D.C. 20007.

Swan, Alice. "Conservation Treatments for Photographs: A Review of Some of the Problems, Literature and Practices." *Image* 21 (June 1978): 24–31.

Weinstein, Robert A., and Booth, Larry. *Collection, Use and Care of Historical Photographs.* Nashville: American Association for State and Local History, 1977.

Wilhelm, Henry. "Color Print Instability: A Problem for Collectors and Photographers." *Afterimage* 6 (Oct. 1978): 11–13.

———. *Processing and Storing Black and White Photographs for Maximum Possible Permanence.* Grinnell, Iowa: East Street Gallery, 1969.

Suppliers

Most cities have large art-supply stores that carry archival-quality products, framing supplies, and other materials useful to photograph collectors. Such suppliers are often the best places to purchase small quantities of these items. Larger quantities or specialized products can be obtained from:

General Suppliers

Light Impressions Corp.
Box 3012
Rochester, N.Y. 14614

Archival-quality materials and supplies. Framing service. Catalogue available.

TALAS
Div. of Technical Library Service
130 Fifth Ave.
New York, N.Y. 10011

Wide range of archival-quality materials and supplies. Catalogue available.

Mounting Board, Papers, Other Materials

Fome-Bord Service Centers
2211 N. Elston Ave.
Chicago, Ill. 60614
and
1860 E. Forty-sixth St.
Los Angeles, Calif. 90058

Lightweight Fome-Cor backing board. Catalogue available.

The Nega-File Co.
Box 78
Furlong, Pa. 18925

Filing systems for film, negatives, slides, etc. Catalogue available.

Print File, Inc.
Box 100
Schenectady, N.Y. 12304

Polyethylene negative files. Catalogue available.

Process Materials Corp.
329 Veterans Blvd.
Carlstadt, N.J. 07072

Archival-quality paper products and adhesives; pH indicators. Literature available.

Spink and Gaborc, Inc.
32 W. Eighteenth St.
New York, N.Y. 10011

Solander boxes and storage cases. Catalogue available.

University Products, Inc.
Box 101
Holyoke, Mass. 01040

Archival-quality papers and products. Catalogue available.

Special Equipment and Supplies

Abbeon Cal, Inc.
123–05A Gray Ave.
Santa Barbara, Calif. 93101

Devices to measure heat and humidity. Catalogue available.

Bendix Corp.
Environmental and Process Instruments Div.
1400 Taylor Ave.
Baltimore, Md. 21204

Devices to measure heat and humidity. Literature available.

Micro Essential Laboratories, Inc.
4224 Ave. H
Brooklyn, N.Y. 11210

pH indicators (pencil style). Literature available.

Rohm and Haas
Plastics Div.
Independence Mall West
Philadelphia, Pa. 19105

Manufacturer of ultraviolet-shielding Plexiglas. Write for name of local supplier.

Solar-Screen Co.
53-11 105th St.
Corona, N.Y. 11740

Ultraviolet-blocking filters for windows and fluorescent light bulbs. Literature available.

Berenice Abbott. *Fifth Avenue at Eighth Street,* ca. 1935. Silver print. (Courtesy the artist)

5

Selected Photographers: A Collector's Compendium

This chapter features illustrated biographical profiles of 234 individual photographers and lists hundreds of others in group entries describing major photographic themes, movements, organizations, and publications. Many photographers whose work is collectible are not mentioned here: since it was impossible to include them all in the space available, selection became unavoidable. The authors have sought to reflect the widest possible range of photographers and types of work. Numerous photographers not listed here appear elsewhere in *The Photograph Collector's Guide;* see chapter 7, the appendixes, and the index.

The nine group entries treat some of the many categories of special interest to collectors: artists (that is, photographers who identify themselves primarily with the traditional art world), *Camera Work,* Farm Security Administration (FSA), fashion, Group *f/*64, photojournalists, Photo League, pictorialists, and travel and regional photographers (19th century). The reader, especially the beginning collector seeking an overview of the field, may find it useful to read these group entries first for general background.

The entries about individuals list the photographer by last name or pseudonym, followed by country of major activity or residence (country of birth, if known to be different, appears in parentheses) and by life dates when available. A narrative summary of the photographer's life and career is given next. When quoted matter is cited, a last name plus a

short title in parentheses after the quotation refers to books listed in the general bibliography that begins on page 419. Other shortened citations (a name or a title only) refer to sources in the SELECTED BIBLIOGRAPHY that concludes each entry.

After the text portion, every entry contains data organized as follows:

WORK   This section lists significant subjects and types of photography done by the artist; it may include cross-references to illustrated examples elsewhere in the book.

MEDIA   Lists processes known to be employed by the photographer or used by others directly under his or her supervision in creating original works. (Collectible *reproductions* such as *Camera Work* gravures appear in the AVAILABILITY AND PRICE section, the SELECTED BIBLIOGRAPHY, or both.)

In addition to the kind of print, the kind of negative made by the photographer is listed when known, except for modern silver prints, in which case film negatives are assumed. Information about signature, stamping, mounting, and size or format is sometimes given here (it may also be mentioned in AVAILABILITY AND PRICE). Unless otherwise specified, all dimensions are given in inches, height before width.

AVAILABILITY AND PRICE   Lists *sources* through which the photographer's collectible work is available — for example, through galleries, at auction, or through the photographer, his or her agent or publisher, or an estate. Only the most significant sources are given; for example, the entry for a contemporary photographer whose work is readily available through galleries but is offered at auction only occasionally will usually mention just galleries as a source.

The relative *availability* of collectible work is also often indicated, by such phrases as "rare," "frequently available," et cetera. (Unless otherwise stated, "readily available" may be assumed for contemporary photographers whose work is offered through galleries.)

The authors' assessment of the *price* of individual works by the photographer — based on the auction and gallery market, prices set by the artist (or an estate or publisher), and data from other published sources — is also listed, broken down into the following ranges:

> extremely low = under $50
> low = $50–$100
> moderate = $100–$250
> moderately high = $250–$500
> high = $500–$1,000
> extremely high = $1,000 or more

Prices of collectible photographic works are constantly changing, most often upward; the values listed in this chapter reflect the general market as of early 1979. Prices of books and of reproductions such as posters are as a rule not included; for prices of portfolios, see chapter 6.

The term *vintage print,* used in this section and elsewhere, refers to a print made a number of years ago, at around the same time as its negative; *modern print* refers to a print made more recently, much later than its negative.

Other factors affecting price — such as signatures or mounting, special formats, or irregularities in print condition — may also appear here (or in the MEDIA section). A general discussion of pricing factors appears in chapter 1.

SIGNATURE / OTHER IDENTIFICATION Illustrates, when available, examples of signatures, stamps, imprints, logos, handwriting, and other marks useful in identifying or helping to authenticate collectible items. Older examples shown are usually taken directly from original works; contemporary examples were generally provided especially for this book. No attempt has been made to reproduce every variant signature or identifying mark, nor has it always been possible to reflect the actual size. (Further details about identification occasionally appear in the MEDIA or AVAILABILITY AND PRICE sections.)

PORTFOLIOS Selectively indicates contemporary, limited-edition portfolios of original photographic prints (most are listed and described in chapter 6). Portfolios of gravures or of other reproductions are excluded here, as are nineteenth-century albums; when listed, they appear instead in the SELECTED BIBLIOGRAPHY.

COLLECTIONS Lists selected public collections of the photographer's work. Most are held by museums, libraries, university archives, or historical societies that may be visited at fixed hours or by appointment. An attempt has been made to list mainly the largest or most significant collections of the photographer's work, especially when many exist. Collections are given alphabetically, usually in an abbreviated form, in two groups (separated by a semicolon): collections located in the United States appear first, followed by those in other countries. *A key*

to the abbreviations appears on pages 412–418. Full addresses and, in some cases, descriptive material about holdings can be found in appendix C.

SELECTED BIBLIOGRAPHY Lists not only collectible items such as books by the photographer, but also critical assessments and material that is useful for reference or because it contains illustrations of the artist's work. Books (including exhibition catalogues), albums, portfolios of reproductions, and unpublished research material are listed first, chronologically; periodicals follow, also listed chronologically (references to *Camera Work* reproductions are included at the end). When an item is listed by title only, the photographer is usually the author; sometimes, however, the name of the author is not available or there is no specific author — as in the case of many exhibition catalogues.

In compiling these bibliographies from various sources, the authors were unable to examine every item; hence some data may be missing and transliterations may vary.

The *"See also"* references consisting of a last name and a short title cite books listed in the general bibliography (page 419) or, if so specified, cite sources about color photography included in the "color bibliography" (page 422). Some *See also* references cite exhibition catalogues listed in chapter 7; they can be located by finding the photographer's alphabetical listings there. The following four comprehensive histories that are listed in the general bibliography treat many of the photographers with main entries in this chapter, so they have been excluded from the *See also* listings: Cecil Beaton and Gail Buckland, *The Magic Image;* Helmut and Alison Gernsheim, *The History of Photography . . . to 1914;* Beaumont Newhall, *The History of Photography from 1839 to the Present Day;* and Peter Pollack, *The Picture History of Photography.*

The following abbreviations for publishers are used throughout:

> GEH   George Eastman House
> IMP/GEH   International Museum of Photography at George Eastman House
> MOMA   Museum of Modern Art

In addition to the above information, almost every entry includes a representative *illustration* of the photographer's work. Illustrations separated from their actual entry — such as the eight color plates that follow page 310 — are noted most often in the section WORK. Photographers often print an image in varying sizes; however, when the actual print of the image illustrated here is especially small or large, its dimensions are usually mentioned in the caption (in inches, height before width). The title of some images is given variously from source to source; the authors have tried to reflect common usage or the photographer's preference in regard to the title. The size of the illustrations was dictated solely by design requirements of the book.

Abbott, Berenice
United States 1898–

Abbott, originally a student of painting and sculpture, lived in Paris in the 1920s, learned photography as an assistant to Man Ray, then opened her own photographic studio. Her portraits of intellectuals and artists in Paris are incisive and penetrating images free of sentiment or gloss. She met Eugène Atget shortly before his death in 1927, made the only known portraits of him, and was instrumental in rescuing his work and promoting it. She returned to the United States in 1929.

Her documents of New York City made in the 1930s are cool and detached in their portrayal of the scale and power of the city. This quality, combined with the detail and clarity of her 8×10-inch negatives, enhances the viewer's belief in their accuracy and realism. Her third major concentration has involved creating photographs to illustrate scientific principles; many of these have great photographic beauty in addition to their scientific interest.

"The challenge for me has first been to see things as they are, whether a portrait, a city street, or a bouncing ball. In a word, I have tried to be objective. What I mean by objectivity is not the objectivity of a machine, but of a sensible human being with the mystery of personal selection at the heart of it. The second challenge has been to impose order onto the things seen and to supply the visual context and the intellectual framework — that to me is the art of photography" (foreword, *Ten Photographs*, portfolio listed in chapter 6).

WORK   Includes portraits from 1920s Paris (e.g., Cocteau, Gide, Joyce), extensive documentation of changing New York City (1930s, partly funded by a WPA Federal Art Project grant) when many old buildings were being torn down to make room for skyscrapers, Greenwich Village (1940s), science series (mid-1940s to early 1960s) illustrating laws of physics (e.g., multiple exposure of a swinging ball in an elliptical orbit), a smaller body of work of scenes along Route 1 on the Atlantic Coast (1950s) and of Maine (early 1960s). (See illustration, page 62.)

MEDIUM   Silver prints. Most are contact printed from 8×10 negatives; late in 1960s the photographer began to enlarge more frequently to 11×14, 16×20. When mounted, signature appears at lower right under print; unmounted prints are signed, stamped on verso, or both. Stamp with Commerce Street (New York City) address dates a print before her move to Maine in mid-1960s. Federal Art Project prints are identified by a stamp on the back.

AVAILABILITY AND PRICE   Most frequently found are prints made in the 1960s and later by Abbott with various assistants. Prints bought from her 1930s-1960s exhibitions appear from time to time, particularly at auction. Vintage prints from her own collection as well as modern prints are available through galleries. Modern prints moderately high; vintage prints high to extremely high.

PORTFOLIOS   *See* chapter 6 entry.

COLLECTIONS   New York (Federal Art Project work), other major collections.

SIGNATURE/OTHER IDENTIFICATION

[signatures of Berenice Abbott]

SELECTED BIBLIOGRAPHY
Changing New York. Text by Elizabeth McCausland. New York: Dutton, 1939. Reprint, *New York in the Thirties.* New York: Dover, 1973.
A Guide to Better Photography. New York: Crown, 1941. Rev. ed., *A New Guide to Better Photography,* 1953.
The View Camera Made Simple. Chicago: Ziff-Davis, 1948.
Greenwich Village Today and Yesterday. With Henry W. Lanier. New York: Harper, 1949.
The World of Atget. Text and ed. by Abbott. New York: Horizon, 1964. Reprint, 1975.
Magnet. Text by E. G. Valens. Cleveland: World, 1964.
Motion. Text by E. G. Valens. Cleveland: World, 1965.
A Portrait of Maine. With Chenoweth Hall. New York: Macmillan, 1968.
The Attractive Universe. Text by E. G. Valens. Cleveland: World, 1969.
David Vestal. *Berenice Abbott: Photographs.* New York: Horizon, 1970.
"It Has to Walk Alone." *Album,* no. 7 (1970), pp. 16–32. Reprint of a 1951 essay.
"New York in the Thirties." *Creative Camera,* Apr. 1977, pp. 114–121. From a 1951 talk.
See also Edey, *Essays;* Lyons, *Photographers;* Newhall, *Masters;* Mann, *Women;* Szarkowski, *Looking;* Travis, *Julien Levy;* Tucker, *Eye.*

Adams, Ansel
United States 1902–

Adams's dramatic landscape images are probably known to more people than the work of any other contemporary American photographer. His strong attraction to nature began at age fourteen when he visited Yosemite Valley for the first time. The beauty of the landscape was, in his words, "a culmination of experience so intense as to be almost painful. From that day in 1916 my life has been colored and modulated by the great earth gesture of the Sierra" (quoted in Muir). Adams (shown on page 155) began to photograph on regular trips to the Sierra Nevada, became interested in mountaineering and conservation, and commenced a lifelong association with the Sierra Club. He was simultaneously training for a career as a concert pianist but by 1930 decided to devote his full energies to photography.

In 1932 he helped found Group f/64, which sought to promote the "straight," unmanipulated photograph as an art form. He met Alfred Stieglitz in New York in 1933 and was given a one-man show in 1936 at An American Place. Adams subsequently helped establish the department of photography at New York City's Museum of

Modern Art (1940), founded the department of photography at what is now the San Francisco Art Institute (1946), and was instrumental in the founding of Friends of Photography in Carmel, California (1966).

During his long and active career, Adams has published many books, including several on photographic technique, and has formulated his unique and well-known Zone System method of exposure and development control. He has stressed — and achieved — mastery of the technical aspects of photography in order to enhance the photographer's concept of an image: "A great photograph is a full expression of what one feels about what is being photographed in the deepest sense, and is, thereby, a true expression of what one feels about life in its entirety. And the expression of what one feels should be set forth in terms of simple devotion to the medium — a statement of the utmost clarity and perfection possible under the conditions of creation and production" (quoted in Lyons, *Photographers*, p. 29).

WORK   Chiefly natural landscape (see illustration, page 2) and details of nature. Also includes portraits, architecture, industrial objects and scenes, social documentation, commercial photography.

MEDIA   Silver prints (4×5 to 16×20 and, until 1973, up to mural size for private commissions and exhibitions). Also Polaroid prints. The term *parmelian print* refers to silver prints in the photographer's first portfolio (1927). Mount board changed in

early 1970s to pure rag; before then heavyweight illustration board used. Signed variously (e.g., "Ansel E. Adams," "A. E. Adams") until about 1934, thereafter only "Ansel Adams." Stamped on back; dates of negative and of print included in stamp as of January 1978.

AVAILABILITY AND PRICE   Through galleries and at auction; small prints moderately high to high, large prints extremely high. Silver prints produced in quantity since the 1960s and through 1978 by Adams; earlier prints rarer. After 1975 Adams stopped taking orders for prints for sale.

Special editions of 8×10 Yosemite prints for Best's Studio / Ansel Adams Gallery, Yosemite, were made by Adams in the late 1950s, and by assistants thereafter (full signature to early 1970s, initialed until fall 1975); extremely low to moderate.

SIGNATURE/OTHER IDENTIFICATION

PORTFOLIOS   *See* chapter 6 entry.

COLLECTIONS   Most major collections in U.S. and Canada; Antwerp, BN, RPS, VA. The Center for Creative Photography (Tucson, Ariz.) will eventually house Adams's negatives, prints, and personal papers.

SELECTED BIBLIOGRAPHY
Taos Pueblo. Text by Mary Austin. San Francisco: privately printed, 1930. 12 silver prints. Facsimile reprint (with duotone plates), afterword by Weston J. Naef. Boston: New York Graphic Society, 1977.
Making a Photograph. New York: Studio, 1935.
Sierra Nevada: The John Muir Trail. Berkeley, Calif.: Archetype Press, 1938. 500 copies, signed.
Born Free and Equal: Photographs of the Loyal Japanese-Americans at Manzanar Relocation Center, Inyo County, California. New York: U.S. Camera, 1944.
Ansel and Virginia Adams. *Illustrated Guide to Yosemite Valley.* San Francisco: H. S. Crocker, 1946. Rev. ed., San Francisco: Sierra Club, 1963.
John Muir. *Yosemite and the Sierra Nevada.* Ed. by Charlotte Mauk. Boston: Houghton Mifflin, 1948.
Basic Photo Series. Hastings-on-Hudson, N.Y.: Morgan & Morgan. 1. *Camera and Lens,* 1948. Rev. ed., 1970. 2. *The Negative,* 1948. 3. *The Print,* 1950. 4. *Natural-Light Photography,* 1952. 5. *Artificial-Light Photography,* 1956. Series presently published Boston: New York Graphic Society.
Mary Austin. *The Land of Little Rain.* Boston: Houghton Mifflin, 1950.
My Camera in Yosemite Valley. Yosemite, Calif.: Virginia Adams, and Boston: Houghton Mifflin, 1950.
My Camera in the National Parks. Yosemite, Calif.: Virginia Adams, and Boston: Houghton Mifflin, 1950.
Death Valley. Text by Nancy Newhall. Redwood City, Calif.: 5 Associates, 1954.
Mission San Xavier del Bac. Text by Nancy Newhall. Redwood City, Calif.: 5 Associates, 1954.

Ansel Adams. *Nasturtiums, Big Sur, California,* 1951. Silver print. (Courtesy the artist)

The Pageant of History in Northern California. Text by Nancy Newhall. San Francisco: American Trust Co., 1954.

Yosemite Valley. Ed. by Nancy Newhall. San Francisco: 5 Associates, 1959.

This Is the American Earth. Text by Nancy Newhall. San Francisco: Sierra Club, 1960. Photographs by Adams and others.

Edwin Corle. *Death Valley and the Creek Called Furnace.* Los Angeles: Ward Ritchie, 1962.

These We Inherit. San Francisco: Sierra Club, 1962.

Polaroid Land Photography Manual. Hastings-on-Hudson, N.Y.: Morgan & Morgan, 1963. Rev. ed., *Polaroid Land Photography.* Boston: New York Graphic Society, 1978.

Ansel Adams: Volume I, The Eloquent Light. Text by Nancy Newhall. San Francisco: Sierra Club, 1963. Only volume.

An Introduction to Hawaii. Text by Edward Joesting. San Francisco: 5 Associates, 1964.

Fiat Lux: The University of California. Text by Nancy Newhall. New York: McGraw-Hill, 1967.

The Tetons and the Yellowstone. Text by Nancy Newhall. Redwood City, Calif.: 5 Associates, 1970.

Ansel Adams. Ed. by Liliane De Cock. Foreword by Minor White. Hastings-on-Hudson, N.Y.: Morgan & Morgan, 1972. Bibliography.

Ansel Adams: Singular Images. Texts by Adams, Edwin Land, David H. McAlpin, Jon Holmes. Dobbs Ferry, N.Y.: Morgan & Morgan, 1974.

Ansel Adams: Images 1923–1974. Foreword by Wallace Stegner. Boston: New York Graphic Society, 1974. Bibliography. Also signed deluxe ed. with 1 print. 1,000 copies.

Photographs of the Southwest. Text by Lawrence Clark Powell. Boston: New York Graphic Society, 1976.

The Portfolios of Ansel Adams. Foreword by John Szarkowski. Boston: New York Graphic Society, 1977.

Yosemite and the Range of Light. Intro. by Paul Brooks. Boston: New York Graphic Society, 1979. Also signed deluxe ed. with 1 print. 250 copies.

See also Edey, *Essays;* Hume, *The Great West;* Naef, *Collection;* Szarkowski, *Looking;* chapter 7 catalogues.

Adams, Robert
United States 1937–

Adams lives and works in Colorado, where his photographs have concentrated on the sprawl of housing tracts, drive-ins, and shopping centers that every year extends its boundaries farther over the land. After teaching English for several years, he began to photograph seriously in 1967. Adams is a describer: his images are objective, spare, and informational. Social issues involving ecology, urban chaos, and the quality of the human environment are central to his work, but he provides no answers — only the data about what is actually happening and the implication that underneath it is a final beauty.

"Paradoxically," he wrote about his work, "we also need to see the whole geography, natural and man-made, to experience a peace; all land, no matter what has happened to it, has over it a grace, an absolutely persistent beauty. The subject of these pictures is, in this sense, not tract homes or freeways but the source of all Form, light. The Front Range is astonishing because it is overspread with light of such richness that banality is impossible. Even subdivisions, which we hate for the obscenity of the

Robert Adams. *Outdoor Theater and Cheyenne Mountain,* 1968. Silver print. (Courtesy Castelli Graphics)

speculator's greed, are at certain times of day transformed to a dry, cold brilliance" (*The New West*).

WORK Chiefly suburban and urban landscapes. Also includes some interiors and people in their environments.

MEDIUM Silver prints. (The photographer tends to print his work flatter in contrast and lighter than the typical full-scale modern silver print.)

AVAILABILITY AND PRICE Through galleries; moderately high.

SIGNATURE/OTHER IDENTIFICATION

COLLECTIONS Colorado, MMA, MOMA, Princeton (Art Museum).

SELECTED BIBLIOGRAPHY
The New West: Landscapes Along the Colorado Front Range. Intro. by John Szarkowski. Boulder: Colorado Associated University Press, 1974.

Denver: A Photographic Survey of the Metropolitan Area. Boulder: Colorado Associated University Press, 1977.

See also Hume, *The Great West;* Life Library, *Year 1977;* Szarkowski, *Mirrors;* chapter 7 catalogues.

Adamson, Robert
See Hill, David Octavius / Adamson, Robert.

Alinder, Jim
United States 1941–

Alinder headed the photography department at the University of Nebraska (Lincoln) before becoming director of Friends of Photography (Carmel, California) in 1977. That same year he was elected president of the Society for Photographic Education (SPE), and he is a contributing editor to *Exposure,* the SPE journal.

Since 1969 Alinder has photographed primarily using a panoramic camera with a 150-degree angle of view. In the exaggerated perspective of the panorama format, he casually places a figure or figures (his wife and children) as if in a straightforward snapshot; the contrast between the ordinary humans and the looming landscape sets up a curious counterpoint in his work.

According to James L. Enyeart: "His subjects most often reflect the excesses evident in our commercial edifices and sharpen our eye for those things taken for granted because of their everyday presence. A common midwestern grain elevator takes on a significance comparable to the tallest tree or the oldest pyramid documented by his 19th century counterparts" (*Fine Photographic Slide Sets* catalogue, Rochester, N.Y.: Light Impressions, 1976, p. 14).

WORK   Chiefly wide-angle views of figures in mid-America landscapes.

MEDIUM   Silver prints (averaging about 8 × 17¾).

AVAILABILITY AND PRICE   Through galleries; moderate.

SIGNATURE/OTHER IDENTIFICATION

COLLECTIONS   Chicago, IMP/GEH, Kansas, MIT (Hayden), MOMA, New Mexico, Smithsonian, VSW; BN, NGC.

SELECTED BIBLIOGRAPHY
Kansas Album. Ed. by Alinder. Danbury, N.H.: Addison House, for the Kansas Bankers' Association, 1977.
"Spirit Documents." *Creative Camera,* July 1970, pp. 214–217.
U.S. Camera Annual 1970.
See also Hume, *The Great West;* chapter 7 catalogues.

Jim Alinder. *David, Palace of Living Art, Los Angeles,* 1974. Silver print. (Courtesy the artist)

Alvarez Bravo, Manuel
Mexico 1902–

Alvarez Bravo began his photographic career in 1924. In 1929 at Tina Modotti's suggestion he sent a portfolio of prints to Edward Weston, who encouraged him to continue his work. He became friendly with Diego Rivera and other artists active during the 1930s ferment in the arts in Mexico. Alvarez Bravo was also aware of the European surrealists, and their influence can be felt in the intensely personal, dreamlike quality that many of his images suggest. In 1945 Diego Rivera said, "Profound and discreet poetry, desperate and refined irony emanate from the photographs of Manual Alvarez Bravo, like those particles suspended in the air which render visible a ray of light as it penetrates a dark room" (quoted in *Manuel Alvarez Bravo* [1971]).

Alvarez Bravo has recorded what many feel to be the essence of Mexican life and culture. Paul Strand wrote: "His work is rooted firmly in his love and compassionate understanding of his own country, its people, their problems and their needs. These he has never ceased to explore and to know intimately. He is a man who has mastered a medium which he respects meticulously and which he uses to speak with warmth about Mexico as Atget spoke about Paris" (*Aperture* [1968], p. 2).

Manuel Alvarez Bravo. *Portrait of the Eternal (Isabel Villaseñor)*, 1937. Silver print. (Courtesy the artist)

WORK Chiefly scenes of life and death in Mexico, metaphorical images. Also includes photographs of works of art.

MEDIA Silver prints, color.

AVAILABILITY AND PRICE Through galleries in small quantities; moderately high. Vintage prints rare; high.

SIGNATURE/OTHER IDENTIFICATION

PORTFOLIOS *See* chapter 6 entry.

COLLECTIONS IMP/GEH, MOMA, New Mexico, New Orleans, Norton Simon; BN, Mexico City.

SELECTED BIBLIOGRAPHY
Bertram D. Wolfe and Diego Rivera. *Portrait of Mexico.* New York: Covici Friede, 1937. Photographs by Alvarez Bravo, Tina Modotti, Lupercio.
Emily Edwards. *Painted Walls of Mexico: From Prehistoric Times until Today.* Austin: University of Texas Press, 1966.
William Philip Spratling. *More Human Than Divine.* Mexico City: Universidad Nacional Autonome de Mexico, 1966.
Manuel Alvarez Bravo Fotografías 1928–1968. Poems by Juan García Ponce. Mexico City: Instituto Nacional de Bellas Artes, 1968.
Manuel Alvarez Bravo. Text by Fred R. Parker. Pasadena, Calif.: Pasadena Art Museum, 1971. Bibliography.
"Manuel Alvarez Bravo." *Aperture* 1, no. 4 (1953): 28–36.
"Manuel Alvarez Bravo." *Aperture* 13, no. 4 (1968): 2–9.
"Manuel Alvarez Bravo." *Album*, no. 9 (1970), pp. 2–12.
A. D. Coleman. "The Indigenous Vision of Manuel Alvarez Bravo." *Artforum* 14 (Apr. 1976): 60–63.
Gerry Badger. "The Labyrinth of Solitude — The Art of Manuel Alvarez Bravo." *The British Journal of Photography*, 21 May 1976, pp. 424 ff.
Jane Livingston et al. *M. Alvarez Bravo.* Boston: Godine, and Washington, D.C.: Corcoran Gallery, 1978.
See also Life Library, *Great Photographers*; Szarkowski, *Looking*; Travis, *Julien Levy*; Witkin, *Julien Levy*; chapter 7 catalogue.

Annan, James Craig
Scotland 1864–1946

Like his father, Thomas Annan (see following entry), J. Craig Annan was a well-known portrait photographer in Glasgow. J. Craig worked in his father's printing factory and in their portrait studio. His personal work was pictorial in style and he was an early experimenter in the serious use of hand-held cameras. Jonathan Green wrote, "His best work anticipates the decisive moment esthetic in which an actual event is given formality and meaning by the strength of the visual organization" (Green, *Camera Work*, p. 334).

In the 1890s Annan made gravure prints from the calotypes of D. O. Hill and Robert Adamson, creating renewed interest in their work. Annan was active in the late-nineteenth-century pictorial movement and was a member of The Linked Ring. He was first president of the International Society of Pictorial Photographers (1904).

WORK   Includes portraits, street and genre scenes.

MEDIA   Best known for gravures. Also made carbon prints.

AVAILABILITY AND PRICE   Vintage prints rare; high. *Camera Work* gravures low to moderate.

COLLECTIONS   IMP/GEH, MMA, Smithsonian; RPS.

SELECTED BIBLIOGRAPHY
Joseph T. Keiley. "J. Craig Annan." *Camera Work,* no. 8 (Oct. 1904), pp. 17–18.
F. C. Lambert. "The Pictorial Work of J. Craig Annan." *Practical Photographer,* Library Series, no. 13 (1904).
"Photography as a Means of Artistic Expression." *Camera Work,* no. 32 (Oct. 1910), pp. 21–24.
Camera Work: Gravures in nos. 8, 19, 26, 32, 45.
See also Green, *Camera Work;* Naef, *Collection.*

Annan, Thomas
Scotland 1829–1887

Thomas Annan set up a calotype studio in Glasgow in 1855 and became well known for his photographic reproductions of paintings and for his other copy work, landscapes, and architectural views. He was also a fine portrait photographer, with a simple, direct style not unlike Nadar's. Between 1868 and 1877 he photographed the Glasgow slums for the Glasgow City Improvement Trust, a project believed to be the earliest commissioned documentation of this type. Annan was interested in permanent printing processes, and his printing factory near Glasgow, T. and R. Annan and Sons, introduced the photogravure process into Great Britain. His factory published carbon prints of Hill and Adamson negatives, fine-art gravures (including work by P. H. Emerson), as well as his own work. He was the father of the photographer J. Craig Annan (see preceding entry).

WORK   Chiefly documentation of the Glasgow slums. Also includes architecture of Glasgow and its environs, portraits (e.g., professors at Glasgow University), landscapes, art reproductions.

MEDIA   Calotypes; collodion wet-plate negatives, albumen prints; carbon prints; gravures. May bear monogram.

AVAILABILITY AND PRICE   Gravure prints from books frequently found; low to moderate. Carbon prints rare; moderately high. Calotypes and albumen prints seldom found; moderate to moderately high.

COLLECTIONS   IMP/GEH, LOC; Mitchell Library.

Thomas Annan. *Close No. 83, High Street No. 10.* From *The Old Closes and Streets of Glasgow,* 1900. Gravure. (Courtesy The Witkin Gallery)

SIGNATURE/OTHER IDENTIFICATION

SELECTED BIBLIOGRAPHY
Sir Walter Scott. *Marmion: A Tale of Flodden Field.* London: A. W. Bennett, 1866. 15 albumen prints.
The Painted Windows of the Glasgow Cathedral. Glasgow: Maclehose, 1867.
Photographs of Glasgow. Intro. by A. G. Forbes. Glasgow: Duthie [1868]. 13 albumen prints.
The Old Country Houses of the Old Glasgow Gentry. Glasgow: Maclehose, 1870. 100 albumen prints. 120 copies. 2d ed., 1878. 225 copies.
Memorials of the Old College of Glasgow. Glasgow: Maclehose, 1871. Carbon prints.
Hugh Macdonald. *Days at the Coast: or the Frith of Clyde.* Glasgow [ca. 1876]. 12 albumen prints.
Photographs of Old Closes, Streets, &c., 1868–1877. Glasgow City Improvement Trust, 1877. 40 carbon prints.
The Old Closes and Streets of Glasgow. Intro. by William Young. Glasgow: T. & R. Annan, 1900. 50 gravures, including 38 from Annan's photographs taken in 1868. 100 copies. Another ed., Glasgow: Maclehose. 100 copies.
Thomas Annan's Old Streets and Closes of Glasgow. Intro. by Anita V. Mozley. New York: Dover, 1977.
Margaret F. Harker. "Annans of Glasgow." *The British Journal of Photography,* 12 and 19 Oct. 1973, pp. 932–935, 966–969.
Anita V. Mozley. "Thomas Annan of Glasgow." *Image* 20 (June 1977): 1–12.

Anthony, Edward
United States 1818–1888

The Anthony name is frequently seen on cartes de visite and stereographs published by the firm of E. and H. T. Anthony and Company, New York City, under its own logo, from the 1850s to 1874. Anthony took his first daguerreotype lesson from Samuel F. B. Morse and is believed to be the first to have used photography in a government survey: in the 1840s he joined an expedition covering the border between the eastern United States and Canada. Afterward he and a fellow photographer, J. M. Edwards, traveled to Washington, D.C., where they made daguerreotype portraits of members of Congress and other notables.

In 1847 Anthony became an importer of daguerreotype materials and, shortly thereafter, a manufacturer and distributor of the same, supplying photographers such as Mathew Brady and many others with equipment and chemicals. The company later acquired a complete set of Brady's Civil War negatives as a result of Brady's default of payment for supplies. Anthony's prints from these negatives, especially carte-de-visite portraits, are frequently found, as are works he commissioned from other photographers and published under the Anthony name. Anthony's "instantaneous" stereographs of people and vehicles on the streets of New York City were among the first to record clearly such activity. In 1901 E. and H. T. Anthony merged with Scovill and Adams Company to become Anthony and Scovill Company; in 1907 the firm became Ansco Company, and later Agfa.

WORK Includes portraits (Civil War and trade), street scenes, travel views, etc.

MEDIA Daguerreotypes; collodion wet-plate negatives, albumen prints.

AVAILABILITY AND PRICE Significant daguerreotypes rare; extremely high. Mass-produced stereographs and cartes de visite (both identifiable by studio name) frequently found; low.

SIGNATURE/OTHER IDENTIFICATION

COLLECTIONS IMP/GEH, LOC, many other historical archives.

SELECTED BIBLIOGRAPHY
[Firm of E. Anthony.] *Comprehensive . . . Catalogue of Photographic Apparatus.* New York: Snelling, 1854.
E. and H. T. Anthony & Co. *New Catalogue of Stereoscopes and Views.* New York [ca. 1867]. Lists 2,000 views.
————. *Illustrated Descriptive Price List of Photographic Apparatus,* 1872.
————. *Illustrated Catalogue of Photographic Equipment and Materials for Amateurs,* 1891. Reprint, Hastings-on-Hudson, N.Y.: Morgan & Morgan, 1970.
See also Taft, *Photography.*

Arbus, Diane
United States 1923–1971

The daughter of well-to-do parents, Arbus grew up in a comfortable, middle-class world, married young, and became, with her husband, Allan, a successful fashion photographer. After almost twenty years of a conventional career, she began in the late 1950s to explore her personal view of the world. She took a class with Lisette Model, who encouraged her unorthodox vision. Arbus herself best conveyed the feeling of her prints: "Once I dreamed I was on a gorgeous ocean liner, all pale, gilded, cupid-encrusted, rococo as a wedding cake. There was smoke in the air, people were drinking and gambling. I knew the ship was on fire and we were sinking, slowly. They knew it too but they were very gay, dancing and singing and kissing, a little delirious. There was no hope. I was terribly elated. I could photograph anything I wanted to" (*Artforum*, May 1971).

Arbus found unsettling oddities of life-style and personality among "normal" people as often as she did among those who are defined by society as deviates. Transvestites, people in the park, inmates in an insane asylum, frolickers at a masked ball, nudists — Arbus's subjects are poignant in their willingness to reveal themselves to the camera. Arbus's own personality also shaped these images, as did her style of posing people facing square into the camera and her lighting, frequently with direct frontal flash, which isolated her subjects in pitiless clarity. Within ten years, Arbus produced a body of compelling, controversial, and influential work. After her suicide, her photographs became even more fascinating to those who reinterpreted them in terms of her death.

WORK Chiefly portraits (e.g., close-ups of people on the street or at home, children, nudists, midgets, carnival performers, twins or people in matching costumes). Also includes a few environments without people (e.g., a castle at Disneyland), early fashion work. Her last series was of inmates in a home for retarded women.

MEDIUM Silver prints (images printed as large as 14×14 on 16×20 photographic paper, unmounted). Any large, unmounted print may ripple slightly at the edges, and Arbus said she liked this effect, even if the print was framed.

Diane Arbus. *Patriotic Boy with Straw Hat, Buttons and Flag, Waiting to March in a Pro-War Parade, N.Y.C.,* 1967. Silver print. (Courtesy Doon Arbus / Diane Arbus Estate)

AVAILABILITY AND PRICE   Arbus made few prints from each negative, and often she left them unsigned, so her own signed prints are priced extremely high. Estate prints made by Neil Selkirk are available through galleries; moderate. (The back of these prints carries identification of printer, title, and signature by Arbus's daughter Doon.) Images from the photographer's ten-print *Portfolio* (on 16×20 paper) are available individually from the estate and through galleries on 11×14 paper only; moderate.

SIGNATURE/OTHER IDENTIFICATION

PORTFOLIO   *See* chapter 6 entry.

COLLECTIONS   Minneapolis, MOMA, New Orleans, other major collections.

SELECTED BIBLIOGRAPHY
Diane Arbus. Millerton, N.Y.: Aperture, 1972.
Doon Arbus. "Diane Arbus — Photographer." *Ms.* 1 (Oct. 1972): 44 ff.
Peter C. Bunnell. "Diane Arbus." *Print Collector's Newsletter* 4 (Jan.-Feb. 1973): 128–130.
Susan Sontag. "Freak Show." *New York Review of Books,* 15 Nov. 1973, pp. 13–19.
Robert B. Stevens. "The Diane Arbus Bibliography." *Exposure* 15 (Sept. 1977): 10–19.

See also Life Library, *Documentary, Year 1973;* Mann, *Women;* Szarkowski, *Looking, Mirrors;* Tucker, *Eye;* chapter 7 catalogue.

ARTISTS

The interplay between "art" and photography is complex and varied and immediately snarled in semantic difficulties. As David Bourdon wrote in a catalogue introduction to a show combining works by artists in traditional media and works by photographers: "Many established prejudices, as well as the English language, encourage an elitist distinction between artists and photographers (who are also artists). It is often thought, at least in some quarters of the art world, that artists' photographs are inherently 'high art,' that is, somehow superior to 'mere' photography. Some conceptual-type artists, it should be noted, make their photographs in all but total ignorance of the craft, history and expressive possibilities of photography. It is hoped all . . . works . . . will be judged by the same standards and evaluated on their individual merits" [*(photo) (photo)²* . . . *(photo)"* catalogue, listed in chapter 7].

Artists have taken or used photographs for a variety of reasons. Some, like Charles Sheeler, took them as studies for other works. Ben Shahn and others used photography as an independent expressive medium, in addition to their other work. Dadaists, such as Hannah Höch, made photocollages or mixed-media collages, as have Robert Rauschenberg and many other contemporary artists. László Moholy-Nagy and other Bauhaus photographers of the 1920s explored the "new vision" that photography brought to the visual arts.

Artists, here, means those who use photographs but identify themselves primarily with the art world and its concerns. Not included are those who use photographs only as a step in the production of some completely different art form, for example photo realist painters such as Chuck Close. The dividing lines are often hazy: it can be argued that Moholy-Nagy's photographs, for example, are at least as significant as the other work he produced; Robert Heinecken uses found imagery and takes few photographs himself, yet is linked to the world of photography. So, with apologies to all who believe their favorite photographer/artist should be listed here but isn't — or vice versa — we give the following names. (*Italicized* photographers have separate entries in this chapter.)

Anschutz, Thomas. U.S. 1851–1912
Antin, Eleanor. U.S. 1935–
Baldessari, John. U.S. 1931–
Bayer, Herbert, U.S. (b. Austria). 1900–
Bearden, Romare. U.S. 1914–
Becher, Bernhard / Becher, Hilla
Beckley, Bill. U.S. 1946–
Bellmer, Hans. France (b. Germany). 1902–1975
Berman, Wallace. U.S. 1926–
Citroën, Paul. Netherlands (b. Germany). 1896–

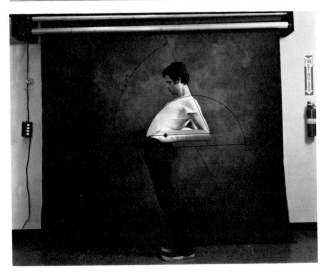

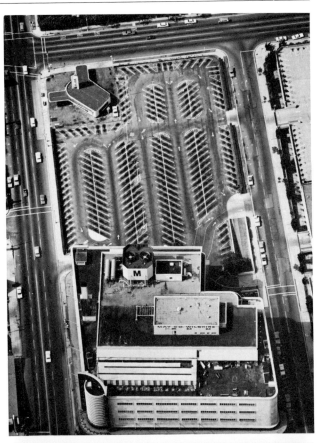

ABOVE: Robert Cumming. *Pen-Point Choreography,* 1976. Unique silver print. (Courtesy the artist)

TOP RIGHT: Edward Ruscha. *May Company, 6067 Wilshire Blvd.* From his book *Thirtyfour Parking Lots,* 1967. Silver print. (Courtesy Heavy Industry Publications)

BOTTOM RIGHT: Thomas Anschutz. *Aunt Em Tarrey of Wheeling, West Virginia, with "Ris," an Old Retainer,* ca. 1881. Cyanotype. (Courtesy The Witkin Gallery)

BELOW: Barbara Kasten. Untitled, 1977. Cyanotype (photogenic painting on paper, oil pastel), 29×42 inches. (Courtesy the artist)

Cumming, Robert. U.S. 1943–
Degas, (Hilaire Germain) Edgar. France. 1834–1917
Dibbets, Jan. Netherlands. 1941–
Eakins, Thomas
Ernst, Max. France (b. Germany). 1891–1976
Groover, Jan
Grosz, George. Germany. 1893–1959
Hausmann, Raoul. France (b. Austria). 1886–1971
Haxton, David. U.S. 1943–
Heartfield, John
Höch, Hannah. Germany. 1889–
Hockney, David. England. 1937–
Kasten, Barbara. U.S. 1936–
Kepes, Gyorgy. U.S. (b. Hungary). 1906–
Le Gac, Jean. France. 1936–
McMillan, Jerry. U.S. 1936–
Magritte, René. Belgium. 1898–1966
Man Ray
Marsh, Reginald. U.S. (b. France). 1898–1954
Moholy-Nagy, László
Mucha, Alphonse Marie. France (b. Moravia). 1860–1939
Nash, Paul. England. 1889–1946
Rauschenberg, Robert. U.S. 1925–
Rodchenko, Alexander. Russia. 1891–1956

Ruscha, Edward. U.S. 1937–
Samaras, Lucas
Schad, Christian. Germany. 1894–
Shahn, Ben
Sheeler, Charles
Warhol, Andy. U.S. 1930–
Wegman, William. U.S. 1943–
Wells, Lynton. U.S. 1940–
Wesselmann, Tom. U.S. 1931–

WORK/MEDIA/AVAILABILITY AND PRICE/SIGNATURE–OTHER IDENTI-
FICATION/PORTFOLIOS/COLLECTIONS *See* individual entries.

SELECTED BIBLIOGRAPHY
Kunstlerphotographien im XX. Jahrhundert. Hannover, Ger-
    many: Kestner-Gesellschaft, 1977.
Hector Maclean. *Photography for Artists.* London: P. Lund, 1896.
W. Rotzler. *Photography as Artistic Experiment: From Fox Tal-
    bot to Moholy-Nagy.* New York: Amphoto, 1976.
Robert Doty. "The Value of Photography to the Artist, 1839."
    Image 11, no. 6 (1962): 25–28.
See also Coke, *Painter;* Scharf, *Art;* Stelzer, *Kunst;* Vigneau,
    Histoire; chapter 7 catalogues.

Alexander Rodchenko. *Assembling for a Demonstration,* 1928.
Silver print. (Collection, The Museum of Modern Art, New York
City)

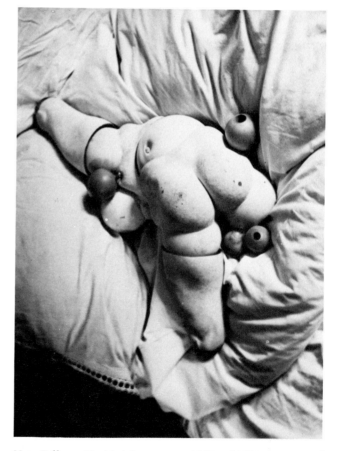

Hans Bellmer. Untitled, between ca. 1947 and 1951. A variant of
Plate XI in his book *Le Jeu de la pupée,* 1949. Silver print with
some hand-tinting. (Courtesy Mark Kelman Works of Art)

Atget, Jean-Eugène-Auguste
France 1857–1927

In his youth, Eugène Atget was a sailor, and later an actor eking out a living playing minor roles. In his early forties, faced with the need to earn a living in some other way, he tried painting and then turned to photography. A friend wrote of him: "For some time he had had the ambition to create a collection of all that which both in Paris and its surroundings was artistic and picturesque. An immense subject" (quoted in *The World of Atget,* p. xi). With a single-minded devotion, Atget began his collection: architecture, trees, statues, shop windows, street vendors, fountains, urns — thousands of photographs in dozens of categories. The sign on Atget's door read *Documents pour Artistes* and his notebook showed that he sold photographs to designers, painters (Braque, Utrillo, and Vlaminck among them), editors, architects, stage designers, and others who used his pictures as resources for their own work.

It was not until just before his death that Atget's photographs began to be appreciated in their own right. Man Ray published a few (without credit) in 1926 in his periodical *La Révolution surréaliste.* Berenice Abbott recognized Atget's genius and it was largely through her efforts after his death that his work was preserved and promoted. She predicted, "He will be remembered as an urbanist historian, a genuine romanticist, a lover of Paris, a Balzac of the camera, from whose work we can weave a large tapestry of French civilization" (ibid., p. xxxi).

John Szarkowski described the unique poetry of Atget's vision: "His pictures are as plain and transparent and precious as water. Individually they are like short beautiful sentences made of small and common words. Collectively they are a testament to the simplicity of genius" ("Eugène Atget: The Simplicity of Genius," *Modern Photography,* Jan. 1973, p. 73).

WORK   About 10,000 photographs of Paris and its surroundings — streets, buildings, monuments, architectural details, parks, vendors, prostitutes, vehicles, farms and farmers, trees, flowers, rivers, ponds, and many other categories.

MEDIA   Gelatin dry-plate negatives (7⅛×9⅜). Vintage prints (most have the photographer's written identification on verso at top and/or name stamp — see examples) are contact prints made on a silver-chloride printing-out paper and toned in gold chloride (sometimes called aristotypes). No platinum prints are known, though some prints have the soft look of platinum.

AVAILABILITY AND PRICE   Through galleries and at auction. Vintage prints rare; extremely high. Various modern gold-toned silver prints made by Abbott (1930–1968; verso has Atget/Abbott stamps) are frequently found; moderate to high. Limited-edition modern prints from the Museum of Modern Art (New York City) moderately high.

PORTFOLIO   *See* chapter 6 entry.

COLLECTIONS   The Museum of Modern Art holds the prints (4,000) and negatives (1,280) acquired by Abbott. Also Chicago,

IMP/GEH, MMA, New Mexico, New Orleans, NGC, San Francisco; Antwerp, Archives Photographiques, BN.

SIGNATURE/OTHER IDENTIFICATION

E. ATGET
Rue Campagne-Premiere, 17e

Photograph by Eugene Atget
Copyright: Berenice Abbott
Reproduction rights reserved

EUGENE ATGET PHOTOGRAPH
COLLECTION BERENICE ABBOTT

EUGÈNE ATGET
PHOTOGRAPH
Printed by
Berenice Abbott

(Handwriting sample)

Jean-Eugène-Auguste Atget. *Marche de Carmes, Place Maubert,* ca. 1910. Silver print made by Berenice Abbott from the original plate. (Courtesy The Witkin Gallery)

SELECTED BIBLIOGRAPHY

Atget, Photographe de Paris. Preface by Pierre MacOrlan. Paris: Jonquières, 1930. U.S. ed., New York: Weyhe, 1930.

Yvan Christ. *Atget, Photographie de Saint Germain des Près.* Paris, 1951.

A Vision of Paris . . . . Text by Marcel Proust. Ed. by A. D. Trottenberg. New York: Macmillan, 1963. French ed., *Paris de temps perdu.*

The World of Atget. Text and ed. by Berenice Abbott. New York: Horizon, 1964. Reprint, 1975.

Jean Leroy. *Atget: Magicien du vieux Paris en son époque.* Paris: Jean Balbo, 1975.

La Révolution surréaliste, June and Dec. 1926. Uncredited photographs by Atget.

B. J. Kosposth. "Eugène Atget." *Transition,* no. 15 (Feb. 1929), pp. 122–124.

Le Crapouillot, May 1929. Special issue on Paris with selection of photographs by Atget.

John Szarkowski. "Atget." *Album,* no. 3 (1970), pp. 4–12. Excerpt from an exhibition catalogue.

Camera, March 1978. Entire issue.

William Johnson. "Eugène Atget: A Chronological Bibliography." *Exposure* 15 (May 1977): 13–15.

See also Life Library, *Documentary;* Szarkowski, *Looking;* Travis, *Julien Levy;* Witkin, *Julien Levy.*

Jean-Eugène-Auguste Atget. *Newsstand, Paris,* October 1910. Silver print made by Berenice Abbott from the original plate. Cracks such as those visible here are the result of deterioration of Atget's plates. In order to preserve endangered images before they were lost entirely, Abbott often chose to print the plates that were in the worst condition. (Courtesy The Witkin Gallery)

Avedon, Richard
United States 1923–

A student and protégé of Alexey Brodovitch, the influential former art director of *Harper's Bazaar,* Avedon was a photographer for that magazine from 1945 until 1965, when he went to *Vogue.* His fashion work has been innovative and much copied; his photographs anticipated several trends, such as using black high-fashion models and showing models crying, engaged in erotic foreplay, and in other formerly unfashionable poses. His subjects are often in motion — either shot at slow shutter speeds so that the image is blurred or, at the other extreme, frozen sharp in the mid-movement of song, speech, or gesture.

Avedon's portraits of the famous are stark, often grim close-ups isolated against bare studio backgrounds, harshly lit and angled to emphasize every detail of aging anatomy. Enlarged to life size and larger, these portraits are noble and revealing, or grotesque and malicious, depending on one's interpretation of them.

Avedon wrote: "Youth never moves me. I seldom see anything very beautiful in a young face. I do, though: in the downward curve of Maugham's lips. In Isak Dinesen's hands. So much has been written there, there is so much to be read, if one could only read" (quoted in *Observations*). "My photographs don't go below the surface. They don't go below anything. They're readings of what's on the surface. I have great faith in surfaces. A good one is full of clues" (*Avedon,* Minneapolis Institute of Arts exhibition catalogue, 1970).

WORK Includes fashion and advertising, portraits (e.g., the Duke and Duchess of Windsor, Truman Capote, the Chicago Seven, Igor Stravinsky, Andy Warhol), stage and ballet. (See illustration, page 140.)

MEDIA Silver prints (up to mural size), color.

AVAILABILITY AND PRICE Silver prints available through galleries in limited editions and various sizes; moderate to extremely high (prices are raised as editions sell out). Color work is not offered for sale.

SIGNATURE/OTHER IDENTIFICATION

PORTFOLIOS *See* chapter 6 entry.

COLLECTIONS Minneapolis, MMA, MOMA, Philadelphia, Smithsonian, other major collections.

SELECTED BIBLIOGRAPHY

Observations. Text by Truman Capote. New York: Simon & Schuster, 1959.

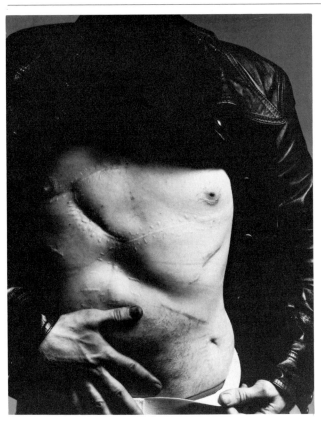

Richard Avedon. *Andy Warhol, Artist, New York City, 8·20·69.* Silver print. (Courtesy the artist)

dium with simplicity and directness. Much of his work documented architecture in France: he was commissioned by the Comité des Monuments Historiques to photograph monuments in Paris, Fontainebleau, Burgundy, and the Dauphiné (1851); he photographed monuments in Arles, Nîmes, and Avignon (1853); he made 1,500 detailed photographs of a new wing of the Louvre (1854–1855). With Marville and Bayard he photographed sculpture at the Louvre and Versailles.

Baron James de Rothschild commissioned Baldus to photograph along railroad lines in France and these works created, according to Robert Sobieszek, "a new type of landscape, an industrial landscape whose terminals, tracks, and bridges are treated with as much understanding and picturesqueness as any purely natural view. [They were significant because] the by-products of industrialization were as much a part of man's environment as nature itself" (Jammes and Sobieszek, *Primitive*). Baldus was a founding member of the Société Héliographique (1851).

WORK   Chiefly monuments and architecture throughout France. Also includes sculpture and paintings, landscape, documentation of the floods in southern France (1865).

MEDIA   Calotypes (1851); improved waxed-paper negatives (by 1852); collodion wet-plate negatives, albumen prints (by 1856); albumenized salt prints. From about 1854, pioneered with heliogravure, an early photomechanical process. Often worked in large format (some prints as large as 17½×23). May be signed "E. Baldus" in negative or have name on mount.

AVAILABILITY AND PRICE   Relatively rare; moderate to high.

SIGNATURE/OTHER IDENTIFICATION

E. Baldus.

COLLECTIONS   IMP/GEH, New Mexico; Archives Beaux-Arts (Comité work), BN.

Nothing Personal. Text by James Baldwin. New York: Atheneum, 1964.

Alice in Wonderland: The Forming of a Company and the Making of a Play. Text by Doon Arbus. New York: Merlin House, 1973.

Avedon. New York: Marlborough Gallery, 1975.

Portraits. Text by Harold Rosenberg. New York: Farrar, Straus & Giroux, 1976.

Avedon: Photographs 1947–1977. New York: Farrar, Straus & Giroux, 1978.

"The Family." *Rolling Stone,* 21 Oct. 1976. Portraits of 73 American political leaders.

See also Life Library, *Art, Studio;* Szarkowski, *Looking.*

Baldus, Edouard-Denis
France 1820–1882

Originally a painter, Baldus was one of those who are sometimes called French primitive photographers. Like Charles Marville, Henri Le Secq, Gustave Le Gray, Hippolyte Bayard, Maxime Du Camp, and others, he pioneered in the early years of photography, using the me-

Edouard-Denis Baldus. *Chemin de Fer du Nord,* ca. 1850s. Albumenized salt print. (Private collection)

SELECTED BIBLIOGRAPHY
Several albums of albumen prints exist (ca. 1853–1855), including:
Chemin de fer de Paris à Lyon et à la Mediterranée. 69 prints.
Chemin de fer du nord: Ligne de Paris à Boulogne. 50 prints.
Chemin de fer du nord: Ligne de Paris à Compiègne par Chantilly. 74 prints.
Paris. 3 vols. (Paris, France, Belgium and Germany). 129 prints (by Baldus and others).
Vues de Paris en Photographie.
See also Jammes and Sobieszek, *Primitive;* Marbot, *Invention.*

Baltz, Lewis
United States 1945–

Baltz considered studying architecture, but ultimately decided to specialize in art, receiving his M.F.A. from Claremont Graduate School in 1971. He is interested in contemporary art issues and his work addresses the concerns of minimal and informational artists. Baltz takes as his subject matter what has been called "the new topographics" — works whose information content is not modulated by overtones of emotion or pictorial beauty. Baltz said of his Maryland photographs, "I hope that these photographs are sterile, that there's no emotional content" (*Nation's Capital*). However, a tension does exist between the documentary aspect of his images and their formal elements; his prints are rich and full scale in tonality and they are obviously intentionally composed, with objects carefully organized and aligned within the image area. Like Walker Evans, who was one photographic influence, Baltz often records architectural facades with a flat frontality that enhances the coolness and objectivity of the image.

WORK Includes images of buildings and their settings (e.g., housing tracts and industrial-park landscapes).

MEDIUM Silver prints.

AVAILABILITY AND PRICE Through galleries; moderate.

Lewis Baltz. *Tract House #4,* 1971. Silver print. (Courtesy Castelli Graphics)

SIGNATURE/OTHER IDENTIFICATION

PORTFOLIOS *See* chapter 6 entry.

COLLECTIONS Baltimore, Chicago, Corcoran, Houston, IMP/GEH, La Jolla, LOC, MMA, New Mexico, Norton Simon, Seattle.

SELECTED BIBLIOGRAPHY
The New Industrial Parks near Irvine, California. New York: Castelli Graphics, 1974.
The Nation's Capital in Photographs, 1976. Washington, D.C.: Corcoran Gallery of Art, 1976.
Manfred Willmann, ed. *American Photographers.* Graz, Austria: Fotogalerie im Forum Stadtpark, 1977.
"Notes on Recent Industrial Developments in Southern California." With William Jenkins. *Image* 17 (June 1974): 1–9.
Carter Ratcliff. "Route 66 Revisited: The New Landscape Photography." *Art in America* 64 (Jan./Feb. 1976): 86–91.
See also Szarkowski, *Mirrors;* Wise, *Choice;* chapter 7 catalogues.

Barnard, George N.
United States 1819–1902

During the Civil War Barnard did photographic work for the Union Army. His usual assignments probably consisted of copying maps and plans, but he also took a number of photographs in the field. In *Photographic Views of Sherman's Campaign* he published photographs that he made along the route followed by General Sherman's army on its campaign at the end of the war and on its famous March to the Sea. E. and H. T. Anthony published some of Barnard's stereo views, *Harper's Weekly* used his photographs as the basis for line engravings, and several photographs that he made with James F. Gibson were published in *Gardner's Photographic Sketch Book of the War.*

The complexities of the wet-plate process made it all but impossible to photograph during actual battles; Barnard usually worked far behind the front lines photographing bridges, railroads, and other engineering installations; famous battle sites; informal scenes with soldiers; as well as the devastation and ruins left by the war. His views of battlefields taken long after the soldiers had gone are as carefully composed as still lifes; their quietness contrasts with the viewer's mental image of what must have happened there. Dramatic clouds added from a second negative during printing are characteristic of Barnard's work.

WORK Chiefly the Civil War (especially Sherman's campaign). Also includes some of the earliest surviving news photographs (daguerreotypes of an 1853 mill fire in Oswego, N.Y.), street scenes (especially vendors, Charleston, S.C., ca. 1875).

MEDIA Collodion wet-plate negatives, gold-toned albumen prints (Civil War photographs; prints from *Sherman's Campaign* are 10×14). Also daguerreotypes.

George N. Barnard. *Chattanooga Valley from Lookout Mountain No. 2.* From *Photographic Views of Sherman's Campaign* [1866]. Albumen print. (Courtesy The Witkin Gallery)

AVAILABILITY AND PRICE   Individual prints occasionally available at auction and through galleries; moderately high to high. Complete copies of *Sherman's Campaign* are very rare; a fine copy was offered by a dealer in 1976 for $14,500. Daguerreotypes rare; extremely high.

SIGNATURE/OTHER IDENTIFICATION

Photo from nature By. G.N. Barnard.

COLLECTIONS   IMP/GEH, LOC, New Mexico; NGC; other major museums.

SELECTED BIBLIOGRAPHY
Photographic Views of Sherman's Campaign. New York [1866]. 61 albumen prints, inscribed "Photo from nature by G. [or Geo.] N. Barnard." (A 30-page supplementary pamphlet, unillustrated, was published separately [New York: Wynkoop & Hallenbeck, 1866].) Reprint, preface by Beaumont Newhall. New York: Dover, 1977.
Alexander Gardner. *Gardner's Photographic Sketch Book of the War.* 2 vols. Washington, D.C.: Philp & Solomons, 1866. Plates 4–11 by Barnard with James F. Gibson. Reprint, 1 vol. New York: Dover, 1959.
See also Life Library, *Great Photographers*; Szarkowski, *Looking.*

Barrow, Thomas F.
United States 1938–

Barrow, who studied with Aaron Siskind in the 1960s and counts him as an important influence in his work, has been active in photography as a curator, editor, writer, and teacher. Originally interested in graphic design, printmaking, and film, he has worked to augment the standard range of photographic materials, format, and imagery.

Describing Barrow's "cancelled" prints, William Jenkins wrote: "These are toned, monochromatic prints made from negatives which, after normal exposure and development, have been 'cancelled.' . . . The product issued to us as viewers is a print from the cancelled negative, with the evidence of the negative having been viciously gouged, punched or scratched meticulously rendered on the toned, signed and titled print. The final result is incredibly complex and multi-layered. . . . The slashes and holes in Barrow's negatives, like Brecht's insistent proscenium arch, are constant reminders that we are not looking at reality but at a *photograph*; a useful but extremely vulnerable extension of our experience" (*Extended Document* catalogue, p. 3, listed in chapter 7).

WORK   Includes documentation of library shelves, cancellation series, Verifax (office copy machine) montages, double-frame sequenced photographs, multiple exposures of television images.

MEDIA   Silver prints (some toned), Verifax prints.

AVAILABILITY AND PRICE   Through galleries; moderate.

COLLECTIONS   IMP/GEH, New Mexico; NGC.

SELECTED BIBLIOGRAPHY
Album, no. 4 (1970), pp. 40–48.
Untitled 9 (1975).
See also Coke, *100 Years*; Hume, *The Great West*; Life Library, *Art*; Wise, *Choice*; chapter 7 catalogues.

SIGNATURE/OTHER IDENTIFICATION

Thomas F. Barrow. *Tucson Palm.* From the series "Cancellations," 1975. Silver print. (Courtesy the artist and Light Gallery)

Bayard, Hippolyte
France 1801–1887

Bayard, an early experimenter with the action of light upon chemicals, investigated various photographic procedures before 1836. Within a month of hearing the announcement of Daguerre's discovery in 1839, he produced negative images on paper. Learning that Daguerre made direct positives, he devised within a few weeks a positive process on paper, too. In exchange for a small grant from the French government he agreed not to make his process public, perhaps so that Daguerre's discovery would not be diminished.

Bayard never received the public recognition or financial rewards that he felt he deserved as much as Daguerre. In protest he made a photograph of himself posing as a drowned man, with the caption: "The body that you see here is that of M. Bayard. . . . The government which had given too much to M. Daguerre said it was able to do

nothing for M. Bayard and the unfortunate man drowned himself."

Bayard remained an enthusiastic and accomplished photographer, nevertheless, who produced carefully composed work as fine as that of contemporaries such as Gustave Le Gray, Henri Le Secq, Charles Marville, and Edouard-Denis Baldus. In the early 1850s he was commissioned by the Comité des Monuments Historiques to record monuments in Normandy. He was a founding member of the Société Héliographique (1851) and the Société Française de Photographie (1854).

WORK Includes architecture and cityscapes (e.g., Normandy, Montmartre), still lifes (e.g., plaster casts, garden scenes), genre scenes, self-portraits, street barricades in Paris (1848).

MEDIA Direct positives on paper; daguerreotypes; waxed-paper negatives, albumen-on-glass negatives, collodion wet-plate negatives, albumen prints.

AVAILABILITY AND PRICE Vintage work very rare; extremely high. Modern limited-edition prints from Bayard's negatives, made by Claudine Sudre in 1972 for the Société Française de Photographie (Paris), are occasionally available; moderate.

SIGNATURE/OTHER IDENTIFICATION (Examples from letters)

PORTFOLIO *See* chapter 6 entry.

COLLECTIONS Chicago, IMP/GEH; Société Française (about 600 prints).

SELECTED BIBLIOGRAPHY
Lo Duca. *Bayard.* Paris: Prisma, 1943.
Hippolyte Bayard: Ein Erfinder der Photographie. German text by O. Steinert. French text by P. Harmant. Essen: Museum Folkwang, 1960.
André Jammes. *Hippolyte Bayard: Ein verkannter Erfinder und Meister der Photographie.* Lucerne: Bucher, 1976.
See also Life Library, *Great Photographers;* Marbot, *Invention.*

Hippolyte Bayard. *Self-Portrait as a Corpse,* ca. 1840. Modern silver print from the original waxed-paper negative. (Courtesy Société Française de Photographie)

Beato, Felice A.
See Robertson, James / Beato, Felice A.

Beaton, Cecil
England 1904–

Born and educated in the upper stratum of English society, Cecil Beaton has had a long and active career in theatrical design and in fashion photography, portraiture, and reportage. As a leading photographer for *Vogue* in the 1930s and later for *Harper's Bazaar,* his fashion and portrait work reflected his interest in the theater. He used elaborate sets, props, shadow projections, and other stage devices in photographing and often created stylized tableaux of mystery or amour. He frankly stated his view of the purpose of fashion photography: "The dressmaker provides the dress, but the photographer must make the woman in that dress appear in a manner that will give all other women a feeling of covetousness" (Life Library, *Studio,* p. 106).

During World War II, Beaton was a photographer for the British Ministry of Information. His documentation of the effects of war at home and in foreign campaigns contrasts sharply with his glamourous fashion fantasies. In addition, Beaton designed scenery and costumes for a number of theatrical productions, including the stage and screen versions of *My Fair Lady.* He often photographed the royal family, making many official portraits as well as less formal studies.

Cecil Beaton. *Nancy Cunard,* late 1920s. Silver print. (Courtesy Sotheby's, London)

WORK Chiefly fashion photographs and portraits of celebrities (e.g., Marlene Dietrich, Elizabeth II, Churchill, Gertrude Stein). Also includes travel photographs (e.g., Morocco, China, Japan, India), reportage of World War II (e.g, London's bombed churches, blitz victims, the war in the Libyan Desert).

MEDIA Silver prints, color.

AVAILABILITY AND PRICE Frequently available at auction, also through galleries; moderate to high. Sotheby's, Belgravia (London), holds Beaton's negatives as a picture library and sells modern and vintage prints at auction, with the exception of royal family portraits.

SIGNATURE/OTHER IDENTIFICATION

COLLECTIONS LIFE, New Orleans; Imperial War Museum (about 40,000 World War II images), NPG.

SELECTED BIBLIOGRAPHY
The Book of Beauty. London: Duckworth, 1930.
Cecil Beaton's Scrapbook, 1937.
Cecil Beaton's New York. London: Batsford, 1938. Rev. ed., *Portrait of New York,* 1948.
Air of Glory. London: HMSO, 1941.
Time Exposure. Text by Peter Quennell. London: Batsford, 1941.
James Pope-Hennessy. *History under Fire.* London: Batsford, 1941.
Winged Squadrons. London: Hutchinson, 1942.
Near East. London: Batsford, 1943.
British Photographers. London: Collins, 1944.
Far East. London: Batsford, 1945.
India. Bombay: Thacker, 1945.
Harold B. Rattenbury. *Face to Face with China.* London: Harrap, 1945.
Chinese Album. London: Batsford, 1946.
An Indian Album. London: Batsford, 1946.
Ashcombe: The Story of a Fifteen-Year Lease. London: Batsford, 1949.
Ballet. London: Wingate, 1951.
Photobiography. London: Odhams, 1951.
Persona Grata. With Kenneth Tynan. London: Wingate, 1953.
Glass of Fashion. Garden City, N.Y.: Doubleday, 1954. Not photographically illustrated.
It Gives Me Great Pleasure. London: Weidenfeld & Nicolson, 1955. U.S. ed., *I Take Great Pleasure.* New York: Day, 1956.
The Face of the World. London: Weidenfeld & Nicolson, 1957.
Japanese. London: Weidenfeld & Nicolson, 1959.
Diaries. London: Weidenfeld & Nicolson. *The Wandering Years: 1922–1939,* 1961. *The Years Between: 1939–1944,* 1965. *The Happy Years: 1944–1948,* 1972. *The Strenuous Years: 1948–1955,* 1973.
Images. Preface by Edith Sitwell. Intro. by Christopher Isherwood. London: Weidenfeld & Nicolson, 1963.
Royal Portraits. Intro. by Peter Quennell. London: Weidenfeld & Nicolson, 1963.
Cecil Beaton's 'Fair Lady.' New York: Holt, Rinehart & Winston, 1964.
Beaton Portraits. London: National Portrait Gallery, 1968.

The Best of Beaton. Intro. by Truman Capote. London: Weidenfeld & Nicolson, 1968.

Cecil Beaton: Memoirs of the 40's. New York: McGraw-Hill, 1972.

The Magic Image: The Genius of Photography from 1839 to the Present Day. With Gail Buckland. London: Weidenfeld & Nicolson, and Boston: Little, Brown, 1975.

Charles Spencer. *Cecil Beaton: Stage and Film Designs.* New York: St. Martin, 1976.

See also Liberman, *Art* (in color bibliography); Life Library, *Studio.*

Becher, Bernhard
Germany 1931–

Becher, Hilla
Germany 1934–

When the Bechers began their collaboration in 1959, Hilla was a photographic archivist and Bernhard (Bernd) a painter and lithographer who had begun to photograph (and to collect photographs of) industrial complexes in Germany. They are best known for their documentation of the typology of structures: photographic comparisons of structures such as lime kilns and gasholders that serve the same, usually industrial, function. As Robert Sobieszek described their work: "The pictures are perfect models of good industrial and architectural photography. They are, however, more. . . . The similarity of the structures . . . and the sameness of the style all contribute to a monotonic effect. But it is this monotony that is so surprisingly refreshing. . . . The similitude of the plates somehow draws the reader into a closer observation of the particulars; a more refined awareness of the details subsumed within an apparent oneness then takes place" (Sobieszek, p. 12).

The Bechers' work is related to that of conceptual artists who seek to record rather than interpret a scene. In some ways it is analogous to the direct and naturalistic renderings of architecture made by early French photographers such as Henri Le Secq and Gustave Le Gray.

WORK Includes residential architecture and industrial structures such as cooling towers, silos, pithead gears, etc., presented as a series of images of different structures that serve the same function or as a series of the same structure seen from different sides.

MEDIUM Silver prints. Often four or more prints are mounted on one panel.

AVAILABILITY AND PRICE Through galleries; moderately high. Series and single images are both sold.

PORTFOLIO *See* chapter 6 entry.

COLLECTIONS MOMA, Oberlin; Wallraf-Richartz.

Bernhard and Hilla Becher. *Cooling Towers,* 1972. Nine silver prints, 60×40 inches, mounted as one piece. (Courtesy Sonnabend Gallery)

SIGNATURE/OTHER IDENTIFICATION

SELECTED BIBLIOGRAPHY

Anonyme Skulpturen: Eine Typologie technischer Bauten. Düsseldorf: Art-Press, 1970. U.S. ed., *Anonyme Skulpturen: A Typology of Technical Constructions.* New York: Wittenborn, 1970.

Die Architektur der Förder- und Wassertürme. Munich: Prestel, 1971.

Framework Houses of the Siegen Industrial Region. Munich: Schirmer Mosel, 1977.

Kunst-Zeitung, no. 2 (Jan. 1969). Entire issue.

Robert A. Sobieszek. "Two Books of Ultra-Topography." *Image* 14 (Sept. 1971): 11–13.

Carl Andre. "A Note on Bernhard and Hilla Becher." *Artforum* 11 (Dec. 1972): 59–61.

Joseph Masheck. "Unconscious Formalism: A Response to Andre's Note on the Bechers." *Artforum* 11 (Mar. 1973): 74–75.

See also Kahmen, *Art History;* chapter 7 catalogues.

Bedford, Francis
England 1816–1894

Originally a lithographer, Bedford was active in photography in the 1850s–1860s. His work, which concentrated on the architecture and landscape of Great Britain, was held in very high repute by his contemporaries and was widely published. As a result, in 1862 he was commanded by Queen Victoria to accompany the young Prince of Wales (the future Edward VII) on an educational tour of the Middle East. Bedford later published views from the trip, some of which included the royal party. He was active in the formation of the (Royal) Photographic Society of Great Britain (1853).

Graham Ovenden wrote: "The soft caressing tone of the prints, the unassuming nature of pastoral life is seldom bettered in Victorian photography. Bedford's photographs illustrate what is perhaps one of the most important qualities in Pre-Raphaelite art, the harmonious existence of the natural and the human world" (Ovenden, *Pre-Raphaelite*).

WORK Chiefly topographical views of Britain (e.g., landscapes, castles, cathedrals). Also scenes from Palestine, Syria, Constantinople, Athens, and the Mediterranean islands (made while accompanying the Prince of Wales, 1862).

MEDIA Collodion wet-plate, collodion dry-plate negatives, albumen prints. Prints are often small — cartes de visite, stereographs, 4×6½ — but larger sizes, 10×12, exist from Near East tour. May bear name and negative number in plate (see below).

AVAILABILITY AND PRICE Printed in large numbers for travel-view collections and as book illustrations. Several sets of stereo views issued (e.g., *Devonshire Illustrated, Herefordshire Illustrated, North Wales Illustrated*). Prints may be found unmounted or pasted on album pages. Priced extremely low to low.

SIGNATURE/OTHER IDENTIFICATION

COLLECTIONS Found in many museums, libraries, and educational institutions, often filed by subject matter.

SELECTED BIBLIOGRAPHY
The Sunbeam. Ed. by Philip Delamotte. London, 1857. Photographs by Bedford and others.
Pictorial Illustrations of Torquay and Its Neighborhood. Chester: Catherall & Pritchard [1860s]. 30 prints.
Tour in the East: Photographic Pictures Made by Mr. Francis Bedford [accompanying] *His Royal Highness, The Prince of Wales.* London: Day, 1862. 3 portfolios containing 172 prints.
William and Mary Howitt. *Ruined Abbeys and Castles of Great Britain.* London: Bennett, 1862. 27 prints by Bedford and others. Vol. 2 (1864) has no photographs by Bedford.
———— *The Wye: Its Ruined Abbeys and Castles.* London: Bennett, 1863. 4 prints by Bedford, 2 by Russell W. Sedgfield. Extracted from the preceding entry.
Charles Piazzi Smyth. *Our Inheritance in the Great Pyramid.* London: Alexander Strahan, 1864. Frontispiece by Bedford.

Photographic Views of Chester. Chester, 1865. 10 prints.
Photographic Views of Tintern Abbey and Chepstow. Chester [ca. 1865]. 10 prints.
The Stones of Palestine. Text by Mrs. Mentor Mott, 1865. 12 prints.
The Holy Land, Egypt, Constantinople, Athens, etc. Text by W. M. Thompson. London: Day, 1866. 48 prints.
Photographic Views of Exeter.
Photographic Views of North Wales. 20 prints.
Photographic Views of Warwickshire. Chester: Catherall & Pritchard. 15 prints (some sources list 12 or 30).
See also Ovenden, *Pre-Raphaelite.*

Francis Bedford. Untitled English scene, ca. 1860s. Albumen print. (Courtesy The Witkin Gallery)

Bellocq, E. J.
United States 1873–1949

Little is known about Bellocq, a commercial photographer who worked in New Orleans from about 1895 to 1940. An unattractive man — even misshapen — Bellocq had few friends. After his death, eighty-nine glass-plate negatives of prostitutes from the Storyville district in New Orleans were found in his desk. They date from about 1912 and are the only part of his work known to exist. John Szarkowski speculated that the photographs may have been a commercial assignment. "But the pictures themselves suggest that they were not made on assignment, but as a personal adventure. They possess a sense of leisure in the making, and a variety of conception not typical of photographic jobs done at the customer's request. It is more likely that Bellocq photographed the women of Storyville because he found them irresistibly compelling" (*E. J. Bellocq*, p. 13). Credit goes to photographer Lee Friedlander for saving, printing, and promoting Bellocq's work, much as Berenice Abbott did for Eugène Atget. Deterioration of the glass plates, which had occurred before Friedlander acquired them, has added interest to Bellocq's images rather than detracted from them. The movie *Pretty Baby* (1978) by Louis Malle portrays Bellocq photographing women in a Storyville brothel.

E. J. Bellocq. *Girl on the Wicker Chaise Longue,* ca. 1913. Modern silver print (on printing-out paper) made by Lee Friedlander from the original plate. (Courtesy Lee Friedlander)

WORK Portraits of prostitutes in their rooms, plus a few in outdoor settings.

MEDIUM Gelatin dry-plate negatives. Friedlander makes modern silver prints (identified by his stamp on the back) using printing-out paper and gold-chloride toning to reproduce the delicate tonal range of the negatives.

AVAILABILITY AND PRICE Small quantities of Friedlander's modern prints are available through galleries; moderately high.

COLLECTIONS MOMA, New Orleans. Many collections have one or two of Friedlander's prints from Bellocq's negatives.

SELECTED BIBLIOGRAPHY
E. J. Bellocq: Storyville Portraits. Ed. by John Szarkowski. Preface by Lee Friedlander. New York: MOMA, 1970.
Al Rose. *Storyville, New Orleans: Being an Authentic, Illustrated Account of the Notorious Red-Light District.* University: University of Alabama Press, 1974.
See also Life Library, *Caring;* Szarkowski, *Looking.*

Bernhard, Ruth
United States (b. Germany) 1905–

The daughter of graphic artist Lucien Bernhard, Ruth Bernhard studied art history and typography in Berlin, came to the United States in 1927, and began photographing in 1930. Self-taught as a photographer, she has said that the most important influences on her work were Edward Weston, the poet Rainer Maria Rilke, and Michelangelo. Though, like Weston, she photographs natural forms in a sharp-focus, straight style, she is more sensual and romantic in her interpretation of nature than he was.

The photographer once wrote: "My photographs are the result of intense reaction to my daily experiences. I do not wish to record, but to search for the elusive fragments of meaning according to my perceptiveness and awareness of the universe. Is a blade of grass not as miraculous as the firmament and of equal value? Life and death are two words for the same thing — all part of the living order, the illumination of which leads to the underlying philosophy of the creative artists in every medium" (*The Photograph as Poetry,* Pasadena Art Museum exhibition catalogue, 1960).

WORK Includes female nudes, natural objects (e.g., shells, leaves) symbolic imagery dealing with the nature of life and death, portraits. Some are multiple exposures. (See illustration, page 280.)

MEDIUM Silver prints.

AVAILABILITY AND PRICE Vintage prints occasionally available; moderately high. Modern prints available through galleries; moderate.

SIGNATURE/OTHER IDENTIFICATION

Ruth Bernhard

PORTFOLIOS *See* chapter 6 entry.

COLLECTIONS MOMA, Oakland, other major collections.

SELECTED BIBLIOGRAPHY
Melvin Van [Peebles]. *The Big Heart.* San Francisco: Fearon, 1957.
"Portfolio: Ten Reproductions." *Aperture* 7, no. 3 (1959): 109–121.
Photo-Image 1, no. 1 (1976).
See also Lacey and LaRotonda, *Nude;* Mann, *Women;* chapter 7 catalogues.

Bing, Ilse
United States (b. Germany) 1899–

After a long period of neglect, in the mid-1970s Bing's work began to regain the attention it received when she was an active young photographer in Paris in the 1930s. Bing studied art history in Frankfurt in the late 1920s. To complete her dissertation, she obtained a camera and taught herself photography, and in 1928 decided to become a photographer. In 1930 she settled in Paris, where she free-lanced and exhibited in leading galleries and in major shows. The rise of Nazism forced her to flee to America.

Bing has always experimented freely with new techniques: in the 1930s she was one of the first to work exclusively with a small camera (the Leica); in 1948 she switched to a Rolleiflex 2¼-inch negative at a time when all the other photographers she knew were using the 35mm Leica. She was one of the first to photograph extensively at night, to use portable electronic-strobe lighting, and to solarize negatives. In 1959 her interest turned to drawing and she ceased photographing. In 1976 she explained: "Photography is based on reality with all its integral parts: time, space, and chance. I gave up still photography because a different aspect of time interests me now: no more the single moment in its lasting significance but the flow of time with its permanent change" (statement to the authors).

WORK Includes portraits; people and streets, Paris; nature; scenes in Holland.

MEDIUM Silver prints.

AVAILABILITY AND PRICE Through galleries; moderately high. Vintage prints returned to Bing after World War II are few in number, as are prints made in United States.

SIGNATURE/OTHER IDENTIFICATION

COLLECTIONS Brooklyn, MOMA, New Orleans.

SELECTED BIBLIOGRAPHY
See Travis, *Julien Levy;* Witkin, *Julien Levy.*

Ilse Bing. *My Shadow in Amsterdam Graacht*, 1933. Silver print. (Courtesy the artist and The Witkin Gallery)

Bishop, Michael
United States 1946–

An active exhibitor, Bishop was a founding member of the Visual Dialogue Foundation (Carmel, California). He studied photography with Henry Holmes Smith and has taught photography at UCLA, the Visual Studies Workshop (Rochester, New York), and elsewhere. He photographs very ordinary objects and landscapes but presents each image with a unique and subjective interpretation that contradicts the apparently inconsequential nature of the subject matter. William Jenkins observed: "Each of these objects is photographed with great care as though it occupied all of the photographer's attention at the time

of exposure. Yet . . . Bishop simultaneously provides us with all the necessary input to perceive that his interests lie not with the subjects, but only with the photographs themselves" (*Extended Document* catalogue, p. 3, listed in chapter 7). Many aspects of the prints — their variable toning, their odd perspective or cropping, their deliberate vignetting — call attention to the photographic process itself as the true subject of Bishop's work.

Michael Bishop. *#74-1143*, 1974. Silver print. (Courtesy Light Gallery. Copyright © 1974 by Michael Bishop)

WORK Includes landscapes, views of common objects, rephotographed collages, photograms.

MEDIA Silver prints (often toned), color, gum-bichromate prints.

AVAILABILITY AND PRICE Through galleries; moderate.

SIGNATURE/OTHER IDENTIFICATION

COLLECTIONS Harvard (Fogg), IMP/GEH, New Mexico, St. Petersburg, Tennessee.

SELECTED BIBLIOGRAPHY
Esquire, Feb. 1976.
Modern Photography, July 1976, p. 104.
See also chapter 7 catalogues.

Bisson, Auguste-Rosalie
France b. 1826

Bisson, Louis-Auguste
France b. 1814

The Bisson *frères* are best known for their views of the Alps made from the 1850s to 1860s. In addition, Helmut and Alison Gernsheim call them the leading architectural photographers in France during the 1860s.

In 1841 the brothers opened one of the first daguerreotype studios in Paris, and it soon became a popular meeting place for Parisian artists and intellectuals. They began using the new collodion wet-plate process in 1851 and by 1855 had begun making their dramatic views of alpine scenery. They commemorated the 1860 visit of Napoleon III and the Empress Eugénie to Switzerland by producing an album of spectacular mountain views. In 1861 August-Rosalie made an arduous climb of Mont Blanc — a difficult feat even without attempting the cumbersome wet-plate process — and returned with images again impressive in their revelation of the stark alpine landscape.

The Bissons' studio neighbor Nadar is reported to have said of them: "Anyone who had experienced the horrors of the collodion process can only be filled with admiration at the immaculate execution of the immense plates that used to be made. The Bisson brothers had discovered and trained as a darkroom assistant a former policeman who could coat with collodion a glass plate forty inches by thirty-two, in one movement of his arm and without a run, bubble or a speck of dust" (Braive, *Photograph*, p. 66).

The brothers retired in 1865; some attribute this to the craze for cartes de visite, which undermined their business.

WORK   Chiefly travel views of the Alps; architectural views of historical buildings in France, Italy, and Belgium; portraits. Also includes reproductions of artworks.

MEDIA   Daguerreotypes; calotypes; collodion wet-plate negatives (up to 40×30¼), albumen prints, salt prints. May bear name in plate.

AVAILABILITY AND PRICE   Through galleries and at auction. Daguerreotypes and calotypes rare; other media, including gravures, can be found; moderately high to extremely high.

COLLECTIONS   IMP/GEH, MOMA, NYPL, Princeton (Library); BN, Société Française, VA.

SELECTED BIBLIOGRAPHY
Choix d'ornements arabes de l'Alhambra. . . . Paris: J. Baudry, 1853. 12 prints processed by Lemercier.
Monographie de Notre Dame de Paris et de la Nouvelle Sacristie de Mm. Lassus et Viollet-le-Duc. Paris: A. Morel [ca. 1853–57]. 12 prints by Bisson *frères*.
L'Oeuvre de Rembrandt reproduit par la photographie. Text by Charles Blanc. 3 vols. Paris: Gide and Gide et J. Baudry, 1853–57. Reproduces over 90 etchings; the first book to be illustrated from glass-plate negatives.
The Knight, Devil and Death: Oeuvre d'Albert Dürer photographié [ca. 1854].
Emile Leconte. *La Napoleonium: Monographie du Louvre et des Tuileries . . . .* Paris: Grim, 1856. 2 albumen prints.
Untitled album of architectural studies by Ed. Renaud presented to M. Le Comte F. Baciocchi. Paris, 1858. 21 albumen prints, plus title page, by Bisson *frères*.
Le Mont Blanc et ses glaciers: Souvenir du voyage de L.L. M.M. L'Empereur et L'Impératrice. Paris, 1860. 24 prints.
See also Colnaghi, *Photography*; Jammes and Sobieszek, *Primitive*; Life Library, *Great Photographers, Travel*.

Bisson *frères*. *Rome. Arch of Constantine. Detail*, ca. 1860. Albumen print. (Courtesy Samuel Wagstaff Collection)

Blanquart-Evrard, Louis-Désiré
France 1802–1872

Blanquart-Evrard, a pioneer of photographic publishing, convinced photographers that he could produce quality prints on a scale and at a cost that made them practical as book illustrations. In 1851 he established the Imprimerie Photographique in Lille, France; this large-scale printing house employed forty women on an assembly line to process as many as 300 prints a day. Because he was a good craftsman as well as a promoter, prints made in his plant are found in a good state of preservation. He was one of the earliest archival printers — double fixing, double washing, toning, and thorough washing were standard procedures to ensure permanence.

Blanquart-Evrard's first publishing effort, *Album photographique de l'artiste et de l'amateur*, which reproduced works of art, was offered in September 1851 and was a success. He thereafter made the prints for many books, among them Maxime Du Camp's *Egypte, Nubie, Palestine et Syrie* (1852), John B. Greene's *Le Nil: Monuments, paysages, explorations photographiques* (1854), and Auguste Salzmann's *Jerusalem* (1856). In 1855 he established another printing operation, on the island of Jersey, in partnership with Thomas Sutton (1819–1875). He retired from an active role in photography in 1857, but the magazine *Photographic Notes,* which he founded in 1856 with Sutton, continued to appear until 1867.

Describing the Du Camp prints, Gerda Peterich wrote: "Blanquart-Evrard's photographic prints . . . are superb. Of a slate-grey image tone with an occasional purple tint, on a warm-tone paper, they have preserved all their detail and depth. The matte surface adds richness. The prints bear out Blanquart-Evrard's claim for permanence" (Peterich [1957], p. 84).

WORK Because Blanquart-Evrard commissioned and printed work by other photographers, it is difficult to determine which, if any, may be his own images. According to André Jammes, some proofs from 1846 or 1847 are known to be taken by him — for example, the marketplace at Ypres, Belgium.

MEDIA Calotypes, Blanquart-Evrard's own improved calotypes, salt prints, albumen prints. Many prints bear Blanquart-Evrard's name as publisher but identify no photographer. Prints from albums such as *Etudes photographiques, Mélanges photographiques,* and *Paris photographique* (all ca. 1852–1854) are about 6×8 on mounts about 14×18. Prints from other albums range up to about 16½×23. (See illustrations, pages 16 and 188.)

AVAILABILITY AND PRICE Prints bearing the imprint "Imprimerie Photographique Blanquart-Evrard, à Lille" are rare; can be high to extremely high, depending on condition, interest of scene, and importance of photographer.

SIGNATURE/OTHER IDENTIFICATION

IMPRIMERIE PHOTOGRAPHIQUE Blanquart-Evrard, à Lille.

COLLECTIONS IMP/GEH; BN, NGC.

SELECTED BIBLIOGRAPHY
Procédés employés pour obtenir les épreuves photographiques sur papier. Paris: Charles Chevalier, 1847.
Album photographique de l'artiste et de l'amateur, 1851.
Traité de photographie sur papier. Paris: Roret, 1851.
La Photographie: Ses origines, ses progrès, ses transformations. Lille: L. Danel, 1869.
Thomas Sutton. [An account of the operations at Lille.] *The British Journal of Photography* 19 (1872): 308–309.
Gerda Peterich. "The Calotype in France and Its Uses in Architectural Documentation." Master's thesis, University of Rochester (N.Y.), 1956.
James Borcoman. *Charles Nègre.* Ottawa: National Gallery of Canada, 1976.
Gerda Peterich. "Louis Désiré Blanquart-Evrard: The Gutenberg of Photography." *Image* 6 (Apr. 1957): 80–89.
Camera, Dec. 1978. Entire issue (text by Isabelle Jammes).
See also Jammes and Sobieszek, *Primitive;* Marbot, *Invention;* Scharf, *Art;* Taft, *Photography;* bibliography in Marville entry.

Blumenfeld, Erwin
United States (b. Germany) 1897–1969

A successful fashion photographer in the 1940s and '50s, Blumenfeld was, at his peak, one of the most sought-after commercial photographers. He also pursued personal imagery, especially studies of women. Discussing Blumenfeld's work in 1948, Ebria Feinblatt wrote that he showed "a powerful grasp of the psychological as well as artistic effects of photography. . . . His quest is not reality but the mystery of reality" (*Seventeen American Photographers*).

After his discharge from the German army in 1918, Blumenfeld opened a leather-goods shop in Amsterdam, where he exhibited his photographs. In 1934 he had his first major exhibition in Amsterdam, and the following year his work appeared in *Photographie, XXe Siècle, Sculpture,* and *Verve.* He had a large exhibition in Paris in 1936 and remained there to work for *Harper's Bazaar* and *Vogue.* Blumenfeld and his family were imprisoned in Nazi concentration camps in France and Algiers in 1941. Finally reaching the United States, he worked as a free-lance photographer, producing in all over a hundred color covers for *Vogue, Harper's Bazaar, Look, Cosmopolitan,* and *Popular Photography.*

Blumenfeld made skillful use of darkroom techniques such as solarization, reticulation of negatives, and combining a negative with a positive, and gained other effects by using mirrors, reflectors, and lenses. According to Jacob Deschin, "his talent was a combination of experimental and commercial approaches, often raising the latter to a level of art by his natural inventiveness" ("Viewpoint," *Popular Photography,* March 1970, pp. 22 ff.).

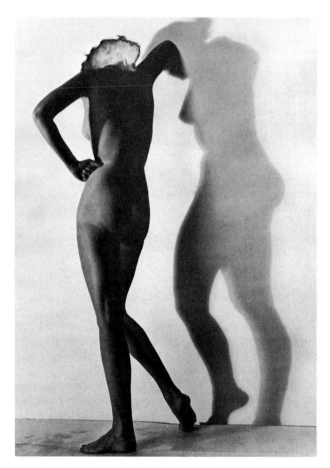

Erwin Blumenfeld. Untitled nude, ca. late 1930s. Silver print. (Courtesy The Witkin Gallery)

WORK Chiefly female nudes; distortions; faces; portraits of prominent people (e.g., Eugene O'Neill, Matisse, Rouault). Also includes commercial photography, especially fashion, as well as views of architecture and sculpture.

MEDIA Glass-plate negatives and film negatives, silver prints. Also color prints and transparencies. Most silver prints are 11×14; the photographer reprinted his early glass negatives to this size after most of the original prints had been destroyed. Prints seldom carry his signature but may be stamped on verso. Prints from his estate may also be signed by his widow, Marina Schinz, who holds the estate.

AVAILABILITY AND PRICE Vintage prints offered by the photographer's estate available through galleries; moderate to moderately high.

SIGNATURE/OTHER IDENTIFICATION

COPYRIGHT 1957 BY
ERWIN BLUMENFELD

(Signature of Marina Schinz)

COLLECTIONS CCP, FIT (all negatives and color transparencies), MOMA, New Mexico, New Orleans, San Antonio, Smith.

SELECTED BIBLIOGRAPHY
Ebria Feinblatt. *Seventeen American Photographers.* Los Angeles: Los Angeles County Museum, 1948.
Durch Tausenjahrige Zeit. Frauenfeld, Switzerland: Huber, 1976. Autobiography. Reviewed: Alfred Andersch. "Refreshment through Hate." *Times Literary Supplement,* 11 Mar. 1977.
See also Liberman, *Art* (in color bibliography).

Bonfils, Félix
France 1829–1885

Little is known about this photographer whose name appears on mass-produced nineteenth-century photographs of ancient cities and historical landscapes. Based in his studio in Beirut, he worked in the Middle East during the 1870s. The appeal of his views was summed up in the preface to one of his books: "The traveler and the artist departing for this enchanted region, those returning or those spirits curious about and enamored of beautiful things will be unable to forgo perusing the marvelous series of plates which make up this remarkable publication. Those who for reasons of health, fortune or station in life can not undertake such long journeys will consider themselves happy to accomplish them without giving up their regular habits" (Gratien Charvet, *Souvenirs*

Félix Bonfils. *Dead Sea,* 1870s. Albumen print. (Courtesy The Witkin Gallery)

d'Orient, quoted in Weinberg, p. 12). "As more of Bonfils' works come to light," wrote Adam D. Weinberg, "it becomes increasingly evident that he is one of the great photographers of 'views' and ethnography in the 19th century" (p. 16).

Photographs by Bonfils were included in books published around 1868 in Alais (now Alès), France. He also produced his own albums. Because his images and publications were issued in a variety of sizes and editions (deluxe and regular), their exact number and titles are presently uncertain. There is evidence that Bonfils followed the common practice of printing negatives by various other, earlier photographers, such as E. Béchard; all images bearing his name are not necessarily his work.

WORK Includes views of Egypt, Greece, Turkey, and the Holy Land; costume studies.

MEDIA Collodion wet-plate negatives, albumen prints (ranging from 3×3¾ to 11×14; usually about 6×8). Often signed in the negative.

AVAILABILITY AND PRICE Found in abundance in old albums, on loose boards, or unmounted; extremely low to moderate.

COLLECTIONS BPL (*Souvenirs d'Orient*), Brandeis, Harvard (Semitic), IMP/GEH, MMA, New Mexico. Also found in many libraries, often filed by subject matter.

SIGNATURE/OTHER IDENTIFICATION (Detail from above image)

SELECTED BIBLIOGRAPHY
Catalogue des vues photographiques de l'Orient, Egypte, Palestine (Terre-Sainte), Syrie, Grèce, et Constantinople. A. Brugeroille, 1876.
Albums photographiques des sites les plus célèbres de l'Orient. Paris: J. Baudry, 1878.

Souvenirs d'Orient: Album pittoresque des sites, villes et ruines les plus remarquables de la Terre-Sainte. Preface by Gratien Charvet. Alais, France: Bonfils, 1878.
Nazareth et ses environs. St. Petersburg, 1894. 12 prints by Bonfils, among others.
Souvenir de Jerusalem. Leipzig: Dr. Trenkler [ca. 1895].
Adam D. Weinberg. *Majestic Inspirations, Incomparable Souvenirs.* Waltham, Mass.: Brandeis University, 1977.
See also Life Library, *Travel.*

Boubat, Edouard
France 1923–

Boubat first became acquainted with photography at a trade school, then worked as a phototechnician. His personal work began after World War II with such images as a little child in the Luxembourg Gardens wearing a coat made of leaves, and Lella, a woman in a white blouse. A chance meeting with Picasso and the latter's encouragement led Boubat to give up his plant job and concentrate on his own photography. A 1951 exhibition in Paris with Robert Doisneau, Izis, and Brassaï resulted in a fifteen-year association with the magazine *Réalités.*

Boubat's vision concentrates on the graces of humanity. He sees life everywhere — in old-fashioned villages as well as in modern cities — as unified and meaningful. The rituals of planting and harvesting, the expressions of the human face, and the relationship of mother and child are themes that dominate his work. He has documented the life of people of all classes in China, India, France, Portugal, Italy, Africa, and America.

Boubat points out that while a painter sits in front of his subject for hours, a photographer has to perceive an image, select the best vantage point, and make the exposure with the speed of a hunter. "A characteristic of Boubat's working method," wrote Bernard George, "is that he releases the shutter comparatively seldom. . . . He watches and waits, and when the moment comes, he reacts with lightning speed. Although his photographs are not *prearranged* in the manufactured sense, his work, viewed as a whole, is, in the best sense of the word, premeditated" (*Edouard Boubat*).

WORK   Chiefly humanistic reportage of people the world over.

MEDIA   Silver prints, color. Print sizes vary from 5×7 to 11×14.

AVAILABILITY AND PRICE   Through galleries; moderate.

SIGNATURE/OTHER IDENTIFICATION

COLLECTIONS   MOMA; BN.

SELECTED BIBLIOGRAPHY
Edouard Boubat. Text by Bernard George. Lucerne: Bucher, 1972. U.S. ed., New York: Collier/Macmillan, 1973.

Miroirs, Autoportraits. Paris: Denoël, 1973.
Woman. New York: Braziller, 1973.
Anges. Text by Antoine Blondin. Paris: Atelier d'Expression, 1974.
La Survivance. Paris: Mercure de France, 1976.
Walter Rosenblum. "The Humanistic Eye: Edouard Boubat." *35mm Photography,* Summer 1975, pp. 24–31, 108–109.
Album, no. 12 (1970), pp. 4–16.

Edouard Boubat. Untitled, Paris, 1970. Silver print. (Courtesy The Witkin Gallery)

Boughton, Alice
United States 1865–1943

After first studying painting, Boughton turned to photography and was associated for a time with Gertrude Käsebier. She opened a studio in New York in 1890 and remained active, primarily in portraiture, for over forty years. Her work is characterized by soft focus and a sensitive treatment of her sitters that was in keeping with the photographic style of the day.

Boughton wrote of portrait photography: "The photographer must first of all have ideas. He must understand his tools and his personality must play so prominent a part that it cannot be undervalued. He must have tact, and infinite patience. The photographer should be intuitive, to be able to get in touch with his subject; to be ready when the right instant presents itself. Unlike the painter, the photographer has one moderately short session, and for that reason, he must sharpen his wits. If the photographer has sufficient insight to perceive the interest and character of the sitter, the result may be a real achievement. It is the photographer's business to try and seize upon and bring out the innate quality, the individuality or charm of each" ("Photography, A Medium of Expression," p. 35).

Alice Boughton. *Henry James,* ca. 1910. Silver print. (Courtesy The Witkin Gallery)

WORK   Chiefly portraits of literary and theatrical figures (e.g., George Arliss, Gorki, Eleanora Duse, Henry James). Also includes female nudes in allegorical or natural settings, children (mainly her two daughters).

MEDIA   Platinum prints. Also some silver prints.

AVAILABILITY AND PRICE   Platinum prints and silver prints rare; moderately high. *Camera Work* gravures low to moderate.

SIGNATURE/OTHER IDENTIFICATION   *See* signed menu, page 103.

COLLECTIONS   IMP/GEH, MMA, other major collections.

SELECTED BIBLIOGRAPHY
Charles Rann Kennedy. *The Servant in the House.* New York: Harper, 1908. Eight halftones taken by Boughton expressly to illustrate this play.
Household Arts and Social Lunches. Cleveland: Survey Committee of the Cleveland Foundation, 1912.
Photographing the Famous. Foreword by James L. Ford. New York: Avondale, 1928.
"Photography, A Medium of Expression." *Camera Work,* no. 26 (Apr. 1909), pp. 33–35.
Camera Work: Gravures in no. 26.
See also Green, *Camera Work;* Naef, *Collection.*

Bourke-White, Margaret
United States 1904–1971

Renowned as a photojournalist from the 1930s to the 1950s, Bourke-White studied photography with Clarence H. White, photographed through her college years, and began to take on free-lance assignments in Cleveland in the late 1920s, concentrating on heavy machinery and factories. In 1929 she became the first staff photographer for Henry Luce's *Fortune* magazine, where she continued to make images of business and industry. She joined another Luce publication, *Life,* and her cover photo and picture essay on Fort Peck (Mont.) Dam appeared in its first issue, 23 November 1936.

On assignments for *Fortune* and *Life* she photographed all over the world and eagerly took the toughest assignments: World War II action in Europe, including photographs of Nazi concentration camp survivors and victims; partition hardships in India and Pakistan in the 1940s; and Korean War guerrilla action. Her collaboration with her future husband Erskine Caldwell resulted in *You Have Seen Their Faces,* a classic record of hard times in the southern United States during the Depression. She also wrote a number of books about her assignments and illustrated them with her photographs. Her text has a breezy reporter's tone, relaying information about GIs and foreign lands for the folks back home.

Much of Bourke-White's work, particularly her industrial photography, has a boldly simplified composition. Many of her scenes were deliberately organized, lit, and posed. The huge machines and structures are often monumental, the attending workers relatively small elements. She was skilled in the use of multiple flash: to light cavernous factory interiors she set up several flashbulbs to fire simultaneously when the shutter opened.

An ambitious, hard-driving, dedicated photographer, Bourke-White was determined to go after exactly the picture she wanted. Alfred Eisenstaedt wrote: "At the peak of her distinguished career she was as willing and eager as any beginner on a first assignment. She would get up at daybreak to photograph a bread crumb, if necessary" (*The Eye of Eisenstaedt,* New York: Viking, 1969, p. 36).

Margaret Bourke-White. *Helix: Panel in NBC Mural, Radio City Music Hall,* ca. 1934. Silver print. (Courtesy Lee D. Witkin)

WORK Includes machines and heavy industry, Cleveland, Detroit (1927–1929); industrial photographs for *Fortune* (1929–1936); advertising work (e.g., for Goodyear Tires); Soviet Russia (1930–1932); people and scenes in America during the Depression; picture stories for *Life* in many countries (1936–1957); giant photomurals (e.g., at Radio City, New York City, early 1930s).

MEDIUM Silver prints.

AVAILABILITY AND PRICE Prints from the 1920s to 1930s in a distinctive, rich-toned, black-bordered style were made by Bourke-White's private printer and either have her stamp on the verso or are signed; infrequently available; moderately high to high. Prints made in 1970 by Time-Life are identifiable by the photographer's stamp on the verso and her initials on the print; approved by her for a small edition of 12 classic images from her negatives, these are priced moderate; due to her death the edition was not completed. Gravures from a portfolio of Russian images (ca. 1932) moderate.

SIGNATURE/OTHER IDENTIFICATION

A
MARGARET BOURKE-WHITE
PHOTOGRAPH

Margaret Bourke-White

COLLECTIONS LIFE Picture Collection (New York City) preserves negatives Bourke-White made for Time Inc. The George Arents Research Library, Syracuse (N.Y.) University, holds the largest collection of her prints and manuscripts. Also Brooklyn, Cleveland, IMP/GEH, LOC, MOMA, New Orleans; RPS.

SELECTED BIBLIOGRAPHY
Eyes on Russia. New York: Simon & Schuster, 1931. Reprint, New York: AMS Press, 1968.
Sir Arthur Newsholme and John Adams Kingsbury. *Red Medicine.* New York: Doubleday, Doran, 1933.
U.S.S.R. Photographs. Albany, N.Y.: Argus Press, 1934.
Newsprint. Montreal: International Paper Sales [ca. 1935].
Fred C. Kelly. *One Thing Leads to Another: The Growth of an Industry.* Boston: Houghton Mifflin, 1936.
You Have Seen Their Faces. Text by Erskine Caldwell. New York: Viking, 1937. Reprint, New York: Arno, 1975.
North of the Danube. Text by Erskine Caldwell. New York: Viking, 1939.
Say, Is This the U.S.A. Text by Erskine Caldwell. New York: Duell, Sloan & Pearce, 1941.
Shooting the Russian War. New York: Simon & Schuster, 1942.
They Called It "Purple Heart Valley": A Combat Chronicle of the War in Italy. New York: Simon & Schuster, 1944.
"Dear Fatherland, Rest Quietly": A Report on the Collapse of Hitler's "Thousand Years." New York: Simon & Schuster, 1946.
Halfway to Freedom: A Report on the New India. New York: Simon & Schuster, 1949.
A Report on the American Jesuits. With John La Farge. New York: Farrar, Straus & Cudahy, 1956.
Portrait of Myself. New York: Simon & Schuster, 1963.
Theodore M. Brown. *Margaret Bourke-White: Photojournalist.* Ithaca, N.Y.: Cornell University Press, 1972. Bibliography.
The Photographs of Margaret Bourke-White. Ed. by Sean Callahan. Greenwich, Conn.: New York Graphic Society, 1972. Bibliography.
See also Edey, *Essays;* Mann, *Women;* Stott, *Documentary;* Szarkowski, *Looking;* Tucker, *Eye.*

Bourne, Samuel
England 1834–1912

At about the same time that expeditionary photographers were documenting the far reaches of the American West, Bourne chose to record the even more remote and forbidding Himalaya Mountains. Previously a landscape photographer in England, he arrived in Simla, India, in 1863 and formed a partnership with Charles Shepherd, proprietor of the oldest photographic firm in that country. Their firm of Bourne and Shepherd, which is still active, became the leading supplier of views of India.

Bourne was the first to photograph in many parts of the Himalayas; in the period 1863–1866 he made three major expeditions to elevations as high as 18,600 feet. At such heights, his technically excellent and powerfully composed landscapes were produced under enormous difficulties. The wet-plate process he used was at best awkward to manipulate in the field. In addition, he contended with rarefied atmosphere, freezing weather, storms, treacherous terrain, and less-than-enthusiastic help from bearers who had often been commandeered to begin with and who suffered from Bourne's determination to accomplish his goals at almost any cost. He kept a journal of his travels and described his adventures in a series of lively articles for *The British Journal of Photography.*

Bourne settled in Calcutta, where he opened a branch of Bourne and Shepherd. He returned to England in 1872 and turned to manufacturing for his livelihood, while remaining active as an amateur photographer. He reflected, "To practise photography in England — say on the grassy banks of a stream . . . with every comfort and convenience at hand — is one thing; to practise it on a journey amid the wilds of the Himalayas . . . subject to every inconvenience, is quite another" (quoted in Sprague).

Samuel Bourne. *Palace and Tank Built by Rajah Bulman Singh, Goverdhun,* ca. 1870. Albumen print. (Courtesy Carol Fruchter)

WORK   Chiefly landscapes, architecture, historic sites, and cityscapes, in India, Burma, and Ceylon. Also includes some groups of native peoples. According to Aaron Scharf, Bourne made about 1,500 negatives in the East, of which 800–900 were made on his three Himalayan expeditions.

MEDIA   Collodion wet-plate negatives, albumen prints (about 10×12; may be signed and numbered in the negative, titled on the mount). Also stereographs.

AVAILABILITY AND PRICE   General views from India frequently found in albums, both tipped in and glued; low to moderate. Himalayan photographs rarer; moderately high to high.

SIGNATURE/OTHER IDENTIFICATION

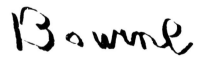

COLLECTIONS   BPL, Harvard (Carpenter), IMP/GEH, New Mexico, NYPL, Texas (Gernsheim); India Records, NGC, RGS, RPS, VA.

SELECTED BIBLIOGRAPHY
"Ten Weeks with the Camera in the Himalayas." *The British Journal of Photography.* In installments beginning 1 Feb. 1864.
"Narrative of a Photographic Trip to Kashmir and Adjacent Dis-
tricts." *The British Journal of Photography.* In installments beginning 19 Oct. 1866.
"A Photographic Journey through the Higher Himalayas." *The British Journal of Photography.* In installments beginning 1869.
Sean Sprague. "Samuel Bourne: Photographer of India in the 1860s." *The British Journal of Photography,* 14 Jan. 1977.
See also Scharf, *Pioneers;* Worswick and Embree, *Last Empire.*

Brady, Mathew B.
United States 1823–1896

Mathew B. Brady's name is linked most often with Civil War photography, but he was also noted for photographing many famous people of his time. He originally aspired to be a painter, then became interested in the daguerreotype process, which he learned from Samuel F. B. Morse and John W. Draper. In 1844 he opened a portrait studio in New York City (see illustration, page 17); later he opened another in Washington, D.C., and a lavish third one, again in New York.

About 1845 he conceived the idea of photographing every notable person of his time. In 1850 he published *Gallery of Illustrious Americans,* illustrated with twelve lithographs made from his daguerreotypes, and he had plans (which never materialized) for a companion volume.

When the Civil War broke out, Brady developed another grand scheme: the complete photographic documentation of the war. He hired and equipped a number of photographers and sent them to various war zones. Though Brady was in the field on a number of occasions, most of the photographs that bear his name were made by the men he hired. His eyesight had never been good and as early as 1858 it was so poor that he rarely operated a camera himself. Most of the photographs credited to him were actually made by his employees, but following a common commercial practice, he used his name as a trademark and did not identify individual photographers. This led to objections from some of them — for example, Alexander Gardner, who eventually left to form an independent photographic unit, hiring away from Brady some of his best photographers.

Brady hoped either to sell his war photographs to the public or to get substantial reimbursement from the United States government. Neither happened. He eventually received a token sum from the government, but not nearly enough to cover his expenses. One complete set of his negatives went to the E. and H. T. Anthony Company, to cover his debts to them for photographic supplies. A duplicate set was sold at auction because he could not pay the storage charges on it. He died virtually penniless.

Brady's chief significance is as a historian. His idea of documenting his era with photographs produced invaluable records of a significant period of United States history. Robert Taft noted that in addition to his war documentation Brady photographed so many famous people that "scarcely a man or woman before the public eye but was recorded first on the silver plate, and later by means of the glass negative. Is it too much to credit Brady with being one of the foremost historians of his day?" (Taft, *Photography*, p. 58).

WORK   Best known for portraits (e.g., Lincoln, John C. Calhoun, Henry Clay, Dolley Madison, P. T. Barnum, Jenny Lind, Edgar Allan Poe, Brigham Young), Civil War scenes (e.g., battles, group and individual portraits, topography, camp life). Also photographed in New York and Washington, D.C.

MEDIA   Daguerreotypes; collodion wet-plate negatives, albumen prints (ranging in size from imperial to cartes de visite and stereographs). Also a few lantern slides. Anthony Co. reprints generally read "From Photographic Negative By Brady." Many images appeared as wood engravings in illustrated journals.

AVAILABILITY AND PRICE   Through galleries and at auction. Good prints moderately rare; high. Cartes de visite and stereographs more easily found, expensive for their category; extremely low to moderate. Carte quality varies; many are second- or third-generation reprints.

SIGNATURE/OTHER IDENTIFICATION   *See also* illustration, page 71.

Mathew B. Brady. *Abraham Lincoln*, 1864. Modern silver print from the original plate. Probably the most famous Brady portrait, ultimately used for the engraving of Lincoln's head on the U.S. five-dollar bill. (Library of Congress)

PORTFOLIOS   *See* chapter 6 entry.

COLLECTIONS   Harvard (Houghton), IMP/GEH, Kalamazoo, LOC, National Archives, NYPL, Smithsonian, Yale (Beinecke).

SELECTED BIBLIOGRAPHY
Gallery of Illustrious Americans. Text by C. Edwards Lester. Lithographs (from Brady's work) by Francis D'Avignon. New York: D'Avignon Press, 1850.
John W. Ehninger. *Illustrations of Longfellow's Courtship of Miles Standish.* New York: Rudd & Carleton, 1859. 8 prints from the original drawings.
New York City Metropolitan Fair, 1864: Recollections of the Art Exhibition. New York, 1864. 20 prints.
Brady's Collection of Historical Portraits. 41st Congress, 3rd session, U.S. House of Rep. Report no. 46, 3 Mar. 1871.
The Photographic History of the Civil War. Ed. by Francis Trevelyan Miller. 10 vols. New York: The Review of Reviews, 1911. Photographs by Brady and others. Various reprints exist.
Roy Meredith. *Mr. Lincoln's Camera Man: Mathew B. Brady.* New York: Scribner, 1946. Reprint, New York: Dover, 1974.
———. *Mr. Lincoln's Contemporaries: An Album of Portraits by Mathew B. Brady.* New York: Scribner, 1951.
J. D. Horan. *Mathew Brady: Historian with a Camera.* New York: Crown, 1955. Bibliography.
Hirst D. Milhollen and Donald H. Mugridge. *Civil War Photographs, 1861–1865: A Catalog of Copy Negatives Made from Originals Selected from the Mathew B. Brady Collection in the Prints and Photographs Division of the Library of Congress.* Washington, D.C.: Library of Congress, 1961.
Dorothy Meserve Kunhardt; Philip B. Kunhardt, Jr.; and the Editors of Time-Life Books. *Mathew Brady and His World.* Alexandria, Va.: Time-Life Books, 1977.
Many Brady photographs appear in books about the Civil War. *See* Donald H. Mugridge. *The Civil War in Pictures 1861–1961.* Washington, D.C.: Library of Congress, 1961.
See also Life Library, *Great Photographers*; Newhall, *Daguerreotype*; Rudisill, *Mirror Image*; Taft, *Photography*.

Brandt, Bill
England 1904–

Largely self-taught in photography, Brandt studied with Man Ray in Paris (1929–1930) and became interested in surrealism. He also admired the work of Eugène Atget, Edward Weston, Brassaï, and the early images of Henri Cartier-Bresson. In 1931 he returned to England, where he began documenting life and mores at a time when serious photographic reportage there was almost nonexistent. His many photographs of this period recorded an era of fixed status and finely tuned manners that disappeared with World War II. "Towards the end of the war," the photographer recalled, "my style changed completely. I have often been asked why this happened. I think I gradually lost my enthusiasm for reportage. Documentary photography had become fashionable. Everybody was doing it. ... Whatever the reason, the poetic trend of photography, which had already excited me in my early Paris days, began to fascinate me again. It seemed to me that there were wide fields still unexplored. I began to photograph nudes, portraits, and landscapes" (*Album*, no. 3, 1970).

Brandt's images became dark, brooding evocations of an uneasily balanced, not quite real, not quite surreal dream world. His nudes are distorted by exaggerated wide-angle perspective; his portraits show the subjects moody and isolated in strangely lit surroundings; his landscapes are not unfriendly ones, but are not always entirely meant for humans. He stated: "I found atmosphere to be the spell that charged the commonplace with beauty. And I am still not sure what atmosphere is. I only know that it is a combination of elements . . . which reveals the subject as familiar yet strange (quoted in *Album,* no. 2, 1970, p. 12).

Before 1951 Brandt made very dark, almost muddy prints. Later prints of both new and old images have very high contrast that heightens their unreality by rendering scenes in chalky whites, inky blacks, and few middle tones. In his words: "Photographers should follow their own judgment and not the fads and dictates of others. Photography is still a very new medium and everything is allowed and everything should be tried" (*Album,* no. 3, 1970, p. 47).

WORK Includes Paris (1929–1930); people and life in London before World War II (e.g., East End children, parlormaids); industrial towns in north England during the depression of the 1930s; wartime London (1939–1945); English landscapes and architecture (e.g., literary sites); portraits of literary, art-world, and theatrical figures (e.g., Alec Guinness, Magritte, the Sitwells); nudes.

MEDIA Silver prints, color. Brandt often does visible pencil retouching on prints.

AVAILABILITY AND PRICE Through galleries. Modern prints moderately high; vintage prints rare, moderately high to high.

SIGNATURE/OTHER IDENTIFICATION

COLLECTIONS IMP/GEH, MOMA; BN, VA.

SELECTED BIBLIOGRAPHY
The English at Home. London: Batsford, 1936.
A Night in London. London: Country Life, 1938.
Camera in London. London and New York: Focal Press, 1948.
Literary Britain. London: Cassell, 1951.
Perspective of Nudes. Preface by Lawrence Durrell. London: Bodley Head, and New York: Amphoto, 1961.
Shadow of Light. Intro. by Cyril Connolly. Notes by Marjorie Beckett. London: Bodley Head, 1966. Rev. ed., intro. by Mark Haworth-Booth. London: Gordon Fraser, and New York: Da Capo, 1977.
Bill Brandt: Photographs. Text by R. Campbell and Aaron Scharf. London: Arts Council of Great Britain, 1970.
Bill Brandt: Early Photographs, 1930–1942. London: Arts Council of Great Britain, 1975.
Ruth Spencer. "Bill Brandt." *The British Journal of Photography,* 9 Nov. 1973.
See also Life Library, *Great Photographers;* Szarkowski, *Looking;* chapter 7 catalogue.

Bill Brandt. Untitled, 1953. Silver print. (Courtesy the artist)

Brassaï
Transylvania (Romania) 1899–

Brassaï (born Gyula Halász) arrived in Paris in 1923, fresh from his painting studies in Budapest and Berlin. "During my first years in Paris," he later recalled, "I lived at night, going to bed at sunrise, getting up at sunset, wandering about the city from Montparnasse to Montmartre. And even though I had always ignored and even disliked photography before, I was inspired to become a photographer by my desire to translate all the things that enchanted me in the nocturnal Paris I was experiencing" (*The Secret Paris of the 30's*).

With advice and a camera borrowed from his friend André Kertész, Brassaï captured the misty streets and smoke-filled cafés inhabited by artists, poets, writers, and other colorful characters. His images are at once poetic and realistic. They are artfully composed and use the mysterious effects that light is capable of, whether on a face or a street at night. His photographs convey a naturalness even when his subjects are aware of his presence. The sense of a time and a place is strong in Brassaï's Paris photographs, and over the years, they have come to virtually define the ambience of the society he documented.

Later Brassaï expanded his vision to include wall graffiti and portraits of artists and writers such as Picasso, Henry Miller, Jean Genet, and Giacometti.

In Brassaï's words: "The photograph has a double destiny. . . . It is the daughter of the world of externals, of the living second, and as such will always keep something of the historic or scientific document about it; but it is also the daughter of the rectangle, a child of the *beaux-arts*, which requires one to fill up the space agreeably or harmoniously with black-and-white spots or colors" (quoted in *Brassaï* [1968], p. 13).

WORK Best known for Paris at night, 1930s–1940s; portraits of famous writers and artists. Also includes life elsewhere in France and in Spain.

MEDIA Silver prints. Also clichés-verres, color.

AVAILABILITY AND PRICE Through galleries and at auction; moderately high to high. Most prints are issued in numbered editions (usually 25 or 40; prices are raised as editions sell out).

SIGNATURE/OTHER IDENTIFICATION

PORTFOLIOS *See* chapter 6 entry.

COLLECTIONS Arizona State, Chicago, Detroit, IMP/GEH, Kansas, Michigan, MOMA, Nebraska, New Mexico, New Orleans, RISD, Worcester, Yale (Art Gallery); Antwerp, BN, Israel Museum.

Brassaï. *Bal Musette*, 1932. Silver print. (Courtesy the artist)

SELECTED BIBLIOGRAPHY

Paris de Nuit. Text by Paul Morand. Paris: Arts et Métiers Graphiques, 1933.
Histoire de Marie. Intro. by Henry Miller. Paris: Point du Jour, 1948. A novel; unillustrated.
Camera in Paris. London and New York: Focal Press, 1949.
Les Sculptures de Picasso. Text by Daniel Henry Kahnweiler. Paris: Chêne, 1948.
Brassaï. Intro. by Henry Miller. Paris: Editions Neuf, 1952.
Dominique Aubier. *Séville en fête.* Paris: Delpire, 1954. U.S. ed., *Fiesta in Seville.* New York: Studio/Crowell, 1956.
Graffiti: 105 Schwarzweiss Fotos. Stuttgart: Belser, 1960.
John Russell. *Paris.* New York: Viking, 1960.
J. Adhémar, et al. *Brassaï.* Paris: Bibliothèque Nationale, 1963.
Conversations avec Picasso. Paris: Gallimard, 1964. U.S. ed., *Picasso and Company.* Garden City, N.Y.: Doubleday, 1966.
Images de Camera. Ed. by Brassaï. Paris: Deux Coqs d'Or; London: Aldus; and Lucerne: Bucher, 1964.
Brassaï. Intro. by Lawrence Durrell. New York: MOMA, 1968. Bibliography.
Henry Miller, Grandeur Nature. Paris: Gallimard, 1975.
The Secret Paris of the 30's. New York: Pantheon, 1976.
Nancy Newhall. "Brassaï: 'I Invent Nothing, I Imagine Everything.'" *Camera,* May 1956, pp. 185–215.
"Language of the Wall." *U.S. Camera Annual 1958,* pp. 6 ff. Includes statement by Edward Steichen.
Album, no. 8 (1970), pp. 24–28.
See also Life Library, *Great Photographers, Year 1977;* Szarkowski, *Looking;* Travis, *Julien Levy;* Witkin, *Julien Levy.*

Braun, Adolphe
France 1811–1877

Braun's first photographs probably were daguerreotypes made in the 1840s. A designer/draftsman for an Alsatian textile manufacturer, in the 1850s and 1860s he made many flower still-life photographs, some of which he used as the basis for designs. "In the field of the photographic still-life, Adolphe Braun has seldom been matched and possibly never exceeded. . . . His studies are reminiscent of the lovely flower paintings by his compatriot and contemporary Henri Fantin-Latour. When seen beside them, the Brauns are often more vigorous" (*Image* 5, Feb. 1956, p. 42).

Braun founded the firm of Braun et Compagnie in Dornach (Alsace) and Paris, and introduced the carbon process into France and Belgium especially for the reproduction of paintings and drawings. He also used the carbon process for his own work, such as for large prints of Alpine panoramas. He was official photographer of the court of Napoleon III and photographed many of its prominent personalities.

WORK Includes still lifes (e.g., flower studies), Paris street scenes, landscapes in Swiss mountains and Black Forest, picturesque scenes (e.g., parks or gardens with elegant ladies and gentlemen), portraits (e.g., Napoleon III, as well as ordinary citizens), art in the major museums of Europe (e.g., the Louvre, Sistine Chapel), a few nudes.

MEDIA   Daguerreotypes (not extant as far as is known); collodion wet-plate negatives, albumen prints (ranging in size from panoramas, about 9×19, to stereographs and cartes de visite); carbon prints.

AVAILABILITY AND PRICE   Through galleries and at auction. Large prints very rare, high to extremely high; stereographs and cartes de visite low to moderate.

COLLECTIONS   BPL, Harvard (Carpenter), IMP/GEH, MMA, New Mexico, Temple; Mulhouse.

SELECTED BIBLIOGRAPHY
Vatican: Museo Vaticano (album). 3 vols. [ca. 1870]. 86 prints.
Catalogue général des photographies. Paris: Braun, 1887. General catalogue of views by Adolphe Braun and his son Gaston. Includes "Vues de Suisse" and listing of the firm's documentation of European art masterpieces.
Claude Roy. "Le Second Empire vous regard." *Le Point,* Jan. 1958.

SIGNATURE/OTHER IDENTIFICATION

Adolphe Braun. *Flower Arrangement,* ca. 1856. Albumen print. (Courtesy IMP/GEH)

Brigman, Anne W.
United States 1869–1950

Anne (Annie) Brigman thought of herself as a pagan and free spirit and expressed her passionate feelings about nature in photographs and poetry. She was raised in Hawaii and later spoke of times in her childhood when she felt the urge for "flight, of the wild, wonderful need to stampede" (quoted in Heyman, p. 2). She moved to California, became interested in photography, and in 1903 had a work displayed at the Third San Francisco Photographic Salon, where she saw for the first time a number of images by members of the Photo-Secession. She herself was elected to the Photo-Secession in 1906.

Brigman's soft-focus, pictorial photographs of her family and friends, and of herself, often posed nude in nature, were attacked by some (and still are) for their romantic sentimentality and careless printing, but they were much appreciated by many others, including Alfred Stieglitz; her images were published in several issues of *Camera Work.* J. Nilsen Laurvik wrote that "her work is kin to the ancient saga lore. Certain of her prints are fraught with that same brooding, elemental feeling that distinguish[es] the speech and gestures of those old viking heroes. While this is the dominant, prevailing characteristic of her work, there are not wanting touches of idyllic, almost lyrical beauty . . ." (quoted in ibid., p. 6).

Brigman once described the moment in the High Sierra that revealed the power of photography to her: "One day during the gathering of a thunder storm when the air was hot and still and a strange yellow light was over everything, something happened almost too deep for me to be able to relate. New dimensions revealed themselves in the visualization of the human form as a part of tree and rock rhythms and I turned full force to the medium at hand and the beloved Thing gave to me a power and abandon that I could not have had otherwise" (quoted in ibid., p. 3).

WORK Best known for figures, usually female, in nature. Also includes figure studies, landscapes. (See illustration, page 105.)

MEDIA Chiefly silver prints. Also gum-bichromate prints, palladium prints, platinum prints.

AVAILABILITY AND PRICE Signed prints, relatively rare, appear at auction; moderate to moderately high. *Camera Work* gravures low to moderate.

SIGNATURE/OTHER IDENTIFICATION

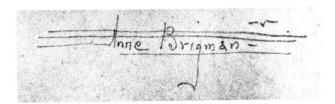

COLLECTIONS IMP/GEH, Oakland; RPS.

SELECTED BIBLIOGRAPHY
Songs of a Pagan. Caldwell, Idaho: Caxton, 1949.
Therese Thau Heyman. *Anne Brigman: Pictorial Photographer/Member of the Photo-Secession.* Oakland: Oakland Museum, 1974. Bibliography.
J. Nilsen Laurvik. "Mrs. Annie W. Brigman — A Comment." *Camera Work,* no. 25 (Jan. 1909), p. 47.
"What 291 Means to Me." *Camera Work,* no. 47 (July 1914), pp. 17–20.
Camera Work: Gravures in nos. 25, 38, 44.
See also Green, *Camera Work;* Mann, *Women;* Naef, *Collection;* Witkin, *Julien Levy.*

Brooks, Ellen
United States 1946–

Brooks studied art and photography at the University of California (Los Angeles) and has been innovative in exploring contemporary art concepts — interestingly, often by using old photographic processes such as the cyanotype. Her oversize *Bread Spreads* (three 8×10-foot cyanotype panels, containing photograms of 380 pieces of bread in various stages from slice to crumb) confront the viewer with unavoidable and delightful insistence on the infinite

variability of bread. She explained: "The physical and psychological space between the image and receiver of the image has always been of primary importance to me. In the past [e.g., *Bread Spreads,* 1974] I was involved in making the photograph into a more three-dimensional configuration to intensify the viewing experience" (statement to the authors, 1977).

Brooks's later work varies this approach: "At the present I am interested in the sculptural elements presenting themselves in a more straightforward manner. I am relying more on the photographic illusion to heighten this physical experience" (ibid.).

Brooks describes her new work as "singular figures in various postures printed one-and-a-half times life. The environment where these photographs exist and their installation are central to the conception of the piece" (ibid.).

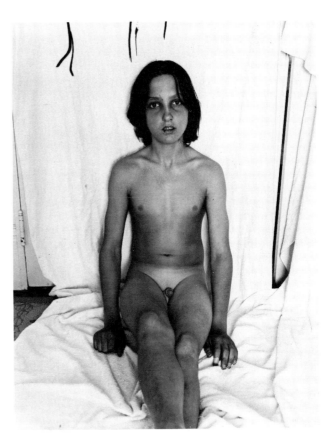

Ellen Brooks. *Keith,* 1977. Silver print. (Courtesy the artist)

WORK Figurative lifesize or over-lifesize pieces, adolescent boys and girls in the nude (20×24 prints on sensitized canvas), Polaroid SX-70 images of erotic fantasies.

MEDIA Prints on various sensitized surfaces; mixed media; cyanotypes; silver prints; Polaroid prints.

AVAILABILITY AND PRICE Most pieces are commissioned privately or by museums; high to extremely high.

SIGNATURE/OTHER IDENTIFICATION

COLLECTIONS   UCLA; NGC.

SELECTED BIBLIOGRAPHY
Bay Area Photography: New Directions. San Francisco: M. H. de
    Young Memorial Museum, 1974.
Gallery as Studio. Claremont, Calif.: Galleries of the Claremont
    Colleges, 1976.
See also Life Library, *Year 1975;* chapter 7 catalogues.

Brown, Dean
United States 1936–1973

Brown began photographing and printing at the age of ten.
After studying and teaching music, he chose photography
as a career and free-lanced for *Opera News, New York,*
Time-Life Books, *Holiday, Redbook,* and other publications before his career was cut short: he died at thirty-
seven from injuries suffered in a fall while on assignment
in New Hampshire's White Mountains.

In 1969 Brown turned from black-and-white subjects to
color landscapes. An exacting craftsman, he learned the
dye transfer color process and built his own lab to make
his dye prints. He chose to make his prints relatively
small, both for technical clarity and for aesthetic value,
and whenever possible used available light only. "I like
to photograph a thing or situation as I find it, without
rearrangement or interference," he once explained (quoted
in introduction, *Photographs of the American Wilderness*).

"The photographs of Dean Brown are clear, concise documents, rendered with exquisite attention to the faithful
representation of the subject," wrote Robert Doty. "The
photographs may be viewed quickly and easily, or they
may be slowly and deliberately studied — each method
will produce its own rewards. There is nothing ephemeral
or forced about Dean's images. They simply illuminate
an intimate experience with the land and its unique properties and elements. The medium is never allowed to
become more important than the subject. Photography is
the means of translating experience, and it was Dean's
constant respect for the basic properties of the medium
that made a significant translation possible" (ibid.,
preface).

WORK   Chiefly color landscapes. Also includes various black-
and-white subjects (e.g., Berlin essay, portraits, Martin Luther
King funeral shot from TV screen). (See color plate 2.)

MEDIA   Dye transfer color prints, silver prints.

AVAILABILITY AND PRICE   Black-and-white prints or color prints
made by the photographer rare; high. Lab prints made for his
estate (both Type C prints and dye transfer prints, from 4×5 to
20×30, bearing the estate stamp and signature of his widow,
Carol Brown) are available through galleries; moderate to high,
depending on size.

SIGNATURE/OTHER IDENTIFICATION

COLLECTIONS   IMP/GEH, Kansas, Virginia; NGC.

SELECTED BIBLIOGRAPHY
James U. Crockett. *Landscape Gardening.* New York: Time-Life
    Books, 1971.
Dale Brown. *Wild Alaska.* New York: Time-Life Books, 1972.
Edward Abbey. *Cactus Country.* New York: Time-Life Books,
    1973.
Ann Sutton and Myron Sutton. *Wild Places: A Photographic
    Celebration of Unspoiled America.* New York: Harper & Row,
    1973.
Ogden Tanner. *New England Wilds.* New York: Time-Life Books,
    1974.
Photographs of the American Wilderness. Preface by Robert
    Doty. Intro. by Carol Brown. Garden City, N.Y.: Amphoto,
    1976.
See also Life Library, *Nature, Print, Year 1974;* chapter 7
    catalogue.

Brown Di Giulio, Lou
See Di Giulio, Lou Brown.

Bruehl, Anton
United States (b. Australia) 1900–

Bruehl, who arrived in the United States in 1910, started
his photographic career as a student of Clarence H. White,
with whom he later taught. After White's death in 1925,
Bruehl made portraits and opened a fashion and advertising studio in New York City, where he made photographs
for *Vogue, Vanity Fair, House and Garden,* and other
magazines. A major figure in photography during his fifty-
year career, Bruehl was one of the first photographers to
work in color. He did most of the early color illustrations
and advertisements for Condé Nast publications. His
heavy use of black as a background became his trademark.
Bruehl's portraits of many famous people of the day —
including Amelia Earhart, Marlene Dietrich, and James
Cagney — are elegant and very typical of the period,
achieving effect through lighting and dramatic posing.

"I think there's an awful lot of nonsense in Art," he
once declared. "Although you can learn technique from
someone else, you must go your own way. I admired much
of the old Käsebier, White, Stieglitz work — *Camera Work*
inspired me a lot. But I quickly found out you can't make
a living except in advertising. People would pay $1,000

for an ad but wouldn't pay that for a photographic print even though it may be better. So I did a lot of advertising" (statement to the authors, 1977).

Anton Bruehl. *Peter Lorre*, ca. 1930s. Silver print. (Courtesy the artist)

WORK Chiefly portraits of the famous, still lifes, fashion, theater scenes, advertising. Also includes views of people and places in Mexico.

MEDIA Chiefly silver prints. Also platinum prints, Type C color prints, carbro prints, chromatones.

AVAILABILITY AND PRICE Vintage prints rare; moderately high to high. Modern color and black-and-white prints available through galleries; moderate.

SIGNATURE/OTHER IDENTIFICATION

Anton Bruehl

COLLECTIONS Chicago, IMP/GEH, MOMA.

SELECTED BIBLIOGRAPHY
Paul T. Frankl. *Form and Re-form: A Practical Handbook of Modern Interiors.* New York: Harper, 1930.
Photographs of Mexico. New York: Delphic Studios, 1933. 25 collotypes. 1,000 copies. Reissue, text by Sally Lee Woodall. New York: U.S. Camera, 1945.
Lowell Thomas. *Magic Dials: The Story of Radio and Television.* New York: Lee Furman, 1939. Another ed., New York: Polygraphic Co. of America, 1939.
Tropic Patterns. Hollywood, Fla.: Dukane Press, 1970.
Vogue, June 1941. Camera issue.
Helen Lawrenso. "The First of the Beautiful People." *Esquire,* Mar. 1973, pp. 98–106.
See also Travis, *Julien Levy;* Witkin, *Julien Levy.*

Bruguière, Francis
United States 1879–1945

Bruguière's first interests were painting, music, and poetry. About 1905 he met Alfred Stieglitz, was influenced by Frank Eugene, and became a member of the Photo-Secession. He began experimenting with abstractions perhaps as early as 1912. He made many multiple exposures, cut-paper and light abstractions, and derivations in the experimental style typical of the 1920s. "The photographer has the choice of either dealing with the things that can be seen (landscapes, portraits, still-lifes), or of creating his own world," he once said. "In making subjects of my own, I have used paper-cut designs brought into low relief, and lit, generally by one small spot lamp of 250 watts: the same lamp has been placed in different positions through a series of exposures. The field is not limited to paper; any plastic material will answer the purpose. Then you can have the pleasure of making your own 'unnatural' world, to which it is not unpleasant to return" (quoted in Lyons, *Photographers,* pp. 34–36).

James L. Enyeart wrote of two styles that had emerged in Bruguière's work by 1923: "From the multiple-exposure technique came a series of surreal images making up a still-photo scenario for a film he hoped to produce, to be called *The Way;* and from his growing obsession with light as the quintessence of the photo image he developed a style and method of 'light abstractions' that were as unique as the photograms of Man Ray and Moholy-Nagy" (Enyeart, pp. 21–22).

Bruguière had opened a studio in New York by 1918. He photographed Theatre Guild productions and was one of the first to photograph actors using only available stage lighting. In addition to his photographs, Bruguière also exhibited his paintings. After moving to England in 1928, he collaborated on the books *Beyond This Point* and *Few Are Chosen,* which were notable for their creative integration of text and images. He also made several films, including *Light Rhythms,* England's first abstract film.

WORK Includes pictorial photographs; cut-paper and light abstractions; solarizations and cliché-verre-like abstractions; stage photography (e.g., John Barrymore as Hamlet); architecture, often multiple exposures (e.g., English cathedrals, New York skyscrapers).

MEDIA Silver prints (some hand-tinted), gum-bichromate prints, autochromes.

Francis Bruguière. *Light Abstraction No. 36,* ca. 1927. Silver print. (Private collection)

AVAILABILITY AND PRICE   Through galleries and at auction. Vintage prints rare; moderately high to high. A limited edition of modern prints from the original negatives is planned; moderate. *Camera Work* gravure moderate.

SIGNATURE/OTHER IDENTIFICATION

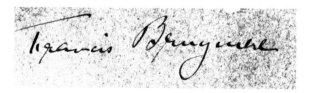

FRANCIS J. BRUGUIERE
Original Print

PLEASE
CREDIT
FRANCIS BRUGUIERE

PORTFOLIO   *See* chapter 6 entry.

COLLECTIONS   Chicago, IMP/GEH, Kansas, LOC, Oakland, San Francisco.

SELECTED BIBLIOGRAPHY
San Francisco. San Francisco: Crocker, 1918.
Norman Bel Geddes. *A Project for a Theatrical Presentation of the Divine Comedy of Dante Alighieri.* New York: Theatre Arts, 1924.
Lance Sieveking. *Beyond This Point.* London: Duckworth, 1929.
Oswell Blakeston. *Few Are Chosen.* London: Eric Partridge, 1931.
James L. Enyeart. *Bruguière: His Photographs and His Life.* New York: Knopf, 1977.
Alan A. Potamkin. "The Work of Francis Bruguière." *Transition,* no. 18 (Nov. 1929).
Walter Chappell. "Francis Bruguière." *Art In America* 47 (Fall 1959): 56–59.
Camera Work: Gravure in no. 48.
See also Green, *Camera Work;* Lyons, *Photographers;* Travis, *Julien Levy;* Witkin, *Julien Levy.*

Bullock, Wynn
United States 1902–1975

Bullock studied music and by the 1930s was pursuing a promising career as a concert tenor when he became gradually more interested in the visual arts, particularly photography. In the late 1930s he studied photography with Edward Kaminski at the Los Angeles Art Center School and by 1949 was concentrating on it as a means of creative expression. He was particularly interested in the photographic work of László Moholy-Nagy and Edward Weston and was in addition profoundly impressed by the work of the semanticist Alfred Korzybski, especially his theory that the names people attach to objects filter and distort human perceptions of reality.

Bullock sought to express his philosophical concepts about reality through his photographs. For example, he explored his interest in time, space and change through long exposures, multiple exposures, and superimposed images. His theory of opposites — that nothing can exist without its opposite — found expression in the juxtaposition of contrasting visual elements. He once commented: "My inner development as a photographer I measure to the degree I am aware of, have developed a sense of, and can symbolize (visually) reality in all of its four dimensions" (*Wynn Bullock* [1971]).

WORK   Chiefly the nude and objects in nature. Also includes interiors, some with nudes. In addition, Bullock worked with less traditional techniques (e.g., negative prints, light abstractions in color, solarization, double printing).

MEDIA   Silver prints, Type C color prints.

AVAILABILITY AND PRICE   Through galleries. Silver prints moderately high to high. Color prints rare; high.

SIGNATURE/OTHER IDENTIFICATION

PORTFOLIO   *See* chapter 6 entry.

COLLECTIONS The Center for Creative Photography (Tucson, Ariz.) houses prints, negatives, personal papers. Also BMFA, California (Santa Cruz), IMP/GEH, Mint, MMA, MOMA, Nebraska, Oakland, Oregon, Ringling, San Francisco, Smithsonian, St. Petersburg; BN, RPS.

SELECTED BIBLIOGRAPHY
Richard Mack. *The Widening Stream.* Carmel, Calif.: Peregrine, 1965. Poetry, with photographs by Bullock.
Wynn Bullock. Text by Barbara Bullock. Notes by Wynn Bullock. San Francisco: Scrimshaw, 1971.
Wynn Bullock: 20 Color Photographs/Light Abstractions. Santa Clara, Calif.: de Saisset Art Gallery & Museum, 1972.
Wynn Bullock: Photography, A Way of Life. Ed. by Liliane DeCock. Text by Barbara Bullock-Wilson. Dobbs Ferry, N.Y.: Morgan & Morgan, 1973. Bibliography.
The Photograph As Symbol. Capitola, Calif.: Artichoke Press, 1976.
Wynn Bullock. Intro. by David Fuess. Millerton, N.Y.: Aperture, 1976. Bibliography.
Jonathan Williams. "Three Phantasts: Laughlin, Sommer, Bullock." *Aperture* 9, no. 3 (1961): 114–119.
Paul Hill and Tom Cooper. "Wynn Bullock." *Camera,* Feb. and Mar. 1976. Interview.
See also Lewis, *Darkroom 1;* Life Library, *Themes;* Lyons, *Photographers;* chapter 7 catalogues.

Wynn Bullock. *Woman and Dog,* 1953. Silver print. (Courtesy The Wynn Bullock Estate)

Callahan, Harry
United States 1912–

A lyrical and personal photographer, Callahan has been influential for many years both as an artist and a teacher. He began to photograph in 1938 as a hobby; in 1941 he saw the work of Ansel Adams, whose sharp, brilliant photographs were the first ones to influence him strongly. In 1946 he joined the faculty of the Institute of Design (Chicago) and has taught and headed the departments of photography there and at the Rhode Island School of De-

Harry Callahan. *Eleanor,* 1948. Silver print. (Courtesy Light Gallery)

sign. He is currently devoting himself full time to his own work.

Callahan has concentrated in his art on the experiences of his daily life and has returned many times to three central themes to record his responses to them. His portraits of his wife express his vision of her as life-giving and symbolically female; he mentions Alfred Stieglitz's cumulative portrait of Georgia O'Keeffe as one tradition behind this series. Pictures made in cities where he has lived seem joyless; in them, people's faces reveal the pressures of the city. In contrast to the cityscapes, his landscapes are rejuvenating; his details of nature are highly graphic in design.

Callahan's work is unique in that it combines a purist's preference for realism, sharpness, and full-scale tonality with a willingness to experiment, specifically with graphic abstraction and camera-made double exposures. His images always serve his own personal expression. "I realize that we all do express ourselves," he once noted, "but those who express that which is always being done are those whose thinking is almost in every way in accord with everyone else. Expression on this basis has become dull to those who wish to think for themselves. I wish more people felt that photography was an adventure the same as life itself and felt that their individual feelings were worth expressing. To me, that makes photography more exciting" (quoted in Lyons, *Photographers,* p. 41).

WORK Includes portraits of his wife Eleanor and daughter Barbara, indoors and out, nude and clothed; cityscapes (e.g., architecture, people on the street); natural landscapes (e.g., trees, grasses, beaches). Some of these are multiple exposures (e.g., figures plus landscapes or cityscapes).

MEDIA Silver prints, color.

AVAILABILITY AND PRICE Through galleries; moderately high.

SIGNATURE/OTHER IDENTIFICATION

Harry Callahan

PORTFOLIOS *See* chapter 6 entry.

COLLECTIONS The Center for Creative Photography (Tucson, Ariz.) holds the Callahan archive: about 50 fine prints, 20,000 work prints, 5,000 color slides, 100,000 negatives, plus correspondence and personal papers. Many major collections have prints.

SELECTED BIBLIOGRAPHY

The Multiple Image: Photographs by Harry Callahan. Intro. by Jonathan Williams. Chicago: Press of the Institute of Design, 1961.

Photographs: Harry Callahan. San Francisco: El Mochuelo Gallery, 1964. Bibliography.

Harry Callahan. Intro. by Sherman Paul. New York: MOMA, 1967. Bibliography.

Callahan. Ed. and intro. by John Szarkowski. Millerton, N.Y.: Aperture, 1976. Bibliography.

Harry Callahan. Intro. by Peter C. Bunnell. New York: American Federation of Arts, and Rizzoli International, 1978.

Peter Worth. "A Note on the Photographs of Callahan." *University of Nebraska Galleries: No. 1, Four Gallery Talks.* Lincoln: University of Nebraska Press, 1952.

See also Life Library, Art, Great Photographers, Themes; Lyons, *Photographers;* Szarkowski, *Looking;* chapter 7 catalogues.

CAMERA WORK

Camera Work, a quarterly magazine published in New York City by Alfred Stieglitz from 1903 to 1917, contained work by major photographers of the period in some of the finest quality reproductions in the history of photographic publishing. Issues of the magazine as well as individual reproductions from it are also important collector's items because of the magazine's association with Stieglitz and the Photo-Secession. In addition, many of the images that appeared in *Camera Work* no longer exist as photographic prints: the magazine's gravures and halftones are the only extant collectible forms of these images.

In addition to photography, *Camera Work* championed other modern arts and reproduced work by Cézanne, Marin, Matisse, Picasso, Rodin, and others. With original articles by George Bernard Shaw, Sadakichi Hartmann (sometimes writing as Sidney H. Allen), Gertrude Stein, Mabel Dodge, and many others, the magazine was a forum for modern critical thinking on photography and other art forms. The fifty issues were produced with consistently fine materials and elegant choices in typography and design, owing to the effort of Edward Steichen; each copy is a splendid example of fine printing. Reproduced in *Camera Work* were photographs by the following individuals. (*Italicized* photographers have separate entries in this chapter.)

Abbot, C. Yarnall
Adamson, Prescott. U.S. Active ca. 1900
Annan, James Craig
Becher, Arthur E.
Boughton, Alice
Brigman, Anne W.
Bruguière, Francis
Cadby, Will. England. Active 1893–1932
Cameron, Julia Margaret
Coburn, Alvin Langdon
Davison, George. England. 1856–1930
Demachy, Robert
de Meyer, Adolf (Gayne)
Devens, Mary. Great Britain. Active ca. 1900
Dugmore, A. Radclyffe. Active ca. 1900
Dyer, William B. U.S. Active ca. 1900
Eugene, Frank
Evans, Frederick H.
French, Herbert Greer. U.S. 1872–1942
Haviland, Paul B. U.S. (b. France). 1880–1950
Henneberg, Hugo. Austria. 1863–1918
Herzog, F. Benedict. U.S. d. 1921
Hill, David Octavius
Hinton, A. Horsley. England. 1863–1908
Hofmeister, Theodor (1868–1943) and Oscar (1871–1937). Germany
Käsebier, Gertrude
Keiley, Joseph T. U.S. 1869–1914
Kernochan, Marshall R. U.S. Active ca. 1900
Kühn, Heinrich
Lamb, H. Mortimer
Le Bègue, René. France. Active ca. 1900
Lewis, Arthur Allen
Muir, Ward
Post, William B. U.S. 1857–1925
Pratt, Frederick H.
Puyo, C. (Emile Joachim Constant Puyo). France. 1857–1933
Renwick, W. W.
Rey, Guido. Italy. Active 1890s–mid-1920s
Rubincam, Harry C. U.S. 1871–1940
Sears, Sarah C. U.S. 1858–1935
Seeley, George H. U.S. 1880–1955
Shaw, George Bernard. Ireland. 1856–1950
Spencer, Ema
Steichen, Edward
Stieglitz, Alfred
Strand, Paul
Strauss, John Francis. U.S. Active ca. 1900
Struss, Karl F. U.S. 1886–
Watson-Schütze, Eva. U.S. 1867–1935
Watzek, Hans. Austria. 1848–1903
White, Clarence H.
Wilmerding, William E.

WORK *See* individual entries.

MEDIA Photographs were reproduced in gravure and halftone; some drawings appeared in collotype. Gravures were hand-pulled, often on fine Japan tissue and frequently mounted on colored paper. Stieglitz considered the gravure illustrations to be fine prints suitable for framing. A *Camera Work* announcement in 1906 reported that in a major international show "the Exhibition Committee . . . took about thirty of the gravures which had been published in Camera Work, mounted and framed them [and these were] the success of the exhibition. . . . This speaks eloquently for the value of the individual Camera Work gravures for mounting and framing." Cover size of the magazine is 12½×9; page size is 11¾×8⅛; sizes of reproductions vary. (*See also* individual entries.)

AVAILABILITY AND PRICE Though as many as 1,000 copies of each issue were printed, complete issues are relatively scarce, particularly those published toward 1917, when subscriptions declined. Illustrations were tipped into the magazine when a copy was mailed or sold; some copies assembled afterward do not have all the illustrations in place. Entire sets of *Camera Work* are very rare but are occasionally available. An almost-complete set was sold at auction in 1976 for $32,000. Single issues range in price from moderately high to extremely high, depending on the material contained within. Single reproductions, which collectors often overmat and display like any fine photograph, are often available; they vary in price considerably, depending on the prominence of the photographer and the importance of the image, from low for an obscure image by a relative unknown to extremely high for Stieglitz's *The Steerage* (page 20), which appeared in 1911 in no. 36. Gravures are generally more valuable than halftones. (*See also* individual entries.)

SIGNATURE/OTHER IDENTIFICATION (Menu [ca. 1905] designed by Steichen for a Photo-Secession dinner, signed by those who attended. Courtesy Lee D. Witkin. *See also* individual entries.)

COLLECTIONS Individual reproductions in many collections; complete individual issues or sets less common. Complete sets: AAA, BPL, Philadelphia, Princeton (Library). (*See also* individual entries.)

PORTFOLIOS *See* individual entries.

SELECTED BIBLIOGRAPHY
Marianne Fulton Margolis, ed. *Camera Work: A Pictorial Guide.* New York: Dover, 1978.
See also Camera Work (facsimile reprint), Doty, *Photo-Secession;* Green, *Camera Work;* Life Library, *Print;* Naef, *Collection.*

Guido Rey. *The Letter.* From *Camera Work*, no. 24, 1908. Gravure. (Courtesy The Witkin Gallery)

Gertrude Käsebier. *The Picture Book.* From *Camera Work*, no. 10, 1905. Gravure. (Courtesy The Witkin Gallery)

Alfred Stieglitz. *The "Flat-Iron."* From *Camera Work,* no. 4, 1903. Gravure. (Courtesy The Witkin Gallery)

Frank Eugene. *Sir Henry Irving.* From *Camera Work,* no. 30, 1910. Gravure. (Courtesy The Witkin Gallery)

Frederick H. Evans. *Height and Light in Bourges Cathedral.* From *Camera Work,* no. 4, 1903. Gravure. (Courtesy The Witkin Gallery)

Paul Strand. *New York (Wall Street)*, 1915. From *Camera Work*, no. 48, 1916. Gravure. (Courtesy The Witkin Gallery)

Edward Steichen. *Steeplechase Day, Paris: Grand Stand*, 1905. From *Camera Work*, no. 42/43, 1913. Duogravure. (Courtesy The Witkin Gallery)

Clarence H. White. *Telegraph Poles*. From *Camera Work*, no. 3, 1903. Gravure. (Courtesy The Witkin Gallery)

Anne W. Brigman. *The Soul of the Blasted Pine*. From *Camera Work*, no. 25, 1909. Gravure. (Courtesy The Witkin Gallery)

Cameron, Julia Margaret
England (b. India) 1815–1879

Cameron was boundlessly energetic, impulsive, unconventional, and passionate about ideas and art. She turned to photography in 1863, at the age of forty-eight, when given a photographic outfit by her daughter, who suggested that it might serve as an amusing diversion. Characteristically, Cameron turned photography into a passion: she converted a coalhouse into a darkroom, a chickenhouse into a studio, and worked tirelessly, pressing into service as models her family, friends, and servants, as well as complete strangers. "I longed to arrest all beauty that came before me, and at length the longing has been satisfied. Its difficulty enhanced the value of the pursuit. I began with no knowledge of the art. I did not know where to place my dark box, how to focus my sitter, and my first picture I effaced to my consternation by rubbing my hand over the filmy side of the glass" ("Annals of My Glass House").

A spontaneous and intuitive artist, Cameron never was much concerned with technique. If the plate was imperfectly coated or the image out of focus, she did not care. What she did care about and what she did splendidly was to capture the personality of her sitters. She made some of the most revealing and powerful portraits that have been produced in any medium. Sir John Herschel, Tennyson, Ellen Terry, Thomas Carlyle, and numerous other eminent Victorians were her friends and sat patiently (because she imperiously commanded them to do so) until she got the effect she wanted: "My whole soul has endeavoured to do its duty . . . in recording faithfully the greatness of the inner as well as the features of the outer man" (ibid.).

She also made religious and allegorical compositions in the style of the Pre-Raphaelites; in these posed and costumed tableaux she indulged freely in the uninhibited sentiment that was acceptable in the nineteenth century but is less so today. Nevertheless, many of these works remain oddly touching if the viewer is willing to accept them on their own terms. The last word Cameron uttered before dying was "Beautiful."

WORK Chiefly portraits; religious, allegorical, and symbolic compositions; illustrations for poetry and drama. Also includes a few photographs of plantation workers in Ceylon (where the photographer lived for several years before her death).

MEDIA Collodion wet-plate negatives (9×11; also 12×15 from 1866 on), albumen prints.

AVAILABILITY AND PRICE Frequently available, at auction and through galleries; moderately high to extremely high, depending on subject and condition. Buyers should exercise discretion since many prints are stained and faded; an authenticated but unsigned fine print is more valuable than a signed poor print of the same image. Prints may be inscribed by the photographer in various ways (e.g., "From life. Copyright Registered Photograph. Julia Margaret Cameron"; sometimes also inscribed "Not enlarged" or "Untouched," or titled. Some sources say she engaged mem-

Julia Margaret Cameron. *Alice Liddell*, 1872. Albumen print. (Courtesy The Metropolitan Museum of Art, David Hunter McAlpin Fund, 1963)

bers of her household to title prints, but copyright lines and signatures are in her hand).

Cameron sold her prints through P. and D. Colnaghi from about 1865; the Colnaghi blind-stamp on the mount is desirable if the print is not signed. Also available are carbon prints made and sold by the Autotype Company after 1875; moderately high to high if signed. Later cabinet photographs and cartes de visite, some printed by her son Henry Herschel Hay Cameron, are priced low. *Camera Work* gravures moderate.

SIGNATURE/OTHER IDENTIFICATION

Julia Margaret Cameron

COLLECTIONS NPG, RPS, VA, most major collections.

SELECTED BIBLIOGRAPHY
Alfred Tennyson. *Idylls of the King and Other Poems*. 2 vols. London: King, 1875. Albumen prints.
Anne Thackeray Ritchie and H. H. H. Cameron. *Alfred, Lord Tennyson and His Friends*. London: T. Fisher Unwin, 1893. Gravures of photographs by Julia Margaret and H. H. H. Cameron.

Victorian Photographs of Famous Men and Fair Women. Intro. by Virginia Woolf and Roger Fry. London: Hogarth Press, and New York: Harcourt, Brace, 1926. Rev. ed., ed. by Tristram Powell. Boston: Godine, 1973.

Helmut Gernsheim. *Julia Margaret Cameron: Her Life and Photographic Work.* London: Fountain, 1948. Reprint, Millerton, N.Y.: Aperture, 1975. Bibliography.

Brian Hill. *Julia Margaret Cameron: A Victorian Family Portrait.* London: Peter Owen, and New York: St. Martin, 1973.

Anita Ventura Mozely. *Mrs. Cameron's Photographs from the Life.* Stanford, Calif.: Stanford University Museum of Art, 1974.

Graham Ovenden, ed. *A Victorian Album: Julia Margaret Cameron and Her Circle.* New York: Da Capo, 1975.

"Annals of My Glass House." Unfinished manuscript. Reprinted in Gernsheim, *Julia Margaret Cameron.*

Camera Work: Gravures in no. 41.

See also Green, *Camera Work;* Life Library, *Camera, Great Photographers;* Mann, *Women;* Naef, *Collection;* Newhall, *Masters;* Szarkowski, *Looking.*

Caponigro, Paul
United States 1932–

Caponigro's earliest artistic interest was in music. He studied piano but gradually became aware of the expressive possibilities of photography, which he studied with Benjamin Chin, Alfred W. Richter, and Minor White. He became a teaching assistant to White in 1959, and has since taught, exhibited, and published extensively. He is interested in the idea that photography can be a teacher and that the process of making photographs can reveal basic truths: "All that I have achieved are these dreams locked in silver. Through this work it was possible, if only for brief moments, to sense the thread which holds all things together. The world, the unity of force and movement, could be seen in nature — in a face, a stone, or a patch of sunlight. The subtle suggestions generated by configurations of cloud and stone, of shape and tone, made of the photograph a meeting place, from which to continue on an even more adventurous journey through a landscape of reflection, of introspection" (*Landscape,* p. 67).

WORK   Includes landscapes, close-ups of natural objects (e.g., an apple, frost on windows, leaves, flowers), English and Irish scenery (e.g., Irish monuments, Stonehenge), negative images.

MEDIUM   Silver prints, 4×5 to 11×14 and larger (*Running White Deer* print, 11×14 and 16×20).

AVAILABILITY AND PRICE   Through galleries; moderate to moderately high.

SIGNATURE/OTHER IDENTIFICATION

Paul Caponigro

PORTFOLIOS   *See* chapter 6 entry.

COLLECTIONS   CCP, Chicago, Florida, IMP/GEH, LOC, Louisville, MOMA, Oregon; BN, NGC, VA.

SELECTED BIBLIOGRAPHY

Paul Caponigro: Photographs. Millerton, N.Y.: Aperture, 1967. Rev. ed., 1972. Bibliography.

Sunflower. New York: Filmhaus, 1974.

Landscape. New York: McGraw-Hill, 1975.

Contemporary Photographer, summer 1973. Caponigro and Jerome Liebling issue.

See also Hume, *The Great West;* Life Library, *Art, Studio;* Szarkowski, *Looking, Mirrors;* chapter 7 catalogues.

Paul Caponigro. *Monument Valley, Utah,* 1970. Silver print. (Courtesy The Witkin Gallery)

Carjat, Etienne
France 1828–1906

A contemporary of Nadar, Carjat took up photography as a hobby, then operated a studio part-time from 1855 to 1875. He was also a caricaturist, journalist, actor, and playwright, and he knew and photographed many theatrical and literary personalities, as well as scientists, politicians, and other famous people of the day. Though Carjat's posing and lighting are similar to Nadar's, he seems at times more acerbic in his portrayal of his sitters, more willing to reveal their foibles. Like Nadar, Carjat contributed to *Galerie Contemporaine,* a serial containing portraits of noteworthy people; he also had portraits in a number of illustrated periodicals of the theater, arts, and letters.

WORK   Portraits (e.g., Baudelaire, Rossini, Sarah Bernhardt, Courbet).

MEDIA   Collodion wet-plate negatives, albumen prints.

AVAILABILITY AND PRICE   Most prints available today are woodburytypes from *Galerie Contemporaine* or similar publications of the period; low to moderate. Cabinet photographs and cartes de visite occasionally available; price varies from low to moderate, depending on condition and subject.

Etienne Carjat. *Victor Hugo.* From *Paris-Artiste*, no. 43, 1885. Woodburytype. (Courtesy The Witkin Gallery)

SIGNATURE/OTHER IDENTIFICATION

COLLECTIONS BPL, IMP/GEH, New Mexico; BM, BN, Caisse Nationale, NGC.

SELECTED BIBLIOGRAPHY

J. Adhémar. "Carjat." *Gazette des Beaux-Arts* 80 (July 1972): 71–81. Bibliography.
See also Life Library, *Great Photographers.*

Carroll, Lewis
England 1832–1898

An Oxford mathematician, don, and clergyman, Carroll (Charles Lutwidge Dodgson) is renowned for *Alice's Adventures in Wonderland* and *Through the Looking-Glass.* He pursued photography as a hobby from 1856, primarily taking portraits of children and distinguished adults. He was often more at ease with children than with adults and particularly enjoyed the company of young girls (as he once put it: "I am fond of children, except boys"). He went to great lengths to make their acquaintance, entertain them, dress them up as beggars, Greeks, Romans, or characters from fiction, and photograph them. He sometimes posed them partially clothed or nude, and to contemporary sensibilities these images often have a sensual, even erotic, flavor. However, any interpretation of Carroll's psychology based on his photographs is purely speculative.

WORK Best known for portraits of children, sometimes in the nude or in costume. Also made portraits of fellow academics and celebrities (e.g., Tennyson, D. G. Rossetti), occasional landscapes, miscellaneous subjects.

MEDIA Collodion wet-plate negatives (five sizes, from 3¼×4¼ to 8×10), albumen prints. According to Helmut Gernsheim, many of Carroll's negatives were sent out for printing, to Joseph Cundall and Co. (London), Hills and Saunders (Oxford), and Henry Peach Robinson's firm (Tunbridge Wells), and it is impossible to tell which prints he made himself. Cartes de visite (portraits of Tennyson, etc.) were published in the 1860s by Cundall and Co.

AVAILABILITY AND PRICE Sometimes available at auction; high to extremely high. (These photographs would be collectible no matter who had taken them, but the fact that they are by a major literary figure adds interest and value.)

SIGNATURE/OTHER IDENTIFICATION

COLLECTIONS Princeton (Library), Texas (Gernsheim); NPG.

SELECTED BIBLIOGRAPHY

Stuart Dodgson Collingwood. *The Life and Letters of Lewis Carroll.* . . . London: T. Fisher Unwin, 1898.
Helmut Gernsheim. *Lewis Carroll: Photographer.* London: Parrish, 1949. Rev. ed., New York: Dover, 1969. Bibliography.
Le Bambine di Carroll: Foto e Lettere di Lewis Carroll a Mary, Alice, Irene, Agnese . . . . Ed. by Guido Almansi. Notes by Brassaï and Helmut Gernsheim. Parma, Italy: Ricci, 1974. U.S. ed., *Photos and Letters of Lewis Carroll to His Child Friends.* New York: Rizzoli, 1975.
Lewis Carroll at Christchurch. London: National Portrait Gallery, 1974.
Jean Gattégno. *Lewis Carroll: Fragments of a Looking Glass.* New York: Crowell, 1976.

Morton N. Cohen. *Lewis Carroll's Photographs of Nude Children.* New York: Potter, 1979.
See also Life Library, *Children.*

Lewis Carroll. *Ellen and Florence Tracy,* ca. 1865. Modern silver contact print (on printing-out paper toned with gold chloride) made from the original plate. (Courtesy Graphics International, Ltd.)

Cartier-Bresson, Henri
France 1908–

Cartier-Bresson influenced a generation of photographers in the 1940s and 1950s with his memorable images of "decisive moments" when a situation crests in a visual configuration. He has had three recurring artistic interests: photography, film, and painting. In 1923 he began studying painting, continuing his studies in 1927 and 1928 with André Lhote, the cubist painter. In 1930 he became seriously committed to photography; the work of Man Ray and Eugène Atget were early influences, and he later credited André Kertész as his "poetic source" (*Le Monde,* 5 Sept. 1974).

Cartier-Bresson's purchase of a Leica 35mm camera formalized his approach to his work. The Leica is small, inconspicuous, and fast-working, and he became skilled at merging into a situation, almost disappearing from the attention of his subjects. With a Leica the photographer views and composes by looking straight ahead through a viewfinder; Cartier-Bresson called his camera an extension of his eye, one through which he could perceive and organize a scene with the speed of vision itself. He made his prints from the entire negative area without cropping.

He wrote: "At the moment of shooting, [composition] can stem only from our intuition, for we are out to capture the fugitive moment, and all the interrelationships involved are on the move. . . . It very rarely happens that a photograph which was feebly composed can be saved by reconstruction of its composition under the darkroom's enlarger; the integrity of vision is no longer there" (*The Decisive Moment*).

In 1937 he began doing picture stories for magazines and newspapers and later, with Robert Capa, David Seymour, and others, founded the Magnum picture agency. From the 1930s he was also intermittently active in film: he worked with Paul Strand, Jean Renoir, and others, and he made documentaries during the Spanish Civil War (1937) and on the return of World War II prisoners of war to France (1945). He worked steadily in photography until the 1970s, when he ceased taking pictures in order to concentrate on painting and drawing.

Cartier-Bresson's finest photographs go beyond simple street reportage to touch some underlying, though usually hard-to-verbalize, reality. He once explained: "Photography, as I understand it, is just another means of taking visual notes. Like all notes, photographic notes are necessarily incomplete in that they may not express the subject with all its angles and facets. The important thing is that each note touches upon the essence of the subject" (*Camera,* p. 4).

Cartier-Bresson was profoundly affected by the concepts of surrealism, but Robert Capa advised him that if his work was labeled as such "you will have an exhibition once in a while and your work will become precious and confidential. Keep on doing what you want, but use the name 'photojournalism,' which will put you in direct contact with what is going on in the world" (quoted in ibid., p. 45).

WORK Photojournalism (e.g., Spain, 1933; coronation crowds, London, 1938; Chinese Civil War, 1948; Gandhi's funeral, 1949; Moscow, 1954).

MEDIUM Silver prints.

AVAILABILITY AND PRICE Through galleries, at auction, and through the photographer's agent. Vintage prints rare; high. Modern prints are made by a private printer and often signed by the photographer; moderate to moderately high.

SIGNATURE/OTHER IDENTIFICATION

Henri Cartier-Bresson

Photo : **HENRI CARTIER-BRESSON**
Mention obligatoire

COLLECTIONS Chicago, Menil (on extended loan to Rice University, Houston), Houston, ICP, IMP/GEH, MOMA, Worcester; BN.

SELECTED BIBLIOGRAPHY

The Photographs of Cartier-Bresson. Intro. by Lincoln Kirstein and Beaumont Newhall. New York: MOMA, 1947. Bibliography.

Images à la sauvette. Paris: Verve, 1952. U.S. ed., *The Decisive Moment.* New York: Simon & Schuster, 1952.

D'une Chine à l'autre. Preface by Jean-Paul Sartre. Paris: Delpire, 1954. U.S. ed., *From One China to the Other.* Text by Han Suyin. New York: Universe, 1956.

Les Européens. Paris: Verve, 1955. U.S. ed., *The Europeans.* New York: Simon & Schuster, 1955.

Moscou, vu par Henri Cartier-Bresson. Paris: Delpire, 1955. U.S. ed., *The People of Moscow.* New York: Simon & Schuster, 1955.

Photographies de Henri Cartier-Bresson. Paris: Delpire, 1963. U.S. ed., *Photographs by Cartier-Bresson.* Intro. by Lincoln Kirstein and Beaumont Newhall. New York: Grossman, 1963.

China. New York: Bantam Gallery, 1964.

Howard Barnstone. *The Galveston That Was.* New York: Macmillan, 1966.

Flagrants délits. Paris: Delpire, 1968. U.S. ed., *The World of Henri Cartier-Bresson.* New York: Viking, 1968.

L'homme et la machine. Intro. by Etiemble. Paris: Chêne, 1968. U.S. ed., *Man and Machine.* New York: Viking, 1968.

Vive la France. Text by François Nourissier. Paris: Laffont, 1970. U.S. ed., *Cartier-Bresson's France.* New York: Viking, 1970.

The Face of Asia. Intro. by Robert Shaplen. New York: Weatherhill, 1972. French ed., *Visage d'Asie.* Paris: Chêne, 1972.

A propos de l'U.R.S.S. Paris: Chêne, 1973. U.S. ed., *About Russia.* New York: Viking, 1974.

Henri Cartier-Bresson. Millerton, N.Y.: Aperture, 1976. Bibliography.

Henri Cartier-Bresson: Photographer. Essay by Yves Bonnefoy. Boston: New York Graphic Society, 1979.

Camera, July 1976. Entire issue.

See also Edey, *Essays;* Life Library, *Art, Camera, Children, Documentary, Great Photographers, Travel, Year 1975;* Lyons, *Photographers;* Newhall, *Masters;* Szarkowski, *Looking;* Travis, *Julien Levy;* Witkin, *Julien Levy.*

Clark, Larry
United States 1943–

Photographer, rock musician, witness to the drug culture of his generation and place, Clark — through his book *Tulsa* — showed the realities of a life-style of which he was part. (The book, out of print, seems unlikely to be reissued because of legal complications involving releases from people he photographed.) The impact of *Tulsa* on photography in the 1970s is comparable to that of Robert Frank's book *The Americans* in the late 1950s. It explores a fringe culture with the realism that only a participant can convey. Clark takes a harsh, semidocumentary, semisubjective look at both his friends and himself.

In the introduction to his portfolio *Teen Lust,* Clark wrote: "since i became a photographer i always wanted to turn back the years. always wished i had a camera when i was a boy. . . . in 1972 and 73, the kid brothers in the neighborhood took me with them in their teen lust scene. it took me back."

WORK   Chiefly portraits and images of the photographer, his friends, and their environment.

MEDIUM   Silver prints (usually to 6½×9½ on 11×14 photographic paper).

AVAILABILITY AND PRICE   Through galleries; moderate.

SIGNATURE/OTHER IDENTIFICATION

Larry Clark

PORTFOLIOS   *See* chapter 6 entry.

COLLECTION   IMP/GEH.

SELECTED BIBLIOGRAPHY

Tulsa. New York: Lustrum, 1971.

"Kid Crump." Autobiographical work in progress.

See also Lewis, *Darkroom 1.*

Larry Clark. *Gun/Flag.* From *Tulsa,* 1971. Silver print. (Courtesy Lustrum Press)

Claudet, Antoine François Jean
France 1797–1867

Initially a glass merchant, Claudet learned the daguerreotype process directly from L. J. M. Daguerre in 1839; he subsequently obtained a license to photograph in Britain and moved there. He began by importing and selling apparatus and daguerreotype views; then, in 1841, three months after Richard Beard opened his, Claudet opened England's second daguerreotype studio, in London.

Among Claudet's technical contributions to the medium was a process for shortening the exposure time required. He is also given credit for making the first daguerreotype stereographs. Hand-colored daguerreotypes featuring elaborate backdrops soon became his trademark. In 1851 he opened his "Temple of Photography" and in 1853 was appointed official photographer to Queen Victoria.

WORK Chiefly portraits. Also includes genre scenes and anecdotal pieces (e.g., *The Geography Lesson*).

MEDIA Daguerreotypes (including stereoscopic daguerreotypes; many hand-colored; usually identified by name and various addresses stamped on case); calotypes; collodion wet-plate negatives, albumen prints (including cartes de visite and stereographs; usually identified by his logo).

AVAILABILITY AND PRICE Through galleries and at auction. Cartes de visite and uncredited daguerreotype portraits infrequently found; low to moderate. Stereoscopic daguerreotypes and portraits of famous persons are rare; high to extremely high.

COLLECTIONS IMP/GEH, other historical collections.

SELECTED BIBLIOGRAPHY
Recherches sur la théorie des principaux phénomènes de photographie dans le procédé du daguerréotype. Paris: Lerebours, 1850.
Nouvelles Recherches sur la différence entre les foyers visuels et photogéniques: . . . Description du dynactinomètre, du focimètre, etc. Paris: Lerebours et Secretan, 1851.
Du Stéréoscope et de ses applications à la photographie, par A. Claudet . . . *et Derniers Perfectionnements apportés au daguerréotype,* par F. Colas. Paris: Lerebours et Secretan, 1853.
A Memoir, 1868. Authorship uncertain; possibly by Jos. Ellis.
Arthur T. Gill. "Antoine François Jean Claudet, 1797–1867." *Photographic Journal* 107 (1967): 405–408.
See also Colnaghi, *Photography;* Darrah, *Stereo Views;* Life Library, *Children.*

Clergue, Lucien
France 1934–

Clergue has been photographing since the age of fourteen and has produced several extensive series of still images. Seldom working away from his native Arles and the nearby Camargue region, he often photographs seaside and marsh scenes. His nudes on the beach, which he began in 1956, glorify and romanticize the volumes and textures of flesh, sand, and surf; in 1970 he began photographing nudes away from the water — for example, suspended on a background of dead branches. In the mid-1970s he photographed posed nudes on rooftops and in windows of New York City skyscrapers.

A protégé of Picasso, Clergue has made many short films, as well as the longer work *Picasso: Guerre, amour et paix* (shown in the United States as *Picasso at 90*). An active lecturer whose efforts have helped gain recognition in France for photography and young photographers, Clergue is responsible for the photography events at the annual Arles Festival held in July.

Lucien Clergue. *Nu de la plage,* 1971. Silver print. (Courtesy The Witkin Gallery. Copyright © by Lucien Clergue)

WORK Includes nudes; images of death (e.g., dead birds and cats, and especially the ritual killing of bulls in the arena); landscapes; abstractions in nature; an early series of acrobats, dancers, and musicians.

MEDIA Silver prints, color.

AVAILABILITY AND PRICE Through galleries; moderate. Prints are usually made in editions of twenty. Clergue has published many books and portfolios with gravures, original prints, or both.

SIGNATURE/OTHER IDENTIFICATION

COLLECTIONS Chicago, MMA, MOMA, Philadelphia, Smithsonian; Arles, BN, NGC.

SELECTED BIBLIOGRAPHY
Paul Eluard. *Corps mémorable.* Paris: Seghers, 1957.
Naissance d'Aphrodite. Poems by F. Garcia Lorca. Paris: Forces Vives, 1963.
Toros mueros. Text and poems by Jean Cocteau. Paris: Forces Vives, 1963.

Douze photographies. Preface by Mario Prassinos. Paris, 1970. 12 reproductions on loose sheets, and 1 original signed print. 200 copies, signed.

Eight Photographs. Arles, 1972. Reproductions on loose sheets. 200 copies, signed.

Genèse. Poem by Saint-John Perse. Paris: Belfond, 1973.

Lucien Clergue. Text by Michel Tournier. Paris: Perceval, 1974.

Camargue secrète. Paris: Belfond, 1976.

Jean-Marie Magnan. *Le Quart d'heure du taureau.* Paris: Chêne, 1976.

J. Brody. "Urban Nudes: Lucien Clergue." *Camera 35* 22 (Apr. 1978): 52–59.

Coburn, Alvin Langdon
Britain (b. United States) 1882–1966

Coburn began to photograph in 1898, encouraged by his distant cousin F. Holland Day, the pictorial photographer. Coburn was a founding member of the Photo-Secession and was also a member of The Linked Ring. His pictorial work was influenced by the painting style of James McNeill Whistler and by tonalism, an American offshoot of impressionist painting. The misty atmosphere painted by Whistler was sought by Coburn in soft-focus effects, which he sometimes pursued to the extent of removing the lens entirely and photographing through a pinhole opening.

In 1917, stimulated by the cubists — specifically, England's vorticists — he made a kaleidoscopic mirror attachment for his camera to produce abstract images he called vortographs. His 1912 series "New York from Its Pinnacles" had already revealed the abstraction of shapes that occurs when objects are seen from directly overhead. He asked, "Why should not the camera artist break away from the worn-out conventions, that even in its comparatively short existence have begun to cramp and restrict his medium, and claim the freedom of expression which any art must have to be alive?" (quoted in Newhall, *History,* p. 161).

Coburn is also known for his photographs of prominent people, especially artists and writers, and for his gravure illustrations for numerous books. In 1919 he began investigating the mysteries of nature as revealed by Freemasonry and he remained interested in the occult until his death. He photographed intermittently into the 1950s.

WORK Includes city scenes (e.g., New York, London, Paris, Venice), portraits (e.g., Rodin, Stieglitz, Ezra Pound), vortographs (abstractions), landscapes (e.g., the Grand Canyon, Yosemite).

MEDIA Platinum prints, gum-bichromate/platinum prints, silver prints, cyanotypes, autochromes, gravures.

AVAILABILITY AND PRICE Reproductions, especially gravures from *Camera Work* and illustrated books, are plentiful; low to moderate. Larger gravures (to 12×16), which the photographer hand-pulled from his own press (see illustration, page 21), are rarer; moderately high. Vintage photographs rare; high.

SIGNATURE/OTHER IDENTIFICATION *See* signed menu, page 103.

Broadway and the Singer Building by night.
From Coburn's "New York"

Advertisement for Alvin Langdon Coburn's *New York.* From *Camera Work,* no. 32, 1910. Gravure. (Courtesy Lee D. Witkin)

PORTFOLIO *See* chapter 6 entry.

COLLECTIONS IMP/GEH received from Coburn's estate over 400 prints and 14,000 negatives. Also Chicago, Detroit, Kansas, Louisville, Maryland, New Mexico, New Orleans, Wellesley; RPS.

SELECTED BIBLIOGRAPHY
Maurice Maeterlinck. *The Intelligence of the Flowers.* New York: Dodd, Mead, 1907. 4 gravures.

Henry James. *Novels and Tales.* 24 vols. New York: Scribner, 1907–09. Gravure frontispiece in each vol.

London. Intro. by Hilaire Belloc. London: Duckworth, and New York: Brentano's, 1909. 20 gravures.

New York. Essay by H. G. Wells. London: Duckworth, and New York: Brentano's [1910]. 20 gravures.

H. G. Wells. *The Door in the Wall and Other Stories.* New York and London: Kennerley, 1911. 10 gravures. 600 copies, including 60 signed by Wells and Coburn. Only 300 sets of the gravures were completed; the remaining 300 copies lack one or more gravure illustrations but supply them in aquatone if at all.

Men of Mark. London: Duckworth, and New York: Kennerley, 1913. 33 gravures.

Moor Park, Rickmansworth. London: Mathews, 1914. 20 gravures. Limited edition.

G. K. Chesterton. *London.* Minneapolis: privately printed, 1914. 10 gravures.

The Book of Harlech. Harlech, Wales: D. H. Parry, 1920. 20 gravures.

More Men of Mark. London: Duckworth, 1922. 33 collotypes.

Robert Louis Stevenson. Edinburgh, Picturesque Notes. London: Hart-Davis, 1954. 23 gravures.

A Portfolio of Sixteen Photographs by Alvin Langdon Coburn. Text by Nancy Newhall. Rochester, N.Y.: GEH, 1962. Bibliography.

Alvin Langdon Coburn, Photographer: An Autobiography. Ed. by Helmut and Alison Gernsheim. London: Faber & Faber, and New York: Praeger, 1966. Bibliography.

Camera Work: Reproductions (gravures, halftones, colored halftone) in nos. 3, 6, 8, 15, 21, 28, 32.

See also Green, *Camera Work;* Lawton and Know, *Knights;* Life Library, *Great Photographers, Print;* Lyons, *Photographers;* Naef, *Collection;* Szarkowski, *Looking;* Witkin, *Julien Levy.*

Cohen, Mark
United States 1943–

Cohen's images mystify and frustrate many viewers. His photographs — parts of people's bodies, fragments of ordinary street scenes taken in his hometown of Wilkes-Barre, Pennsylvania — seem almost accidental. "Cohen's approach is to get so close to whatever he's photographing that his image is necessarily fragmentary," noted A. D. Coleman. "This seems not so much a stylistic device as an internal compulsion, especially when applied to people. Many of Cohen's images involve people, but only small portions thereof: a knee, a hand, a smile which he transforms into a set of bared teeth. . . . Cohen then blows these bits and pieces up to 16×20 inches" (*New York Times,* 27 Jan. 1974, section 2).

Cohen expressed his approach as follows: "A positive photograph must have a quality that is beyond solving the problems of line and texture and subject. It must go far beyond considerations of timeliness and documentation. It must be better than having an underlying sense of balance and organization and symbolism. Its highest positive value must be in its being a medium for an expression of creativity that can not be seen; but was felt by the photographer and recorded" (statement to MOMA, 1969).

WORK Chiefly fragmented images of people, buildings, commonplace objects. Also includes street portraits.

MEDIA Silver prints (usually 16×20), color.

AVAILABILITY AND PRICE Through galleries; moderately high.

SIGNATURE/OTHER IDENTIFICATION

COLLECTIONS Chicago, Harvard (Fogg), IMP/GEH, MOMA, New Mexico, Vassar; Arts Council, NGC, NGV.

SELECTED BIBLIOGRAPHY
Dennis Longwell. "Mark Cohen's Works." *Camera Mainichi,* no. 252 (Oct. 1974), pp. 143–149.

Andy Grundberg. [Review.] *Art in America* 64 (Mar. 1976): 113.
"Mark Cohen." *Creative Camera Yearbook* (ed. by Peter Turner), pp. 124–135. London: Coo Press, 1976.
Kenneth Poli. "Mark Cohen; Persistence of Vision." *Popular Photography* 80 (Apr. 1977): 104 ff.
Carol Squiers. "Mark Cohen: Recognized Moments." *Artforum* 16 (Mar. 1978): 22–25.
See also Szarkowski, *Mirrors;* chapter 7 catalogues.

Mark Cohen. Untitled, December 1974. Silver print. (Courtesy Castelli Graphics)

Coke, Van Deren
United States 1921–

Paul Strand, Man Ray, Ansel Adams, and Edward Weston were early influences on Coke's work. In the 1960s he began to explore ways of creating imagery that went beyond realistic, "straight" photographs. Coke collected diverse images, often from ambrotypes and other old photographs, and combined them to serve personal ideas. He employed toners and solarization techniques to physically alter and transform these found images into new, allusive, mysterious visions in works such as *Recollections of Malvern Hill, Painting from Snapshot,* and *The Man Machine.*

Gerald Nordland wrote: "Fully grounded in the lore and chemistry of the beginnings of photography, [Coke] has sought to keep the 'photographic' part of earlier work even as he has experimented with negative prints, solarization, fogging or flashing, chance, the found negative, and sandwiches of negatives in combination. He responds emphatically to the silvery reflecting surface of Daguerre, and he makes much of the phenomenon of edge reversal. He plainly delights in darkroom adventure" (*Van Deren Coke: Photographs 1956–1973*).

Coke, a noted critic and teacher especially interested in the effect of photography on painters, wrote of his own imagery: "The ideas I deal with are usually simple and autobiographical. Central to any consideration of my work is the fact that I am an art historian as well as a photographer. Many of my prints either make reference to the work of painters I have admired or deal in photographic terms with ideas first explored by artists" (ibid).

Coke was deputy director and then director of the International Museum of Photography at George Eastman House (Rochester, New York) from 1970 to 1972, has been professor of art and director of the art museum at the University of New Mexico (Albuquerque), and is currently curator of photography at the San Francisco Museum of Modern Art.

WORK Includes homages to favorite artists (e.g., Richard Hamilton, Thomas Eakins, Ralph Eugene Meatyard), autobiographical imagery, dead creatures (e.g., birds, snakes, fish), landscapes.

MEDIA Silver prints, color. Also manipulated prints, using toning, staining, montage, flashing with light during processing, etc. (since such prints cannot be identically repeated, each can be considered unique); some gravures from these prints.

AVAILABILITY AND PRICE Through galleries; moderate to moderately high.

SIGNATURE/OTHER IDENTIFICATION

VC '76

COLLECTIONS Arizona State, IMP/GEH, MOMA; NGC.

SELECTED BIBLIOGRAPHY
The Painter and the Photograph. Albuquerque: University of New Mexico Press, 1964. Rev. ed., subtitled *From Delacroix to Warhol*, 1972.
Van Deren Coke: Photographs 1956–1973. Texts by Henry Holmes Smith and Gerald Nordland. Albuquerque: University of New Mexico Press, 1973. Bibliography.
One Hundred Years of Photographic History. Ed. by Coke. Albuquerque: University of New Mexico Press, 1975.
"Van Deren Coke: Portfolio." *Photography*, Nov. 1961, pp. 36–43.
Keith F. Davis. "Photography at the University of New Mexico." *Artspace*, summer 1977, pp. 12–20.
See also Life Library, *Light*; chapter 7 catalogues.

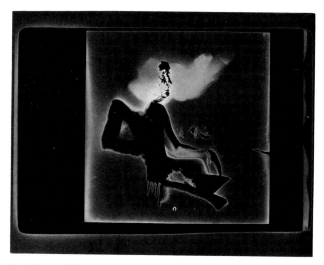

Van Deren Coke. *In Memory of Meatyard*, 1973. Unique flashed silver print. (Courtesy the artist)

Cosindas, Marie
United States   Contemporary

Marie Cosindas is widely recognized as an artist with a unique personal vision who has followed her own path without regard to changes in photographic fashions. Working primarily with Polaroid color materials, she organizes each image with infinite care and patience. She may spend days collecting the fabric, vase, rug, flowers, or other objects in her photograph and more days arranging and rearranging them. Her portraits are also carefully composed; she chooses the clothing for her sitters, poses them, and arranges the background until it is exactly to her satisfaction.

The photographer attended the Modern School of Fashion Design in Boston and later studied painting, drawing, and graphics at the Boston Museum School. She began using the camera as a creative tool in the late 1950s. In the early sixties the Polaroid Corporation offered to let her experiment with their black-and-white film and their about-to-be-released Polacolor film. The near-instant feedback of Polaroid materials allowed her to modify her color balance as she went along — altering lens filters, exposure and development times, even film temperature — until she had just the tones she wanted. She had found the perfect medium to let her express her inner vision.

She recalled: "Whether it was a person, flowers, or objects in front of my camera, the way I worked didn't seem to change very much. A 4×5 view camera on a tripod with a black cloth. The atmosphere quiet and intimate. The soft afternoon light coming into my room, reminiscent of the light in a painting by Rembrandt" (*Marie Cosindas: Color Photographs*).

Perry T. Rathbone observed, "Her images, concrete and of this world, reach us nevertheless from another plane. They are like something remembered, an experience of the eye softened by time. The ephemera of life which flows through her lens is filtered, transformed by her sense of poetry" (*Marie Cosindas: Polaroid Color Photographs*, Museum of Modern Art, 1966).

WORK Chiefly still lifes, portraits. Also includes landscapes, commercial work.

MEDIA Chiefly Polaroid color materials. Also silver prints, other color.

AVAILABILITY AND PRICE Through the photographer; color images moderately high, black and whites moderate.

SIGNATURE/OTHER IDENTIFICATION

Marie Cosindas

COLLECTIONS Addison, BMFA, Chicago, IMP/GEH, Kansas, MMA, MOMA, Nebraska; NGC.

SELECTED BIBLIOGRAPHY
Faces and Facades. Texts by L. Fritz Gruber and Peter C. Bunnell. Cambridge, Mass.: Polaroid Corp., 1977.
Ansel Adams. *Polaroid Land Photography.* Boston: New York Graphic Society, 1978 (rev. ed.).
Marie Cosindas: Color Photographs. Essay by Tom Wolfe. Boston: New York Graphic Society, 1978. Bibliography.
Margaret R. Weiss. "A Show of Color." *Saturday Review,* 24 Sept. 1966, pp. 45–52.
"Beyond Realism." *Life,* 3 May 1968, pp. 46–52.
See also Life Library, *Camera, Children, Color, Light;* Szarkowski, *Mirrors.*

Marie Cosindas. *Dolls,* 1966. Polacolor print. (Courtesy the artist)

Cunningham, Imogen
United States 1883–1976

In the last years of her life Imogen Cunningham occupied the role of grande dame of American photography and loved every moment of it. She began photographing about 1901, some sixty-two years after the invention of the medium, and she continued to shoot and print until shortly before her death. Her career covers one of the longest time spans of any known photographer.

Cunningham learned the platinum process while working for Edward S. Curtis in Seattle from 1907 to 1909. After studying in Germany she opened a portrait studio in Seattle in 1910. Her early photographs were soft-focus and romantic, showing her friends, often nude, in allegorical tableaux. She was possibly the first woman to exhibit photographs of the male nude. With her husband, the etcher Roi Partridge, she moved to San Francisco in 1917. Her friendship and shared photographic concerns with Edward Weston, Ansel Adams, Willard Van Dyke, and other Bay Area photographers resulted in her joining Group f/64, formed in 1932 to champion "straight" photography.

While raising her three sons, Cunningham turned her camera close to home, creating between 1922 and 1929 a series of plant studies that have become classics. After her divorce in 1934 she supported herself by doing portrait photography, commercial assignments, and teaching. In the 1930s she photographed "ugly men" for *Vanity Fair,* including such Hollywood stars as Spencer Tracy, Cary Grant, James Cagney, and Wallace Beery. In 1960 — at the age of seventy-seven — she made a return visit to Europe, photographing, among others, August Sander at his home in Germany.

Cunningham's work was frequently irreverent, always perceptive, and often years ahead of its time. As Margery Mann noted, she had "that rarest of all qualities among photographers, a sense of humor" (*Imogen Cunningham* [1970]). In her last years, Cunningham became something of a celebrity in San Francisco — a familiar figure, with her black cape and camera. This tended at times to overshadow the high quality and seriousness of her art.

"In addition to her photographic achievements," wrote Margaretta Mitchell, "a long life allowed Imogen the time to live out her childhood dream of becoming an actress. Ann Hershey, whose film, *Never Give Up: Imogen Cunningham,* was made by working with Imogen over a four-year period (1970–1974), felt she had the actress's love of center stage, of drawing attention to herself through the character she played, 'the little old lady whose style always defied us to understand her completely'" (*After Ninety,* p. 17). Cunningham was the subject of two other films — one, which also included Wynn Bullock, by Fred Padula (1966), and another by John Korty (1971).

Cunningham was often sought out by young photographers and asked for advice and theory. "There's too much philosophizing about photography already these days," she would say, shrugging her shoulders. "People will just have to look at my stuff and make up their own minds" (quoted in *Imogen Cunningham* [1970]).

WORK Chiefly "straight," sharp images emphasizing shape, form, light (e.g., plants, nudes); portraits (e.g., artists such as Morris Graves, dancers such as Martha Graham and Merce Cunningham, and fellow photographers such as Edward Weston, Margrethe Mather, Ansel Adams, Brassaï, Judy Dater). Also includes early pictorial images (e.g., male nude on Mount Rainier); combination pieces, double images, and manipulated prints (e.g., Duchamp-like portrait of Man Ray); commercial work. (See illustration, page 7.)

MEDIA Platinum prints, silver prints. Also some color (commercial work).

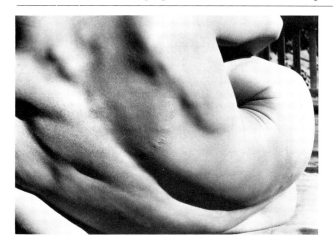

Imogen Cunningham. Untitled, ca. 1930s. Silver print. (Courtesy The Imogen Cunningham Trust)

AVAILABILITY AND PRICE Through galleries and at auction. Vintage prints, which include platinum and warm-toned silver prints, frequently available; high to extremely high. Modern prints made and signed by the photographer or made by The Imogen Cunningham Trust (beginning in 1974) and signed by her are moderately high to high. Prints issued by the trust after her death and bearing her designated oriental-style logo and blind-stamp signature are priced moderate.

SIGNATURE/OTHER IDENTIFICATION

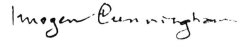

PHOTOGRAPH BY

COLLECTIONS CCP, Chicago, IMP/GEH, Kalamazoo, MMA, MOMA, New Orleans, Oakland, San Francisco, Seattle, Smithsonian, Stanford, Tacoma, UCLA, Washington; Antwerp.

SELECTED BIBLIOGRAPHY
Edna Tartaul Daniel. "Imogen Cunningham: Portraits, Ideas, and Design." Foreword by Beaumont Newhall. University of California at Berkeley, Regional Cultural History Project Interview, 1961. Typescript of interviews conducted in 1959.
Imogen Cunningham: Photographs 1921–1967. Intro. by Beaumont Newhall. Stanford, Calif.: Stanford Art Gallery, 1967.
Imogen Cunningham: Photographs. Intro. by Margery Mann. Seattle: University of Washington Press, 1970. Bibliography.
Imogen! . . . Photographs 1910–1973. Intro. by Margery Mann. Seattle: University of Washington Press, 1974. Bibliography.
After Ninety. Intro. by Margaretta Mitchell. Seattle: University of Washington Press, 1977.
Judy Dater. *Imogen Cunningham: A Portrait.* Boston: New York Graphic Society, 1979.
Flora Huntley Maschmedt. "Imogen Cunningham — An Appreciation." *Wilson's Photographic Magazine* 51 (Mar. 1914): 96 ff.
George M. Craven. "Imogen Cunningham." *Aperture* 11, no. 4 (1964): 134–174.
"Imogen Cunningham." *Album*, no. 5 (1970), pp. 22–38.
Camera, Oct. 1975. Entire issue.
See also Danziger and Conrad, *Interviews*; Life Library, *Print*; Mann, *Women*; Szarkowski, *Looking*; Travis, *Julien Levy*; Witkin, *Julien Levy*; chapter 7 catalogues.

Curtis, Edward Sheriff
United States 1868–1952

Edward S. Curtis's legacy was a monumental record of the vanishing Indian way of life. He first photographed an Indian in 1896 — Princess Angeline, daughter of Chief Seattle, digging clams on the Seattle waterfront. In 1899 he embarked as one of two official photographers on E. H. Harriman's two-month, 9,000-mile steamship exploration of Alaskan waters. Soon thereafter he began pursuing his life's goal: to document, through photograph and written word, Indian traditions, habits, and life-styles west of the Mississippi River before contact with the white man completely destroyed them. Curtis undertook a series of exhibitions and articles to draw attention to his efforts, and he soon had the encouragement of Theodore Roosevelt and the financial support of J. Pierpont Morgan.

The first two volumes of Curtis's *The North American Indian* were published in December 1907; the twentieth and final volume appeared in 1930. The text and illustrations portray the daily life, ceremonies, customs, songs, crafts, stories, and costumes of many tribes. Before making field visits, Curtis spent long hours studying the various tribes' mythologies, histories, and other lore. Often accused of being a romantic, Curtis understood and respected the Indians' concept of nature and their reverence for the gods who controlled it. In his photographs he often deliberately posed his subjects to impart a dignity that reflects his idealized vision of their world view.

T. C. McLuhan observed: "Curtis was an enthusiast for his subject matter to the point of being a fanatic; he also was a perfectionist. Some of his pictures took years of planning to get just the right effect and point of view, a notable example being that of the *Three Chiefs* — Four Horns, Small Leggings and Mountain Chief, all old-time Blackfoot warriors, on the prairies of Montana under a threatening sky. It cost Curtis the expense of three trips to get it. One trip was spent in locating a pool of water, the other two in cultivating the chiefs" (*Portraits from North American Indian Life*, p. xi).

After the fanfare and acclaim that greeted the completion of the sets in 1930, the work was paid little attention for forty years. Issued in an edition projected at 500 sets (only 350 or so were ever assembled), each priced at $3,000, *The North American Indian* was purchased by only a few individuals and institutions. Fashion was a factor in limiting sales: during these years Indian life was not topical. However, awakening interest and concern in the early 1970s for ecology and Indian culture brought a new awareness of Curtis's work that resulted in many books and exhibitions.

WORK Chiefly North American Indians. Also includes Alaskan expedition.

MEDIA Platinum prints, silver prints (some toned), orotones (8×10 to 11×14, also called Curt-tones and goldtones; see illustration, page 39), gravures.

The North American Indian appeared as 20 bound volumes incorporating small full-page gravures, and 20 accompanying portfolios each of 36 or more large gravures. Of the approximately 1,500 images in the complete set, 722 are large gravures (12×16) printed on 18×22 sheets of various papers: tissue, Japan vellum, Holland (Van Gelder), as well as a Linden stock from a later printing (ca. 1956) by the New York printer Soroni, who was commissioned by Lauriat's in Boston to complete ten sets by filling in the missing plates. The small gravures (6½×9¼) are printed on 9×12 sheets, also of various papers.

AVAILABILITY AND PRICE Through galleries and at auction. Vintage platinum prints and silver prints moderate to high, depending on subject, condition, size, and whether signed (the stylized signature may have been put on by staff artists in Curtis's West Coast studios). Orotones, when in the original art nouveau frames of gilded plaster, are priced extremely high.

Both sizes of gravures from the original *North American Indian* sets are frequently available; moderate. Modern (ca. 1956) pulls from the plates, as well as copy prints, are also available; low. In May 1976 a complete set of *The North American Indian* sold at auction for $60,000 (Sotheby's, New York City); in May 1977 a complete set sold for $55,000 plus 10% buyer's fee, making the total price $60,500 (Christie's, New York City).

SIGNATURE/OTHER IDENTIFICATION (Studio signature)

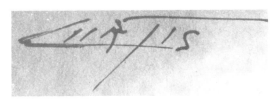

COLLECTIONS LOC (400 toned silver prints), Morgan, New Mexico (complete set of 722 large *North American Indian* gravures), Philadelphia, UCLA (Alaska expedition albums), Washington; BM, Exeter; many other archives.

SELECTED BIBLIOGRAPHY
Harriman Alaska Series. Ed. by C. Hart Merriam. 14 vols. New York: Doubleday, Page, 1901/1902–1905 (vols. 1–5 and 8–13), and Washington, D.C.: Smithsonian Institution, 1910 (vol. 14) and 1933 (vols. 6, 7). Vols. 1 and 2 contain photographs by Curtis and D. G. Inverarity, plus narrative accounts by John Burroughs, John Muir, and George Bird Grinnell. Vols. 3–14 contain technical reports; vol. 3 includes about 4 reproductions of photographs by Curtis and a comment on his contribution to the expedition.
The North American Indian. 20 vols., plus 20 portfolios. Seattle: published by the photographer, 1907–30.
M. E. Ryan. *The Flute of the Gods.* New York: Stokes, 1909.
Indian Days of the Long Ago. Yonkers-on-Hudson, N.Y.: World, 1914.
In the Land of the Head-Hunters. Yonkers-on-Hudson, N.Y.: World, 1915.
Ralph W. Andrews. *Curtis' Western Indians.* New York: Crown, 1962.
Touch the Earth: A Self-Portrait of Indian Existence. Compiled by T. C. McLuhan. New York: Outerbridge & Lazard, 1971.
In a Sacred Manner We Live. Text by Don D. Fowler. Barre, Mass.: Barre Publishing Co., 1972.
The North American Indians. Text by Joseph Epes Brown. Millerton, N.Y.: Aperture, 1972.
Portraits from North American Indian Life. Intros. by A. D. Coleman and T. C. McLuhan. New York: Outerbridge & Lazard, 1972.
Florence Curtis Graybill and Victor Boesen. *Edward Sheriff Curtis: Visions of a Vanishing Race.* New York: Crowell, 1976.
Camera, Dec. 1973. Entire issue.
Alvin M. Josephy, Jr. "The Splendid Indians of Edward S. Curtis." *American Heritage* 25, no. 2 (Feb. 1974): 40 ff.
See also Lawton and Know, *Knights.*

Edward Sheriff Curtis. *Haschelti – Navaho,* 1904. From *The North American Indian.* Gravure. (Courtesy Witkin-Berley, Ltd.)

Daguerre, Louis Jacques Mandé
France 1787–1851

Though there are several claimants to the honor of being the inventor of photography, unquestionably Daguerre perfected the first widely popular photographic process. A painter and stage designer, he had often used the camera obscura in the production of huge paintings for his Diorama, an illusionistic display of painted scenes. About 1824 he began experimenting with attempts to fix the image of the camera obscura and in 1829 entered into partnership with Joseph Nicéphore Niepce, who was conducting similar experiments. After Niepce's death, Daguerre continued working and by 1837 had produced a successful image by a process he called the *daguerréotype.* In return for an annuity from the French government to himself and Niepce's son, Daguerre revealed the process, and it was announced by François Arago to the French Academy of Sciences in 1839. Shortly afterward Daguerre retired.

The public response to Daguerre's process was immediate and overwhelming, and one can still feel some of the astonishment and delight of people responding to these first photographs: "We have seen the views taken in Paris by the 'Daguerreotype' and have no hesitation in avowing that they are the most remarkable objects of curiosity and admiration, in the arts, that we ever beheld. Their exquisite perfection almost transcends the bounds of sober belief. . . . There is not an object even the most minute [in the picture] which was not in the original; and it is impossible that one should have been omitted. Think of that!" (quoted in Taft, *Photography,* p. 3).

WORK Includes still lifes (e.g., with fossils, sculpture), city scenes (e.g., Boulevard du Temple).

MEDIUM Daguerreotypes.

AVAILABILITY AND PRICE Few daguerreotypes by Daguerre are known to exist, and any authenticated image would be of extraordinary value. Even the early editions of his instruction manual are priced extremely high.

COLLECTIONS IMP/GEH, Texas (Gernsheim); Conservatoire National, Société Française.

SELECTED BIBLIOGRAPHY

[François Arago.] *Rapport de M. Arago sur le Daguerréotype lu à la séance de la Chambre des Députés le 3 juillet 1839 et à l'Académie des Sciences, séance du 19 août.* Paris: Bachelier, 1839.

Historique et description des procédés du Daguerréotype et du Diorama. Paris: Giroux, 1839. In English: *History and Practice of Photogenic Drawing on the True Principles of the Daguerreotype with the New Method of Dioramic Painting.* London: Smith, Elder, 1839, and other eds. Reprint, intro. by Beaumont Newhall. New York: Winter House, 1971. Bibliography.

Nouveau Moyen de préparer la couche sensible des plaques destinées à recevoir les images photographiques. Paris: Bachelier, 1844.

Helmut and Alison Gernsheim. *L. J. M. Daguerre: The History of the Diorama and the Daguerreotype.* London: Secker & Warburg, 1956. Bibliography. U.S. ed., New York: Dover, 1968.

Daguerre (1787–1851) et les premiers daguerréotypes français. Paris: Bibliothèque Nationale, 1961.

See also Newhall, *Latent Image.*

Louis Jacques Mandé Daguerre. *Intérieur d'un cabinet de curiosités,* 1837. Daguerreotype, whole plate. (Courtesy Société Française de Photographie)

SIGNATURE/OTHER IDENTIFICATION (Example from a letter)

Dahl-Wolfe, Louise
United States 1895–

A fashion and portrait photographer for *Harper's Bazaar* from 1936 to 1958, Dahl-Wolfe brought a strong consciousness of composition and form to her work. She had studied design with Rudolph Schaeffer at the California School of Fine Arts (now the San Francisco Art Institute) and her interest in painting and decorating is evident in her photographs. Throughout her career she was very much concerned with composition — the exact placement of model and props within the frame of the photograph, plus the use of lighting to accentuate and play off one shape against another. Like Adolf de Meyer, she chose props and backgrounds with care, and she was one of the first fashion photographers to take her models to distant locations to provide authentic and exotic backgrounds.

Dahl-Wolfe was also one of the first to make extensive use of color in fashion work. At a time when color materials were less predictable than they are now, she mastered color both in controlled studio situations and on location. She was able to reproduce the natural effect of available light, and her color images, often 8×10-inch Kodachrome transparencies, are notable for their luminance and clarity.

Louise Dahl-Wolfe. *Portrait of Colette,* 1940s. Silver print. (Courtesy the artist)

WORK Includes fashion, portraits (e.g., Wanda Landowska, Sigrid Undset, Colette), nudes.

MEDIA Silver prints, color.

AVAILABILITY AND PRICE Vintage material (prints made for assignments or as gifts) occasionally appears at auction; moderately high. Most material is still in the photographer's personal collection; current plans call for modern prints to be made to archival and exhibition standards.

SIGNATURE/OTHER IDENTIFICATION

COLLECTIONS FIT, MOMA.

SELECTED BIBLIOGRAPHY
See Mann, *Women;* Life Library, *Studio.*

Dater, Judy
United States 1941–

Judy Dater became involved in photography when she took a course taught by Jack Welpott at San Francisco State College in the early 1960s. She soon found photog-

raphy a means of expressing an emerging awareness of herself and the life around her. Her early work — landscapes, figure studies, interiors — hints at the intense vision that soon followed. In the early 1970s she and Welpott created a major portrait study of women; her photographs tend to be dark, brooding, and psychologically challenging to the viewer. They incorporate details around the subject — clothing, furniture, fabrics — and employ chiaroscuro to capture the singular mystery and strength of each sitter. Dater subsequently expanded her work to include male nudes and portraits of friends such as photographers Harold Jones, Imogen Cunningham, and Linda Connor.

"Dater considers herself within the tradition of interpretive portraiture," according to Anne Tucker. "Her intention is not to document, nor to glamorize. For her the most important thing is that people reveal themselves to the camera and express something about themselves which definitely exists, though it may be hidden — perhaps even from themselves'" (Tucker, *Eye,* pp. 142–143).

Judy Dater. *Summer Bath,* 1975. Silver print. (Courtesy The Witkin Gallery)

WORK Chiefly portraits (mid-1960s and after). Also includes landscapes, with and without figures; interiors.

MEDIUM Silver prints (8×10 to 11×14).

AVAILABILITY AND PRICE Through galleries; moderate.

SIGNATURE/OTHER IDENTIFICATION

PORTFOLIO *See* chapter 6 entry.

COLLECTIONS Harvard (Fogg), Kansas, MOMA, Norton Simon, Oakland, San Francisco; Antwerp.

SELECTED BIBLIOGRAPHY
Clifford S. Ackley. *Private Realities: Recent American Photography*. Boston: Museum of Fine Arts, 1974. Bibliography.
Women and Other Visions. With Jack Welpott. Texts by Welpott and Henry Holmes Smith. Dobbs Ferry, N.Y.: Morgan & Morgan, 1975.
Imogen Cunningham: A Portrait. Boston: New York Graphic Society, 1979.
Leslie Goldberg. "Behind the Lens with Judy Dater." *San Francisco Bay Guardian*, 20 Oct. 1977, pp. 15–17.
See also Hume, *The Great West*; Kelly, *Darkroom 2*; Life Library, *Year 1973*; Mann, *Women*; Szarkowski, *Mirrors*; Tucker, *Eye*; chapter 7 catalogues.

Davidson, Bruce
United States 1933–

Davidson became interested in photography in his early teens and later studied it at the Rochester (N.Y.) Institute of Technology and at Yale University. His work consists of reportage done in a very personal manner — extended portraits and essays of people and ways of life. Davidson's photographs reveal the close rapport he establishes with his subjects: candidness on both sides of the camera and human interaction are evident. In his words, "I look at people with my camera, but as much to find out what's inside me — to reflect my own emotional state, the struggles, the states of consciousness, and to discover who the person was who took the picture" (statement to the authors, 1978).

John Szarkowski pointed out that "Bruce Davidson has done a difficult and valuable thing: he has shown us true and specific people, photographed in those private moments of suspended action in which the complexity and ambiguity of individual lives triumph over abstractions" (*East 100th Street*).

Writing about his photo-essay *East 100th Street*, Davidson said: "The pictures needed to serve the community in some way, and I decided to take the collection of photographs to publishers. They said that they needed a written text, but I refused. I couldn't use words to break the trust that people gave me standing silently before the camera in that still suspended moment when they looked into themselves and out at the world" (*Bruce Davidson Photographs*).

A member of the Magnum photo agency since 1958, Davidson has photographed for many magazines, including *Life*, *Vogue*, and *Esquire*; he has also frequently photographed for corporate annual reports and advertisements. In the early 1970s he began to turn his energies to film; he made *Living off the Land* (1970) and later dramatized and directed two stories by Isaac Bashevis Singer (*Isaac Singer's Nightmare and Mrs. Pupko's Beard*, 1973). He subsequently wrote the screenplay for Singer's *Enemies, A Love Story*.

WORK Photo-essays and single images dealing with the contemporary social scene: "The Dwarf" (1958); "The Brooklyn Gang" (1959); England (1960); "Black Americans" (1962–1965); "The

Bridge" (1963; Verrazano-Narrows construction, New York City); "Los Angeles" (1964); the New Jersey Meadows (1965); a camper trip (1965); a topless restaurant (1965); "Welsh Miners" (1965); New York City's East 100th Street (1966–1968); the Tombs, New York City's jail (1972); the Garden Cafeteria (1976), New York City.

MEDIUM Silver prints.

AVAILABILITY AND PRICE Through galleries and exhibitions; moderate.

SIGNATURE/OTHER IDENTIFICATION

COLLECTIONS Chicago, Harvard (Carpenter, Fogg), Kansas, MMA, MOMA, Nebraska, Smithsonian, Yale (Art Gallery).

SELECTED BIBLIOGRAPHY
East 100th Street. Intro. by John Szarkowski. Cambridge, Mass.: Harvard University Press, 1970.
Subsistence, U.S.A. With Carol Hill. New York: Holt, Rinehart & Winston, 1973.
Bruce Davidson Photographs. Intro. by Henry Geldzahler. New York: Agrinde/Summit/Simon & Schuster, 1979.
"Brooklyn Minority Report." *Esquire*, June 1960, pp. 129–137.
"Gallery." *Life*, 15 Aug. 1969, pp. 4–7.
See also Life Library, *Art*, *Children*; Szarkowski, *Looking*, *Mirrors*; chapter 7 catalogues.

Bruce Davidson (Magnum Photos, Inc.). *South Wales*, 1965. Silver print. (Courtesy the artist)

Day, Fred Holland
United States 1864–1933

An eccentric, independently wealthy Bostonian, F. Holland Day was something of a dilettante but nevertheless produced an interesting body of pictorial photography. In the 1890s he was a "Boston Bohemian," one of a group influenced by the Decadent Movement among artists such as Oscar Wilde and Aubrey Beardsley. From 1893 to 1899 his firm of Copeland and Day, Boston, published fine books of poetry and other literary works.

Fred Holland Day. *The Seven Last Words,* 1898. Sequence of seven platinum prints in elaborate frame, depicting the photographer as Christ. (Courtesy The Metropolitan Museum of Art, The Alfred Stieglitz Collection, 1949)

Day apparently began photographing sometime in the late 1880s, and by 1895 had established a reputation as a pictorial photographer. In 1900 he arranged in London the first major exhibition of American pictorial photography in Europe: The New School of American Photography, with works by himself, Edward Steichen, Gertrude Käsebier, Frank Eugene, Clarence H. White, and others. Day declined to become a member of the American Photo-Secessionists (conflict with Alfred Stieglitz was involved); his work is mentioned in many issues of *Camera Work,* but, by his own choice, none of it was reproduced there. In 1904 Day's studio was destroyed by fire and he lost many prints and most of his negatives. In 1917 he took to his bed, where, as a last eccentricity, he remained for the next sixteen years until his death.

Day's photographs were very carefully composed and lit, at times self-consciously so, and were sometimes modeled after famous paintings. He liked that which he perceived as exotic: themes from classical literature; elaborate costumes; Oriental, black, and foreign-looking models (including the young Kahlil Gibran, a protégé of Day's). Among his best-known work is an 1898 series of 250 photographs on the Passion of Christ — "Sacred stuff," as he called it — with Day posing as Jesus. He also did many male nudes, often in classical poses in woodland settings. Classical "studies" were an accepted pictorial theme, but like the work of some European photographers of the period, Day's nudes also exhibit sexual overtones.

WORK   Includes compositions illustrating legends and the Bible (e.g., the legend of Orpheus, the Crucifixion); nude studies; portraits.

MEDIA   Chiefly platinum prints. Also glycerine-developed platinum prints (capable of more manipulation than standard platinum prints), cyanotypes (as test prints for platinum prints), gumbichromate prints, ozotypes, silver prints. Sizes smaller than 8×10. Before 1898 prints were blind-stamped "FHD." The 1898 religious photographs and those made thereafter were often dated, sometimes signed and titled. Beginning in 1900 the photographer used a red-ink monogram.

AVAILABILITY AND PRICE   Through galleries and at auction but prints very rare; moderately high to extremely high. Gravures (from photo annuals and other publications) moderate.

SIGNATURE/OTHER IDENTIFICATION

 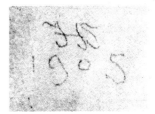

COLLECTIONS   The Library of Congress holds the largest collection (650 prints). Also Chicago, IMP/GEH, MMA, Norwood; RPS.

SELECTED BIBLIOGRAPHY
Hyder Edward Rollins and Stephen Maxfield Parrish. *Keats and the Bostonians: Amy Lowell, Louise Imogen Guiney, Louis Arthur Holman, Fred Holland Day.* Cambridge, Mass.: Harvard University Press, 1951.
Ellen Fritz Clattenburg. *The Photographic Work of F. Holland Day.* Wellesley, Mass.: Wellesley College Museum, 1975. Bibliography.
See also Lawton and Know, *Knights;* Naef, *Collection.*

DeCarava, Roy
United States 1919–

Best known perhaps for his collaboration with Langston Hughes on *The Sweet Flypaper of Life,* DeCarava has turned his camera on life in Harlem and in New York City generally. He began photographing in 1946 after studying painting and printmaking. In 1952 he became the first black artist ever to win a Guggenheim Fellowship. In March 1955 he opened A Photographer's Gallery at 48 West Eighty-fourth Street in New York; he ran it until June 1957, exhibiting the work of Ralph Eugene Meatyard, Harry Callahan, and Ruth Bernhard, among others. In 1975 he began teaching at Hunter College (New York City).

"'It must be good to look at' is the first and only dictum which Roy DeCarava states when asked to note the fundamentals which create a good photograph," wrote Alvia Ward Short. "For DeCarava, essential to creating works which are good to look at is always a sense of underlying order. He is highly conscious of varied elements working together in the reality of nature and human life and he finds beauty in such organization. Many of his photographs show compositional order . . . extracted from a situation reflecting societal disorder. . . . The 'documentary' label which some have affixed to his work, ostensibly because of the subject matter, is a summarily inadequate method of describing his form of art" (*Roy DeCarava: Photographs*, p. 4).

Roy DeCarava. *Man on Stoop*, ca. 1950. Silver print. (Courtesy The Witkin Gallery)

SIGNATURE/OTHER IDENTIFICATION

Roy DeCarava

WORK   Includes life in New York City, jazz artists (e.g., Billie Holiday, John Coltrane).

MEDIUM   Silver prints.

AVAILABILITY AND PRICE   Through galleries; moderately high.

PORTFOLIO   *See* chapter 6 entry.

COLLECTIONS   CCP, Chicago, Houston, MMA, MOMA.

SELECTED BIBLIOGRAPHY
The Sweet Flypaper of Life. Text by Langston Hughes. New York: Simon & Schuster, 1955. Another ed., New York: Hill & Wang, 1967.
Roy DeCarava, Photographer. Lincoln: University of Nebraska, 1970.
Roy DeCarava. Washington, D.C.: Corcoran Gallery of Art, 1976.
Roy DeCarava: Photographs. Text by Alvia Ward Short. Houston: Museum of Fine Arts, 1976.
See also Szarkowski, *Looking, Mirrors.*

Delano, Jack
United States (b. Russia) 1914–

Delano is best known for the work he did for the Farm Security Administration (FSA) in the early 1940s. While studying photography at the Pennsylvania Academy of the Fine Arts in Philadelphia, he photographed in Pennsylvania, New York, and Europe. In 1940 Roy Stryker hired him for the FSA. Delano's first trip was to New England, where Stryker ordered him to "emphasize the idea of abundance — the 'horn of plenty' and pour maple syrup over it — you know; mix well with white clouds and put on a sky-blue platter" (quoted in Hurley, p. 148).

As Stryker remembered him, Delano liked to photographically sum up a situation rather than dissect it: "Jack was the artist, and being an artist would say, 'What one picture could I take that would say Vermont?'"(ibid.). After World War II Delano worked for Stryker documenting the oil industry for Standard Oil of New Jersey. He eventually went into television work and became director of the government television service in Puerto Rico, while continuing his personal photography.

WORK   Chiefly FSA images of the Northeast, South, and Puerto Rico. Also includes documentary work in Puerto Rico (1946–1977). (See illustration, page 137.)

MEDIUM   Silver prints.

AVAILABILITY AND PRICE   Vintage prints rare; moderate to moderately high. Modern prints made by the photographer are available through galleries; moderate. Modern FSA prints from the Library of Congress extremely low.

COLLECTIONS   LOC (FSA work), Minnesota.

SELECTED BIBLIOGRAPHY
Arthur F. Raper. *Tenants of the Almighty.* New York: Macmillan, 1943.
The Emperor's Clothes. New York: Random House, 1971. Drawings by Jack and Irene Delano.
F. Jack Hurley. *Portrait of a Decade: Roy Stryker and the Development of Documentary Photography in the Thirties.* Baton Rouge: Louisiana State University Press, 1972. Bibliography.
See also bibliography in FSA entry.

Demachy, Robert
France 1859–1937

The son of a wealthy Parisian banker, Demachy was financially independent and spent his time pursuing his interests in music and art. He was active in pictorial photography from the 1880s and in 1894 began to use the gum-bichromate process, which allowed considerable handwork to be done on the print. His gum prints, with their greatly softened detail reminiscent of impressionist art, were a great success and he became a prominent and vocal defender of manipulated printing techniques, writing more than a thousand articles and a number of books on the technical processes and aesthetic issues involved.

Prominent brushstrokes and rough-textured papers are characteristic of Demachy's work, which, though manipulated, still respects a naturalism in camera imagery. He once wrote: "Do not say that Nature being beautiful, and photography being able to reproduce its beauty, therefore photography is Art. This is unsound. Nature is often beautiful, of course, but never *artistic* 'per se,' for there can be no art without the intervention of the artist in the *making* of the picture. Nature is but a theme for the artist to play upon. Straight photography registers the theme, that is all — and, between ourselves, it registers it indifferently" (quoted in Jay, pp. 28–29).

Demachy was a leader in French pictorial photography at the turn of the century. He was a founder of the Photo-Club de Paris, a member of The Linked Ring, and an honorary member of the Royal Photographic Society. He gave up his photographic work completely in 1914.

Robert Demachy. *In Brittany.* From *Camera Work,* no. 5, 1904. Gravure. (Courtesy The Witkin Gallery)

WORK Includes portraits, nudes, genre scenes (e.g., ballet dancers, people at work), landscapes (with and without figures), city scenes, (e.g., buildings, harbors), racing cars in motion.

MEDIA Chiefly gum-bichromate prints (1894–1906), oil prints (1906 and after), oil-transfer prints (1910 and after). Also ozotypes, silver prints, platinum prints (earliest images).

AVAILABILITY AND PRICE Through galleries and at auction. Vintage prints rare (most material exists in an estate collection from which some duplicate vintage prints are currently being shown and sold internationally); moderately high to high. *Camera Work* reproductions low to moderate.

SIGNATURE/OTHER IDENTIFICATION

COLLECTIONS MMA; BN, Photo-Club de Paris, RPS, Société Francaise.

SELECTED BIBLIOGRAPHY

Photo-aquatint or the Gum Bichromate Process: A Practical Treatise on a New Process of Printing in Pigment Especially Suitable for Pictorial Workers. With Alfred Maskell. London: Hazell, Watson & Viney, 1897. One of several "how-to" books by Demachy.

Les Procédés d'art en photographie. With C. Puyo. Paris: Photo-Club de Paris, 1906.

Anna Bowman Dodd. *In and Out of a French Country House.* New York: Dodd, Mead, 1910.

Bill Jay. *Robert Demachy 1859–1936: Photographs and Essays.* New York: St. Martin, 1974. Bibliography.

Robert Demachy: Un Portfolio de seize photographies rares. Text by Roméo Martinez. Lausanne, Switzerland: Videografic, 1975 (issued through La Photogalerie, Paris). 16 reproductions. Deluxe ed. includes an original print.

Camera, Dec. 1974. Entire issue.

Camera Work: Reproductions (gravures and halftones) or articles about or by Demachy in nos. 5, 7, 11, 16, 18, 19.

See also Green, *Camera Work;* Life Library, *Great Photographers;* Naef, *Collection.*

de Meyer, Adolf (Gayne)
United States (b. France) 1868–1946

Baron Adolf de Meyer's connections with socially important and fashionable people and his own sense of elegance made him the first great fashion photographer. In pre-World War I London, de Meyer and his wife, Olga, were arbiters of all that was chic and stylish. They were friends of Edward VII (Olga's godfather and rumored to be her natural father), and Adolf was created a baron by the king of Saxony just so the couple could attend Edward's coronation. The de Meyers actively promoted the artistic avant-garde; in 1911, they were aficionados and unofficial publicists of Diaghilev and his Ballet Russe on its first visit to London, where Adolf made a famous series of photographs of the ballet's star, Nijinsky.

De Meyer, who had been photographing his aristocratic friends more as a service to them than as a commercial enterprise, in 1914 accepted an offer to photograph for *Vogue* and *Vanity Fair*. He continued to photograph famous and fashionable people into the 1930s, including the Duke of Windsor and Wallis Simpson, but he gradually became passé in the eyes of a new generation and ultimately died in relative obscurity in Los Angeles.

De Meyer's fashion work has overshadowed his connections with pictorial photography. He became a member of The Linked Ring in 1903, having first exhibited in its salon in 1898; he also exhibited at Alfred Stieglitz's gallery "291." His photographs often swim in light. De Meyer frequently backlit his subjects, making hair a halo of light or rimming a profile in brilliant outline. He used a lens that broke highlights into starry reflections and sometimes photographed through a piece of silk gauze as well. His models are often posed with hand on hip, studies in nonchalant sophistication. His still lifes appear just as carefully posed — every fallen petal perfectly arranged.

WORK Includes celebrity and society portraits (before 1914), Nijinsky and other members of the Ballet Russe (1911–1912), fashion and advertising photography (after 1914), still lifes (e.g., flowers), occasional genre scenes (e.g., *A Street in China*).

Adolf (Gayne) de Meyer. *Still Life.* From *Camera Work*, no. 24, 1908. Gravure. (Courtesy The Witkin Gallery)

MEDIA Platinum prints, silver prints.

AVAILABILITY AND PRICE Through galleries and at auction. Vintage prints rare; moderately high to extremely high. *Camera Work* gravures low to moderate.

SIGNATURE/OTHER IDENTIFICATION

PORTFOLIO *See* chapter 6 entry.

COLLECTIONS IMP/GEH, MMA, NYPL (Lincoln Center); BN.

SELECTED BIBLIOGRAPHY
L'Après-midi d'un faune (Nijinsky album). Texts by Auguste Rodin, Jacques-Emile Blanche, and Jean Cocteau. London: Paul Iribe, 1914. 200 copies, plus 50 on Japan paper.
De Meyer. Ed. by Robert Brandau. Biographical essay by Philippe Jullian. New York: Knopf, 1976. Abridged in *Vogue* (U.S.), Apr. 1976.
"Women as Objets d'Art." *Photo World*, Apr./May 1977, pp. 84–92.
De Meyer's photographs appeared in *The Craftsman*; many were published in *Vogue* and *Vanity Fair*, 1914–1921, and in *Harper's Bazaar*, 1922–1934.
Camera Work: Gravures in nos. 24, 40.
See also Green, *Camera Work*; Life Library, *Studio*; Naef, *Collection*; Szarkowski, *Looking*.

Diamond, Paul
United States 1942–

Diamond did not formally study photography, but he lists Diane Arbus, Arthur Freed, Les Krims, and Robert D'Alessandro as influences. "Humor is very valuable to me," he once wrote. "I treat myself to it as often as possible in my life and my work. Rather like the dentist of reality, digging in the cavities of the world, spreading them liberally with my silver" (Wise, *Choice*, p. 210). Diamond constantly suggests through his work that he is making photographs and not representing reality. He plays with near/far relationships, juxtaposing objects in discordant scale; his locales and subjects appear realistic, yet selectively added flash lighting makes them glow oddly. His prints include the edge of the film frame with the Kodak markings — a device similar to the jump cuts in New Wave films, which remind the viewer: this is a movie.

SIGNATURE/OTHER IDENTIFICATION

WORK Chiefly people and their environments, including self-portraits. Many images are night scenes with flash, or daylight scenes with flash added.

MEDIUM Silver prints. Since 1970 Diamond has been enlarging 2¼×2¼ negatives full-frame to maximum size on 16×20 paper.

AVAILABILITY AND PRICE Through galleries; moderate.

COLLECTIONS Addison, IMP/GEH, Ohio Wesleyan; NGC.

SELECTED BIBLIOGRAPHY
See Hume, *The Great West*; Wise, *Choice*; chapter 7 catalogues

Paul Diamond. *Street Vision, San Francisco, Summer 1974*. Silver print. (Courtesy The Witkin Gallery)

Di Giulio, Lou Brown
United States 1933–

Lou Brown Di Giulio specializes in three-dimensional photographic reconstructions of real objects. Her trompe-l'oeil photosculptures not only amuse but also gently disconcert the viewer because the fabricated art objects are as "real" as the originals. *20 Cabbages* (1972) was Di Giulio's first construction piece in the medium, which allows her to combine her interests in photography and sewing. "I'm interested in seeing where I can push this," she explained, "where I can make it go that it hasn't gone before" (statement to the authors, 1977).

WORK Chiefly objects (e.g., ivy, a large caladium plant, a large tossed salad, cabbages) that are photographed and silkscreened onto canvas, cut out, sewn together, stuffed, wired, and reassembled, with great precision. Also includes pieces for room settings and environmental pieces (e.g., *Tree/Butterfly Construction*, which deals with the destruction of trees by flocks of migrating monarch butterflies). (See color plate 4.)

MEDIUM Photo-silkscreen on fabric, using extensive hand-coloring with oil-based paints.

AVAILABILITY AND PRICE Through galleries and exhibitions; high. Because of the time it takes to make each piece (*20 Cabbages*, e.g., took over a year), Di Giulio's total output is small. Pieces have been shown throughout the United States and illustrated in many catalogues.

SIGNATURE/OTHER IDENTIFICATION

Lou Brown Di Giulio

COLLECTIONS Chiefly private collections.

SELECTED BIBLIOGRAPHY
The Photographic Process. Riverside: University of California Art Gallery, 1974.
The Gallery as Studio. Claremont, Calif.: Lang Art Gallery, Scripps College, 1975.
See also chapter 7 catalogues.

Disdéri, André Adolphe-Eugène
France 1819–1889

After a brief career as a daguerreotypist in Brest and as a genre photographer in Nîmes, Disdéri opened a studio in Paris in 1854 and patented the carte-de-visite photograph in that year. The new carte format became popular (according to Nadar, a rumored visit by Napoleon III to Disdéri's studio in 1859 was responsible) and Disdéri prospered, as did others — in many countries the marketing of cartes de visite of famous people became a rapidly growing industry. Disdéri's full-length views, with their overwrought accessories and dramatic or humorous poses, were an especially appealing novelty at the time, and he became a favorite photographer of the court of Napoleon III. He also photographed theatrical performers and visiting dignitaries, as well as the petite bourgeoisie, who had a new social visibility and wanted photographs to prove it.

In 1861 Disdéri was reputed to be the richest photographer in the world. He was appointed photographer to the imperial courts of France, England, Spain, and Russia. But although he opened a second studio (for equestrian portraits) in Paris in 1863 and a branch in London in 1868, his continued innovations with enlargement processes and carbon prints could not counteract the French public's declining interest in the carte de visite during the late 1860s. Disdéri left Paris and operated a portrait studio in Nice from 1880 to 1889. He died in a poorhouse.

WORK Chiefly portraits. Also includes genre scenes, views of Versailles (1855), Paris and suburbs after the Commune and the Franco-Prussian War, views of Brest (signed by Mme. Disdéri).

MEDIA Daguerreotypes; collodion wet-plate negatives, albumen prints (including cartes de visite, larger-format portraits and landscapes, stereographs).

AVAILABILITY AND PRICE Through galleries and at auction. Daguerreotypes rare; high to extremely high. Cartes de visite frequently found; low. Other formats somewhat rare; generally moderate.

SIGNATURE/OTHER IDENTIFICATION

DISDÉRI
PHOTOGRAPHE de S.M.L'EMPEREUR
8,Boulevart des Italiens ‹   Disdéri Phot.
PARIS

COLLECTIONS BPL, IMP/GEH, MMA, New Mexico, Smithsonian; Antwerp, BN; other historical collections.

SELECTED BIBLIOGRAPHY
Manuel operatoire. Nimes, 1853.
Renseignements photographiques indispensables à tous. Paris, 1855.
Application de la photographie à la reproduction des oeuvres d'art. Paris, 1861.
L'Art de la photographie. Intro. by Lafon de Camarsac. Paris: Disdéri, 1862. Last section translated, London, 1864.
See also Sobieszek, "Photography and the Theory of Realism," in Coke, *100 Years*; Freund, *Société*; Gernsheim, *Creative Photography*; Scharf, *Art*.

Dodgson, Charles Lutwidge
See Carroll, Lewis.

Doisneau, Robert
France 1912–

In the 1930s Doisneau worked as an industrial photographer for Renault and did various other commercial work. Since World War II he has concentrated on photojournalism. His photographic domain is Paris, and he has become known for 35mm images that convey the humor and pathos of Parisian street life. He roams the streets with his camera always handy, seeking the unusual and finding it. In his words, "The marvels of daily life are exciting; no movie director can arrange the unexpected that you find in the street" (quoted in Pollack, *History*, p. 497). Doisneau's special genius is for the oddities of life — chance juxtapositions that comment with wit but never sarcasm on human foibles and adventures. As Blaise Cendrars remarked, Doisneau "fills himself with irony and laughter so your heart is captured" (quoted in ibid., p. 499).

Doisneau in 1977 reflected on the state of photography: "Slowly but surely the time is passing when photography was regarded as the village idiot who brought in, captured in his cap, a bird of unknown species. You will not be surprised if I add that such activity did not yield a very high standing in the art world. The gentlemen of the Beaux Arts held themselves a bit apart.

"But today we prefer the cultivation of images to the gathering of the wild harvest. The classic evolution of all civilizations.

"This represents certain advantages: A saving in time, and, above all — thanks to a codified graphic system — the possibility of finding pictorial or literary references, which greatly facilitates conversation.

"Readmitted to the culture, photographers in exchange learn good manners and become socially acceptable. Some even marry princesses.

"For me, alas, it's too late. I am going to die a village idiot — the later the better. Leave me the hope of finding, tomorrow, the unimaginable image.

"In order to make everyone uncomfortable" (statement to the authors).

Robert Doisneau. *Les Animaux supérieurs*, 1954. Silver print. (Courtesy The Witkin Gallery)

WORK Chiefly incidents of daily life in the streets of Paris. Also includes commercial work (e.g., industrial, advertising, and postcard photography); portraits of artists (e.g., Picasso, Saul Steinberg, Braque, Léger, Giacometti).

MEDIUM Silver prints (usually to 11×16, some to 16×20).

AVAILABILITY AND PRICE Through galleries; moderate.

SIGNATURE/OTHER IDENTIFICATION

COLLECTIONS CCP, Chicago, IMP/GEH, MOMA, New Mexico, New Orleans; Arles.

SELECTED BIBLIOGRAPHY
Blaise Cendrars. *La Banlieue de Paris.* Paris: Seghers, 1949.
Robert Giraud and Michel Ragon. *Les Parisiens tels qu'ils sont.* Paris: Delpire, 1954.
Instantanés de Paris. Preface by Blaise Cendrars. Paris: Arthaud, 1955. U.S. ed., *Paris.* New York: Simon & Schuster, 1956.
1, 2, 3, 4, 5. Lausanne, Switzerland: Guilde du Livre, 1955.

Elsa Triolet. *Pour que Paris soit.* Paris: Cercle d'Art, 1956.
Enfants. Tokyo: Heibon-sha, 1957.
Jean Donguès. *Gosses de Paris.* Paris: Jeheber, 1957.
Epouvantables Epouvantails. Paris: Hors Mesure, 1965.
Maurice Chevalier. *My Paris.* New York: Macmillan, 1972.
Le Paris de Robert Doisneau et Max-Pol Fouchet. With Max-Pol
    Fouchet. Paris: Les Editeurs Français Reunis, 1974.
La Loire: Journal d'un voyage — 2. Paris: Denoël-Filipacchi,
    1978.
James Sage. *The Boy and the Dove.* New York: Workman, 1978.
"The Frenchman's France." *Fortune,* May 1954, pp. 128–133.
"Bistrots." Text by Robert Giraud. *Le Point,* no. 57 (1960). Special
    issue.
Samuel Grafton. "Through the Lens of War: Meaning of a Free
    Press." *Lithopinion* 3, no. 1, issue 9 (1968): 6–19.
See also Life Library, *Year 1975;* Szarkowski, *Looking.*

Dorfman, Elsa
United States 1937–

Elsa Dorfman records the ordinary, daily occurrences in
her own life, especially visits to her home from poets
Allen Ginsberg, Lawrence Ferlinghetti, Robert Creeley,
and other friends. She invests her photographs with seemingly simplistic order and style, captioning and dating
them underneath as they might be in a snapshot album.
Her images are straightforward and unstressed; the sitter
looks easily and directly at the photographer and, by implication, at the viewer as well.

Dorfman's formal training was in English and education. "In 1965 I picked up a camera for the first time,"
she explained, "and from the beginning, without making
a conscious decision, my work became rooted in my relationships. Most of my ideas about photography came
from poetry and the work of my friends. Dailiness. Intimacy. I photograph where I am. I don't worry whether
what I take will bore other people or if/how I will use the
images. I just do it" (statement to the authors, 1977).

Elsa Dorfman. *David O'Connell and Patricia O'Connell,* February 1972. Silver print. (Courtesy the artist)

WORK Chiefly friends and family, in the photographer's Cambridge, Mass., home and elsewhere.

MEDIUM Silver prints (titles are written on the prints by the
photographer).

AVAILABILITY AND PRICE Through galleries; low to moderate.
Less expensive "imperfect" prints are occasionally sold by the
photographer from a shopping cart in Harvard Square (Cambridge,
Mass.).

SIGNATURE/OTHER IDENTIFICATION

COLLECTIONS BMFA, Colby, Portland (Maine), Princeton (Art
Museum), Washington U., Wellesley.

SELECTED BIBLIOGRAPHY
His Idea. With Robert Creeley. Toronto: Coach House Press,
    1973.
Elsa's Housebook: A Woman's Photojournal. Boston: Godine,
    1974.
See also Mann, *Women.*

Du Camp, Maxime
France 1822–1894

Du Camp, a wealthy dilettante interested in literary matters, conceived the idea that a trip to the Middle East
would be a splendid diversion for himself and a friend. He
learned calotyping from Gustave Le Gray and in 1849
persuaded the French Ministry of Education to send him
on a photographic tour of archeological sites, accompanied
by the novelist Gustave Flaubert. On their twenty-one-
month tour, Du Camp made 220 calotypes, 125 of which
were printed by Louis-Désiré Blanquart-Evrard and published as *Egypte, Nubie, Palestine et Syrie,* the first book
about the Middle East illustrated with actual photographs.
After his return, Du Camp gave up photography and devoted his time to writing. Steegmuller's *Flaubert in Egypt*
offers a fascinating and unexpurgated account of Du Camp
and Flaubert on tour in the Middle East — "our heads
more hairless than our knees, smoking long pipes and
drinking coffee on divans" (p. 79).

WORK Chiefly scenes of the Middle East, primarily architecture
and monuments (e.g., the Colossus of Abu Simbel).

MEDIA Calotype negatives, prints on slightly albumenized paper.

AVAILABILITY AND PRICE Through galleries and at auction but
rare; high to extremely high.

COLLECTIONS Chicago, IMP/GEH, NYPL (Rare Book), UCLA;
BN.

SELECTED BIBLIOGRAPHY

Egypte, Nubie, Palestine et Syrie . . . . Paris: Gide et Baudry, 1852. 125 prints.

Le Nil, Egypte et Nubie. Paris: Librairie Nouvelle, 1854. Unillustrated.

Souvenirs littéraires. 2 vols. Paris: 1882, 1883.

Francis Steegmuller, trans. and ed. *Flaubert in Egypt: A Sensibility on Tour — A Narrative Drawn from Gustave Flaubert's Travel Notes and Letters.* Boston: Little, Brown, 1972. Includes photographs and extracts from Du Camp's descriptions of the trip.

See also Life Library, *Great Photographers.*

Eakins, Thomas
United States 1844–1916

Eakins is very well known for his realistic paintings, but it is less known that he made photographs as studies for his works, sometimes painting directly from them, as in *The Wrestlers* (1899). His earliest dated photographs are from 1880 and the last from before 1904. Although any photograph by Eakins has certain collateral value simply because it was made by a famous painter and may illumine his personality or art, many of his photographs are essentially family snapshots. However, some images are of great interest because they reappear in his paintings, and others, especially portraits, have merit as photographs in their own right. According to Lincoln Kirstein, "The camera kept [Eakins] company, a dispassionate tutor, research assistant, playfellow, partner, compass, guide. Its capacity fascinated him, seeming to give him, if not other eyes, at least a visual dimension heightened and strengthened for what he had already seen and known, only less sharply" ("Walt Whitman and Thomas Eakins").

Eakins based his art on an accurate rendering of anatomy and thus became interested in the photographic analysis of motion. In 1883 he supported a project to bring Eadweard Muybridge to the University of Pennsylvania to record motion studies and he even posed for Muybridge. Eakins himself later used a device similar to Etienne Marey's stop-motion "wheel" camera to make photographs of humans and horses in motion.

WORK Includes personal and family scenes (e.g., friends, students, pets), portraits (e.g., Walt Whitman; Eakins's wife and father), landscapes, genre scenes, figure and motion studies.

MEDIA Gelatin dry-plate negatives, platinum prints. Eakins used a 4×5 camera and rarely enlarged beyond that size.

AVAILABILITY AND PRICE Vintage prints available at auction but extremely rare; extremely high. In 1977 *Three Female Nudes* (4⅞×3⅝; illustrated page 8) sold at auction for $11,000. Modern prints from copy negatives of original prints in the collection of Gordon Hendricks are available through galleries; moderate to moderately high. Some images credited to Eakins may be by his wife, Susan Macdowell Eakins, or, rarely, by his friend Samuel Murray.

COLLECTIONS Hirshhorn, MMA, Philadelphia.

SELECTED BIBLIOGRAPHY

Gordon Hendricks. *Thomas Eakins: His Photographic Works.* Philadelphia: Pennsylvania Academy of the Fine Arts, 1969.

———. *The Photographs of Thomas Eakins.* New York: Grossman, 1972.

———. *The Life and Work of Thomas Eakins.* New York: Viking, 1974.

The Olympia Galleries Collection of Thomas Eakins Photographs. Philadelphia, 1976.

Thomas Eakins Photographs. New York: Sotheby Parke Bernet, 1977. Catalogue for Nov. 10 auction.

William I. Homer. "Eakins, Muybridge and the Motion Picture Process." *Art Quarterly,* Summer 1963, pp. 194–216.

Lincoln Kirstein. "Walt Whitman and Thomas Eakins: A Poet's and a Painter's Camera-Eye." *Aperture* 16, no. 3 (1972).

Garnett McCoy. "Some Recently Discovered Thomas Eakins Photographs." *Archives of American Art Journal* 12, no. 4 (1972): 15–22.

Ronald J. Onorato. "Photography and Teaching: Eakins at the Academy." *American Art Review* 3 (July/Aug. 1976): 127–140.

See also Coke, *Painter.*

Thomas Eakins. Unidentified sitter, 1729 Mt. Vernon Street, Philadelphia, ca. 1884. Albumen print. (Courtesy Gordon Hendricks)

Edgerton, Harold
United States 1903–

In 1932, as a graduate student at the Massachusetts Institute of Technology, Harold E. Edgerton devised a "stroboscopic" light to photograph rapidly moving objects. His device emitted a series of brilliant flashes of light that could record on film a series of stopped-action sequential images of objects in motion. A single burst was so brilliant and brief (as short as one three-millionth of a second) that a bullet could be visually halted in flight. Edgerton's achievement provided detailed analyses of a variety of very complex, rapid movements, such as the splash of a drop of milk.

As MIT professor emeritus of electrical measurements, Edgerton continues to develop photographic equipment for investigating natural phenomena. He was associated with the firm that produced timing equipment used by the Atomic Energy Commission in nuclear testing, and in 1954 he developed an early deep-sea camera and an underwater flash lamp. Edgerton later became director of photography for an expedition begun in June 1976 to search for the Loch Ness Monster.

In addition to their scientific value, Edgerton's stop-motion and multiple images are widely admired for their intrinsic beauty — an aspect of his work that was emphasized in a 1961 George Eastman House exhibition organized by Beaumont Newhall. "The 'new vision,'" wrote Newhall, "is . . . the revelation of what the unaided eye cannot see but which has ever existed; as more powerful tools for observation are built, more worlds of form are revealed. They seem new only because we have not seen them before: the forms themselves are basic; . . . it is our acceptance of [scientific photographs] as *esthetic* revelations which is new" (Newhall, *History*, p. 173).

Work High-speed flash photographs that record such phenomena as a bird in flight, the beat of a hummingbird's wing, cups breaking, a golfer's swing.

Media Silver prints, color (both media 8×10 and 11×14).

Availability and Price Through galleries; moderate to moderately high.

Signature/Other Identification

Harold Edgerton

Portfolio *See* chapter 6 entry.

Collections IMP/GEH, MIT (Historical Collections), Plainsman; BN, Fotografiska, Science Museum.

Selected Bibliography
Flash! Seeing the Unseen by Ultra-High-Speed Photography. With J. R. Killian. Boston: Hale, Cushman & Flint, 1939. Another ed., Boston: Charles T. Branford, 1954.

Electronic Flash, Strobe. New York: McGraw-Hill, 1970.
Moments of Vision: The Stroboscopic Revolution in Photography. With James R. Killian, Jr. Cambridge, Mass.: MIT Press, 1979.
See also Life Library, *Tool*; Szarkowski, *Looking*.

Harold Edgerton. *Drop of Milk*, ca. late 1930s. Silver print. (Courtesy the artist and the Center for Creative Photography)

Eggleston, William
United States 1939–

Eggleston had only a moderate interest in photography until about 1962 when the work of Henri Cartier-Bresson came to his attention. Eggleston's photographs, primarily in color, abound in restrained conflicts: he makes large, sensuous, vibrantly colored prints, but of the most ordinary, personal, commonplace subject matter. At first glance, they seem to be casual and unadorned snapshots, but the exactitude of their compositions contradicts their surface resemblance to simple record shots. John Szarkowski wrote in regard to Eggleston's work that "the best photography of today is related in iconography and technique to the contemporary standard of vernacular camera work [that is, the snapshot], which is in fact often rich and surprising. The difference betweeen the two is a matter of intelligence, imagination, intensity, precision, and coherence" (*William Eggleston's Guide*, p. 10).

Work Includes people, objects and places in the American South. (See color plate 5.)

MEDIUM Dye transfer and Type C color prints.

AVAILABILITY AND PRICE Through galleries; dye transfers high; Type C prints moderately high. Prints usually issued in editions of 20.

SIGNATURE/OTHER IDENTIFICATION

William Eggleston

PORTFOLIOS *See* chapter 6 entry.

COLLECTIONS Brooks, Corcoran, MOMA, NCFA, New Orleans.

SELECTED BIBLIOGRAPHY
William Eggleston's Guide. Text by John Szarkowski. New York: MOMA, 1976.
See also Life Library, *Year 1976;* Szarkowski, *Mirrors;* chapter 7 catalogues.

Eisenstaedt, Alfred
United States (b. West Prussia) 1898–

A pioneer in photojournalism, Eisenstaedt first took up photography as a hobby but by the late 1920s had become "a fanatical camera nut," saving all his money and using all his spare time for it. His early work was pictorial in style but he soon realized, along with contemporaries such as Erich Salomon, that there was a new market for reportage of current events and people in the news. He switched to a small camera to capture unposed, candid, existing-light images. "A photographer needs a short-circuit between his brain and his fingertips," he once explained. "Things happen: sometimes expected, more often unexpected. You must be ready to catch the right split second, because if you miss, the picture may be gone forever. . . . Life moves swiftly and unexpectedly; it won't wait for you to fumble with your focusing control or film advance" (*The Eye of Eisenstaedt,* p. 56).

In 1935 Eisenstaedt came to America and soon after joined *Life* magazine as a staff photographer. His subjects were wide-ranging: an aging Winston Churchill flashing his "V for Victory" sign; Joseph Goebbels coldly looking up at the camera; an ice-skating waiter at St. Moritz, debonairly balancing a full tray; the mud-caked bare heel of an Ethiopian soldier; Jacqueline Kennedy reading to her young daughter. "I keep looking and shooting all the time," he related, "not just on the job but between assignments, on weekends, and during vacation. Some of the photographs which have pleased me most were done just for the hell of it. It's really a matter of observing; of coming back again and again if you think you can do the picture better another time, of being ready to stop your car and jump out anywhere, of being constantly alert to the sudden unexpectedness of life, which so often provides you with your best opportunities" (ibid., p. 123).

WORK Includes photojournalism, celebrity portraits, travel views, candid street scenes, many other subjects. (See illustration, page 212.)

MEDIA Silver prints, color.

AVAILABILITY AND PRICE Vintage prints (often bearing magazine stamps such as "Pix Inc." or "Life" on back) occasionally available through galleries and at auction; moderate to moderately high. Recently, LIFE Picture Collection (New York City) has produced under the photographer's supervision signed prints of exhibition quality in limited editions; moderate to moderately high.

SIGNATURE/OTHER IDENTIFICATION

Alfred Eisenstaedt

COLLECTIONS LIFE (which also preserves negatives Eisenstaedt made for Time Inc.); RPS.

SELECTED BIBLIOGRAPHY
Witness to Our Time. New York: Viking, 1966.
The Eye of Eisenstaedt. As told to Arthur Goldsmith. New York: Viking, 1969.
Martha's Vineyard. Text by Henry Beetle Hough. New York: Viking, 1970.
Witness to Nature. New York: Viking, 1971.
John McPhee. *Wimbledon: A Celebration.* New York: Viking, 1972.
People. New York: Viking, 1973.
Eisenstaedt's Album: Fifty Years of Friends and Acquaintances. New York: Viking, 1976.
Eisenstaedt's Guide to Photography. New York: Viking, 1978.
See also Edey, *Essays;* Life Library, *Photojournalism, Travel.*

Emerson, Peter Henry
England (b. Cuba) 1856–1936

A major force in nineteenth-century photography, P. H. Emerson developed a "naturalistic" aesthetic that revivified photography when it was in danger of becoming moribund with academic pictorialism. In his youth he distinguished himself at Cambridge, studying medicine and natural science and earning several degrees. In 1882 he bought his first camera and photographed, studied, and experimented in the medium with a thoroughness and energy that was characteristic of everything he undertook.

Emerson loathed the "high art" photography of H. P. Robinson, O. G. Rejlander, and others then dominant in the Photographic Society of Great Britain. Their work struck him as sentimental and artificial, so he devised his own aesthetic for photography based on what he believed to be scientific and naturalistic theories. He stressed the importance of natural settings and spontaneous poses, and opposed artificial studio setups or excessively contrived combination prints. He also advocated focusing sharply on the central object in a scene, with the other planes of the picture slightly out of focus. He believed this to be the way the eye sees — differentially focused rather than totally sharp from foreground to background as a lens can be made to "see."

In 1885 Emerson exploded onto the photographic scene. With his pictures on display and winning prizes everywhere, he avidly engaged in writing, lecturing, and publishing to support and explain his theories, showing a talent for virulent diatribe against the opposition. He had visited and become familiar with East Anglia, a marshy coastal area of fogs, shimmering waterways, and picturesque residents. Though his photographs of peasants fishing, gathering reeds, or doing other work seem a bit like still lifes when compared to today's images made at $\frac{1}{500}$ of a second or faster, the naturalness of the gestures remains convincing. His landscape and seascape prints are rich in delicate tonalities; platinum-coated paper, with its subtle shadings of soft grays, was the perfect medium for rendering the misty atmosphere of the marshes.

In 1889 Emerson published *Naturalistic Photography*, a handbook describing his approach and the scientific theories that he believed supported it. The following year he reexamined his opinions and published *The Death of Naturalistic Photography*, a black-bordered pamphlet that recanted his earlier statements that photography was capable of being an art. However, it was too late; the idea of photography as an independent art with its own criteria had taken root and begun to flourish.

Emerson himself remained active in photography despite his disclaimer; though he did not exhibit or publish his work after 1900, he continued to photograph. He personally issued medals honoring living and dead photographers whose work he admired, such as Julia Margaret Cameron, Nadar, and Brassaï, sometimes to the bewilderment of the recipient. A few years before his death he completed a history of pictorial photography (the manuscript was never published and remains undiscovered).

WORK Includes landscapes, seascapes, genre scenes of rural life (e.g., hunting, fishing, harvesting).

MEDIA Gelatin dry-plate negatives, platinum prints, gravures (many hand-pulled by the photographer).

AVAILABILITY AND PRICE Through galleries and at auction. Platinum prints rare; high. Gravures, mostly taken from Emerson's limited-edition books, moderate to moderately high. A complete copy of *Life and Landscape* sold for over $20,000 in 1977. The photographer destroyed his negatives after a limited-edition run.

SIGNATURE/OTHER IDENTIFICATION

P.H.EMERSON

COLLECTIONS IMP/GEH, LOC, New Mexico, NYPL, Texas (Gernsheim); Colman and Rye, NGC, RPS.

SELECTED BIBLIOGRAPHY
The sizes of various editions listed here are smaller than in some other published sources: the planned number of copies of an edition was not always printed.
Life and Landscape on the Norfolk Broads. Text by P. H. Emerson and T. F. Goodall. London: Sampson Low, Marston, Searle & Rivington, 1886. 40 platinum prints. 25 deluxe, 175 regular copies.

Pictures from Life in Field and Fen. London: Bell, 1887. 20 gravures. 50 deluxe, 200 regular copies.
Idyls of the Norfolk Broads. London: Autotype Co., 1888. 12 gravures. 100 deluxe, 100 regular copies.
Pictures of East Anglian Life. London: Sampson Low, Marston, Searle & Rivington, 1888. 32 gravures. 75 deluxe, 250 regular copies. Portfolio ed., 9 gravures. 250 copies.
Izaak Walton and Charles Cotton. *The Compleat Angler.* 2 vols. (some bound as 1 vol.). London: Sampson Low, Marston, Searle & Rivington, 1888. 27 gravures by Emerson in vol. 1. 50 copies. Another ed., 750 copies.
Naturalistic Photography for Students of the Art. London: Sampson Low, Marston, Searle & Rivington, 1889. Reprints, New York: Amphoto, 1972; New York: Arno, 1973.
The Death of Naturalistic Photography. Privately printed, 1890. Reprint, New York: Arno, 1973.
Wild Life on a Tidal Water. London: Sampson Low, Marston, Searle & Rivington, 1890. 30 gravures, including 29 by Emerson. 100 deluxe, 300 regular copies.
On English Lagoons. London: David Nutt, 1893. Deluxe ed., 15 gravures, 100 copies. Regular ed. not photographically illustrated.
Birds Beasts and Fishes of the Norfolk Broads. London: David Nutt, 1895. Halftones by T. A. Cotton. Text by Emerson.
Marsh Leaves. London: David Nutt, 1895. 16 gravures. 50 deluxe, 200 regular copies. Rev. ed., unillustrated.
Nancy Newhall. *P. H. Emerson: The Fight for Photography as a Fine Art.* Millerton, N.Y.: Aperture, 1975. Bibliography.
Peter Turner and Richard Wood. *P. H. Emerson: Photographer of Norfolk.* Boston: Godine, 1975.
See also Life Library, *Great Photographers*; Lyons, *Photographers*; Newhall, *Masters*; Szarkowski, *Looking*.

Peter Henry Emerson. *Ricking the Reed.* From *Life and Landscape on the Norfolk Broads*, 1886. Platinum print. (Courtesy Rick Reed)

Engel, Morris
United States 1918–

As a young man, Engel was influenced by the photographers at the Photo League in New York and, most profoundly, by Paul Strand. From 1935 to 1941 Engel produced a widely exhibited series of photographic essays on New York life, including such locales as Coney Island, the Lower East Side, and Harlem. He was also a regular contributor to the newspaper *PM*.

In a statement written for the announcement of Engel's show at the New School for Social Research in 1939, Strand said: "Here is a young man of twenty-one who sees people with compassionate understanding as they move within the city's tumult or relax for a few hours at a nearby beach. . . . Engel sees his subjects very specifically and intensely. They are not types, but people in whom the quality of the life they live is vivid — unforgettable."

From 1941 to 1945 Engel was a photographer in the U.S. Navy (he received a citation for his combat work from Edward Steichen, who was in charge of Navy combat photography for a time). After discharge, Engel did freelance magazine photography, then went on to film. As producer, writer, and cinematographer, he made the award-winning movies *Little Fugitive, Lovers and Lollipops, Weddings and Babies,* and *I Need a Ride to California.* Saul Bellow credited his innovative film work with presaging the New Wave ("The Art of Going It Alone," *Horizon,* Sept. 1962, pp. 108–110). Engel takes photographs only rarely now.

Morris Engel. *Coney Island Embrace,* ca. 1940. Silver print. (Courtesy the artist and The Witkin Gallery)

WORK   Chiefly documentary essays on New York life (e.g., the daily experience of a shoeshine boy, Coney Island crowds, portraits of city people, peddlers, shopkeepers).

MEDIA   Silver prints (8×10 to 11×14). In 1976 Engel produced "light boxes" — 8×10 positive transparencies of some of his early images, illuminated from the rear in a box frame.

AVAILABILITY AND PRICE   Through galleries. Vintage prints few; moderately high. Modern prints moderate. Light boxes, when available, moderately high.

SIGNATURE/OTHER IDENTIFICATION

COLLECTIONS   MMA, MOMA, New Mexico, Worcester.

SELECTED BIBLIOGRAPHY
PM Picture Gallery, 21 July 1940.
U.S. Camera Annual 1941.
See also Life Library, *Documentary.*

Erwitt, Elliott
United States (b. France) 1928–

Erwitt is noted for his sense of humor and humanity in observing daily life. His quick eye often sees amusing relationships between men, women, children, animals, and the world around them. His vision can be comic, without satire or judgment, but he also shows a sensitivity for the sad, tender, and touching.

Erwitt first studied photography in Hollywood during high school. He photographed while in the Army, and after World War II became a member of the photo agency Magnum. He has made several documentary films, including *Beauty Knows No Pain* (about the rigors of life for a college drill team that performs during halftime periods at football games).

"His bearing is such that it allows him to be ever ready to know when a significant gesture might transcend its own circumstances to enter ours," wrote Peter C. Bunnell. "His pictures are a statement of contemporary life, an examination of certain ideas concerning life on a simple human level, but with a very clear eye to our punctilious conduct" (introduction to untitled Erwitt portfolio listed in chapter 6).

WORK   Photojournalism, advertising, and other commercial photography. Some of Erwitt's famous series deal with life in a nudist camp, people and statues, and dogs. His large photomural *The People Wall* in Corning, N.Y., is a 4,000-square-foot color scene showing, in life size, a cross-section of the residents and pets of Corning.

MEDIA   Silver prints, color.

AVAILABILITY AND PRICE   Through galleries; moderate to moderately high.

SIGNATURE/OTHER IDENTIFICATION

PORTFOLIOS   *See* chapter 6 entry.

COLLECTIONS   MOMA, New Orleans, Smithsonian; BN.

SELECTED BIBLIOGRAPHY
Observations on American Architecture. With Ivan Chermayeff. New York: Viking, 1972.
Photographs and Anti-Photographs. Texts by Sam Holmes and John Szarkowski. Greenwich, Conn.: New York Graphic Society, 1972.
The Private Experience: Elliott Erwitt. Text by Sean Callahan. Los Angleles: Alskog, 1974.
Son of Bitch. New York: Grossman, 1974.
Recent Developments. Intro. by Wilfred Sheed. New York: Simon & Schuster, 1978.
"Elliott Erwitt." Intro. by P. G. Wodehouse. *Album,* no. 12 (1970), pp. 20–32.
See also Danziger and Conrad, *Interviews;* Life Library, *Year 1973;* Szarkowski, *Looking, Mirrors;* chapter 7 catalogue.

Elliott Erwitt (Magnum Photos, Inc.). *New York,* 1953. Silver print. (Courtesy The Witkin Gallery)

Eugene, Frank
Germany (b. United States) 1865–1936

Eugene, born Frank Eugene Smith, was a prominent member of the pictorial movement in photography and was associated with Alfred Stieglitz and the Photo-Secession. He studied at City College of New York and later at the Royal Bavarian Academy of Fine Arts in Munich. In 1906 he moved to Germany, dropping the family name Smith. He had been recognized as a portrait painter in New York, and in Germany was well known for his *Jugendstil* (art nouveau) paintings. He was also a skilled etcher and as his interest in photography grew he began to mark and scratch his images to give an effect similar to that of etchings.

Dallett Fuguet, another member of the Photo-Secession, wrote: "Mr. Eugene does not work on the prints in any way, but his negatives must be in a state which the ordinary photographer would consider shocking. He apparently rubs away and scratches the secondary high-lights that he desires to subdue; and he uses pencil and paint on the shadows he would lessen or lighten. He modifies and

changes details in the same way, and all with a frank boldness" (quoted in Doty, *Photo-Secession,* p. 31). Eugene was a founding member of the Photo-Secession and in 1913 was appointed to the first notable academic position in photography: Royal Professor of Pictorial Photography at the Royal Academy of Graphic Arts in Leipzig.

WORK   Includes portraits of photographers (e.g., Alfred Stieglitz, Edward Steichen) and of German artists, intellectuals, and society figures (e.g., H. R. H. Rupprecht, prince of Bavaria); allegorical studies; nudes. (See illustration, page 104.)

MEDIA   Platinum prints, gum-bichromate prints, salt prints, autochromes.

AVAILABILITY AND PRICE   Through galleries and at auction. Vintage prints rare; high to extremely high. *Camera Work* gravures moderate to moderately high.

SIGNATURE/OTHER IDENTIFICATION

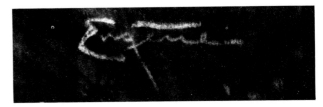

COLLECTIONS   Chicago, MMA; RPS.

SELECTED BIBLIOGRAPHY
Sadakichi Hartmann. "Frank Eugene: Painter-Photographer." *The Photographic Times* 30 (Oct. 1899): 555–561.
Camera Work: Eugene is mentioned in a number of issues; gravures in nos. 5, 25, 30, 31, 48.
See also Green, *Camera Work;* Lawton and Know, *Knights;* Life Library, *Print, Themes;* Naef, *Collection.*

Evans, Frederick H.
England 1853–1943

Frederick Henry Evans is best known for his architectural interiors: much more than mere records, they are luminous images of light, form, and space that exhibit a sensitive creative awareness. Before turning to photography he owned and ran a bookstore in London, where he championed writers and artists, many of whom later became important figures. His first association with photography occurred around 1885, when he made a series of photomicrographs to supplement a scientific text. Around 1895 Evans photographed such personalities as his friends George Bernard Shaw and Aubrey Beardsley. In 1896 he began to photograph English cathedrals and French cathedrals and chateaux. He retired from the bookshop in 1898 and, with a small annuity, was free to use the camera in his "lifelong study of the beautiful."

Evans strongly advocated the techniques of "straight," unmanipulated photography. His platinum prints were praised and widely exhibited, and his cathedral interiors were published by Alfred Stieglitz in *Camera Work* and were shown at his gallery "291." Evans was a member of The Linked Ring and the Royal Photographic Society and wrote articles for the leading photographic magazines of the day. In the 1920s, when commercially made platinum paper became increasingly scarce, he stopped printing upon discovering that his images lacked richness on the newer silver paper.

"Evans must be reckoned as one of the great pictorial photographers," Beaumont Newhall wrote in 1944, after viewing a memorial exhibition. "It can be no exaggeration to write that his architectural photographs are the greatest of their kind, because he was able to combine precision of definition with a softness and delicacy of gradation and because he had an extraordinary sense of scale and of light. Detail is everywhere — every tracing, every lead of the stained glass windows is present — yet the result is far from a record; each print is an interpretation" (quoted in *Frederick H. Evans* [1973]).

Evans's own advice to beginners: "Try for a record of emotion rather than a piece of topography. Wait till the building makes you feel intensely, in some special part of it or other; then try and analyse what gives you that feeling, see if it is due to the isolation of some particular aspect or effect, and then see what your camera can do towards reproducing that effect, that subject."

Frederick H. Evans. *Ingoldmells*, ca. 1900. Platinum print on bordered mount by the photographer. (Courtesy Lee D. Witkin)

WORK   Architecture, portraits, landscapes. (See illustration, page 104.)

MEDIA   Platinum prints, some silver prints. Evans also made glass lantern slides for lectures he gave.

AVAILABILITY AND PRICE   Through galleries and at auction. Platinum prints somewhat rare; moderate to moderately high. Silver prints rare; moderate. Signed lantern slides rare; low to moderate. *Camera Work* gravures moderate.

Many prints are titled and signed by Evans and/or bear his monogram impressed on the mount and/or his ornate bookplate on the back. Evans often mounted his prints on several layers of toned or colored paper and drew single or multiple borders around them. After his death, loose prints were mounted on single-weight white weave stock by his son Evan and the monogram applied.

SIGNATURE/OTHER IDENTIFICATION   (*See also* signed menu, page 103.)

(Bookplate)

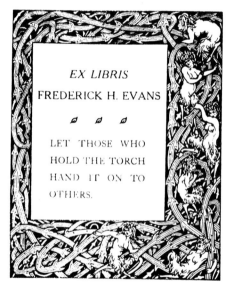

PORTFOLIO   *See* chapter 6 entry.

COLLECTIONS   BMFA, Harvard (Carpenter), IMP/GEH, LOC, New Orleans, Philadelphia; NGC, RPS.

SELECTED BIBLIOGRAPHY

The Dance of Death by Hans Holbein: Enlarged Facsimiles in Platinotype by Frederick H. Evans of Fifty Wood Engravings. . . . Privately printed, 1913. 50 platinotypes, each with Evans's monogram. 15 copies.

Beaumont Newhall. *Frederick H. Evans.* Rochester, N.Y.: GEH, 1964.

————. *Frederick H. Evans.* Millerton, N.Y.: Aperture, 1973. Bibliography.

George Bernard Shaw. "Evans — An Appreciation." *Camera Work*, no. 4 (Oct. 1903), pp. 13–16.

Camera Work: Reproductions (gravures, halftones) in nos. 4, 8.

See also Green, *Camera Work*; Life Library, *Caring, Print*; Naef, *Collection*; Szarkowski, *Looking.*

Evans, Walker
United States 1903–1975

Evans dropped out of college in 1926 and went to Paris, where he developed an interest in literature. He returned to the United States in 1927 and found himself alienated from American society and its mores. In turning to photography, he was influenced by Flaubert's attitude that the artist should be invisible but all-powerful, and he reacted against the pictorialism then in vogue. He moved toward a clear, straightforward, "truthful" style. In John Szarkowski's words: "He thought of photography as a way of preserving segments out of time itself, without regard for the conventional structures of picture-building. Nothing was to be imposed on experience; the truth was to be discovered, not constructed" (*Walker Evans* [1971], p. 12).

In the mid-1930s Evans made photographs for the Farm Security Administration (FSA). After 1938 and through the fifties ne photographed increasingly in subways, in the streets, and from moving trains. During this period he also wrote for *Time* magazine (1943–1945) and wrote and photographed for *Fortune* (1945–1965). When, in later years, he returned to the more formal style of his youth, the images were more personal and autobiographical.

John R. Gossage, describing Evans as "an artist who hides his hand," wrote: "Walker Evans's work, even on a casual reading, consists of facts immediately present to the attention. There are no overt references to symbology or metaphor, no reaching for drama or art, yet all these are achieved. These remarkable photographs coerce, persuade, not to a point of view, but to a deeply felt conviction that these pictured things really did exist — they really looked like that — on that day. . . . But don't let these photographs fool you. There is nothing simple about being this direct, nothing casual about the plainness of these scenes and, most importantly, there is nothing detached or sentimental in this quiet passion. When you start to examine the trick these photographs have played on you — inducing you to believe that the photograph presents the scene 'the way it really was' — a certain complex balance begins to assert itself: intelligence, and, more importantly, passion have allowed the images just the proper amount of space to complete the illusion, while at the same time being sufficiently expressive to sustain their maker. This result can only be achieved by a photographer with the kind of unalterable assurance in command of his art which enables him to permit something merely to *be* while simultaneously retaining involvement and kinship with it" (*14 American Photographers* catalogue, p. 11, listed in chapter 7).

WORK Includes vernacular architecture (ca. 1930 and after), Cuba (1933), African art (1935), FSA images (1935–1938), subway riders (early 1940s), Chicago street portraits (1940s), U.S. industrial landscapes seen from train windows (1950s and earlier), interiors and homes of friends (1930s–1975). (See illustration, page 23.)

MEDIA Silver prints, color (including Polaroid SX-70).

AVAILABILITY AND PRICE Through galleries and at auction. Vintage prints high to extremely high. (Condition of vintage prints varies from faded and stained to good; they were not necessarily printed by Evans, who often had others make them). Signed prints from his 1971 and 1974 portfolios moderately high. Modern FSA prints from the Library of Congress extremely low.

SIGNATURE/OTHER IDENTIFICATION

Walker Evans

PORTFOLIOS *See* chapter 6 entry.

COLLECTIONS Harvard (Fogg), LOC (FSA work), MMA, MOMA, New Mexico, New Orleans, San Francisco, Smith, Wadsworth, Yale (Art Gallery); NGC; most major collections.

Walker Evans. *Billboard, Birmingham, Alabama,* March 1936. Modern silver print from the original negative. (Library of Congress)

SELECTED BIBLIOGRAPHY
Hart Crane. *The Bridge.* Paris: Black Sun, 1930. 3 gravures. 250 deluxe copies, including 50 signed by Crane. Regular ed., New York: Liveright, 1930. 2 halftones.
Carleton Beals. *The Crime of Cuba.* Philadelphia: Lippincott, 1933. Reprint, New York: Arno, 1970.
American Photographs. Essay by Lincoln Kirstein. New York: MOMA, 1938, 1962. Reprint, New York: East River Press, 1975.
James Agee. *Let Us Now Praise Famous Men.* New York: Houghton Mifflin, 1941. Another ed., Boston: Houghton Mifflin, 1960.
Karl Bickel. *The Mangrove Coast.* New York: Coward-McCann, 1942.
Paul Radin and James Johnson Sweeney. *African Folktales and Sculpture.* New York: Pantheon, 1952. Rev. ed., 1964.
Many Are Called. Intro. by James Agee. Boston: Houghton Mifflin, 1966.
Message from the Interior. Afterword by John Szarkowski. New York: Eakins Press, 1966.
"Photography." In *Quality* (pp. 169–211), ed. by Louis Kronenberger. New York: Atheneum, 1969.

Walker Evans. Intro. by John Szarkowski. New York: MOMA, 1971. Bibliography.

Walker Evans: Photographs for the Farm Security Administration, 1935–1938. Intro. by Jerald C. Maddox. New York: Da Capo, 1973.

Carol Lynn Yellin, ed. *Images of the South: Visits with Eudora Welty and Walker Evans.* Memphis: Center for Southern Folklore, 1977.

First and Last. New York: Harper & Row, 1978.

The Presence of Walker Evans. Text by Alan Trachtenberg. Boston: Institute of Contemporary Art, 1978.

Sidney Tillim. "Walker Evans: Photography as Representation." *Artforum* 5 (Mar. 1967): 14–18.

See also Life Library, *Great Photographers;* Newhall, *Masters;* Szarkowski, *Looking;* Travis, *Julien Levy;* Witkin, *Julien Levy;* bibliography in FSA entry; chapter 7 catalogues.

f/64

See Group *f*/64.

FARM SECURITY ADMINISTRATION (FSA)

More than a quarter of a million pictures were made by U.S. Farm Security Administration photographers from 1935 through 1943 in a monumental documentation of the plight of Americans during the Depression years and the results of government programs to assist them. This innovative federal operation, brainchild of Rexford Guy Tugwell, assistant secretary of agriculture, was directly supervised by Roy Stryker, who in 1935 was appointed chief of the Division of Information, Historical Section, in the Resettlement Administration (by 1936, renamed the FSA). Stryker was a former professor of economics who in his classes had used the then somewhat unconventional technique of teaching with pictures: "I got impatient because the bright boys at Columbia had never seen a rag doll, a corn tester, or an old dasher churn. I dug up pictures to show city boys things that every farm boy knows about" (quoted in Stryker and Wood, p. 11).

Stryker was not a photographer himself and left matters of style and technique to the photographers he hired, but he did insist that they know what they were photographing and why. He once described how he sent Carl Mydans to photograph Alabama cotton fields: "We sat down and we talked almost all day about cotton. We went to lunch and we went to dinner and we talked well into the night about cotton. I told him about cotton as an agricultural product, cotton as a commercial product, the history of cotton in the South, what cotton did to the history of the country, and how it affected areas outside the country. By the time we were through, Carl was ready to go off and photograph cotton" (quoted in *The Years of Bitterness and Pride*).

Other photographers and agencies over the years have documented social hardships and the efforts of people to create a better life for themselves, but the size of the FSA project sets it apart, as does the intensity and intelligence of Stryker's direction and the quality and dedication of

his photographers. FSA images such as Dorothea Lange's stoop laborers, Walker Evans's sharecropper families, and many others came to be symbols of the Depression and the human suffering, fortitude, and dignity that it engendered.

Stryker said it was the FSA goal to "record on film as much of America as we could in terms of people and the land. . . . Many of these people were sick, hungry, and miserable. The odds were against them. Yet their goodness and strength survived. What we ended up with was as well-rounded a picture of American life during that period as anyone could get. The pictures that were used were mostly pictures of the dust bowl and migrants and half-starved cattle. But probably half of the file contained positive pictures, the kind that give the heart a tug" (Stryker and Wood, p. 14). Listed here are some of the photographers connected at one time or another with the FSA (all were active in the United States; *italicized* photographers have separate entries in this chapter).

Bubley, Esther
Carter, Paul
Collier, John, Jr. 1913–
Collins, Marjorie
Delano, Jack
Evans, Walker
Jung, Theodor (b. Austria). 1906–
Lange, Dorothea
Lee, Russell
Mydans, Carl
Parks, Gordon, Sr. 1912–
Rosskam, Edwin. 1903–
Rothstein, Arthur
Shahn, Ben
Siegel, Arthur. 1913–1978
Vachon, John. 1914–1975
Wolcott, Marion Post

WORK Includes, according to the Library of Congress, the following major coverage: land use, farms and farming, rural home life, individual family case histories, sharecroppers, migratory agricultural labor, government projects to relieve Depression conditions (especially farm-labor housing), housing projects, small towns, selected large-city studies, Negroes, social conditions, and selected industries (especially coal mining, lumbering, railroad operation, and transportation). (*See also* individual entries.)

MEDIA Chiefly silver prints. Also color (Kodachrome transparencies, 1939 and after). (*See also* individual entries.)

AVAILABILITY AND PRICE Vintage prints are intermittently available through galleries and at auction; moderate to moderately high. Modern FSA prints (black-and-white prints only) are available from the Prints and Photographs Division, Library of Congress, Washington, D.C., 20545; extremely low. Modern prints made by the photographers from their FSA negatives (which they may borrow from the Library of Congress) are sometimes available through galleries; moderate.

The photographer of each image is almost always identifiable, but exactly who printed a particular photograph is seldom known. According to Hank O'Neal, film was usually turned into the FSA lab for processing and printing, but there were excep-

Marion Post Wolcott. *Jitterbugging in Negro Juke Joint, Memphis, Tennessee, November 1939.* Modern silver print from the original negative. (Library of Congress)

Carl Mydans. *Interior of Ozark Cabin Housing Six People, Missouri, May 1936.* Modern silver print from the original negative. (Library of Congress)

Russell Lee. *Tenant Purchase Clients at Home in Hidalgo County, Texas, February 1939.* Modern silver print from the original negative. (Library of Congress)

Arthur Rothstein. *School, Skyline Farms, Alabama, February 1937.* Modern silver print from the original negative. (Library of Congress)

Jack Delano. *In the Convict Camp in Greene County, Georgia, May 1941.* Modern silver print from the original negative. (Library of Congress)

ABOVE: John Collier, Jr. *Maclovia Lopez, wife of the mayor, spinning wool by the light of the fire. . . . Trampas, New Mexico, January 1943.* Modern silver print from the original negative. (Library of Congress)

TOP LEFT: Ben Shahn. *Roadside Inns, Central Ohio, Summer 1938.* Modern silver print from the original negative. (Library of Congress)

BOTTOM LEFT: John Vachon. *Office of John W. Dillard, Real Estate and Insurance Agent, Washington, Indiana, June 1941.* Modern silver print from the original negative. (Library of Congress)

tions. Lange developed her own film and made prints for herself before she sent in her negatives. Evans, Lee, Shahn, and Rothstein did some of their own processing and printing. However, copies that went out as press prints were made by the staff, not by the photographers (except for Lange, who did make some press prints).

Vintage prints are identifiable by early stamp or handwritten information; signs of age also help distinguish them. O'Neal reports seeing a Resettlement Administration stamp only on a few early prints of Shahn and Rothstein. Prints from about 1936 to 1942 are identified by an FSA stamp on the back. In the period 1942 to 1944 the FSA prints were made under the supervision of the Office of War Information (OWI); however, the old FSA stamp was still sometimes used and prints stamped OWI are scarce. Since 1945, the Library of Congress has done the government's printing of FSA images; these prints usually have a catalogue number and caption on the back and may also be stamped "Library of Congress." (*See also* individual entries.)

SIGNATURE–OTHER IDENTIFICATION/PORTFOLIOS *See* individual entries.

COLLECTIONS LOC (an estimated 272,000 negatives, 150,000 prints, 640 color transparencies), NYPL (a reference set of prints). Detailed descriptions of the photographs are on file at: California, U. of Chicago, Harvard, MOMA, New Orleans, North Carolina. The University of Louisville Photographic Archives preserves Stryker's picture collection. (*See also* individual entries.)

SELECTED BIBLIOGRAPHY

Archibald MacLeish, ed. *Land of the Free.* New York: Harcourt, Brace, 1938.

Sherwood Anderson. *The Face of America: Home Town.* New York: Alliance, 1940.

Richard Wright and Edwin Rosskam. *12 Million Black Voices.* New York: Viking, 1941.

Carl Sandburg. *Poems of the Midwest.* 2 vols. in 1. New York: World, 1946. Also limited ed.

Edward Steichen, ed. *The Bitter Years: 1935–1941. Rural America as Seen by the Photographers of the Farm Security Administration.* New York: MOMA, 1962.

Arthur Rothstein, John Vachon, and Roy Stryker. *Just Before the War: Urban America from 1935 to 1941 as Seen by Photographers of the Farm Security Administration.* Ed. by Thomas Garver. New York: October House, 1968.

F. Jack Hurley. *Portrait of a Decade: Roy Stryker and the Development of Documentary Photography in the Thirties.* Baton Rouge: Louisiana State University Press, 1972. Bibliography.

Roy Emerson Stryker and Nancy Wood. *In This Proud Land: America 1935–1943 as Seen in the FSA Photographs.* Greenwich, Conn.: New York Graphic Society, 1973. Bibliography.

The Years of Bitterness and Pride: FSA Photographs 1935–1943. Text by Hiag Akmakjian. New York: McGraw-Hill, 1975.

Hank O'Neal. *A Vision Shared: A Classic Portrait of America and Its People (1935–1943).* New York: St. Martin, 1976.

See also Life Library, *Documentary, Photojournalism;* Stott, *Documentary;* bibliographies in individual entries.

FASHION

Fashion photographers record current styles for illustrations in the mass media, and women are both their prime subject and audience. Since fashion photographers both reflect and amplify social trends in their work, it is interesting to trace the transitions in their images of women, from the idealized and glossy mannequins of the 1930s to the healthy outdoor types that were often portrayed in the 1950s to the sexually ambiguous creatures of the 1970s. There is a new interest in fashion photographs as collectible works, both as cultural documents and as visually exciting images. Among the photographers active in the field of fashion are the following (*italicized* photographers have separate entries in this chapter):

Abbé, James. U.S. 1883–1973
Arbus, Diane
Avedon, Richard
Bailey, David. England. 1933–
Barr, Neil
Barré. France. Active 1930s
Beaton, Cecil
Blumenfeld, Erwin
Bourdin, Guy. France. Contemporary
Brookman, F. W. Active ca. 1900–1910
Bruehl, Anton
Cecil, Hugh. England. Active 1920s
Clarke, Henry. France (b. U.S.). Active 1950s–1960s
Coffin, Clifford
Cunningham, Bill. U.S. Contemporary
Dahl-Wolfe, Louise
Danielson, Emilie. U.S. Active 1940s
de Meyer, Adolf (Gayne)
Durst, André. Active 1930s
Engstead, John. U.S. Active 20th c.
Feder, Joel. Active 1910s
Felix. Active 1910s
French, John. Great Britain. Active 1960s
Frissell, Toni. U.S. 1907–
Henle, Fritz
Hiro (Yasuhiro Wakabayashi). U.S. (b. China). Contemporary
Horst (Horst P. Horst). U.S. (b. Germany). 1906–
Hoyningen-Huene, George. U.S. (b. Russia). 1900–1968
Kane, Art. U.S. 1925–
Kertész, André
Klein, William. U.S. 1926–
Landshoff, Hermann. U.S. Active 1930s–1950s
Lynes, George Platt
MacWeeney, Alen. U.S. 1939–
Man Ray
Matter, Herbert. U.S. (b. Switzerland). 1907–
Meerson, Harry O. France. Active 1930s
Miller, Lee. U.S. 1907–1977
Moon, Sarah. France. Contemporary
Munkacsi, Martin. U.S. (b. Hungary). 1898–1963
Muray, Nickolas. U.S. (b. Hungary). 1892–1965
Newton, Helmut. France (b. Germany). Contemporary
Parkinson, Norman. England. 1913–
Parks, Gordon, Sr. U.S. 1912–
Penn, Irving
Pulham, Peter Rose. England. Active 1930s
Rawlings, John. Active 1940s–1960s
Reutlinger (Mlle.). France. Active 1900–1910s

Deborah Turbeville. Untitled, 1975. Silver print. (Courtesy Sonnabend Gallery)

Helmut Newton. *Elsa Peretti as Bunny*, ca. 1972. Silver print. (Courtesy the artist. Copyright by Helmut Newton)

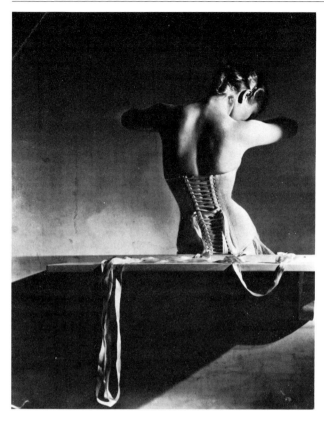

Horst. Untitled, 1939. Silver print. (Courtesy Sonnabend Gallery)

Richard Avedon. *Carmen (Homage to Munkacsi), Paris,* 1957. From *Avedon* [1978] portfolio, listed in chapter 6. Silver print. (Courtesy the artist)

Reynal, Kay Bell (b. Beall). U.S. 1905–1977
Richards, Matsy Wynn. Active 1920s
Richardson, Bob. Active 1960s
Ronsard
Scaioni, Edigio. Active 1930s
Sieff, Jeanloup. France. 1933–
Steichen, Edward
Stern, Bert. U.S. 1930–
Székessy, Karin
Turbeville, Deborah. U.S. Contemporary
Wagenheim, Chris von. Contemporary
Wildman, Shaw. Great Britain. Active 20th c.

WORK/MEDIA *See* individual entries.

AVAILABILITY AND PRICE Vintage prints turn up frequently from sources such as magazine files and private collections. They may be found through galleries and at auction, priced low to moderately high, depending on photographer, condition, etc. Some photographers make prints from their early negatives for exhibition and sale. (*See also* individual entries.)

SIGNATURE–OTHER IDENTIFICATION/PORTFOLIOS *See* individual entries.

COLLECTIONS The Fashion Institute of Technology's Resource Center (New York City) is assembling a large collection for permanent exhibition and study. Many major collections also include such work. In 1977 IMP/GEH mounted and circulated a survey show of fashion photography. (*See also* individual entries.)

SELECTED BIBLIOGRAPHY
Peter Quennell. *Victorian Panorama: A Survey of Life and Fashion from Contemporary Photographs.* London: Batsford, 1937.
Alison Gernsheim. *Fashion and Reality.* London: Faber & Faber, 1963.
American Fashion. Ed. by Sarah Tomerlin Lee. New York: Fashion Institute of Technology, and Quadrangle, 1975.
Fashion 1900–1939. Text by Madge Garland et al. Edinburgh: Scottish Arts Council, 1975.
Diana Vreeland. *Inventive Paris Clothes, 1909–1939: A Photographic Essay by Irving Penn.* New York: Viking, 1977.
Nancy Hall-Duncan. *The History of Fashion Photography.* New York: Abrams, 1979.
See also Beaton and Buckland, *Magic Image;* Life Library, *Studio, Year 1975, Year 1976;* bibliographies in individual entries.

Kay Bell Reynal. *Two Models with Sunshields, Nassau,* 1948. Silver print. (Courtesy The Witkin Gallery)

George Hoyningen-Huene. Untitled, ca. 1930. Silver print. (Courtesy Sonnabend Gallery)

Feininger, Andreas
United States (b. France) 1906–

A prolific photographer since 1936, Andreas Feininger cannot be easily classified. He has produced sizable bodies of work on forms in nature, industry, cities, architecture, and sculpture. It is his sense of a unity of structure in all these diverse forms that imposes his particular stamp on the images.

"Andreas Feininger is one of the great architects who helped create photography as we know it today," wrote Ralph Hattersley. "He is a specialist in visible and non-visible structures, whose great language is photography" (*Andreas Feininger*). "Precise, clear, absolutely connected with reality, Feininger's pictures also communicate on the intuitive level of symbol-imagery . . ." (ibid.).

The son of artist Lyonel Feininger, Andreas was educated in Germany, attended the Bauhaus in Weimar, and worked for a while as a cabinetmaker. He became interested in photography, which he began to study and explore on his own. From 1929 to 1933, while he worked as an architect, the sale of his photographs supplemented his income. He moved his family to Sweden in 1933 and there turned totally to photography as a profession in 1936. In 1939 he came to New York City, where his association with the Black Star Picture Agency and *Life* magazine led to a wide variety of assignments around the world. He completed 346 *Life* assignments while producing dozens of books and articles, both on his own photographs and on the technical aspects of the craft.

WORK Germany (1929–1931), Paris streets (1932–1933), architectural and industrial images in Sweden (1936–1939), New York City (1940s–1950s), nature studies, shells, trees, sculpture, motion studies, places and people worldwide.

MEDIA Silver prints, color.

AVAILABILITY AND PRICE Through galleries. Vintage prints rare, moderately high; modern prints moderate.

SIGNATURE/OTHER IDENTIFICATION

PORTFOLIOS *See* chapter 6 entry.

COLLECTIONS Delaware, Harvard (Carpenter), ICP, IMP/GEH, LIFE (which also preserves negatives Feininger made for Time Inc.), MMA, MOMA, Newark, New Orleans, New York, Smithsonian, Wellesley; BN, VA.

SELECTED BIBLIOGRAPHY
Menschen vor der Kamera. Halle, Germany: Heering, 1934.
Fotografische Gestaltung. Harzburg, Germany: Heering, 1937.
New Paths in Photography. Boston: American Photographic, 1939.

New York. Intro. by John Erskine. Chicago: Ziff-Davis, 1945.

Feininger on Photography. Chicago: Ziff-Davis, 1949. Rev. ed., New York: Crown, 1953.

Advanced Photography. New York: Prentice-Hall, 1952.

The Face of New York. Text by Susan E. Lyman. New York: Crown, 1954.

Successful Color Photography. New York: Prentice-Hall, 1954.

The Creative Photographer. Englewood Cliffs, N.J.: Prentice-Hall, 1955.

The Anatomy of Nature. New York: Crown, 1956.

Maids, Madonnas and Witches. New York: Abrams, 1961.

Andreas Feininger: Fotografeert Steen. Haarlem, Netherlands: Gottmer, 1962.

The World through My Eyes. New York: Crown, 1963.

The Complete Photographer. Englewood Cliffs, N.J.: Prentice-Hall, 1965. Rev. ed., 1978.

Lyonel Feininger: City at the Edge of the World. Text by T. Lux Feininger. New York: Praeger, 1965.

Forms of Nature and Life. New York: Viking, 1966.

Trees. New York: Viking, 1968.

Shells. New York: Viking, 1972.

Andreas Feininger. Text by Ralph Hattersley. Dobbs Ferry, N.Y.: Morgan & Morgan, 1973.

Roots of Art. New York: Viking, 1975.

Andreas Feininger: Experimental Work. New York: Amphoto, 1979.

See also Life Library, *Camera, Caring;* chapter 7 catalogue.

Andreas Feininger. *Ninth Avenue Elevated between 14th Street and 19th Street,* 1940. Silver print. (Courtesy the artist)

Fellig, Arthur H.
See Weegee.

Fenton, Roger
England 1819–1869

Fenton is best known for his Crimean War photographs, the earliest surviving extensive photographic documentation of a war. The son of a wealthy English manufacturer and banker, he studied art, including several years in Paris with the painter Paul Delaroche. Fenton became interested in photography and on his return to England in 1844 experimented with the calotype process. His attraction to photography grew and by 1851 he was actively engaged in it. He became acquainted with the royal family, and beginning in 1854 made many photographs of Queen Victoria, Prince Albert, and their children.

In 1855 Fenton arrived in the Crimea to record British war activities there. His expedition had the patronage of Thomas Agnew, a publisher who wished to sell pictures of the campaign, and the semiofficial sanction of British government officials, who hoped the photographs would prove that conditions in the Crimea were not as bad as they were reported to be. Fenton photographed the general landscape and scenes in camp but not actual battles; Agnew had ordered him not to photograph combat scenes, but even had he wanted to, the collodion process he was using was too cumbersome and slow. Fenton wrote home about the execrable conditions he saw but recorded only the milder views in his photographs. However, the implications of carnage are evident in a few scenes; in *The Valley of the Shadow of Death,* shown here, one realizes that the litter of cannonballs fell among horses and men.

After his return to Great Britain in 1855, Fenton pho-

Roger Fenton. *The Valley of the Shadow of Death,* 1855. Albumen print. (Courtesy Leland D. Rice)

tographed extensively in England, Scotland, and Wales. Although the historical importance of his Crimean photographs overshadows his other work, these landscape, architectural, and still-life photographs are also of considerable merit. Fenton almost entirely avoided the burgeoning industrial and urban aspects of English life and concentrated on picturesque and charming views of winding streams, leafy woods, castles, ruined abbeys, and noble cathedrals. In 1862, for reasons that are not quite clear, he abandoned photography and resumed a legal career — possibly he felt that the craze for cartes de visite had cheapened photographic standards too much. Fenton was a founding member in 1847 of the Photographic Club (also known as the Calotype Club) and in 1853 was a prime organizer of the Photographic Society of Great Britain (now the Royal Photographic Society).

WORK Includes views of Russia (1851; e.g., Kiev, St. Petersburg, Moscow); portraits of the royal family; the Crimean War (1855); art, archeological artifacts, and general views of galleries (for the British Museum); architecture and landscapes in Great Britain; still lifes (e.g., fruit, flowers, game); anecdotal and costume pieces (e.g., "*Hush, lightly tread, still tranquilly she sleeps*").

MEDIA Calotypes, waxed-paper negatives, and collodion wet-plate negatives; chiefly salt prints and albumen prints (ranging from stereographs to 16×20). Also photogalvanographic prints and carbon prints.

AVAILABILITY AND PRICE Through galleries and at auction but somewhat rare; moderately high to extremely high.

COLLECTIONS Chicago, Harvard (Carpenter), IMP/GEH, LOC, New Mexico, Texas (Gernsheim). In Great Britain: Cambridge, Liverpool, Manchester, National Army Museum, Royal Library, RPS, Science Museum, Scottish Museum, Stonyhurst College, VA.

SELECTED BIBLIOGRAPHY

Fenton's Crimean War photographs (about 360 in all) were published singly and in various editions, each mounted on a folio card bearing the T. Agnew blind-stamp, the printed title, the photographer's credit, and the word "Depose."
Photographic Art Treasures. London: Photo-galvanographic Co., 1856. Portfolios including several Fenton photogalvanographic prints.
The Conway in the Stereoscope. Notes by J. B. Davidson. London: Reeve, 1860.
William and Mary Howitt. *Ruined Abbeys and Castles of Great Britain and Ireland.* 2 vols. London: Bennett, 1862, 1864. 2 prints by Fenton in vol. 1.
Helmut and Alison Gernsheim. *Roger Fenton: Photographer of the Crimean War.* London: Secker & Warburg, 1954. Reprint, New York: Arno, 1973.
John Hannavy. *Roger Fenton of Crimble Hall.* Boston: Godine, 1976.
"Narrative of a Photographic Trip to the Seat of the War in the Crimea." *Journal of the Photographic Society,* 21 Jan. 1856, pp. 284–291. Reprinted in Hannavy.
Stereoscopic Magazine (London). Issues for 1859–1863 contain a number of albumen stereographs by Fenton.
See also Life Library, *Great Photographers, Light.*

Fichter, Robert W.
United States 1939–

Robert Whitten Fichter studied painting and printmaking at the University of Florida and photography and printmaking at Indiana University, working under Henry Holmes Smith. He was an assistant curator at the International Museum of Photography at the George Eastman House from 1964 to 1966, when he turned to teaching photography.

Characteristic of Fichter's work is the playful and often humorous freedom with which he uses found imagery to create collages, often drawing and painting on the image and adding verbal messages to fabricate one-of-a-kind prints. In a 1977 statement to the authors he wrote: "I began with silver prints. Then, after graduate school, I began combining printmaking, drawing and photography — up to that point I was relatively 'pure.' My work has been an attempt to synthesize all of my interest in 'mark-making.' If you want to express yourself, you have to make some kind of 'mark' — drawing, printmaking — photography is the ultimate in terms of speed. . . . Today there are machines — Verifax, videotape. It's a challenge to bring to bear the full range of your expressive possibilities.

"When I grew up, Abstract Expressionism was the vocabulary of the period. I had to work through this. I found that I was drawn to artists like Goya — I was interested in rendering that kind of 'Renaissance space.' I've had to read everything about painters and sculptors. The vocabulary I use is not drawn from the photographer's vocabulary."

WORK Explorations, puns, and play in the visual world, incorporating multiple imagery, Sabattier effect, found imagery, typography, and handwork.

MEDIA Works (5×7 to 30×40) on paper and fabric, including silver prints, gum-bichromate prints, cyanotypes, Inko dyes, de-

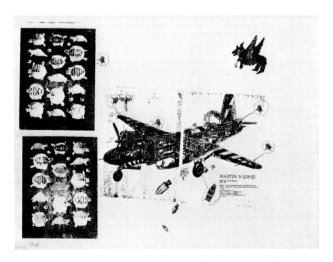

Robert W. Fichter. *Turtle Bomber Complex,* 1973. Verifax transfer with hand-coloring and decal transfers. (Courtesy Light Gallery)

cal transfers, Verifax (office copy machine) prints. Fichter often adds handwork.

AVAILABILITY AND PRICE   Through galleries; moderately high.

SIGNATURE/OTHER IDENTIFICATION

R.W.F.

Robert Whitten Fichter

PORTFOLIOS   *See* chapter 6 Schools and workshops entry.

COLLECTIONS   BMFA, IMP/GEH, New Mexico, Norton Simon, UCLA, VSW; NGC.

SELECTED BIBLIOGRAPHY
See Hume, *The Great West*; chapter 7 catalogues.

Fox Talbot, William Henry
See Talbot, William Henry Fox.

Frank, Robert
United States (b. Switzerland) 1924–

Though Frank is best known for images of the American milieu in the 1950s, he has been active in photography since 1942, including fashion photography, photojournalism, and film. He was the first European photographer to receive a Guggenheim Fellowship (1955); the work he produced while traveling in the United States on this grant, published as *Les Américains* (*The Americans*), documented his reactions to the eateries, highways, jukeboxes, and other commonplaces of 1950s American life. These things had so surrounded the native born that it took an outsider to reveal them as extra-ordinary and worth recording. Jack Kerouac wrote: "The humor, the sadness, the EVERYTHING-ness and American-ness of these pictures! . . . Anybody doesnt like these pitchers dont like potry, see? Anybody dont like potry go home see Television shots of big hatted cowboys being tolerated by kind horses. Robert Frank, Swiss, unobtrusive, nice, with that little camera that he raises and snaps with one hand he sucked a sad poem right out of America onto film, taking rank among the tragic poets of the world" (*The Americans*, pp. ii, vi).

By 1966 Frank had stopped making still photographs, concentrating on filmmaking instead, but his vision had established a new style in documentary still photography: openly subjective rather than ostensibly objective, interpretive rather than factual. Frank once stated: "I have been frequently accused of deliberately twisting subject matter to my point of view. Above all, I know that life for a photographer cannot be a matter of indifference.

Opinion often consists of a kind of criticism. But criticism can come out of love. It is important to see what is invisible to others. . . . It is always the instantaneous reaction to oneself that produces a photograph" (quoted in Evans).

WORK   Best known for images of 1950s American life (e.g., cafeterias, automobiles, the American flag). Also Europe, Peru, and Bolivia; reportage; fashion; advertising.

MEDIUM   Silver prints.

AVAILABILITY AND PRICE   Through galleries; moderately high. According to the photographer's representative, an archive of prints is being established. Once this archive is established the negatives will be retired (no further prints made from them).

SIGNATURE/OTHER IDENTIFICATION

Robert Frank

COLLECTIONS   Chicago, IMP/GEH, MOMA, Philadelphia, Smithsonian; NGC.

SELECTED BIBLIOGRAPHY
New York Is. New York: New York Times [ca.1950s]. Reprint of advertisements with photographs by Frank.
Indiens pas morts. Text by Georges Arnaud. Paris: Delpire, 1956. U.S. ed., *From Incas to Indias.* Intro. by Manuel Tuñan de Lara. New York: Universe, 1956. Photographs by Frank, Werner Bischof, Pierre Verger.
Les Américains. Ed. by Alain Bosquet. Paris: Delpire, 1958. U.S. ed., *The Americans.* Intro. by Jack Kerouac. New York: Grove, 1959. Rev. eds., Millerton, N.Y.: Aperture, 1969, 1978.
Pull My Daisy. With Jack Kerouac and Alfred Leslie. New York: Grove, 1961.
Zero Mostel Reads a Book. New York: New York Times, 1963.
The Lines of My Hand. Tokyo: Kazuhiko Motomura, 1971. U.S. ed., Los Angeles: Lustrum, 1972. Deluxe ed., Tokyo: Yugensha, 1972.
Robert Frank. Intro. by Rudolph Wurlitzer. Millerton, N.Y.: Aperture, 1976. Bibliography.
Walker Evans. "Robert Frank." *U.S. Camera Annual 1958.*
Edna Bennett. "Black and White Are the Colors of Robert Frank." *Aperture* 9, no. 1 (1961).
See also Life Library, *Art, Documentary*; Szarkowski, *Looking*; chapter 7 catalogues.

Freund, Gisèle
France (b. Germany) 1912–

Freund, who earned a doctorate at the Sorbonne with her dissertation on nineteenth-century French photography, began photographing in order to support herself as a student. Later she became a reporter/photographer for *Life* magazine, which published her first picture story in 1936. She traveled extensively and is particularly noted for her sensitive portraits of artists and literary figures, including James Joyce, H. G. Wells, Leonard and Virginia Woolf, George Bernard Shaw, Colette, Marcel Duchamp, André Malraux, and André Gide (some are the only color photographs ever taken of the subject). She was associated with the photo agency Magnum from 1948 to 1954; currently she free-lances.

Freund once wrote: "In its social function, the photograph today is a mass medium of prime importance, for nothing is as persuasive or as accessible to everyone. For a small number of photographers — and I am among them — a picture is far more than a mere means of giving information: by way of the camera, we express ourselves. A photographer is asked, not to create forms, but to reproduce them. In the hierarchy of artists he is closest to the translator, and a good translator must himself know how to write" (*The World in My Camera*, p. 250).

Gisèle Freund. *Virginia Woolf*, 1939. Silver print. (Courtesy the artist)

WORK   Portraits of writers and artists, picture essays (e.g., English slums, Paris, Buenos Aires, Eva Perón).

MEDIA   Silver prints (most about 9⅛ × 11¾), color.

AVAILABILITY AND PRICE   Through galleries; moderately high.

SIGNATURE/OTHER IDENTIFICATION

Gisèle freund

PORTFOLIO   *See* chapter 6 entry.

COLLECTIONS   IMP/GEH.

SELECTED BIBLIOGRAPHY
La Photographie en France au dix-neuvième siècle: Essai de sociologie et d'esthetique. Paris: Monnier, 1936.
James Joyce in Paris: His Final Years. With V. B. Carleton. New York: Harcourt, Brace & World, 1965.
Au Pays des visages: 1938–1968. Paris: Musée d'Art Moderne, 1968.
Photographie et société. Paris: Seuil, 1974. U.S. ed., *Photography and Society.* Boston: Godine, in preparation.
The World in My Camera. New York: Dial, 1974.
Gisèle Freund: Fotografien 1932–1977. Bonn: Habelt, 1977.
The Sunday Times Magazine (London), 22 Dec. 1963.
Photography Italiana, July/Aug. 1969.
Geraldine Fabrikant. "The Key to Inner Character." *Ms.* 3 (Mar. 1975): 60 ff.
See also Mann, *Women.*

Friedlander, Lee
United States 1934–

Friedlander, who began photographing in 1948, records the American social landscape in what at first appear to be snapshots. His work in fact reveals a complex formal structure that captures transitory events, often with a sly wit. "He was one of the first to perceive and render with assurance the odd visual juxtapositions which are a basic condition of the contemporary urban environment," commented Renato Danese. "His pictures are wry and persuasive; they are without drama or narration, and we are often forced to examine details around us which we would prefer to ignore" (*14 American Photographers* catalogue, p. 6, listed in chapter 7).

Friedlander wrote of his own work: "I suspect it is for one's self-interest that one looks at one's surroundings and one's self. This search is personally borne and is indeed my reason and motive for making photographs. The camera is not merely a reflecting pool and the photographs are not exactly the mirror, mirror on the wall that speaks with a twisted tongue. Witness is borne and puzzles come together at the photographic moment which is very simple and complete. The mind-finger presses the release on the silly machine and it stops time and holds what its jaws can encompass and what the light will stain. That moment when the landscape speaks to the observer" (introduction, *Self Portrait*).

Friedlander discovered E. J. Bellocq's work, printed it, and was responsible for its publication (see Bellocq entry).

WORK   Chiefly people, things, and environments (e.g., street scenes, parks, parties). Also includes self-portraits as part of the social landscape; landscapes. (See illustration, page 284.)

MEDIUM   Silver prints.

AVAILABILITY AND PRICE   Through galleries; moderately high.

PORTFOLIOS   *See* chapter 6 entry.

COLLECTIONS BMFA, Harvard (Fogg), Kansas, MOMA, New Mexico, New Orleans, San Francisco, Smithsonian, UCLA; NGC.

SELECTED BIBLIOGRAPHY
Work from the Same House. With Jim Dine. New York: Wittenborn, 1969.
Self Portrait. New City, N.Y.: Haywire Press, 1970.
The American Monument. Text by Leslie George Katz. New York: Eakins Press, 1976. Also limited eds. with 1 or 10 original prints.
The Nation's Capital in Photographs, 1976. Washington, D.C.: Corcoran Gallery of Art, 1976.
Manfred Willmann, ed. *American Photographers.* Graz, Austria: Fotogalerie im Forum Stadtpark, 1977.
Lee Friedlander Photographs. New City, N.Y.: Haywire Press, 1978.
Gerry Badger. "Lee Friedlander." *The British Journal of Photography,* 5 Mar. 1976, pp. 198–200.
See also Hume, *The Great West*; Life Library, *Camera, Documentary*; Szarkowski, *Looking, Mirrors*; chapter 7 catalogues.

Francis Frith. *The Sphinx and Great Pyramid, Giza,* 1857. Albumen print. (Courtesy The Witkin Gallery)

Lee Friedlander. *New Street,* early 1970s. Silver print. (Courtesy the artist)

Frith, Francis
England 1822–1898

The owner of a printing company, Frith began taking photographs around 1850. In the period 1856 to 1860 he made three trips to the Middle East, including one 1,500 miles up the Nile, beyond its Fifth Cataract, where few travelers ventured. He experienced all the torments of a wet-plate photographer working in the desert: temperatures above 120°F. in his airless dark-tent, collodion that boiled when it hit the glass plate, then dust and flies settling on the sticky coated plate.

On his final return to England he opened a photographic business — F. Frith and Company, in Reigate, Surrey — to publish his pictures; it was the first and, at the time, the largest photographic publishing firm in Britain. Middle Eastern views were novel and popular in his day, and Frith's travel photographs were published in numerous books, portfolios, sets of stereographs, and as individual prints. Frith subsequently photographed and published his own scenes of Britain and the Continent, and his company published other work from all over the world. His own work, like that of many other travel and regional photographers of the period, consisted primarily of realistic records of scenic attractions.

WORK Includes the Middle East (e.g., pyramids, temples, landscapes), Western Europe in the 1860s (e.g., Swiss views), Great Britain (1864 and after; e.g., towns, churches, historic monuments, palaces, the countryside).

MEDIA Collodion wet-plate negatives (in Middle East: stereographs, 8×10, 16×20; in Europe: 6×8, 8×12), albumen prints.

AVAILABILITY AND PRICE Through galleries and at auction. Large prints of Egypt rare; extremely high. Smaller prints from various series frequently found; extremely low to moderate. Frith's work bears his name (sometimes with number and date) in the negative or as an embossed stamp on the mount; since he purchased photos by others and issued them under his company's name, however, such identification does not necessarily authenticate his images.

SIGNATURE/OTHER IDENTIFICATION

Frith. Photo. 1857.

COLLECTIONS Chicago, IMP/GEH, MMA, New Mexico, NYPL, Princeton, UCLA, Worcester; Antwerp, BM, RPS, VA. Also found in many libraries, often filed by subject matter.

SELECTED BIBLIOGRAPHY
A definitive Frith bibliography is difficult to compile because some of the same images were bound in more than one volume and the variant combinations of prints were given different titles. The following list has been distilled from many sources.
Charles Henry Cooper. *Memorials of Cambridge.* 2 vols. 1858. 16 albumen prints attributed to Frith.
Cairo, Sinai, Jerusalem and the Pyramids of Egypt. Commentary by Mr. and Mrs. Reginald Poole. 1860. 60 albumen prints (each dated 1857). Smaller-size prints issued in periodical series and remainder of the plates bound into a 2-volume set entitled *Egypt and Palestine.* London: Virtue [ca. 1858–59]. 76 albumen prints.

Views of Sinai, Palestine, Egypt, Ethiopia . . . . 4 sets of 2 vols.
each. London: MacKenzie. In each set there is no date on the
first volume and an 1862 seal on the second volume. Probable
dates: first volumes, 1860–61; second volumes, 1862–63. All
prints are albumen.

Egypt, Sinai and Palestine. Vol. 1: frontispiece self-portrait
plus 15 prints. Supplementary vol.: 21 prints.

Upper Egypt and Ethiopia. Vol. 1: title page photograph plus
18 prints. Vol. 2: 18 prints.

Sinai and Palestine. Vol. 1: title page photograph plus 19 prints.
Vol. 2: 18 prints.

Lower Egypt and Thebes. Vol. 1: title page photograph plus 18
prints. Vol. 2 (titled *Lower Egypt, Thebes, and the Pyramids*):
18 prints.

Egypt, Nubia and Ethiopia. Notes by Samuel Sharpe. Engravings
by Joseph Bonami. London: Smith, Elder, 1862. 100 albumen
stereographs.

The Holy Bible (or *The Queen's Bible*). London: MacKenzie,
1862. 55–57 albumen prints. 170 copies. Another ed., reduced
format.

Photo-Views of Canterbury. Canterbury, 1863. 20 albumen
prints.

The Gossiping Photographer at Hastings. Reigate, England: Frith,
1864. 18 albumen prints.

The Gossiping Photographer on the Rhine. Reigate, England:
Frith, 1864. 15 albumen prints.

Henry Wadsworth Longfellow. *Hyperion: A Romance.* London:
A. W. Bennett, 1865. 24 albumen prints.

Mr. and Mrs. Samuel Carter Hall. *The Book of the Thames from
Its Rise to Its Fall.* London: A. W. Bennett, 1867. 15 albumen
prints.

Liverpool: Its Public Buildings, Docks, Churches, Etc. Liverpool:
Philip, Son & Nephew [1870s]. 35 prints.

Canterbury Cathedral. Privately printed, 1875. 20 albumen
prints.

R. D. Blackmore. *Lorna Doone.* 2 vols. Philadelphia: Winston
[ca. 1882–95]. 38 gravures by Frith & Co. and 13 by Charles L.
Mitchell.

Bill Jay. *Victorian Cameraman: Francis Frith's Views of Rural
England, 1850–1898.* Newton Abbot, England: David &
Charles, 1973.

See also Life Library, *Great Photographers.*

FSA

See Farm Security Administration.

Gagliani, Oliver
United States 1917–

Oliver L. Gagliani's images are highly personal: peeling
walls, a deserted piano, vines, broken panes of glass that
have not so much to do with the reality of the subjects as
they do with Gagliani's use of them to convey his own
mood and feeling. A masterful photographic technician,
he applies his craft to reveal tones, textures, and contrasts
in a way he finds analogous to classical music. "[As] in
music a fortissimo will sound louder if it is preceded by
a soft passage," he has said, "so in photography a tone
will appear lighter if it is surrounded by dark tones"
(*Oliver Gagliani,* p. 15).

Gagliani did not take up photography until his thirties
when, unable to continue his pursuit of music because of
a hearing loss, he began traveling through the parks of
California. The images he saw and photographed became
substitutes for and equivalents of the music he loved. He
began to develop his skills through workshops and his
own technical experimentation; a Minor White seminar
he attended in 1964 influenced him strongly. Years later
an operation restored most of his hearing, but by this time
his life's work was photography.

Gagliani wrote of his work: "I feel that first you must
connect with the subject, in the sense that you recognise
that a meaningful image can be created, to convey as well
as document, the interplay which occurs between yourself
and the discovered image. One must wait until the hidden
meaning is revealed. Then the spirituality of the image
will come through more strongly" (Witkin Gallery press
release no. 48B, Jan. 1974).

Oliver Gagliani. Untitled, 1963. Silver print. (Courtesy the artist)

WORK Landscapes, close-up studies of details of nature, studies
of objects such as peeling walls or broken windows.

MEDIA Silver prints (up to 8×10), color.

AVAILABILITY AND PRICE Through galleries, exhibitions, and the
photographer; high.

SIGNATURE/OTHER IDENTIFICATION

COLLECTIONS Chicago, IMP/GEH, MIT (Hayden), MOMA, San
Francisco.

SELECTED BIBLIOGRAPHY
Oliver Gagliani. Intros. by Van Deren Coke and Leland Rice.
Afterword by Jack Welpott. Menlo Park, Calif.: Ideograph Pub-
lications, 1975. Also limited ed. with 1 original print.
See also Hume, *The Great West;* chapter 7 catalogues.

Gardner, Alexander
United States (b. Scotland) 1821–1882

Gardner is less well known than Mathew Brady, though both produced major photographic documents of the Civil War and a number of photographs commonly attributed to Brady are actually by Gardner. Relatively little information is available about his early life; it is known that he trained as a jeweler and had a strong amateur interest in chemistry, optics, and astronomy. It is not clear exactly how or where he learned photography, but by 1858 he was proficient enough to be placed in charge of Brady's Washington, D.C., studio. He was one of Brady's Civil War photographers before resigning in 1862 over a dispute about copyrights and attribution. Some of Brady's best photographers resigned with Gardner, and he organized them to document the war as Brady was doing. Gardner himself became an official photographer for the Army of the Potomac. In 1866 he published 100 original prints, in two volumes, as *Gardner's Photographic Sketch Book of the War*. The photographs were taken by Gardner and others, to whom he gave the individual credit that Brady did not. The text, which contains extensive background information on each photograph, was probably written by Gardner. Like Brady, Gardner was not successful in selling his photographs to the public, nor could he interest Congress in purchasing his collection.

In 1867 Gardner became an official photographer for the Union Pacific Railroad, Eastern Division, and documented scenes of life and landscape along the U.P. lines in Kansas and westward as far as California.

Gardner was conscious of himself as a historian and of the strength of photography as a recording medium. He observed in the *Sketch Book*: "Verbal representations of [the sites of the war] may or may not have the merit of accuracy; but photographic representations of them will be accepted by posterity with an undoubting faith." His objective, almost anonymous, style concentrated on recording the scene in front of the camera and he seldom introduced compositional devices to make a picture visually more interesting than it already was. In Gardner's work, the fact is more important than the style in which it was photographed.

WORK Includes Civil War scenes (e.g., aftermath of the Battle of Gettysburg); portraits (e.g., many of Lincoln, including the last ever taken); the hanging of the Lincoln assassination conspirators; Kansas along the Union Pacific Railroad in 1867 (e.g., towns, farms, railway structures, army and engineer camps, Indians, settlers); Indian-U.S. peace conference and Indian delegates to Congress; rogues' gallery for Washington, D.C., police (1873).

MEDIA Collodion wet-plate negatives, albumen prints (ranging from stereographs to 11×14). Stereos bear imprint on mount: "Gardner's Photographic Art Gallery, 511 Seventh St., Washington."

AVAILABILITY AND PRICE Through galleries and at auction. The complete *Sketch Book* has sold at auction for as high as $18,000. Prints from the *Sketch Book* are infrequently found (condition varies); moderate to moderately high. Other large-size work is more difficult to find and more expensive. A set of prints (6×8 on 12×18 mounts) titled *Across the Continent on the Kansas Pacific Railroad* was issued in 1868. Sterographs (a set was issued as *Across the Continent on the Union Pacific Railroad, Eastern Division*) are relatively rare, somewhat expensive for their category; low to moderate.

SIGNATURE/OTHER IDENTIFICATION

Positive by A. GARDNER, 511 7th st., Washington.

COLLECTIONS BPL, Chicago, Harvard (Houghton), IMP/GEH, Kansas Historical, LOC, Missouri, National Archives, New Mexico, Princeton, Smithsonian; BM, NGC.

SELECTED BIBLIOGRAPHY
Rays of Sunlight from South America. Washington, D.C.: Philp & Solomons, 1865. 69 prints. Negatives by Henry Moulton, printed by Gardner.
Gardner's Photographic Sketch Book of the War. 2 vols. Washington, D.C.: Philp & Solomons, 1866. 100 albumen prints, about 7×9, each mounted on a letterpress card with the lithographed name of the photographer, date, and title. Credits read Alex. Gardner or A. Gardner (16 prints), his son James Gardner or J. Gardner (10), T. H. O'Sullivan (45), Barnard & Gibson (8), John Reekie or J. Reekie (7), Wood & Gibson (5), David Knox (4), Wm. R. Pywell (3), W. Morris Smith (1), D. B. Woodbury (1). Reprint, 1 vol. New York: Dover, 1959.
J. Cobb. "Alexander Gardner." *Image* 7 (June 1958): 124–136.
Robert Sobieszek. "Alexander Gardner's Photographs along the 35th Parallel." *Image* 14 (June 1971): 6–13.
See also Newhall, *Masters*; Szarkowski, *Looking*; Taft, *Photography*.

Alexander Gardner. *President Lincoln on Battle-Field of Antietam,* October 1862. From *Gardner's Photographic Sketch Book of the War,* 1866. Albumen print. (Courtesy Sotheby Parke Bernet, Inc.)

Garnett, William A.
United States 1916–

Well known for his aerial photographs, Garnett first worked as an architectural and advertising photographer, as a police photographer in Pasadena, California, and as an Army Signal Corps cameraman during World War II. Garnett once related how he became interested in making photographs from the air: "In 1945, like every other GI, I was anxious to get home as quickly as possible. I went out to Newark (N.J.) airport to hitch a ride back on a troop transport. The plane was full, but the crew let me sit in the navigator's seat, and the view was perfect. It was my first cross-country flight, and I decided right then that I had to photograph this great and beautiful land from the air" (*Life,* 15 Mar. 1968, p. 3).

Garnett, who teaches design at the University of California (Berkeley), has used the aerial view to capture the abstract shapes, patterns, colors, and textures of nature and cities. These become, independent of their origins, complex and beautiful images. He conceived and executed the largest project by a single photographer on one subject in *Life*'s history — nine twenty-page essays on the beauty of the United States as seen from the air (1965).

John Szarkowski wrote: "If technically competent, aerial photographs are seldom truly uninteresting; no matter how thoughtlessly made they almost always contain in their details or their patterns some surprising revelation that enriches our knowledge and our sense of landscape. On the other hand, aerial photographs that possess true coherence of intention and resolution are rare, and a remarkable number of those that hold firm in our memories were made by William A. Garnett. Garnett is not a flyer who makes photographs, but a photographer who flies. His plane's function is to hold his camera in precisely the right spot at precisely the right moment, in order to achieve not a map but a picture" (Szarkowski, *Looking,* p. 170).

WORK Aerial photography.

MEDIA Silver prints, Type C color prints (both media 8×10 to 11×14).

AVAILABILITY AND PRICE Since 1975 prints have been available through the photographer; modern prints moderately high, vintage prints (early 1950s aerial views) high. From 1953 to 1974 very few prints were made, and these were sold to museums. Color work is not presently offered for sale. Prints made before 1975 bear only the photographer's stamp; prints made thereafter are signed by him on the verso.

SIGNATURE/OTHER IDENTIFICATION

Garnett

WILLIAM A. GARNETT ⟶

PHOTOGRAPHER

1286 CONGRESS VALLEY ROAD, NAPA, CA 94558

COLLECTIONS IMP/GEH, LIFE, MOMA, Smithsonian.

SELECTED BIBLIOGRAPHY

John Szarkowski. *The Photographer and the American Landscape.* New York: MOMA, 1963.

Hanns Reich. *The World from Above.* New York: Hill & Wang, 1966.

Beaumont Newhall. *Airborne Camera.* New York: Hastings House, 1969.

Nathaniel Alexander Owings. *The American Aesthetic.* New York: Harper & Row, 1969.

Walker Evans. "Over California." *Fortune,* Mar. 1954, pp. 105–112.

Edward Parks. "The Eye of Bill Garnett Looks Down on the Commonplace and Sees Art." *Smithsonian,* May 1977, pp. 74–81.

See also Life Library, *Camera, Tool*; Szarkowski, *Looking.*

William A. Garnett. Aerial view of sand dune, Death Valley, 1954. Silver print. (Courtesy the artist. Copyright © 1954 by William A. Garnett)

Genthe, Arnold
United States (b. Germany) 1869–1942

A scholar trained in philology, Genthe came to America in 1895. He began photographing as a hobby and became well known for a series of photographs showing life at the turn of the century in San Francisco's Chinatown, where old Chinese customs were still evident. To record the natural flow of life, he usually worked on the street with a concealed camera, capturing fleeting moments before his subjects became aware of the black box they disliked.

Genthe lost all his equipment in the San Francisco earthquake and fire of 1906, but realizing the spectacular opportunity he borrowed a camera to document the shattered buildings, the devastating fire that followed the quake, and the stunned survivors. These photographs have an immediacy that is still compelling. In 1911 Genthe moved to New York, where he was a popular photographer of dancers, actors and actresses, and other celebrities. His portraits are in the soft-focus, romantic style popular at the time. Of particular interest and value today are his photographs of Isadora Duncan and her troupe.

Arnold Genthe. *The Street of the Gamblers, Chinatown, San Francisco*, between 1896 and 1906. Silver print. (Collection, The Museum of Modern Art, New York City)

WORK Includes San Francisco Chinatown (1896–1906); the aftermath of the San Francisco earthquake and fire (1906); portraits (e.g., Garbo, Theodore Roosevelt, Jack London); dancers (e.g., Isadora Duncan and the Duncan Dancers, Pavlova); scenes from stage plays; Japan, Korea, Europe, Guatemala, Cuba, Morocco (including daily life, scenic views, architecture); Yosemite Valley; California missions; pueblos of the Southwest; architecture in Charleston, S.C., and New Orleans; nude studies.

MEDIA Gelatin dry-plate negatives and film negatives, platinum prints and silver prints; autochromes.

AVAILABILITY AND PRICE Through galleries and at auction. Early prime images (Chinatown or earthquake) rare; extremely high. Other vintage prints more commonly found; moderate to high. Condition, subject matter, signature strongly affect price.

SIGNATURE/OTHER IDENTIFICATION

Arnold Genthe (signature)

COLLECTIONS California Palace of the Legion of Honor holds original negatives of the San Francisco earthquake and fire; the Library of Congress holds 20,000 glass-plate negatives and film

negatives, 500 prints, 384 autochrome plates, and a few later film transparencies; New-York Historical Society holds about 4,000 prints. Also Chicago, IMP/GEH, MMA, New Orleans, Oakland, Smithsonian.

SELECTED BIBLIOGRAPHY
Will Irwin. *Pictures of Old Chinatown*. New York: Moffat, Yard, 1908. 47 halftones. Expanded ed., *Old Chinatown*. New York: Kennerley, 1913. 91 halftones (of better quality).
George C. Hazelton, Jr., and J. Harry Benrimo. *The Yellow Jacket: A Chinese Play Done in a Chinese Manner*. Indianapolis: Bobbs-Merrill, 1913.
Percy MacKaye. *Sanctuary: A Bird Masque*. New York: Stokes, 1913. 16 halftones, including 4 in color.
The Book of the Dance. New York: Kennerley, 1916. Also deluxe limited ed., 100 copies on Japan vellum. Later ed., Boston: International Publishers, 1920.
Impressions of Old New Orleans. Foreword by Grace King. New York: Doran, 1926. Also limited ed., 200 copies, signed.
Isadora Duncan. Foreword by Max Eastman. New York: Kennerley, 1929.
As I Remember. New York: Reynal & Hitchcock, 1936. Also limited ed.
Highlights and Shadows. New York: Greenburg, 1937. Nude studies by Genthe and others.
Walt Whitman in Camden: A Selection of Prose from Specimen Days. Preface by Christopher Morley. Camden, N.J.: Haddon Craftsmen, 1938. 3 Genthe gravures, including one mounted on the cover. 1,100 copies.
See also Lawton and Know, *Knights*; Naef, *Collection*; Szarkowski, *Looking*.

Gibson, Ralph
United States 1939–

Gibson, who studied at the San Francisco Art Institute, became an assistant to Dorothea Lange in 1962. In 1969 he moved to New York City to assist Robert Frank on a film. That same year Gibson founded Lustrum Press, which has published his own books as well as those of other photographers.

For a number of years Gibson's work was in black and white. He often moved in close to his subject, separating it from its surroundings, and he increased the graininess of the image to further reduce the subject to a graphically simple shape and surface. These isolated aspects of real, identifiable objects suggest surrealistic fragments of half-remembered dreams. About this work he wrote: "A surrealist is someone who prefers to live in his subconscious as a more rewarding place to be. . . . For me, surrealism has centered around a deeper perception of the nature of reality (*Popular Photography*, Mar. 1976, p. 139).

Gibson also stated: "An important aspect to the nature of photography is its capacity to reduce a large three-dimensional universe to a much smaller two-dimensional plane. I've always been concerned with how to suggest the third dimension in my two-dimensional art. At one time I used wide lenses for their distorted spatial effects. Now [mid-1970s] I prefer the 50mm lens, which is virtually free of distortion in its ability to render three-dimensional objects in space" (Lewis, *Darkroom 1*, p. 65).

Gibson's recent color work, such as his photographs of brick walls, is less intensely personal. In it he explores the concerns of minimal art — specifically, color as sensation. He commented: "Color is in many ways autonomous, and color film is somewhat inflexible. I very much admire the independence of this material, and I prefer to bend my will to its greater intelligence. Evolving from black-and-white into color has manifested more of what my eye actually sees. I'm no longer interested in pronouncing fact or myth. I would rather produce works that look at me" (*Camera,* Apr. 1977, p. 13).

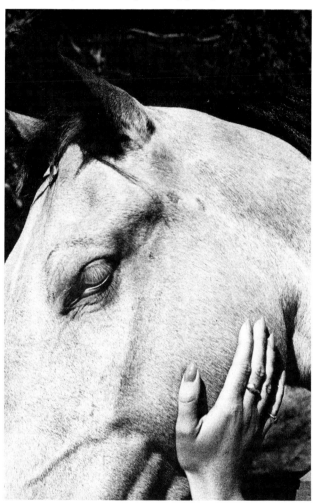

Ralph Gibson. *Horse's Head and Hand.* From *Days at Sea,* 1974. Silver print. (Courtesy the artist and Castelli Graphics)

WORK   Chiefly fragmentary images of the world. Also includes color abstractions and early black-and-white street photography (e.g., Sunset Strip).

MEDIA   Silver prints, color.

AVAILABILITY AND PRICE   Through galleries. Black-and-white prints, issued in editions of 25, moderately high. Color prints, issued in editions of 10, also moderately high. Diptychs (two Type C color images side by side), issued in editions of 15, high.

SIGNATURE/OTHER IDENTIFICATION

PORTFOLIOS   *See* chapter 6 entry.

COLLECTIONS   California, IMP/GEH, MOMA, New Mexico, Norton Simon, U. of Florida, VSW; BN, Fotografiska, NGC.

SELECTED BIBLIOGRAPHY
The Strip. Los Angeles: Roger Kennedy, 1966.
Somnambulist. New York: Lustrum Press, 1970.
Deja-Vu. New York: Lustrum Press, 1973.
Days at Sea. New York: Lustrum Press, 1974.
Manfred Willmann, ed. *American Photographers.* Graz, Austria: Fotogalerie im Forum Stadtpark, 1977.
"Ralph Gibson: La Sintesi Fotografica." *Progresso Fotografico,* Dec. 1976, pp. 26–30.
Camera, Apr. 1977, pp. 4–13. Interview by Allan Porter.
See also Lewis, *Darkroom 1;* Szarkowski, *Mirrors;* chapter 7 catalogues.

Gidal, Tim N.
Israel (b. Germany) 1909–

Tim Nachum Gidal (born Ignaz Gidalewitsch) emerged as a photojournalist in Munich and Berlin in the late 1920s and early 1930s, a time when the appearance of two small-format cameras (the Ermanox and the Leica) coincided with fast-breaking world events and the need for a new kind of visual reporting to capture them. He soon established a reputation for himself, along with other talented young photographers of the period — Felix H. Man (Hans Baumann), Walter Bosshard, Alfred Eisenstaedt, Kurt Hutton, André Kertész, Neudin (Neudatschin), Umbo (Otto Umbehr), Wolfgang Weber, and George Gidal (Tim's brother, who died on assignment in 1931). Elizabeth Claridge wrote that Tim Gidal and most of the others "came from an intellectual background rather than one of professional photography" and "shared the quality of matching a way of seeing to the capacity of the new cameras to record with the minimum of technical barriers" ("Tim Gidal: Before the Storm," p. 23).

Gidal's first published photoreportage, a study of vagabonds in a wood near Stuttgart, appeared in 1929 in the *Münchner Illustrierte Presse,* a picture magazine that was one of the forerunners of periodicals such as *Life* and *Look.* During this time Gidal became associated with writer/editor Stefan Lorant, and when Lorant, in 1938, became editor in chief of the *Picture Post* in London, Gidal found himself often on assignment for him. In 1936 Gidal emigrated to Palestine, where he remained until 1938. During World War II he served as a photoreporter in Britain's Eighth Army; from 1948 to 1954 he worked for *Life.* Since then he has created a series of children's books.

Gidal's long career has taken him throughout Europe, India, Palestine, and the United States, where he taught at the New School for Social Research in New York City.

Many of his images record "menace and fear, anxiety and optimism, bleak deprivation and blind privilege" (ibid.). Gidal has asserted that the photoreporter's only proper subject matter is the human condition, and he believes that to be worthy of his camera the photojournalist must experience empathy with his subject matter.

Tim N. Gidal. *Petit Bourgeois* [Hitler], 1929. Silver print. (Courtesy The Witkin Gallery)

WORK Chiefly photojournalism. Also includes *My Village in . . .* series (children's books about life in different countries).

MEDIA Silver prints; some color.

AVAILABILITY AND PRICE Through galleries; vintage prints moderately high to high, modern prints moderate.

SIGNATURE/OTHER IDENTIFICATION

COLLECTIONS IMP/GEH; Agfa-Gevaert, BN, Israel Museum, NGV, VA.

SELECTED BIBLIOGRAPHY
Jüdische Kinder in Eretz Israel. Berlin: Brandus, 1936.
This Is Israel. With Robert Capa, Jerry Cooke, and Isador F. Stone. New York: Boni & Gaer, 1948.
Bilderberichterstattung und Presse. Tübingen, Germany, 1956.
My Village in . . . series. Photographs by Tim Gidal. Text by Tim and Sonia Gidal. 23 vols. New York: Pantheon, 1956–1970.
Sons of the Desert. New York: Pantheon, 1960.
Goldweights of the Ashanti. Jerusalem, 1971.
Everyone Lives in Communities. Boston, 1972.
Modern Photojournalism: Origin and Evolution, 1910–1933. New York: Collier/Macmillan, 1973.
Elizabeth Claridge. "Tim Gidal: Before the Storm." *London Magazine* 16 (Dec. 1976/Jan. 1977): 23–30.

Gilpin, Laura
United States 1891–

Gilpin was born and raised in the western United States and had an early introduction to photography: W. H. Jackson's photographs of cattle roundups, in which her father appeared as a cowboy on horseback. She received a Brownie box camera when she was twelve, and during World War I went to New York City and entered the Clarence H. White School of Photography. Her early images are soft-focus landscapes, portraits, and still lifes that reflect the pictorial mood of the time. In 1918 she returned to the West and opened a portrait studio.

In the 1930s Gilpin became fascinated by the Navaho Indians. She became friendly with many of them and this winning of their trust enabled her to enter their world and photograph them. Her images, no longer soft focus, depict the Navaho with simplicity and grace in an intimate relationship with the land, and she captures the special light of the Southwest both in close-ups and vast landscapes. Her book *The Enduring Navaho* is the result of many years of work. A. D. Coleman wrote that Gilpin's photographs of Indians are "truly a continuation of [Edward S.] Curtis's labor of love" (*Portraits from North American Indian Life*, New York: Outerbridge & Lazard, 1972).

During World War II Gilpin was a public-relations photographer with Boeing Airplane Company in Wichita, Kansas. Afterward she moved permanently to Santa Fe. At the age of eighty-one she began a major study of the spectacular land and ruins of the Canyon de Chelly in Arizona, traveling through the isolated region by jeep and light airplane to gain access to it in all seasons. In 1975 she was awarded a Guggenheim Fellowship to continue her work with platinum prints, a process she has used since her days at the Clarence H. White School.

WORK Chiefly Indian life and artifacts in the Southwest: Indian pottery (for the Museum of New Mexico); the Navaho; landscape in Colorado, New Mexico, and Arizona (e.g., Canyon de Chelly). Early work includes Yucatan (particularly architecture), the Rio Grande, commercial work (e.g., portraits, architecture), still lifes, Central Park, New York City (ca. 1920).

MEDIA Platinum prints, silver prints.

AVAILABILITY AND PRICE Through galleries. Vintage platinum prints (4×5 to 8×10) rare; high. Modern prints (8×10, 11×14, 16×20) moderate.

SIGNATURE/OTHER IDENTIFICATION

Laura Gilpin

COLLECTIONS Arizona, CCP, Kansas, MMA, MOMA, Museum of New Mexico, New Mexico, New Orleans, Oakland, Princeton (Art Museum).

SELECTED BIBLIOGRAPHY

Federal Writers' Project. *New Mexico: A Guide to the Colorful State.* New York: Hastings House, 1940.

The Pueblos: A Camera Chronicle. New York: Hastings House, 1941.

Temples in Yucatan; A Camera Chronicle of Chichén Itzá. New York: Hastings House, 1948.

The Rio Grande: River of Destiny. New York: Duell, Sloan & Pearce, 1949.

The Enduring Navaho. Austin: University of Texas Press, 1968.

Claire Morrill. *A Taos Mosaic: Portrait of a New Mexico Village.* Santa Fe: University of New Mexico Press, 1973.

Laura Gilpin Retrospective: 1910–1974. Santa Fe: Museum of New Mexico, 1974.

"Laura Gilpin, Photographer." *New America* 1 (Spring 1975): 28–32.

Gilpin's photographs appeared in *Platinum Print: A Journal of Personal Expression* (published 1913–1916) and in the monthly Boeing Company magazine.

See also Hume, *The Great West*; Mann, *Women*; chapter 7 catalogue.

Laura Gilpin. *Francis Nakai and Family*, 1950. From *The Enduring Navaho*, 1968. Silver print. (Courtesy The Witkin Gallery)

Gowin, Emmet
United States 1941–

Gowin, a teacher of photography at Princeton University, has said that he learned photography from books and has listed among his important influences Henri Cartier-Bresson, Robert Frank, Harry Callahan, and Frederick Sommer. Gowin's wife and family appear in nearly all of his work. He uses them repeatedly — so often that they become a motif, deeply personal but taking on larger meanings. Strange relationships between people and objects are implied in his photographs, and a direct interaction between the subject and the photographer/camera is always apparent. His images are not "captured": they are quite consciously "made." "It is Gowin's sensibility, rather than any specific visual style or carefully plotted ideational thrust which is the hallmark and unifying force of his oeuvre," according to A. D. Coleman, writing in the *New York Times.*

Gowin once reflected: "I had set out to describe the world within my domain, to live a quality with things. Enrichment, I saw, involves a willingness to accept a changing vision of the nature of things — which is to say, reality. Often I had thought that things teach me what to do. Now I would prefer to say: As things teach us what we already are, we gain a vision of the world" (*Emmet Gowin: Photographs*, p. 101).

WORK Chiefly portraits of his wife Edith and other family members; children; nudes; landscapes. Recent work includes images of decayed books and of other objects.

MEDIA Silver prints, color.

Emmet Gowin. *Nancy, Edith and Dwayne, Danville, Virginia*, 1966. Silver print. (Courtesy Light Gallery)

AVAILABILITY AND PRICE   Through galleries; silver prints moderately high, color moderate.

SIGNATURE/OTHER IDENTIFICATION

PORTFOLIO   *See* Chapter 6 Schools and workshops entry.

COLLECTIONS   Chicago, Cincinnati, Dayton, Harvard (Fogg), Kansas, Minneapolis, MOMA, New Mexico, RISD; NGC.

SELECTED BIBLIOGRAPHY
Clifford S. Ackley. *Private Realities: Recent American Photography.* Boston: Museum of Fine Arts, 1974. Bibliography.
Emmet Gowin: Photographs. New York: Knopf, 1976.
"Emmet Gowin." *Album,* no. 5 (1970), pp. 40–48.
"Photographs/Emmet Gowin." *Aperture* 16, no. 2 (1971): 38 ff.
Camera Mainichi, Oct. 1972.
See also Kelly, *Darkroom 2;* Life Library, *Art, Children;* Szarkowski, *Mirrors;* chapter 7 catalogues.

Groover, Jan
United States 1943–

Groover studied painting and drawing at Pratt Institute (Brooklyn) and Ohio State University and now teaches painting, drawing, and photography. In her serial color images of city and highway scenes she records chance activity as conceptual art. She does not seek out action but selects a place and records matter-of-factly what passes before the lens.

Groover's photographs seek to avoid both the heightened realism and the sentiment often associated with color. They entail her response to available light, the framing of the subject matter by the camera, and the recording of the movement that occurs before the lens. When she presents the photographs in a sequence on a single mount, the presentation creates a new overall work in which the elements of design and color become as important as image content.

Groover remarked: "In photography there is the idea — endlessly, variable, but inevitably — that one is stuck with the real world. But if you are stuck with something, it certainly isn't the world, or the mechanics of the camera; simply, you are stuck with whatever your mind makes of things. The rules are yours, how else could it be?" (statement to the authors, 1977).

WORK   Chiefly urban landscapes, including vehicles on highways and city streets; houses; highly patterned closeup studies of kitchen objects and flora.

MEDIUM   Type C color prints (ranging from 6×9 to 16×20), presented in multiples of two, three, four, or more on a single mount.

AVAILABILITY AND PRICE   Through galleries; high to extremely high.

SIGNATURE/OTHER IDENTIFICATION

COLLECTIONS   IMP/GEH; Pompidou.

SELECTED BIBLIOGRAPHY
Jan Groover. Intro. by Jane Livingston. Washington, D.C.: Corcoran Gallery of Art, 1976.
The Nation's Capital in Photographs, 1976. Washington, D.C.: Corcoran Gallery of Art, 1976.
"The Medium Is the Use." *Artforum* 12 (Nov. 1973): 79–80.
See also Szarkowski, *Mirrors;* Wise, *Choice;* chapter 7 catalogues.

Jan Groover. *Piscataway: Green House, Hedge, Pink House,* 1977. Three 9×6-inch Type C color prints. (Courtesy Sonnabend Gallery)

GROUP f/64

Group *f*/64 was an informal group of U.S. photographers active on the West Coast during the 1930s. The work of its members consisted of sharply focused, unmanipulated, "straight" photography rather than the old soft-focus pictorialism. Group *f*/64 took its name from the small lens-aperture setting that produced the detailed images its members preferred.

Willard Van Dyke (1906–) conceived of the idea in 1932. "It came about one day as I was returning from a trip on U.S. [highway] 256 with a college buddy," he recalled. "We were drinking wine and feeling marvelous and young. I had the idea of local photographers getting together and exhibiting. I asked Edward [Weston] and Imogen [Cunningham]. It was Ansel [Adams]'s idea to use the name *f*/64. I wanted to call it U.S. 256, an equivalent aperture setting on another system. Weston's old rapid rectilinear lens had a U.S. system. But the '*f*' system made more sense. The group also included Sonya Noskowiak [b. Germany; 1900–1975], Henry Swift [1891–1960], and John Paul Edwards [1883–1958]. Lloyd Rollin of the de Young Museum was interested in photography and gave us a group show in 1932. It was the only time, as far as I can remember, that we exhibited together. The group actually had more influence than body. Edward at one point wanted to withdraw, but I persuaded him not to. It was amorphous enough; without him it would have been nothing" (statement to the authors, 1977).

The group remained active for several years. Afterward, "*f/64*" remained a descriptive term applied to all straight photography. "It is interesting to observe how this 'straight' mode of photography has changed for us since its first appearance in the 30's," wrote Hilton Kramer. "Its preoccupation with formal definition, with a certain kind of light and precision, now looks almost as 'esthetic' to our eyes as the pictorial style it supplanted" (*New York Times*, 3 June 1977, p. C14).

Willard Van Dyke. *Ansel Adams*, 1934. Silver print. (Courtesy the artist)

WORK/MEDIA/AVAILABILITY AND PRICE/SIGNATURE–OTHER IDENTIFICATION/PORTFOLIOS/COLLECTIONS *See* individual entries (Adams, Ansel; Cunningham, Imogen; Weston, Edward).

SELECTED BIBLIOGRAPHY
Group f.64. Texts by Jean S. Tucker and Willard Van Dyke. St. Louis: University of Missouri, 1978.

Hahn, Betty
United States 1940–

Ever experimenting with the photographic medium and producing amusing and intriguing results, Hahn is best known for her gum-bichromate images on fabrics embellished by stitchery. She studied with Henry Holmes Smith and received an M.F.A. degree from Indiana University in graphic design and photography. She has taught at the Rochester (New York) Institute of Technology and is currently associate professor of art at the University of New Mexico (Albuquerque).

"Responding to the possibilities of the 'new' [gum-bichromate] process," she wrote, "was, for me, like changing from a simple declarative sentence, however carefully rendered, to a compound, complex statement of fact and fantasy. The picture was no longer synonymous with the subject because I could manipulate the process and exercise some intellectual control over those details recorded by the camera while incorporating other ideas. Photographic information could be provided where details were included, or it could remain hidden where details were obscured. The quality and quantity of information could be expanded upon as long as the total picture didn't become too cluttered" (Lewis, *Darkroom 1*, pp. 79–80).

In a 1977 statement to the authors, Hahn wrote of her work: "The fabric with color thread added represents a distinct preference for mixed-media and an attempt to unite the imagery of photography to that of traditional figurative stitchery. My wish was to reach a balance between the two media which allowed the pictures to acquire some of the detail and space of photography and the color, surface and unique quality of handworked textiles."

WORK   Includes nudes, vegetables, fruits, landscapes, portraits, series of flamingos and of the Lone Ranger and Tonto on horseback.

MEDIA   Prints (gum-bichromate, cyanotype, vandyke) on paper or on fabric, sometimes with stitching or collaged; color prints made with a very inexpensive plastic Mick-A-Matic camera; silver prints.

AVAILABILITY AND PRICE   Through galleries; moderate.

SIGNATURE/OTHER IDENTIFICATION

PORTFOLIO   *See* Chapter 6 Schools and workshops entry.

COLLECTIONS   Akron, Chicago, IMP/GEH, Indiana, MOMA, Nebraska, New Mexico, Smithsonian; NGC.

SELECTED BIBLIOGRAPHY
Abby Eden. "Betty Hahn." *Artspace*, Winter 1976/77, pp. 14–16. Interview.

Thelma R. Newman. *Innovative Printmaking.* New York: Crown, 1977.
See also Colors (in color bibliography); Hume, *The Great West;* Lewis, *Darkroom 1*, Mann, *Women;* chapter 7 catalogues.

Betty Hahn. Untitled, 1976. From the series "Who Was That Masked Man? I Wanted to Thank Him." Cyanotype with Flair pen. (Courtesy The Witkin Gallery)

Hallman, Gary L.
United States 1940–

The photographs of Hallman, who studied under Jerome Liebling at the University of Minnesota, exemplify an important shift in contemporary photography — namely, to a philosophy in which the photographer is more concerned with the formal or fictive characteristics of a photograph than with the specific information it contains.

E. William Peterson wrote that "Hallman's photographs, like the paintings of Newman and Olitski, are in essence about experience and sensation. The content of his works is not the overt subject matter, but is located instead in the experience of perception — or the process of seeing itself. In composition and tone, they are occasionally reminiscent of early snapshots and participate in the same pureness and spontaneity of vision — a kind of seeing that surprises itself in the act. The selective toning of the large 22×33-inch prints renders luminous and metallic golds, browns, purples, and suggests silvers. Like the effects obtained by Olitski and others using the spraygun in recent painting, the diffusion of the image by focus and the stippled character of over-enlargement in Hall-

man's photographs combines with the toning to give an impression that everything is somehow collecting on the surface rather than appearing to be behind it" ("Review," p. 26).

WORK Landscapes, "Press Pull" series (ca. 1972; enlarged extreme close-ups of people poking and grabbing flesh), "Salad under Glass" series (1975; arrangements created in the photographer's loft/studio), "The Studio" series (1975; 20 photographs of locations in the photographer's loft/studio).

MEDIUM Silver prints (some selectively toned). Hallman often draws on the image.

AVAILABILITY AND PRICE Through galleries; moderate. Recent prints are issued in small numbered editions.

SIGNATURE/OTHER IDENTIFICATION

[signature]

COLLECTIONS IMP/GEH, MOMA, New Mexico.

SELECTED BIBLIOGRAPHY
E. William Peterson. "Review: Photography of Gary Hallman." *Image* 17 (Sept. 1974): 26–27.
See also Szarkowski, *Mirrors;* chapter 7 catalogues.

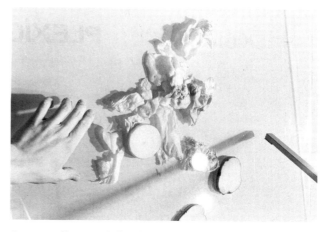

Gary L. Hallman. *Salad under Glass,* 1975. Silver print. (Courtesy Light Gallery)

Halsman, Philippe
United States (b. Latvia) 1906–1979

Halsman, a professional photographer in Paris in the 1930s, emigrated to the United States in 1940 and established his reputation photographing celebrities. Many of his pictures appeared in *Life, Time,* and other magazines. Self-taught in photography, he has said he has been influenced less by photographers or painters than by writers such as Tolstoy and Dostoevski. His style varies considerably; in each portrait he attempts to reveal something unique about the sitter. "Lighting and photographic equipment are less important for the portraitist than psychology and conversation," he once observed. "If he uses them effectively, sometimes in the short span of a sitting a miracle happens. A fragment of evanescent truth is captured and instant eternity (simply add hypo!) is born. The end result is another surface to be penetrated, this time by the sensitivity of the onlooker" (*Sight and Insight*).

In addition to his more conventional portraits, Halsman devised one unusual way to reveal his subjects' personalities: he asked to photograph each of them jumping. "In a jump, the subject, in a sudden burst of energy, overcomes gravity," he explained. "He cannot simultaneously control his expressions, his facial and his limb muscles. The mask falls. The real self becomes visible. One has only to snap it with the camera" (*Jump Book*).

Philippe Halsman. *Albert Einstein*, 1954. Silver print. (Courtesy Rinhart Galleries, Inc. Copyright © by Philippe Halsman)

WORK Chiefly portraits (e.g., Einstein, Dali). Also includes magazine illustrations, advertising, jump pictures (e.g., the duke and duchess of Windsor, Richard Nixon, Marilyn Monroe).

MEDIA Silver prints, color.

AVAILABILITY AND PRICE Through galleries; moderately high.

SIGNATURE/OTHER IDENTIFICATION

COLLECTIONS LIFE, MMA, MOMA, New Orleans, Smithsonian; RPS.

SELECTED BIBLIOGRAPHY
The Frenchman: A Photographic Interview with Fernandel. New York: Simon & Schuster, 1949.
The Candidate. New York: Simon & Schuster, 1952.
Piccoli. New York: Simon & Schuster, 1953.
Dali's Mustache: A Photographic Interview with Salvador Dali. New York: Simon & Schuster, 1954.
Jump Book. New York: Simon & Schuster, 1959.
Halsman on the Creation of Photographic Ideas. New York: Ziff-Davis, 1961.
Sight and Insight. New York: Doubleday, 1972.
Ruth Spencer. "Philippe Halsman." *The British Journal of Photography*, 10 Oct. 1975, pp. 898 ff.
See also Life Library, *Great Photographers, Studio, Themes.*

Harbutt, Charles
United States 1935–

Harbutt began his career as a writer and editor for *Jubilee* (from 1956 to 1959) and made photographs to accompany articles such as those on migrant farmworkers and the civil-rights movement in the American South. By the late 1950s he was devoting himself full time to photography.

Harbutt's images document reality, but in a personal, emotional, and tautly composed way; he often uses contrasts and juxtaposition to suggest contemporary ironies. Of his work in *Travelog* he wrote: "My photographs are both real and surreal. . . . The loneliness, alienation, and fears, the lusts and sexual sorrows, the difficulties of sustaining emotional relationships. The damage people do to each other and the delight they can and do give one another. Throughout the desire to break free. At the same time it is about what is specifically photographic about photography" (*Travelog*).

A member of the Magnum photo agency, Harbutt in the 1970s began to teach photography. He directed the use of photographs for the New York City Planning Commission's *Plan for New York City* and in 1975 created the photographs for the U.S. Bicentennial Commission touring exhibition. His other works have included films that employ still photographs, and *Picture Bandit*, a projection device that displayed three images at random when played like a slot machine.

WORK "35mm work with roots in the documentary tradition, subjects being the world, the flesh, the devil and home" (Harbutt statement to the authors, 1977).

MEDIUM Silver prints.

AVAILABILITY AND PRICE Through galleries and the photographer; moderate.

SIGNATURE/OTHER IDENTIFICATION

PORTFOLIO *See* chapter 6 Schools and workshop entry.

Charles Harbutt (Magnum Photos, Inc.). *Building, rue Schoelcher,* 1975. Silver print. (Courtesy the artist)

COLLECTIONS MOMA, Nebraska, Smithsonian; BN.

SELECTED BIBLIOGRAPHY
America in Crisis: Photographs for Magnum. Ed. by Harbutt and Lee Jones. Text by Mitchell Levitas. New York: Holt, Rinehart & Winston, 1969.
New York City Planning Commission. *Plan for New York City.* 6 vols. Cambridge, Mass.: MIT Press, 1970-71.
Travelog. Cambridge, Mass.: MIT Press, 1974.
Album, no. 9 (1970), pp. 16 ff.
See also Kelly, *Darkroom 2;* Life Library, *Children;* chapter 7 catalogue.

Hawes, Josiah Johnson
See Southworth, Albert Sands/Hawes, Josiah Johnson.

Haynes, Frank Jay
United States 1853-1921

F. Jay Haynes traveled widely in the Midwest in the late nineteenth century and made many photographs of life and landscape there. He was appointed the official photographer for the Northern Pacific Railway in 1881, holding a position similar to A. J. Russell's with the Union Pacific Railroad. He is best known as the official photographer of Yellowstone National Park (1884–1916), a post in which his son J. E. Haynes succeeded him. Haynes photographed Yellowstone scenery in a way that is somewhat similar to Eadweard Muybridge's treatment of Yosemite (though Haynes's images are generally less powerful): dramatic clouds, rushing waters, juxtaposition of near and far objects to give the illusion of deep space. Views made by Haynes's Yellowstone studio were immensely popular with tourists. Mount Haynes in Yellowstone is named for him.

WORK Landscapes and scenic views: the Midwest (ca. 1877–1880; e.g., the mining town of Deadwood, Dakota Territory); along the Missouri River to Fort Benton, Montana; the Northern Pacific Railway and adjacent territory between Lake Superior and the Missouri River; along the Canadian Pacific Railway, including Alaska; Yellowstone National Park.

MEDIA Collodion wet-plate negatives, gelatin dry-plate negatives, film negatives; albumen prints and (later) silver prints. Many different formats, often hand-tinted: stereographs, cabinet photographs, 8×10, enlargements up to 30×48, lantern slides. Also lithographed postcards of Yellowstone (ca. 1900 and after). Various stamps on verso.

AVAILABILITY AND PRICE Through galleries and at auction. Large-size albumen prints rare; moderate to high. Later silver prints mass-issued for travelers, postcards, etc., frequently found; low.

SIGNATURE/OTHER IDENTIFICATION

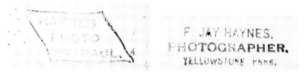

COLLECTIONS Haynes Museum (Bozeman, Montana). Also found in many schools and libraries, often filed by subject matter.

SELECTED BIBLIOGRAPHY
Albert Brewer Guptill. *All about Yellowstone Park: A Practical Guide.* St. Paul: Haynes [1890s].
Yellowstone National Park in Photo Gravure. St. Paul: Haynes, 1891.
Hiram Martin Chittenden. *The Yellowstone National Park.* Cincinnati: Robert Clarke, 1895.
Albert Brewer Guptill. *Haynes' Guide to Yellowstone Park.* Haynes, 1897.
Clyde Max Bauer. *Yellowstone Geysers.* Yellowstone Park, Wyo.: Haynes, 1937. Rev. ed., 1947.
Tilden Freeman. *Following the Frontier with F. Jay Haynes, Pioneer Photographer of the Old West.* New York: Knopf, 1964.
See also Taft, *Photography.*

Frank Jay Haynes. *Gibbon Falls, 84 Feet, Yellowstone,* ca. 1886. Albumen print. (Private collection)

Heartfield, John
Germany 1891–1968

Heartfield (born Helmut Herzfeld) is known for his powerful satiric photomontages directed at political and social conditions in Nazi Germany. After studying at the Arts and Crafts School in Berlin in 1913, he became a commercial artist. In 1917, with his brother Wieland Herzfelde, he formed Malik Verlag, which published the work of left-wing writers and artists; Heartfield designed book jackets for these publications and also designed works for the German Communist Party. In the 1920s he was a member of the Berlin Dadaists, a more politically oriented group of artists than other Dadaists.

From 1921 to 1923 Heartfield was scenic director for Max Reinhardt's Berlin theaters. He also edited the satirical magazine *Der Knüppel* (1923–1927), and designed covers for and contributed to AIZ (*Arbeiter-Illustrierten Zeitung* — published in Berlin 1929–1933, in Prague 1933–1938). In 1933 Heartfield was forced to flee Germany because of the reaction to his vitriolic photomontages aimed against the Third Reich. He worked in Prague until 1938, when he was again forced to move, this time to London, where he made book covers and illustrations. In 1950 he returned to Germany and designed theatrical scenery and posters.

"As images, Heartfield's photomontages are immediately clear and direct, however subtle the message may be," according to Dawn Ades. ". . . When works done for AIZ were exhibited, Heartfield always insisted on having a copy of the paper on show beside the original to underline the fact that his works were political propaganda aimed at a wide public, not private works of art" (*Photomontage*, p. 13). Seldom making his own photographs, he often had others print them or used pictures from books, magazines, photographic agencies, and newspapers. He "always called his works photomontages, even when using photographs unaltered or specially posed. . . . In the end, remarkably, whether montaged or not, they still *look* like newspaper photographs" (ibid.).

WORK Includes political satire; book jackets, covers, and illustrations; theatrical posters.

MEDIA Photomontages and photomechanical reproductions of photomontages in newspapers, magazines, and in poster form; silver prints.

AVAILABILITY AND PRICE Through galleries and at auction. Book designs and broadsides (e.g., posters, flyers) low to moderate. Original photomontages very rare; extremely high.

SIGNATURE/OTHER IDENTIFICATION

John Heartfield

COLLECTIONS Akademie der Künste, Nationalgalerie.

SELECTED BIBLIOGRAPHY

H. K. Frenzel. "John Heartfield und seine photographische-graphischen Arbeiten." In *Gebrauchsgraphik*, vol. 7 (1927).

Kurt Tucholsky. *Deutschland, Deutschland, über Alles*. Berlin: Neuer Deutscher Verlag, 1929. Reprint, Hamburg: Rowohlt, 1964. U.S. ed., subtitled *A Picture-book*. Trans. by Anne Halley. Afterword and notes by Harry Zohn. Amherst: University of Massachusetts Press, 1972.

Sergei Tretyakov. *John Heartfield: Eine Monographie*. Moscow, 1936.

Konrad Farner, ed. *John Heartfield: Photomontagen zur Zeitgeschichte*. Zurich: Kultur und Volk, 1945.

Bodo Uhse. "John Heartfield und seine Fotomontagen." In *John Heartfield und die Kunst der Fotomontage*. Berlin: Deutsche Akademie der Künste, 1957.

Wieland Herzfelde. *John Heartfield: Leben und Werk*. Dresden: Verlag der Kunst, 1962.

John Heartfield: Photomontages. London: Institute of Contemporary Arts, 1969.

John Heartfield. Dresden: VEB, 1970.

John Heartfield, Krieg im Frieden: Fotomontagen zur Zeit, 1930–1938. Munich: Karl Hanser, 1972.

John Heartfield: 33 Photomontages. Dresden: VEB, 1974.

John Heartfield 1891–1968: Fotomontages. Eindhoven, Netherlands: Abbemuseum, 1975.

Dawn Ades. *Photomontage*. New York: Pantheon, 1976.

Heartfield. Intro. by Roland März. Berlin: Staatliche Museen (Nationalgalerie), 1976.

Photomontages of the Nazi Period: John Heartfield. New York: Universe, 1977.

See also Life Library, *Print*.

John Heartfield. *The Nazis Play with Fire*, 2/28/35. Photomontage. (Courtesy Gertrud Heartfield and Miriam Grossman Cohen)

Heinecken, Robert F.
United States 1931–

Since the early 1960s, Heinecken's work has helped to revitalize the experimental tradition in photography and to explore the boundaries of the medium. He has been drawing and painting since he was a child, and his work shows the influence of his studies in painting, printmaking, and film: he often draws on or adds color to his work; he issues some works in lithographic editions and overprints images in other pieces; he segments some images like frames in a film.

Heinecken mixes graphic and photographic techniques in two- and three-dimensional works that break down the once-traditional separation of art media. His subject matter is also a mix — of erotic, pornographic, advertising, and found imagery: "I am interested in what I term *gestalts*; picture circumstances which bring together disparate images or ideas so as to form new meanings and new configurations" (*Untitled 7/8*).

John Upton wrote: "The most assertive single characteristic of his work is the assault on conventional gestalt formations. He has compared himself with someone engaged in guerilla warfare: 'With a strange sense of propriety or humor, I like to go into something, shake it up, and disappear,' [which] suggests the planting of booby traps designed to do violence to habitual patterns of perception and identification" (*Minor White, Robert Heinecken, Robert Cumming*).

WORK   Includes images of female forms cut into squares and rearranged as picture puzzles, cubes, or stacked blocks; altered magazines, sometimes re-bound; print-through magazine images,

Robert F. Heinecken. *Cliche Vary/Autoeroticism,* 1974. Photosensitized linen and color chalk, 42×42 inches. (Courtesy Light Gallery)

using a magazine page instead of a negative and exposing photographic paper underneath (e.g., "Are You Rea" series); assemblages; mixed-media compositions.

MEDIA   Include film, paper, photosensitized linen, plastics, metals, canvas, acrylics, colored chalk, magazine images, real objects. Reproduction processes include lithography, offset printing, etching.

AVAILABILITY AND PRICE   Through galleries; low to extremely high, depending on the object.

SIGNATURE/OTHER IDENTIFICATION

PORTFOLIOS   *See* chapter 6 Schools and workshops entry.

COLLECTIONS   IMP/GEH, MOMA, New Mexico, many other collections.

SELECTED BIBLIOGRAPHY
Are You Rea, 1964–68. Los Angeles: published by the photographer, 1968.
John Upton. *Minor White, Robert Heinecken, Robert Cumming.* Long Beach: California State University Fine Arts Gallery, 1973.
James L. Enyeart. *Heinecken.* Danbury, N.H.: Addison House, 1979.
Carl I. Belz. "Robert Heinecken." *Camera,* Jan. 1968, pp. 6–13.
"I Am Involved in Learning to Perceive and Use Light." *Untitled* 7/8 (1974) pp. 44–46.
Charles Hagen. "Robert Heinecken: An Interview." *Afterimage* 3 (Apr. 1976): 8–12.
Candida Finkel. "Space-Time and the Syzygy." *Exposure* 15 (Dec. 1977): 16–19.
See also Colors (in color bibliography); Hume, *The Great West;* Life Library, *Art, Print;* Szarkowski, *Mirrors;* chapter 7 catalogues.

Henle, Fritz
Germany 1909–

After studying photography with Hannah Seewald in Munich, Henle left in 1931 to earn his living traveling and photographing. His first assignment, which influenced his strong sense of design and composition in later years, was with an art historian in Italy, photographing works of the Italian Renaissance. He toured India, the Far East, and the United States, and his photographs from these travels were published in magazines such as *Fortune* and *Life.* Working with Alexey Brodovitch, he also made fashion photographs for *Harper's Bazaar.* Interested in people and their life-styles, Henle becomes well acquainted with his subjects. He often does extensive projects for publication in book form.

WORK   Chiefly studies of countries, with emphasis on the culture and people (e.g., his longtime friend Pablo Casals). Also includes fashion, industrial photography, guides to photography.

Fritz Henle. *Exit* [in painter Georges Braque's home], ca. 1946. Silver print. (Courtesy the artist. Copyright © by Fritz Henle)

MEDIUM Silver prints.

AVAILABILITY AND PRICE Through galleries. Vintage prints infrequently available, moderately high; modern prints moderate.

SIGNATURE/OTHER IDENTIFICATION

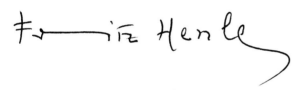

COLLECTIONS Mint, MOMA, Smithsonian.

SELECTED BIBLIOGRAPHY
Takayasu Senzoku. *Das ist Japan* (and English ed., *This Is Japan*). Harzburg, Germany: Heering, 1937.
Fung Kwok-ying. *China*. New York: Holt, 1943.
Mexico. Chicago: Ziff-Davis, 1945.
Elliot Paul. *Paris*. New York: Ziff-Davis, 1947.
Norman J. Wright. *Hawaii*. New York: Hastings House, 1948.
Vivienne Tallal Winterry. *The Virgin Islands*. New York: Hastings House, 1949.
———. *Fritz Henle's Rollei*. New York: Hastings House, 1950.
Fritz Henle's Figure Studies. Intro. by Jacquelyn Judge. New York: Crowell, 1954.
Norman Hall and Basil Burton, eds. *Fritz Henle*. London: Photography, 1955.
George B. Wright. *Fritz Henle's Guide to Rollei Photography*. New York: Crowell, 1956.
P. E. Knapp. *The Caribbean: A Journey with Pictures*. New York: Crowell, 1957.
H. M. Kinzer. *Photography for Everyone*. New York: Viking, 1959.
Anne Freemantle. *A Holiday in Europe*. Intro. by Patrick Dennis. New York: Viking, 1963.
H. M. Kinzer. *A New Guide to Rollei Photography*. New York: Viking, 1965.
Casals. New York: American Photographic Book, 1975.
Fritz Henle. Foreword by Allan Porter. New York: Fritz Henle Publishing, 1975.

Hill, David Octavius
Scotland 1802–1870

Adamson, Robert
Scotland 1821–1848

Robert Adamson wanted a career in engineering, but when ill health ended his apprenticeship, he turned to photography. He learned the calotype process in 1842, opened a portrait studio in Edinburgh, and began a five-year partnership with D. O. Hill in 1843. Hill was a landscape painter who had become interested in photography while planning a large commemorative painting of the founders of the Free Church of Scotland; he sought the help of Adamson in the belief that the calotype process would aid in rendering the likenesses of the 474 clergymen and dignitaries involved. The partners soon expanded their subject matter to include genre and other scenes, and between them made about 1,500 images before the partnership ended when Adamson died in 1848. Hill then returned to painting until 1860 when he tried — not very successfully — to resume photography, with A. McGlashan as his camera operator. Though Hill was ostensibly the artist and Adamson only the technician, together they created finer work than either did by himself.

Hill and Adamson are notable for the dignity and presence they gave to their subjects and for their subtle use of simple gestures and props to portray individuality of character. They exploited the best inherent qualities of the calotype by boldly subordinating details into strongly massed areas of brightness and shadow. David Bruce wrote: "This was the measure of their achievements: that they took an infant medium, grasped at once its virtues and limitations and made it their own. Where others had played with photography as a toy, they were able to draw it into the mainstream of artistic expression" (*Sun Pictures*, p. 22). Their work was almost forgotten between the 1860s and late 1880s, but was rediscovered by pictorialists in the 1890s.

WORK Chiefly portraits (e.g., clergy, artists, children). Also includes genre scenes of life in Scotland (e.g., fishing boats, fisherfolk, old cottages); architectural and landscape views, many with figures.

MEDIA Calotypes (about 5⅝ × 7⅞). Hill's work with McGlashan used the collodion wet-plate process.

David Octavius Hill and Robert Adamson. *Mrs. Anne Rigby and Miss Elizabeth Rigby,* ca. 1845. Carbon print, ca. 1916, made by Jessie Bertram from the original calotype negative. (Courtesy The Witkin Gallery)

AVAILABILITY AND PRICE Through galleries and at auction. Calotypes in first-rate condition (unfaded and rich in color) of prime subjects are rare; high to extremely high. Poorer prints or less interesting subjects moderate to high. Carbon prints and gravures from Hill-and-Adamson negatives printed in the 1890s and after by Thomas and J. C. Annan, Alvin Langdon Coburn, Jessie Bertram, and others are somewhat rare; moderate to high. *Camera Work* gravures moderate.

COLLECTIONS Albright-Knox, Chicago, IMP/GEH, MMA, New Mexico, Texas (Gernsheim); NGC. In Edinburgh: Edinburgh Photographic Society, Edinburgh Public Library, Royal Scottish Museum, Scottish NPG. In London: BM, NPG, RPS, Science Museum, VA.

SELECTED BIBLIOGRAPHY
Andrew Elliot. *Calotypes by D. O. Hill and R. Adamson Illustrating an Early Stage in the Development of Photography, Selected from His [Elliot's] Collection.* Edinburgh: privately printed (by Jessie Bertram), 1928. 38 copies.
Heinrich Schwarz. *David Octavius Hill.* Leipzig: Insel, and New York: Viking, 1931.
A Centenary Exhibition of the Work of David Octavius Hill and Robert Adamson. Text by Katherine Michaelson. Edinburgh: Scottish Arts Council, 1970.
Hill and Adamson Photographs. Ed. by Graham Ovenden. Intro. by Marina Henderson. New York: St. Martin, 1973.

David Bruce. *Sun Pictures: The Hill-Adamson Calotypes.* Boston: New York Graphic Society, 1974.
An Early Victorian Album: The Hill/Adamson Collection. Ed. and intro. by Colin Ford. Commentary by Roy Strong. London: Cape, 1974. U.S. ed., New York: Knopf, 1976.
Camera Work: Reproductions (gravures, halftones) in nos. 11, 28, 37.
See also Green, *Camera Work;* Life Library, *Camera, Great Photographers;* Naef, *Collection;* Newhall, *Masters;* Scharf, *Pioneers;* Szarkowski, *Looking.*

Hillers, John K.
United States (b. Germany) 1843–1925

Jack Hillers was hired in 1871 as an oarsman and general helper on John Wesley Powell's second survey of the Colorado River. He became interested in photography while on the trip and received instruction from the survey's photographers, including E. O. Beaman. Another expedition member described what happened in the spring of 1872 after Beaman and his various successors left the expedition: "We could not find anyone else who desired to do the Grand Canyon with us. . . . There was nothing for it but to make Jack Hillers photographer-in-chief. He was equal to the job. In spite of enormous difficulties, great fatigue, shortage of grub, etc., he made a number of first class negatives" (quoted in Taft, *Photography,* pp. 290–291).

Hillers continued as Powell's photographer on several more expeditions, and later was hired by Powell to work for the U.S. Bureau of Ethnology and the U.S. Geological Survey, where he worked as late as 1919. Hillers made many views of the western landscape (including early views of the Grand Canyon) and of Southwest American Indian life. Mount Hillers in Utah is named for him.

WORK Includes views of the Grand Canyon and vicinity; Southwest American Indian portraits and daily life.

John K. Hillers. *Tewa. Cicomavi. Wolpi. Mokitowns, Arizona,* ca. 1873 or 1874. Albumen print. (Courtesy The Witkin Gallery)

MEDIA Collodion wet-plate negatives, albumen prints (including stereographs). Also large glass transparencies (up to 4×5 feet), some hand-colored, made for various government exhibits.

AVAILABILITY AND PRICE Through galleries and at auction. Prints about 11×14 on 16×20 Smithsonian mounts (gray with ornate border; also identifiable by name scratched in plate) are rare; moderately high. Prints larger than 11×14 are rarest; extremely high. Various smaller unsigned prints on heavy board mounts can also be found; low to moderate. Stereographs rare, expensive for their category; extremely low to low.

SIGNATURE/OTHER IDENTIFICATION

COLLECTIONS BPL, California (Bancroft), Denver, IMP/GEH, LOC, Museum of New Mexico, National Archives, New Mexico, NYPL, Smithsonian (Anthropological Archives), Utah.

SELECTED BIBLIOGRAPHY
Frederick S. Dellenbaugh. *The Romance of the Colorado River.* New York and London: Putnam, 1902.
———. *A Canyon Voyage.* New Haven, Conn.: Yale University Press, 1926.
Julian H. Steward. *Notes on Hillers' Photographs of the Paiute and Ute Indians Taken on the Powell Expedition of 1873.* Washington, D.C.: Smithsonian Institution, 1939.
"Photographed All the Best Scenery": Jack Hillers' Diary of the Powell Expeditions, 1871–1875. Ed. by Don D. Fowler. Salt Lake City: University of Utah Press, 1972.
See also Taft, *Photography.*

Hine, Lewis Wickes
United States 1874–1940

Hine was one of the first and greatest of those who used photography for social reform. As a youth he worked for a while in a furniture factory, then studied at the University of Chicago, New York University, and Columbia University. In 1903, while he was teaching botany and nature studies at the Ethical Culture School in New York, he received a camera from the head of the school to use as a teaching aid and to record school activities.

Hine's interest in social welfare and in reform movements led him in 1905 to begin his first documentary series, immigrants on Ellis Island. In 1908 he left teaching to become an investigator and photographer for the National Child Labor Committee (NCLC), and between 1908 and 1916 he traveled extensively photographing child-labor abuses. He would inveigle his way into factories, take notes on conditions, record the children's names and ages, surreptitiously measure their heights against the buttons on his vest, and then, if he could, photograph them at work. He visited children and families who worked at home and he wrote with impassioned sarcasm of "'opportunities' for the child and the family to enlist in the service of industry" (quoted in Gutman [1967], p. 23).

Hine's photographs were used to make lantern slides for lectures and to illustrate pamphlets, magazine articles, and exhibitions. Hine himself arranged layouts, wrote reports based on his field interviews, and was in charge of NCLC exhibitions (ca. 1915). His images helped win passage of child-labor laws — they constituted proof that the conditions the NCLC wrote about actually existed and they made the plight of the children real.

Hine strove to photograph positive qualities in life, especially the dignity of labor. From 1930 to 1931 he took hundreds of pictures of the Empire State Building under construction; they were published in *Men at Work* along with photographs of factory workers and other laborers. He wrote: "Some of them are heroes; all of them persons it is a privilege to know" (quoted in Stott, *Documentary*, p. 213).

Though early in Hine's career his photographs were often published, by the 1930s interest in his work had declined. In 1938 he was denied a grant to photograph American craftspeople at work. The Photo League in New York publicized his work but it was not until a number of years after his death that he again received wide recognition. Hine referred to his photographs as "photo-interpretations." As Judith Mara Gutman observed: "Hine shaped a new art form. . . . a kind of photography he called 'interpretive,' later schools called documentary. . . . a flat fiery arrangement of people, light, and form that became a timeless humanist art" (*Lewis W. Hine and the American Conscience*, p. 47).

WORK Includes immigrants at Ellis Island before World War I; life and work of slum dwellers; many scenes of children in mines, factories, agriculture, street trades; street scenes in numerous cities; people at work (e.g., in factories, constructing the Empire State Building); American Red Cross relief in Europe and America (1918 and after); small towns and rural America (1930s); Tennessee Valley Authority projects (1933).

MEDIA Gelatin dry-plate negatives (5×7) and (later) film negatives (4×5); silver prints.

AVAILABILITY AND PRICE Through galleries and at auction. Duplicate vintage prints from both the IMP/GEH and NCLC collec-

Lewis Wickes Hine. *Young Coal Mine Workers, Pennsylvania,* 1911. Silver print. (Courtesy The Witkin Gallery)

tions frequently found (usually 5×7, but also 8×10 to 16×20). Most not signed but may have description on back in Hine's or another's handwriting. Condition varies; most were work prints, not exhibition quality, but still are powerful images. Moderate to moderately high.

SIGNATURE/OTHER IDENTIFICATION

LEWIS W. HINE
INTERPRETIVE PHOTOGRAPHY
HASTINGS-ON-HUDSON, NEW YORK

PORTFOLIOS *See* chapter 6 entry.

COLLECTIONS Gutman rates as "the best single survey of Hine's life and work" the IMP/GEH holdings (Hine's personal collection of negatives, prints, correspondence, etc., which went to the Photo League after his death). Other major collections include: Maryland (NCLC work); Minnesota Archives (small-town and rural photographs); Columbia (Empire State Building and other photographs); NYPL (Genealogy, Picture); American Red Cross Headquarters, Washington, D.C. (work after 1930, not identified by photographer); LOC (NCLC work and an uncatalogued American Red Cross collection of work up to 1930); National Archives (Works Progress Administration collection); TVA. Also Chicago, Detroit, Minneapolis, Minnesota, MOMA, New Mexico, New Orleans, Princeton, Smithsonian.

SELECTED BIBLIOGRAPHY
Paul Underwood Kellog, ed. *The Pittsburgh Survey: Findings in Six Volumes.* New York: Charities Publication Committee (later New York Survey Association), Russell Sage Publication [ca. 1911].
Homer Folks. *The Human Cost of War.* New York: Harper, 1920.
Men at Work: Photographic Studies of Modern Men and Machines. New York: Macmillan, 1932. Rev. ed., New York: Dover, 1977.
Through the Threads: An Interpretation of the Creation of Beautiful Fabrics. New York: Blumenthal, 1933.
Else H. Naumburg, Clara Lambert, and Lucy Sprague Mitchell. *Skyscraper.* New York: John Day, 1933.
Judith Mara Gutman. *Lewis W. Hine and the American Social Conscience.* New York: Walker, 1967. Bibliography.
Thomas F. Barrow. *In Ordering Use This Number 1756 Hine Photo Company . . . .* Rochester, N.Y.: GEH, 1970. 12 Hine reproductions in portfolio.
Judith Mara Gutman. *Lewis W. Hine, 1874-1940.* New York: Grossman, 1974.
Walter Rosenblum, Naomi Rosenblum, and Alan Trachtenberg. *America & Lewis Hine: Photographs 1904-1940.* Millerton, N.Y.: Aperture, 1976. Bibliography.
The Lewis W. Hine Document. Intro. by Naomi Rosenblum. Brooklyn Museum, 1977. 16 reproductions in portfolio.
Many of Hine's photographs were published in the early 1900s in *Charities and Commons, Red Cross Magazine, Survey, Survey Graphic,* and other periodicals.
See also Life Library, Documentary, Great Photographers; Szarkowski, *Looking.*

Hofer, Evelyn
United States (b. Germany) Contemporary

Hofer planned to become a musician but later changed her profession to photography and apprenticed in two commercial studios in Switzerland. She came to the United States in 1947 and began working with Alexey Brodovitch as a fashion photographer for *Harper's Bazaar.* Later she worked for *Vogue.*

Hofer's career took a decisive turn when the painter Eugene Berman introduced her to writer Mary McCarthy, with whom she collaborated on the book *The Stones of Florence;* this work led to other books on famous cities of the world. In the 1960s Hofer began doing her many photographic essays for Time-Life Books; she has done numerous assignments for the "*Life* Special Reports" series, and for *The New York Times Magazine* and *The Sunday Times Magazine* (London).

Hofer's work with a 4×5 view camera is serenely straightforward and characterized by clarity of detail. Hilton Kramer wrote: "Distinguished, above all, for the exalted sense of form that characterizes her every image, Miss Hofer's pictures are also miracles of visual nuance. She has an extraordinary eye for subtle differences in the quality of life and in the details of texture and shape, whether her subject is the Duomo in Florence or two young waiters in a Dublin restaurant, and she has extraor-

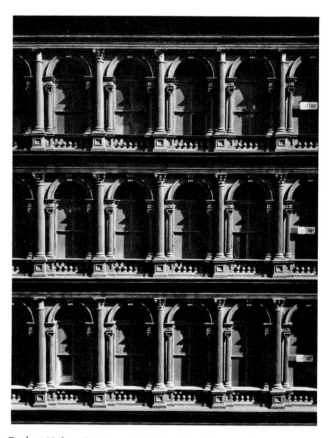

Evelyn Hofer. *Cast-Iron Building, Broadway and Broome,* ca. 1965. Silver print. (Courtesy The Witkin Gallery)

dinary patience, too, in capturing from every subject the exact image she intends to wrest from it" (*New York Times*, 25 Feb. 1977).

WORK   Includes architecture and people of cities and countries of the world, photographic essays (e.g., ghost towns; the history of the Irish Cross; the Negro in Washington, D.C.; Samuel Pepys's London; J. M. W. Turner's home in Petworth, England; Watergate; Gerald Ford's hometown of Grand Rapids, Michigan; life in English prisons; Michelangelo; Arthur Rubinstein).

MEDIA   Silver prints, color.

AVAILABILITY AND PRICE   Modern prints available through galleries; silver prints (about 11×14) moderate, limited-edition dye transfer color prints moderately high.

SIGNATURE/OTHER IDENTIFICATION

COLLECTIONS   Indiana, MMA, Smith.

SELECTED BIBLIOGRAPHY
Maurice Sandoz. *The Pleasures of Mexico*. New York: Kamin, 1957.
Mary McCarthy. *The Stones of Florence*. New York: Harcourt, Brace & World, 1959.
V. S. Pritchett. *London Perceived*. New York: Harcourt, Brace & World, 1962.
James Morris. *The Presence of Spain*. New York: Harcourt, Brace & World, 1964.
V. S. Pritchett. *New York Proclaimed*. New York: Harcourt, Brace & World, 1965.
William Walton. *The Evidence of Washington*. New York: Harper & Row, 1966.
V. S. Pritchett. *Dublin: A Portrait*. New York: Harper & Row, 1967.
Time-Life Books. Essays and individual photographs appear in Charles Blitzer, *Age of Kings* (1967); Gerald Simons, *Barbarian Europe* (1968); *The District of Columbia* (1968); Diana Hirsh, *The World of Turner* (1969); Peter S. Feibleman, *The Bayous* (1973).
See also Life Library, *Color*.

Hoppé, Emil Otto
Germany 1878–1972

E. O. Hoppé worked for a number of years as a banker before he turned to photography in 1907. He was a prolific and well-known portrait photographer in England in the 1910s and 1920s and many members of London high society sat for him. From the 1930s on he concentrated on travel views, which he took on his many trips throughout the world. He exhibited frequently, wrote extensively, and published numerous books in England and Germany. He was a founding member of The London Salon of Photography, a 1910 outgrowth of the pictorialist group The Linked Ring. Although Hoppé retouched his portraits and used soft focus, he did so less than many of his then-fashionable contemporaries, and today his work seems less romanticized and more modern than theirs.

WORK   Includes portraits, travel views.

MEDIA   Silver prints, platinum prints.

AVAILABILITY AND PRICE   Frequently available through galleries and at auction; low to moderately high. Fine gravures found in some books.

SIGNATURE/OTHER IDENTIFICATION

COLLECTIONS   IMP/GEH, Texas (Gernsheim). In England: Kodak, Mansell, RPS.

Emil Otto Hoppé. *Sinclair Lewis, London*, July 1921. Silver print. (Courtesy Lee D. Witkin)

SELECTED BIBLIOGRAPHY
Studies from the Russian Ballet, 1911.
Arthur St. John Adcock. *Gods of Modern Grub Street: Impressions of Contemporary Authors.* London: Sampson Low, Marston, 1913. Another ed., *The Glory That Was Grub Street,* 1928.
The Book of Fair Women. Intro. by Richard King. New York: Knopf, 1922. 500 copies.
Taken from Life. With J. D. Beresford. London: Collins, 1922.
Picturesque Great Britain: The Architecture and the Landscape. Intro. by Charles F. G. Masterman. New York: Brentano's, 1926, and Berlin: Wasmuth, 1926.
The United States of America. London: Studio, 1927. U.S. ed., *Romantic America: Picturesque United States.* New York: Westermann, 1927.
Deutsche Arbeit: Bilder von Wiederaufstieg Deutschlands. Berlin: Ullstein, 1930.
Round the World with a Camera. London: Hutchinson, 1934.
The Image of London. London: Chatto & Windus, 1935.
A Camera on Unknown London. London: Dent, 1936.
Hundred Thousand Exposures: The Success of a Photographer. Intro. by Cecil Beaton. London: Focal Press, 1945.
Camera Portraits by E. O. Hoppé. Text by Terence Pepper. London: National Portrait Gallery, 1978. Bibliography.
Blaue Berge von Jamaica. Berlin: Safari, n.d.
See also Gernsheim, *Creative Photography.*

SIGNATURE/OTHER IDENTIFICATION

COLLECTIONS   IMP/GEH, MOMA, Nebraska, Smithsonian; BN, Tokyo.

SELECTED BIBLIOGRAPHY
Man and Woman. Japan: Camerart, 1961.
Killed by Roses. Text by Yukio Mishima. Tokyo: Shuei-sha, 1963. Reissued in different form as *Ordeal by Roses,* 1971.
Miyuki Futata. *Why, Mother, Why? The Tragedy and Triumph of a Little Girl — in Poetry and Pictures.* Tokyo: Kodan-sha, 1965.
Kamaitachi: A Tragic Comedy. Preface by Shuzo Takiguchi. Poem by Toyoichiro Miyoshi. Tokyo: Gendaishicho-sha, 1969.
Embrace. Preface by Yukio Mishima. Tokyo: Shashin Hyoron-sha, 1971.
Camera, Oct. 1970.
"Ordeal by Roses." Text by Yukio Mishima. *Aperture,* no. 79 (1977), pp. 44–63.
See also Lewis, *Darkroom 1;* Lyons, *20th Century;* Szarkowski, *Japanese.*

Hosoe, Eikoh
Japan 1933–

Very active and well-known internationally, Hosoe graduated from the Tokyo School of Photography in 1954. He has free-lanced since then and periodically exhibits, gives lectures, and teaches workshops in the United States and elsewhere. Much of Hosoe's work freely explores fantasies and dreams, in a blend of sexuality, mystery, and allegory. High contrast and other stylized printing choices further enhance his images and separate them from reality. His series "Man and Woman" and "Embrace" explore human bodies in abstracted yet sensual images.

Yukio Mishima, the Japanese writer who posed for Hosoe's *Killed by Roses,* commented in the text: "I had seen some of the magical work produced with the camera, but Hosoe's work is not so much simple magic as a kind of mechanical sorcery; it is the use of this civilized precision instrument for purposes utterly opposed to civilization. The world to which I was abducted under the spell of his lens was abnormal, warped, sarcastic, grotesque, savage, and promiscuous . . . yet there was a clear undercurrent of lyricism murmuring gently through its unseen conduits."

WORK   Surreal evocations of personal worlds and landscapes. (See illustration, page 25.)

MEDIUM   Silver prints.

AVAILABILITY AND PRICE   Through galleries; under 20×24 moderate, 20×24 moderately high.

Eikoh Hosoe. *Kamaitachi,* 1969. Silver print. (Courtesy Light Gallery. Copyright © by Eikoh Hosoe)

Hujar, Peter
United States 1934–

A successful fashion and advertising photographer for many years, Hujar decided in 1968 to concentrate on his personal work. He has cited Richard Avedon, Irving Penn, and Bill Brandt as influences.

On a trip to the catacombs in Palermo, Italy, in 1966, he photographed the mummified remains there and began thinking of their application to portraiture. His book *Portraits in Life and Death*, in which he juxtaposes photographs of the living with the catacomb images, is the result of this exploration. Susan Sontag wrote: "His fleshed and moist-eyed friends stand, sit, slouch, mostly lie — and are made to appear to meditate on their own mortality. The Palermo photographs — which precede these portraits in time — complete them, comment upon them" (*Portraits in Life and Death*). Hujar prints his portraits of the living in large format. Shot from the waist up, his subjects either address the camera directly or look away in a tranquil, pensive, serious mood.

WORK Portraits of friends and acquaintances, and corpses in Palermo catacombs. Also early commercial work.

MEDIUM Silver prints.

AVAILABILITY AND PRICE Through galleries; moderate.

SIGNATURE/OTHER IDENTIFICATION

COLLECTION Princeton (Art Museum).

Peter Hujar. *Susan Sontag,* 1975. Silver print. (Courtesy Marcuse Pfeifer Gallery)

SELECTED BIBLIOGRAPHY
Portraits in Life and Death. Intro. by Susan Sontag. New York: Da Capo, 1976.

Hyde, Scott
United States 1926–

From 1947 to 1949, while studying art at the Art Students League in New York City, Scott Hyde photographed for Condé Nast Publications. In 1950 he left Condé Nast to do free-lance commercial work, which he continues in addition to teaching. His personal work explores color imagery, although he seldom uses color films. He explained: "I do my original photography on black-and-white films. I print several of these images together, each in a different color for the final multicolor picture. . . . One major concern is finding ways to render the effects of color and light that I see in nature. . . . Another area of interest is the relationship between a given subject, seen in nature, and the same subject seen in print, and the transformations that can occur in the image-making process.

"My choices for subject matter are made from a visual/esthetic attitude; that is, my subjects have beauty for me. Although photography is rich in anecdotal, documentary and commentary possibilities, these do not concern me currently. The conceptual possibilities, however, as well as experiments with various print processes, do play a minor role in my work" (statement to the authors, 1977).

WORK Includes superimposed images (e.g., a painting and street scenes, several views of a kitchen table), often printed in high contrast.

MEDIA Silver prints, silkscreen prints, color photo-offset lithographs, gum-bichromate prints (and variations). Sizes range from about 8×10 to 22×28.

AVAILABILITY AND PRICE Through galleries; extremely low for press prints to moderately high for unique multiple gum prints.

SIGNATURE/OTHER IDENTIFICATION

COLLECTIONS High, IMP/GEH, Kansas, MMA, MOMA, New Mexico, New York, Norton Simon, Pomona, UCLA; BN, NGC.

SELECTED BIBLIOGRAPHY
CAPS Book. New York: published by the photographer, 1975. 10 original color photo-offset lithographs.
Gallery Association of New York State. *On the Offset Press.* Syracuse, N.Y.: Lightwork, 1977. Includes 1 color offset print by Hyde.
Modern Photography Annual 1974.
"Pictures by Scott Hyde." Text by Hyde and Syl Labrot. *Aperture* 15, no. 2 (1970).
See also Szarkowski, *Mirrors;* chapter 7 catalogue.

1917 PENNY BRIDGE AND COUNTY ROAD, Stony Point, N. Y. *1968*

Scott Hyde. *1917 Penny Bridge and County Road, Stony Point, N.Y.,* 1968. Montage combining a 1917 picture postcard view and a 1968 photograph from the same viewpoint. (Courtesy The Witkin Gallery)

Jackson, William Henry
United States 1843–1942

Jackson was a prolific photographer who during his long life actively published and wrote about his work, and he is to many people the best known of the nineteenth-century western-landscape photographers. He began as a photographic retoucher in the East. In 1866 he made his first trip to the West, as a trail drover, and sketched scenes of camp life but did not photograph. In 1867, with his brother, he established a photographic portrait studio in Omaha, but he soon found he preferred outdoor work. By 1869 he was traveling with A. C. Hull westward along the Union Pacific Railroad from Omaha, photographing towns, settlers, railroad workers, and some landscapes (work that has survived almost entirely as stereographs).

Jackson's artistic growth as a landscape photographer began in 1870 when he was hired by F. V. Hayden as the official photographer for the U.S. Geological and Geographical Survey of the Territories. According to Weston J. Naef, within a few years Jackson fully matured as a landscape photographer: "Consciously or not, he had absorbed the esthetic of picturesque romanticism. The inherent drama of a panorama extending miles into the distance was his preference, and wherever possible a figure was tastefully introduced.... The photographs have a self-conscious artfulness that is as evident as naïveté was in the 1869 series" (Naef and Wood, *Era,* p. 224).

Jackson's photographs of Yellowstone, made on one of the surveys, were shown in Washington, D.C., and helped influence Congress to establish Yellowstone National Park. In 1879 he left government service and established the Jackson Photographic Company in Denver, which specialized in commissioned landscapes for the railroads. He began regularly to use a mammoth-plate camera to document the landscape and natural wonders with which

the railroads hoped to entice travelers and settlers. In 1898 he became part owner of the Detroit Publishing Company, which published many of his landscapes as well as views by other photographers. He photographed primarily in the West, though he also worked in other parts of the United States and the world.

In 1942 Jackson visited the Department of Photography at the Museum of Modern Art in New York City, linking — as incredible as that seems — the expeditionary photographers of the Old West and "modern" photography.

WORK Includes views of Omaha and along the Union Pacific Railroad route (1867–1869); Hayden Survey scenes (1870–1879; e.g., Yellowstone region, Colorado Rockies, ethnological studies of Indians); genre scenes and scenic views of natural wonders in the West (1879–1896; on railroad assignment); foreign scenes — primarily India, Far East, Siberia (1894) — for "World's Transportation Commission"; scenes of eastern United States, Mexico, Central America, and the Caribbean (1883–1884, 1900–1905).

MEDIA Early work: collodion wet-plate negatives, albumen prints (ranging from stereographs to 20×24; almost always mounted on board of the period). Later work: gelatin dry-plate negatives and film negatives; silver prints. Often identifiable by number and title in plate, plus (after 1880) "W. H. Jackson & Co., Denver, Col." in plate. May also be identified on mount (e.g., government-issued Hayden Survey prints, which are 11×14 on 16×20 white mounts with gold borders). Also lithographed postcards.

AVAILABILITY AND PRICE Through galleries and at auction. Large rich-tone albumen prints (ca. 16×20 on 22×28 mounts) of prime subject matter are rare; extremely high. Cabinet photographs frequently found; low. Many other prints are available, varying in size, quality, and price.

COLLECTIONS The National Archives preserves Hayden Survey albumen prints. The Library of Congress holds: a portion of the working files of the Detroit Publishing Company (including 20,000 prints and 30,000 glass-plate negatives, many by Jackson);

William Henry Jackson. *Old Acqueduct* [sic] *at Querétaro, Mexico,* ca. 1880s. Albumen print. (Courtesy Lee D. Witkin)

800 prints plus many glass plates from Central America and the Caribbean; 350 film negatives of India, Far East, Siberia. The State Historical Society of Colorado (Denver) holds 7,000 negatives (civilian work west of the Mississippi, 1880–1902) plus other material. The Bureau of Ethnology (Washington, D.C.) holds 2,000 negatives of Pawnee and Omaha Indians. Also Academy of Natural Sciences, Antiquarian Society, Amon Carter, BPL, California (Bancroft), Denver, Harvard, IMP/GEH, Museum of New Mexico, New Mexico, Princeton (Library), Smithsonian, UCLA, Yale (Beinecke).

SIGNATURE/OTHER IDENTIFICATION

W.H.JACKSON & C? DENVER.COL.

SELECTED BIBLIOGRAPHY

U.S. Dept. of the Interior, U.S. Geological Survey. *Photographs of the Yellowstone National Park and Views in Montana and Wyoming Territories.* Washington, D.C., 1873. 37 prints, ca. 11×14, on 16×20 mounts, each with descriptive letterpress guardsheet.

———. *Views of the Yellowstone.* Washington, D.C., 1871. 81 prints.

Portraits of American Indians: 1876. Washington, D.C.: privately printed, 1876. 616 prints, selected from Hayden Survey.

Denver & Rio Grande Railroad Co. Rocky Mountain Scenery. New York: American Bank Note Co. [ca. 1885]. 12 albertype prints, 9 with Jackson name in plate.

Grand Cañon of the Arkansas. Denver: Jackson [1880s]. 12 ills.

The White City (as it was . . .). Chicago: White City Art Co., 1894. 80 photoetchings of the World Centennial Exposition.

Wonder-Places: The Most Perfect Pictures of Magnificent Scenes in the Rocky Mountains. Denver: Great Divide, 1894. 21 ills.

Jackson's Famous Pictures of the World's Fair, 1893. Chicago: White City Art Co., 1895. 80 ills.

Among the Rockies: Pictures of Magnificent Scenes in the Rocky Mountains. Denver: Great Divide, 1900.

The Cañons of Colorado. Denver: Thayer, 1900.

The Pioneer Photographer: Rocky Mountain Adventures with a Camera. With Howard R. Driggs. Yonkers-on-Hudson, N.Y.: World Book, 1929.

Drawings of the Oregon Trail. New York [?], 1929–30. 6 ills.

Time Exposure. New York: Putnam, 1940. Reprint, New York: Cooper Square, 1970. Autobiography.

Clarence S. Jackson. *Picture Maker of the Old West: William Henry Jackson.* New York: Scribner, 1947.

———. *Pageant of the Pioneers: The Veritable Art of William H. Jackson, "Picture Maker of the Old West."* Minden, Nebr.: Harold Warp Pioneer Village, 1958.

The Diaries of William Henry Jackson, Frontier Photographer. Ed., intro., and notes by LeRoy R. Hafen and Ann W. Hafen. Glendale, Calif.: Clarke, 1959.

Aylsea Forsee. *William Henry Jackson: Pioneer Photographer of the West.* New York: Viking, 1964.

Helen Markley Miller. *Lens on the West: The Story of William Henry Jackson.* New York: Doubleday, 1966.

Beaumont Newhall and Diana E. Edkins. *William Henry Jackson.* Dobbs Ferry, N.Y.: Morgan & Morgan, 1974. Bibliography.

William C. Jones and Elizabeth Jones. *William Henry Jackson's Colorado.* Boulder, Colo.: Pruett, 1975. Also limited ed.

See also Andrews, *Pioneers;* Life Library, *Great Photographers, Light;* Naef and Wood, *Era;* Szarkowski, *Looking;* Taft, *Photography.*

Jacobi, Lotte
United States (b. Germany) 1896–

Jacobi is a fourth-generation photographer, her great-grandfather having learned the art from L. J. M. Daguerre. After studying at the Bavarian State Academy of Photography and the University of Munich, she took over the responsibility for her father's Berlin studio in 1927 and became one of Germany's best-known portrait photographers. Her work was widely exhibited and in 1931 she received the silver medal at the Royal Photography Salon in Tokyo. In 1935 she fled Nazi Germany, settled in New York City, and there opened a studio. Among her sitters were Albert Einstein, Eleanor Roosevelt, W. H. Auden, Marianne Moore, and Robert Frost, as well as photographers Alfred Stieglitz, Edward Steichen, and Paul Strand. "I love to photograph," she once said. "I love people and like to find out about them through the photographs I take of them. I try not to have a preconceived idea of how anybody should look. In a way, I exclude myself from the photographs . . ." (statement to the authors, 1977).

In addition to her portraits, Jacobi is noted for works she calls "photogenics," with which she began experimenting in the 1950s; these are cameraless, nonobjective photographic prints that she creates directly on paper under an enlarger or with a flashlight by passing translucent or opaque materials, or both, between the light beam and

Lotte Jacobi. Untitled, ca. 1950. "Photogenic" print. (Courtesy Kimmel/Cohn Photography Arts)

the light-sensitive material. The results are lyrical and evocative abstractions.

In 1963 she opened Lotte Jacobi Place in Deering, New Hampshire, where she exhibited the work of various artists, including photographers such as Minor White, Robert and Frances Flaherty, and Albert Renger-Patzsch. She continued actively photographing and has had many one-woman shows, particularly during the mid-seventies.

WORK Includes portraits; abstract "photogenics" (generally unique) and photomontages; nature.

MEDIA Chiefly silver prints. Also bromoil-transfer prints, platinum prints. Recent (1970s) palladium prints, titled and signed by Jacobi, have been made by Carlos Richardson from her negatives.

AVAILABILITY AND PRICE Through galleries and at auction. Most work before 1935 was left in Berlin and destroyed. Vintage and unique images high; other images, including modern silver prints made under the photographer's supervision, moderate to high.

SIGNATURE/OTHER IDENTIFICATION

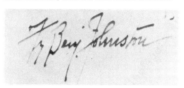

PORTFOLIO *See* chapter 6 entry.

COLLECTIONS Maryland, MOMA; Folkwang, Schiller.

SELECTED BIBLIOGRAPHY
Lotte Jacobi: Menschen von Gestern und Heute — Fotografische Porträts, Skizzen und Dokumentationen. Essen: Museum Folkwang, 1973.
James A. Fasanelli. *Lotte Jacobi.* Danbury, N.H.: Addison House, 1979. Also limited ed. with 1 original print.
Albert Einstein: 100th Anniversary, March 14, 1979. Deering, N.H.: published by the photographer, 1979. 25 reproductions on loose sheets.
Infinity, Apr. 1960.
"Lotte Jacobi — Photogenics." *Aperture* 10, no. 1 (1962): 4–15.
Camera, Apr. 1967.
Popular Photography, July 1967.
Richard M. Bacon. "Lotte Jacobi." *Yankee,* Aug. 1976, pp. 60–67.
See also Mann, *Women;* chapter 7 catalogue.

Johnston, Frances Benjamin
United States 1864–1952

Johnston studied art in Paris and Washington, D.C., and in the late 1880s began to write for magazines, first illustrating her articles with her own drawings, then with photographs. In the early 1890s she opened a studio in Washington and was quickly a success, active and resourceful in pursuit of photographs she wanted. She published extensively, received many important assignments, and traveled and lectured widely.

Known as the first woman press photographer, Johnston encouraged other women to become photographers, writing articles about them and arranging exhibitions of their work. In the latter part of her long career she concentrated on architectural photography, extensively documenting historic American buildings in the South, which she realized had not been recorded as had early architecture in the Northeast.

Johnston produced and exhibited some pictorial work (in the style of her friend Gertrude Käsebier), but she is best known as a journalist and documentary photographer; her direct and detailed images are an important record of her time. Lincoln Kirstein described Johnston's style in the best of her work as "a simple monumentality in miniature, a sober austere placement of figures" (*The Hampton Album,* p. 9).

WORK Includes photojournalism for the popular press and various official commissions (e.g., Pennsylvania coalfields; Mammoth Cave; Washington, D.C., school system; U.S. Mint and Bureau of Engraving and Printing; Hampton Institute, Virginia), portraits (e.g., U.S. presidents from Cleveland to Taft, other Washington notables and their families), pictorial photographs, architectural photographs (1909 and after, including historic architecture and gardens of the South, beginning in the late 1920s).

MEDIA Gelatin dry-plate negatives (6½ × 8½) and film negatives (5 × 7; also 4 × 5, 8 × 10); platinum prints, silver prints.

AVAILABILITY AND PRICE Most vintage prints are in museum collections and relatively few come on the market; moderate to moderately high when available. Modern prints from the Library of Congress extremely low (not all negatives are in good condition, however).

SIGNATURE/OTHER IDENTIFICATION

Frances Benjamin Johnston. *Science Class Studying Water Vapor, Second Division School, Washington, D.C.,* 1899. Modern silver print from the original negative. (Library of Congress)

COLLECTIONS The Library of Congress received from Johnston most of her negatives plus many prints. The Henry E. Huntington Library and Art Gallery (San Marino, Calif.) holds about 1,200 portrait negatives (ca. 1880-1910). Also Carnegie, Harvard (Carpenter), MMA, MOMA.

SELECTED BIBLIOGRAPHY
Booker T. Washington. *Working with the Hands.* New York: Doubleday, Page, 1904.
Colonial Churches in Virginia. With Henry Irving Brock. Richmond: Dale Press, 1930.
Plantations of the Carolina Low Country. Text by Samuel Gaillard Stoney. Charleston, S.C.: Carolina Art Association, 1939.
The Early Architecture of North Carolina. With Thomas Tileston Waterman. Chapel Hill: University of North Carolina Press, 1941.
The Mansions of Virginia, 1706-1776. Text by Thomas Tileston Waterman. Chapel Hill: University of North Carolina Press, 1945.
The Dwellings of Colonial America. Text by Thomas Tileston Waterman. Chapel Hill: University of North Carolina Press, 1950.
The Early Architecture of Georgia. With Frederick Doveton Nichols. Chapel Hill: University of North Carolina Press, 1957.
The Hampton Album. Text by Lincoln Kirstein. New York: MOMA, 1966.
Pete Daniel and Raymond Smock. *A Talent for Detail: The Photographs of Miss Frances Benjamin Johnston 1889-1910.* New York: Harmony, 1974.
Demorest's Family Magazine, Dec. 1889 and Jan. 1890, contains Johnston's first photographically illustrated articles. Many photographs were published in *Demorest's Ladies' Home Journal,* *Lester's Magazine,* *Town and Country,* and other periodicals of the time.
See also Mann, *Women;* Szarkowski, *Looking;* Tucker, *Eye.*

Josephson, Kenneth
United States 1932–

Ken Josephson studied photography at the Rochester (N.Y.) Institute of Technology, and at the Chicago Institute of Design under Harry Callahan and Aaron Siskind. At one time a photographer for Chrysler Corporation, he turned to free-lancing and teaching photography. In his personal work Josephson explores the overlaps and differences between photography and reality, often playing with juxtapositions — for example, holding up a print of a scene within his lens's view of the same scene. For *The Bread Book* he photographed the front and back sides of the slices of a loaf of bread and arranged the images in order, one side of each slice to a page, compressing the entire loaf into a thin booklet.

"Kenneth Josephson's photographs successfully combine humour and a gentle surrealism," Marie Czach pointed out. "They are, essentially, pictures about picture-making, taking as their point of departure the idiom of the amateur snapshot. Capitalizing upon the 'mistakes' found in almost every family photograph album [he] refines these phenomena and skilfully makes them a part of his visual vocabulary" (quoted in "Kenneth Josephson").

Kenneth Josephson. *New York State,* 1970. Silver print. (Courtesy the artist)

WORK Includes the following, as described by the photographer: "Expression of visual ideas made possible by the photographic medium; the special reality of photographs; humor and surrealism; chance and accident; manipulative photography; snapshots" (ibid., p. 4).

MEDIA Silver prints, photocollage and assemblage.

AVAILABILITY AND PRICE Through galleries; moderate to moderately high.

SIGNATURE/OTHER IDENTIFICATION

PORTFOLIOS See chapter 6 entry.

COLLECTIONS Chicago, Harvard (Fogg), IMP/GEH, MOMA, Nebraska, Norton Simon, UCLA; BN, NGC.

SELECTED BIBLIOGRAPHY
The Bread Book. Chicago: published by the photographer, 1973.
"Kenneth Josephson." *Camera,* May 1974, pp. 4-11.
Creative Camera, Aug. 1974.
Alex Sweetman. "Reading the Bread Book . . . ." *Afterimage* 2 (Mar. 1974): 10-11.
Max Kozloff. "Photos within Photographs." *Artforum* 14 (Feb. 1976): 34-39.
See also Hume, *The Great West;* Life Library, *Children;* Szarkowski, *Looking, Mirrors;* Wise, *Choice;* chapter 7 catalogues.

Karsh, Yousuf
Canada (b. Armenia) 1908–

Karsh, who originally wanted to be a physician, was brought to Canada by his uncle, a photographer. He apprenticed in Boston to the portrait photographer John Garo, and in 1932 opened his own portrait studio in Ottawa. In 1941 he became internationally known when his portrait of a stern Winston Churchill appeared on the cover of *Life* magazine. The story behind the portrait is now legendary: the photograph captured Churchill's reaction when Karsh pulled a freshly lit cigar from the prime minister's mouth.

Since then Karsh has photographed thousands of illustrious men and women — Elizabeth II, John F. Kennedy, Pablo Picasso, Georgia O'Keeffe, Edward Steichen, Jawaharlal Nehru, Pablo Casals, Nikita Khrushchev, Ernest Hemingway, plus many others — and each portrait is a synthesis of the personality and public role of the subject. Karsh prefers to photograph people in their own environment and travels widely doing so. His portraits, usually made with an 8×10-inch view camera, are carefully posed and lit, and his prints typically have deep, rich blacks, often with the subject's face and hands highlighted.

WORK Best known for portraits, chiefly of well-known figures in the arts, science, and government. Also includes still lifes, children in a hospital, cities.

MEDIUM Silver prints (about 14×17 and 16×20).

AVAILABILITY AND PRICE Through galleries; moderately high to high.

COLLECTIONS Chicago, IMP/GEH, MMA, MOMA, St. Louis; NGC, NPG.

SIGNATURE/OTHER IDENTIFICATION

SELECTED BIBLIOGRAPHY
Faces of Destiny. New York: Prentice-Hall, 1946.
This Is the Mass. Text by Fulton J. Sheen and Henri Daniel-Rops. New York: Hawthorn, 1958.
Portraits of Greatness. Toronto: University of Toronto Press, 1959.
This Is Rome. Text by Fulton J. Sheen and H. V. Morton. New York: Hawthorn, 1959.
This Is the Holy Land. Text by Fulton J. Sheen and H. V. Morton. New York: Hawthorn, 1960.
In Search of Greatness: Reflections of Yousuf Karsh. Toronto: University of Toronto Press, and New York: Knopf, 1962.
These Are the Sacraments. Text by Fulton J. Sheen. New York: Hawthorn, 1962.
The Warren Court. Text by John P. Frank. New York: Macmillan, 1965.
Karsh Portfolio. Toronto: University of Toronto Press, and New York: Nelson, 1967.
Faces of Our Time. Toronto: University of Toronto Press, 1971.
Karsh Portraits. Toronto: University of Toronto Press, and Boston: New York Graphic Society, 1976.
Karsh Canadians. Toronto: University of Toronto Press, 1978.
See also Danziger and Conrad, *Interviews*; Life Library, *Great Photographers, Themes.*

Käsebier, Gertrude
United States 1852–1934

Käsebier turned to art and photography relatively late in life, after raising a family. Beginning about 1888 she studied painting in New York City and Paris, but by 1893 was concentrating on photography. In 1897 she opened a studio in New York and successfully introduced natural poses and a creative style into the relatively stereotyped commercial portrait photography common at the time. A founding member of the Photo-Secession (1902), she was also a member of The Linked Ring. Her Photo-Secession tie to Alfred Stieglitz was broken over his commitment to straight photography, and she was instrumental in founding the Pictorial Photographers of America (1916). Her photographs appeared in a number of magazines, including *McClure's, Scribner's, Camera Notes, The Craftsman, The Monthly Illustrator, The Photographic Times,* and *Camera Work*.

Käsebier's work often depicts the relationships between women and children. She once described a photo session with her grown daughter, herself a mother: "There suddenly seemed to develop between us a greater intimacy than I had ever known before. Every barrier was down. We were not two women, mother and daughter, old and young, but two mothers with one feeling . . . the tremendous import of motherhood which we had both realized seemed to find its expression in this photograph" (quoted in Edgerton). For Käsebier, motherhood included both loving rewards and the penalty of conflict between home and

Yousuf Karsh. *Georgia O'Keeffe,* 1956. Silver print. (Courtesy the artist. Copyright © Karsh, Ottawa)

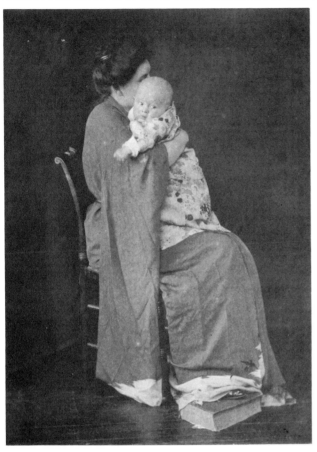

Gertrude Käsebier. *Nancy and Bubby (at Five Months), Autumn of 1900.* Platinum print. (Courtesy The Witkin Gallery)

career. Her images show children as sweet, even cherubic, and mothers as nurturing, but some of her photographs' titles, such as *Marriage: Yoked and Muzzled,* reveal an unsentimental view of the complexities involved.

WORK Includes pictorial work dealing with womanhood and motherhood (ca. 1898 and after), portraits (e.g., Rodin, Stieglitz, American Indians in Buffalo Bill's Wild West Troupe), illustrations of fiction. (See illustration, page 103.)

MEDIA Platinum prints, gum-bichromate prints, gum-platinum prints, bromoil prints, silver prints. Print or mount often bears Käsebier's distinctive signature, her monogram, or both.

SIGNATURE/OTHER IDENTIFICATION *See also* signed menu, page 103.

AVAILABILITY AND PRICE Through galleries and at auction, but most of the photographer's work was donated by her heirs to museums. Platinum and gum prints moderately high to high. *Camera Work* reproductions low to moderate.

COLLECTIONS Chicago, IMP/GEH, Kansas, LOC, MMA, MOMA, New Mexico, New Orleans, Princeton, Smithsonian; RPS.

SELECTED BIBLIOGRAPHY
Charles H. Caffin. "Mrs. Käsebier's Work — An Appreciation." *Camera Work,* no. 1 (1903), p. 17.
Frances Benjamin Johnston. "Gertrude Käsebier, Professional Photographer." Ibid., p. 20.
Giles Edgerton [Mary Fanton Roberts]. "Photography as an Emotional Art: A Study of the Work of Gertrude Käsebier." *The Craftsman,* 1907. Reprinted in *Image* 15 (Dec. 1972): 2–12.
Joseph T. Keiley. "Gertrude Käsebier." *Camera Work,* no. 20 (Oct. 1907), pp. 27–31.
Jane Cleland O'Mara. "Gertrude Käsebier . . . ." *Feminist Art Journal,* Winter 1974/75, pp. 18–20.
Barbara L. Michaels. "Rediscovering Gertrude Käsebier," *Image* 19 (June 1976): 20–32.
Mary Ann Tighe. "Gertrude Käsebier Lost and Found." *Art in America* 65 (Mar./Apr. 1977): 94–98.
Camera Work: Reproductions (gravures, halftone) in nos. 1, 10.
See also Green, *Camera Work;* Lawton and Know, *Knights;* Life Library, *Print;* Mann, *Women;* Naef, *Collection;* Tucker, *Eye;* Witkin, *Julien Levy.*

Kertész, André
United States (b. Austria-Hungary) 1894–

In the 1970s Kertész began to receive recognition as one of the major photographers of his time. He started photographing while a young man in Austria-Hungary, seeking to make a visual diary of his life. In 1925 he decided to devote himself to photography and left his business in Budapest to settle in Paris. There he did free-lance reportage and began his personal studies of daily experience. He pioneered in the use of the small-format camera and in photojournalism, influencing such photographers as Henri Cartier-Bresson and Brassaï. He was one of the first to photograph Paris at night.

"I began selling my pictures back in '26 in Paris," he recalled. "Julien Levy, the dealer, came in '29, and he wanted to sell my pictures in America. . . . He bought maybe 20 or 30 of my pictures; he sold maybe one or two. The selling price was twenty dollars" (quoted in McCabe, p. 285).

Kertész was widely known by the time he came to New York City in 1937. He did not plan to remain in America, but World War II forced him to stay. He supported himself by taking on commercial assignments — it was a period of his life that still frustrates him — yet he continued to enlarge and enrich his body of personal work, making many pictures from his apartment overlooking Washington Square Park.

Kertész's photographs are characterized by a keen perception of design and composition, by a curiosity about people, and by a great affection for human dignity found in the trivial details of daily existence. He photographs only what attracts him: "If I do not have the contact, I do not touch," he once explained (Life Library, *Documentary*, p. 125).

"Perhaps more than any other photographer, André Kertész discovered and demonstrated the special aesthetic of the small camera," wrote John Szarkowski. "Kertész had never been much interested in deliberate, analytical description; since he had begun photographing in 1912 he had sought the revelation of the elliptical view, the unexpected detail, the ephemeral moment — not the epic but the lyric truth. . . . He loved the play between pattern and deep space; the picture plane of his photographs is like a visual trampoline, taut and resilient. . . . In addition to this splendid and original quality of formal invention, there is in the work of Kertész another quality less easily analyzed, but surely no less important. It is a sense of the sweetness of life, a free and childlike pleasure in the beauty of the world and the preciousness of sight" (Szarkowski, *Looking*, p. 92).

André Kertész. *Distortion No. 147*, 1933. Silver print. (Courtesy the artist. Copyright © 1933 by André Kertész)

WORK Chiefly scenes of everyday life. Also includes distorted nudes (1930s), portraits of artists (e.g., Chagall), still lifes, reportage, fashion, architecture, landscapes. (See illustration, page 9.)

MEDIA Silver prints, some color (commercial work). Because of an allergy to chemicals, Kertész has been unable to print his negatives since the 1940s. Modern prints (8×10 and 11×14; signed on verso) are made to his approval by his private printer.

AVAILABILITY AND PRICE Through galleries and at auction. Modern prints moderately high to high, vintage prints extremely high.

SIGNATURE/OTHER IDENTIFICATION

A. Kertész

PORTFOLIOS *See* chapter 6 entry.

COLLECTIONS Detroit, Harvard (Carpenter), Kansas, Mint, MOMA, Nebraska, New Orleans, Smithsonian, Wellesley, Worcester; Pompidou.

SELECTED BIBLIOGRAPHY
Enfants. Text by Jaboune. Paris: Editions d'Histoire et d'Art, 1933.
Paris vu par André Kertész. Text by Pierre MacOrlan. Paris: Editions d'Histoire et d'Art, 1934.
Nos Amies les bêtes. Text by Jaboune. Paris: Editions d'Histoire et d'Art, 1936.
Les Cathédrals du vin. Text by Pierre Hamp. Paris: Sainrapt et Brice, 1937.
Day of Paris. Ed. by George Davis. New York: Augustin, 1945.
André Kertész, Photographer. Intro. by John Szarkowski. New York: MOMA, 1964. Bibliography.
Robert E. Hood, ed. *12 at War: Great Photographers under Fire.* New York: Putnam, 1967.
The Photographs of André Kertész. New York: Grossman, 1967.
Cornell Capa, ed. *The Concerned Photographer.* New York: Grossman, 1968.
On Reading. New York: Grossman, 1971.
André Kertész: Sixty Years of Photography, 1912-1972. Ed. by Nicolas Ducrot. New York: Grossman, 1972.
J'aime Paris: Photographs since the Twenties. Ed. by Nicolas Ducrot. New York: Grossman, 1974.
Distortions. Intro. by Hilton Kramer. New York: Knopf, 1976.
Of New York. New York: Knopf, 1976.
Washington Square. Intro. by Brendan Gill. New York: Grossman/Viking, 1976.
Cynthia Jaffe McCabe. *The Golden Door: Artist-Immigrants of America, 1876-1976.* Washington, D.C.: Hirshhorn Museum and Sculpture Garden, 1976.
André Kertész. Intro. by Carole Kismaric. Millerton, N.Y.: Aperture, 1977. Bibliography.
Brassaï. "My Friend Kertész." *Camera*, Apr. 1963.
Ruth Spencer. "André Kertész." *The British Journal of Photography*, 4 Apr. 1975, pp. 290-291.
Kertész's work appeared frequently in Condé Nast magazines (1940s-1950s).
See also Liberman, *Art* (in color bibliography); Life Library, *Documentary, Year 1973*; Szarkowski, *Looking*; Travis, *Julien Levy*; Witkin, *Julien Levy*; chapter 7 catalogue.

Kossoy, Boris
Brazil 1941–

Kossoy is a major artistic force and innovator in photography in Brazil. Head of the department of photography at the Museu de Arte in São Paulo, he has also run a gallery in São Paulo and has written extensively on the history of photography in Brazil.

Of his own work, which explores surrealistic imagery, Kossoy said: "I try to photograph individuals in their daily proceedings, anonymous or otherwise, which in [some] way or other cross my way in this world. There is an essence that I try to reach that is usually symbolized by beings (alive or otherwise), places, and things" (statement to the authors, 1976).

In his photographs, he wrote elsewhere, "people, real

and contrived, embark on fantastic journeys, searching futilely for a peace they will never find, submitting to the incongruous and the exceptional. . . . The 'Viewer' will interpret [the images] in his own fashion, identifying, perhaps, with his own thoughts, contritions, aspirations, follies and all that goes through his mind" (*Journey into the Fantastic*).

Boris Kossoy. *The Visit*, 1974. Silver print. (Courtesy the artist)

WORK   Surrealistic images.

MEDIUM   Silver prints.

AVAILABILITY AND PRICE   Through galleries; moderate.

SIGNATURE/OTHER IDENTIFICATION

COLLECTIONS   IMP/GEH, MMA, MOMA, Smithsonian; BN, São Paulo.

SELECTED BIBLIOGRAPHY
Journey into the Fantastic. Preface by P. M. Bardi. São Paulo: published by the photographer, 1971.

Koudelka, Josef
Czechoslovakia 1938–

Koudelka trained as an aeronautical engineer. He has been active as a theater photographer in Prague and has also spent much time studying and photographing the Gypsies of eastern Czechoslovakia. John Szarkowski commented: "Although many of Koudelka's pictures contain information concerning the specific daily details of Gypsy life, such anthropological data does not seem their real point. They seem instead to aim at a visual distillation of a pattern of human values: a pattern that involves theater, large gesture, brave style, precious camaraderie, and bitter loneliness. The pattern and texture of his pictures form

the silent equivalent of an epic drama" (Szarkowski, *Looking*, p. 202). Koudelka became a resident of Britain in 1970 and a member of the Magnum photo agency in 1971.

WORK   Includes Gypsies of Europe, the theater.

MEDIUM   Silver prints.

AVAILABILITY AND PRICE   Through galleries, at auction, and through the photographer's agent; moderate.

SIGNATURE/OTHER IDENTIFICATION

COLLECTIONS   MOMA; RPS.

SELECTED BIBLIOGRAPHY
Gypsies. Text by Willy Guy. Millerton, N.Y.: Aperture, 1975.
See also Life Library, *Year 1976*; Szarkowski, *Looking*; chapter 7 catalogue.

Krause, George
United States 1937–

Krause's interest in photography evolved while he attended the Philadelphia College of Art in the 1950s. During the late fifties he taught lithography, painting, and drawing, and later worked as a graphic designer and advertising photographer, while continuing to produce images on his own. In the early 1970s he abandoned commercial work to teach photography and explore his personal photographic interests. Except for a year off teaching at the American Academy in Rome, he has taught photography since 1975 at the University of Houston.

"I have noticed in some of my work a hint of a kind of fantasy," Krause once remarked. "To me real images such as photographic images give a more powerful feeling of fantasy than a manufactured one a painter might make. I plan to explore the medium of fantasy with the medium of photography" ("Young Talent," p. 54).

Mark Power wrote: "In many of George's pictures there's that finger pointing to the fantasy in our real past. His work is like the obverse side of Cartier-Bresson's coin; his strongest photographs for me capture those indecisive moments when man's persona takes over, moments when the spirit transcends the flesh: girls walking up stairs and changing to Alice-in-Wonderland, doors turning into faces, men metamorphosing into gods, gargoyles stepping off walls, tenuous moments when stone turns to flesh, or flesh to stone, and myth and legend walk among us" (*George Krause*).

WORK   Includes "Qui Riposa" series (gravestones in Italian-American cemeteries; 1960 and after); "Saints and Martyrs" series (statues in Mexican and Spanish churches; 1964 and after); street scenes, landscapes, portraits, and interiors from throughout the world; unusual nude studies (1976 and after).

George Krause. Untitled. From the series "Saints and Martyrs," 1964 and after. Silver print. (Courtesy the artist)

MEDIUM   Silver prints (some brown in tone; about 4×6 to 5×7).

AVAILABILITY AND PRICE   Through galleries; moderate.

SIGNATURE/OTHER IDENTIFICATION

George Krause

PORTFOLIO   *See* chapter 6 entry.

COLLECTIONS   Addison, BMFA, Houston, IMP/GEH, LOC, MOMA, Philadelphia; BN, Caracas.

SELECTED BIBLIOGRAPHY
George Krause. Intro. by Mark Power. Haverford, Pa.: Toll & Armstrong, 1972.
"Two Young Philadelphians: Don Donaghy, George Krause." Intro. by Murray Weiss. *Contemporary Photographer,* Fall 1962.
"Young Talent." *Art in America* 51 (June 1963): 54–55.
Art in America, Dec. 1964.
Camera, Aug./Sept. 1964.
"Malagueña." *Camera,* Jan. 1966, pp. 4–15.
Life, 23 Oct. 1970.
See also Lewis, *Darkroom 1;* Life Library, *Art, Children;* Szarkowski, *Looking, Mirrors.*

Krims, Leslie
United States 1943–

Trained as a painter, Krims became a self-taught photographer. He creates fictions, staged for the camera, of unlikely interactions of people with each other or with their environment — for example, a nude woman with her breast in a meat grinder, or a man's half-body screaming from a pedestal. The images reveal black humor, and like the art of other humorists who attack social conventions violently, Krims's photographs sometimes generate alarm and even stronger reactions. "Krims holds the distinction of being the only photographer ever to cause a kidnaping:

when four of his half-comic, half-scatological pictures of nudes were displayed at the Memphis (Tenn.) Academy of Arts, an enraged spectator kidnaped the son of one of the academy instructors at gunpoint, demanding the removal of Krims' images as ransom. The gallery complied and the little boy was returned safely — but Krims' work is still on the loose" (Douglas Davis, *Newsweek,* 2 June 1975).

Krims stated: "I am not a Historian, I create History. [My] images are anti–decisive moment. It is possible to create any image one thinks of; this possibility, of course, is contingent on being able to think and create. The greatest potential source of photographic imagery is the mind" (*Camera Mainichi,* Aug. 1970).

WORK   Metaphorical and satirical images (e.g., mother with snapshots of her son pasted on her chest), documentary projects (e.g., *The Little People of America 1971, The Deerslayers*).

MEDIA   Silver prints (some on Kodalith paper, some toned), color (including manipulated Polaroid SX-70).

AVAILABILITY AND PRICE   Through galleries; unique SX-70 prints high, uranium-toned and Kodalith prints (generally made in editions of 5) moderately high.

Leslie Krims. *Mom's Snaps,* 1971. Silver print (on Kodalith paper). (Courtesy the artist)

SIGNATURE/OTHER IDENTIFICATION

PORTFOLIO *See* chapter 6 entry.

COLLECTIONS BMFA, Cornell, IMP/GEH, Kansas, LOC, Minneapolis, MOMA, New Mexico, VSW; NGC, Tokyo.

SELECTED BIBLIOGRAPHY
The Deerslayers (boxed reproductions). Rochester, N.Y.: published by the photographer, 1972.
The Incredible Case of the Stack O'Wheat Murders (boxed reproductions). Rochester, N.Y.: published by the photographer, 1972.
The Little People of America 1971 (boxed reproductions). Rochester, N.Y.: published by the photographer, 1972.
Making Chicken Soup. Buffalo: Humpy Press, 1972.
Clifford Ackley. *Private Realities: Recent American Photography.* Greenwich, Conn.: New York Graphic Society, 1974.
Fictcryptokrimsographs. Buffalo: Humpy Press, 1975.
Manfred Willmann, ed. *American Photographers.* Graz, Austria: Fotogalerie im Forum Stadtpark, 1977.
"Leslie Krims — Portfolio." Intro. by Peter C. Bunnell. *Aperture* 13, no. 3 (1967).
"Leslie Krims." *Album,* no. 4 (1970), pp. 16–24.
Camera Mainichi, Aug. 1970.
See also Szarkowski, *Mirrors;* chapter 7 catalogues.

Kühn, Heinrich
Austria (b. Germany) 1866–1944

Best known now for his impressionistic gum-bichromate prints, which Helmut and Alison Gernsheim compared to watercolors by John Singer Sargent, Kühn first studied science and medicine, but by 1888 was devoting himself to photography. He worked on a multiple gum-bichromate process for color prints with Hugo Henneberg and Hans Watzek, whom he had met at the Vienna Camera Club. The three men, known as the Trifolium (*Das Kleeblatt*), were leaders of the pictorial movement in Austria.

Kühn liked the manipulative control of the image that is possible with gum printing, a process in which the photographer "can subdue or entirely suppress anything too prominent in the less important parts of the picture [and can] emphasize all the subtleties where they are interesting and of importance for a pictorial effect.... The apparatus, the soulless machine, must be subservient, the personality and its demands must dominate. The craftsman becomes an artist" (Kühn, quoted in Matthies-Masuren). In the 1920s Kühn changed his aesthetic approach considerably: he advocated previsualization and the production of a negative that would not require any manipulation of the print.

WORK Includes portraits, landscapes, genre scenes.

MEDIA Gum-bichromate prints, oil-transfer prints, platinum prints, autochromes.

AVAILABILITY AND PRICE Through galleries and at auction. Gum-bichromate prints and other original prints rare; high. *Camera Work* reproductions low to moderate.

SIGNATURE/OTHER IDENTIFICATION

COLLECTIONS Chicago, IMP/GEH, MMA, Smithsonian, Texas (Gernsheim), Yale (Beinecke); NGC.

SELECTED BIBLIOGRAPHY
Technik der Lichtbildnerei. Halle, Prussia: Knapp, 1921.
Heinrich Kühn (1866–1944), Photographer. Text by Peter Weiermair. Innsbruck: Allerheiligen Presse, 1978.
F. Matthies-Masuren. "Hugo Henneberg — Heinrich Kühn — Hans Watzek." *Camera Work,* no. 13 (Jan. 1906), pp. 21–40.
Robert A. Sobieszek. "Heinrich Kühn." *Image* 14 (Dec. 1971): 16–18.
Camera, June 1977. Entire issue.
Camera Work: Reproductions (gravures, halftones) in nos. 13, 33.
See also Green, *Camera Work;* Life Library, *Art;* Naef, *Collection.*

Heinrich Kühn. *Study.* From *Camera Work,* no. 33, 1911. Gravure. (Courtesy The Witkin Gallery)

Lange, Dorothea
United States 1895–1965

Lange is best known for her documentary photographs, particularly of the Depression in 1930s America. Encouraged by Arnold Genthe to become a photographer, she studied in New York City with Clarence H. White at Columbia University, and in 1919 opened a portrait studio in San Francisco. By the 1930s, however, she had become dissatisfied with the limitations of commercial portraiture, and she started to photograph on San Francisco streets. Drawn to the poor and the unemployed, who were suffering from the collapse of the nation's economy, she began to notice and photograph how people's lives and feelings were translated into body gesture.

As a result of her street work she was hired by Paul S. Taylor to photograph migratory workers for the California State Emergency Relief Administration. In 1935 she went to work for the U.S. Resettlement Administration (later renamed the Farm Security Administration) and produced photographs in every part of the country except New England. Lange was sensitive to the words people used as well as to their gestures and she recorded the comments of her subjects, particularly the migrants. Later, in *An American Exodus*, these quotes were innovatively combined with the pictures.

Lange's work from the 1930s and after is characterized by empathy for her subjects and by her desire to photograph them exactly as she saw them. On her darkroom door she posted the following statement by Francis Bacon: "The contemplation of things as they are / Without error or confusion / Without substitution or imposture / Is in itself a nobler thing / Than a whole harvest of invention."

Dorothea Lange. *Texas Drought Refugees in California, August 1936.* Modern silver print from the original negative. (Library of Congress)

WORK Chiefly FSA and Depression-related images. Also includes early portraits (some soft-focus); U.S. internment of Japanese-Americans after Pearl Harbor bombing (1942); photoessays in *Life* and other publications — e.g., "Three Mormon Towns" (1954; with her son Daniel Dixon and Ansel Adams), "The Public Defender" (1955), "Death of a Valley" (1956–1957; with Pirkle Jones); Ireland, Asia, Venezuela, Ecuador, Egypt (1954–1963).

MEDIUM Silver prints. Many were made by Lange's printer or one of Lange's assistants; very few are signed.

AVAILABILITY AND PRICE Vintage prints available through galleries and at auction but infrequently found; high. Exhibition-quality prints available from Oakland Museum; low. Modern FSA prints from the Library of Congress extremely low.

SIGNATURE/OTHER IDENTIFICATION

COLLECTIONS Oakland Museum holds about 50,000 prints and negatives, plus personal papers. Also Amon Carter, IMP/GEH, LOC (FSA work), Minnesota, Mint, MOMA, Nebraska, New Mexico, NYPL, San Francisco, Smithsonian, Worcester.

SELECTED BIBLIOGRAPHY
An American Exodus: A Record of Human Erosion. With Paul Schuster Taylor. New York: Reynal & Hitchcock, 1939. Rev. ed., New Haven: Yale University Press, and Oakland: Oakland Museum, 1969. Reprint, New York: Arno, 1975.
Dorothea Lange. Intro. by George P. Elliott. New York: MOMA, 1966. Bibliography.
Dorothea Lange Looks at the American Country Woman. Text by Beaumont Newhall. Fort Worth, Tex.: Amon Carter Museum, and Los Angeles: Ward Ritchie, 1967.
The Making of a Documentary Photographer. Berkeley: University of California Press, 1968. Interviews by Suzanne Reiss.
Maisie Conrat and Richard Conrat. *Executive Order 9066: The Internment of 110,000 Japanese Americans.* San Francisco: California Historical Society, 1972.
To a Cabin. With Margaretta K. Mitchell. New York: Grossman, 1973.
Milton Meltzer. *Dorothea Lange: A Photographer's Life.* New York: Farrar, Straus & Giroux, 1978.
"Death of a Valley." With Pirkle Jones. *Aperture* 8, no. 3 (1960).
See also Edey, *Essays*; Life Library, *Great Photographers*; Lyons, *Photographers*; Mann, *Women*; Newhall, *Masters*; Tucker, *Eye*; bibliography in FSA entry.

Langenheim, Frederick
U.S. (b. Germany) 1809–1879

Langenheim, William
U.S. (b. Germany) 1807–1874

The Langenheim brothers were active in various aspects of photography beginning in the early 1840s, when they opened a daguerreotype studio in Philadelphia. According to historian Robert Taft, they were the first to daguerreotype Niagara Falls; in 1845 they made five-panel panoramas of the falls, sets of which were sent to L. J. M. Daguerre and several European monarchs.

In 1849 the Langenheims purchased the U.S. rights to William Henry Fox Talbot's calotype process, but they totally failed to popularize the medium with American photographers, who preferred the sharp detail of the daguerreotype. In 1849 they also introduced what they called hyalotypes — glass or paper stereograph images. The Langenheims were the first to commercially produce stereographs, and their American Stereoscopic Company became one of the leading producers of stereo views. In 1861 they sold their interest in the company to E. and H. T. Anthony and Company and concentrated on the production of stereopticon slides (glass transparencies used for projection).

Frederick and William Langenheim. Unidentified sitter, ca. 1850. Salt print copy of a daguerreotype. (Courtesy IMP/GEH)

WORK   Includes portraits (e.g., President Tyler, Henry Clay), scenic views (e.g., Niagara Falls, Philadelphia).

MEDIA   Daguerreotypes, calotypes, hyalotypes, salt prints, stereographs (bearing Langenheim name), stereopticon slides.

AVAILABILITY AND PRICE   Authenticated prints occasionally found at auction or through a knowledgeable dealer; moderately high to high. Prints have also been sold unnoticed at auction in lots with less valuable work; they may turn up at swap meets, flea markets, or other outlets priced low. Stereographs occasionally found; low to moderate (for unique images). Glass stereos are more expensive than paper ones.

SIGNATURE/OTHER IDENTIFICATION

by W. & F. Langenheim Philad. Exchange

COLLECTIONS   IMP/GEH, LOC, Missouri.

SELECTED BIBLIOGRAPHY
See Newhall, *Daguerreotype*; Taft, *Photography*.

Lartigue, Jacques Henri
France 1894–

Lartigue, who received his first camera from his father at age five, represents that rare instance of an artist who precociously produced a major body of work — in his case between the ages of seven and twelve. His main interest was to capture the fun and games enjoyed by his well-to-do family in France in the dozen or so years before World War I. Young Lartigue was fascinated by movement and recorded it all — cars racing; people jumping, falling, caught in midair — with a wonderful freshness and sense of the ridiculous. Although he still photographs — personal images as well as for magazines — painting has been Lartigue's main activity throughout his adult career. His photography did not receive public attention until the mid-1960s.

John Szarkowski wrote: "The persuasive charm of a vanished world may hide [his photographs'] deeper beauty. For these pictures are the observations of a genius: fresh perceptions, poetically sensed and graphically fixed" ("The Photographs of Jacques Henri Lartigue").

WORK   Chiefly early images: the photographer's relatives at play, racing autos, flying their planes, etc.; people strolling in Paris parks, at the seashore, and at the races. Also includes later images (e.g., his wife Bibi; fashion; stills taken on movie sets; official portrait of Valéry Giscard d'Estaing, May 1974).

MEDIA   Chiefly glass-plate negatives and (later) film negatives; silver prints (some sepia toned). Also some autochromes and, in the 1960s and 1970s, much other color.

AVAILABILITY AND PRICE   Vintage prints exist only in Lartigue's personal collection. Modern prints made to his approval and signed by him are available through galleries; high. Minor flaws from deterioration of early negatives are considered part of the images and are therefore left unretouched.

Jacques Henri Lartigue. *Cousin "Bichonade" in Flight*, 1905. Silver print. (Courtesy The Witkin Gallery)

SIGNATURE/OTHER IDENTIFICATION

PORTFOLIOS   *See* chapter 6 entry.

COLLECTIONS   MOMA, New Orleans, San Francisco; BN; many other major collections.

SELECTED BIBLIOGRAPHY
Boyhood Photos of J. H. Lartigue: The Family Album of a Gilded Age. Lausanne, Switzerland: Guichard, 1966.
Diary of a Century. Ed. by Richard Avedon. New York: Viking, 1970. Reprint, New York: Penguin, 1978.
J.-H. Lartigue et les femmes. Paris: Chêne, 1973. U.S. ed., New York: Dutton, 1974.
J.-H. Lartigue et les autos. Paris: Chêne, 1974.
Lartigue 8 × 80. Text by Michel Frizot. Paris: Musée des Arts Décoratifs, 1975.
Mémoires sans mémoire. Preface by Michel Tournier. Paris: Laffont, 1975.
Jacques-Henri Lartigue. Intro. by Ezra Bowen. Millerton, N.Y.: Aperture, 1976. Bibliography.
John Szarkowski. "The Photographs of Jacques Henri Lartigue." *MOMA Bulletin* 30, no. 1 (1963).
See also Szarkowski, *Looking.*

Laughlin, Clarence John
United States 1905–

A fantast, a poet, and one of the most prolific and idiosyncratic of American photographers, Laughlin has tirelessly pursued his own vision with total disregard for the shifting winds of critical fashion. He once declared, "I especially want it made clear that I am an *extreme romanticist* — and I don't want to be presented as some kind of goddamned up-to-the-minute version of a semiabstract photographer" (*Clarence John Laughlin*, p. 8).

Born in Louisiana, Laughlin has lived most of his life in New Orleans. He was early influenced by Baudelaire and the French Symbolists. In 1934 he began to photograph and has mentioned Alfred Stieglitz, Paul Strand, Edward Weston, Man Ray, and Eugène Atget as important to his development. Laughlin's first large project was photographing architecture in New Orleans, and he has earned his living primarily as an architectural photographer. Jonathan Williams remarked that "there is no one else in the history of photography who has his feeling for the animate life of architecture" (ibid., p. 6). Laughlin wrote of his personal work: "The physical object, to me, is merely a stepping-stone to an inner world where the object, with the help of subconscious drives and focused perceptions, becomes transmuted into a symbol whose life is beyond the life of the objects we know and whose meaning is a *truly human* meaning. By dealing with the object in this way, the creative photographer sets free the *human contents* of objects; and imparts humanity to the inhuman world around him" (ibid., p. 14).

WORK   Unmanipulated prints as well as negative and/or multiple imagery, including still lifes, architecture, landscapes, and such subjects, according to the photographer, as "Metal Magic (the sinister beauty of the metal forms evolved by our society), Glass Magic (the exploration of space in glass. Made in homage to Eugène Atget), Satires (the camera used as a weapon against our society), Poems of the Inner World (the symbolic use of the camera)," and others.

MEDIA   Silver prints. Also some 1943–1946 work using color dyes. Laughlin coated many early prints with wax, which has yellowed with age.

AVAILABILITY AND PRICE   Through galleries and at auction. Vintage prints rare; moderate to high. Modern prints moderate to moderately high.

SIGNATURE/OTHER IDENTIFICATION

COLLECTIONS   The University of Louisville Photographic Archives holds the bulk of Laughlin's work: over 17,000 negatives and an equal number of prints. Also Harvard (Fogg), LOC, MMA, MOMA, New Orleans, Philadelphia, Phillips, Smithsonian; BN.

SELECTED BIBLIOGRAPHY
New Orleans and Its Living Past. Text by David L. Cohn. Boston: Houghton Mifflin, 1941. Signed limited ed., 1,030 copies.
Ghosts along the Mississippi. New York: Scribner, 1948. Reprint, New York: Crown, 1962.
Photographs of Victorian Chicago. Washington, D.C.: Corcoran Gallery of Art, 1968.
Clarence John Laughlin: The Personal Eye. Intro. by Jonathan Williams. Millerton, N.Y.: Aperture, 1973. Bibliography.
Jonathan Williams. "Three Phantasts: Laughlin, Sommer, Bullock." *Aperture* 9, no. 3 (1961): 98–106.
Mary Louise Tucker. "Clarence John Laughlin: Phantoms and Metaphors." *Modern Photography,* Apr. 1977, pp. 100 ff.
See also Edey, *Essays;* Life Library, *Year 1975;* Travis, *Julien Levy;* Witkin, *Julien Levy.*

Clarence John Laughlin. *The Spectre of Coca-Cola,* 1962. Silver print. (Courtesy the artist. Copyright © 1973 by Clarence John Laughlin)

Lee, Russell
United States 1903–

Lee trained and worked as a chemical engineer, then studied painting for several years before finally finding his true vocation in 1935, when he acquired a small 35mm camera. Initially intending to use it for capturing facial expressions as an aid in painting, Lee began to photograph on New York City streets at the height of the Depression years. In 1936 he was introduced by Ben Shahn to Roy Stryker of the Farm Security Administration (FSA) and was soon hired to join the agency's staff of photographers documenting conditions across America.

Lee liked the people he photographed and quickly gained their trust. He told one woman who was reluctant to have her picture made: "Lady, you're having a hard time and a lot of people don't think that you're having such a hard time. We want to show them that you're a human being, a nice human being, but you're having troubles" (quoted in Life Library, *Documentary,* p. 83). Lee not only got his picture, but an introduction to the woman's friends and an invitation to supper.

In 1942 Lee joined an aerial photographic unit of the U.S. Air Transport Command and worked in South Amer-

ica, Europe, and the Far East. After World War II he did a series of photographs on bituminous-coal miners for the U.S. government, took on various commercial and photojournalism assignments, and taught photography at the University of Texas at Austin.

A notable characteristic of Lee's work, especially evident in his FSA photographs, is the harsh illumination from on-camera flash lighting, which he liked for its simplicity of use and its sharp rendering of details. He often shot extensive series of photographs, thus portraying many aspects of each situation. Roy Stryker commented: "Russell was the taxonomist with a camera. . . . He takes apart and gives you all the details of the plant. He lays it on the table and says, 'There you are, Sir, in all its parts'" (quoted in Hurley [1972], p. 148).

WORK   Includes New York City (ca. 1935); FSA images (some color), principally in the Midwest; U.S. internment of Japanese-Americans after bombing of Pearl Harbor (1942); coal miners (1946–1947); industrial, commercial, photojournalism assignments. (See illustration, page 137.)

MEDIA   Silver prints, color.

AVAILABILITY AND PRICE   Vintage prints rare; moderate to moderately high. Modern prints made and signed by the photographer available through galleries; moderate. Modern FSA prints (black and white only) from the Library of Congress extremely low.

COLLECTIONS   BMFA, CCP, LOC (FSA work), Minnesota, St. Petersburg, Texas, U.S. Dept. of Interior (coal miners).

SELECTED BIBLIOGRAPHY
J. T. Boone. *A Medical Survey of the Bituminous Coal Industry.* Washington, D.C.: U.S. Department of the Interior, 1947. Section by Lee later reissued as *The Coal Miner and His Family.*
Russell Lee: Retrospective Exhibition, 1934–1964. Austin, Tex., 1965.
Maisie Conrat and Richard Conrat. *Executive Order 9066: The Internment of 110,000 Japanese Americans.* San Francisco: California Historical Society, 1972.
F. Jack Hurley. *Russell Lee: Photographer.* Dobbs Ferry, N.Y.: Morgan & Morgan, 1978.
William Arrowsmith, ed. "Image of Italy." *Texas Quarterly,* no. 4 (1961).
F. Jack Hurley. "Russell Lee." *Image* 16 (Sept. 1973): 1–32.
Lee's photographs appeared in various issues of *The Lamp* (publication of Standard Oil Company of New Jersey; 1947 and after), *Fortune* (1940s–1960s), and *Texas Observer* (Austin).
See also bibliography in FSA entry (includes Hurley [1972]).

Le Gray, Gustave
France 1820–ca. 1882

Originally a painter who studied with artist Paul Delaroche, Le Gray turned to photography and in 1848 opened a portrait studio in Paris. He introduced his waxed-paper adaptation of the calotype process in 1850 and used the technique in his photographic documentation of historical

Gustave Le Gray. *Seascape,* 1856. Albumen print. (Courtesy Christie's, London)

monuments in the Aquitaine and the Touraine. One of the first to suggest the use of collodion, Le Gray also developed a method for producing cloud effects in landscapes by combining a separate negative of clouds with the original scene, thus solving the problem of blank skies inherent in collodion photography. He is well known for his seascapes, in which he used this cloud technique.

Le Gray recorded scenes of military life at the camp at Châlons, covered Napoleon III's visit there in 1858, and photographed at the barricades at Palermo. He also did some portraiture and photographed landscapes, but his lack of interest in the popular vogue for cartes de visite caused him to close his studio, which he sold in 1859. He then disappeared from sight. He apparently left Paris by 1864, and in 1865 was reported in Cairo, where he served as professor of drawing and painting at the viceroy's school while continuing to make photographs, chiefly for copying by engravers. He died in Cairo.

WORK Chiefly architecture, landscapes, seascapes, scenes of military life. Also includes portraits.

MEDIA Waxed-paper negatives and collodion wet-plate negatives; salt prints and albumen prints.

AVAILABILITY AND PRICE At auction but rare (seascapes especially sought after); high to extremely high. In 1978 six Le Gray albumen prints sold for $7,700 at auction (Argus, Ltd., New York City).

SIGNATURE/OTHER IDENTIFICATION

COLLECTIONS Chicago, IMP/GEH, MMA, New Mexico, Smithsonian, Texas (Gernsheim); Société Francaise.

SELECTED BIBLIOGRAPHY
Photographie: Traité pratique de photographie sur papier et sur verre. Paris: Ballière, 1850.
Nils Ramstedt. "Gustave Le Gray . . . ." Ph.D. dissertation, University of California (Santa Barbara), 1977.
See also Colnaghi, *Photography;* Gernsheim, *Creative Photography;* Jammes and Sobieszek, *Primitive;* Marbot, *Invention.*

Le Secq, Henri
France 1818–1882

Like many other painters during the early years of photography, Le Secq was fascinated by the new medium. At first he pursued it merely as a hobby; indeed, throughout his career he directed his main energies toward his paintings (which he exhibited at the Paris Salon from 1842 to 1880). Like Charles Nègre, Gustave Le Gray, and Roger Fenton — also photographic pioneers — Le Secq was a student of the academic painter Paul Delaroche.

In 1851 Le Secq (shown on page 201) was one of five photographers employed by the Comité des Monuments Historiques to document historical architecture throughout France. He was assigned primarily to the regions of Alsace, Lorraine, and Champagne, where he thoroughly documented the cathedrals of Reims, Chartres, Amiens, Bourges, and Strasbourg, in addition to making landscape photographs and genre scenes. Meanwhile, in Paris he continued to photograph historic buildings, many of which were later destroyed during Baron Haussmann's modernization of the city. Le Secq's enthusiasm for photography is said to have "dwindled with the advent of the collodion process" (*Camera,* p. 47).

A contemporary of Le Secq wrote of him: "The young artist has recorded, stone by stone, the cathedrals of Strasbourg and Reims in over a hundred different prints. Thanks to him we have clim[b]ed all the steeples . . . what we never could have discovered through our own

Henri Le Secq. *Windmills,* ca. 1850s. Modern silver print from the original calotype negative. (Courtesy IMP/GEH)

eyes, he has seen for us . . . one might think the saintly artists of the Middle Ages had foreseen the daguerreotype in placing on high their statues and stone carvings where birds alone circling the spires could marvel at their detail and perfection. . . . The entire cathedral is reconstructed, layer on layer, in wonderful effects of sunlight, shadow, and rain. M. Le Secq, too, has built his monument" (quoted in Jammes and Sobieszek, *Primitive*).

WORK Chiefly documentation of French cathedrals, architectural monuments in Paris, landscapes. Also includes still lifes, genre scenes.

MEDIA Waxed-paper negatives, calotypes (often signed), some cyanotypes.

AVAILABILITY AND PRICE Vintage prints available through galleries and at auction but rare; high to extremely high. Modern prints made by Claudine Sudre from a selection of Le Secq's negatives available through her publisher; moderate.

SIGNATURE/OTHER IDENTIFICATION

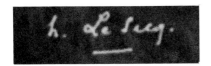

COLLECTIONS IMP/GEH; BN, Musée des Arts Décoratifs.

SELECTED BIBLIOGRAPHY
G. Cromer. "Henri Le Secq." *Bulletin de la Société Française de Photographie*, 1930, pp. 287–295.
Camera, Feb. 1974. Issue on French photography, 1840–1940, in the collection of the Bibliothèque Nationale.
Eugenia Parry Janis. "The Man on the Tower of Notre Dame: New Light on Henri Le Secq." *Image* 19 (Dec. 1976): 13–25.
See also Jammes and Sobieszek, *Primitive*; Marbot, *Invention*.

Levitt, Helen
United States 1918–

Levitt began photographing on the streets of New York City in the late 1930s, particularly concentrating on children and their games. Her small-camera documentary approach was influenced by Henri Cartier-Bresson, and she also studied with Walker Evans. She has worked in film and collaborated with James Agee on the award-winning films *The Quiet One* (1949) and *In the Street* (1952).

Ben Maddow wrote of her work: "I once saw a dragonfly in New York City: it was caught between bundles of black plastic trash. The color of this astonishment is in all of Helen Levitt's photographs. She sees, trails, hunts and seizes hold of those dances that ordinary people do on their own turf. The sidewalk is raised like a stage. The gestures of arm and face and walk are stills from a marveling film. . . . Helen Levitt walks about in the slums of this city, greedy, discriminating, bold, secret. In her transparencies we feel an emotion, only too justified these days, that somehow vibrates between love and fear" ("Helen Levitt," p. 36).

Helen Levitt. *Gypsy Boy, New York*, ca. 1945. Silver print. (Courtesy the artist)

WORK Chiefly street life (e.g., Harlem, Mexico City).

MEDIA Silver prints, color.

AVAILABILITY AND PRICE Through galleries. Modern black-and-white prints moderate to moderately high; dye transfer color prints moderately high. Vintage prints infrequently available; moderately high.

SIGNATURE/OTHER IDENTIFICATION

COLLECTIONS MMA, MOMA, NYPL, Springfield (Mo.).

SELECTED BIBLIOGRAPHY
A Way of Seeing. Essay by James Agee. New York: Viking, 1965.
"Helen Levitt: Photographs of New York City." Intro. by Ben Maddow. *Aperture* 19, no. 4 (1975): 36–43.
See also Szarkowski, *Mirrors*.

Lynes, George Platt
United States 1907–1955

The male nude is relatively seldom used as a subject by photographers. George Platt Lynes, however, is one who made a number of works in this genre. Lynes displayed artistic and literary interests early. In 1926 he published booklets by Gertrude Stein, René Crevel, and Ernest Hemingway under the imprint of As Stable Publications. Self-taught in photography, he took up professional portraiture in the mid-1920s. He opened a New York studio in 1933 and for about three years during the mid-1940s worked in Hollywood.

Lynes was well known for his photographs of literary and artistic personalities, dance, and fashion. His work appeared regularly in *Town and Country, Harper's Bazaar,* and *Vogue*. His nudes, which are today the most sought after of all his work, are at once cool and erotic, often skillfully cross-lit to reveal flesh textures and musculature. With Julien Levy, the New York City gallery owner whom he met in 1931, Lynes also made surrealistic still lifes.

WORK Includes male nudes, portraits of literary and artistic personalities, ballet, fashion, advertising, surrealistic still lifes.

MEDIUM Silver prints (usually 8×10).

AVAILABILITY AND PRICE Through galleries and at auction; moderately high to extremely high. Nude studies highest.

George Platt Lynes. *Serge Lifar — Spectre de la Rose (on point),* ca. 1930s. Silver print. (Courtesy Russell Lynes and The Witkin Gallery)

SIGNATURE/OTHER IDENTIFICATION

G. P. LYNES

COLLECTIONS Chicago, IMP/GEH, Institute for Sex Research, MMA, MOMA, NYPL (Lincoln Center), Smith.

SELECTED BIBLIOGRAPHY
International Photographers. Brooklyn: Brooklyn Museum, 1932.
Murals by American Painters and Photographers. New York: MOMA, 1932.
Ebria Feinblatt. *Seventeen American Photographers.* Los Angeles: Los Angeles County Museum, 1948.
Lincoln Kirstein. *The New York City Ballet.* New York: Knopf, 1973. Photographs by Lynes and Martha Swope.
Jeffrey Weschler. *Surrealism and American Art, 1931–1947.* New Brunswick, N.J.: Rutgers University Press, 1977.
Philip Andrews. "Studio Fashions: George Platt Lynes — Fashion and Portrait Photographer." *The Complete Photographer* 6, no. 26 (1942): 1690–1698.
Dance Index, vol. 3, Dec. 1944. Entire issue illustrated with photographs by Lynes.
"George Platt Lynes." *Camera,* Feb. 1956, pp. 45–54.
See also Travis, *Julien Levy;* Witkin, *Julien Levy.*

Lyon, Danny
United States 1942–

Lyon attended the University of Chicago and received his B.A. in history in 1963, the same year he joined the Student Non-violent Coordinating Committee as a photographer documenting the U.S. civil-rights movement. The resulting photographs form a significant part of the book *The Movement* and mark the beginning of his personal involvement recording various social and cultural aspects of American life during the 1960s and 1970s. As a member of a motorcycle club, for instance, Lyon photographed fellow cyclists. The prisoners in his book *Conversations with the Dead* are both the photographer's subjects and his collaborators in creating the book.

Thomas H. Garver described the link between Lyon and his work: "A certain feeling (compassion would be a weak substitute perhaps) must involve him utterly before a project is undertaken, and the photos resulting from such a project are less images than totemic surrogates for those lives, events and experiences which he has endured. Photography is reality for Lyon because he does not wish to separate his art from the life matrix which formed it" (*Danny Lyon*).

Also active in cinema since 1960, Lyon has directed four films.

WORK Chiefly social and cultural images of life in the United States. Also includes the life of street urchins in Santa Marta and Cartagena, Colombia.

MEDIA Silver prints, color.

AVAILABILITY AND PRICE Through galleries; silver prints moderate, color moderately high.

Danny Lyon. *Men on the Cornwagon — Ramsey Prison,* 1968. From *Conversations with the Dead,* 1971. Silver print. (Courtesy The Witkin Gallery)

SIGNATURE/OTHER IDENTIFICATION

PORTFOLIO *See* chapter 6 Schools and workshops entry.

COLLECTIONS Houston, IMP/GEH, MOMA, New Mexico.

SELECTED BIBLIOGRAPHY
The Movement. Text by Lorraine Hansberry. New York: Simon & Schuster, 1964. U.K. ed., *A Matter of Colour.* London: Penguin.
The Bikeriders. New York: Macmillan, 1968.
The Destruction of Lower Manhattan. New York: Macmillan, 1969.
Conversations with the Dead. New York: Holt, Rinehart & Winston, 1971.
Danny Lyon: Ten Years of Photographs. Text by Thomas H. Garver. Newport Beach, Calif.: Newport Harbor Art Museum, 1973. Bibliography.
Camera, Feb. 1977, pp. 4–13.
See also Life Library, *Children;* Szarkowski, *Mirrors;* chapter 7 catalogues.

Lyons, Nathan
United States 1930–

Lyons separates his involvement with photography into three periods. The first, 1946–1950, was as an amateur, and the second, 1950–1954, was as a senior photographer for the U.S. Air Force, photographing everything from criminal investigations to evidence of UFOs. The third period, which began while he was majoring in English literature at Alfred (New York) University, involves his major exploration of the medium: the relationship of poetry to photography. He reflected in 1971: "Environment and landscape have always been central to a thought process or process of experience that words did not always parallel or satisfy. . . . Distinct images, directly perceived, began to replace the need for verbal orientation" ("Notations in Passing").

In 1957 Lyons went to work for the George Eastman House in Rochester, New York, where he developed many major exhibitions and publications. He edited or otherwise helped publish eighteen titles, including *The Daybooks of Edward Weston.* He was also instrumental in founding the Society for Photographic Education in 1962 and was its first chairman. In 1969 he left the George Eastman House to form the Visual Studies Workshop, also in Rochester, and to program photographic studies for the State University of New York at Buffalo.

"Photography," he wrote, "is primarily a means of retaining the impressions that an individual deems significant. . . . The photograph exists not only as evidence of a given moment of response, . . . but becomes a reflection of, or commitment to, a continuity of moments" (*Photography in the Twentieth Century,* pp. vii–viii).

WORK Includes street scenes, store windows, buildings, landscapes, all showing the mark of society.

MEDIUM Silver prints.

AVAILABILITY AND PRICE Through galleries; early work using a 4×5 view camera moderately high, recent 35mm images moderate.

SIGNATURE/OTHER IDENTIFICATION

COLLECTIONS Addison, IMP/GEH, Minnesota, MOMA, UCLA; BN, NGC.

SELECTED BIBLIOGRAPHY
Under the Sun. With Syl Labrot and Walter Chappell. New York: Braziller, 1960. Another ed., Millerton, N.Y.: Aperture, 1972.

Nathan Lyons. Untitled, Outer Banks, North Carolina, 1976. Silver print. (Courtesy the artist)

Contemporary Photographers: Toward a Social Landscape. Ed. and text by Lyons. New York: Horizon, and Rochester, N.Y.: GEH, 1966.

Photographers on Photography. Ed. by Lyons. Englewood Cliffs, N.J.: Prentice-Hall, and Rochester, N.Y.: GEH, 1966.

Photography in the Twentieth Century. Ed. by Lyons. New York: Horizon, and Rochester, N.Y.: GEH, 1967.

Vision and Expression: An International Survey of Contemporary Photography. Ed. by Lyons. New York: Horizon, and Rochester, N.Y.: GEH, 1969.

Notations in Passing. Cambridge, Mass.: MIT Press, 1974.

"Notations in Passing." *Aperture* 16, no. 2 (1971).

See also Hume, *The Great West;* chapter 7 catalogues.

Man Ray
United States and France 1890–1976

"I paint what can not be photographed. I photograph what I do not wish to paint," Man Ray once said in an apt description of his work. During his long and varied career he felt free to move from medium to medium — painting, photography, sculpture, collage, constructed objects, film — as his needs of the moment changed. Though he considered his photography to be less important than his painting, it is his photographs that appear fresh and original today.

Born Emmanuel Rudnitsky (?) in Philadelphia, Man Ray decided at age seven to be an artist. In his early twenties, visits to Stieglitz's "291" gallery in New York City acquainted him with the artists who were breaking with old traditions. He lived for many years as an émigré in Paris, with poets, painters, and writers as friends, particularly dadaists and surrealists such as Marcel Duchamp, Tristan Tzara, Max Ernst, and Francis Picabia. He photographed them at his studio and supported himself by commercial photographic jobs in fashion and portraiture. From 1940 to 1951 Man Ray lived and worked in Hollywood. In 1951 he moved back to Paris, where he lived with his wife Juliet (the subject of many of his paintings and photographs) until his death.

Man Ray's personal work encompassed many types of photographic manipulation. In the early 1920s, following an accidental discovery in his darkroom, he explored the results possible with photograms — rayographs, as he called them. He also mastered the Sabattier effect, using it subtly to enhance, outline, and emphasize nude studies and other images. His experiments were always, he insisted, a means of extended expression and not fascination with the technique itself: "Seized in moments of visual detachment during periods of emotional contact, these images [rayographs] are oxidized residues, fixed by light and chemical elements, of living organisms. No plastic expression can ever be more than a residue of an experience. The recognition of an image that has tragically survived an experience, recalling the event more or less clearly, like the undisturbed ashes of an object consumed by flames, the recognition of this object so little representative and so fragile, and its simple identification on the part of the spectator with a similar personal experi-

ence, precludes all psycho-analytical classification or assimilation into an arbitrary decorative system" (quoted in *Man Ray* [1966], p. 21).

A. D. Coleman observed that "usually unexpected and frequently shocking proximity, always based upon an acute sense of distance, scale, and proportion, is . . . a hallmark of all of Man Ray's photographic imagery. He will often force the viewer to confront at point-blank range a face, an eye, a pair of disembodied lips, or some peculiar arrangement of common objects whose relationship and significance is established by their precise placement in and occupation of space. From a diametrically opposite standpoint, Man Ray uncovered the same truth as the combat photographer Robert Capa: 'If your pictures are no good, you're not in close enough'" (*Man Ray Photographs 1920–1934*).

WORK Chiefly portraits, nudes, abstractions (some using Sabattier effect). Also includes landscapes, still lifes, self-portraits, much commercial work (e.g., portraits, fashion). (See illustration, page 22.)

MEDIA Silver prints (some manipulated, on print and/or negative), rayographs, clichés-verres. Also some photo-silkscreens.

AVAILABILITY AND PRICE Through galleries and at auction; moderately high to extremely high. Rayographs from the 1920s and 1930s command the highest prices.

SIGNATURE/OTHER IDENTIFICATION

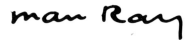

COLLECTIONS Chicago, IMP/GEH, Kansas, MOMA, New Mexico, New Orleans, Oakland, RISD, Yale (Art Gallery); Antwerp.

SELECTED BIBLIOGRAPHY

Les Champs délicieux: Album de photographies. Preface by Tristan Tzara. Paris: Société Générale d'Imprimerie et d'Edition, 1922.

Georges Ribemont-Dessaignes. *Man Ray.* Paris: Gallimard, 1924.

Kiki Souvenirs. Paris: Henri Broca, 1929.

Electricité (portfolio). Intro. by Pierre Bost. Paris: La Compagnie Parisienne de Distribution d'Electricité, 1931. 10 gravures from rayographs. 500 copies.

Photographies, 1920–1934, Paris. Paris: Cahiers d'Art, for James Thrall Soby, Hartford, Conn., 1934. Essays and poems by André Breton, Paul Eluard, "Rrose Selavy" (Marcel Duchamp), Tristan Tzara, and Man Ray. Reprint, *Man Ray Photographs 1920–1934:* Intro. by A. D. Coleman. New York: East River Press, 1975.

Facile. Poems by Paul Eluard. Paris: G.L.M., 1935.

La Photographie n'est pas l'art. Paris: G.L.M., 1937. Foreword by André Breton. 17 loose pages in folder, containing 12 reproductions.

Self-Portrait. Boston: Little, Brown, 1963. French ed., *Autoportrait.* Paris: Laffont, 1964.

Man Ray. Intro. by Jules Langsner. Los Angeles: Los Angeles County Museum of Art, 1966.

Les Invendables. Vence, France: Galerie Alphonse-Chave, 1969. 50 copies. Contains Man Ray's only photocollage.

Mr. and Mrs. Woodman. The Netherlands: Unida, 1970. Reproductions of 27 photographs of mannequins printed from negatives made in 1947, plus one engraving; boxed, signed, and numbered. 65 copies.

Oggetti d'Affezione. Turin: Einaudi, 1970.

Man Ray. Intro. by Alain Jouffroy. Paris: Musée National d'Art Moderne, 1972.

Man Ray. Chicago: J. Philip O'Hara, 1973.

Man Ray. New York: Alexander Iolas Gallery, 1974.

Roland Penrose. *Man Ray.* Boston: New York Graphic Society, 1975.

Janus. *Man Ray's Photography.* Milan: Electa, 1977.

Arturo Schwarz. *Man Ray: The Rigour of Imagination.* New York: Rizzoli, 1977.

See also Life Library, *Great Photographers, Studio, Year 1974;* Szarkowski, *Looking;* Travis, *Julien Levy;* Witkin, *Julien Levy.*

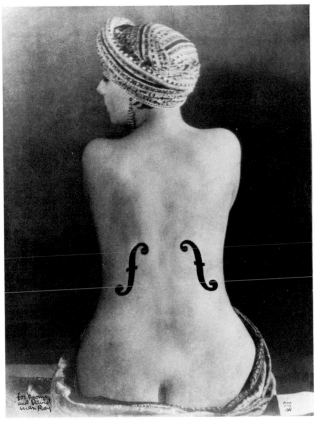

Man Ray. *Le Violon d'Ingres,* 1924. Silver print with hand-alterations. (Courtesy the artist; collection Naomi and David Savage)

Marcus, Elli
Germany 1899–1977

Marcus was a famous photographer of theatrical personalities in Berlin in the 1920s and early 1930s, active there at the same time as Lotte Jacobi. In addition to her advertising and fashion photography, Marcus photographed Marlene Dietrich, Paul Wegener, Albert Basserman, Lucie Hoeflich, Kaethe Dorsch, Hans Albers, and almost every other noted stage figure of the period.

"I was the first female photographer on the stage," she recollected in 1976. "I created something new — the portrait on the stage — the expression of the art of the mask. There were at least ten male stage photographers. They photographed the entire stage from the orchestra. I made close-up portraits *on* the stage during rehearsal. I was not given too much time, and I often worked under very difficult circumstances, and therefore the actors appreciated it" (statement to the authors).

Widowed, she left Nazi Germany with her son in 1933 and moved to Paris, where she set up a studio. To escape the Nazi occupation of France, they fled to the United States in 1941. In New York City she continued to photograph for the next fifteen years, making portraits of Alfred Stieglitz, Georgia O'Keeffe, Paul Robeson, Lotte Lenya, and many other well-known personalities. Because many of her commercial clients demanded heavy retouching of their portraits, Marcus ultimately gave up photography. She turned to graphology (the study of handwriting) and at the time of her death was a professional graphologist.

Elli Marcus. *Marlene Dietrich* [second from left] *in Chorus Line of "Broadway," Berlin,* 1927. Silver print. (Courtesy The Witkin Gallery)

WORK   In Germany and France (1920s, 1930s): portraits of stage personalities; advertising and fashion photography. In the United States (1940s, early 1950s): portraits, including some that experimentally combine graphology and photography (e.g., the handwriting of the subject superimposed on the image).

MEDIUM   Silver prints.

AVAILABILITY AND PRICE   Through galleries; moderately high. Much of Marcus's European work — the original negatives and many prints — was lost in the war. She reached the United States with about 150 prints (portraits and stage scenes), some of which are available. In the early 1970s Marcus lent all existing prints to the Photographic Center (Landesbildstelle) of the Free City of Berlin, which made copy negatives and offers prints from them. Vintage portraits made in the United States are also available, but because Marcus stopped printing in the mid-1950s, they exist in small numbers.

Bill Jay. *Victorian Candid Camera: Paul Martin 1864–1944.* Intro. by Cecil Beaton. Newton Abbot, England: David & Charles, 1973.

Roy Flukinger, Larry Schaaf, and Standish Meacham. *Paul Martin: Victorian Photographer.* Austin: University of Texas Press, 1977.

"Paul Martin." *Album,* no. 7 (1970), pp. 4–12.

See also Life Library, *Great Photographers.*

SIGNATURE/OTHER IDENTIFICATION

COLLECTIONS   NPG (U.S.), Princeton (Art Museum).

SELECTED BIBLIOGRAPHY

In Germany, Marcus's work appeared in *Welt Spiegel, Berliner Illustrierte Zeitung, Muenchen Illustrierte Zeitung, Hamburg Illustrierte Zeitung, Die Dame, Elegante Welt, Sport in Bild,* and other periodicals (1920s–1930s). In the United States, it appeared in *U.S. Camera* (1940s–1950s).

Martin, Paul
England (b. France) 1864–1944

Martin was one of the first photographers to exploit the potential of small, hand-held cameras and was the first to make an extensive series of unposed photographs of English daily life. As early as the 1890s he was making snapshots of London street life, people on holiday at the beach, and other candid subjects, using a Facile detective camera that he concealed as a parcel. It was impossible to frame the image exactly with this camera, but Martin was interested in capturing the activities of his subjects, not in the formal composition of the picture.

Though photographs in imitation of paintings were very popular when Martin began his work, he said that such pictorial photography "never had the same interest for me as the real snapshot — that is, people and things as the man in the street sees them" ("Paul Martin"). Martin was also one of the first to experiment with making photographs at night. He worked mainly as a press photographer and later made studio portraits, but his snapshots, which are of prime interest to viewers today, gained little recognition until after his death.

WORK   Best known for unposed snapshots of English life. Also includes London at night; English countryside; professional press work (e.g., Victoria's Diamond Jubilee); a few pictorial, posed, and double-printed pieces (e.g., one titled *Don't Tell Me, Let Me Guess*); studio portraits.

MEDIA   Gelatin dry-plate negatives, silver prints. Also carbon prints, platinum prints, lantern slides.

AVAILABILITY AND PRICE   Through galleries and at auction. Though Martin produced a large body of work, prints are found rather infrequently; most low to moderate.

COLLECTIONS   Chicago, Texas (Gernsheim); Kodak, Radio Times, RPS, VA.

SELECTED BIBLIOGRAPHY

Victorian Snapshots. London: Country Life, 1939. Reprint, New York: Arno, 1973.

Marville, Charles
France 1816–ca. 1880

Originally a painter, Marville in the 1850s was commissioned by the city of Paris to document with photographs the old quarters of the French capital before Napoleon III and Baron Haussmann cut great boulevards through them. Marville's photographs of historic landscapes and architecture were also included in L.-D. Blanquart-Evrard's publications.

According to André Jammes, "Marville achieved documentary perfection: precise rendition of materials, perfect focus, exact perspective, luminous shadows. [He] loved the picturesque and knew how to lend dignity to sordid old streets. With feeling he recorded the old Paris quarters that Haussmann pitilessly tore down. Deliberately, he chose rainy days when cobblestones glistened and the light was evenly distributed" (Jammes and Sobieszek, *Primitive*).

Charles Marville. *Eglise de St. Wulfrand à Abbeville.* From *Souvenirs photographiques,* 1853–1854. Calotype made by L.-D. Blanquart-Evrard. (Courtesy Lee D. Witkin)

WORK Chiefly scenes of streets and buildings in Paris and Germany (1850s), cathedrals and their treasures. Also includes landscapes, "news" photographs (1856; the arrival of Napoleon III's carriage and the scene outside Notre Dame at the baptism of the prince imperial).

MEDIA Calotypes; collodion wet-plate negatives, salt prints, albumen prints.

AVAILABILITY AND PRICE Through galleries and at auction but rare; moderately high to high. Many images were published by Blanquart-Evrard with Marville credited as photographer.

SIGNATURE/OTHER IDENTIFICATION

CH. MARVILLE PHOT.

COLLECTIONS IMP/GEH, New Mexico; BN, Paris, Société Française.

SELECTED BIBLIOGRAPHY
Calotypes from Marville's negatives are included in the following publications by Blanquart-Evrard: *Album photographique de l'artiste et de l'amateur*, 1851; *Mélanges photographiques*, 1852–54; *Paris photographique*, 1852–54; *Art religieux*, 1853–54; *Etudes photographiques*, 1853–54; *Souvenirs photographiques*, 1853–54; *Variétés photographiques*, 1853–54; *Bords du Rhin*, 1854; *Etudes et paysages*, 1854–55.
See also Jammes and Sobieszek, *Primitive*; Marbot, *Invention*.

Margrethe Mather. *Pierrot* [Otto Matiesen], ca. 1917. Platinum print. (Courtesy San Francisco Museum of Modern Art)

Mather, Margrethe
United States 1885–1952

Though principally known because of her affiliation with Edward Weston, Mather was a talented photographer in her own right. Little has been recorded or is known about her (information about her in various books about Weston is not always reliable). An orphan, she ran away from her foster parents while a teenager. When she met Weston, possibly as early as 1912, she was already an accomplished photographer, though he was still formulating his style. She worked with him for ten years in his Glendale, California, studio and eventually became his creative partner, running the studio when he went to Mexico in 1922. She frequently modeled for him during the early days of their acquaintance (see illustration, page 270); in 1923 she posed for a series of nude studies by him. In that year they also posed together for a series of portraits by Imogen Cunningham.

Mather and Weston frequented art-oriented circles (Ramiel McGehee and photographer Johan Hagemeyer were among their friends) and, according to Weston, her portraits of many of these associates were highly regarded. Mather's images — still lifes, romantic portraits, studies of interiors — possess an elegant pictorial style and express a keen sense of design.

On several occasions Mather and Weston created images together, such as their portrait of Carl Sandburg (both signed the prints). In 1925 Weston referred to her as "the first important person in my life, and perhaps even now, though personal contact has gone, the most important" (*The Daybooks*, vol. 1, p. 145).

With her friend William Justema, Mather had an exhibition, Patterns by Photography, at the de Young Museum (San Francisco) in 1931. Afterward her interest in photography declined, as did her health.

WORK Chiefly portraits of friends and celebrities (e.g., Pablo Casals, Sadakichi Hartmann). Also natural and artificial forms (e.g., still lifes); some commissioned work (including documentation of Frank Lloyd Wright homes and interior decoration by Harold Grieve). (See illustration, page 215.)

MEDIA Platinum prints, silver prints (mostly contact printed from 8×10 negatives).

AVAILABILITY AND PRICE Through galleries and at auction but rare; moderate to high. All of Mather's negatives are believed destroyed as a result of careless storage.

SIGNATURE/OTHER IDENTIFICATION

PORTFOLIOS In the 1920s Mather made two portfolios — platinum prints of erotic drawings by William Justema — to sell to Los Angeles collectors.

COLLECTIONS CCP, IMP/GEH, MOMA, New Mexico, New Orleans, San Francisco.

SELECTED BIBLIOGRAPHY
Edward Weston. *The Daybooks.* 2 vols. Millerton, N.Y.: Aperture, 1971.
Ben Maddow. *Edward Weston: Fifty Years.* Millerton, N.Y.: Aperture, 1973.
Margery Mann. *California Pictorialism.* San Francisco: San Francisco Museum of Modern Art, 1977.
Mather's work appeared in various photography magazines and annuals from 1912 to 1925.

Meatyard, Ralph Eugene
United States 1925–1972

An optician by profession, Meatyard pursued photography mostly on weekends. He was a student of Van Deren Coke and credited Coke as a strong influence. He also studied briefly with Henry Holmes Smith and with Minor White.

Meatyard's photographs deal with contradictions: the motion of subjects in an otherwise solid setting; partly sharp and partly out-of-focus scenes; children and others, sometimes masked, in seemingly normal situations that are oddly disquieting. His images create a world of mystery, one concerned with the ineffability of reality.

Ralph Eugene Meatyard. Untitled, 1975. Silver print. (Courtesy Madelyn O. Meatyard)

Meatyard wrote: "I work in several different groups of pictures which act on and with each other — ranging from several abstracted manners to a form for the surreal. I have been called a preacher — but, in reality, I'm more generally philosophical. I have never made an abstracted photograph without content. An educated background in Zen influences all of my photographs. It has been said that my work resembles, more closely than any photographer, 'Le Douanier' Rousseau — working in a fairly isolated area and feeding mostly on myself — I feel that I am a 'primitive' photographer" (*Photographer's Choice*, no. 1, Spring 1959, Bloomington, Ind.).

WORK Includes figures in rooms and in landscapes.

MEDIUM Silver prints.

AVAILABILITY AND PRICE Through galleries. Vintage prints (usually not signed by Meatyard but bearing the estate stamp and signature of his widow, Madelyn Meatyard) rare; moderately high. Posthumous prints made by his son Christopher Meatyard (bearing his name and date of printing) low to moderate.

SIGNATURE/OTHER IDENTIFICATION

R. E. Meatyard   *Rem 55*

RALPH EUGENE MEATYARD
Lexington, Kentucky

(Signature of Madelyn Meatyard)

madelyn meatyard

PORTFOLIOS *See* chapter 6 entry.

COLLECTIONS BMFA, IMP/GEH, Louisville, MIT (Hayden), MMA, MOMA, Nebraska, New Mexico, New Orleans, Norton Simon, Smithsonian, UCLA.

SELECTED BIBLIOGRAPHY
Five Photographers. Intro. by Michael McLoughlin. Lincoln: Sheldon Memorial Art Gallery, University of Nebraska, 1968.
Wendell Berry. *The Unforeseen Wilderness: An Essay on Kentucky's Red River Gorge.* Lexington: University Press of Kentucky, 1971.
James Baker Hall. *Ralph Eugene Meatyard.* Millerton, N.Y.: Aperture, 1974.
The Family Album of Lucybelle Crater. Ed. by Jonathan Williams. Millerton, N.Y.: Jargon Society, 1974.
Van Deren Coke. *Ralph Eugene Meatyard: A Retrospective.* Normal: Center for the Visual Arts Gallery, Illinois State University, 1976.
Susan Dodge Peters. *The Photographs of Ralph Eugene Meatyard.* Williamstown, Mass.: Williams College Museum of Art, 1977.
Van Deren Coke. "The Photography of Eugene Meatyard." *Aperture* 7, no. 4 (1959): 154–168.
See also Life Library, *Art, Children, Year 1973*; chapter 7 catalogues.

Mertin, Roger
United States 1942–

Mertin is one of a group of photographers who explore ways the camera can create statements about the process of photography itself. He studied at the Rochester (New York) Institute of Technology with Nathan Lyons and Minor White from 1963 to 1966, and then at the Visual Studies Workshop in Rochester, where he now teaches.

Mertin often adds electronic flash to basic daylight illumination so that objects in the foreground of his images glow or cast unexpected shadows. The objects themselves are quite ordinary — trees, for example — but their relation to their environment is ambiguous. R. Reep commented: "Photographers are fascinated with light and the possibilities it provides for experimentation. Mertin works in the tradition of the straight silver print but . . . transform[s] the reality before his camera by means of light to arrive at a highly personal vision" (*Light & Substance* catalogue, listed in chapter 7).

WORK "Plastic Love Dream" series (1968), "Couples" series (1969–1972), "Trees" series (1971–).

MEDIUM Silver prints.

AVAILABILITY AND PRICE Through galleries; moderate. Usually printed in very small editions (e.g., one or two prints).

SIGNATURE/OTHER IDENTIFICATION

COLLECTIONS Baltimore, Chicago, IMP/GEH, MIT (Hayden), MOMA, Nebraska, New Mexico, VSW; NGC.

SELECTED BIBLIOGRAPHY
Records 1976–78. Chicago: Chicago Center for Contemporary Photography, Columbia College, 1978.

Roger Mertin. *Rochester, New York,* 1975. Silver print. (Courtesy the artist)

Camera, Sept. 1959.
Album, no. 8 (1970), pp. 4–21.
See also Hume, *The Great West;* Life Library, *Print;* Lyons, *20th Century;* Szarkowski, *Mirrors;* chapter 7 catalogues.

Metzker, Ray K.
United States 1931–

Metzker, who himself became a teacher, attended the Institute of Design (Chicago) in the 1950s and has cited Harry Callahan, with whom he studied, as a major influence. In the 1960s Metzker produced assemblages, some as large as 4×5 feet and containing more than fifty images. Each work can be read in a variety of ways — as repeated fragments of reality, as patterns of black against white or white against black, and so forth; orchestrated as a single visual entity, the whole is entirely different and more exciting than its parts.

Metzker in 1967 explained the direction of this work: "Discontented with the single, fixed frame image (the isolated moment), my work has moved into something of the composite, of collected and related moments. . . . I employ methods of combination, repetition and superimposition. Where photography has been primarily a process of selection and extraction, I wish to investigate the possibilities of synthesis.

"To date my works have formed three categories: repetition with tonal variations in prints; juxtaposed images formed at different moments but linked in the camera by the interval between frames; and overlapping successive exposures on roll film so that the entire strip is seen as one print. . . . I intend the elements to be presented like a mosaic or mural for simultaneous viewing" ("Ray K. Metzker" [1967]).

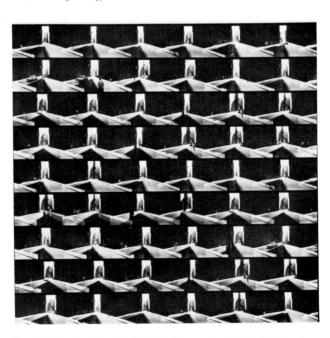

Ray K. Metzker. Untitled, 1966. Silver print, 32¼ × 34¾ inches. (Courtesy The Museum of Modern Art, New York City)

In a 1976 interview Metzker discussed more recent interests: "I guess more and more I am picking up on the word *drawing*, a kind of concern for line. I know what happens when I am working with solarized prints particularly. The flat areas become nothing and it is the edges that count" (Bondi and Misani, p. 3).

WORK   In the 1960s: chiefly multiple imagery — 2 images to 50 or more (sizes from 5×7 inches to 4×5 feet) — of street scenes, nudes, beach scenes. In the 1970s: single images of landscapes, buildings.

MEDIUM   Silver prints.

AVAILABILITY AND PRICE   Most of the large "mosaics" of the 1960s are unique pieces and are in museum collections. Single-image prints and other works are sometimes available through galleries and the photographer; moderate.

SIGNATURE/OTHER IDENTIFICATION

COLLECTIONS   BMFA, Chicago, Harvard (Fogg), IMP/GEH, MMA, MOMA, Smithsonian; BN.

SELECTED BIBLIOGRAPHY
Bennett, Steichen, Metzker: The Wisconsin Heritage in Photography. Milwaukee: Milwaukee Art Center, 1970.
Discovery: Inner and Outer Worlds. Portfolio II. Carmel, Calif.: Friends of Photography, 1970.
"Ray K. Metzker." *Aperture* 9, no. 2 (1961).
"Ray K. Metzker." *Contemporary Photographer* 2, no. 2 (1961).
"Ray K. Metzker." *Aperture* 13, no. 2 (1967).
Inge Bondi and Marco Misani. "Ray K. Metzker — An American Photographer and Teacher." *Printletter* 3 (May/June 1976).
Peter C. Bunnell. "Ray Metzker." *The Print Collector's Newsletter* 9 (Jan./Feb. 1979): 177–179.
See also Life Library, *Art*; Szarkowski, *Looking, Mirrors*; Wise, *Choice*; chapter 7 catalogues.

Meyerowitz, Joel
United States 1938–

Meyerowitz, a graduate of Ohio State University, began his career as a medical illustrator and a painter. He started photographing in 1963 when he was working as an art director and was assigned to accompany Robert Frank on a job.

"Of course, I didn't know he was Robert Frank and I didn't know the world of photography existed," Meyerowitz related in 1978. "When I saw Robert take pictures, I quit my job and went out on the street with a camera and started shooting.

"I started with color. After a year of learning how to use the camera, I put a darkroom together and taught myself to make black-and-white prints. In a sense I've spent the last twelve years getting back to the thing I started with. Color makes everything more interesting. Color suggests more things to look at. Color suggests that the light itself is a subject. Color describes more things, there is more content. The form for the content is more complex, more interesting to work with" (statement to the authors).

WORK   Street scenes and other images of the social landscape; Cape Cod landscapes and other scenes, often using very long exposures to photograph during dusk; views of St. Louis and the Gateway Arch; Florida. (See color plate 8.)

MEDIA   Silver prints (early work), color (Ektacolor RC 74 and dye transfer prints, ranging from 8×10 to 40×60). Meyerowitz prints the 8×10 RC 74 prints from 8×10 negatives; the dye transfers are made from 35mm negatives at a commercial lab, under his supervision.

AVAILABILITY AND PRICE   Through galleries. Silver prints and RC 74 prints moderate; dye transfers moderate to high, depending on size.

SIGNATURE/OTHER IDENTIFICATION

PORTFOLIO   *See* chapter 6 entry.

COLLECTIONS   BMFA, IMP/GEH, MOMA, Philadelphia, St. Louis, Virginia.

SELECTED BIBLIOGRAPHY
Alan Trachtenberg, Peter Neill, Peter C. Bunnell, eds. *The City: American Experience.* New York: Oxford University Press, 1971.
The Snapshot. Ed. and intro. by Jonathan Green. Millerton, N.Y.: Aperture, 1974.
Cape Light: Color Photographs. Boston: Museum of Fine Arts, 1978. Includes interview by Bruce K. MacDonald.
Max Kozloff. "Photography: The Coming to Age of Color." *Artforum* 13 (Jan. 1975): 30–35.
———. "Joel Meyerowitz." *Aperture*, no. 78 (1977), pp. 32–45.
"Joel Meyerowitz." *Camera*, Sept. 1977.
"Joel Meyerowitz." *American Photographer*, Aug. 1978, pp. 60–67.
See also Life Library, *Year 1973*; Lyons, *20th Century*; Szarkowski, *Looking, Mirrors*; chapter 7 catalogue.

Michals, Duane
United States 1932–

Though he works extensively as a commercial photographer, Duane Michals has created a distinct — and distinctive — body of personal images. An important influence on contemporary photography, he is best known for his sequences, which are sometimes accompanied by a handwritten narrative (as are some single images). His

1

2

3

4

5

6

Duane Michals. *The Human Condition,* 1969. Sequence of six
silver prints. (Courtesy the artist)

subject is himself: his feelings, understandings, perceptions, philosophies. Michals uses models and props to tell a sort of story that usually subverts the viewer's ordinary perceptions of reality, and to that extent he can be considered a surrealist. His images are emotionally charged, often humorous and sexually provocative.

"Nothing is what I once thought it was," he has written. "You are not what you think you are. You are nothing you can imagine . . . I use photography to help me explain my experience to myself . . . I am the limits of my work; you are the limits of yours . . . I believe in the imagination. What I cannot see is infinitely more important than what I can see . . . When you look at my photographs, you are looking at my thoughts . . . Never try to be an artist. Just do your work and if the work is true, it will become art" (*Real Dreams*).

WORK   Chiefly surreal, invented situations (single images and sequences ranging from about 5 to 15 images; e.g., *Journey of the Spirit after Death, Something Strange Is Happening*). Also portraits (e.g., René Magritte, Joseph Cornell, Warren Beatty), street photographs in the Soviet Union (1958), scenes of empty spaces in New York City (ca. 1964), fashion, advertising.

MEDIUM   Silver prints (may be accompanied by handwritten text).

AVAILABILITY AND PRICE   Through galleries. Single images with no text moderate, with text moderately high. Sequences vary in price, depending on the number of images in each; moderately high to extremely high.

SIGNATURE/OTHER IDENTIFICATION

Duane Michals

PORTFOLIOS   *See* chapter 6 entry.

COLLECTIONS   Chicago, IMP/GEH, MOMA, Museum of New Mexico, New Mexico, Norton Simon, Smithsonian, UCLA.

SELECTED BIBLIOGRAPHY
Sequences. Garden City, N.Y.: Doubleday, 1970.
Journey of the Spirit after Death. New York: Winter House, 1972.
Things Are Queer. Cologne: Galerie Wilde, 1972.
Chance Meeting. Cologne: Galerie Wilde, 1973.
Duane Michals: The Photographic Illusion. New York: Crowell, 1975.
Real Dreams. Danbury, N.H.: Addison House, 1976.
Take One and See Mt. Fujiyama and Other Stories. Rochester, N.Y.: Light Impressions/Stefan Mihal, 1976.
Manfred Willmann, ed. *American Photographers*. Graz, Austria: Fotogalerie im Forum Stadtpark, 1977.
Homage to Cavafy. With Constantine Cavafy. Danbury, N.H.: Addison House, 1978.
Album, no. 7 (1970), pp. 34–41.
See also Lewis, *Darkroom 1*; Life Library, *Art, Themes*; Szarkowski, *Looking, Mirrors*; Wise, *Choice*; chapter 7 catalogues.

Modotti, Tina
Mexico (b. Italy) 1896–1942

Although Modotti's images were admired and published in the 1920s, her reputation for the past few decades has been based on her role as companion and model for Edward Weston. In recent years, with the rediscovery and exhibition of her photographs, she is being recognized for her own work — sharply focused, unmanipulated, "straight" images. Most of it is scattered, however, and there is no major collection of her prints known at this time. A small group of her negatives that remained intact were printed by Richard Benson for an exhibition at New York City's Museum of Modern Art in 1977.

After emigrating from Italy to the United States about 1918, Modotti appeared in several early Hollywood films. She and Weston lived and photographed together in Mexico in the early 1920s, and she produced most of her work between 1922 and 1930. Intensely opposed to Fascism, Modotti was part of the militant revolutionary movement in Mexico and was friendly with Diego Rivera and other left-wing cultural and political figures. Her political activism caused her expulsion from the country in 1930, and for the next ten years she was involved in the political unrest in Europe. She eventually returned under a false passport to Mexico, where she died.

WORK   Chiefly portraits (e.g., artists and other friends in Mexico, Mexican peasants, mothers with children), abstract compositions from patterns made by objects (e.g., wine glasses, telephone wires), still lifes (e.g., bullets, corn, and a sickle).

MEDIA   Silver prints, platinum prints.

AVAILABILITY AND PRICE   Through galleries and at auction but very rare; high to extremely high. Modern prints by Richard Benson are not offered for sale.

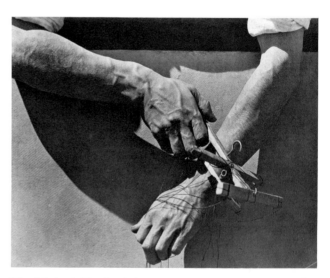

Tina Modotti. *Hands of the Marionette Player*, 1926. Platinum print. (Collection, The Museum of Modern Art, New York City. Anonymous gift)

COLLECTIONS IMP/GEH, MOMA, Oakland.

SELECTED BIBLIOGRAPHY
Anita Brenner. *Idols behind Altars*. New York: Harcourt, Brace, 1929. Photographs by Modotti and Edward Weston.
Bertram D. Wolfe and Diego Rivera. *Portrait of Mexico*. New York: Covici Friede, 1937. Photographs by Modotti, Manuel Alvarez Bravo, Lupercio.
Mildred Constantine. *Tina Modotti: A Fragile Life*. New York: Paddington, 1975.
Forma: Revista de Artes Plásticas 1, no. 4 (1927).
Transition, Feb. 1929. Selected images.
David Vestal. "Tina's Trajectory." *Infinity*, Feb. 1966, p. 4.
"Ten Photographs by Tina Modotti." *Massachusetts Review*, no. 13 (1972), pp. 113–124.
"Sesso, Arte, Violenza e Marxismo." *Bolaffiarte*, 1977, pp. 54–55. Special issue.
See also Mann, *Women*; Szarkowski, *Looking*.

Moholy-Nagy, László
United States (b. Austria-Hungary) 1895–1946

A prolific and versatile artist and theoretician whose work has been influential in numerous creative areas, Moholy-Nagy is well known as a painter allied with the constructivist movement, but he also sculpted, made films, designed and wrote books, taught (at the Bauhaus, Germany, 1920s; at the New Bauhaus School of Design, later the Institute of Design, Chicago, 1930s–1940s), and, not least, photographed and explored the potential of the photographic medium.

It is not known when he started photographing, but by 1922 he and Lucia Moholy, his first wife, were collaborating on photograms and he was simultaneously exploring photomontage and camera-made imagery. Lucia Moholy reports that almost all photographs produced prior to 1928 were the result of their collaboration. The photograms were directly related to his "transparent" paintings, which gave the effect of abstract superimposed patterns of light. Leland D. Rice described the similar treatment of light in the photograms: "The photographic paper acted as a neutral surface which complemented his intention to 'dematerialize' the precise looks of an arrangement of objects to obtain a 'new vision.' The observer . . . stares at a series of flat, abstract patterns floating in a deep, plastic space" (*Photographs of Moholy-Nagy*).

Moholy-Nagy's camera images are significant for their free exploration of vantage point. He shot from overhead, underneath, and at oblique angles, often violating the eye-level point of view that had dominated Western art from the Renaissance until the twentieth century. He knew unusual viewpoints were disconcerting and he once observed: "The photographic camera reproduces the purely optical image . . . whereas the eye, together with our intellectual experience, supplements perceived optical phenomena by means of association. . . . Thus in the photographic camera we have the most reliable aid to a be-ginning of objective vision" (*Painting, Photography, and Film*).

Because photography as an art in America was dominated from the 1920s to the 1950s by "straight" photography — by the work of Paul Strand, Edward Weston, Ansel Adams, and others — many of Moholy-Nagy's ideas about the creative use of photography have only relatively recently gained wide acceptance. He once declared: "The enemy of photography is the convention, the fixed rules of the 'how-to-do.' The salvation of photography comes from the experiment. The experimenter has no preconceived idea about photography. . . . He dares to call 'photography' all the results which can be achieved with photographic means with camera or without . . ." (*Vision in Motion*).

László Moholy-Nagy. *Fotoplastik*, ca. 1925. Photomontage. (Courtesy Robert Schoelkopf Gallery)

WORK Includes photograms, photomontages (which he called *fotoplastik* pieces), camera images showing "a new way of seeing" (e.g., strong shadows on objects, negative images, scenes from unusual angles), documentary images (e.g., London street markets).

MEDIA Silver prints, color transparencies. Moholy-Nagy was not interested in darkroom labor and did little, if any, himself. Lucia Moholy did the technical work in their collaborations, and other prints were commercially processed. Much of his later work was on Kodachrome slides. Beaumont Newhall reported that Moholy-Nagy "once said . . . that if his seeing was not strong enough to stand up to the routine processing of the corner drugstore then he wasn't seeing in a challenging way" (quoted in *Photographs of Moholy-Nagy*).

AVAILABILITY AND PRICE Through galleries and at auction but infrequently found; high to extremely high. The original assemblages of Moholy-Nagy's montages are extremely rare, priced accordingly.

COLLECTIONS IMP/GEH, MOMA; Antwerp.

SIGNATURE/OTHER IDENTIFICATION

and capture specifically for the camera the gestures that were the most significant and most expressive of each dance's meaning. "In photographing action," Morgan explained, "I don't merely react to the surface form in motion, but basic[al]ly to the invisible axis of the form in motion, in its space relation to other forms. The serene harmony of a tree comes from its vertical axis responding to gravity. The excitement of a leap comes from our empathy with another person whose axis is no longer 'safe with gravity' . . ." (*Barbara Morgan*, p. 155).

Morgan has created strongly realized work in several distinctly different areas. For example, the photomontages she created as metaphors of the rigors of New York City life seem quite unlike her sensitive and touching photographs of children or her abstract light drawings (images of a light source in motion). But underlying all her images, according to Anne Tucker, are Morgan's "own impressions about life's rhythms. These concerns with rhythm, motion, dynamism, and harmony, all pivotal to her work, have served to unify the diverse subjects of her art" (Tucker, *Eye*, p. 93).

SELECTED BIBLIOGRAPHY

Malerei, Fotographie, Film. Munich: Langen, 1925. U.S. ed., *Painting, Photography and Film.* Cambridge, Mass.: MIT Press, 1969.

Von Material zu Architektur. Munich: Langen, 1929. U.S. ed., *The New Vision.* New York: Brewer, Warren & Putnam, 1932. Also later variant eds.

L. Moholy-Nagy: 60 Fotos / 60 Photos / 60 Photographies. Ed. by Franz Roh. Berlin: Klinkhardt & Biermann, 1930.

Mary Benedetta. *The Street Markets of London.* London: Miles, 1936. Reprint, New York: Blom, 1972.

Eton Portrait. Text by Bernard Fergusson. London: Miles, 1937. Rev. ed., *Portrait of Eton.* London: Muller, 1949.

An Oxford University Chest. Text by John Betjeman. London: Miles, 1938.

Vision in Motion. Chicago: Theobald, 1947.

Sibyl Moholy-Nagy. *Moholy-Nagy: Experiment in Totality.* Intro. by Walter Gropius. New York: Harper, 1950. Reprint, Cambridge, Mass.: MIT Press, 1969.

Moholy-Nagy. Ed. by Richard Kostelanetz. New York: Praeger, 1970. Bibliography.

Lucia Moholy. *Moholy-Nagy: Marginal Notes; Documentary Absurdities.* Krefeld, Germany: Scherpe, 1972.

Photographs of Moholy-Nagy. Ed. by Leland D. Rice and David W. Steadman. Claremont, Calif.: Galleries of the Claremont Colleges, 1975. Bibliography.

Telehor: The International Review [for] New Vision (Brno, Czechoslovakia: Kalivoda), 1936. Special issue.

Caroline Fawkes. "Photography and Moholy-Nagy's Do-it-yourself Aesthetic." *Studio International,* July 1975, pp. 18–26.

See also Life Library, *Great Photographers, Print;* Lyons, *Photographers;* Travis, *Julien Levy;* Witkin, *Julien Levy.*

Morgan, Barbara
United States 1900–

Barbara Morgan's continued and enthusiastic involvement in the arts well into her seventies confirms an early, somewhat precocious dedication: she was only four when she decided to become an artist. Trained in art, she taught at the University of California at Los Angeles, and with considerable encouragement from her husband, writer/photographer (and later publisher) Willard D. Morgan, she added photography to her painting and drawing activity. The work of Edward Weston, which she first saw in 1925, eventually convinced her that photography could be a medium of artistic expression — one that she could use to reveal the underlying essence and rhythm of life.

Morgan is best known for her images of dancers such as Martha Graham, José Limón, and Merce Cunningham. She did not photograph performances; instead, she studied the dances and then worked with the performers to distill

Barbara Morgan. *Letter to the World (Kick),* 1940. Silver print. (Courtesy the artist)

WORK   Dancers (mid-1930s to 1940s); photomontages as metaphors of New York City life; abstract light drawings; trees and natural forms; children; portraits.

MEDIUM   Silver prints.

AVAILABILITY AND PRICE   Through galleries. Modern prints (ranging from 11×14 to 16×20, printed by Morgan with assistants) are priced moderately high. Vintage prints (in the photographer's personal collection) are not offered for sale.

SIGNATURE/OTHER IDENTIFICATION

Barbara Morgan

PORTFOLIOS   *See* chapter 6 entry.

COLLECTIONS Addison, IMP/GEH, LOC, MIT, MMA, MOMA, New Orleans, NPG (U.S.), NYPL (Lincoln Center), Philadelphia, Princeton (Art Museum), Smithsonian.

SELECTED BIBLIOGRAPHY
Martha Graham: Sixteen Dances in Photographs. New York: Duell, Sloan & Pearce, 1941.
Prestini's Art in Wood. Text by Edgar Kaufmann, Jr. Lake Forest, Ill.: Pocahontas Press, 1950. 1,000 copies.
Summer's Children: A Photographic Cycle of Life at Camp. Scarsdale, N.Y.: Morgan & Morgan, 1951.
Barbara Morgan. Intro. by Peter C. Bunnell. Hastings-on-Hudson, N.Y.: Morgan & Morgan, 1972. Bibliography.
"Kinetic Design in Photography." *Aperture* 1, no. 4 (1953): 18–27.
Aperture 11, no. 1 (1964). Entire issue.
Ruth Spencer. "Barbara Morgan." *The British Journal of Photography,* 13 June 1975, pp. 512–515.
New York Times, 19 June 1975. Interview.
Morgan's work appeared in many issues of *The Complete Photographer* (1941–1943).
See also Life Library, *Art, Children, Studio, Tool;* Mann, *Women;* Szarkowski, *Looking;* Tucker, *Eye;* chapter 7 catalogues.

Morris, Wright
United States 1910–

More widely known as a writer than as a photographer, Wright Morris has contributed to photography a unique combination of pictures and prose. Born in Nebraska, Morris lived there and in Illinois until he left in 1930 to attend college in California. Though he returned only intermittently to the Midwest, its influence on the subject matter and style of his art has remained strong.

Morris's serious concern with photography began in 1935, paralleling his growth as a writer. In 1939 he realized that a powerful relationship could exist between his writing and photographs. *The Inhabitants* and Morris's similar works are photo/text documents of ·rural and small-town life, although the prose does not explicitly describe the images. He once indicated, "I wanted each medium to exist independently, in its unique separateness, until joined in the mind's eye of the reader" (*Wright Morris: Structures and Artifacts*). People are deliberately omitted from the human environment Morris records. He noted that "the absence of people in [my] photographs enhances their presence in the objects — the structures, the artifacts, even the landscape suggest its appropriate inhabitant" (ibid.).

James Alinder wrote that "the photographs of Wright Morris present with formal elegance, precision and clarity an emotional and intellectual commitment to the commonplace, to the structures and artifacts of a time now disappeared. These pictures are the visible essence of that era, and they may begin to indicate to us what of the present needs to be salvaged" ("Wright Morris," p. 193).

WORK Landscapes, buildings, interiors, and objects in the United States; Venice.

MEDIA Silver prints, color (Venice images).

AVAILABILITY AND PRICE Through galleries but rare; moderately high. Morris seldom prints; while he was teaching at Princeton University in 1971/72 he had access to a darkroom and printed some of his old negatives.

SIGNATURE/OTHER IDENTIFICATION

COLLECTIONS BMFA, MOMA, Nebraska, San Francisco.

SELECTED BIBLIOGRAPHY
The Inhabitants. New York: Scribner, 1946. Reprint, New York: Da Capo, 1973.
The Home Place. New York: Scribner, 1948. Reprint, Lincoln: University of Nebraska Press, 1968.
God's Country and My People. New York: Harper & Row, 1968.
Love Affair: A Venetian Journal. New York: Harper & Row, 1972.
The Cat's Meow. Los Angeles: Black Sparrow Press, 1975. 325 copies, signed, with original photographic frontispiece.
Wright Morris: Structures and Artifacts. Photographs 1933–1954. Intro. by Norman A. Geske. Lincoln: University of Nebraska Press, 1975.
Robert E. Knoll, ed. *Conversations with Wright Morris: Critical Views and Responses.* Lincoln: University of Nebraska Press, 1977.
James Alinder. "Wright Morris: An Introduction and Photographic Chronology." *Exposure* 14, no. 1 (Feb. 1976): 14–17.
———. "Wright Morris: You Can Go Home Again." *Modern Photography,* Mar. 1978, pp. 116 ff.
See also Szarkowski, *Looking.*

Wright Morris. *Drawer with Silverware,* 1947. Silver print. (Courtesy the artist)

Muybridge, Eadweard
United States (b. England) 1830–1904

Muybridge (born Edward James Muggeridge) is notable in that he made major contributions to two distinctly different areas in photography — western landscapes and motion studies. He arrived in America about 1852 and by 1856 was the proprietor of a bookstore in San Francisco. For several years he photographed a variety of California scenes, gaining his first real fame with views of Yosemite in 1867. His 1872 Yosemite mammoth plates were praised even above Carleton E. Watkins's celebrated views of 1861–1866. Muybridge's landscape work was much more romantic than that of Watkins. He intentionally chose dramatic lighting and camera angles and often exaggerated the distances between near and far objects so as to emphasize the impression of deep space. To add clouds (absent from the overly blue-sensitive wet-plate emulsion), he printed them in from separate negatives; later he used a "skyshade" to shield the negative so that the sky would not be overexposed.

In 1872 Muybridge was commissioned to photograph Leland Stanford's horse Occident as it moved past the camera. Stanford had wagered that a horse trotting at full speed had all four feet off the ground at some point in its stride and he thought photographs might prove his point. Muybridge succeeded in recording a silhouette of the fast-moving horse and won the wager for Stanford — as well as Stanford's continuing support for motion studies.

In 1884, under the auspices of the University of Pennsylvania, Muybridge began his major work — an estimated 20,000 negatives, arranged in 781 plates, of animals and humans in motion. Muybridge simultaneously photographed each subject from several different points of view, with batteries of as many as twelve cameras making exposures in sequence. His subjects engaged in myriad activities: tigers paced, birds flew, horses leaped; men, women, and children (clothed and unclothed) walked, ran, jumped, poured tea, boxed, et cetera. The images are valuable both as scientific data (Muybridge's intention) and as interesting visual imagery in themselves. To complement his still pictures of motion, Muybridge devised his Zoöpraxiscope (1879), a machine that projected in rapid sequence drawings made from his photographs, thus giving them the illusion of motion. His device was an important forerunner of the motion-picture film projector.

WORK   Includes daily life in California (1867 and after; e.g., industry, agriculture, missions, railroads, waterfront scenes), Alaska (1868), Yosemite (1867, 1872), route of the Central Pacific Railroad (1870), Modoc Indian War (1873), landscape and daily life in Central America (1875), panorama of San Francisco from California Street Hill (1877), studies of humans and animals in motion (Sacramento, Calif., 1872; Palo Alto, Calif., 1878–1879; University of Pennsylvania, Philadelphia, 1884–1885).

MEDIA   Until 1881 collodion wet-plate negatives (ranging from stereographs to 20×24), albumen prints. Also gelatin dry-plate negatives; lantern slides. Until 1872 Muybridge signed his work "Helios."

AVAILABILITY AND PRICE   Through galleries and at auction. Large Yosemite views very rare; extremely high. Individual collotypes from *Animal Locomotion* frequently available; low to moderate. In 1978 a complete set of *Animal Locomotion* (11 folio volumes) sold at auction for $66,000, including 10% buyer's fee (Argus Ltd., New York City). Stereographs relatively rare, expensive for their category; low to moderate. All other work rare; high to extremely high.

SIGNATURE/OTHER IDENTIFICATION

Eadward Muybridge. *Woman Pirouetting (.277 second)*. Sequence of twelve images, collotype plate 187 from *Animal Locomotion*, 1887. (Courtesy The Witkin Gallery)

PORTFOLIO *See* chapter 6 entry.

COLLECTIONS AMNH, California (Bancroft), CHS, CSL, Harvard (Carpenter, Widener), IMP/GEH, LOC, MMA, New Mexico, NYHS, NYPL, Oakland, Philadelphia, Philadelphia Civic Center, Philadelphia Library, Princeton, Smithsonian, Stanford, UCLA; Kingston-on-Thames, NGC, RPS, Science Museum, VA.

SELECTED BIBLIOGRAPHY
John Shertzer Hittell. *Yosemite: Its Wonders and Its Beauties.* San Francisco: Bancroft, 1868. 20 albumen prints by Muybridge.
The Pacific Coast of Central America and Mexico; the Isthmus of Panama; Guatemala; and the Cultivation and Shipment of Coffee. San Francisco, 1876. The 6 known extant copies generally contain from 136 to 144 albumen prints.
Panorama of San Francisco from California Street Hill. San Francisco: Morse's Gallery, 1877. 11 albumen prints mounted on cloth (entire panorama nearly 8 feet long). Includes a separate photo-key index listing 220 locations.
J. D. B. Stillman. *The Horse in Motion.* Boston: Osgood, 1882.
Animal Locomotion: An Electro-Photographic Investigation of Consecutive Phases of Animal Movement. 11 vols. Philadelphia: University of Pennsylvania, 1887. 781 collotypes.
Animals in Motion. London: Chapman & Hall, 1899. Selected plates from *Animal Locomotion.* Reprint, ed. by Lewis S. Brown. New York: Dover, 1957.
The Human Figure in Motion. London: Chapman & Hall, 1901. Selected plates from *Animal Locomotion.* Reprint, intro. by Robert Taft. New York: Dover, 1955.
Kevin MacDonnell. *Eadweard Muybridge: The Man Who Invented the Moving Picture.* Boston: Little, Brown, 1972.
Eadweard Muybridge: The Stanford Years, 1872–1882. Stanford University Museum of Art, 1972.
Gordon Hendricks. *Eadweard Muybridge: The Father of the Motion Picture.* New York: Grossman, 1975. Bibliography.
Robert Bartlett Haas. *Muybridge: Man in Motion.* Berkeley: University of California Press, 1976.
Timo Tauno Pajunen. "Eadweard Muybridge." *Camera,* Jan. and Feb. 1973.
See also Andrews, *Pioneers;* Naef and Wood, *Era;* Scharf, *Pioneers;* Taft, *Photography.*

Mydans, Carl
United States 1907–

Mydans first worked as a reporter for the Boston *Globe* and Boston *Herald,* then in 1931 joined *American Banker,* a Wall Street newspaper. In that year he bought a 35mm camera and began to do free-lance photographic work. In 1935 he won his first major assignment: taking photographs for a book (never published) for the Resettlement Administration in Washington, D.C. The agency — which later became the Farm Security Administration (FSA) — soon reassigned him to Roy Stryker's staff of photographers documenting conditions across America during the thirties.

Mydans's first photographic trip for Stryker was to "do cotton" in the South, but he was drawn more to people, particularly the rural poor, than to cotton production. Mydans later recollected: "All of the staff members of the FSA felt strongly about people. If you go through the files, you will know that of all things these photographers felt strongly about the people around them" (O'Neal, p. 94).

Mydans's 35mm technique produced more photographs than most people were used to seeing in the 1930s, when "miniature" camera work was still relatively new. Stryker recalled: "Carl came in with hundreds of feet of 35mm film. I had never seen anybody take so many pictures! We had to spread everything out on the floor of the office just to see what he had. It was wonderful!" (Hurley, p. 44). In 1936 Mydans left the FSA to join the newly forming *Life* magazine; he eventually became head of the Time-Life bureau in Tokyo.

WORK FSA images; numerous assignments for Time-Life, including extensive coverage of World War II and the Korean War. (See illustration, page 137.)

MEDIA Silver prints, color.

AVAILABILITY AND PRICE Modern FSA prints (black and whites only) from the Library of Congress extremely low. Few other prints available.

COLLECTIONS LOC (FSA work). LIFE Picture Collection (New York City) preserves negatives Mydans made for Time Inc.

SELECTED BIBLIOGRAPHY
Marguerite Higgins. *War in Korea: The Report of a Woman Combat Correspondent.* New York: Doubleday, 1951.
More Than Meets the Eye. New York: Harper, 1959.
J. G. Lootens. "The Story of Carl Mydans." *U.S. Camera,* Dec. 1939, pp. 22–23.
See also bibliography in FSA entry (includes O'Neal and Hurley).

Nadar
France 1820–1910

Nadar (Gaspard-Félix Tournachon) was a journalist and caricaturist who is best known for his photographs of the intelligentsia of mid-nineteenth-century Paris. He began to photograph about 1853 and his studio soon became a meeting place for numerous writers and artists. His portraits of them are simple — characteristically three-quarter length, with a plain background, and with lighting high and from the side. More complex is his insight into their characters and his ability to capture revealing images of them. He wrote of the importance of "the instinctive understanding of your subject — it's this immediate contact which can put you in sympathy with the sitter . . . and enables you to make not just a chancy, dreary, cardboard copy typical of the merest hack in the darkroom, but a likeness of the most intimate and happy kind, a speaking likeness" (quoted in Scharf, *Pioneers,* p. 106).

Nadar's exuberant personality and exploits made him as well known as many of the famous people who came to his studio. He was one of the first to photograph using electric illumination; in 1861 he made an extensive series of photographs with carbon arc lights in the catacombs and sewers of Paris. He was an enthusiastic aeronaut: in

Nadar. *Sarah Bernhardt,* 1859. Modern silver print from the original plate. (Courtesy IMP/GEH)

1858 he took the first photographs from a balloon — a formidable feat, since the collodion technique that he used involved coating and processing on the spot; the Daumier lithograph caricature of Nadar in a balloon "elevating photography to a high art" (*Nadar élevant la photographie à la hauteur de l'Art*) is a collector's item. In 1886 Nadar conceived the idea of a picture interview in which each photograph would be accompanied by the words spoken when the picture was taken, and he had his son Paul photograph him interviewing the centenarian scientist Michel-Eugène Chevreul "On the Art of Living a Hundred Years." From about 1886 until 1939 Nadar's studio was operated by his son, who continued to use his father's signature as a trademark.

WORK   Chiefly portraits (e.g., Sarah Bernhardt, Liszt, Daumier, Baudelaire). Also includes aerial views, catacombs, and sewers of Paris; photo interviews; portraits of the insane (ca. 1858–1860).

MEDIA   Collodion wet-plate negatives, albumen prints (ranging from cartes de visite to 8×10).

AVAILABILITY AND PRICE   Through galleries and at auction. Most often found are cartes de visite and cabinet photographs with Nadar's ornate signature logo; low to moderately high. Also available are woodburytypes (see illustration, page 45) of his images from *Galerie Contemporaine* (1876–1885) and other publications (e.g., *Paris-Théâtre*); moderate to moderately high. Unique prints (large format or not mass produced) very rare; extremely high. (Prints signed "Nadar Jeune" were taken by Nadar's brother Adrien Tournachon.)

SIGNATURE/OTHER IDENTIFICATION

PORTFOLIO   *See* chapter 6 entry.

COLLECTIONS   IMP/GEH, New Mexico; Antwerp, Archives Photographiques (negatives), BN (prints and personal papers), Caisse Nationale, Société Française.

SELECTED BIBLIOGRAPHY
A Terre et en l'air . . . Mémoires du Géant. Paris: E. Dentu, 1864.
Le Droit au vol. Paris: Hetzel, 1865. 3rd ed. has preface by George
    Sand. U.K. ed., *The Right to Fly.* London: Cassell, 1866.
Les Ballons en 1870. Paris: Chatelain, 1870.
Quand j'étais Photographe. Paris: E. Flammarion, 1900.
Nadar. Paris: Bibliothèque Nationale, 1965.
Jean Prinet and Antoinette Dillasser. *Nadar.* Paris: Colin, 1966.
Nadar: 50 Photographies de ses illustrés contemporains. Paris:
    Barret, 1975.
Nigel Gosling. *Nadar.* New York: Knopf, 1976.
Camera, Dec. 1960. Entire issue.
See also Newhall, *Masters*; Scharf, *Pioneers*; Witkin, *Julien Levy.*

Nègre, Charles
France 1820–1880

Nègre, a student of J. A. D. Ingres and Paul Delaroche, initially used photography to aid his efforts as a painter. He wrote: "Henceforth, photography will replace that category of drawing requiring rigorous accuracy. . . . In giving us perspective and geometric precision, however, photography does not destroy the personal feeling of the artist: he must always know how to choose his subject; he must know how to choose the most advantageous point of view; he must choose the effect that will be most in harmony with his subject" (Borcoman, p. 6).

In the 1850s Nègre made a number of unposed photographs of tradespeople on Paris streets; he was one of the first photographers to concentrate on such subject matter. He also photographed in Provence and made a number of images of monuments such as Chartres Cathedral. He experimented with permanent-ink processes, including photogravure (in 1865 he made sixty-four gravure plates of photographs taken the previous year by Lieutenant L. Vigne during the Duc de Luynes's geological expedition to the Dead Sea). Nègre lost contact with his fellow artists when failing health forced him to leave Paris permanently for Nice in 1863. In his last years he produced commissioned portraits and views of the Riviera for the tourist trade.

WORK   Chiefly monuments of Paris (e.g., Notre Dame, Hôtel de Ville), views of events in the streets, tradespeople (e.g., organgrinders, chimney sweeps, musicians), genre scenes. Also archeological ruins, scenery of the Midi and the Riviera, portraits (e.g., Maxime Du Camp, Théophile Gautier), interiors and personnel of Vincennes Imperial Asylum, art reproductions.

Charles Nègre. *The Vampire* [portrait of Henri Le Secq], ca. 1853. From *Charles Nègre, Photographe,* 1963. Salt print. (Courtesy Lee D. Witkin)

MEDIA Waxed-paper negatives, calotypes and salt prints (up to 20×29); collodion wet-plate negatives, albumen prints. A single extant daguerreotype is attributed to Nègre.

AVAILABILITY AND PRICE Through galleries and at auction but very rare; high to extremely high.

SIGNATURE/OTHER IDENTIFICATION

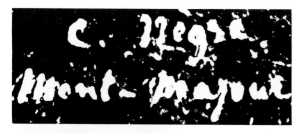

COLLECTIONS The National Gallery of Canada (Ottawa) holds the largest public collection of Nègre's work. Also IMP/GEH, RISD, Smithsonian; BN, Société Française.

SELECTED BIBLIOGRAPHY
"Le Midi de la France photographié." Unpublished manuscript (ca. 1854) held by Rhode Island School of Design. It may have been meant to serve as an introduction to Nègre's *Midi de la France* album, which was never completed (two installments were issued in 1854).

De la Gravure héliographique, son utilité, son origine, son application à l'étude de l'histoire, des arts et des sciences naturelles. Nice, 1867.

Erika Billeter and Hans Finsler. *Pioniere der Photographie: Edward Steichen, Charles Nègre.* Zurich: Kunstgewerbemuseum, 1963.

André Jammes. *Charles Nègre, Photographe.* Paris: André Jammes, 1963.

Max Heib and André Jammes. *Charles Nègre, 1820–1880.* München: Münchner Stadtmuseum, 1966.

James Borcoman. *Charles Nègre.* Ottawa: National Gallery of Canada, 1976.

See also Coke, *Painter*; Jammes and Sobieszek, *Primitive*; Life Library, *Great Photographers.*

Nettles, Bea
United States 1946–

Nettles's body of highly personal work consists of old photographs of her family and herself, an ongoing series of photographs of her friends, and recent self-portraits. She uses various processes to physically transform the images into evocative interpretations of her past and present.

"In my images," she explained, "I am attempting to make fantasies visible. Through them I am investigating and sharing myself, my life, and the landscape that is around and within me. Family ties, twenty years spent in the green and growth of Florida, and dreams that I remember in the morning are elements in my work. I feel that rather than 'taking' photographs, I am making them. I freely use any materials to make my images: . . . thread, dust, cloth, plastic, pencil, mirrors, as well as photographic paper and film. I'm trying to stretch and share the limits of my imagination: that is why and how I continue to work" (quoted in Tucker, *Eye,* p. 155).

WORK Chiefly a series of self-published limited-edition books and unique nonsilver images dealing with landscapes and people in the photographer's life. Also includes a series of prints from negatives made with a Diana, an inexpensive plastic camera that unpredictably introduces distortion, variations in sharpness, and other changes in the image. (See color plate 6.)

MEDIA Cyanotypes, gum-bichromate prints, Kwik-Prints, photosilkscreen, photosensitized fabrics. Also mixed media, silver prints.

AVAILABILITY AND PRICE Through galleries; moderate to high, depending on size and process.

PORTFOLIO *See* chapter 6 Schools and workshops entry.

COLLECTIONS IMP/GEH, MMA; NGC.

SIGNATURE/OTHER IDENTIFICATION

B. Nettles

SELECTED BIBLIOGRAPHY

Ten works were published by the photographer, in Rochester, N.Y.: *Events in the Water,* 1972; *Events in the Sky,* 1973; *The Imaginary Blowtorch* (with Grace N. Nettles), 1973; *A Is for Applebiting Alligators,* 1974; *The Elsewhere Bird,* 1974; *The Nymph of the Highlands,* 1974; *Dream Pages,* 1975; *Mountain Dream Tarot,* 1975; *Swamp Lady,* 1975; *Of Loss and Love,* 1976.

Breaking the Rules: A Photo Media Cookbook. Rochester, N.Y.: Inky Press/Light Impressions, 1977.

See also Colors (in color bibliography); Tucker, *Eye;* chapter 7 catalogues.

Newman, Arnold
United States 1918–

Best known for his experimental portraits of people mainly in the arts, sciences, and politics, Newman began photographing as an apprentice in a chain portrait studio in Philadelphia. Shortly afterward, he began making environmental portraits — as he put it, simply "pictures of people in their natural surroundings." In 1941 he moved to New York City and became acquainted with various painters and sculptors, whom he photographed in their studios. In 1945 his first one-man show, Artists Look Like This, gained him much attention and he began to freelance for *Life, Harper's Bazaar,* and other major magazines; since then his work has been widely published and exhibited and his style has been very influential on portraiture.

Newman's portraits tend to be symbolic as well as abstract at times, succinctly presenting the subject's working life in a combination of powerful graphic design and significant environmental detail. According to him, "a good portrait must first be a good photograph. Its concept is always changing, and the inquiry into the abstraction and symbolism of the subject is only a part of it. A creative person is always looking, seeking, and trying to work out new ideas" (statement to the authors, 1978).

WORK Chiefly portraiture (e.g., Alfred Stieglitz and Georgia O'Keeffe, Stravinsky). Also includes early documentary work, abstractions, industrial photography, still lifes.

MEDIA Silver prints; color; some use of collage, cut-out images, shaped assemblages.

AVAILABILITY AND PRICE Through galleries; moderately high.

SIGNATURE/OTHER IDENTIFICATION

Arnold Newman

PORTFOLIO *See* chapter 6 entry.

COLLECTIONS Chicago, IMP/GEH, MMA, MOMA, Phoenix, Smithsonian, Worcester; Israel Museum.

SELECTED BIBLIOGRAPHY

Bravo Stravinsky. Text by Robert Craft. Cleveland: World, 1967.

One Mind's Eye. Foreword by Beaumont Newhall. Intro. by Robert Sobieszek. Boston: Godine, 1974. Bibliography. Another ed., Boston: New York Graphic Society, 1978.

Faces U.S.A. Foreword by Thomas Thompson. Garden City, N.Y.: Amphoto, 1978.

The Great British. London: Weidenfeld & Nicolson, 1979, and Boston: New York Graphic Society, 1979.

Arthur Goldsmith. "On Assignment with Arnold Newman." *Popular Photography,* May 1957, pp. 80 ff.

Ruth Spencer. "Arnold Newman." *The British Journal of Photography,* 18 Apr. 1975.

See also Danziger and Conrad, *Interviews;* Life Library, *Great Photographers, Light, Studio.*

Arnold Newman. *Alfred Krupp,* 1963. Silver print. (Courtesy the artist. Copyright © 1974 by Arnold Newman)

Niepce, Joseph Nicéphore
France 1765–1833

Niepce is today honored in his native country as the father of photography, although he died without having attained the goal for which he spent much of his life and fortune:

the discovery of a practical means of fixing a continuous-tone photographic image taken from nature.

As a young man Niepce was intrigued by the camera obscura. In 1814 his interest in the new art of lithography led him to experiment with reproducing engravings on plates coated with light-sensitive varnishes. In 1826 Niepce made the earliest surviving permanent photograph from a camera-made image — a view from a window of his house Le Gras at Saint-Loup-de-Varennes. The process involved, which he called heliography, used bitumen of Judea (a substance that hardens on exposure to light) coated on a polished pewter plate.

Niepce went to England at this time, but because of his secretiveness about details was unable to interest the Royal Society in his discoveries. Through the offices of the Paris lensmaker Chevalier, he came in contact with L. J. M. Daguerre in 1826, but again he was unwilling to divulge much information. Finally, in 1829 Niepce entered into a partnership agreement with Daguerre. Niepce died in 1833, however, and Daguerre developed an entirely different means of fixing an image — the daguerreotype — which won him popular attention as the inventor of photography.

WORK/MEDIUM Heliographs. Chiefly contact prints made from engravings (e.g., of Pope Pius VII, Cardinal d'Amboise). Also includes a few camera-made images (e.g., *Table Laid for a Meal*). (See illustration, page 14.)

AVAILABILITY AND PRICE Exceptionally rare; would be extremely high. Authentication by experts is essential.

SIGNATURE/OTHER IDENTIFICATION (Example from a letter)

COLLECTIONS The Gernsheim Collection at the University of Texas (Austin) holds "the world's first photograph" (which Helmut Gernsheim found in England) — the view at Le Gras — and two manuscripts by Niepce describing his invention of heliography. Also Musée Nicéphore Niepce, Science Museum, Société Française.

SELECTED BIBLIOGRAPHY
L. J. M. Daguerre. *Historique et description des procédés du Daguerréotype et du Diorama*. Paris: Giroux, 1839. Includes "Notice sur l'héliographie." Reprint, intro. by Beaumont Newhall. New York: Winter House, 1971. Bibliography.

Isidore Niépce. *Historique de la découverte improprement nommée daguerréotype; précedé d'une notice sur son véritable inventeur, feu M. Joseph-Nicéphore Niepce . . . .* Paris: Astier, 1841.

Victor Fouque. *La Vérité sur l'invention de la photographie: Nicéphore Niepce, sa vie, ses essais, ses travaux, d'après sa correspondance et autres documents inédits*. Paris: Librairie

des Auteurs et de l'Académie des Bibliophiles, 1867. U.S. ed., *The Truth concerning the Invention of Photography: Nicéphore Niepce, His Life and Works*. New York: Tennant & Ward, 1935. Reprint, New York: Arno, 1973.

Ernouf [Baron Alfred Auguste]. *Les Inventeurs du gaz et de la photographie*. Paris: Hachette, 1877.

A. Davanne. *Nicéphore Niepce; Inventeur de la photographie*. Paris, 1885.

Joseph-Nicéphore Niepce: Lettres, 1816-1817. Correspondance conservée à Chalon-sur-Saône. Rouen, France: Pavillon de la Photographie, 1973.

Joseph-Nicéphore Niepce: Correspondances, 1825-1829. Rouen, France: Pavillon de la Photographie, 1974.

Pierre G. Harmant and Paul Mariller. "Some Thoughts on the World's First Photograph." *Photographic Journal* 107 (1967): 130-140.

Helmut Gernsheim. "The 150th Anniversary of Photography." *History of Photography* 1 (Jan. 1977): 3-8.

See also Newhall, *Latent Image*.

Notman, William
Canada (b. Scotland) 1826-1891

The work of William McFarlane Notman, who settled in Montreal in 1856, is an invaluable record of life in Canada from that year until his death. For many years Canada's most famous photographer, he was its first to have an international reputation. He made many portraits — of Indians, voyageurs, trappers, social and cultural personages, visiting British nobility, and others. In his studio he re-created outdoor scenes with hunters, skaters, and the like, often as detailed tableaux realistically arranged with trees and bushes, rocks, camp gear, and stuffed animals. Notman claimed he could "build cottages, form sandy beaches with boats drawn up, erect tents, plant trees . . . form snow-wreathed plains or introduce a frozen lake or stream" (Life Library, *Great Photographers*, p. 81); he made skillful simulations of campfire lighting in some of these scenes.

William Notman. *From Custom House, Montreal, Looking East*, ca. 1885. Albumen print. (Courtesy The National Gallery of Canada, Ottawa)

Beginning about 1870 Notman also produced composite imagery (his first effort was a scene from *The Merchant of Venice* as performed by a junior theatrical group). Of considerable interest are his beautifully detailed landscapes and records of activities in many parts of Canada. At various times his Notman Photographic Company had studios in Montreal, Ottawa, Toronto, and Halifax, as well as in Boston, Albany, and New York City. (Not all photographs issued under its trademark are by Notman himself, however.) The firm's business was continued after his death by his sons.

WORK Chiefly portraits (e.g., Sitting Bull, Buffalo Bill); scenes in various parts of Canada, including documentation along the Canadian Pacific Railway. Also includes outdoor scenes re-created in the studio; composite imagery.

MEDIA Daguerreotypes; 8×10 collodion wet-plate negatives (before 1880) and gelatin dry-plate negatives (after 1880), albumen prints, platinum prints (1890 and after). Sizes range from stereographs to 8×10 (also some 16×20 enlargements). Some mammoth-sized composites also exist.

AVAILABILITY AND PRICE Through galleries and at auction. Cartes de visite, cabinet photographs, and stereographs also frequently found through antique stores, at rummage sales, etc., often in albums. Prime landscapes, portraits, and composites are rarer. Prices range from extremely low for cartes to high for major images.

SIGNATURE/OTHER IDENTIFICATION

COLLECTIONS BPL, Chicago, IMP/GEH, Smithsonian; McGill, NGC.

SELECTED BIBLIOGRAPHY
Photographic Selections by William Notman, Vol. 1. Foreword by the Rt. Hon. Viscount Monck. Montreal: John Lovell, 1863.
Notman's Photographic Selections. Montreal: Notman, 1865.
Fennings Taylor. *Portraits of British Americans by W. Notman.* 3 vols. Montreal: Notman, 1865-68.
Henry Beaumont Small. *Canadian Handbook and Tourist's Guide . . . .* Ed. by J. Taylor. Montreal: M. Longmoore, 1866.
Henry G. Vennor. *Our Birds of Prey; or, the Eagles, Hawks and Owls of Canada.* Montreal: Dawson Brothers, 1876.
Through Mountains and Canyons: The Canadian Rockies. . . . Toronto: MacFarlane [between 1900 and 1909].
48 Specially Selected Views of the Canadian Rockies on the Line of the Canadian Pacific Railway. Montreal: Valentine, 1907.
J. Russell Harper and S. Triggs, eds. *Portrait of a Period: A Collection of Notman Photographs, 1865-1915.* Montreal: McGill University, 1967.
See also Greenhill, *Canada*; Life Library, *Great Photographers.*

Orkin, Ruth
United States 1921–

Active for many years as a photojournalist, Orkin has produced sensitive, humanistic views of the world that have appeared in numerous national magazines, photography annuals, books, and advertisements. She has also worked in cinematography, co-directing the award-winning 1950s films *The Little Fugitive* and *Lovers and Lollipops.*

The daughter of a silent-movie actress, Orkin first became interested in films at the age of four. As a teenager she collected autographs from celebrities in Hollywood, where she was raised, but soon decided that photographing them was more interesting. In 1944 she moved to New York City and began to free-lance as a photojournalist. Her work has appeared in magazines such as *Life, Look, Esquire, Cosmopolitan, New York, Ms., This Week, Collier's,* and *Ladies' Home Journal.*

Orkin has a special talent for photographing people, and she is comfortable working up close — a danger zone for many photographers, who prefer the safety of distance and noninvolvement. She is tenacious in pursuit of her subject: "I can outwait anyone. People do loosen up after a while because they want to go on with their lives" (quoted in Stevens). As a result, many of her photographs of celebrities capture intimate and revealing moments that seem to go beyond a public image.

WORK Chiefly photojournalism (e.g., personalities, classical musicians, women, children, New York City window views, Israel, Europe). Also includes a personal picture diary.

MEDIA Silver prints, color.

AVAILABILITY AND PRICE Through galleries, low to moderate.

COLLECTIONS MMA, MOMA.

Ruth Orkin. *Opening Night Party of "The Member of the Wedding"* [from left: Ethel Waters, Carson McCullers, Julie Harris], 1950. Silver print. (Courtesy The Witkin Gallery. Copyright 1950 by Ruth Orkin)

SIGNATURE/OTHER IDENTIFICATION

SELECTED BIBLIOGRAPHY

A World through My Window: Photographs by Ruth Orkin. Ed. by Arno Karlin. New York: Harper & Row, 1978.
Nancy Stevens. "Ruth Orkin." *Popular Photography,* June 1977.

O'Sullivan, Timothy H.
United States ca. 1840–1882

Relatively little is known about the life of O'Sullivan, who made some of the most memorable photographs of the Civil War and the American West. Before the war he worked at Mathew Brady's New York gallery, then at Brady's Washington, D.C., gallery under Alexander Gardner. During the Civil War he photographed war scenes — first for Brady, then for Gardner — at Bull Run, Gettysburg, Appomattox, and elsewhere. Though O'Sullivan, like other Civil War photographers, generally worked after battles had taken place, he twice had his camera hit by shell fragments.

From 1867 to 1875 he accompanied various U.S. governmental expeditionary surveys, primarily in western America but also at the site of the proposed Panama Canal. On his expeditions O'Sullivan experienced the rou-

tine rigors of a photographer using wet-collodion plates in the desert: temperatures high enough to boil the chemical solutions, swarms of mosquitoes thick enough to extinguish candles, near starvation when boats carrying supplies capsized, and negatives ruined by accidents during their transportation. Little is known of him after 1875, when he returned from his last expedition suffering from the tuberculosis that eventually took his life. He died not long after his 1880 appointment as chief photographer for the U.S. Treasury Department.

In his Civil War photographs O'Sullivan developed the style that he perfected in his expeditionary photographs. His mature work appears distinctly modern, combining a cool objectivity with an understated use of design and composition. He never romanticized his landscapes (for example, by choosing dramatic camera angles), but he could exploit the aesthetic possibilities in the most barren of landscapes. He used blank, white skies as backgrounds against which he traced the jagged lines of rocky hilltops, and in many of his images the sky becomes a powerful and independent shape itself. Weston Naef wrote: "O'Sullivan's views are among the least picturesque of all western landscape photographers. . . . The modernity his images hold for us . . . derives from the austerity of his preferred subjects and the intense esthetic consciousness of his vision" (Naef and Wood, *Era,* pp. 135–136).

WORK   Includes Civil War scenes (e.g., battle sites, the dead, war machinery) and expeditionary photographs, chiefly landscapes: Clarence King expedition (1867–1869) along the fortieth parallel in Nevada, California, and Utah, including the earliest mine interiors (taken with magnesium flash lighting); Thomas O. Selfridge expedition (1870) to the Isthumus of Darien (Panama); George M. Wheeler expeditions (1871–1875) to California, Nevada, Arizona, including the Grand Canyon of the Colorado.

MEDIA   Collodion wet-plate negatives, albumen prints (ranging from stereographs to 11x14).

Timothy H. O'Sullivan. *Black Canyon, Colorado River,* 1871. Albumen print. The covered cubicle visible on this boat was a small darkroom used for coating and developing photographic plates. (Courtesy Lee D. Witkin)

AVAILABILITY AND PRICE Through galleries and at auction. The most frequently found large prints are from Wheeler's expeditions or from Gardner's *Sketch Book*; high to extremely high, depending on condition and subject matter. Stereographs relatively rare, expensive for their category; low.

SIGNATURE/OTHER IDENTIFICATION

T. H. O'Sullivan, Phot.

COLLECTIONS AGS, BPL, California (Bancroft), Chicago, Harvard (Carpenter, Fogg), IMP/GEH, LOC, Museum of New Mexico, National Archives, New Orleans, NYHS, Princeton, UCLA; NGC.

SELECTED BIBLIOGRAPHY
Alexander Gardner. *Gardner's Photographic Sketch Book of the War.* 2 vols. Washington, D.C.: Philp & Solomons, 1866. 45 albumen prints by O'Sullivan. Reprint, 1 vol. New York: Dover, 1959.
U.S. Geographical Surveys West of the 100th Meridian. *Annual Report 1871-72: Photographs.* Washington, D.C. [ca. 1874]. 50 albumen prints by O'Sullivan and W. Bell.
———. *Photographs Showing Landscapes, Geological and Other Features, of Portions of the Western Territory of the United States . . . 1871, 1872, and 1873.* Washington, D.C., 1874. 35 albumen prints by O'Sullivan on mounts with the Survey imprint.
James D. Horan. *Timothy O'Sullivan: America's Forgotten Photographer.* New York: Crown, 1966. Bibliography.
Beaumont Newhall and Nancy Newhall. *T. H. O'Sullivan: Photographer.* Rochester, N.Y.: GEH, 1966.
See also Andrews, *Pioneers*; Life Library, *Great Photographers*, *Light*; Naef and Wood, *Era*; Newhall, *Masters*; Taft, *Photography.*

Outerbridge, Paul, Jr.
United States 1896–1958

Outerbridge studied art and worked in theatrical design before taking up photography in 1921. That same year he enrolled at the Clarence H. White School of Photography (New York City), where he soon became a teacher of composition and aesthetics. He made mostly studio still-life photographs, including abstractions of commonplace objects. Some of these photographs appeared as commercial illustrations in magazines such as *Vogue, Vanity Fair,* and *Harper's Bazaar.*

In 1925, Outerbridge moved to Europe where he was friendly with Man Ray, Brancusi, Picasso, Picabia, and other artists. He worked for a short time as a staff photographer for Paris *Vogue* but essentially free-lanced, doing commercial illustrative work.

After returning to the United States in 1929, he began working with the carbro process and used it to produce many color illustrations for magazines. He also began to make photographs of the female nude, exploring surrealism, sexual fetishism, and decadence — work which remained unexhibited and unpublished until recently.

John Szarkowski wrote of Outerbridge's early abstrac-

tions: "These pictures exhibit an original sense of abstract photographic form, which remains impressive even in the work of the twenties — a decade in which pure graphics was a central preoccupation of adventurous photography" (Szarkowski, *Looking,* p. 80).

Paul Outerbridge, Jr. *Mormon Crankshaft,* 1923. Platinum print. (Courtesy Mark Kelman Works of Art)

WORK Includes abstractions, still lifes, nudes, portraits, travel, advertising, editorial photography.

MEDIA Platinum prints, carbro color prints.

AVAILABILITY AND PRICE Through galleries and at auction but rare; high to extremely high.

SIGNATURE/OTHER IDENTIFICATION

COLLECTIONS Laguna Beach (Calif.) Museum of Art holds the largest collection of Outerbridge's work. Also BMFA, Cleveland, LOC, MMA.

SELECTED BIBLIOGRAPHY
Photographing in Color. New York: Random House, 1940.
Paul Outerbridge, Jr. Text by Graham Howe. Los Angeles: Los Angeles Center for Photographic Studies, 1976. Bibliography.

M. F. Agha. "Paul Outerbridge, Jr." *Advertising Arts*, May 1931, pp. 42–45.

M. Burcel. "Paul Outerbridge, Jr." *Creative Art* 12 (Feb. 1933): 108–115. Bibliography.

Graham Howe. "Outerbridge from Cubism to Fetishism." *Artforum* 15 (Summer 1977): 51–55.

See also Life Library, *Year 1978*; Szarkowski, *Looking*; Travis, *Julien Levy*; Witkin, *Julien Levy*.

Owens, Bill
United States 1938–

Owens's chief subject matter has been middle-class suburban life and groups in the United States. He grew up on a farm, went to college, hitchhiked around the world, and served in the Peace Corps before taking a job in 1968 as a photographer for the Livermore (California) *Independent*. He was close enough to middle-class life to quickly become a part of the community but distant enough to perceive the photographic potential in his environment.

Owens's first book, *Suburbia*, recorded the life-style of his new friends. As *Camera* magazine described the work, "the images are human, factual, and sincere and reveal the thread of genuine humor which holds suburbia together" ("Bill Owens," p. 4). About his method of working, Owens said: "I consider myself a 'documentary' photographer. I am not setting out to be critical of Instant America, but rather to make an honest statement with my camera about what it is" (*U.S. Camera/Camera 35 Annual 1972*, p. 105).

Bill Owens. *Beauty Contest*, ca. 1975. Silver print. (Courtesy The Witkin Gallery)

WORK Includes suburban life-styles; groups, associations, clubs; people at work.

MEDIUM Silver prints.

AVAILABILITY AND PRICE Through galleries; moderate.

SIGNATURE/OTHER IDENTIFICATION

Bill Owens

PORTFOLIO *See* chapter 6 entry.

COLLECTIONS Oakland, MOMA, San Francisco.

SELECTED BIBLIOGRAPHY
Suburbia. San Francisco: Straight Arrow, 1973.
Our Kind of People: American Groups and Rituals. San Francisco: Straight Arrow, 1975.
Working: I Do It for the Money. New York: Simon & Schuster, 1977.
Documentary Photography: A Personal View. Danbury, N.H.: Addison House, 1978.
U.S. Camera/Camera 35 Annual 1972.
"Bill Owens." *Camera*, Mar. 1974, pp. 4–13.
See also Life Library, *Year 1974*; Szarkowski, *Mirrors*.

Palfi, Marion
United States (b. Germany) 1907–1978

Palfi, the daughter of Hungarian theatrical producer Victor Palfi, was already a well-known model by her teens and had appeared in films. Dissatisfied with praise that she felt was based on her image rather than her actual accomplishments, she turned to photography. For several years she ran a portrait studio in Amsterdam, then left for the United States as Hitler rose to power.

After working in a photo-finishing lab, she began on her own to photograph social injustices in order "to inspire people everywhere that such horrors [as Nazism] should never happen again" (statement to the authors, 1976). In her work over the years she examined such subjects as segregation in the North and the South, the plight of the relocated American Indian, abandoned children, a southern town where a black man had just been lynched (1949), and the problems of the aged. Her images are straightforward and simply framed. Some convey pain with a sensibility that is raw in its unflinching view of hardship (much of Palfi's work remains unpublished because of her uncompromising approach). Her photographs, taken for many social agencies, facilitated legislative reforms in the areas of housing, foster-child care, and civil rights.

"I am a social research photographer who is trying to combine an art form with social research," she once said. ". . . I want to make people aware — aware that a discriminator destroys himself; that the diversity of people in America is their strength" (Pasadena Museum press release, 1974).

WORK Chiefly social documentation: deprived children across the United States ("Suffer Little Children," 1946–1949); three studies dealing with racism from Florida to Oregon ("There Is No More Time," "Civil Rights," "The South," 1949–1964); the aged in New York ("You Have Never Been Old," 1956–1958);

American Indian life on and off reservations ("First I Liked the Whites, I Gave Them Fruits," 1967–1969); a study of prison life in Trenton, N.J. (1973–1976).

MEDIUM   Silver prints.

AVAILABILITY AND PRICE   Through galleries; moderate.

SIGNATURE/OTHER IDENTIFICATION

Marion Palfi

PORTFOLIO   *See* Chapter 6 Schools and workshops entry.

COLLECTIONS   The Menninger Foundation (Topeka, Kans.) preserves the Palfi archive. Also Kansas, MOMA.

SELECTED BIBLIOGRAPHY
Suffer Little Children. New York: Oceana Publications, 1952.
James L. Enyeart. *Invisible in America.* Foreword by Lee D. Witkin. Lawrence: University of Kansas Museum of Art, 1973.
See also Mann, *Women.*

Marion Palfi. *In the Shadow of the Capitol, Washington, D.C.,* ca. 1947. Silver print. (Courtesy The Witkin Gallery. Copyright by Marion Palfi)

Parker, Bart
United States 1934–

Born in Iowa, Parker grew up in Mississippi and Colorado. He owned several cameras during childhood and high school and became intrigued by the difference between what things meant to him and how the photographs of those things looked. Encouraged to draw and paint, he also studied music and writing. He applied to a daily newspaper for work as a reporter but was hired as a photojournalist and thus began to concentrate on the possibilities of photography.

Much of Parker's work assembles images of separate bits of reality into a new reality. He commented: "A synthesis such as multiple printing was necessary in order to answer the compulsion — strengthened by writing — to assemble separate times and places into one photographic object" (statement to the authors, 1977).

Van Deren Coke wrote about the dreamlike dislocations in Parker's work: "Transformed and muted by various means are commonplace objects that, when juxtaposed in an unexpected context, evoke the sleeping state" (*Image* 15, Mar. 1972, p. 6).

WORK   Includes multiple printing that joins previously unrelated realities or constructs illogical realities; individual prints, collaborations, and series that explore discrepancies among perceptions, camera evidence, and verbal meanings; large-format pieces.

MEDIA   Chiefly silver prints. Parker occasionally uses large-size roll paper, transparency material, Polacolor, color prints, and color Xerox.

AVAILABILITY AND PRICE   Through galleries; moderate to moderately high.

COLLECTIONS   Chicago, IMP/GEH, Norton Simon, RISD.

SELECTED BIBLIOGRAPHY
Lew Thomas, ed. *Photography and Language.* San Francisco: Camerawork Press, 1976.
Bulletin of the Rhode Island School of Design, Dec. 1974. Includes selected images by Parker.
"Bart Parker: 'I Subsist on Analogy.'" *Afterimage* 4 (Nov. 1976): 10–12.
See also Life Library, *Print*; chapter 7 catalogues.

SIGNATURE/OTHER IDENTIFICATION

Bart Parker. *Gladys and Yvonne in Urbana, Illinois,* 1971. Silver print. (Courtesy the artist)

Penn, Irving
United States 1917–

Penn's first creative interest was in drawing and painting. In the late 1930s he studied under Alexey Brodovitch at the Philadelphia Museum School of Industrial Art, published drawings in *Harper's Bazaar,* then in 1942 spent a year painting in Mexico. In 1943 he was hired by *Vogue* to suggest covers but was soon making a cover photograph himself — a purse, gloves, and scarf, with lemons, oranges, and a huge topaz — the first of over a hundred he did for the magazine.

In his fashion photographs and portraits of celebrities, Penn's preference has been for plain, almost clinical backgrounds and neutral illumination from indirect north light. He has also traveled to many parts of the world to photograph people against plain backgrounds that simulate the neutral atmosphere of a bare studio; the isolation of the subject concentrates the viewer's attention on whatever clues face, posture, and outfit reveal about the sitter's life and personality. Penn wrote: "I found pictures trying to show people in their natural circumstances generally disappointing. At least I knew that to accomplish such a result convincingly was beyond *my* strength and capabilities. . . . I preferred the limited task of dealing only with the person himself, away from the accidentals of his daily life, simply in his own clothes and adornments, isolated in my studio. From himself alone I would distill the image I wanted, and the cold light of day would put it onto the film" (*Worlds in a Small Room,* p. 8).

Penn's current work is an extension of his portraiture: very large platinum prints of refuse, such as cigarette butts, that are photographed like his portraits — isolated against plain backgrounds and bathed in cool, revealing light. The enlargements are so great and the tonal range of the hand-coated platinum paper is so sensuous that the viewer is forced to acknowledge the possibilities of beauty even in such unlikely subject matter.

WORK   Includes fashion (early 1940s and after); portraits of celebrities (e.g. Picasso, Colette); portraits of tradespeople and workers (e.g., coal man, motorcycle policeman); documentary portraits, photographed in neutral settings, of people from different parts of the world (e.g., San Francisco Hell's Angels, Peruvian Indians, Saharan nomads); still lifes; very large close-ups of cigarette butts.

MEDIA   Silver prints, platinum prints, dye transfer color prints.

AVAILABILITY AND PRICE   Through galleries; high to extremely high.

COLLECTIONS   IMP/GEH, MMA, MOMA, Smithsonian.

SELECTED BIBLIOGRAPHY
Moments Preserved: Eight Essays in Photographs and Words. New York: Simon & Schuster, 1960.
Worlds in a Small Room. New York: Grossman/Viking, 1974.
Diana Vreeland. *Inventive Paris Clothes, 1909–1939: A Photographic Essay by Irving Penn.* New York: Viking, 1977.
"Photographs by Irving Penn." *America* (Russian-text U.S. Information Agency publication), no. 25 (1958).
R. E. Martinez. "Irving Penn." *Camera,* Nov. 1960, pp. 4–34.
J. Malcolm. "Certainties and Possibilities." *The New Yorker,* 4 Aug. 1975, pp. 56–59.
Thomas B. Hess. "Irving Penn: New Platinum Photographs." *Vogue,* Aug. 1975, pp. 128–129.
See also Liberman, *Art* (in color bibliography); Life Library, *Camera, Great Photographers, Studio, Year 1975;* Szarkowski, *Looking.*

Irving Penn. *Woman in Black — Man in White/Morocco,* 1971. Silver print. (Courtesy the artist. Copyright © 1974 by Irving Penn)

PHOTOJOURNALISTS

Photojournalists cover topical events for the mass media, recording the current affairs that make news or that editors simply think might make interesting copy. Their aim is often to convey information in a kind of pictorial shorthand that sums up person, place, and situation at a glance. W. Eugene Smith wrote: "The most important thing in photography is knowing what the subject is about. Often the 'straight' news photographer doesn't know. That is why so many newspictures look so monotonously alike. To know who's who and what's what is to get the significances of a scene or event" (quoted in Hicks, p. 89).

Modern photojournalism began in the 1920s and early 1930s with the introduction of the Ermanox, Leica, and other small, hand-held cameras that could record a situation as it was occurring. *Life, Look,* the *Weekly Illustrated* (London), *Berliner Illustrierte Zeitung, Münchner Illustrierte Presse,* and other picture magazines of the 1930s–1960s period once dominated the market for picture news, a function now largely provided by television. With the demise of many general picture magazines, many photojournalists turned to special-interest magazines such as *Sports Illustrated* or to self-generated projects published as books and portfolios. Many compelling images have been made by unknown or little-known photojournalists: often, being in the right place at the right time produced a unique opportunity. Among the better-known photojournalists are the following (*italicized* photographers have separate entries in this chapter):

Bischof, Werner. Switzerland. 1916–1954
Bosshard, Walter. Switzerland. 1892–1975
Bourke-White, Margaret
Burrows, Larry. England. 1926–71
Capa, Cornell. U.S. (b. Hungary). 1918–
Capa, Robert. U.S. (b. Hungary). 1913–1954
Cartier-Bresson, Henri
Davidson, Bruce
Doisneau, Robert
Duncan, David Douglas. U.S. 1916–
Eisenstaedt, Alfred
Elisofon, Eliot. U.S. 1911–1973
Erwitt, Elliott
Frank, Robert
Gidal, George. Germany. 1908–1931
Gidal, Tim N.
Goro, Fritz. U.S. Contemporary
Griffiths, Philip Jones. England. (b. Wales). 1936–
Haas, Ernst. U.S. (b. Austria). 1921–
Hutton, Kurt. England. 1893–1960
Johnston, Frances Benjamin
Kertész, André
Kessel, Dmitri. U.S. (b. Russia). b. 1902
Lechenperg, Harald
Lee, Russell
Loengard, John. U.S. Contemporary
McAvoy, Thomas D. U.S. d. 1966
McCombe, Leonard. U.S. Contemporary
McCullin, Donald. England. 1935–
Magubane, Peter. South Africa. 1932–
Man, Felix H. (Hans Baumann). Germany (b. Switzerland). 1893–

David Seymour (Magnum Photos, Inc.). *Bernard Berenson at Ninety, Visiting the Borghese Gallery, Rome,* 1955. Silver print. (Courtesy Magnum)

Mark, Mary Ellen. U.S. 1941–
Martinez, Romeo
Mili, Gjon. U.S. (b. Albania). 1904–
Miller, Wayne. U.S. 1918–
Moore, David. Australia. 1927–
Munkacsi, Martin. U.S. (b. Hungary). 1898–1963
Mydans, Carl
Neudin (Neudatschin)
Orkin, Ruth
Parks, Gordon, Sr. U.S. 1912–
Phillips, John. Contemporary
Riboud, Marc. France. 1923–
Rodger, George. England. 1908–
Rothstein, Arthur
Ruge, Willi
Salomon, Erich
Schaal, Eric. U.S. Contemporary
Seymour, David ("Chim"). U.S. (b. Poland). 1911–1965
Silk, George. U.S. (b. New Zealand). 1916–
Smith, W. Eugene
Stackpole, Peter. U.S. 1913–
Umbo (Otto Umbehr). Germany. 1902–
Uzzle, Burk
Vandivert, William. U.S. 1912–
Vestal, David. U.S. 1924–
Weber, Wolfgang. Germany. 1902–
Weegee

WORK *See* individual entries.

MEDIA Prints, usually black and white, range from glossy 4×5s and 8×10s (often in poor condition) to quality exhibition prints, some in larger sizes. (*See also* individual entries.)

AVAILABILITY AND PRICE Through galleries and at auction. If the photographer exhibited and sold prints, some can usually be found. If the photographer turned film over to his or her publisher, most likely only the original lab prints exist. Price depends on condition, size, whether or not signed or stamped, vintage of print, etc. (*See also* individual entries.)

Marc Riboud (Magnum Photos, Inc.). *Hanoi, North Vietnam,* 1968. Silver print. (Courtesy Magnum. Copyright © by Marc Riboud)

Robert Capa (Magnum Photos, Inc.). *Medical Corpsmen Treat a Wounded Infantry in Sicily,* 1943. Silver print. (Courtesy Magnum. Copyright © 1964 by Robert Capa)

Mary Ellen Mark (Magnum Photos, Inc.). *Acadian Couple,* 1973. Silver print. (Courtesy the artist)

David Moore. *Pitjantjatjara Children, South Australia,* 1963. Silver print. (Courtesy the artist)

David Seymour (Magnum Photos, Inc.). *Mykonos, Greece,* 1951. Silver print. (Courtesy Magnum)

Ernst Haas. *Invalid, Vienna,* 1948. Silver print. (Courtesy the artist)

Alfred Eisenstaedt. *Dr. Joseph Goebbels, Hitler's Minister of Culture and Propaganda, League of Nations Assembly in Geneva, Sept. 1933.* (Courtesy Alfred Eisenstaedt, *Life* magazine. Copyright © 1954 by Time Inc.)

SIGNATURE–OTHER IDENTIFICATION/PORTFOLIOS *See* individual entries.

COLLECTIONS The International Center of Photography (New York City) has a large collection of photojournalism. Historical societies, libraries, newspaper and magazine files, and stock picture agencies are often repositories for prints. LIFE Picture Collection (New York City) preserves negatives made for Time Inc. The Library of Congress holds news pictures from many countries and periods (including the *Look* magazine archives). (*See also* individual entries.)

SELECTED BIBLIOGRAPHY

Laura Vitray, John Mills, Jr., and Roscoe Ellard. *Pictorial Journalism.* New York: McGraw-Hill, 1939.

John Floherty. *Shooting the News: Careers of the Camera Men.* Philadelphia: Lippincott, 1949.

Edward Steichen. *Memorable LIFE Photographs.* New York: MOMA, 1951.

Wilson Hicks. *Words and Pictures: An Introduction to Photojournalism.* New York: Harper & Row, 1952. Reprint, New York: Dover, 1973.

Stanley Rayfield. *How LIFE Gets the Story: Behind the Scenes in Photojournalism.* New York: Doubleday, 1955.

Arthur Rothstein. *Photojournalism: Pictures for Magazines and Newspapers.* New York: American Photographic Book, 1956.

Stanley Rayfield. *LIFE Photographers: Their Careers and Favorite Pictures.* New York: Doubleday, 1957.

Ake Meyerson and Sven Ulric Palme. *Als die neue Zeit anbrach.* Zurich: Atlantis, 1958.

John Faber. *Great Moments in News Photography.* New York: Nelson, 1960.

Helmut Gernsheim and Alison Gernsheim. *The Recording Eye: A Hundred Years of Great Events as Seen by the Camera, 1839–1939.* New York: Putnam, 1960.

Raymond Smith Schuneman. *The Photograph in Print: An Examination of New York Daily Newspapers, 1890–1937.* Ann Arbor, Mich.: University Microfilms, 1966.

Robert E. Hood. *12 at War: Great Photographers under Fire.* New York: Putnam, 1967.

James L. C. Ford. *Magazines for Millions.* Carbondale: Southern Illinois University Press, 1969.

Tim N. Gidal. *Modern Photojournalism: Origin and Evolution, 1910–1933.* New York: Collier/Macmillan, 1973.

André Barret. *Les Premiers Reporters photographes 1848–1914.* Paris: André Barret, 1977.

Harold Evans. *Pictures on a Page: Photo-Journalism, Graphics and Picture Editing.* London: Heinemann, 1978, and New York: Holt, Rinehart & Winston, 1978.

Sheryle Leekley and John Leekley. *Moments: The Pulitzer Prize Photographs.* New York: Crown, 1978.

See also Edey, *Essays;* Life Library, *Photojournalism;* Szarkowski, *Picture Press.*

PHOTO LEAGUE

The photographers of New York City's Photo League were committed to using documentary photography to effect social change. An early statement of purpose declared: "Photography has tremendous social value. Upon the photographer rests the responsibility and duty of recording a true image of the world as it is today" (quoted in Life Library, *Documentary*).

Organized in 1936 by still photographers who broke away from the Film and Photo League (ca. 1930–1937), the group served as a gathering place for amateur and professional photographers. The League offered lectures and classes, provided darkrooms, produced photographic projects (on areas such as Park Avenue North and South, Chelsea, and Harlem), and published *Photo Notes,* an irregular monthly bulletin. Sid Grossman, a photographer, teacher, and director of the Photo League School, was a powerful force in mobilizing League activities in documentary photography. Photo exhibitions included the first for Weegee and the first in the United States for John Heartfield and Lisette Model.

When labeled "subversive" in 1947 by the U.S. Department of Justice for alleged Communist ties, the Photo League was at first buoyed by a surge of new memberships, as photographers from all over the country came to its support. Although the League firmly maintained that it was a purely photographic organization, the intensifying climate of political suspicion made continued membership too difficult for too many photographers and the League ceased functioning in 1951. Among the Photo League photographers were the following (all were active in the United States; *italicized* photographers have separate entries in this chapter):

Bernstein, Lou
Burkhardt, Rudolph
Cole, Barney. 1911–
Corsini, Harold. 1919–
Delano, Jack
Eagle, Arnold. 1914–
Ehrenberg, Mike
Elisofon, Eliot. 1911–1973
Engel, Morris
Fenn, Albert
Gildstein, Leo
Grossman, Sid. 1913–1955
Gwathmey, Rosalie. 1908–
Huberland, Morris
Kalisher, Clemens
Kanaga, Consuelo. 1894–1978
Kattelson, Sy
Kerner, Sidney
Leipzig, Arthur
Lepkoff, Rebecca
Lessinger, Jack
Libsohn, Sol. 1914–

Liebling, Jerome. 1924–
Lyon, Richard
Mahl, Sam
Manning, Jack. 1920–
Meyer, Sonia Handelman
Moser, Lida
Orkin, Ruth
Robbins, David
Rosenblum, Walter
Rothman, Henry
Schwartz, Joe
Siskind, Aaron
Smith, W. Eugene
Stettner, Louis
Stoumen, Louis. 1917–
Tarkington, Lester
Tessler, Ted
Vestal, David. 1924–
Weiner, Dan. 1919–1959
Witt, Bill
Yavno, Max. 1921–

WORK/MEDIA/AVAILABILITY AND PRICE/SIGNATURE–OTHER IDENTIFICATION/PORTFOLIOS/COLLECTIONS *See* individual entries.

SELECTED BIBLIOGRAPHY
Photo Notes. Published monthly (but irregularly) by the Photo League, New York, 1938–1951. Reprint, Rochester, N.Y.: Visual Studies Workshop, 1977. 200 copies.
This Is the Photo League. Intro. by Nancy Newhall. 1948/1949.
Anne Tucker. *Photographic Crossroads: The Photo League.* Ottawa: National Gallery of Canada, 1978. Special supplement to *Afterimage.*
See also Life Library, *Documentary.*

PHOTO-SECESSION
See Camera Work; Pictorialists; Stieglitz, Alfred.

PICTORIALISTS

Photographers who consider themselves artists have always striven to produce photographs of aesthetic merit and have them accepted as a valid art form; the *style* accepted as "artistic," however, has changed over the years. In the 1890s and early 1900s many photographers formed groups devoted to what was variously called pictorial, aesthetic, salon, or simply art photography, and they organized groups such as The Linked Ring Brotherhood (London, 1892), the Photo-Club de Paris (1894), the Vienna Camera Club (1891), and the Photo-Secession (New York City, 1902) to exhibit, publish, and promote those works they felt were of artistic quality.

Since the pictorialists thought of themselves as a part of the art world, it is understandable that their photographs reflected and at times imitated the styles popular in other art media of their period. In particular, the pictorialists often sought to achieve the atmospheric effects of the impressionists — for example, landscapes veiled in the soft light of dusk, dawn, or mist. There was a revival of interest in Hill and Adamson's calotype prints, with their muted detail and compositions based on broad tonal masses. Some pictorialists actually made salt prints using a method similar to the calotype process. Many made platinum prints rather than ordinary silver prints because they preferred the platinum prints' longer tonal scale, delicate gradations of grays, and evidence of paper texture. A softened image could be achieved in other ways, such as by photographing through gauze, by using a special soft-focus lens, or by employing a pinhole aperture instead of a lens. Controlled printing processes such as gum-bichromate or bromoil printing were favored by pictorialists because they gave the photographer the ability to control tonal values, alter or omit details, add color, or introduce visible handwork.

Pictorialism is sometimes thought to be completely different from "straight," sharp-focus, unmanipulated photography, but not all pictorialists made soft-focus or manipulated prints: Frederick H. Evans's photographs of English cathedrals, for example, are sharply focused, detailed images. In general, however, pictorialists tended to make prints that looked like some other art medium (such as a charcoal drawing or an etching), and the less that pictorial work looked like, photography, the more some critics praised it.

By 1914 pictorialism had passed its creative peak and its formulas for composition and tonality became increasingly rigid and contrived. Though pictorialism continued for a number of years, especially in amateur camera clubs, later imagery seldom had the vitality of earlier work. Listed here, categorized roughly by place of major activity, are some of the photographers who worked in the pictorial style at one time or another (*italicized* photographers have separate entries in this chapter).

UNITED STATES

Armer, Laura Adams. 1874–1963
Boughton, Alice
Brigman, Anne W.
Buehrmann, Elizabeth. ca. 1866–after 1962
Clark, Rose (1852–1942) and Wade, Elizabeth Flint (d. 1915)
Coburn, Alvin Langdon
Connell, Will. 1898–1961
Dassonville, William E. 1879–1957
Day, Fred Holland
Eugene, Frank
Hanscom, Adelaide. 1876–1932
Haviland, Paul B. (b. France). 1880–1950
Hiller, Lejaren à. b. 1880
Hussey, Henry A. 1887–1959
Kales, Arthur F. 1882–1936
Käsebier, Gertrude
Keiley, Joseph T. 1869–1914
Kemmler, Florence B. 1900–1972
Mather, Margrethe
Mortensen, William. 1897–1965
Pitchford, Emily. 1878–1954
Reece, Jane. ca. 1869–1961
Rubincam, Harry C. 1871–1940
Schneider, (Dr.) Roland E. 1884–1934
Sears, Sarah C. 1858–1935
Seeley, George H. 1880–1955
Steichen, Edward
Stieglitz, Alfred
Strauss, Julius C. 1857–1924
Struss, Karl F. 1886–
Watson-Schütze, Eva. 1867–1935
Weston, Edward
White, Clarence H.

AUSTRIA

Henneberg, Hugo. 1863–1918
Kühn, Heinrich
Pichier, Paul. Active ca. 1900
Spitzer, (Dr.) Friedrich. Active ca. 1900
Watzek, Hans. 1848–1903

BELGIUM

Bourgeois, A. Active early 20th c.
Bovier, L.
Ickx, Romaine. Active early 20th c.
Misonne, Léonard. 1870–1943
Puttemans, C. Active ca. 1900
Vanderkindere, M. Active ca. 1900

FRANCE

Bergon, Paul. Active ca. 1900
Bucquet, Maurice. d. 1921
Demachy, Robert
Le Bègue, René. Active ca. 1900
Puyo, C. (Emile Joachim Constant Puyo). 1857–1933

GERMANY

Dührkoop, Rudolf. 1848–1918
Einbeck, Georg. Active ca. 1900
Erfurth, Hugo. 1874–1948
Grainer, Franz. 1871–1948
Hofmeister, Theodor (1868–1943) and Oscar (1871–1937)
Nothmann, (Frau) E. Active ca. 1900
Perscheid, Nicola. 1864–1930
Weimer, Wilhelm

GREAT BRITAIN

Annan, James Craig
Craigie, Reginald
Davison, George. England. 1856–1930
de Meyer, Adolf (Gayne)
Evans, Frederick H.
Hinton, A. Horsley. England. 1863–1908
Hollyer, Frederick H. England. 1837–1933
Keighley, Alexander. England. 1861–1947
Moss, Charles
Sawyer, Lyddell. England. 1856–1895
Sutcliffe, Frank M.
Warburg, J. C. England. d. 1932
Wellington, J. B. B. England. d. 1939
Wilkinson, Benjamin Gay. England. 1857–1927

ITALY

Casazza, Gatti. Active ca. 1900
Grosso, Giacomo. Active ca. 1900
Rey, Guido. Active 1890s–mid-1920s

NETHERLANDS

Polak, Richard. 1870–1957

RUSSIA

Mazurin, Aleksei Sergeevich. b. 1846

SWITZERLAND

Boissonnas, Fred. 1858–1947

WORK *See* individual entries.

MEDIA Range from unmanipulated prints on platinum or silver paper to controlled media such as gum prints in color with considerable added handwork; autochromes. (*See also* individual entries.)

AVAILABILITY AND PRICE Fine-quality reproductions from *Camera Work* are found more frequently than original prints. (*See also* individual entries and *Camera Work* entry.)

SIGNATURE-OTHER IDENTIFICATION/PORTFOLIOS/COLLECTIONS *See* individual entries.

Karl F. Struss. *Sunday Morning, Chester, Nova Scotia.* From *Camera Work*, no. 38, 1912. Gravure. (Courtesy The Witkin Gallery)

Margrethe Mather and Edward Weston. Untitled, 1921. Platinum print. (Courtesy Shirley Burden)

William Mortensen. *Human Relations*, 1932. Silver print. (Courtesy Mrs. William Mortensen)

George H. Seeley. *The Firefly.* From *Camera Work*, no. 20, 1907. Gravure. (Courtesy The Witkin Gallery)

SELECTED BIBLIOGRAPHY

Heyworth Campbell, ed. *Pictorialists*. Modern Masters of Photography, series 1. New York: Galleon Press [ca. 1900].

W. I. Lincoln Adams. *In Nature's Image: Chapters on Pictorial Photography*. New York: Baker & Taylor, 1898.

Charles H. Caffin. *Photography as a Fine Art*. New York: Doubleday, 1901. Reprint, intro. by Thomas F. Barrow. Dobbs Ferry, N.Y.: Morgan & Morgan, 1971. Reprint, intro. by Peter Pollack. New York: Amphoto, 1972.

Charles Holme, ed. *Art in Photography*. London: The Studio, 1905.

———, ed. *Colour Photography*. London: The Studio, 1908.

Photo Pictorialists of Buffalo. *Pictorial Landscape Photography*. Boston: American Photographic, 1921.

John Wallace Gillies. *Principles of Pictorial Photography*. New York: Falk, 1923.

F. C. Tilney. *The Principles of Photographic Pictorialism*. Boston: American Photographic, 1930.

Marilies v. Brevern. *Künstlerische Photographie: Von Hill bis Moholy-Nagy*. Berlin: Mann, 1971.

Wanda M. Corn. *The Color of Mood: American Tonalism 1880–1910*. San Francisco: M. H. de Young Memorial Museum & California Palace of the Legion of Honor, 1972.

Weston Naef. *The Painterly Photograph 1890–1914*. New York: Metropolitan Museum of Art, 1973.

Margery Mann. *California Pictorialism*. San Francisco: San Francisco Museum of Modern Art, 1977.

Camera, Dec. 1970. Entire issue.

James Borcoman. "Purism versus Pictorialism." *Artscanada*, Dec. 1974, pp. 69–81.

See also Doty, *Photo-Secession*; Green, *Camera Work*; Lawton and Know, *Knights*; Naef, *Collection*.

Plowden, David
United States 1932–

After studying economics and American history at Yale University, Plowden traveled extensively and in 1960 began to use photography to document the ways that people create, destroy, and alter their environment. In essence, he photographs as a historical and sociological record. He was influenced by long discussions with his close friend Walker Evans, with whom he shared many common photographic concerns.

Plowden records both urban and rural landscapes, showing the ideal as well as the sadly altered and blighted. His images are carefully composed, presenting each scene in a simple, straightforward manner. He has published a number of books that reflect his concern with the environment.

WORK   Chiefly the face of the United States: rural America, urban blight, old architecture. Also includes a day in the "life" of a New York harbor tugboat (for a children's book).

MEDIA   Silver prints, color.

AVAILABILITY AND PRICE   Through galleries; moderate.

COLLECTIONS   MOMA, Smithsonian.

SIGNATURE/OTHER IDENTIFICATION

SELECTED BIBLIOGRAPHY

Farewell to Steam. Brattleboro, Vt.: Stephen Greene, 1966.

Lincoln and His America. New York: Viking, 1970.

The Hand of Man on America. Washington, D.C.: Smithsonian Institution Press, 1971.

Nantucket. With Patricia Coffin. New York: Viking, 1971.

Floor of the Sky: The Great Plains. New York: Sierra Club, 1972.

Cape May to Montauk. New York: Viking, 1973.

Bridges: The Spans of North America. New York: Viking, 1974.

Commonplace. New York: Dutton, 1974.

Desert and Plain; the Mountains and the River: A Celebration of Rural America. New York: Dutton, 1975.

Tugboat. New York: Macmillan, 1976.

See also Hume, *The Great West*.

David Plowden. Untitled, 1975. Silver print. (Courtesy The Witkin Gallery. Copyright © 1975 by David Plowden)

Porter, Eliot
United States 1901–

Eliot Furness Porter's photographs of nature have been widely published and exhibited for their scientific and aesthetic value. He began to photograph birds and landscape on the Maine island where his family spent summers. After graduating from Harvard Medical School in

1929, he taught biochemistry and bacteriology at Harvard until 1939. In 1938/39 he had an exhibition at Alfred Stieglitz's gallery An American Place and, encouraged by Stieglitz and Ansel Adams, decided to devote his full time to photography. Stieglitz wrote to him in 1939: "I must thank you for having given me the opportunity to live with your spirit in the form of those photographs that for three weeks were on our walls. . . . Some of your photographs are the first I have ever seen which made me feel 'there is my own spirit'" (quoted in *Summer Island*, p. 74).

Porter was awarded two Guggenheim Fellowships to photograph birds, and his pictures have appeared in a number of books on wildlife, including *Living Birds of the World* and *Land Birds of America*. His interest in conservation led to several projects with the Sierra Club, such as a book about Glen Canyon that was produced just before the area was submerged by a dam project on the Colorado River. Unlike most photographers using color, Porter makes his own separation negatives and dye transfer prints so that the color values of the final print are more fully under his control.

WORK   Includes the natural landscape, wildlife (especially birds). (See color plate 3.)

MEDIA   Silver prints, dye transfer color prints.

AVAILABILITY AND PRICE   Through galleries; moderate to extremely high, depending on size and medium.

SIGNATURE/OTHER IDENTIFICATION

Eliot Porter

PORTFOLIOS   *See* chapter 6 entry.

COLLECTIONS   IMP/GEH, MMA, MOMA, Nebraska, New Mexico.

SELECTED BIBLIOGRAPHY
Henry David Thoreau. *"In Wildness Is the Preservation of the World."* Intro. by Joseph Wood Krutch. San Francisco: Sierra Club, 1962.
The Place No One Knew: Glen Canyon on the Colorado. Ed. by David Brower. San Francisco: Sierra Club, 1963.
Summer Island: Penobscot Country. Ed. by David Brower. San Francisco: Sierra Club, 1966.
Forever Wild: The Adirondacks. Text by William Chapman White. New York: Harper & Row, 1966.
Baja California and the Geography of Hope. Text by Joseph Wood Krutch. Ed. by Kenneth Brower. San Francisco: Sierra Club, 1967.
Galapagos: The Flow of Wildness. Text by Loren Eisley. Ed. by Kenneth Brower. San Francisco: Sierra Club, 1968.
John Wesley Powell. *Down the Colorado: Diary of the First Trip Through the Grand Canyon, 1869.* Additional text by Don D. Fowler. New York: Dutton, 1969. Photographs and epilogue by Porter.
Appalachian Wilderness: The Great Smoky Mountains. Text by Edward Abbey and Harry M. Caudill. New York: Dutton, 1970.
Peter Matthiessen. *The Tree Where Man Was Born: The African Experience.* New York: Dutton, 1972.
Birds of North America: A Personal Selection. New York: Dutton, 1972.
Portraits from Nature: A Portfolio. Intro. by Beaumont Newhall. New York: Dutton, 1973. 8 color reproductions of photographs from earlier books.
Moments of Discovery: Adventures with American Birds. New York: Dutton, 1977.
Brian Davies. *Seal Song.* New York: Viking, 1978.
Antarctica. New York: Dutton, 1978.
See also Hume, *The Great West*; Naef, *Collection*; Szarkowski, *Mirrors*; chapter 7 catalogues.

Post Wolcott, Marion
See Wolcott, Marion Post.

Prince, Douglas
United States 1943–

Doug Prince is known for his boxed Plexiglas photosculptures incorporating photographic images displayed as planes of varying transparency. Similarly, he makes silver prints with multiple imagery that overlays one reality onto another. His single-negative images are primarily environmental portraits, usually of family and friends (including a continuing series of his two sons).

He commented: "The techniques which I use all share a basic concern for synthesizing elements within an image; and the personal significance is derived from the

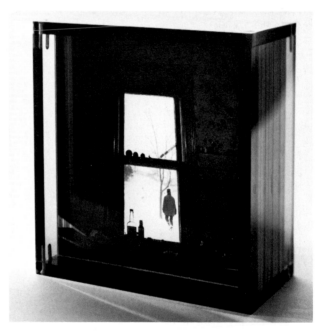

Douglas Prince. *Kitchen Window*, 1969. Plexiglas photosculpture (three separate images printed on individual sheets of graphic-arts film, each sandwiched between two pieces of Plexiglas and arranged at different levels inside a Plexiglas box to create a three-dimensional effect). (Courtesy the artist and The Witkin Gallery)

relationships of those elements. The arrangements of these elements involve the same concerns and sensitivities, regardless of whether they are in the context of single, multiple, or photosculpture images. I want to avoid making artificial boundaries between categories of techniques or subjects. Whether I create an image in the darkroom or on the beach, the same principles of creativity and perception apply. My creative processes do not begin or end at the darkroom door" (statement to the authors, 1978).

WORK Chiefly composite imagery. Also includes unmanipulated images, portraits, prints using Sabattier effect.

MEDIA Silver prints, Plexiglas photosculptures.

AVAILABILITY AND PRICE Through galleries; silver prints moderate, photosculptures moderately high.

SIGNATURE/OTHER IDENTIFICATION

DougPrince

COLLECTIONS MOMA, Princeton (Art Museum), Worcester.

SELECTED BIBLIOGRAPHY
Aspects of American Photography. Intro. by Jean S. Tucker. St. Louis: University of Missouri, 1976.
Camera International, Nov. 1965.
Peter C. Bunnell. "Photographs as Sculpture and Prints." *Art in America* 57 (Sept. 1969): 56–61.
———. "Photography into Sculpture." *Artscanada,* June 1970.
"Photography Takes Shape." *Modern Photography,* July 1970.
See also Kelly, *Darkroom 2;* Szarkowski, *Mirrors;* chapter 7 catalogues.

Ray, Man
See Man Ray.

Ray-Jones, Tony
England 1941–1972

In his brief but active career Tony Ray-Jones created a large body of work that with an often kindly wit reveals much about British character, daily life, and tradition. As a student of graphic design at the London College of Printing, he was particularly impressed by Bill Brandt's early photographs of English life. After winning a scholarship to Yale University, where he did graduate work in design in 1961/62, Ray-Jones studied with Alexey Brodovitch and Richard Avedon at the Design Laboratory in New York City. He worked with Brodovitch as associate art director on *Sky* magazine until 1964, when he decided to turn his eye on his native country. He roamed everywhere with his camera: to beach resorts, festivals, dog shows, beauty contests — to every kind of public gathering.

He stated, "My aim is to communicate something of the spirit and the mentality of the English, their habits and their way of life, the ironies that exist in the way they do things, partly through tradition and partly through the nature of their environment and mentality" (*Creative Camera,* Oct. 1968).

Ainslie Ellis wrote: "Tony sensed the natural eccentricity which has always been a quality of life in [England]. He was immediately at home with eccentrics because he had a naturally warm disposition and that rare quality of genuine interest, as opposed to crude curiosity, that is the key to positive contact and relationship" (*A Day Off,* p. 7).

WORK Scenes of English life.

MEDIA Silver prints, color.

AVAILABILITY AND PRICE Through galleries; prints made by the photographer moderately high, prints made by his estate moderate.

Tony Ray-Jones. *Durham Miners' Gala,* 1969. Silver print. (Courtesy Photographic Collections Limited, London)

PORTFOLIOS *See* chapter 6 entry.

COLLECTIONS Dallas, IMP/GEH, MOMA, Norton Simon, San Francisco, VSW; Arts Council, BN, British Council, RPS, VA.

SELECTED BIBLIOGRAPHY
A Day Off: An English Journal. Intro. by Ainslie Ellis. London: Thames & Hudson, 1974. U.S. ed., *A Day Off.* Boston: New York Graphic Society, 1977.
Creative Camera, Oct. 1968, Jan. 1971, Oct. 1974.
Album, no. 3 (1970), pp. 16–32.
The British Journal of Photography Annual 1970.
See also Life Library, *Art, Print, Themes;* chapter 7 catalogue.

Rejlander, Oscar Gustave
England (b. Sweden?) 1813–1875

O. G. Rejlander studied painting, worked as a portraitist and copyist in Rome, then settled in England in the early 1840s. He learned the rudiments of photography in an afternoon's instruction in 1853, apparently to use as an aid in his painting, but soon opened a photographic studio. He began to produce genre scenes — tableaux that told little stories of daily life, such as *A Secret* (shown here). The open sentiment of Rejlander's photographs appealed to many viewers of the period: "Well thought out, most ingenious in their subjects, and most wonderful in their truth and exactness of expression," observed one commentator (quoted in Jones, p. 14).

Rejlander began to make combination prints as a way of surmounting the difficulties he encountered using the relatively slow collodion process to photograph posed groups for his tableaux. Individuals or small groups were photographed separately, then printed onto a single sheet of paper. The culmination of this technique was *Two Ways of Life* (1857), a combination of some thirty negatives into an allegorical image contrasting the effects of Industry and Dissipation. The print was received with much controversy: some viewers, like Prince Albert, applauded its moral message; others objected to its supposed indelicacy in showing nude models in a photograph. Rejlander particularly opposed the criticism that photography was machine made, hence could not be considered true art: "We photographers have a good ground of complaint against you art critics for the sneering and overbearing manner in which you assign limits to our powers. . . . Who disputes that photography is not engraving or lithography, wood engraving or etching? We are satisfied that it is an art in itself, only guided by the general canons of art for successful combination to produce an art-looking result" (quoted in ibid., p. 37).

WORK Includes genre and anecdotal compositions; allegorical, symbolical, and religious compositions; portraits (e.g., Lewis Carroll, Gustave Doré); studies for artists (e.g., figures, drapery); character and child studies; studies of emotions (some of which Rejlander posed for as well as photographed) for Darwin's *The Expression of the Emotions in Man and Animals.*

MEDIA Collodion wet-plate negatives, albumen prints (frequently combination prints — two or more negatives printed separately onto the photographic paper).

AVAILABILITY AND PRICE Through galleries and at auction but infrequently found. Cartes de visite low; other prints moderately high to extremely high.

SIGNATURE/OTHER IDENTIFICATION

Oscar Gustave Rejlander. *A Secret,* ca. 1860. Albumen print. (Courtesy IMP/GEH)

COLLECTIONS IMP/GEH, New Mexico, Smithsonian, Texas (Gernsheim); Edinburgh Photographic Society, Kodak, RPS.

SELECTED BIBLIOGRAPHY
Charles Darwin. *The Expression of the Emotions in Man and Animals.* London: John Murray, 1872. 7 heliotypes (one of the first books to be illustrated by this process).
Edgar Yoxall Jones. *Father of Art Photography: O. G. Rejlander, 1813–1875.* Greenwich, Conn.: New York Graphic Society, 1973.

"Cuthbert Bede and O. J. [sic] Rejlander." *History of Photography* 1 (July 1977): 213–214.

John Fuller. "O. G. Rejlander: From Philistine to Forerunner." *Exposure* 14 (Dec. 1976): 32–36.

See also Life Library, *Camera, Great Photographers.*

Renger-Patzsch, Albert

Germany 1897–1966

Renger-Patzsch was a pioneer in the new objectivity (*Neue Sachlichkeit*) movement in German painting, film, and still photography of the 1920s, which developed at the same time as the realistic "straight" photography of Paul Strand and Edward Weston in the United States. The son of an amateur photographer, Renger-Patzsch was already taking pictures by the age of fifteen. He opposed the double exposures and photographic manipulations of László Moholy-Nagy and Man Ray as well as the sentimentalism and artificiality of the pictorialists, asserting that photographs were nothing if they were not objective reports about reality.

Renger-Patzsch was able to find design and beauty in many objects, as he indicated in the title of his best-known book, *Die Welt ist schön* (The World Is Beautiful). His close-ups of natural and manufactured objects are sharp and crisply textured; each object in them is isolated from its surroundings so that its shape and substance become the entire subject of the photograph. He photographed from unusual points of view, transforming each scene into a design of shapes yet preserving its link to realism. He once remarked, "Let us leave art to artists and let us try by means of photography to create photographs that can stand alone on account of their photographic quality — without borrowing from art" (quoted in H. and A. Gernsheim, *Concise History*, p. 205).

WORK   Chiefly recognizable subjects, often seen in an unfamiliar way to stress their shape and form, including natural objects (e.g., forests, marshes, water, plants); industrial products, structures, and machines (e.g., glassware, slag pile); architecture (e.g., vaulting, facades). Also includes portraits.

MEDIUM   Silver prints.

AVAILABILITY AND PRICE   Vintage prints available through galleries and at auction but rare; moderately high to extremely high. Modern prints made from the photographer's negatives by his estate available through galleries; moderate.

SIGNATURE/OTHER IDENTIFICATION

PORTFOLIO   *See* chapter 6 entry.

COLLECTIONS   Chicago, FOP, IMP/GEH, MOMA, New Mexico; Antwerp, BN, Cologne, RPS.

Albert Renger-Patzsch. *Church in Elsass* [Alsace], 1941. Silver print. (Courtesy Friends of Photography, Inc.)

SELECTED BIBLIOGRAPHY

Das Chorgestühl von Kappenberg. Berlin: Auriga, 1925.

Das Gesicht einer Landschaft, 1926.

Die Halligen. Berlin: Albertus, 1927.

Die Welt ist schön. Intro. by Carl Georg Heise. Munich: Wolff, 1928.

Lübeck. Berlin: Wasmuth, 1928.

Rudolf Schwarz. *Wegweisung der Technik.* Potsdam: Müller & Kiepenheuer, 1928.

Kurt Wilhelm-Kästner. *Das Münster in Essen.* Essen: Fredebeul & Koenen, 1929.

Sylt-Bild einer Insel. Munich: Bruckmann [1930s].

Werner Burmeister. *Norddeutsche Backsteindome.* Berlin: Deutscher Kunstverlag, 1930.

Hamburg: Photographische aufnah-men. Hamburg: Gebrüder Enoch, 1930.

Eisen und Stahl. Berlin: Reckendorf, 1931.

Albert Lange. *Leistungen deutscher Technik.* Leipzig: Seemann, 1935.

Deutsche Wasserburgen. Königstein: Langewiesche, 1941.

Land am Oberrhein, 1944.

Beständige Welt. Münster: Quell, 1947.

Friedrich Schnack. *Dresden wie es war und wurde.* Munich: Knorr & Hirth, 1956.

Michael Meier. *Oberrhein.* Munich: Deutscher Kunstverlag, 1959.

Hanno Hahn. *Hohenstaufenburgen in Süditalien.* Ingelheim am Rhein: Boehringer, 1961.

Im Wald. Wamel-Möhnesee: Hermann Kätelhöln, 1965.

Klaus Honnef. *Fotografien 1925-1960 von Albert Renger-Patzsch.* Bonn: Rheinisches Landesmuseum, 1977. Bibliography.

Beaumont Newhall. "Albert Renger-Patzsch." *Image* 8 (Sept. 1959): 138–155.

Allan Porter and Bernd Lohse. "Deutschland 1920-1933." *Camera,* Apr. 1967.

Untitled 12, Aug. 1977. Entire issue.

See also H. and A. Gernsheim, *Concise History;* Life Library, *Great Photographers.*

Rice, Leland D.
United States 1940–

Rice was a business major at Arizona State University (Tempe) until he happened to take a photography course from Van Deren Coke that completely changed the direction of his career. In addition to pursuing his personal photography, Rice has been active as a teacher and writer and has organized a number of photographic exhibitions. He was a member of the short-lived yet influential Visual Dialogue Foundation — an informal group of San Francisco area photographers, including Jack Welpott and Judy Dater, who met for discussions and exhibited together (ca. 1968-1973).

In his images Rice explores tonal variation, pattern, and texture; through the use of simple elements such as chairs, empty rooms, and light on walls, he explores the relationship between commonplace objects and the space they occupy. "In reviewing Rice's development . . . , one is struck by how rapidly he has moved toward broader effects of tone and scale and how painterly his work is, without in any way becoming unphotographic," wrote Charles W. Millard. "In that respect, it recalls the work of Aaron Siskind more than that of any other contemporary photographer" (*Leland Rice*). In 1977 the photographer reported: "Drawing has influenced my more recent color work. I approach my work as making marks or defining space; a schematic approach to the selection and relationships of objects" (statement to the authors).

WORK   Chiefly abstracted walls and other objects in space. Also includes portraits of women, "portraits" of chairs.

MEDIA   Silver prints, color.

AVAILABILITY AND PRICE   Through galleries; silver prints (8×10, 11×14, 16×20) moderate, color prints (16×20, 20×24) moderately high.

SIGNATURE/OTHER IDENTIFICATION

Leland Rice

PORTFOLIOS   *See* chapter 6 Schools and workshops entry.

COLLECTIONS   CCP, Chicago, Harvard (Fogg), IMP/GEH, Kansas, Los Angeles (Art), MMA, MOMA, New Mexico, Norton Simon, Oakland, Princeton (Art Museum), VSW; Arles, BN, NGC.

SELECTED BIBLIOGRAPHY

The Visual Dialogue Foundation. Intro. by Jack Welpott. Davis, Calif.: Visual Dialogue Foundation and Friends of Photography, 1971.

Charles W. Millard. *Leland Rice.* Washington, D.C.: Hirshhorn Museum and Sculpture Garden, 1977.

"Visual Dialogue Foundation: Members' Portfolio." *Album,* no. 10 (1970), pp. 34–45.

See also Doty, *America;* Life Library, *Year 1978;* Szarkowski, *Mirrors;* chapter 7 catalogues.

Leland D. Rice. *Wall Site,* 1977. Type C color print. (Courtesy the artist)

Riis, Jacob August
United States (b. Denmark) 1849-1914

An immigrant to the United States in 1870, Riis struggled for a number of years to earn a living. After holding a variety of jobs, he became a police reporter for the New York *Tribune* and later for the *Evening Sun.* His work took him to the center of New York's Lower East Side slums, where he had lived himself, and he began to crusade in print against the wretched conditions there. He later recalled: "It was upon my midnight trips with the sanitary police that the wish kept cropping up in me that there was some way of putting before the people what I saw there. A drawing might have done it, but I cannot draw. . . . anyway, a drawing would not have been evidence of the kind I wanted" (*The Making of an American*). The evidence that Riis sought was made possible by the introduction of flash powder in 1887. One of the first American photographers to use it, he brought light to show the murky cellars and hallways in which the poor lived and worked.

At first Riis's photographs could be printed with his articles only by converting them to line drawings. His images received wider distribution with the development of the halftone process, which permitted photographs to be printed on the same press with letterpress type. His book *How the Other Half Lives* was the first to have a number of photographic halftone illustrations. He also made photographic lantern slides for illustrated lectures that he gave on slum conditions. Riis's persistent reportage led to much needed social reform, but he was matter of fact about his photography: "I had use for it, and beyond that I never went" (ibid.). The use that he put it to, however, produced a number of powerful and moving documents.

WORK Social conditions in New York slums (late 1880s–1898 at the latest).

MEDIA Gelatin dry-plate negatives, silver prints.

AVAILABILITY AND PRICE Vintage prints available through galleries and at auction but extremely rare; high to extremely high. Modern prints made by Alexander Alland available through galleries; moderately high. Modern prints from the Museum of the City of New York, made from its collection of Riis negatives, extremely low.

COLLECTIONS Minnesota, New York, NYHS.

Jacob August Riis. *Tenement Child: Baby in Slum Tenement*, ca. 1890. Silver print. (Courtesy Museum of the City of New York)

SIGNATURE/OTHER IDENTIFICATION (Example from letter)

Jacob A Riis

SELECTED BIBLIOGRAPHY

How the Other Half Lives: Studies among the Tenements of New York. New York: Scribner, 1890. Reprint, with 100 photographs from the Riis collection of the Museum of the City of New York. New York: Dover, 1971.
The Children of the Poor. New York: Scribner, 1892. Reprint, New York: Arno, 1971.
Out of Mulberry Street. New York: Century, 1898.
A Ten Years' War. Boston: Houghton Mifflin, 1900.
The Making of an American. New York: Macmillan, 1901. Many reprints.
The Battle with the Slum. New York: Macmillan, 1902. Reprint, New York: MSS Information Corp., 1972.
Children of the Tenements. New York: Macmillan, 1903.
The Peril and the Preservation of the Home. Philadelphia: Jacobs, 1903.
Is There a Santa Claus? New York: Macmillan, 1904.
The Old Town. New York: Macmillan, 1909.
Hero Tales of the Far North. New York: Macmillan, 1919.
Christmas Stories. New York: Macmillan, 1923.
Louise Ware. *Jacob A. Riis: Police Reporter, Reformer, Useful Citizen.* New York: Appleton-Century, 1938. Bibliography includes newspaper and magazine articles.
Jacob Riis Revisited. Ed. and intro. by Francesco Cordasco. Garden City, N.Y.: Doubleday, 1968.
Alexander Alland, Sr. *Jacob A. Riis: Photographer and Citizen.* Millerton, N.Y.: Aperture, 1974.
See also Life Library, *Documentary*.

Robertson, James
Middle East and India (b. England)   Active mid-1800s

Beato, Felice A.
Middle and Far East (British citizen, b. Italy) d. 1903

It is not known just how and when these photographers joined forces, but as Robertson and Beato they produced many images of nineteenth-century life in the Middle East and elsewhere. Their work is well composed and sharp, yet can be said to be distinguished more by content than style. They were active as a team from 1852 to 1865, initially making travel views in Athens, Constantinople, and Egypt. In 1855 they photographed scenes of the Crimean campaign (after Roger Fenton, who had done so earlier, had returned to England). Their war scenes are "aftermaths" — the complexities of processing wet plates in the field precluded photographing battlefield action.

At the close of the Crimean War, Robertson and Beato worked in Malta, where Beato, who may have been an assistant until this time, apparently assumed equal partnership. Prints made by their firm — Robertson Beato and Company — include some attributed variously to Antonio Beato, Alphonse Beato, or A. Beato, whose relationship to Felice is uncertain and who may even have been the same person.

James Robertson and Felice A. Beato. *Petit champs de morts et l'Arsenal, Constantinople, Turkey,* ca. 1858. Albumen print. (Courtesy The Witkin Gallery)

The pair traveled to India in 1857/58 and photographed scenes of the Indian Mutiny. Beato alone is usually given credit for the photographs of the aftermath of the Siege of Lucknow. In 1860 their partnership disintegrated as Beato went to China to document the Opium War, while Robertson stayed in India as official photographer to the British military forces. Beato's is the sole signature on a series of views taken in Japan in the 1860s; thereafter, he apparently made trips to China and England before he returned to Egypt, where he was active until at least 1886.

Work Chiefly travel views (e.g., Constantinople, Malta, Athens, Cairo, biblical sites in Palestine), Crimean War and other war views of the period. Also includes Japan (e.g., customs, landscapes, architecture).

Media Calotypes (possibly); collodion wet-plate negatives, salt prints, albumen prints. Print sizes range from 6×9½ to 10×12; panoramas composed of many separate views also exist. Prints may be signed in the plate in a variety of ways: "Robertson Beato & Co.," "J. Robertson," "F. Beato," "A. Beato." Prints signed in ink by either Beato or Robertson exist but are rare.

Availability and Price Through galleries and at auction. Travel views frequently available; low to moderate. War scenes and signed prints rarer; moderate to high.

Signature/Other Identification

A. Beato

Collections IMP/GEH, MOMA, New Mexico. In London: Imperial War Museum, India Records, National Army Museum, VA.

Selected Bibliography
Scenes of the Mutiny. Robertson Beato & Co., 1857. 61 prints.
Indian Mutiny. Robertson Beato & Co., 1857–58. 48 prints.
Photographic Views and Costumes of Japan (album). Yokohama [1868].
19th Century Photographs from the Collection. Preface by Van Deren Coke. Santa Fe: Art Museum, University of New Mexico, 1976.
Marie-Thérèse Jammes and André Jammes. *En Egypte au temps de Flaubert.* Paris: Kodak-Pathé [ca. 1976].
Walter Chappell. "Robertson Beato & Co.: Camera Vision at Lucknow, 1857–1858." *Image* 7 (Feb. 1958): 36–40.

Robinson, Henry Peach
England 1830–1901

The most prominent "high art" photographer of Victorian England, H. P. Robinson was first a bookstore clerk and painter; in 1857 he opened a commercial photographic portrait studio in Reigate. O. G. Rejlander's composite tableau *Two Ways of Life* created a sensation that year in photographic circles, and Robinson began making combination prints also. His first composition, *Fading Away,* created a sensation of its own: he combined five separate negatives to create a scene of a dying girl surrounded by her grieving relatives — "calculated to excite painful emotions," as he said (*The Elements of a Pictorial Photograph*). Anecdotal, narrative paintings, often with sentimental themes, were immensely popular at the time. Rejlander and Robinson were among the first of many genre photographers to make photographs in imitation of such paintings; these carefully posed scenes of idyllic peasant life, domestic tranquillity, and moral instruction became a staple of fashionable photographic art of the period.

One of the most popular and influential photographers of his time, Robinson won numerous competition medals. He wrote extensively on photography, staunchly defending his point of view that if photography were to be an art it must go beyond factual recording: "No possible amount of scientific truth will in itself make a picture. Something

Henry Peach Robinson. *Primrose Time,* ca. 1880s. Platinum combination print. (Courtesy IMP/GEH)

more is required. The truth that is wanted is artistic truth — quite a different thing" (quoted in Lyons, *Photographers*). Robinson believed that "any 'dodge, trick, and conjuration' of any kind is open to the photographer's use. . . . It is his imperative duty to avoid the mean, the bare and the ugly, and to aim to elevate his subject, to avoid awkward forms, and to correct the unpicturesque" (*Pictorial Effect in Photography.*) In addition to his combination prints, Robinson also made a number of single-negative pictures, and he eventually suggested that combination printing be used only when an effect was impossible to achieve otherwise.

WORK   Includes anecdotal and genre compositions, illustrations of poetry (e.g., Tennyson's *The Lady of Shalott*), portraits, landscapes.

MEDIA   Collodio-albumen negatives; albumen prints, platinum prints, carbon prints. Robinson's combination prints were produced by assembling separate prints, blending the edges, and rephotographing the entire work. Sizes range to as large as 22×30.

AVAILABILITY AND PRICE   Through galleries and at auction but infrequently found; high to extremely high.

PORTFOLIO   *See* chapter 6 entry.

COLLECTIONS   IMP/GEH, Smithsonian, Texas (Gernsheim); NGC, RPS.

SELECTED BIBLIOGRAPHY
Pictorial Effect in Photography: Being Hints on Composition and Chiaroscuro for Photographers. London: Piper & Carter, 1869. Reprint, Pawlet, Vt.: Helios, 1971.
The Art and Practice of Silver Printing. London: Piper & Carter, 1881. Reprint, New York: Arno, 1973.
Picture-Making by Photography. London: Piper & Carter, 1884. Rev. ed., with a chapter disputing P. H. Emerson, 1889. Reprint, New York: Arno, 1973. French ed., *La Photographie en plein air.* 2 vols. Paris: Gauthier-Villars, 1899.
The Studio and What to Do in It. London: Piper & Carter, 1885.
Letters on Landscape Photography. London: Piper & Carter, 1888. Reprint, New York: Arno, 1973.
Art Photography in Short Chapters. London, 1890.
The Elements of a Pictorial Photograph. Bradford, England: Lund, 1896. Reprint, New York: Arno, 1973.
See also Life Library, *Camera, Great Photographers*; Lyons, *Photographers.*

Rosenblum, Walter
United States 1919–

Rosenblum learned photography at a Boys' Club, then in 1937 joined the Photo League in New York City to make use of its darkroom. Through the League he met and was influenced by Sid Grossman, Eliot Elisofon, and Paul Strand. The League became a major part of Rosenblum's life — he worked for it in various capacities, became editor of its publication *Photo Notes,* and was president several times between 1941 and 1951.

The Photo League philosophy, which envisioned photography as a tool to document social conditions, found intense expression in Rosenblum's work. His first major photographic project with the League, a document of life on Pitt Street on the Lower East Side, is a powerful evocation of the resilience and strength of human character.

During World War II Rosenblum served as a still- and motion-picture photographer for the U.S. Army Signal Corps in combat, including at the D-Day landing in Normandy, and was the most decorated American photographer in the war. He later became influential as a teacher and has taught in the art department of Brooklyn College since 1947.

Milton W. Brown wrote: "A child of the New York slums, Rosenblum has no profound feeling for nature and responds to it only in its relationship to man; nor for beauty, except as he finds it in people, young or old, black or white, in the most unlikely places. Then he reacts with tenderness, as if having discovered a rare blossom. His abiding passion is for humanity, about which he is incurably optimistic and to which he offers himself as an artist" (*Walter Rosenblum: Photographer*).

Walter Rosenblum. *Haitian Woman,* 1959. Silver print. (Courtesy the artist)

SIGNATURE/OTHER IDENTIFICATION

WORK Chiefly documentary photography: Pitt Street, Lower East Side (1940); Spanish refugee camps in France (1946); Mexican migrant workers in Texas (1946); Gaspé Peninsula, Canada (1949); Knickerbocker Village (1949); 105th Street in Spanish Harlem (1951); Haiti (1958–1959); France, Spain, Italy (1973). Also includes war photography for the Signal Corps (1943–1945).

MEDIUM Silver prints.

AVAILABILITY AND PRICE Through galleries; moderately high.

COLLECTIONS Brooklyn, IMP/GEH, MOMA; BN.

SELECTED BIBLIOGRAPHY
Wilfred Carty. *The West Indies: Islands in the Sun.* Camden, N.J.: Nelson, 1967.
Walter Rosenblum: Photographer. Text by Milton W. Brown. Cambridge, Mass.: Fogg Art Museum, 1974.
A Walter Rosenblum Retrospective. Intro. by Paul Strand. Flushing, N.Y.: Queens Museum, 1976.
See also Life Library, *Documentary.*

Rothstein, Arthur
United States 1915–

Rothstein's long career in photojournalism started when he took a class in contemporary civilization from Roy Stryker at Columbia University. Rothstein began working with him, copying pictures for a book Stryker was doing on agriculture, and in 1935 became the first photographer Stryker hired for the U.S. Resettlement Administration (later renamed the Farm Security Administration [FSA]).

During World War II Rothstein photographed for the Office of War Information and the Army, then for the United Nations in China. In 1946 he rejoined *Look* magazine, where he had worked briefly in 1940, and rose from staff photographer to director of photography. Rothstein helped found the American Society of Magazine Photographers and served as editor of its journal, *Infinity.* He then became associate editor of the national Sunday newspaper supplement *Parade.*

William Saroyan wrote: "Arthur Rothstein is a professional photographer. His work is straight, not arty. At their best, however, his pictures are works of art. Understanding the mechanics of the camera is likelier to make art than trying to understand the truth about God. The value of camera-pictures lies in their aesthetic neutrality. Before it is anything else a photograph is a fact. Then, comes its subject. And finally its identification — the picture is a work of art, a work of history, or both. It isn't necessary for a photograph to be both, but many of Rothstein's photographs are" (*Look at Us . . .*).

WORK Includes FSA images (1935–1940), photojournalism (e.g., John F. Kennedy's funeral). (See illustration, page 137.)

MEDIA Silver prints, color.

AVAILABILITY AND PRICE Vintage FSA prints infrequently found; moderately high. Modern FSA prints (black and white only) from the Library of Congress extremely low. Modern prints made and signed by Rothstein available through galleries; moderate.

SIGNATURE/OTHER IDENTIFICATION

[signature: Arthur Rothstein]

PORTFOLIO *See* chapter 6 entry.

COLLECTIONS IMP/GEH, LOC (FSA work), MOMA, San Francisco, Smithsonian; RPS.

SELECTED BIBLIOGRAPHY
Photojournalism: Pictures for Magazines and Newspapers. New York: American Photographic Book, 1956.
Creative Color in Photography. Philadelphia: Chilton, 1963.
Look at Us, Let's See, Here We Are. . . . Text by William Saroyan. New York: Cowles, 1967.
———, John Vachon, and Roy Stryker. *Just Before the War: Urban America from 1935 to 1941 as Seen by Photographers of the Farm Security Administration.* Ed. by Thomas Garver. New York: October House, 1968.
Color Photography Now. New York: Amphoto, 1970.
The Depression Years. New York: Dover, 1978.
See also bibliography in FSA entry.

Rubinstein, Eva
United States (b. Argentina) 1933–

Born of Polish parents, Rubinstein lived as a child in Paris and Warsaw, then emigrated to the United States at the beginning of World War II. She trained in dance and acting and appeared in several productions on and off Broadway and in Europe. She began to photograph in 1968 with Sean Kernan and also studied with Lisette Model, Jim Hughes, Ken Heyman, and Diane Arbus. She recalled: "I had been an actress and a dancer. Photography appealed to me because it didn't go away in the morning — it was so much less ephemeral than what I had been doing. I wanted to hold on to what I had created" (statement to the authors, 1976).

Rubinstein does free-lance editorial, documentary, and portrait work, plus her own more personal images. She often photographs light — glowing through windows, on flesh, on the brilliant linen of a bed or in the corner of a room. She once wrote: "For me, in its best moments, photography has an element of falling in love with the subject, be it mouse or man, female nude or empty house, for, however brief the moment may be, what it really means is some sort of giving out from oneself to whoever or whatever you are photographing — so it is *not* just a taking. Something a little different, something private, occurs each time — never repeated or even repeatable" ("Eva Rubinstein," p. 24).

WORK Includes portraits, interiors, nudes.

MEDIUM Silver prints.

AVAILABILITY AND PRICE Through galleries; moderate.

Eva Rubinstein. *Cousins, Spain,* 1973. Silver print. (Courtesy the artist)

PORTFOLIOS *See* chapter 6 entry.

COLLECTIONS ICP, MMA; Antwerp, Arles, BN.

SELECTED BIBLIOGRAPHY
Eva Rubinstein. Intro. by Sean Kernan. Dobbs Ferry, N.Y.: Morgan & Morgan, 1974.
"Eva Rubinstein." *Camera,* Jan. 1973, pp. 24–32.

Russell, A. J.
United States 1830–1902

Best known as a railroad photographer, Andrew Joseph Russell in his early career practiced both painting (including many landscapes) and photography. During the Civil War he was a captain in the U.S. Military Railroad Construction Corps and in that capacity photographed primarily railroad equipment, fortifications, and the like, rather than battles or their aftermath.

Andrew Joseph Russell. *Citadel Rock — Green River Valley,* 1869. Albumen print. (Courtesy University of New Mexico, University Art Museum)

After the war Russell was appointed official photographer for the Union Pacific Railroad. In 1868/69 he recorded the westward progress of the railroad, making a number of views of scenes along the route and of construction, including photographs in 1869 of the driving of the spike that joined the Union Pacific with the Central Pacific Railroad at Promontory Point, Utah. Later, Russell established a studio in New York City.

Russell often used human figures, tiny in the distance, as a clue to the monumental scale of the western landscape. The minuscule figures draw the viewer into the scene and vividly convey the vast emptiness of the West as it must have appeared to early settlers.

WORK Civil War images, primarily related to the railroad; landscapes and scenes taken during construction of the Union Pacific Railroad; views made on a trip to Sacramento, Calif. (See illustration, page 6.)

MEDIA Collodion wet-plate negatives, albumen prints (in varying sizes, including stereographs).

AVAILABILITY AND PRICE Through galleries and at auction. Prints from *Sun Pictures of Rocky Mountain Scenery* frequently found; moderate. Other images rare; moderate to extremely high.

COLLECTIONS AGS, BPL, LOC, National Archives, New Mexico, Oakland.

SELECTED BIBLIOGRAPHY
The Great West Illustrated in a Series of Photographic Views across the Continent; Taken along the Line of the Union Pacific Railroad, West from Omaha, Nebraska. New York, 1869. 50 albumen prints.
Ferdinand V. Hayden. *Sun Pictures of Rocky Mountain Scenery.* New York: Bien, 1870. 30 albumen prints (smaller versions of some of the photographs in *The Great West*).
Barry B. Combs. *Westward to Promontory.* Palo Alto, Calif.: American West, 1969.

Photographs from the Coke Collection. Intro. by Van Deren
Coke. Santa Fe: Museum of New Mexico, 1973.
E. D. Pattison. "The Pacific Railroad Rediscovered." *Geographical Review* 53, no. 1 (1962): 25–36.

Salomon, Erich
Germany 1886–1944

Salomon was one of the first photographers to use a small, hand-held camera to make unposed photographs of statesmen and other celebrities; the term "candid camera" was coined by the London *Graphic* to describe his innovative work.

Salomon's career as a photojournalist began around 1928. He worked first with an Ermanox, a small camera that exposed single glass plates; later he was one of the first to use a Leica. He sometimes concealed his camera, but more often he simply used it inconspicuously, working with available light rather than flash.

Salomon regarded himself as a historian documenting high-level political and cultural events. He was often invited to photograph at official functions, and when he wasn't, was ingenious in finding some way to record the event. He was so well known that in 1930 Aristide Briand, prime minister of France, jokingly advised the participants at a conference to await Salomon's arrival before convening since the meeting might not be considered important unless photographed by him. Salomon's work appeared in *Berliner Illustrierte Zeitung* and other picture magazines. He and his family left Germany for Holland in the thirties. During the war they were arrested and taken to Auschwitz, where he, his wife, and a son died.

Walker Evans wrote of Salomon: "His speciality was a kind of photographic spy work in the higher corridors of international diplomacy. This extraordinary man was not to be stopped. His phenomenal gift lay in mastery of entrée far exceeding any mere reporter's gall. Somehow he was taken for granted in the rather ghoulish atmosphere of flummery and cunning, duplicity and swordplay that is one side of foreign affairs. . . . Though Salomon's work stimulated and inspired countless imitators, his style has never been successfully counterfeited" ("Photography," in *Quality,* ed. by Louis Kronenberger [New York: Atheneum, 1969]).

SIGNATURE/OTHER IDENTIFICATION

Photo Dr. Erich Salomon

Dr. Erich Salomoh
CHARLOTTENBURG 9
Hölderlinstrasse 11
Amt Westend 441

PHOTO DR. ERICH SALOMON.

Flat Duinwijck, Den, Haag
van Alkemadelaan 350. Tel.774570

Erich Salomon. *Conférence européenne interministérielle, La Haye,* 1929 or 1930. Silver print. (Courtesy La Photogalerie)

WORK Candid photographs of conferences, meetings, trials, parties, lectures, concerts, etc., throughout Europe and the United States (e.g., signing the Kellogg-Briand Pact, 1928; inside the League of Nations; inside the White House; the U.S. Supreme Court in session; Stravinsky conducting).

MEDIA Gelatin dry-plate negatives (before 1932) and film negatives thereafter, silver prints.

AVAILABILITY AND PRICE Through galleries and at auction. Vintage prints infrequently available; moderately high to high. Modern prints made by or under the supervision of Salomon's son Peter Hunter in Amsterdam are moderate in price.

COLLECTIONS LIFE, MOMA, New Orleans, Texas (Gernsheim); Antwerp.

SELECTED BIBLIOGRAPHY
Berühmte Zeitgenossen in unbewachten Augenblicken. Stuttgart: J. Engelhorns, 1931.
Porträt einer Epoche. Berlin: Ullstein, 1963. U.S. ed., *Portrait of an Age.* New York: Collier/Macmillan, 1966.
Erich Salomon. Intro. by Peter Hunter. Millerton, N.Y.: Aperture, 1978. Bibliography.
K. Safranski. "Dr. Salomon." *Popular Photography,* Aug. 1948.
Peter Hunter. "Salomon." *Photography* (London), Jan. 1957, pp. 32–37.
———. "Dr. Erich Salomon: Father of Modern Photojournalists." *Camera* 35, no. 4, 1958, pp. 268–277.
See also Life Library, *Camera, Photojournalism;* Newhall, *Masters;* Szarkowski, *Looking.*

Samaras, Lucas
United States (b. Greece) 1936–

Samaras had been a painter, sculptor, and mixed-media artist when in 1969 he began photographing himself with Polaroid instant-picture materials. His subject matter is his own body, photographed from every angle and in every position, usually nude but also in various outfits, including wigs and makeup. The background is his kitchen, which he shares with the television set that stimulates his vision. He manipulates his prints to create patterns and distortions that overlay, transfigure, and sometimes all but destroy the nominal subject. The overall effect is of erotic playacting — sometimes comic, sometimes grotesque, always intentional.

"My body is one of the materials I work with," Samaras said in his "Autointerview." "I use myself and therefore I don't have to go through all the extraneous kinds of relationships like finding models and pretending artistic distance or finding some symbol of geometry. I use myself also because it is still unorthodox to use one's self. . . . I formulated myself, I mated with myself, and I gave birth to myself. And my real self was the product — the polaroids" (*Samaras Album*, pp. 3–4).

Arnold Glimcher wrote that Samaras's "photo-transformations are divided into two types: images in which the figure is transformed by actual physical contortion and extravagantly illuminated or painted with colored lights; and others in which the posed and lighted image is later distorted by altering the process of the film's development. As the image begins to appear, Samaras tests the limits of his fantasies' credibility by manually blending or mixing the photo-emulsion pigments using the surface itself as a palette in a kind of expressionistic finger-painting" (*Lucas Samaras: Photo-Transformations* [1974]).

WORK Self-portrait fantasies. (See color plate 7.)

MEDIA Polaroid prints, including SX-70, usually with hand-manipulated surfaces that make each a unique print.

AVAILABILITY AND PRICE Through galleries; high.

SIGNATURE/OTHER IDENTIFICATION

COLLECTIONS Harvard (Fogg), MOMA, Philadelphia.

SELECTED BIBLIOGRAPHY
Samaras Album: Autointerview/Autobiography/Autopolaroid. New York: Whitney Museum of American Art, and Pace Editions, 1971. Also limited ed. with signed Polaroid print. 100 copies.
Lucas Samaras: Photo-Transformations. Intro. by Arnold B. Glimcher. New York: Pace Gallery, 1974.
Kim Levin. *Lucas Samaras.* New York: Abrams, 1975.
Lucas Samaras: Photo-Transformations. Text by Arnold B. Glimcher. Long Beach: California State University, and New York: Dutton, 1975. Bibliography.
"Autopolaroids." *Art in America* 58 (Nov./Dec. 1970): 66–83.
Max Kozloff. "The Uncanny Portrait: Sander, Arbus, Samaras." *Artforum* 11 (June 1973): 58–66.
See also Doty, *America*; Life Library, *Frontiers*; Szarkowski, *Mirrors*; chapter 7 catalogue.

Sander, August
Germany 1876–1964

Sander's portraits comprise a revealing document of the social strata in Germany before World War II. After working for various commercial photographers early in his career, he was able in 1910 to establish his own studio in Cologne. In order to get more work, Sander began to travel through the countryside around his studio making portraits of the peasants of Westerwald in their natural surroundings. At the same time, he was exhibiting and winning medals for pictorial-style prints and was experimenting with the new three-color process.

In 1918 he made friends among contemporary artists of Cologne, including the Marxist painter Franz Wilhelm Seiwert, who believed that art should reveal the structure of society. Stimulated by discussions with Seiwert, Sander conceived the idea of a vast photographic project he called "People of the 20th Century." To his collection of photographs of peasants he planned to add images of people from all walks of life. He also changed his style of work: he stopped retouching his portraits, removed the retouching he had added previously, and began to print on a glossy paper that revealed every detail of the images. In 1929 he published *Antlitz der Zeit* (Face of the Time) as the first installment in his project. In the accompanying text, the novelist Alfred Döblin spoke of the new, objective realism of Sander's work — a kind of comparative photography in the sense of comparative anatomy. In 1934, after Sander's son Erich came under suspicion for his political activities, *Antlitz der Zeit* was confiscated by the Nazis and the printing plates destroyed; the negatives, however, survived. Sander photographed little after the war, concentrating instead on assembling and printing his existing negatives.

Artists, intellectuals, bureaucrats, merchants, workers, the unemployed, soldiers, industrialists — all passed before Sander's camera. Often the subjects face the camera squarely, as if both photographer and subject are totally straightforward and objective. Yet Sander was also subtly interpreting his subjects and their social roles: a circus performer with just a trace of seductive slouch stands in the mud outside her wagon, a laborer stolidly shoulders his load of brick, a pastry cook's roly-poly physique is echoed in his round bowl and round, bald head. Sander wrote: "It is not my intention either to criticize or to describe these people, but to create a piece of history with my pictures" (*Men without Masks*).

WORK Chiefly people in various trades, classes, and social roles. Also includes landscapes.

MEDIA Chiefly gelatin dry-plate negatives and film negatives, silver prints. Also gum-bichromate prints, pigment prints, three-color prints. Vintage prints may be signed or bear blind-stamp or ink-stamp on verso.

AVAILABILITY AND PRICE Through galleries. Vintage prints, also available from collections owned by Sander's relatives and his estate, high to extremely high. Modern prints, made by his son Gunther from the original negatives (and also available through him), are moderate in price.

SIGNATURE/OTHER IDENTIFICATION

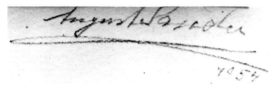

PORTFOLIOS   *See* chapter 6 entry.

August Sander. *Pastry Cook Franz Bremer, Cologne,* 1928. Modern silver print made by Gunther Sander from the original negative. (Courtesy Thomas Halsted and The August Sander Estate)

COLLECTIONS   IMP/GEH, MOMA, New Mexico, New Orleans, RPS.

SELECTED BIBLIOGRAPHY
Antlitz der Zeit. Text by Alfred Döblin. Munich: Transmare, 1929. Reprint, Munich: Schirmer Mosel, 1976.
Deutschenspiegel: Menschen des 20 Jahrhunderts. Intro. by Heinrich Lützeler. Munich, 1929. Another ed., Gütersloh, Germany: Sigbert Mohn, 1962.
Land an Rhein und Ruhr. Frankfort: Umschau, 1955.
Menschen ohne Maske. Lucerne: Bucher, 1971. U.S. ed., *Men without Masks: Faces of Germany, 1910–1938.* Foreword by Golo Mann. Text by Gunther Sander. Greenwich, Conn.: New York Graphic Society, 1973. U.K. ed., *August Sander: Photographer Extraordinary.* London: Thames & Hudson, 1973.
Rheinlandschaften. Text by Wolfgang Kemp. Munich: Schirmer Mosel, 1975.
August Sander. Intro. by John von Hartz. Millerton, N.Y.: Aperture, 1977. Bibliography.
Max Kozloff. "The Uncanny Portrait: Sander, Arbus, Samaras." *Artforum* 11 (June 1973): 58–66.
Ulrich Keller. "Photographs in Context." *Image* 19 (Dec. 1976): 1–12.
See also Life Library, *Great Photographers.*

Sarony, Napoleon
United States (b. Canada) 1821–1896

Sarony owned a successful lithographic printing company in New York until 1858, then studied art in Europe, where he apparently learned photography from his brother Oliver François Xavier Sarony (1820–1879), a successful portrait photographer in England. Napoleon Sarony opened his own photographic studio in Birmingham, England, in 1864, but by 1866 he had returned to the United States and had opened a studio in New York City.

Sarony was well known for his theatrical portraits (he is reported to have made some forty thousand of them), and expressive and unconventional poses were his specialty. He was given to theatrical dress and behavior himself and was a gifted storyteller. No taller than the Little General whose namesake he was, Sarony enjoyed strutting around in hussar's uniforms and the like. He tried to elicit animated expressions from his sitters — a difficult achievement given the thirty-second or longer exposures required for indoor portraits at the time — and his showmanship was no doubt an asset in engaging their attention. The character Julius Bianchi in F. Hopkinson Smith's novel *The Fortunes of Oliver Horn* (1902) is based on Sarony.

WORK   Chiefly portraits.

MEDIA   Collodion wet-plate negatives, albumen prints.

AVAILABILITY AND PRICE   Through galleries and at auction. Cabinet-photograph portraits (also frequently found at flea markets, antique shops, etc.) extremely low. Larger prints are rarer and more expensive. Sarony's flowing signature identifies his work.

COLLECTIONS   IMP/GEH, New Mexico, New York.

Savage, Charles R.
United States (b. England) 1832–1909

Savage is best known for his photographs of the Rocky Mountains, of life on the Great Plains, and of Salt Lake City. He came to New York in 1856 and after some training in photography set up a studio in Nebraska in 1859, then in 1860 moved to Salt Lake City. In 1866 he traveled to San Francisco, where he spent some time with Carleton E. Watkins. Savage photographed the joining of the Union Pacific and Central Pacific railroads at Promontory Point, Utah, in 1869. His views of western scenes were widely distributed by his firm, Savage and Ottinger, particularly as stereographs. In 1883 his studio burned down and he lost many years' worth of negatives.

WORK Chiefly Rocky Mountain landscapes, life on the plains, Salt Lake City. Also includes scenes of California, Oregon, and along the wagon trail from Nebraska City, Neb., to Salt Lake City.

MEDIA Collodion wet-plate negatives, albumen prints (including stereographs).

AVAILABILITY AND PRICE Through galleries and at auction. Small prints mass-produced for albums, many with "Savage and Ottinger" printed in the negative, are frequently found; low to moderate. Large prints extremely rare; extremely high.

Napoleon Sarony. *James O'Neill* [father of playwright Eugene O'Neill], early 1870s. Albumen cabinet photograph. (Courtesy IMP/GEH)

SIGNATURE/OTHER IDENTIFICATION

630 Broadway,
New York

SELECTED BIBLIOGRAPHY

Washington Irving. *Rip Van Winkle: A Legend of the Katskill Mountains.* New York: Putnam, 1870. Variant editions may have 5 albumen, 4 carbon, or other prints of actor Joseph Jefferson as Rip Van Winkle.
Sarony's Living Pictures: Photographed from Life. New York: Chasmar, 1894–95.
Ben L. Bassham. *The Theatrical Photographs of Napoleon Sarony.* Kent, Ohio: Kent State University Press, 1978.
See also Taft, *Photography.*

Charles R. Savage. *North Portal of Castle Gate, Price Cañon, Utah,* early 1870s. Albumen print. (Private collection)

COLLECTIONS The Office of the Historian of the Church of Jesus Christ of Latter-Day Saints (Salt Lake City) preserves many thousands of Savage's photographs. Also BPL, Harvard (Carpenter), IMP/GEH, New Mexico.

SELECTED BIBLIOGRAPHY

[Thomas] Nelson and Sons. *Salt Lake City.* New York: Nelson, 1869.

Views of Utah and Tourists' Guide (folder). Salt Lake City: Savage, 1887.

Virginia [Donaghé] McClurg. *Picturesque Utah.* Denver: F. S. Thayer, 1888.

Gems of Utah Scenery (portfolio). Salt Lake City: Savage [1890s].

The Reflex of Salt Lake City and Vicinity. Salt Lake City: Savage [1890s]. Also later variant eds.

Nelson B. Wadsworth. *Through Camera Eyes.* Provo, Utah: Brigham Young University Press, 1975.

"A Photographic Tour of near 9,000 Miles." *The Philadelphia Photographer,* Sept./Oct. 1867, pp. 287 ff.

See also Naef and Wood, *Era;* Taft, *Photography.*

Savage, Naomi
United States 1927–

Savage first studied photography with Berenice Abbott at the New School for Social Research (New York City) in 1943 and later continued her studies at Bennington College in Vermont. In 1947/48 she assisted Man Ray, her uncle, in Hollywood.

Starting with a photographic image, Savage carries it through various processes such as photoengraving, collaging, and solarization. For example, she has photographed pieces of fruit, printed the images in high contrast, cut them out, and grouped them in a collage. She also explores and expands the boundaries of the photographic medium by creating photographic images etched and deeply bitten on metal plates, onto which patinas are applied; these photoengravings are then framed as the art object.

"Pictures like Savage's differ from traditional photographs," wrote John Szarkowski, "chiefly in that the photographer must be able to enjoy a different kind of adventure. Rather than attempting to anticipate as precisely as possible the look of one's finished picture, the photographer arranges a procedure that will result in interesting surprises. It is less a matter of getting what one wants, and more a matter of being open to the possibility of wanting what one gets" (Szarkowski, *Looking,* p. 190).

In 1971 Savage was commissioned to make a photo-engraved mural wall (shown here) for the Lyndon Baines Johnson Library in Austin, Texas. This work, composed of a sequence of five deeply etched magnesium plates, 8×10 feet each, uses well-known photographs that show Johnson as president and with each of his four immediate predecessors (Roosevelt, Truman, Eisenhower, Kennedy). Her latest work includes porcelain dishes and plaques — some using engravings, some using photographs as decals — and gum-bichromate prints using muted watercolors.

WORK Portraits and other subject matter, often highly abstracted (1949 and after); streets and sculpture of Paris (1950).

MEDIA Savage makes or uses collage, solarization, high-contrast toning, intaglio printing, texture screening, silkscreen, negatives between Plexiglas, photograms, line-cut photoengravings on metal, gum-bichromate prints, images on porcelain. Many of her works are unique objects. Sizes range from 3½×4½ inches to mural size.

AVAILABILITY AND PRICE Through galleries and by commission. Intaglio prints (issued in small editions), small engraved pieces, and unique gum prints moderate to moderately high. Larger pieces extremely high.

SIGNATURE/OTHER IDENTIFICATION

COLLECTIONS Harvard (Fogg), Kansas, MOMA, New Jersey, Princeton.

SELECTED BIBLIOGRAPHY

Two Generations of Photographs: Man Ray and Naomi Savage. Trenton: New Jersey State Museum, 1969.

Art: A Woman's Sensibility. Ed. by Miriam Schapiro. Valencia: California Institute of the Arts, 1975.

Annie Gottlieb. *Women See Women.* New York: Crowell, 1976.

Peter C. Bunnell. "Photography as Sculpture and Prints." *Art in America* 57 (Sept. 1969): 56–61.

"Naomi Savage." *Album,* no. 10 (1970), pp. 2–10.

OvoPhoto (Montreal), no. 17/18 (Sept./Oct. 1974).

"Visual Answers to Verbal Questions." *Untitled* 7/8 (1974), pp. 68–79.

See also Mann, *Women;* Szarkowski, *Looking, Mirrors;* chapter 7 catalogues.

Naomi Savage. Mural wall, LBJ Library, Austin, Texas, 1971. Sequence of five 8×10-foot photoetchings on magnesium plates. (Courtesy the artist and The Witkin Gallery)

Shahn, Ben
United States (b. Lithuania) 1898–1969

Shahn is well known as a painter and graphic artist. Less known is his large body of work as a photographer for the Farm Security Administration (FSA) in the 1930s. He was already active as an artist when he became interested in photography as an aid in sketching details and was given a Leica by his brother. He shared a studio with Walker Evans at the time — and later recounted the only lesson he ever had from Evans: "Well, it's very easy, Ben. F-9 on the sunny side of the street. F-4.5 on the shady side of the street. For 1/20th of a second hold your camera steady" (quoted in Maddow, *Faces*, p. 316). Shahn particularly admired the work of Henri Cartier-Bresson, as well as that of Mathew Brady, Eugène Atget, and Lewis W. Hine. In 1946 he remarked: "I am a social painter or photographer. I paint or photograph for two reasons: either because I like certain events, things, or people with great intensity or because I dislike others with equal intensity" (quoted in *The Photographic Eye of Ben Shahn*, p. vii).

In 1934/35 Shahn collaborated with the artist Lou Block on a planned Rikers Island (New York City) Penitentiary mural (never completed) and made studies for it by photographing local street and prison scenes. From 1935 to 1938 he worked for the FSA as an artist, designer, and photographer. Roy Stryker, head of the FSA photographic unit, wrote: "I was taken by Ben's photos because they were so compassionate. Ben's were warm. Ben's had the juices of human beings and their troubles and all those human things" (ibid., p. ix). Shahn made more than six thousand photographs during the Depression — of the unemployed, of the poor, of government homestead projects, and of small-town life.

In 1938, when he left the FSA, his serious involvement with photography ended, though he continued to use photographs as aids in his paintings and graphic work. Shahn was never interested in the fine points of photographic technique; he was concerned with the social implications of the pictures he took and with picture content — the ability of the camera to discover and record compelling visual material.

WORK   Includes street and prison scenes (1932–1935), FSA images of the South and Midwest (1935–1938), photographs made as studies for paintings and other works. (See illustration, page 138.)

MEDIUM   Silver prints.

AVAILABILITY AND PRICE   Vintage prints available through galleries and at auction but rare; moderately high to extremely high. Modern FSA prints from the Library of Congress extremely low.

COLLECTIONS   Harvard University's Fogg Art Museum holds 3,000 of Shahn's vintage prints. Also Harvard (Carpenter), IMP/GEH, LOC (FSA work), Louisville, Minnesota, RISD, San Francisco.

SELECTED BIBLIOGRAPHY
Selden Rodman. *Portrait of the Artist as an American: Ben Shahn. A Biography with Pictures.* New York: Harper, 1951.

Ben Shahn, Photographer: An Album from the Thirties. Ed. and intro. by Margaret R. Weiss. New York: Da Capo, 1973.
The Photographic Eye of Ben Shahn. Ed. by Davis Pratt. Cambridge, Mass.: Harvard University Press, 1975.
See also bibliography in FSA entry.

Sheeler, Charles
United States 1883–1965

Charles Sheeler is best known as a painter in the American precisionist movement, which concentrated on the graphic shapes of urban and industrial scenes. The powerful forms in Sheeler's paintings are also evident in the photographs he began to make in 1912, when he was an art student looking for a way to support himself. He earned income photographing new houses and buildings for architectural firms, and on his own time used the camera to study details of his Doylestown, Pennsylvania, home and the surrounding countryside.

In 1919 Sheeler moved to New York City, where he became friendly with Alfred Stieglitz, Edward Steichen, Paul Strand, and other photographers and painters. During the 1920s he photographed the skyscrapers of New York, sometimes using double exposure and tilting his camera to produce an unusual perspective. In 1921, with Paul Strand, he made a six-minute film titled *Manahatta* (also called *New York the Magnificent*). The success of Shee-

Charles Sheeler. *Funnel,* 1927. Silver print. (Courtesy IMP/GEH)

ler's canvases allowed him to give up commercial photography in the early 1930s and devote most of his time to painting. He deemphasized his personal photography, having had something of a love/hate relationship with it. His last exhibition of photographs for sale was in 1931, though he continued to photograph after that time.

Charles Millard wrote: "Although his pictures shared a 'straight,' sharp-focused, uncropped quality with the work of other important photographers of his time, Sheeler's photographs are differentiated from those of his contemporaries by their lack of dramatic assertiveness and by their tendency toward surface composition. . . . Sheeler did not use light and dark contrast to dramatize his subjects, but rather for the abstract two-dimensional cohesiveness the resulting patterns gave his pictures" (*Charles Sheeler* [1968], p. 85).

WORK Chiefly industrial and architectural photographs (e.g., the Ford Motor Co. River Rouge [Mich.] plant, 1927). Also includes still lifes (e.g., *Zinnia and Nasturtium Leaves,* 1915); African tribal sculpture (1918); cityscapes; barns; Chartres Cathedral (1929); commercial work, including fashion and portraits (1923–1929).

MEDIUM Silver prints (some sepia-toned).

AVAILABILITY AND PRICE At auction occasionally but extremely rare; extremely high. Prints from Sheeler's estate, purchased by a private collector, are not currently available.

SIGNATURE/OTHER IDENTIFICATION

Sheeler

COLLECTIONS Chicago, IMP/GEH, LIFE, MOMA, New Mexico, Princeton, RISD, Whitney.

SELECTED BIBLIOGRAPHY
Constance Rourke. *Charles Sheeler: Artist in the American Tradition.* New York: Harcourt, Brace, 1938. Reprint, New York: Da Capo, 1969.
Charles Sheeler: Paintings, Drawings, Photographs. Intro. by William Carlos Williams. New York: MOMA, 1939.
Charles Sheeler. Essays by Martin Friedman, Bartlett Hayes, Charles Millard. Washington, D.C.: Smithsonian Institution Press, 1968.
Martin Friedman. *Charles Sheeler: Paintings, Drawings, Photographs.* New York: Watson-Guptill, 1975.
Samuel M. Kootz. "Ford Plant Photos of Charles Sheeler." *Creative Art* 8 (Apr. 1931): 246–267.
Charles W. Millard. "Charles Sheeler: American Photographer." *Contemporary Photographer* 6, no. 1 (1967).
See also Coke, *Painter;* Naef, *Collection;* Travis, *Julien Levy.*

Shore, Stephen
United States 1947–

Shore is representative of the burgeoning interest in color photography that began in the 1970s. At the age of six he

Stephen Shore. *Dewdney Ave., Regina, Saskatchewan, 8/17/74.* Type C color print. (Courtesy Light Gallery)

was already experimenting in the darkroom and by nine had started taking color images. After actively photographing for several years, he began in the early 1970s to work almost exclusively in color. His subject matter is mostly the urban landscape — ordinary buildings and streets whose muted and glowing colors are unexpectedly beautiful.

"Every object has a psychological resonance," Shore once commented. "The things I photograph have a resonance that attracts me. I don't let it dominate me, but I don't fight it either. I try to find a balance not unlike the balance I try to find in their form" (Life Library, *Year 1977,* p. 100).

Maria Morris observed: "By dwelling on the spaces between things, Shore reveals the character of a place quietly and without rhetoric, like the well-timed pause of a skilled actor. Just as the actor makes his pause meaningful by isolating it within the flow of word and gesture, so Shore controls and articulates his intervals with frames of finite dimensions and real substance. Elegant fields of colored light, immaterial in the real world, are caught and contained by scaffoldings of lampposts and ligatures of telephone wire" (quoted in *Contemporary Photographs,* New York: Light Gallery, 1976).

WORK Chiefly U.S. landscapes and cityscapes (in color, 1970s). Also includes portraits (in color and in black and white), events at Andy Warhol's "Factory" (in black and white, 1965–1967).

MEDIA Type C color prints (from 8×10 negatives), silver prints.

AVAILABILITY AND PRICE Color prints available through galleries; moderate (for 8×10 size) to moderately high (for 16×20).

SIGNATURE/OTHER IDENTIFICATION

STEPHEN SHORE

PORTFOLIO *See* chapter 6 entry.

COLLECTIONS Delaware, Everson, Houston, IMP/GEH, MMA, MOMA, Princeton (Art Museum), Seattle, Vassar, Yale (Art Gallery).

SELECTED BIBLIOGRAPHY
Andy Warhol. Boston: Boston Book and Art, 1968.
Manfred Willmann, ed. *American Photographers.* Graz, Austria: Fotogalerie im Forum Stadtpark, 1977.
Richard Pare, ed. *Court House: A Photographic Document.* New York: Horizon, 1978.
Max Kozloff. "Photography: The Coming to Age of Color." *Artforum* 13 (Jan. 1975): 30–35.
Venturi & Rauch. "Signs of Life: Symbols in the American City." *Aperture,* no. 77 (1976), pp. 49–65.
Camera, Jan. 1977, pp. 14–22.
See also Hume, *The Great West;* Life Library, *Year 1977;* Szarkowski, *Mirrors;* chapter 7 catalogues.

Silvy, Camille (de)
England (b. France) Active 1857–1869

A French aristocrat, Silvy had been a diplomat before opening a London portrait studio in 1859. In that same year he won acclaim for his landscapes, which effectively blended images from two negatives — one for the landforms and another for a cloud-filled sky. During his ten years of studio work he became a leading society photographer, producing carte-de-visite portraits of English nobility, including Prince Albert and almost every noblewoman except Queen Victoria.

Silvy's portrait work had a particular refinement of taste, enhanced by his personal arrangements of props and settings appropriate to the sitter. His series of cartes of women entitled "The Beauties of England" was a great success. In 1867 he marketed a roller-slide device for exposing one section of film at a time, one of the several precursors of the roll-film camera.

WORK Chiefly portraits, landscapes. Also includes animals.

MEDIA Collodion wet-plate negatives, albumen prints (chiefly cartes de visite).

AVAILABILITY AND PRICE Through galleries and at auction. Cartes de visite low; single images moderate to high; landscapes in good condition rare, extremely high.

SIGNATURE/OTHER IDENTIFICATION

PHOTOGRAPHED BY

38 Porchester Terrace
BAYSWATER W.

COLLECTIONS New Mexico; NPG, Société Française, VA.

SELECTED BIBLIOGRAPHY
Camera, Feb. 1974. Issue on French photography, 1840–1940, in the collection of the Bibliothèque Nationale.
See also Life Library, *Camera;* Marbot, *Invention.*

Camille (de) Silvy. Unidentified sitter, Bayswater West, London, ca. 1865. Albumen carte de visite. (Courtesy The Witkin Gallery)

Siskind, Aaron
United States 1903–

Influential as both a photographer and a teacher, Siskind made his first earnest attempts at photography in 1931/32. Moved by documentary photographs on display in New York City at the Film and Photo League (the forerunner of the Photo League), he joined the group and became active in the production of such projects as "Harlem Documentary" and "Portrait of a Tenement." But, he later recalled, "for some reason or other there was in me the desire to see the world clean and fresh and alive, as primitive things are clean and fresh and alive. The so-called documentary picture left me wanting something" (*Minicam Photography,* vol. 8, no. 9 [1945]). In the early 1940s a major change took place in his work. He photographed organic objects — for example, rocks — as flat shapes on the surface of the picture plane, rather than as objects with the pictorial illusion of possessing three dimensions. "For the first time in my life, subject matter, as such, had ceased to be of primary importance," he explained. "Instead, I found myself involved in the relationships of these objects, so much so that these pictures turned out to be deeply moving and personal experiences" (ibid.).

Siskind also photographed walls, portions of signs, graffiti, peeling posters, and other objects; his primary interest was in the flat graphic messages that they contained. At first his most sympathetic audience consisted of abstract-expressionist painters he knew, such as Willem de Kooning and Franz Kline, who understood the problems of space, line, and planarity that he was addressing. But in time the new subject matter that Siskind delineated began to be explored by other photographers. Carl Chiarenza wrote, "It is true that many people have photographed material similar to Siskind's walls (a testament to his influence), but Siskind's photographs have never been surpassed for sheer presence, power and continuous experiential possibilities" (*Photographs of Aaron Siskind . . .*). In 1951, at the invitation of Harry Callahan, Siskind joined the faculty of the Institute of Design (Chicago) and in 1961 became head of its photography department. From 1971 to 1976 he served as a faculty member at the Rhode Island School of Design.

WORK   Chiefly surfaces abstracted from their normal context (e.g., peeled and chipped paint on walls; torn posters; rocks; sculpture fragments; tree limbs). Also includes documentary studies of New York (1930s), architectural studies (late 1930s; e.g., Tabernacle City in Bucks County, Pa.), unexpectedly calligraphic forms (e.g., boys jumping, in "Terrors and Pleasures of Levitation" series), close-ups of feet.

MEDIUM   Silver prints.

AVAILABILITY AND PRICE   Through galleries; moderate to moderately high.

SIGNATURE/OTHER IDENTIFICATION

Aaron Siskind

PORTFOLIOS   *See* chapter 6 entry.

COLLECTIONS   The Center for Creative Photography (Tucson, Ariz.) will preserve the Siskind archive: 50 fine prints, 2,000 work prints, 300 early documentary photographs, 30,000 negatives, plus correspondence and personal papers. Also Chicago, Harvard (Carpenter, Fogg), Houston, IMP/GEH, Minneapolis, MOMA, Nebraska, New Mexico, New Orleans, RISD, San Francisco, Smithsonian, UCLA; BN, NGC.

SELECTED BIBLIOGRAPHY
Aaron Siskind: Photographs. Intro. by Harold Rosenberg. New York: Horizon, 1959.
Aaron Siskind: Photographer. Ed. and intro. by Nathan Lyons. Essays by Henry Holmes Smith and Thomas B. Hess. Rochester, N.Y.: GEH, 1965. Bibliography.
Bucks County: Photographs of Early Architecture. Text by William Morgan. New York: Horizon, 1974.
Photographs of Aaron Siskind in Homage to Franz Kline. Essay by Carl Chiarenza. Chicago: David and Alfred Smart Gallery, University of Chicago, 1975. Essay reprinted in *Afterimage* 3 (Dec. 1975): 8–13.
Places: Aaron Siskind Photographs. Intro. by Thomas B. Hess. New York: Light Gallery and Farrar, Straus & Giroux, 1976.
See also Kelly, *Darkroom 2*; Life Library, *Art, Documentary, Great Photographers*; Lyons, *Photographers*; chapter 7 catalogues.

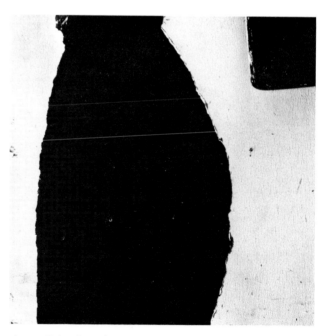

Aaron Siskind. *Hudson #41,* 1971. Silver print. (Courtesy Light Gallery)

Slavin, Neal
United States 1941–

Slavin became interested in photography while pursuing studies in Renaissance painting and sculpture, and his photographs of groups of people sometimes call to mind pictures of saints formally posed with their identifying emblems. He first worked as a free-lance photographer and graphic designer, then traveled in the United States as a commercial postcard photographer. His first personal work was a documentation of black people in the rural South; subsequently, in 1968, he spent a year photographing in Portugal. Since 1972 he has been working extensively with color materials.

Slavin's group photographs reveal the commonality of the purpose that unifies the group without sacrificing the individuality of the members that comprise it. The groups may be dignified or slightly zany, but Slavin treats them all with documentary respect. He once commented: "In an anthropological sense, [the photographs] explore and convey one of the strongest of American social tendencies — belonging. Secondly, because the selection of each organization and the execution of each photograph is without prejudicial bias, the pictures will afford a pictorial anthology of American organizations and associations in context of the 1970s. From an aesthetic point of view, the use of color in the photographs is concerned not with prettiness or colorfulness but rather with rendering as accurately as possible precise pieces of visual information, usually unavailable in black and white" (quoted in "Neal Slavin," p. 29).

Neal Slavin. *Group Portrait: Staten Island Ferry, Narrows Bay, New York*, 1974. Type C color print. (Courtesy Light Gallery)

SIGNATURE/OTHER IDENTIFICATION

WORK   Chiefly associations and professional groups (e.g., American Begonia Society, staff of the Statue of Liberty). Also includes people of Portugal, black people of the rural South, commercial work.

MEDIA   Color, silver prints.

AVAILABILITY AND PRICE   Through galleries; moderate to moderately high.

PORTFOLIO   *See* chapter 6 Women's Campaign Fund entry.

COLLECTIONS   CCP, Maryland, MMA, MOMA, NYPL (Photography), UCLA; Lisbon.

SELECTED BIBLIOGRAPHY
Portugal. Afterword by Mary McCarthy. New York: Lustrum, 1971.
When Two or More Are Gathered Together. New York: Farrar, Straus & Giroux, 1976.
Manfred Willmann, ed. *American Photographers.* Graz, Austria: Fotogalerie im Forum Stadtpark, 1977.
"Neal Slavin." *Camera*, May 1974, pp. 20 ff.
Max Kozloff. "Photography: The Coming to Age of Color." *Artforum* 13 (Jan. 1975): 30–35.
Du, Jan. 1976. Entire issue.
Sheila Turner Seed. "When Two or More Are Gathered Together." *Popular Photography*, Feb. 1976.
See also Kelly, *Darkroom 2*; Life Library, *Art, Light, Year 1974.*

Smith, Frank Eugene
See Eugene, Frank.

Smith, Henry Holmes
United States 1909–

Smith has long been fascinated by the possibilities of abstract color and shape, which he produces in an unconventional way: he combines syrup and water on glass to create a noncamera image that he then prints photographically. He stated, "In my work I would like to praise heroes and enable some persons to remember the firm link between past and future that acts of the imagination provide us" (quoted in Hahn). Castor and Pollux, the phoenix, giants, and angels are among the beings he has found in his abstractions.

A meeting in 1937 between Smith and László Moholy-Nagy led to a teaching job for Smith at the New Bauhaus School of Design in Chicago. In 1947 he began teaching at Indiana University (Bloomington). He is an influential teacher of photography whose students have included Robert W. Fichter, Betty Hahn, Jerry Uelsmann, and Jack Welpott.

WORK   Chiefly abstract color prints. Also includes "Mother and Son" series of 42 variations of a single image.

MEDIA   Cliché-verre "refraction prints" made from syrup and water on glass and printed as silver prints and dye transfer prints

Henry Holmes Smith. *Death of Punch,* 1975. Four-color dye transfer print. (Courtesy the artist)

(8×10 to 11×14 inches). Also (since 1973) silkscreen prints (to 36½×52 inches.)

AVAILABILITY AND PRICE Through galleries and exhibitions; moderate.

SIGNATURE/OTHER IDENTIFICATION

henry holmes smith

Henry Holmes Smith

PORTFOLIOS *See* chapter 6 entry.

COLLECTIONS IMP/GEH, New Mexico, New Orleans.

SELECTED BIBLIOGRAPHY
Henry Holmes Smith's Art: Fifty Years in Retrospect. Bloomington: Indiana University Art Museum, 1973.
Betty Hahn. "Henry Holmes Smith: Speaking with a Genuine Voice." *Image* 16 (Dec. 1973): 1–6.
See also Colors (in color bibliography); chapter 7 catalogues.

Smith, Keith A.
United States 1938–

Smith studied at the Art Institute of Chicago and the Illinois Institute of Technology and has taught painting, drawing, photography, and photographic printmaking. For him the camera image is only the beginning of the photographic process. Often starting from seemingly casual snapshots, he uses a sophisticated mix of old and new photographic techniques (see MEDIA) to fragment, serialize, color, texture, or otherwise modify and manipulate his images. The results are rich in visual, if not factual, information. He has worked extensively with generative systems — such as the 3M Color-in-Color and other photocopy machines — and the instant feedback they give is a perfect match for his prolific visual inventiveness. Robert Frank once wrote to him, "Your work comes out of you like a Rainbow and someone else would say like Poetry and who cares whether it's photography or sculpture" (quoted in *Aspects of American Photography* catalogue, listed in chapter 7).

WORK Portraits and other images in various formats, including multiple and serial imagery.

MEDIA Among the work Smith has exhibited: cyanotypes on cloth (quilted), photoetchings on paper and cloth, 3M Color-in-Color copying, cyanotypes and silkscreens with stitching, silver prints with applied color and drawing, color transparencies (stitched), hand-bound books using multiple photographic techniques.

Keith A. Smith. *The Game of Solitaire, 7 May 1976.* Photoetching with hand-coloring. (Courtesy Light Gallery)

AVAILABILITY AND PRICE Through galleries; prices vary, depending on the piece, and range from extremely low for small works on paper to high for large silkscreens on cloth.

SIGNATURE/OTHER IDENTIFICATION

Keith A Smith

PORTFOLIO *See* chapter 6 Schools and workshops entry.

COLLECTIONS Houston, IMP/GEH, MOMA; Geelong.

SELECTED BIBLIOGRAPHY
See Life Library, *Art, Print*; Szarkowski, *Mirrors*; chapter 7 catalogues.

Smith, W. Eugene
United States 1918–1978

Smith is renowned for his powerful photo-essays — a form he helped develop and raise to a major creative level. In the 1940s and early 1950s his works were published primarily in *Life* magazine; "Spanish Village," "Country Doctor," "Nurse Midwife," and "A Man of Mercy" (Albert Schweitzer) are some of his best-known essays that appeared in those years. John Szarkowski wrote that "Gene Smith was perhaps the photographer who tried most heroically to make the magazine photostory meet the standards of coherence, intensity, and personal accountability that one expects of a work of art" (Szarkowski, *Looking*, p. 150).

While still in high school in Wichita, Kansas, Smith took up news photography and contributed to local newspapers. He moved to New York City and in 1937 joined the staff of *Newsweek* for a while, then free-lanced for the Black Star agency. He became active in the Photo League (and later, from 1948 to 1950, served as its presi-

W. Eugene Smith. *Tomoko and Mother, Minamata, Japan,* 1972. Silver print. (Courtesy the artist and Witkin-Berley, Ltd.)

dent). In 1939 he signed with *Life* — an affiliation that was periodically disrupted by his discontent over editorial decisions affecting his pictures.

During World War II Smith covered military action for the Ziff-Davis publishing company; for a brief time he recorded the Atlantic campaign, but he took most of his photographs in the Pacific. Assigned to various aircraft carriers, he flew on many combat missions. His war photographs, although taken for American audiences, were so focused on the brutality and human cost of war and were so free of propaganda that they were also published by the Japanese. In 1944 the photographer quit Ziff-Davis and rejoined *Life*.

On 22 May 1945, during the invasion of Okinawa, Smith was severely injured in the face and hand by shell fire. After prolonged treatment, he returned to photography almost two years later, determined to make his first exposure a meaningful one. The resulting image was *The Walk to Paradise Garden* (page 24), showing his two small children emerging from a wooded area into the sunlight. It was Smith's statement of affirmation (Edward Steichen used it as the last image in his 1955 exhibition and book *The Family of Man*).

In 1956 Smith resigned from *Life*. He continued to produce photo-essays, to teach, and to write numerous articles on photography. In the early 1970s he lived in Minamata, a Japanese fishing and farming town, where he and his wife Aileen photographed the effect of industrial mercury poisoning on the inhabitants. Convinced that pollution in Minamata reflected a worldwide problem, he sought to increase public concern by showing the alarming plight of the town: "To cause awareness is our only strength," he remarked. ". . . Photography is a small voice. . . . I believe in it" (*Minamata*, pp. 7, 8).

"Always," Smith once said, "I want to comment with 'reasoned' passion. Passion, yes, for passion is in all great searches and it is necessary to all creative endeavors. . . . I am a compassionate cynic, yet I believe I am one of the most affirmative photographers around. I have tried to let truth be my prejudice. It has taken much sweat. It has been worth it" (foreword, *Ten Photographs* portfolio, listed in chapter 6).

A three-time recipient of Guggenheim Fellowships, Smith in 1978 moved to Tucson to teach at the University of Arizona and to arrange his archive at the Center for Creative Photography.

WORK Chiefly photo-essays (e.g., "Minamata," "Pittsburgh," "Haiti," "Ku Klux Klan"). Also includes World War II battle scenes, portraits of personalities (e.g., Tennessee Williams, Thelonious Monk, Charlie Chaplin, Harry S. Truman, Charles Ives). (See illustration, page 294.)

MEDIA Chiefly silver prints (mostly 8×10 to 11×14, some 16×20). Also color. The tonality of Smith's images is distinctive: he exposed his film for highlights and let the shadows go black; prints are usually dark, and white highlights are often hand-bleached (as in the eyes of the mad woman in "Haiti").

Smith signed on his prints in the lower left or right with a stylus and also titled and/or signed below them on the mounts.

AVAILABILITY AND PRICE Through galleries and at auction; high to extremely high. Smith's concern for perfect prints from his 35mm negatives resulted in much darkroom labor; he produced relatively few prints, except for his most famous images (e.g., *The Walk to Paradise Garden, Tomoko and Mother.*)

SIGNATURE/OTHER IDENTIFICATION (Example from letter)

W. Eugene Smith

PORTFOLIO *See* chapter 6 entry.

COLLECTIONS LIFE Picture Collection (New York City) holds a major body of Smith's prints. Also BMFA, Chicago, Dayton, Harvard (Carpenter), ICP, IMP/GEH, Kansas, MOMA, U. of Colorado; BN, Canberra, VA. The Center for Creative Photography (Tucson, Ariz.) is organizing the Smith archive, which it holds.

SELECTED BIBLIOGRAPHY
Japan . . . A Chapter of Image. With Carole Thomas. Tokyo: Hitachi, 1963.
Stefan Lorant, ed. *Pittsburgh: The Story of an American City.* Garden City, N.Y.: Doubleday, 1964.
W. Eugene Smith: His Photographs and Notes. Afterword by Lincoln Kirstein. Millerton, N.Y.: Aperture, 1969. Bibliography.
Minamata: Life — Sacred and Profane. With Aileen M. Smith. Text by Michiko Ishimure. Japan: Sojusha, 1973. 12 reproductions in paper portfolio.
Minamata. With Aileen M. Smith. New York: Holt, Rinehart & Winston, 1975.
"Pittsburgh." *Modern Photography Annual 1959.*
Album, no. 2 (1970), pp. 12–29.
Jim Hughes. "Rebel with a Camera." *Quest/77,* Mar./Apr. 1977, pp. 48 ff.
"Images of Truth: A Photographer's Creed." Ibid., pp. 40–47.
See also Edey, *Essays;* Lewis, *Darkroom 1;* Life Library, *Documentary, Great Photographers, Photojournalism;* Lyons, *Photographers;* Szarkowski, *Looking.*

Sommer, Frederick
United States (b. Italy) 1905–

Raised in Rio de Janeiro, Sommer studied landscape architecture at Cornell University (Ithaca, New York). After working a few years in Rio, he settled in Arizona in 1930 for health reasons and turned from architecture to fine arts. His interest in photography took root in 1935, after a meeting with Alfred Stieglitz in New York. Basically self-taught, Sommer has been influenced by Edward Weston, Charles Sheeler, and, particularly, Max Ernst.

Sommer's surrealistic approach is evident in images that have dreamlike and sometimes nightmarish associations. He photographs assemblages and collages consisting of dolls, reproductions from books, weathered wood, and other found objects arranged with exquisite attention to detail. The layers of surfaces often give an illusion of three-dimensionality that adds to the surreal quality.

Sommer's diverse subject matter includes abstractions, objective and nonromantic studies of desert landscapes, and reminders of the mortality of living things — an amputated human foot, desiccated coyotes, and bird entrails. His output is very small and he sometimes takes months to execute an image. According to John Szarkowski, "Sommer has studied . . . unprepossessing souvenirs of human and geological time with patience and concentration, and has photographed them only when they seem to have shared a portion of their secret" (Szarkowski, *Looking,* p. 162). Sommer himself stated: "It is the time you spend setting up and considering the scene that is the art of photographing; it's really of very small consequence whether you press the button or not" (Center for Creative Photography, p. 24).

Frederick Sommer. *Coyotes,* 1945. Silver print. (Courtesy Light Gallery)

WORK Includes photographs of assemblages and collages; Arizona landscapes (1936 and after); abstractions photographed from cut-paper constructions (1961 and after), or by printing images of smoke on glass (1961 and after) or paint on cellophane (1955 and after); plus some deliberately out-of-focus images.

MEDIA Chiefly silver prints (contact printed from 8×10 negatives). Also some color.

AVAILABILITY AND PRICE Through galleries; extremely high. Sommer makes only a few prints of each image.

SIGNATURE/OTHER IDENTIFICATION

Frederick Sommer

COLLECTIONS CCP, Chicago, Dayton, Harvard (Fogg), IMP/GEH, MOMA, New Mexico.

SELECTED BIBLIOGRAPHY
Alfred H. Barr, Jr. *Masters of Modern Art.* New York: MOMA, 1954.
Frederick Sommer. Text by Gerald Nordland. Philadelphia: Philadelphia College of Art, 1968.

Jonathan Williams. "Three Phantasts: Laughlin, Sommer, Bullock." *Aperture* 9, no. 3 (1961): 106–113.

Aperture 10, no. 4 (1962). Entire issue.

Dave Heath. "Frederick Sommer: 1939–1962 Photographs." *Contemporary Photographer,* Summer 1963.

"Frederick Sommer . . ." *Aperture* 16, no. 2 (1971): 18–25.

Center for Creative Photography (Tucson, Ariz.). *Special Report,* Summer 1976, pp. 23–25.

"A Frederick Sommer Portfolio." *Exposure* 15 (Feb. 1977): 4–7.

See also Szarkowski, *Looking;* chapter 7 catalogues.

Southworth, Albert Sands
United States 1811–1894

Hawes, Josiah Johnson
United States 1808–1901

Southworth was operating a drugstore and Hawes was an itinerant portrait painter when, in 1840, each became enthusiastic about the new art of daguerreotyping. In 1843 they became partners in a commercial daguerreotype portrait studio in Boston. Their emphasis was always on carefully individualized posing and lighting; unlike the straightforward likenesses made by most other daguerreotypists, Southworth and Hawes often produced portraits that are sensitive characterizations of their sitters. The difference between the average daguerreotype and work such as theirs was evident to their contemporaries: "In the former everything is hard, dry, rigid, and disagreeable, the flesh, mere blotches of light and shade, the eyes glaring or completely dead, the action of the figures stiff and constrained, the folds of the draperies, hard as though carved in wood. In the latter, the flesh is preserved in all the beautiful gradations of form and texture, the most delicate lights playing over its surface in a thousand different degrees of intensity, the fabrics are soft, easy, and graceful, the action and expression natural and refined" (quoted in *The Spirit of Fact,* pp. xi–xii).

Nancy Southworth Hawes (Southworth was her brother, Hawes her husband) also contributed to the quality of their product, by hand-coloring many of the plates with more refinement and care than was customary at most other studios. The high standards of creativity maintained by the studio made it popular with the intellectual and social elite of the time. Most of the approximately 1,500 Southworth and Hawes portraits that survive are not even what they themselves considered their finest work: the best exposures made at each sitting were taken by the customer, while the studio retained the rejects, which eventually passed into the possession of various museums and ultimately established the partners' reputation for creative portraiture.

In addition to portraiture, the pair made views of Boston and a few other areas, sold daguerreotype supplies, and patented various photographic devices, such as the Grand Parlor Stereoscope, a viewer for large, full-plate stereo daguerreotypes. By 1862 the partnership had dissolved, and though both Southworth and Hawes continued photographic careers, their best-known work was produced during the period of their joint efforts.

Work Chiefly portraits of well-known people (e.g., Harriet Beecher Stowe, Daniel Webster, Lola Montez), plus many unidentified sitters. Also includes scenes of Boston and vicinity (e.g., shipyards, Mount Auburn Cemetery, schoolrooms, operating room at Massachusetts General Hospital); Niagara Falls and Niagara suspension bridge (also attributed to Platt D. Babbitt); some views of San Francisco (ca. 1853) made by Southworth. (See illustration, page 36.)

Media Best known for daguerreotypes (generally quarter plates and whole plates; also stereographs).

Positive identification of Southworth and Hawes's work is difficult. They did not use imprinted cases or mats. Longhand inscriptions appear on the back of some plates. It is never good practice to open a sealed daguerreotype, but if a plate is already out of the case, a collector might consult *The Spirit of Fact* for illustrations of platemakers' hallmarks that can help identify Southworth and Hawes's plates; such markings do not necessarily authenticate their work (many other photographers used the same platemakers), but the hallmark may provide additional evidence.

Availability and Price At auction but authenticated plates extremely rare; extremely high.

Collections The Museum of Fine Arts (Boston), the International Museum of Photography at George Eastman House (Rochester, N.Y.), and the Metropolitan Museum of Art (New York

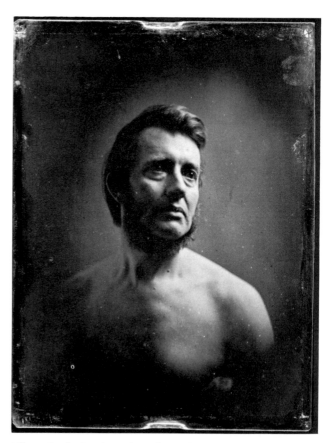

Albert Sands Southworth and Josiah Johnson Hawes. *Albert Sands Southworth,* ca. 1845. Daguerreotype, half plate. (Courtesy IMP/GEH)

City) hold the majority of extant plates by Southworth and Hawes. Also BPL (Hawes prints).

SELECTED BIBLIOGRAPHY
I. N. Phelps Stokes. *The Hawes-Stokes Collection of American Daguerreotypes by Albert Sands Southworth and Josiah Johnson Hawes.* New York: Metropolitan Museum of Art, 1939.
The Legacy of Josiah Johnson Hawes: 19th Century Photographs of Boston. Ed. and intro. by Rachel Johnston Homer. Barre, Mass.: Barre Publishing Co., 1972.
The Spirit of Fact: The Daguerreotypes of Southworth & Hawes, 1843–1862. Text by Robert A. Sobieszek and Odette M. Appel. Boston: Godine, and Rochester, N.Y.: IMP/GEH, 1976.
See also Life Library, *Great Photographers;* Newhall, *Masters, Daguerreotype;* Rudisill, *Mirror Image.*

Steichen, Edward
United States (b. Luxembourg) 1879–1973

Steichen's long life and prolific career stretched from pictorialism at the turn of the century to the "straight" photography of mid-century. Born Eduard Jean Steichen (the name he used before World War I), he came to the United States with his family in 1881. He studied art and then at the age of fifteen apprenticed as a designer in a lithographic company. He took his first photograph in 1896 and shortly thereafter began to make pictures for use as lithographic design models. "So my first real effort in photography was to make photographs that were useful," he recalled. ". . . Gradually, an interest in photographing things that had more personal appeal began to take over" (*A Life in Photography*). The mix between personal and "useful" became characteristic of his photographic career.

His early personal work, pictorial in style, was often extremely soft-focus. He explored pictorial techniques for diffusing an image, such as deliberately setting the lens out of focus, and he added a few of his own — for example, sprinkling water on the lens. His work was first exhibited in 1899 and within a few years he had become prominent in the pictorial movement; he exhibited his photographs in Europe and the United States, was elected to membership in The Linked Ring (1901), and became one of the founders of the Photo-Secession (1902). He was also instrumental in the establishment and operation of the Little Galleries of the Photo-Secession ("291") and in the design of *Camera Work* magazine.

Steichen continued to paint and had a number of successful shows, but after World War I (in which he supervised aerial photographic operations for the U.S. Army), he gave up painting to concentrate on photography. He related: "The wartime problem of making sharp, clear pictures from a vibrating, speeding airplane ten to twenty thousand feet in the air had brought me a new kind of technical interest in photography completely different from the pictorial interest I had had . . . in Photo-Secession days. Now I wanted to know all that could be expected from photography" (ibid.). During this postwar period he experimented with the photographic representation of tone, form, and volume — as in his close-ups of plant

forms and in over a thousand negatives exploring the photographic possibilities of a white cup and saucer.

Steichen's talent for incisive, sophisticated portraiture led to an offer to become chief photographer for Condé Nast publications, and his celebrity portraits and fashion photographs consequently appeared regularly in *Vanity Fair* and *Vogue* from 1923 to 1938. During World War II Steichen served with the U.S. Navy: he formed a unit to photograph naval aviation, created the photographic exhibit Road to Victory, served as director of the U.S. Navy Photographic Institute, and in 1945 was placed in command of all Navy combat photography. In 1947 he was appointed director of the photography department at New York City's Museum of Modern Art, and in that capacity he organized many exhibitions for the museum, including the 1955 show The Family of Man (see illustration, page 24). In 1959 he commenced his last major photographic project — a motion-picture study of a shad-blow tree near his Connecticut home.

Edward Steichen. *Heavy Roses, Voulangis, France,* 1914. Palladium print. (Courtesy Grace M. Mayer)

WORK   Includes pictorial images (ca. 1890s–1910s), especially landscapes, portraits, city scenes, nudes; abstract and close-up photographs (1910s–1920s); fashion for *Art et Décoration* (1911) and celebrity portraiture and fashion for *Vanity Fair* and *Vogue* (1923–1938; e.g., Garbo, Chaplin); New York City (1920s–1930s); advertising and publicity photographs (1920s–1930s; e.g., for Eastman Kodak Company, Jergens Lotion, Travelers Aid Society); photographs for U.S. Navy (World War II); shad-blow tree. (See illustration, page 105; *A Life in Photography* contains examples of all of Steichen's work.)

MEDIA   Until ca. 1920s, included platinum prints, palladium prints, gum-bichromate prints, pigment prints; thereafter, silver prints. Also color (autochromes and Kodachrome transparencies; dye transfer prints).

AVAILABILITY AND PRICE   Through galleries and at auction. Very few examples of early work exist; extremely high. After Steichen began magazine work in the 1920s, most of his printing was done by others; these prints, also rare, are less expensive than early work, but also extremely high. *Camera Work* reproductions moderate to moderately high. War scenes from the photographer's World War II navy career can also be found, though these are very difficult to attribute and were seldom made by him. Collectors should carefully evaluate the quality of Steichen prints — some poor ones were made at the end of his life and after his death. Steichen's signature or stamp on a print enhances its value.

SIGNATURE/OTHER IDENTIFICATION *See also* signed menu, page 103.

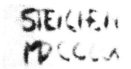

COLLECTIONS The Museum of Modern Art (New York City) preserves Steichen photographs and related material it received during his lifetime. The International Museum of Photography at George Eastman House (Rochester, N.Y.) holds prints and negatives received from his estate. Also Chicago, LOC, MMA, New Orleans; RPS.

SELECTED BIBLIOGRAPHY

Carl Sandburg. *Steichen the Photographer.* New York: Harcourt, Brace, 1929. 925 numbered copies, signed by Steichen and Sandburg.

Mary Steichen Martin. *The First Picture Book: Everyday Things for Babies.* New York: Harcourt, Brace, 1930.

———. *The Second Picture Book.* New York: Harcourt, Brace, 1931.

Henry David Thoreau. *Walden, or Life in the Woods.* Intro. by Henry S. Canby. Boston: Limited Editions Club, 1936. 1,500 copies, signed by Steichen.

Richard Pratt. *The Picture Garden Book and Gardener's Assistant.* New York: Howell, Soskin, 1942. Reprint, *Gardens in Color.* Garden City, N.Y.: Garden City Pub., 1944.

The Blue Ghost: A Photographic Log and Personal Narrative of the Aircraft Carrier USS Lexington. New York: Harcourt, Brace, 1947.

The Family of Man. Ed. by Steichen. New York: MOMA, 1955. Reprint, Garden City, N.Y.: Doubleday, 1967.

Steichen the Photographer. New York: MOMA, 1961.

The Bitter Years: 1935–1941. Rural America as Seen by the Photographers of the Farm Security Administration. Ed. by Steichen. New York: MOMA, 1962.

A Life in Photography. Garden City, N.Y.: Doubleday, 1963. Includes color plates. Later eds., all in black and white.

Sandburg: Photographers View Carl Sandburg. Ed. and intro. by Steichen. New York: Harcourt, Brace & World, 1966.

Dennis Longwell. *Steichen: The Master Prints, 1895–1914. The Symbolist Period.* New York: MOMA, 1978. Bibliography.

Edward Steichen. Intro. by Ruth Kelton. Millerton, N.Y.: Aperture, 1978. Bibliography.

William Innes Homer. "Eduard Steichen as Painter and Photographer, 1897–1908." *American Art Journal* 6 (Nov. 1974).

Camera Work: Reproductions (gravures, hand-toned gravures, halftones, colored halftones, letterpress poster) in nos. 2, 7, 9, 11, 13, 14, 15, 19, 22, 34/35, 42/43, 44, special Steichen supplement, Apr. 1906.

See also Green, *Camera Work;* Lawton and Know, *Knights;* Life Library, *Great Photographers, Print, Studio, Themes, Year 1974;* Lyons, *Photographers;* Naef, *Collection;* Newhall, *Masters.*

Steiner, Ralph
United States 1899–

Steiner began photographing in 1918 while a student at Dartmouth College (Hanover, New Hampshire). He attended the Clarence H. White School of Photography in New York City in 1921/22 and worked the following year as a photogravure technician. For many years he alternated between his personal photographic work and earning a living doing mostly advertising photography.

Steiner's 1920s and 1930s work, like that of Paul Strand and Walker Evans in that period, used the commonplace objects of urban society — billboards, details of automobiles, and so forth — in semiabstract compositions. He considered lighting important to achieve strong textures and tones.

A well-known filmmaker, Steiner brought a similarly fresh cinematic vision to many subjects. *H₂O* (1929), an abstract study of the rhythms of light and shadow on water, was described in a Museum of Modern Art catalogue as one of the most distinguished of avant-garde films. He was a cameraman with Paul Strand on Pare Lorentz's *The Plow That Broke the Plains* (1935). A series of films begun in 1967 on the theme "The Joy of Seeing" includes *Motion on a Quiet Island, A Look at Laundry,* and *Light.*

Ralph Steiner. *Typewriter Keys,* ca. 1921. Silver print. (Courtesy the artist)

"All my life," Steiner said in 1975, "I have been troubled by what is a greater problem of young photographers today: 'How to be happy and free as a creative person and, at the same time, earn a living?' Edward Steichen, at the height of his highly remunerative career, used to advise young photographers to get a job wrapping packages at Macy's. Weekends were to be spent photographing for oneself. At the time I thought it was all too easy for Steichen to give such advice . . . but I certainly have no better answer" (statement to the authors).

WORK Chiefly compositions of ordinary objects and architecture (1920s–1930s; e.g., wicker chair on porch, ham and eggs). Also includes The Group Theater (New York City, 1930s), portraits (e.g., S. J. Perelman), nature studies (e.g., Monhegan Island, Maine), advertising.

MEDIA Silver prints, platinum prints.

AVAILABILITY AND PRICE Through galleries and at auction. Vintage prints from the 1920s and 1930s (mostly signed) rare; moderately high. Later prints made by Steiner from these negatives are moderate in price, as are his prints of nature studies. In 1974 George A. Tice made five prints each of eight 1920s Steiner negatives; signed by both Tice and Steiner, these 4×5 palladium contact prints are priced moderately high.

SIGNATURE/OTHER IDENTIFICATION

ralph steiner

PORTFOLIO *See* chapter 6 entry.

COLLECTIONS Chicago, MMA, MOMA, Princeton (Art Museum).

SELECTED BIBLIOGRAPHY
Ralph Steiner: A Point of View. Intro. by Willard Van Dyke. Middletown, Conn.: Wesleyan University Press, 1978.
See also Szarkowski, *Looking*; Travis, *Julien Levy*; Witkin, *Julien Levy.*

Stieglitz, Alfred
United States 1864–1946

It is hard to overstate the influence Stieglitz had on photography as an art in America. Through his own images, writings, publications, and galleries, and by the sheer power of his personality, he gave strong impetus first to pictorialism at the turn of the century, then to its successor, "straight" photography.

The son of prosperous German immigrants, Stieglitz (shown on page 246) spent his youth in New York City, then in the early 1880s went to Germany to study mechanical engineering at Berlin's Technische Hochschule. He began to photograph in 1883 and later wrote of his first camera: "I bought it and carried it to my room and began to fool around with it. It fascinated me, first as a passion, then as an obsession. The camera was waiting for me by predestination and I took to it as a musician takes

to a piano or a painter to canvas" (quoted in Bry [1965], p. 9). The intensity of these early feelings about photography were typical of Stieglitz throughout his life. His first official photographic recognition came in Europe, including a first prize (awarded by P. H. Emerson) for genre work entered in an 1887 competition.

In 1890 Stieglitz returned to New York, and after several disillusioning years in a commercial photoengraving enterprise, he left the world of business to devote himself to promoting photography as an art form. He had been an editor of *American Amateur Photographer,* and in 1897 founded and edited *Camera Notes,* the journal of the Camera Club of New York. In 1902 Stieglitz established the Photo-Secession, a group of the leading pictorial photographers of the day, and so that he would be free to exercise the control he felt was essential to his editorial efforts, he founded and published its influential quarterly *Camera Work.* In 1905 he opened the Little Galleries of the Photo-Secession (later known as the "291," for its address on Fifth Avenue), the first of a series of galleries — including The Intimate Gallery and An American Place — that he maintained until his death. At these galleries he exhibited photography and modern art, and avant-garde artists from all fields found challenge, encouragement, and like minds.

Alfred Stieglitz. *Portrait of Kitty,* ca. 1905. Gravure. (Courtesy The Witkin Gallery)

Although Stieglitz showed and published soft-focus pictorial photographs by others, his own work (with a few early exceptions) had always been straight, unmanipulated imagery. When he first began to photograph New York in 1892, he actually worked in the fog or rain to achieve the same atmospheric effects that other pictorialists produced with soft-focus lenses or handwork on the print.

Stieglitz's subject matter was varied (see WORK). He eventually came to believe that his photographs could be metaphorical equivalents of his internal feelings. "I have to have experienced something that moves me, and is beginning to take form within me, before I can see what are called 'shapes.' Shapes, as such, mean nothing to me, unless I happen to be feeling something within, of which an *equivalent* appears, in outer form. . . . My cloud photographs, my *Songs of the Sky,* are *equivalents* of my life experience. All of my photographs are equivalents of my basic philosophy of life. All art is but a picture of certain basic relationships; an *equivalent* of the artist's most profound experience of life" (quoted in Norman [1960], pp. 36–37). Stieglitz promulgated the idea that a straight, unaltered photograph could be a means of personal expression and thus helped to confirm as art the work of Paul Strand, Edward Weston, Ansel Adams, Minor White, and other photographers in the straight style that dominated photography as an art in the 1920s–1960s period.

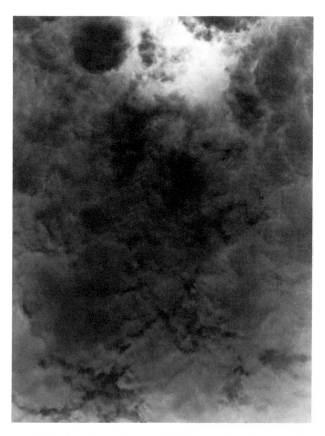

Alfred Stieglitz. *Equivalent,* ca. 1929. Silver print. (Courtesy The Witkin Gallery)

Stieglitz's charismatic personality and his uncompromising rejection of anything that did not meet his standards have made him almost a mythic figure in the history of photography. In his own words: "I was born in Hoboken. I am an American. Photography is my passion. The search for Truth my obsession" (quoted in Green, *Camera Work,* p. 341).

WORK Early genre scenes in Europe (1880s–1890s); New York City street scenes and city life (1890s–1900s, including many of the earliest photographs at night and in rain or snow); portraits (e.g., John Marin, Marsden Hartley, and a series of hundreds of photographs, beginning in 1918, of Stieglitz's wife, Georgia O'Keeffe); clouds (1923 and after); scenes from Lake George, N.Y. (e.g., trees, grasses, porch); New York City viewed from the windows of An American Place and from Stieglitz's apartment in the Shelton Hotel. Stieglitz also collaborated with Clarence H. White on a series of figure studies (ca. 1909). (See color plate 1 and illustrations on pages 20 and 104.)

MEDIA Platinum prints, palladium prints, carbon prints, silver prints, autochromes. Stieglitz used his signature sparingly, particularly after 1900. ("God did not sign the sky," he once pointed out.) He sometimes signed simply "291." Some early work bears his embossed signature on the mount.

AVAILABILITY AND PRICE Through galleries and at auction. Prime vintage platinum prints very rare; priced up to $10,000 and more. Other prints high to extremely high. Privately issued gravures and those from *Camera Notes* and *Camera Work* more frequently found; moderately high to extremely high.

SIGNATURE/OTHER IDENTIFICATION *See* signed menu, page 103.

COLLECTIONS The National Gallery of Art (Washington, D.C.) holds a master set of all images in Stieglitz's personal collection, received at the time of his death. Also BMFA, Chicago, Cleveland, IMP/GEH, LOC, MMA, MOMA, New Mexico, Philadelphia, Princeton (Art Museum), San Francisco, Yale (Beinecke); RPS.

SELECTED BIBLIOGRAPHY

Picturesque Bits of New York and Other Studies. New York: Russell, 1898. Portfolio of 12 gravures.
America and Alfred Stieglitz: A Collective Portrait. Ed. by Waldo Frank et al. Garden City, N.Y.: Doubleday, 1934. Bibliography. Reprint, new intro. by Dorothy Norman. New York: Arno, 1977.
History of an American. Alfred Stieglitz: '291' and After. Philadelphia: Philadelphia Museum of Art [1945].
Dorothy Norman, ed. *Stieglitz Memorial Portfolio 1864–1946.* New York: Twice A Year Press, 1947. 18 loose reproductions on 12×16 sheets, 72 prose tributes in bound booklet. 1,500 copies.
Catalogue of the Alfred Stieglitz Collection for Fisk University. Nashville: Fisk University, Carl Van Vechten Gallery of Fine Arts, 1949.
Doris Bry. *Exhibition of Photographs by Alfred Stieglitz.* Washington, D.C.: National Gallery of Art, 1958.
Dorothy Norman. *Alfred Stieglitz: Introduction to an American Seer.* New York: Duell, Sloan & Pearce, 1960. See also *Aperture* 8, no. 1 (1960).
Doris Bry. *Alfred Stieglitz: Photographer.* Boston: Museum of Fine Arts, 1965.

Herbert Jacob Seligmann. *Alfred Stieglitz Talking: 1925–31.* New Haven, Conn.: Yale University Library, 1966.

Bram Dijkistra. *The Hieroglyphics of a New Speech: Cubism, Stieglitz, and the Early Poetry of William Carlos Williams.* Princeton, N.J.: Princeton University Press, 1969.

Dorothy Norman. *Alfred Stieglitz: An American Seer.* New York: Random House, 1973. Bibliography.

Alfred Stieglitz. Intro. by Dorothy Norman. Millerton, N.Y.: Aperture, 1976. Bibliography.

William Innes Homer. *Alfred Stieglitz and the American Avant-Garde.* Boston: New York Graphic Society, 1977. Bibliography.

Helen Gee. *Stieglitz and the Photo-Secession: Pictorialism to Modernism 1902–1917.* Trenton: New Jersey State Museum, 1978.

Weston J. Naef. *The Collection of Alfred Stieglitz: Fifty Pioneers of Modern Photography.* New York: Metropolitan Museum of Art, 1978. Bibliography.

Georgia O'Keeffe by Alfred Stieglitz. Text by O'Keeffe. New York: Viking, 1979.

Camera Notes. Journal of the Camera Club of New York. Ed. by Stieglitz, 1897–1902.

Camera Work: Published and ed. by Stieglitz, 1903–17. Reproductions (gravures, halftones) in nos. 1, 3, 4, 12, 14, 20, 27, 36, 41, 44, 48.

Dorothy Norman, ed. *Twice A Year: A Semi-Annual Journal of Literature, the Arts, and Civil Liberties.* New York, 1938–1948. 15 numbers in 9 issues plus a tenth-anniversary issue. Includes numerous articles by and about Stieglitz, several photographs of and by Stieglitz.

"An American Collection." *The Philadelphia Art* [Museum] *Bulletin* 40 (May 1945).

See also Camera Work (facsimile reprint); Doty, *Photo-Secession;* Green, *Camera Work;* Lawton and Know, *Knights;* Life Library, *Great Photographers, Print;* Lyons, *Photographers;* Newhall, *Masters.*

John Benjamin Stone. *Inner View of Big Ben's Dial.* From the series "Parliamentary Scenes and Portraits," 1895–1909. Platinum print. (Courtesy National Portrait Gallery, London)

Stone, John Benjamin
England, 1838–1914

A wealthy manufacturer and a member of Parliament, Sir Benjamin Stone first pursued photography by collecting pictures of traditional English ways of life that he feared were vanishing. He was particularly interested in "history photography" that depicted vestiges of ancient customs, such as those surrounding Guy Fawkes Day. He was the founder and principal force behind the National Photographic Record Association, which between 1897 and 1910 undertook the photographic documentation of England. Stone photographed omnivorously himself and produced thousands of pictures with, as he pointed out, "always the same object — to show those who will follow us not only our buildings, but our everyday life, our manners and customs. Briefly, I have aimed at recording history with the camera, which, I think, is the best way of recording it." He was also an enthusiastic traveler who collected and took photographs in many parts of the world.

WORK   Includes traditional English customs, festivals, ceremonies (e.g., ox roastings, May dances); workers (e.g., charcoal burner); portraits of members of Parliament and other government officials (e.g., "Parliamentary Scenes and Portraits," 1895–1909); coronation of George V; foreign views.

MEDIA   Gelatin dry-plate negatives, platinum prints.

AVAILABILITY AND PRICE   Through galleries and at auction but infrequently found; moderate.

SIGNATURE/OTHER IDENTIFICATION

J. Benjamin Stone

COLLECTIONS   The Birmingham (England) Reference Library holds the bulk of Stone's personal collection (more than 14,000 negatives, 20,000 photographs). Also, in London: BM, Commons, NPG.

SELECTED BIBLIOGRAPHY
A Tour with Cook through Spain. London: Sampson Low, Son & Marston, 1873. 4 autotype views.

Sir Benjamin Stone's Pictures: Records of National Life and History. 2 vols. London: Cassell, 1906.

Bill Jay. *Customs and Faces: Photographs of Sir Benjamin Stone.* London: St. Martin, 1972.

Colin Ford. *Sir Benjamin Stone, 1838–1914, and the National Photographic Record Association, 1897–1910.* London: National Portrait Gallery, 1974.

Sir Benjamin Stone, Photographer. Intro. by Barry Lane. London: Arts Council of Great Britain, 1974. Portfolio of reproductions.

"Sir Benjamin Stone." *Album,* no. 1 (1970), pp. 2–10.

See also Life Library, *Documentary.*

Strand, Paul

United States 1890–1976

Strand first studied photography at the Ethical Culture School (New York City) with Lewis W. Hine, who introduced him to Alfred Stieglitz and the "291" gallery. He received encouragement from Stieglitz and was strongly influenced by the work shown in his gallery, particularly that of Picasso, Cézanne, and other modern artists. Strand had briefly worked in the soft-focus pictorial style that was still dominant in art photography, but in 1915 he began his first experiments with abstraction. His close-ups of kitchen bowls and other works of this early period (*The White Fence,* for example) were studies in design; sharply delineated shapes and patterns were of prime importance, though the images never completely lost touch with reality. Stieglitz recognized the power of these works and saw that they pointed toward a new realism; he gave Strand a one-man show at "291" and published his photographs in the last two issues of *Camera Work* (the final issue was devoted exclusively to Strand's work). Pictorialism had reached the end of its creative period and Strand's new images shaped the aesthetic of "straight" photography that was soon to dominate photography as an art form in America.

In 1919 Strand began to explore nature as a source of imagery — trees, leaves, grasses, rock formations, and landscapes — and it became an enduring theme in his work. His other major concern was people. From his early photographs on the streets of New York City, to documents of New England, Europe, Egypt, Africa, and elsewhere, he portrayed a sympathetic and direct appreciation of the humanity of his subjects.

As Strand's work matured it lost its early abstraction. He photographed directly, often using a flat, frontal viewpoint. He no longer searched for effect in unusual points of view or in expanded contrast, and he became almost self-effacing in his attempt to reveal objects without introducing overt comment. "No picture of Strand's is brilliant for brilliance's sake," observed Leo Hurwitz. "To him the object is all important. His photograph is his best effort to render the emotional significance of the object. His approach is one of utmost simplicity. In this sense his photographs are impersonal, selfless; yet they are characterized by a strong emotion" (*The Mexican Portfolio*).

In the 1920s–1940s Strand pursued his concurrent interest in film. The films on which he worked included *Manahatta* (also called *New York the Magnificent*), made in 1921 with Charles Sheeler; *The Wave,* made in 1933 for the Mexican government; and Pare Lorentz's *The Plow That Broke the Plains,* made in 1935 for the U.S. Resettlement Administration.

Paul Strand. *Alfred Stieglitz,* 1920s. Silver print. (Courtesy Philadelphia Museum of Art)

WORK   Chiefly the landscape, architecture, and people of various locales (e.g., Canada's Gaspé Peninsula, Mexico, New England, France, Italy, Outer Hebrides, Egypt, Morocco, Ghana). Also includes portraits (e.g., Stieglitz, Cocteau, Picasso), abstractions (ca. 1915), unposed street portraits and scenes of life in New York City (ca. 1915–1916), close-ups of machines (1917–1923; e.g., a lathe, the inside of a motion-picture camera), nature forms (1919 and after; e.g., trees, rocks, roots), still lifes, city structures, and architecture (1920–1923). (See illustration, page 105).

MEDIA   Platinum prints, palladium prints, silver prints.

AVAILABILITY AND PRICE   Chiefly through galleries. Vintage prints rare; extremely high. Prints made under the photographer's supervision in 1976 for portfolios sometimes available; high to extremely high. *Camera Work* gravures moderate to high (especially valuable are *The White Fence* and *Wall Street*). Gravures from the *Photographs of Mexico* portfolio and its reissued edition frequently available; low.

SIGNATURE/OTHER IDENTIFICATION

PORTFOLIOS *See* chapter 6 entry.

COLLECTIONS The Center for Creative Photography (Tucson, Ariz.) preserves the Strand archive: many prints, plus correspondence, personal papers, and memorabilia. The Philadelphia Museum of Art also holds a large collection of prints. Also BMFA, IMP/GEH, MMA, MOMA, New Mexico, New Orleans, San Francisco, Yale (Beinecke); BN, NGC. Many museums hold gravures from *Photographs of Mexico*.

SELECTED BIBLIOGRAPHY

Photographs of Mexico (portfolio). Intro. by Leo Hurwitz. New York: Virginia Stevens, 1940. 20 gravures. 250 copies. Reissue, *The Mexican Portfolio*. Preface by David Alfaro Sigueiros. New York: Da Capo, 1967. 1,000 copies.

Paul Strand: Photographs 1915–1945. Text by Nancy Newhall. New York: MOMA, 1945. Bibliography.

Time in New England. With Nancy Newhall. New York: Oxford University Press, 1950.

La France de Profil. Text by Claude Roy. Lausanne, Switzerland: La Guilde du Livre, 1952.

Un Paese. Text by Cesare Zavattini. Turin, Italy: Einaudi, 1954.

Frantisek Vrba. *Paul Strand*. Prague: SNKLHU, 1961.

Tir a'Mhurain: Outer Hebrides. Text by Basil Davidson. London: MacGibbon & Kee, 1962. U.S. ed., New York: Grossman, 1968.

Living Egypt. Text by James Aldridge. New York: Horizon, 1969.

Paul Strand: A Retrospective Monograph. 2 vols. (*The Years 1915–1946* and *The Years 1950–1968*.) Millerton, N.Y.: Aperture, 1971, 1972. Bibliography. Also issued as 2 vols. in 1, 1971.

Ghana: An African Portrait. Text by Basil Davidson. Millerton, N.Y.: Aperture, 1976.

Paul Strand: A Retrospective Exhibition of His Photographs, 1915–1968. London: National Portrait Gallery, 1976.

Paul Strand: Sixty Years of Photographs. Profile by Calvin Tomkins. Millerton, N.Y.: Aperture, 1976. Bibliography.

Hollis Frampton. "Meditations around Paul Strand." *Artforum* 10 (Feb. 1972): 52–57.

Camera Work: Gravures in nos. 48, 49/50.

See also Green, *Camera Work*; Life Library, *Documentary, Great Photographers, Print, Year 1973, Year 1977*; Lyons, *Photographers*; Naef, *Collection*; Newhall, *Masters*; chapter 7 catalogue.

Sudek, Josef
Bohemia (Czechoslovakia) 1896–1976

A lyrical imagemaker, Sudek had a long career in photography and produced an abundance of poetic landscapes and still lifes. He was Czechoslovakia's most famous photographer — a *národní umèlec* (national artist). The year 1913 marked the beginning of his photographic output (the loss of his right arm in World War I barely impeded his work — he taught himself to switch film in a changing bag with one hand), but it wasn't until 1922/23 that he studied formally at the State School of Graphic Art in Prague. He earned his living thereafter at his craft, using an 1899 panoramic camera that had been modified to take individual sheets of film.

Sudek once said: "When I began photographing my window during the Second World War, I discovered that very often something was going on under the window which became more and more important to me. An object of some kind, a bunch of flowers, a stone — in short, some-

thing separated this still-life and made an independent picture. I believe that photography loves banal objects. I am sure you know the fairy tales of Andersen: when the children go to bed, the objects come to life, toys, for example. I like to tell stories about the life of inanimate objects, to relate something mysterious: the seventh side of a dice" (*Camera*, Apr. 1976).

Elsie Taussig, a visitor to Sudek's studio in 1974, described it as small and cluttered. Sudek used an old shirt to clear off a chair so she could sit down. Despite his reputation as somewhat of a recluse, she related, he was very friendly: "Sudek looked bedraggled and old, but showed me boots with mud on them and said, 'Look, I'm still working hard.' His sister, with whom he lived, told me he disappeared with his camera when the weather was fine — sometimes for a week. When it rained, he stayed home and printed" (statement to the authors, 1976).

WORK Panoramas of Prague, still lifes, landscapes, series of views of and from window, commercial work (e.g., advertising, portraits).

MEDIUM Silver contact prints (2¼×5½ to 12×15, some toned).

Josef Sudek. Untitled. From the series "Windows of My Studio," 1944–1953. Silver print. (Courtesy the artist and Museum of Decorative Arts, Prague)

AVAILABILITY AND PRICE   Through galleries, but difficult to obtain because of governmental restrictions; moderately high to high.

SIGNATURE/OTHER IDENTIFICATION

PORTFOLIO   *Josef Sudek.* Intro. by Petr Tausk. Prague: Pressfoto, 1976. 13 prints (not printed by Sudek). 3,000 copies.

COLLECTIONS   IMP/GEH, New Mexico; Prague; RPS.

SELECTED BIBLIOGRAPHY

Svaty Vit (Saint Vitus), 1928. 15 original prints. 120 copies.
Magic in Stone. Text by Martin S. Briggs. London: Lincolns, 1947.
Pražský Hrad (The Prague Castle). Text by Rudolf Rouček. Prague: SFINX, 1947.
Nas Hrad (Our Castle). Text by A. Wenig. Prague: Vilímek, 1948.
Praha (Prague). Text by Vitežslav Nezval. Prague: Svoboda, 1948.
Joseph Sudek: Fotografie. Intro. by Lubomir Linhart. Prague: SNKLHU, 1956.
Praha Panoramaticka (Prague Panoramic). Prague: SNKLHU, 1959.
Karluv Most (Charles Bridge). Text by Emanuel Poche. Prague: SNKLHU, 1961.
Sudek: 96 Photographs. Intro. by Jan Rezac. Prague: Artia, 1964.
Five Photographers. Lincoln: Sheldon Memorial Art Gallery, University of Nebraska, 1968.
Janacek: Hukvaldy. Prague: Supraphon, 1971.
Josef Sudek. Aachen, Germany: Lichttropfen, 1976.
Sonja Bullaty. *Sudek.* Intro. by Anna Fárová. New York: Potter, 1978. Bibliography. Also limited ed.
Camera, Mar. 1966, July 1967, June 1973, Apr. 1976 (entire issue).
Carter Ratcliff. "Josef Sudek: Photographs." *The Print Collector's Newsletter* 8 (Sept./Oct. 1977): 93–95.
See also Life Library, *Great Photographers,* Year 1977; chapter 7 catalogue.

Sutcliffe, Frank M.
England 1853–1941

Frank Meadow Sutcliffe was active in photography beginning in the early 1870s. He spent most of his life in the Yorkshire coastal town of Whitby, where he established a successful portrait studio. His personal interest was photographing harbor and landscape scenes in and around Whitby and genre scenes of the activities of fisherfolk, farmers, and children. A friend called him the "pictorial Boswell of Whitby." He wrote extensively on all aspects of photography, exhibited frequently, and in 1892 became a founding member of The Linked Ring.

Sutcliffe advocated natural poses and realistic atmospheric effects, and some of his early photographs foreshadowed P. H. Emerson's theories of naturalistic photography. In 1875, not long after he had begun to photograph, Sutcliffe described his method: "When photographing rustic figures out of doors, I think the best plan is to quietly

Frank M. Sutcliffe. *River Rats,* 1886. Modern silver print from the original plate. (Courtesy Bill Eglon Shaw, The Sutcliffe Gallery)

watch your subjects as they are working or playing, or whatever they are doing, and when you see a nice arrangement to say, 'Keep still just as you are a quarter of a minute,' and expose, instead of placing an arm here and a foot there, which is sure to make your subject constrained, and consequently stiff" (quoted in Arts Council, *Painting,* p. 55).

WORK   Includes portraits, genre scenes, landscapes, harbor scenes.

MEDIA   Collodion wet-plate negatives (until the 1880s) and gelatin dry-plate negatives (1880s and after); albumen prints, platinum prints, carbon prints, silver prints. Sutcliffe made pictures with a Kodak hand-camera late in his career. Some prints are signed; others have initials in plate.

AVAILABILITY AND PRICE   Through galleries. Vintage prints, also available at auction, frequently found; moderate to high. Modern prints from the original plates, some toned to match Sutcliffe's prints, made by Bill Eglon Shaw (operator of the Sutcliffe Gallery in Whitby) are priced low. These prints bear a stamp (see detail below) that reads in part, "One of a series of Photographs, many of which were awarded over sixty Gold, Silver and Bronze Medals at International Exhibitions during the last century."

SIGNATURE/OTHER IDENTIFICATION

(Detail from Shaw stamp)

W. EGLON SHAW, THE SUTCLIFFE GALLERY,
1 FLOWERGATE, WHITBY, YORKSHIRE, ENGLAND.

COLLECTIONS IMP/GEH, New Mexico, Philadelphia, Texas (Gernsheim), Yale (Art Gallery); RPS, Sutcliffe, Whitby.

SELECTED BIBLIOGRAPHY
Michael Hiley. *Frank Sutcliffe: Photographer of Whitby.* London: Gordon Fraser, 1974. U.S. ed., Boston: Godine, 1975.
Frank Meadow Sutcliffe. Ed. by Bill Eglon Shaw. Whitby: Sutcliffe Gallery, 1974.
Frank Meadow Sutcliffe: A Second Selection. Ed. by Bill Eglon Shaw. Whitby: Sutcliffe Gallery, 1978. Also limited ed., 750 copies, signed by Shaw.
See also Life Library, *Children.*

Székessy, Karin
Germany   Contemporary

Székessy has built her reputation photographing dolls and doll-like human nudes. Better known in Europe than in the United States, she and her husband, artist Paul Wunderlich, have exhibited together, and they acknowledge that each has influenced the other's art. Székessy studied photojournalism in Munich from 1957 to 1959. She first began collecting and photographing dolls in 1959. From 1960 to 1966 she was a photographer for the German magazine *Kristall* and thereafter did free-lance photography for a number of magazines. From 1967 to 1969 she taught fashion photography at the Arts School in Hamburg.

Székessy's dolls and nudes are precisely arranged, sometimes surreal, tableaux. "She took her dolls to pieces, dissected them and arranged them freely according to her wish," observed Fritz Kempe. ". . . Her nudes are also imbued with this high artificiality which is intrinsic in old dolls" (*Karin Székessy*).

WORK   Dolls, female nudes, fashion.

MEDIA   Silver prints, color.

AVAILABILITY AND PRICE   Through galleries; silver prints and color work moderate (usually editions of 15), collotypes and gravures low.

SIGNATURE/OTHER IDENTIFICATION

COLLECTIONS   Information not available.

SELECTED BIBLIOGRAPHY
Les Filles dans l'atelier. Paris: Denoël, 1969.
Karin Székessy. Text by Fritz Kempe. Hamburg: Galerie Levy, 1975.
Medium Photographie. Kiel, Germany: Kunsthalle, 1976.
Paul Wunderlich und Karin Székessy Correspondenzen. Text by Fritz J. Raddatz. Zurich: Belser, 1977.

Karin Székessy. *Two Cutouts,* 1970. Silver print. (Courtesy the artist)

Talbot, William Henry Fox
England 1800–1877

Talbot not only invented the negative/positive process that was the forerunner of modern photographic materials, but he also produced the first books to be illustrated with photographs. He had made some unsuccessful attempts at drawing and as a result in 1834 began experimenting with ways for, as he stated, "natural images to imprint themselves durably, and remain fixed upon the paper" (*The Pencil of Nature*). By 1835 he had devised his imperfect but workable photogenic-drawing process and had produced paper negatives from which paper positives could be printed.

Talbot's first images were photograms — light-sensitive paper darkened by exposure beneath leaves, lace, or other objects. He also recorded some very small camera-obscura images, describing them "as might be supposed to be the work of some Lilliputian artist" (quoted in Newhall, *History*, p. 31). Other interests caused him to put this work aside until 1839, when, hearing of L. J. M. Daguerre's invention of the daguerreotype, he immediately put in a claim for the priority of his own process. In 1840 Talbot worked out an improved version of it — the calotype (also called the talbotype). He took many photographs with his improved process and in 1843 at Reading set up the first photographic-printing establishment to mass-produce prints. In 1844 he began publication of the first major book to be photographically illustrated, *The Pencil of Nature.*

Talbot foresaw many of the concerns of nineteenth-century photographers. He realized the medium's aesthetic possibilities and likened his photograph *The Open Door* to compositions of the Dutch masters. He also understood the documentary potential of the medium; most of his own images, like the majority of nineteenth-century photographs, are factual records, carefully arranged to report believable visual information about the subject. He contemplated the use of photographs as legal evidence, and he speculated on scientific applications such as photographing with light beyond the visible spectrum. He was interested in image-reproduction processes, too, and another of his inventions, the photoglyphic-engraving process, was the prototype for photogravure printing. After the 1850s, however, Talbot largely turned from photography to his other scientific and scholarly interests — botany, electromagnetism, and archeology.

WORK Includes photograms of botanical specimens and lace; objects enlarged through the microscope (e.g., insect wings); scenes in and around his home, Lacock Abbey (e.g., architecture, still lifes, residents); art reproductions; genre studies (e.g., chess players); architecture and landscape in Britain and Europe.

MEDIA Photogenic drawings, calotypes (talbotypes), photoglyphic engravings.

AVAILABILITY AND PRICE Through galleries and at auction. Prints and paper negatives frequently available; high to extremely high, depending on condition and subject matter. Positive identification is difficult and authentication is essential. In 1977 *The Pencil of Nature* sold at auction for $30,960 (Sotheby's, London), the highest price to date for a photographically illustrated book.

William Henry Fox Talbot. *Group in the Lacock Abbey Cloister,* ca. 1844. Calotype. (Courtesy The Witkin Gallery)

SIGNATURE/OTHER IDENTIFICATION

PORTFOLIO *See* chapter 6 entry.

COLLECTIONS Chicago, IMP/GEH, LOC, MMA, New Mexico, Princeton, Smithsonian, Texas (Gernsheim), UCLA, Wellesley; NGC, RPS, Science Museum. Talbot's estate at Lacock Abbey (Wiltshire, England) has been turned into the Fox Talbot Museum, where visitors can view Talbot's work as well as the latticed window, tower, garden, and other objects he photographed.

SELECTED BIBLIOGRAPHY

Talbot's establishment at Reading produced the first five publications listed here.

Record of the Death Bed of C. M. W., 1844. Contains a calotype of a statue of Catherine M. Walter. Strictly speaking, this is the first book to be illustrated with a photograph.

The Pencil of Nature, 1844–46. 24 calotypes in 6 installments containing from 3 to 7 prints each. Sold by Longman, Brown, Green & Longmans, London. Facsimile reprint, intro. by Beaumont Newhall. New York: Da Capo, 1969.

Sun Pictures in Scotland. London, 1845. 23 calotypes.

The Talbotype Applied to Hieroglyphics, 1846. 3 calotypes.

Talbotype Illustrations to the Annals of the Artists of Spain, 1847. 66 calotypes of sculpture and engravings.

D. B. Thomas. *The First Negatives.* London: Science Museum, 1964.

Arthur Booth. *William Henry Fox Talbot: Father of Photography.* London: Arthur Barker, 1965.

André Jammes. *William H. Fox Talbot: Inventor of the Negative-Positive Process.* New York: Macmillan, 1974.

12 Unpublished Calotypes from the Lacock Abbey Collection (portfolio). Intro. by R. E. Lassam. Lacock (Wiltshire), England: Fox Talbot Museum, 1976. Facsimiles of Talbot calotypes taken between 1839 and 1846. 50 copies.

H. J. P. Arnold. *William Henry Fox Talbot: Pioneer of Photography and Man of Science.* London: Hutchinson Benham, 1977. Bibliography.

WHF Talbot . . . A Further Assessment. Lacock (Wiltshire), England: Fox Talbot Museum, 1977.

Beaumont Newhall. "William Henry Fox Talbot." *Image* 8 (June 1959): 60–75.

Camera, Sept. 1976. Entire issue.

See also Life Library, *Great Photographers;* Newhall, *Latent Image;* Scharf, *Pioneers.*

Teske, Edmund
United States 1911–

Teske is an innovator in the use of multiple imagery, solarization, and color toning to explore personal experience. He began to photograph in his youth in Chicago, and his interest in the arts extended to painting, music, and theater. In 1936/37 he began to photograph for Frank Lloyd Wright. Before Teske settled in Hollywood in 1943, he taught at the New Bauhaus School of Design in Chicago and for the Federal Arts Project, and assisted Berenice Abbott in New York City.

In 1958/59 he evolved a duotone (two-color toning) and solarization technique and began using it to produce multiple imagery. His continued juxtaposition of key personal images — some new, some old — expands the romantic, mystical vision Teske has of his life, past and present. His composite prints incorporate portraits of his family and friends, houses, landscapes, male nudes, and even such images as the Brooklyn Bridge and drawings by Leonardo da Vinci. Teske's major autobiographical work, "Song of Dust," is a sequence of seventy-two images begun in the early 1950s and completed in 1974.

"A meditative quality of feeling is a dominant note of Teske and his work," wrote Gerald Nordland. "He seems to be unhurriedly seeking to understand the evolution of his life and art. His process is intuitive rather than scientific. He seeks to experience his sympathy and respect for persons, places, and things without sentimentality. He often senses feelings of melancholy and loneliness in his subjects and frequently may overlay their images with significant selections from his landscape work giving unexpected poignancy to the new creation" (*Edmund Teske*, p. 22). Teske has long been an active teacher of photography in the Los Angeles area.

WORK   Chiefly multiple imagery (e.g., male nude superimposed over the Brooklyn Bridge or a mountain landscape). Also includes a series of portraits of streetcar riders (Chicago, 1930s), other portraits, Frank Lloyd Wright architecture.

MEDIUM · Silver prints (often solarized, duotoned, or both; 4×6 to 10×14).

AVAILABILITY AND PRICE   Through galleries. Unmanipulated prints moderate; duotoned, solarized prints moderately high.

SIGNATURE/OTHER IDENTIFICATION

PORTFOLIO   *See* Chapter 6 Schools and workshops entry.

COLLECTIONS   CCP, Chicago, Kansas, MMA, Nebraska, New Orleans, Norton Simon, Oakland, St. Louis.

SELECTED BIBLIOGRAPHY
Edmund Teske. Text by Gerald Nordland. Los Angeles: Municipal Art Gallery, Barnsdall Park, 1974.
"Edmund Teske." *Aperture* 12, no. 3 (1965): 14–35.
See also Life Library, *Art, Print;* chapter 7 catalogues.

Edmund Teske. Untitled, 1976. Silver combination print. (Courtesy The Witkin Gallery)

Thomson, John
Scotland 1837–1921

Active in photography beginning in the mid-1860s, Thomson used his camera to document social problems as well as to photograph landscape, architecture, and travel views. Upon leaving England in 1865, he spent about ten years in the Far East and issued several photographically illustrated volumes on its people, culture, geography, architecture, and antiquities. Some of his Chinese street scenes foreshadow his later and better-known *Street Life in London* (1877–1878), the first work documenting social problems to be illustrated with photographs.

Thomson posed his subjects as naturally as possible, in their everyday surroundings; his photographs have an authenticity that convincingly describes aspects of life in the London slums of the period. In the introduction to *Street Life*, Thomson and Adolphe Smith wrote: "The unquestionable accuracy of photography will enable us to present true types of the London Poor and shield us from the accusation of either underrating or exaggerating individual peculiarities of appearance." After 1880 Thomson became a portrait photographer in London.

John Thomson. *An Old Clothes Shop, Seven Dials.* From *Street Life in London,* 1877–1878. Woodburytype. (Courtesy The Witkin Gallery)

WORK Workers and poor people in London streets (mid-1870s; e.g., peddlers, street musicians, local characters). Also includes views of the Far East and its people (mostly late 1860s to early 1870s), portraits.

MEDIA Through the 1880s: collodion wet-plate negatives, albumen prints.

AVAILABILITY AND PRICE Through galleries and at auction. Individual woodburytypes from *Street Life* frequently found; moderate. Albumen prints of Far East scenes and autotypes from *Illustrations of China* rarer; moderately high to high.

COLLECTIONS BPL, IMP/GEH, New Mexico; RGS, RPS.

SELECTED BIBLIOGRAPHY
Antiquities of Cambodia. Edinburgh: Edmonston & Douglas, 1867. 16 albumen prints.
William R. Beach, ed. *Visit of His Royal Highness, The Duke of Edinburgh, to Hong Kong in 1869.* Hong Kong: Noronha, and London: Smith, Elder, 1869. 7 albumen prints.
Foo Chow and the River Min. London: Autotype Co., 1872. 80 autotypes.
Illustrations of China and Its People. 4 vols. London: Sampson Low, Marston, Low & Searle, 1873–74. 218 autotypes.
The Straits of Malacca, Indo-China and China. London: Sampson Low, Marston, Low & Searle, and New York: Harper, 1875. Illustrated with woodcuts from Thomson's photographs.

Street Life in London. Text by Adolphe Smith. London: Sampson Low, Marston, Searle & Rivington, 1877–78. 36 woodburytypes. Reprint, New York: Blom, 1969. Abridged ed., *Street Incidents.* London: Sampson Low, Marston, Searle & Rivington, 1881. 21 plates.
Through Cyprus with the Camera. 2 vols. London: Sampson Low, Marston, Searle & Rivington, 1879. 59 woodburytypes, 1 autotype.
A Description of the Works of Art Forming the Collection of Alfred de Rothschild. Ed. by Charles Davis. 2 vols. London, 1884. Over 200 prints.
Through China with a Camera. Westminster, England: Constable, 1898.
Robert Doty. "Street Life in London." *Image* 6 (Dec. 1957): 240–245.
———. "John Thomson: Street Life in London." *Album,* no. 9 (1970), pp. 18–32.
See also Life Library, *Light, Documentary, Great Photographers.*

Tice, George A.
United States 1938–

Tice has been working in photography since the age of fourteen. Active in New Jersey camera clubs during his late teens and early twenties, he was a leading international salon exhibitor; in the late 1950s he served as an official Navy photographer. He left the camera clubs in order to pursue the medium on his own; self-taught in his use of the view camera and platinum printing, he sought to emulate the work of Frederick H. Evans.

Tice's first extended photo-essay was on the Amish farmers of Pennsylvania. He had grown up in the region and returned many times over a period of eight years to photograph the traditional life of the sect. Millen Brand wrote: "Going with George, I began to feel his relationship to the place too, I began to get his sensitivity. He drove and drove, watching, waiting, spying (if I can use that word), leaving himself exposed to something that might or might not eventually come" (*Fields of Peace,* p. 10). Other Tice photo-essays, such as those on Paterson, New Jersey, and, most recently, on Artie Van Blarcum, a camera-club friend, also show his sensitivity to and close involvement with his subject.

Tice is acknowledged to be a masterful technician. He often uses an 8×10-inch view camera and his prints made from its large-size negatives have a rich luminance and extraordinary rendering of fine detail. An original print cannot be even approximated in a halftone book illustration. When Tice became interested in the near-obsolete process of platinum printing, long known for the beauty of its tonality, he experimented and devised a way to hand-coat papers with platinum emulsion. In addition to teaching platinum printing to others, he is active in photographic restoration. He has also printed the negatives of other photographers (including Eugène Atget, Francis Bruguière, Frederick H. Evans, Ralph Steiner, and Edward Weston) for museums and portfolios.

George A. Tice. *Oak Tree, Holmdel, New Jersey,* 1970. Silver print. (Courtesy The Witkin Gallery)

Work Pennsylvania Germans; landscapes and nature (e.g., trees); the urban landscape of New Jersey (e.g., Paterson); inhabitants and seascape of Maine; the ghost town Bodie, Calif.; an indepth study of Artie Van Blarcum. (See illustrations, pages 11 and 296.)

Media Silver prints, platinum prints, and palladium prints, often from 8×10 negatives.

Availability and Price Through galleries; moderate (for 8×10, 11×14 sizes) to moderately high (for 16×20).

Signature/Other Identification

George A. Tice   GEO. A. TICE

Portfolios *See* chapter 6 entry.

Collections Amon Carter, Chicago, IMP/GEH, Kansas, Michigan, Minneapolis, MMA, MOMA; BN, VA.

Selected Bibliography
Millen Brand. *Fields of Peace: A Pennsylvania German Album.* Garden City, N.Y.: Doubleday, 1970.
Goodbye, River, Goodbye. Poetry by George Mendoza. Garden City, N.Y.: Doubleday, 1971.
Paterson. New Brunswick, N.J.: Rutgers University Press, 1972.
Seacoast Maine: People and Places. Text by Martin Dibner. Garden City, N.Y.: Doubleday, 1973.
George A. Tice: Photographs 1953–1973. New Brunswick, N.J.: Rutgers University Press, 1975. Bibliography.
Urban Landscapes: A New Jersey Portrait. New Brunswick, N.J.: Rutgers University Press, 1976.
Artie Van Blarcum. Danbury, N.H.: Addison House, 1977.
Gerry Badger. "Recent Books — *Urban Landscapes.*" *The British Journal of Photography,* 25 Mar. 1977, pp. 268–269.
See also Lewis, *Darkroom 1;* Life Library, *Art, Caring, Nature, Year 1973;* Szarkowski, *Mirrors;* chapter 7 catalogues.

Tournachon, Gaspard-Félix
See Nadar.

Trager, Philip
United States 1935–

Trager, a graduate of Columbia University School of Law, is self-taught in photography. He photographed for a number of years as a youth, stopped for a period, then began an earnest commitment to the medium in 1966. He works primarily with a view camera (negatives up to 11×14 inches), making precisely detailed and formally composed personal interpretations of landscape and architecture in the Northeast and Southwest. According to Samuel Green, "Trager's photographs illustrate a profound grasp of the self-contained identity of the object — 'respect for the thing in front of him,' to use Paul Strand's words" (*Photographs of Architecture*). In 1976, after completing a three-year project photographing Connecticut architecture, Trager began a view-camera essay on New York City buildings.

Work Chiefly landscape and architecture. Also includes portraits.

Medium Silver prints.

Availability and Price Through galleries; moderate.

Signature/Other Identification

Philip Trager

Collections MMA, MOMA, St. Petersburg, Smithsonian, Wesleyan, Yale (Art Gallery).

Selected Bibliography
Echoes of Silence. Danbury, Conn.: Scroll Press, 1972.
Photographs of Architecture. Intro. by Samuel M. Green II. Middletown, Conn.: Wesleyan University Press, 1977.
Creative Camera, Sept. 1975.
See also Life Library, *Art.*

Philip Trager. *House, Litchfield Avenue, Torrington, Connecticut,* 1975. Silver print. (Courtesy The Witkin Gallery)

TRAVEL AND REGIONAL PHOTOGRAPHERS (19th century)

One of the first uses of photography was to make scenic travel views. Within a few months of the announcement of L. J. M. Daguerre's process in 1839, photographers were in Egypt, writing back to French publisher N.-M. P. Lerebours: "We keep daguerreotyping away like lions, and from Cairo hope to send home an interesting batch" (quoted in H. and A. Gernsheim, *History*, p. 115).

The intention of early travel and regional photographers was to make images that served as believable records of the locales they documented. Armchair travelers purchased these photographs to experience places they had only read about or seen in engravings, and those intrepid enough to actually visit places far from home bought views as souvenirs. Travel views were reproduced as line drawings, were sold as individual photographs, were published in albums, and, by 1854, were extremely popular as stereographs. It was a common nineteenth-century practice for a photographer to buy exposed plates or swap with colleagues, then to make prints from the plates and sell them under his own name (consequently, collectors may find it difficult to precisely identify the actual photographer of some images).

Listed here, roughly categorized by place of major activity, are some of the many nineteenth-century photographers who produced travel and regional views, plus some of the publishers who issued and distributed views (*italicized* photographers have separate entries in this chapter).

UNITED STATES

Anderson, George Edward. 1860–1928. Active Utah
Babbitt, Platt D. Active Niagara Falls, 1854–ca. 1870
Barker, George. Active Niagara Falls
Barnard, George N.
Barnum, DeLoss. Active Boston and Roxbury, Mass.
Beaman, E. O. Active Grand Canyon, ca. 1871
Bell, William Abraham. Active Nevada, Arizona, Utah, 1860s–1870s
Bennett, Henry Hamilton. 1843–1908. Active Wisconsin Dells
Bierstadt, Albert (b. Germany). 1830–1902. Active Rocky Mountain region, 1859
Bierstadt, Charles (b. Germany). before 1832–1903. Active New Bedford, Mass.
Britt, Peter (b. Switzerland). 1819–1905. Active Oregon, New York City, 1844–1905
Brown, W. Henry. Active Santa Fe, 1870s
Buehman, H. Active Tucson
Carbutt, John. 1832–1902. Active Rocky Mountain region, 1860–1875
Carvalho, Solomon N. 1815–1899. Active Baltimore; New York City; Rocky Mountain region, 1853–1854
Chamberlain, William G. Active Denver, 1860s
Collier, J. Active Colorado, 1880s
Feldman, Arthur
Fiske, George. Active 1880s
Flagg, Wilson
Gage, Franklin B. 1824–1874. Active St. Johnsbury, Vt., 1851 and after

Gardner, Alexander
Glover, Ridgeway
Gurnsey, B. H. Active Colorado Springs, Colo., 1872–1880
Hart, Alfred A. 1816–1869. Active California
Haynes, Frank Jay
Hayward and Muzzall. Active 1870s–1890s
Hesler, Alexander. 1823–1895. Active Madison, Wis.; Galena, Ill.
Hillers, John K.
Hines, T.
Huffman, Layton Alton. 1854–1931. Active Montana
Illingworth, W. H. Active St. Paul, 1868–1876
Jackson, William Henry
Jarvis, J. F. Active Washington, D.C., 1868–1900
Jones, J. Wesley. Active the West, 1850s
Kilburn, Benjamin W. 1827–1909. Active New England's White Mountains; also China and elsewhere
Kinsey, Darius. 1871–1945
Langenheim, Frederick / Langenheim, William
Lea, Carey
Lummis, Charles Fletcher. 1859–1928. Also active Peru, 1890s
McKee, Thomas M.
Moran, John. 1832–1903. Active Philadelphia
Muybridge, Eadweard
Nowell, Frank H. Active ca. 1908
O'Sullivan, Timothy H.
Peabody, Henry Goddard. b. 1855. Active Boston and elsewhere, 1870s–1940
Price, Andrew. Active Geyser Springs, Calif.
Purviance, W. T. Active Pittsburgh
Reilly, J. J. Active Marysville, Calif.
Russell, Andrew Joseph
Savage, Charles R.
Sellers, Coleman. Active Philadelphia
Soule, John P. Active Boston, ca. 1859–1900
Soule, Will
Thurlow, J.
Varela, A. C. Active Los Angeles
Walker, S. C., and Fagersteen, G. Active Stockton, Calif.
Watkins, Carleton E.
Weed, Charles L. Active 1865–1875
Weitfle, Charles. Active Central City, Calif.
Whitney, Joel Emmons. 1822–1886. Active St. Paul, 1851–1871
Wilson, E. L.
Wittick, Ben. 1845–1903. Active the Southwest

CANADA

Henderson, Alexander (b. Scotland). 1831–ca. 1913. Active Montreal, 1850s–1860s
Notman, William

LATIN AMERICA

Auchincloss, William S.
Beecher, H. C.
Charnay, Désiré (French). 1828–1915
De Rosti, Paul

GREAT BRITAIN

Bedford, Francis
Cundall, Joseph. 1818–1895
Delamotte, Philip Henry. 1820–1889
England, William. d. 1896. Active England and elsewhere, 1850s–1870s
Harrington, John. Active Brighton, ca. 1868

James Valentine. *Lime Walk, Trinity College,* ca. 1870s. Albumen print. (Courtesy Carol Fruchter)

Unidentified photographer. *Kakubezishi (Yong Boys) Who Go About from Place to Place, Wearing a Masks Like a Lion's Head, and Practising Some Tricks* [sic], late nineteenth century. Albumen print with hand-tinting. Images such as this one of costumed people, as well as foreign scenic views, were very popular. The quality of hand-tinting and toning varies tremendously; the photographer in most cases is not designated. (Courtesy Lee D. Witkin)

Jennings, J. Payne. Active 1880s
Keith, Thomas. 1827–1895
Valentine, James. 1815–1880. Active Scotland
Wilson, George Washington. 1823–1893. Active Scotland

CONTINENTAL EUROPE

Alinari, Giuseppe (1836–1890) and Leopoldo (d. 1865). Active Florence
Anderson, James (b. England). 1813–1877. Active Rome
Baldus, Edouard-Denis
Bisson, Auguste-Rosalie/Bisson, Louis-Auguste
Braun, Adolphe
Civiale, Aimé. 1821–1893. Active the Alps, 1859–1869
Clifford, Charles (English). d. 1863. Active Spain and Crimea
Dyer, Thomas
Fenton, Roger
Ferrier, Alexandre. Active Paris, 1850s–1890s
Ferrier, Claude-Marie. 1811–1889. Active France
Howard, W. D., and Lloyd, F. H. (both English). Active Dolomite Mountains, 1860s
MacPherson, Robert (Scottish). 1811–1872. Active Rome
Martens, Friedrich von (German). 1809–1875. Active France
Naya, Carlo. 1816–1882. Active Italy, 1858–1875
Neurdein, E. Active France, 1875–1900
Ponti, Carlo. Active Venice, 1860s
Sommer, Georgio (b. Germany). d. 1914. Active Italy
Soulier, Charles. Active France

NEAR EAST

Abdullah *frères.* Active Turkey, 1870s
Beato, Felice A.
Bedford, Francis

Bonfils, Félix
Du Camp, Maxime
Frith, Francis
Robertson, James
Salzmann, Auguste (German). 1824–1872. Active Palestine
Sebah, Pascal. Active Turkey, ca. 1860s–1880s (also Sebah and Joaillier)
Smith, John Shaw. 1811–1873. Also active Europe

INDIA

Biggs, T. Active ca. 1855
Bourne, Samuel
Burke, John. Active 1860s–1907
Clarke, Melville (b. England). Active before 1862
Egerton, Philip H. (b. England). Also active China
Gill, Robert (b. England). Active 1850s–1860s
Glover, T. G. (b. England)
Johnston and Hoffman
Lyon, E. D. Active 1860s
Murray, John. 1808–1898
Rust, T. A.
Scott, Allan N.
Tripe, Linneaus (b. England). Active 1850s; also active Burma

FAR EAST

Merlin, Henry Beaufoy. 1830–1873
Thomson, John
Woodbury, Walter Bentley (English). 1834–1885

NEW ZEALAND

Valentine, George D. (b. Scotland). d. 1890

George Washington Wilson. *A Skye Crofter's House*, ca. 1870s. Albumen print. (Courtesy Lee D. Witkin)

[Pascal] Sebah and Joaillier. *Turkish Woman*, from negative made ca. 1870s. Silver print (earlier prints are albumen). (Courtesy Lee D. Witkin)

Carlo Ponti. *Customhouse and Salute Church, Venice*, 1860s. Albumen cabinet photograph. (Courtesy The Witkin Gallery)

PUBLISHERS OF VIEWS

American Stereoscopic Co., Philadelphia (see *Langenheim, Frederick / Langenheim, William*)

E. and H. T. Anthony and Co., New York City (see *Anthony, Edward*)

D. Appleton and Co., New York

Bourne and Shepherd, India (see *Bourne, Samuel*)

Bradley and Rulofson, San Francisco

John Carbutt, Chicago and Philadelphia

Imprimerie Photographique Blanquart-Evrard, Lille, France (see *Blanquart-Evrard, Louis-Désiré*)

Keystone View Co., Meadville, Pa.

Kilburn Brothers, Littleton, N.H.

Lawrence and Houseworth (later Thomas Houseworth and Co.), San Francisco

N.-M. P. Lerebours, Paris

London Stereoscopic Co., London

W. L. H. Skeen and Co., Ceylon

I. W. Taber, San Francisco

Underwood and Underwood, Ottawa, Kansas

James Valentine and Sons, Dundee, Scotland

H. C. White and Co., U.S.

WORK   *See* individual entries.

MEDIA/AVAILABILITY AND PRICE   Albumen prints from collodion wet-plate negatives (ranging in size from stereographs to mammoth plates) are found most often. Daguerreotype landscapes are rare, calotypes somewhat less so. Mass-produced postcards are frequently found. Prices vary, depending on the fame of the photographer, the uniqueness of the view, the size and condition of the print, and the type of medium. (*See also* individual entries.)

SIGNATURE–OTHER IDENTIFICATION/PORTFOLIOS   *See* individual entries.

COLLECTIONS   Found in every historical photographic collection, often filed by subject matter. Libraries and historical societies are rich in unexplored collections of regional photographers. (*See also* individual entries.)

SELECTED BIBLIOGRAPHY

See Andrews, *Photographers, Pioneers*; Bull and Lorimer, *Nile*; Darrah, *Stereo Views, World*; Goodrich and Cameron, *China*; Greenhill, *Canada*; Helsted, *Rome*; Jammes and Sobieszek, *Primitive*; Loetscher, *Switzerland*; Naef and Wood, *Era*; Taft, *Photography*; Worswick and Embree, *Empire*.

Chamonix traversée de la mer de glace, ca. mid- or late 1870s. Albumen print. This French view bears the initials *ND* in the plate; the photographer's identity has remained a mystery to historians for many years. Recently the work has been attributed to the French photographer E. Neurdein. (Courtesy Lee D. Witkin)

Henry Hamilton Bennett. *Lone Rock, Dells of the Wisconsin River,* 1897. Albumen print. (Courtesy The H. H. Bennett Studio)

Frank H. Nowell. *Elks Club Day, Nome, Alaska,* 10 January 1908. Silver print. (Courtesy The Witkin Gallery)

Carleton E. Watkins. *California Street from Sansome Street, San Francisco, Looking West,* 1860s. Albumen print. Issued by I. W. Taber, San Francisco. (Courtesy Lee D. Witkin)

Tress, Arthur
United States 1940–

Interested in graphic arts, painting, sculpture, and photography since high school, Tress continued his studies in art and art history in college and graduate school, then spent several years traveling, painting, and photographing in Europe, Africa, Asia, Mexico, and California. He is best known for compelling and often disturbing photographs in which he explores children's and his own dream imagery.

"If Arthur Tress comes to photograph you, beware," Duane Michals wrote in the introduction to Tress's portfolio *The Dream Collection.* "Do not be taken in by that innocent smile and shy demeanor. They are his disguises. Arthur sees rather than looks. I don't know quite how he does it. . . . Tress will upset you. When he photographs you with a friend or lover, you will become an actor. You will perform in his theater and that drama one soon realizes is one's own. Don't be surprised if Arthur suddenly asks you to put your mother in a wheelbarrow, and don't be amazed to find yourself doing it. It all seems a joke, but when our smiles fade we are quietly shocked by what we are experiencing."

"A photographer in touch with him/herself makes photographs about what is essential in his/her experience," observed A. D. Coleman. "For Arthur Tress this involves the premeditated creation of images symbolizing the darker side of human nature. It is paradoxical and somewhat unnerving that he does so in a peculiarly forthright and even cheerful way, but that seems always to have been an aspect of his style" (*Theater of the Mind*).

WORK Chiefly portraits of people in peculiar settings with strange objects and costumes (e.g., nude man in bed with a sheep standing over him, a man dressed as a groom on his right side and as a bride on his left). Also includes children acting out their dreams, male homosexual fantasies.

MEDIUM Silver prints (usually square, about 7½ × 7½ to 10¾ × 10¾).

AVAILABILITY AND PRICE Through galleries; low to moderate.

SIGNATURE/OTHER IDENTIFICATION

Arthur Tress

PORTFOLIO See chapter 6 entry.

COLLECTIONS MMA, MOMA; BN, Stedelijk.

SELECTED BIBLIOGRAPHY
Songs of the Blue Ridge Mountains. New York: Oak Press, 1968.
Open Space and the Inner City. New York: State Council on the Arts, 1970.
The Dream Collector. Richmond: Westover, 1972.
Shadow. Intro. by John Minahan. New York: Avon, 1975.
Theater of the Mind. Intro. by A. D. Coleman. Dobbs Ferry, N.Y.: Morgan & Morgan, 1976.
See also Life Library, *Children;* chapter 7 catalogue.

Arthur Tress. *Father Time,* 1977. Silver print. (Courtesy The Witkin Gallery)

Uelsmann, Jerry N.
United States 1934–

Although Uelsmann studied with Ralph Hattersley, Minor White, and Henry Holmes Smith and has cited their influence on him, he has been exploring and evolving composite photographs since the late 1950s in a style uniquely his own. He joined the art department faculty at the University of Florida (Gainesville) in 1960, later becoming a full professor.

Uelsmann creates multiple imagery in the darkroom using as many as seven enlargers to produce the combined image he wants on a single piece of paper; to reproduce each image he reprints using the same complicated process rather than making a copy negative of a finished print. As creator of his own universe, he makes all things possible: huge rocks hang in the sky over serene landscapes, disembodied human eyes stare from sweeping lawns, positive and negative figures roam through a wood, human forms float on ocean surfaces, hands emerge from the floors of empty rooms. Where the fragments of Uelsmann's images are manipulated and where they are intact is visually impossible to tell — and unimportant.

"Creators of Jerry Uelsmann's stature may be seen to have altered the language, the substance, and the direction of their art," wrote Peter C. Bunnell. "He personally has been the recipient of considerable critical praise, though the general field of synthetic photography remains only cautiously embraced. Critics have been transfixed by the rational and the realistic in photography while the irrational and the imaginary have remained foreign to most. . . . Uelsmann [represents a] rebellious breed and in his approach he strives for his senses to reveal, for his mind to re-create, a quintessential structure reflective of how he views the photographic process itself. In one sense his art may be considered conceptual; however, this is not wholly accurate for the otherness of the outside world is affirmed, not mitigated, by the intrusion of this artist's mind and hand" (*Jerry N. Uelsmann: Silver Meditations*).

WORK   Chiefly surreal, personal multiple-image compositions.

MEDIUM   Silver prints (some hand-colored).

AVAILABILITY AND PRICE   Through galleries; most images made after 1970 moderate, images made before 1970 and recent 16×20 prints moderately high (Uelsmann dislikes reprinting old work), hand-colored prints high.

SIGNATURE/OTHER IDENTIFICATION

PORTFOLIOS   *See* chapter 6 entry.

COLLECTIONS   CCP, Chicago, Harvard (Fogg), IMP/GEH, Kansas, LOC, Louisville, Minneapolis, MOMA, Nebraska, New Mexico, New Orleans, Philadelphia, Ringling, Smithsonian, U. of Florida, Yale (Art Gallery); Antwerp, NGC, RPS.

SELECTED BIBLIOGRAPHY
Nathan Lyons, ed. *The Persistence of Vision.* New York: Horizon, and Rochester, N.Y.: GEH, 1967.
Eight Photographs: Jerry N. Uelsmann. Intro. by William E. Parker. New York: Doubleday, 1970.
Jerry N. Uelsmann. Intro. by Peter C. Bunnell. Fables by Russell Edson. Millerton, N.Y.: Aperture, 1970. Bibliography. Rev. ed., 1973.
John L. Ward. *The Criticism of Photography as Art: The Photographs of Jerry N. Uelsmann.* Gainesville: University of Florida Press, 1970.
Clifford S. Ackley. *Private Realities: Recent American Photography.* Boston: Museum of Fine Arts, 1974. Bibliography.
Jerry N. Uelsmann: Silver Meditations. Intro. by Peter C. Bunnell. Dobbs Ferry, N.Y.: Morgan & Morgan, 1975.
"Jerry Uelsmann." *Infinity,* May 1972, pp. 22–26.
"Jerry N. Uelsmann." *Camera,* Jan. 1967.
William E. Parker. "Notes on Uelsmann's Invented World." *Infinity,* Feb. 1967, pp. 4 ff.
———. "Uelsmann's Unitary Reality." *Aperture* 13, no. 3 (1967): 2–22.
See also Hume, *The Great West;* Lewis, *Darkroom 1;* Life Library, *Art, Camera, Color, Print, Year 1976;* Szarkowski, *Looking, Mirrors;* Wise, *Choice;* chapter 7 catalogues.

Jerry N. Uelsmann. Untitled, 1975. Silver combination print. (Courtesy The Witkin Gallery)

Ulmann, Doris
United States 1884–1934

Ulmann's serious interest in photography began in 1914. She studied with Clarence H. White, at Columbia University and later at his school of photography (where Laura Gilpin was one of her classmates). Her early photographs were still lifes, pictorial landscapes, and portraits of editors, doctors, and other professional people. About 1925 her interest in handicrafts led her to document rural life in Appalachia and the South. Ulmann was an extremely wealthy woman, but was accepted by her impoverished subjects even though she traveled right up to their cabin doors in a chauffeured limousine. Her second main study was of black people of the South, particularly the Gullahs who lived and worked on Lang Syne Plantation in South Carolina.

Rural America soon became the domain of the Farm Security Administration (FSA) photographers, whose sharply focused, direct style is often assumed to be the only kind of documentary photography that exists. But Ulmann was a pictorialist as well as a documentarian: she used a soft-focus lens and made prints that are generally muted, even hazy at times. Her photographs are not stricken with the contrived sentimentality of late pictorialism, however, but are as honest as those of the "tougher" FSA photographers. Ulmann simply saw her soft imagery as an acceptable medium for the records of rural life that she wanted to make. She wrote about the subjects that particularly appealed to her: "A face that has the marks of having lived intensely, that expresses some phase of life, some dominant quality or intellectual power, constitutes for me an interesting face. For this reason the face of an older person, perhaps not beautiful in the strictest sense, is usually more appealing than the face of a younger person who has scarcely been touched by life" (quoted in *The Darkness and the Light*).

Doris Ulmann. Untitled, ca. 1930. Platinum print. (Courtesy The Witkin Gallery and John Jacob Niles)

WORK Chiefly rural life in Appalachia and South Carolina (e.g., portraits, people at work, handicraft artisans, church activities). Also still lifes, landscapes, portraits of professionals.

MEDIA Gelatin dry-plate negatives (8×10 and 6½×8½); platinum prints, some gum-bichromate prints and carbon prints.

AVAILABILITY AND PRICE Through galleries. Vintage prints from the collection of John Jacob Niles, Ulmann's friend and assistant, moderately high (most are signed; prints ca. 1917 may bear the signature "Doris Jaeger," her married name at the time). Gravures from the deluxe edition of *Roll, Jordan, Roll* low.

SIGNATURE/OTHER IDENTIFICATION

Doris Ulmann

COLLECTIONS The University of Oregon (Eugene) Library holds 10,000 proof prints (representing Ulmann's entire output from ca. 1915–1934), 2,700 glass-plate negatives, 200 original prints. Also Berea, IMP/GEH, LOC, New Mexico.

SELECTED BIBLIOGRAPHY
The Faculty of the College of Physicians and Surgeons, Columbia University. Foreword by Samuel W. Lambert. New York: Hoeber, 1918. Published under the name Doris Jaeger.
Portraits of the Medical Faculty of the Johns Hopkins University. Baltimore: Johns Hopkins, 1922.
A Portrait Gallery of American Editors. Text by Louis Evan Shipman. New York: Rudge, 1925.
Julia Peterkin. *Roll, Jordan, Roll.* New York: Ballou, 1933. Also deluxe ed., 90 gravures. 350 copies, signed.
Allen Hendershott Eaton. *Handicrafts of the Southern Highlands.* New York: Sage Foundation, 1937.
The Appalachian Photographs of Doris Ulmann. Text by John Jacob Niles and Jonathan Williams. Penland, N.C.: Jargon Society, 1971.
The Darkness and the Light. . . . Text by Robert Coles and William Clift. Millerton, N.Y.: Aperture, 1974.
See also Mann, *Women.*

Uzzle, Burk
United States 1938–

Uzzle has explored several areas in photography, producing work ranging from photojournalism, to surreal-funny-sad-tender observations of modern life, to pictures that are primarily concerned with formal visual relationships. After holding a variety of photographic jobs, including making door-to-door baby portraits, Uzzle became staff photographer for the Raleigh (North Carolina) *News and Observer.* After a period of free-lancing, he worked as a *Life* magazine photographer for six years doing mainly news reportage. He later recounted that "after about 4 years with *Life*, I became aware that I had little of myself invested in my *Life* photography. I then took a summer's leave from *Life* and hitchhiked across America . . . only photographing matters of personal interest" (quoted in Witkin Gallery press release no. 40, Dec. 1973).

Uzzle's photographs organize reality into new, sometimes bizarre, conjunctions. In his words: "I am trying to photograph a certain look, a certain feeling, in which factual subject matter seems not to be of principal interest. Nevertheless, my pictures are children of colliding, circumstantial facts, wrapped in visual intuition. They aspire to order and beauty" (written for *Zoom*).

WORK Includes Americans and their environment (e.g., people at the beach, waitresses), studio images of arranged objects, series of oversize plastic animals placed in unlikely locations, industrial landscapes as near-abstractions.

MEDIUM Silver prints.

AVAILABILITY AND PRICE Through galleries; moderate.

Burk Uzzle (Magnum Photos, Inc.). *Tank Top,* 1975. Silver print. (Courtesy The Witkin Gallery)

SIGNATURE/OTHER IDENTIFICATION

COLLECTIONS   Detroit, MMA, MOMA, Smithsonian, Virginia; BN.

PORTFOLIO   *See* Chapter 6 Schools and workshops entry.

SELECTED BIBLIOGRAPHY
Landscapes. New York: Magnum, 1973.
Camera, Oct. 1970 and Nov. 1973.
James Baker Hall. "Burk Uzzle: The Hustle Comes of Age." *Aperture,* no. 77 (1976), pp. 40–48.
Zoom, Apr. 1976.
See also chapter 7 catalogue.

Van Der Zee, James
United States 1886–

Van Der Zee's parents worked as maid and butler for Ulysses S. Grant in New York City. In 1883 they moved to Lenox, Massachusetts, where James was raised and educated, with music and art an important part of his family life. His interest in photography began in 1900 when he won a small camera outfit for selling twenty packages of sachet. After moving to New York City and marrying, he resettled for two years in Phoebus, Virginia. There, while working in a hotel dining room, he photographed his neighbors as well as pupils and teachers in the Whittier School, a preparatory school for the Hampton Institute. Returning to New York, he opened his first studio in 1916 on 135th Street in Harlem. While occupying various other Harlem locations over the years, he continued to photograph the weddings, funerals, anniversaries, graduations, and other social events of that community for over fifty years.

"The designation 'naive' does not apply to Van Der Zee although he is essentially a self-taught photographer . . . and is still entirely unaware of the photography of his prominent Anglo-American contemporaries," wrote Regenia A. Perry in 1973. ". . . From the beginning of his career, Van Der Zee approached photography as an art rather than a craft. His portraits represent an incredible repertoire of poses and settings, often effected with painted backdrops — many of which he executed himself — studio stock objects, and painting directly on the print. There is rarely an unflattering portrait in Van Der Zee's work. His idealism was manifested through the perfecting of a retouching technique which was used in almost all of his portraits" (*James Van Der Zee*).

Van Der Zee was the largest single contributor to the exhibition Harlem on My Mind, held in 1969 at the Metropolitan Museum of Art in New York City, and this show generated new interest in his career. Shortly afterward, the James Van Der Zee Institute (now under the auspices of the museum) was founded to preserve his work.

James Van Der Zee. Untitled, ca. 1920s. Silver print. (Courtesy James Van Der Zee Institute)

WORK   Chiefly studio portraits, parades, weddings, etc., in Harlem, N.Y. (1916–1969). Also includes portraits made in Virginia (1907–1909), early scenes in Lenox, Mass.

MEDIUM   Silver prints (4×5 to 11×14; often toned, retouched, or hand-painted; usually signed).

SIGNATURE/OTHER IDENTIFICATION

AVAILABILITY AND PRICE   Through galleries and at auction; vintage prints moderately high, modern prints made from Van Der Zee's negatives moderate.

PORTFOLIOS *See* chapter 6 entry.

COLLECTIONS MMA, New Orleans, San Antonio.

SELECTED BIBLIOGRAPHY
Allon Schoener, ed. *Harlem on My Mind: Cultural Capital of Black America 1900-1968.* New York: Metropolitan Museum of Art, 1969.
The World of James Van Der Zee. Intro. by Reginald McGhee. New York: Grove Press, 1969.
James Van Der Zee. Intro. by Regenia A. Perry. Dobbs Ferry, N.Y.: Morgan & Morgan, 1973.
The Harlem Book of the Dead. With Owen Dodson and Camille Billops. Dobbs Ferry, N.Y.: Morgan & Morgan, 1978.

Vishniac, Roman
United States (b. Russia) 1897–

Vishniac is known both for his documentation of Eastern European Jews in the 1930s and for his natural-science photographs. He took his first photograph, through a microscope, when he was seven — a section of a cockroach's leg. The son of a prominent Moscow umbrella manufacturer, he remained in Moscow to complete his university studies in zoology and medicine when the revolution forced his family to flee Russia, then rejoined them in Berlin.

Vishniac recalled his reasons for photographing Jewish life in the 1930s: "My friends assured me that Hitler's talk was sheer bombast. But I replied that he would not hesitate to exterminate those people when he got around to it. And who was there to defend them? I knew I could be of little help, but I decided that, as a Jew, it was my duty to my ancestors, who grew up among the very people who were being threatened, to preserve — in pictures, at least — a world that might soon cease to exist" (Kinkead, p. 17). Many of his contemporaries, including Erich Salomon, told Vishniac no one would ever be interested in such pictures, but he persisted, traveling widely, often in danger, taking over five thousand shots, mostly unposed, sometimes using a camera hidden under his coat or in a large handkerchief.

Edward Steichen later proclaimed Vishniac's photographs of Jews in Eastern European ghettos before World War II "among photography's finest documents of a time and place. . . . Vishniac took with him on this self-imposed assignment . . . a rare depth of understanding and a native son's warmth and love for his people" (quoted in ibid., p. 18).

In 1940 Vishniac moved to New York City, where, while free-lancing as a portrait photographer, he began to concentrate on photographing through microscopes. His achievements in this field have earned him recognition as one of the world's foremost photomicrographers. Aside from their scientific significance, many of the images are fascinating color abstract designs. "Vishniac feels that the microscope conveys intimations of divinity . . . and regards himself as the spiritual descendent of Anton van Leeuwenhoek, the famous seventeenth-century Dutch naturalist and microscopist" (ibid., p. 42).

Also a lecturer, filmmaker, and teacher, Vishniac has taught at Yeshiva and Fordham universities in New York City and at the Rhode Island School of Design. He is currently working on his autobiography.

WORK Eastern European Jews (1933–1939); natural-science images, especially color photomicrography (e.g., human skin, anthrax bacteria, vitamins). Also portraits (e.g., Einstein, Chagall).

MEDIA Silver prints, Type C color prints.

AVAILABILITY AND PRICE Modern prints made under the photographer's supervision available through galleries. Black-and-white prints (8×10, 11×14, 16×20) moderate to moderately high, depending on size. Color prints (microscope studies) moderately high. Vintage prints not available.

SIGNATURE/OTHER IDENTIFICATION

PORTFOLIO *See* chapter 6 entry.

COLLECTIONS LOC, MOMA, Smithsonian.

Roman Vishniac. *The Jewish Scholar,* 1936. Silver print. (Courtesy The Witkin Gallery)

SELECTED BIBLIOGRAPHY
Polish Jews: A Pictorial Record. Text by Abraham Joshua Heschel. New York: Schocken, 1942, 1965.
Isaac Bashevis Singer. *A Day of Pleasure.* New York: Farrar, Straus & Giroux, 1969.
Michael Edelson. *The Concerned Photographer 2.* New York: International Center for Photography, and Grossman, 1972.
Eugene Kinkead. *Roman Vishniac.* New York: Grossman, 1974.
Francene Sabin. "The Photomicrographic World of Roman Vishniac." *Omni,* Oct. 1978, pp. 72–81.
See also Szarkowski, *Looking.*

Vroman, Adam Clark
United States 1856–1916

Vroman's major contribution to photography is his extensive documentation of Southwest American Indian life at the turn of the century. Originally a Pasadena, California, book collector and dealer, Vroman around 1892 became interested in photography. In 1895 he attended a Hopi Indian snake ceremony and was profoundly affected by the intensity of the ritual and the devotion of the participants. He wrote in his journal: "How I should like to speak their language and witness the entire ten days' ceremonies and have someone explain it all to me. Join the order if possible, to be initiated, as it were" (quoted in *Untitled 2/3,* 1972/73, p. 31).

Adam Clark Vroman. *Two Zuni Women with Ollas, 30 August 1897.* Modern silver print from the original negative. (Courtesy William Webb)

Vroman returned many times over the next ten years to the Indian villages of the Southwest. He crusaded against attempts during the period to assimilate the Indians forcibly into the white culture by suppressing their native religions and ways of life. He photographed, lectured, and wrote in an effort to call attention to the dignity and values of the various Indian cultures. The best of Vroman's photographs are powerful and direct, showing the specifics of Indian life with a genuine respect for the subjects.

WORK Best known for Indians of the Southwest (1895–1904; e.g., ceremonies, portraits, people at work). Also includes illustrations for *Ramona* (a romantic tale of Indian life); California missions; Yosemite Valley (ca. 1901) and other scenes of the Southwest (e.g., New Mexico churches, Canyon de Chelly, mountain canyons near Pasadena); Pennsylvania rural life.

MEDIA Chiefly gelatin dry-plate negatives and some film negatives; platinum prints, solio prints. Also lantern slides.

AVAILABILITY AND PRICE Through galleries and at auction but infrequently found; moderately high.

SIGNATURE/OTHER IDENTIFICATION (Sample photograph title)

COLLECTIONS The Pasadena Public Library holds the only large collection of original platinum prints. Also Bureau of Ethnology, FOP, IMP/GEH, Los Angeles (Natural History), New Mexico, Southwest.

SELECTED BIBLIOGRAPHY
Mission Memories. Los Angeles: Kingsley-Barnes & Neuner, 1898.
The Genesis of the Story of Ramona. With T. F. Barnes. Los Angeles: Kingsley-Barnes, 1899.
Helen Hunt Jackson. *Ramona.* Boston: Little, Brown, 1913. Intro. and 24 halftones by Vroman.
Photographer of the Southwest: Adam Clark Vroman 1856–1916. Ed. by Ruth I. Mahood with Robert A. Weinstein. Intro. by Beaumont Newhall. Los Angeles: Ward Ritchie, 1961.
Dwellers at the Source: Southwestern Indian Photographs of A. C. Vroman, 1895–1904. Text by William Webb and Robert A. Weinstein. New York: Grossman, 1973.
See also Life Library, *Great Photographers.*

Waldman, Max
United States 1919–

Known chiefly for his widely published photographs of theater and dance, Waldman spent twenty years as an advertising, fashion, and editorial photographer before turning to stage work. Discussing his first important excursion into theatrical photography, he recollected: "When I did *Marat/Sade* [1966], I realized this was a serious thing. I gave up advertising work to devote myself full time to the performing arts, and I never looked back" (statement to the authors, 1977).

Waldman simplifies and eliminates extraneous props in his images, isolating figures with dramatic gestures and light, to get at the essence of a movement or emotion. The extreme graininess he uses as a stylistic device is characteristic of his photographs. He once related: "I've heard one hundred times, 'Max, I don't know how you knew exactly what I had in my mind!' I reply, 'I don't know what you had in your mind at all, but I know what I had in mine!'" (ibid.).

Max Waldman. *Glenda Jackson as Charlotte Corday in "Marat/Sade," New York City,* 1966. Silver print. (Courtesy the artist. Copyright © 1966 by Max Waldman)

WORK Best known for images of theater and dance performances. Also includes nudes, portraits of sports figures and other personalities, commercial photographs.

MEDIUM Silver prints, some color (commercial work).

AVAILABILITY AND PRICE Silver prints available through galleries; moderate to moderately high (some prints issued in limited editions, in both 11×14 and 16×20 sizes).

SIGNATURE/OTHER IDENTIFICATION

Max Waldman

COLLECTIONS LOC, MMA, MOMA.

SELECTED BIBLIOGRAPHY
Zero Mostel. *Zero on Mostel.* New York: Horizon, 1966.
Waldman on Theatre. Texts by Clive Barnes and Peter C. Bunnell. New York: Anchor, 1972.
Waldman on Dance. Intro. by Clive Barnes. New York: Morrow, 1977.
"Illusions Etched in Anguish." *Life,* 12 Dec. 1969, pp. 60–66.
R. Hattersley. "Artistry of Max Waldman." *Popular Photography,* Jan. 1970, pp. 102–111.
"Lovely New Swan Alights: Natalya Makarova." *Life,* 22 Jan. 1971, pp. 38–43.
"Swinging Shakespeare." Ibid., 9 Apr. 1971, pp. 64–67.
See also Szarkowski, *Mirrors*; chapter 7 catalogues.

Walker, Todd
United States 1917–

Before deciding in 1970 to devote full time to teaching and his personal work, Walker was for twenty-five years a successful free-lance commercial photographer (among his many jobs was putting the Hertz Rent-a-Car flying man in the driver's seat). In 1965 he began printing and publishing small books and portfolios that combine reproductions of his own images with prose and poetry. He recalled in 1976: "Being a photographer of long-standing persuasion who lost interest in the inane literary, commercial uses for which I was making pictures, I began to finally make my own photographs and about that time acquired a 1250 [Multilith] offset duplicator. For me these share a symbiotic relationship" (*"For Nothing Changes"*).

"My working process [has] to do with initially confronting the world with my camera, observing, allowing myself to respond," he explained elsewhere. "With a myriad of images to select from, I try to find a single image to clarify my responses to that world. The print, by whatever process, silver, pigment or ink, attempts to clearly state that response. Color is extremely important to me. Scientifically correct color seems less correct than I feel. I separate the continuous tonal values of the photograph by means of photographic and graphic process methods into many alternatives, then reassemble these in arbitrary color. The color, too, becomes a means to more clearly and strongly state my response" (quoted in *Contemporary Trends,* Chicago: The Chicago Photographic Gallery of Columbia College, 1976, p. 50).

Todd Walker. Untitled, 1976. Offset lithograph. (Courtesy the artist)

SIGNATURE/OTHER IDENTIFICATION

Todd Walker

T Walker

WORK Chiefly the female nude, often incorporating Sabattier effect and posterization (separation of the continuous tones of a photograph into flat, posterlike colors or tones). Also includes early portraiture and street photography; commercial photographs.

MEDIA Silver prints, offset lithographs, gum-bichromate prints, silkscreen prints, collotype prints.

AVAILABILITY AND PRICE Through galleries; moderately high. Early commercial work is not available.

PORTFOLIOS *See* chapter 6 Schools and workshops entry.

COLLECTIONS Harvard (Fogg), IMP/GEH, Madison, Minneapolis, Norton Simon, Philadelphia, St. Petersburg, UCLA, Virginia; BN.

SELECTED BIBLIOGRAPHY
Fourteen works were published by the photographer (Los Angeles: Thumbprint Press): *8 Shakespeare Sonnets/8 Todd Walker Photographs,* 1965; *John Donne,* 1966; *The Story of an Abandoned Shack in the Desert,* 1966; *An Abandoned Shack* (portfolio), 1967; *How Would It Feel to be Able to Dance Like This,* 1967; *John Donne* (portfolio), 1968; *Melancholy,* 1968; *Portfolio III* (portfolio), 1974; *Twenty-Seven Photographs,* 1975; *"For Nothing Changes,"* 1976; *The Edge of the Shadow,* 1977; *A Few Notes,* 1977; *Three Soliloquies,* 1977; *See,* 1978.
Gallery Association of New York State. *On the Offset Press.* Syracuse, N.Y.: Lightwork, 1977. Includes 1 color offset print by Walker.
"Advertising's Natural Look." *Infinity,* Oct. 1959, pp. 16–19.
"Colour Photography in the Service of Advertising." *Graphis,* no. 60 (1955), pp. 307 ff.
Camera, Dec. 1971/Jan. 1972.
Creative Camera, May 1973.
Charles Kelly. "Todd Walker." *Afterimage* 2 (Mar. 1974). Interview.
Ed Scully. "Beyond the Negative." *Modern Photography,* Nov. 1975.
Michael Lonier. "Two from Todd." *Exposure* 15 (May 1977): 42–43.
See also Colors (in color bibliography); Doty, *Photography;* Szarkowski, *Mirrors;* Wise, *Choice;* chapter 7 catalogues.

Watkins, Carleton E.
United States 1829–1916

Watkins learned the daguerreotype process from Robert Vance in California in 1854 and became the operator of one of Vance's galleries. He opened his own gallery in San Francisco around 1858 after learning the collodion process, and in 1861 he visited the Yosemite Valley and made a number of mammoth-size wet-plate views that astounded viewers with their size and beauty.

Watkins returned to Yosemite several times and by 1867 was considered by his contemporaries to be the best of the California landscape photographers. According to Weston Naef, Watkins's Yosemite photographs are "the first body of [American photographs] to systematically present the landscape as a wilderness before the arrival of man. They are not the first landscape photographs, but they are the first to present nature from a deliberately assumed artistic posture" (Naef and Wood, *Era,* p. 79). Watkins's studio, his plates, and his file of prints were destroyed in the San Francisco earthquake and fire of 1906.

Carleton E. Watkins. *The Valley from the Mariposa Trail, Yosemite,* ca. 1866. Albumen print. (Private collection)

WORK Best known for landscapes (e.g., Yosemite, 1861 and after; Oregon, ca. 1868; Mts. Shasta and Lassen, ca. 1870; along the Union Pacific Railroad route, ca. 1873, 1880). Also includes views of California missions (ca. 1880), San Francisco (including street scenes), commercial work (before ca. 1859 and after 1875; e.g., portraits, farms).

MEDIA Daguerreotypes (none known to be extant); collodion wet-plate negatives, albumen prints (ranging from stereographs to 18×22).

AVAILABILITY AND PRICE Through galleries and at auction. Large-plate views rare; extremely high. Smaller prints, including stereographs, are more frequently found; low to moderately high, depending on size, etc. The firms of Bradley and Rulofson, Lawrence and Houseworth, and I. W. Taber issued Watkins prints under their own names; Watkins issued under his own name stereo prints by Alfred A. Hart.

COLLECTIONS BPL, California (Bancroft), CHS, CSL, Huntington, IMP/GEH, LOC, MMA, New Mexico, NYPL (Rare Book), Oakland, Stanford, UCLA.

SELECTED BIBLIOGRAPHY
Yosemite Views [early 1860s]. 30 albumen prints.
Yosemite. San Francisco: Watkins, 1867. 15 albumen prints.
The Yosemite Book. New York: Bien, 1868. 24 albumen prints by Watkins, 4 by W. Harris.
William R. Bentley. *Bentley's Hand-book of the Pacific Coast.* Oakland: Pacific Press, 1884. 31 albumen prints.
Paul Mickman. "Carleton E. Watkins." *Northlight* (issued by Arizona State University Art Dept.), Jan. 1977. Entire issue.
See also Naef and Wood, *Era;* Taft, *Photography.*

Weegee
United States (b. Austria-Hungary) 1899–1968

The stereotype of the tough, wisecracking news photographer — chewing a cigar stub, hat propped on the back of his head, and holding a Speed Graphic with a No. 5 flashbulb — had its real-life counterpart in Weegee. The son of a rabbi, Weegee (born Arthur H. Fellig) immigrated to America at the age of ten. He left school at fourteen and supported himself for a number of years at odd jobs, including as an itinerant street photographer. In the 1930s he acquired his first Speed Graphic, a 4×5 hand-held camera that was then the standard model used by newspaper photographers. He habitually used on-camera flash lighting, which isolated his subjects in a blast of light against a dark background and gave a stark, punchy quality to his pictures.

Weegee's newsbeat was New York City. He received his nickname — an allusion to the Ouija board — because he arrived early so often at the scenes of news-making crimes or catastrophes (it was a radio constantly tuned in to police calls, not a mystical connection, that got him there). His 1945 book *Naked City,* from which the title for a movie and popular television series was later taken, made him a celebrity; in his book he recorded bleeding corpses, gawking onlookers, firemen with body bags, and other daily events in New York. Documenting violence was his specialty in the early part of his career, and he was fond of displaying a check from Time Inc. with the notation "Two Murders, $35" neatly typed on the stub. But Weegee also photographed more benign scenes — children playing in the spray of a fire hydrant, Frank Sinatra's fans swooning, Hollywood and New York City celebrities, and similar subjects. His photographs have a spontaneity and often a wit that go far beyond ordinary news photography.

One of Weegee's notable encounters (described in *Naked City*) was with the aging Alfred Stieglitz, almost a mythical figure in the world of art photography. "You Stieglitz? I'm Weegee," went the introduction. "You may have read about me in magazines or seen my pictures in *PM.*" Then he photographed Stieglitz — with his flash shifted to the side instead of on-camera, making the lighting even harsher than usual.

Weegee once explained: "Here's my formula — dealing as I do with human beings, and I find them wonderful: I leave them alone and let them be themselves — holding hands with love-light in their eyes — sleeping — or merely walking down the street. The trick is to be where the people are. One doesn't need a scenario or shooting script, all one needs to do is to be on the spot, alert and human. One never knows what will happen. . . . I am often asked what kind of Candid Camera I use — there really is no such thing — it's the photographer who must be candid" (*Weegee's People*).

WORK Chiefly crimes and disasters (e.g., fires, murder scenes, victims, suspects, excited onlookers); other images of New York City (e.g., people sleeping on a tenement fire escape on a hot

Weegee. Untitled. From *Weegee's People,* 1946. Silver print. (Courtesy The Witkin Gallery)

night); infrared photography (e.g., theater audiences). Also includes photocaricatures and distortions, advertising, fashion, society photography.

MEDIUM Silver prints. May bear signature or one of several stamps used by the photographer (e.g., "Arthur Fellig," "A. Fellig," "Weegee," "Weegee the Famous"). Also often found with his handwritten description on the back (see example).

AVAILABILITY AND PRICE Through galleries and at auction but infrequently found (and usually in bad condition — creased, torn, scraped); moderately high. Weegee printed quickly and passed out his prints casually to newspapers, friends, and others.

SIGNATURE/OTHER IDENTIFICATION

(Handwriting sample)

COLLECTIONS The Center for Creative Photography (Tucson, Ariz.) holds a relatively large Weegee collection (142 prints). Also ICP, IMP/GEH, MMA, MOMA; BN.

SELECTED BIBLIOGRAPHY
Naked City. New York: Essential Books, 1945. Reprint, New York: Da Capo, 1975.
Weegee's People. New York: Duell, Sloan & Pearce, 1946. Reprint, New York: Da Capo, 1975.
Naked Hollywood. With Mel Harris. New York: Pellegrini & Cudahy, 1953. Reprint, New York: Da Capo, 1975.
Weegee's Secrets of Shooting with Photo Flash. With Mel Harris. [New York?]: Designers 3, 1953.
Weegee's Creative Camera. With Roy Ald. Garden City, N.Y.: Hanover House, 1959.
Weegee by Weegee: An Autobiography. New York: Ziff-Davis, 1961. Reprint, New York: Da Capo, 1975.
Weegee. Ed. by Louis Stettner. New York: Knopf, 1977.
Weegee (Arthur Fellig). Intro. by Allene Talmey. Millerton, N.Y.: Aperture, 1977. Bibliography.
John Coplans. "Weegee the Famous." *Art in America* 65 (Sept./Oct. 1977): 37–41.

Welpott, Jack
United States 1923–

As a photographer and teacher, Welpott has been a major influence in the San Francisco area since 1959. After military service during World War II, he began his formal study of photography upon entering Indiana University. Henry Holmes Smith was one of his teachers, and Welpott soon met Aaron Siskind, Minor White, Harry Callahan, Roy Stryker, Jerry Uelsmann, and other figures active in the medium. In 1950 he began exhibiting his own photographs.

For several years in the early seventies Welpott and Judy Dater worked together making portraits, mostly of women whom they found "fascinating and who, in some manner, expressed something about the 'feminine mystique.' Most were strangers to us," Welpott wrote. "We discovered them in cafes, banks, shops, and on the streets. . . . We usually spent several hours photographing them in their own environment" (*Women and Other Visions*). The photographs are intense and highly personal, and although Welpott and Dater photographed the same subjects, the results were quite different. "Jack liked to use a wide-angle lens," Dater explained. "He would get further away. The women were frequently seen more as objects in the rooms. Women responded to Jack as a man, whereas with me, of course, they did not" (quoted in "Behind the Lens with Judy Dater," *San Francisco Bay Guardian*, 20 Oct. 1977, p. 15).

"The psychological landscape" and the "attempt to define changing reality in terms of human psychology" are how Welpott has described his themes (Wise, *Choice*, p. 11). He once observed: "Part of the fascination that photography holds is its ability to unlock secrets kept even from ourselves" (*Women and Other Visions*).

WORK Portraits (e.g., women, photographers), "metaphorical" landscapes and interiors.

MEDIUM Silver prints (8×10, 11×14).

AVAILABILITY AND PRICE Through galleries; moderate.

SIGNATURE/OTHER IDENTIFICATION

PORTFOLIO *See* chapter 6 Schools and workshops entry.

COLLECTIONS Chicago, IMP/GEH, Minneapolis, MOMA, Nebraska, New Mexico, Oakland, San Francisco.

SELECTED BIBLIOGRAPHY
Jack Welpott: The Artist as Teacher, the Teacher as Artist. Photographs 1950–1975. Texts by Rodney C. Stuart and Henry Holmes Smith. San Francisco: San Francisco Museum of Modern Art, 1975.
Women and Other Visions. With Judy Dater. Texts by Welpott and Henry Holmes Smith. Dobbs Ferry, N.Y.: Morgan & Morgan, 1975.
See also Hume, *The Great West*; Life Library, *Print*; Wise, *Choice*; chapter 7 catalogues.

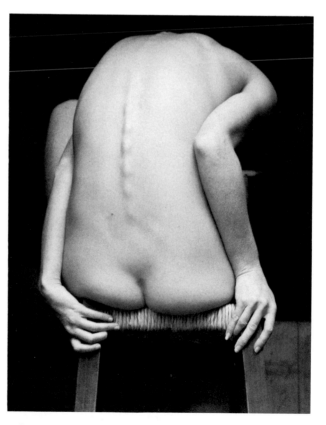

Jack Welpott. *Twinka's Back*, 1975. Silver print. (Courtesy The Witkin Gallery. Copyright © by Jack Welpott)

Wessel, Henry, Jr.
United States 1942–

Wessel's photographs are ordinary scenes of the human environment: the camera's role is simply to record what is there, while Wessel's role is to be extremely selective about just where he places the camera. The camera and photographer together impose a visual rationale by isolating or emphasizing certain elements in the scene. In Wessel's words: "My primary function as a photographer is to describe, with a camera, how something looks as a photograph" ("Henry Wessel jun."). Wessel often plays with near/far relationships in order to shift emphasis, impose new proportions, manipulate space, or allot major attention to seemingly inconsequential objects.

Ben Lifson analyzed the Wessel photograph shown here: "The scene which this apparently huge man dwarfs, largely obstructs, and perhaps surveys is a sunlit bay. Sand, shoreline, water; across the bay a distant pier; mist rises from the pier and mountains from the mist. All this stuff is the subject matter of earlier heroic landscape photographs. Yet although it stretches off into the far distance beyond the wall, it . . . is seen in pieces, occupying those portions of the frame the human figure doesn't. Only the man is seen whole, uniting the fragmented landscape by his contingency to its several parts" (*Henry Wessel, Jr.*).

WORK The human environment (e.g., beaches, parks, streets, houses, roadsides, etc.).

MEDIUM Silver prints (8×12).

AVAILABILITY AND PRICE Through galleries; moderate.

SIGNATURE/OTHER IDENTIFICATION

Henry Wessel. Jr.

COLLECTIONS IMP/GEH, MOMA, Nebraska, Philadelphia, VSW; NGC.

SELECTED BIBLIOGRAPHY
Snapshot. Ed. and intro. by Jonathan Green. Millerton, N.Y.: Aperture, 1974.
Henry Wessel, Jr. Intro. by Ben Lifson. El Cajon, Calif.: Grossmont College Art Gallery, 1976.
"Henry Wessel jun." *Camera,* May 1974, pp. 12–19.
See also Hume, *The Great West*; Szarkowski, *Looking, Mirrors*; chapter 7 catalogues.

Henry Wessel, Jr. *San Francisco, California,* 1973. Silver print. (Courtesy the artist)

Weston, Brett
United States 1911–

The second son of Edward Weston (see following entry) Brett Weston has, in his own right, occupied a major place in photography. He apprenticed with his father in Mexico in 1925 and has continued to work prolifically since. Upon returning to the Weston portrait studio in Glendale, California, in 1927, he participated in the business and also began to exhibit his prints. His early work differs from his later images: softer in tone, it is concerned with constructing dramatic compositions from such recognizable forms as factories, cars, sand dunes, plants, and rooftops.

In 1930 Weston set up his own studio in Santa Barbara. Drafted into the Army in 1941, he was stationed in New York City. One of his commanding officers, Arthur Rothstein, allowed him time to photograph the city with an 11×14-inch view-camera; the resulting portfolio *New York* was issued in 1951. After using a 1947 Guggenheim Fellowship to photograph along the East Coast, Weston moved to Carmel, California, to assist his father, who was increasingly incapacitated from Parkinson's disease. He printed Edward Weston's *50th Anniversary Portfolio* (1951/52) and made other prints from many of his father's negatives.

In the 1940s and thereafter Brett Weston's style changed sharply as he found his own eye. His images became more abstract, textured, hard-edged — more intellectually involved with visual problems and space, and less with emotion. He does all his own darkroom work and is a masterful printer who produces rich, brilliant images that pull the maximum tonal range from photographic materials.

"Brett Weston has characteristically seen the world graphically, in terms of pattern," wrote John Szarkowski. "When Edward and Brett photographed the same sand dune, the father made photographs that showed the sensuous, plastic sculpture of natural forms; the son's sand dunes emerged as constructions of flat planes, straight lines, and sharp angles" (Szarkowski, *Looking*, p. 122).

Brett Weston. *Palmetto, Mexico,* 1973. Silver print. (Courtesy the artist)

WORK   Early studies of plants, cars, buildings, etc. Since 1950 chiefly abstracts from nature; landscapes. (See illustration, page 297.)

MEDIUM   Silver prints. Weston most often makes 8×10 view-camera negatives, but also uses 11×14 and 5×7 sizes. In later years he has used a 2¼×2¼ camera. Most prints bear his signature.

AVAILABILITY AND PRICE   Through galleries and the photographer; vintage prints high, modern prints moderate (for 8×10 size) to moderately high (for 11×14, 16×20).

SIGNATURE/OTHER IDENTIFICATION

PORTFOLIOS   *See* chapter 6 entry.

COLLECTIONS   Amon Carter, Arizona State, Chicago, Harvard (Carpenter, Fogg), IMP/GEH, Kansas, LOC, Louisville, MOMA, New Mexico, New Orleans, Norton Simon, Oakland, Portland (Ore.), San Francisco, Yale (Art Gallery).

SELECTED BIBLIOGRAPHY
Merle Armitage. *Brett Weston: Photographs.* New York: E. Weyhe, 1956.
Brett Weston: Photographs. Intro. by Nancy Newhall. Fort Worth, Tex.: Amon Carter Museum of Western Art, 1966.
Beaumont Newhall and Nancy Newhall. *A Collection of Photographs.* Millerton, N.Y.: Aperture, 1969.
Brett Weston: Voyage of the Eye. Afterword by Beaumont Newhall. Millerton, N.Y.: Aperture, 1975.
F. H. Halliday [Charis Wilson Weston]. "Brett Weston, Photographer." *Camera Craft* 47 (Mar. 1940): 113–122.
Dody Warren [Dody Weston Thompson]. "Brett Weston, Photographer." *American Photography* 46 (Sept. 1952): 32–39.
"Brett Weston." *Aperture* 7, no. 4 (1959): 136–150.
Roger Aikin. "Brett Weston and Edward Weston: An Essay in Photographic Style." *Art Journal* 32 (Summer 1973): 394–404.
See also Danziger and Conrad, *Interviews;* Hume, *The Great West;* Szarkowski, *Looking;* Witkin, *Julien Levy;* chapter 7 catalogue.

Weston, Edward
United States 1886–1958

One of the most original and renowned photographers of the twentieth century, Edward Weston made his first photographs in 1902 with a Bulls-Eye No. 2 camera. Born in Illinois, Weston moved to California in 1906. He began to earn his living in photography by doing house-to-house portraiture, and in 1911 opened a studio in Tropico (now Glendale).

Weston was an active exhibitor in salon shows of the period but he became increasingly dissatisfied with his soft-focus, pictorial work. An exhibition of modern painting he saw at the 1915 San Francisco World's Fair had a major effect upon his photographic vision, and by 1922 he had reached a turning point in his work. In that year, on a trip back to the Midwest, he photographed the Armco Steel plant in Ohio using a direct, sharply focused, strongly composed style. Later in his life he destroyed most of the negatives he had made before 1922, wishing to preserve only his nonpictorial work and base his reputation on it.

Once he found his own style, Weston advocated "straight" photography. He painstakingly composed the final image on the camera's ground glass, sometimes devoting an entire day to making a single exposure. Aside from minor controls in the darkroom, he did not manipulate his negatives. His darkroom equipment was a testament to simplicity: only a simple contact frame, a light bulb, and the necessary chemicals — all he needed to produce prints of the highest quality.

Weston's life-style was simple, due as much to his ascetic values as to his meager income. His reputation began to be established as early as 1925, but his photographs never sold well — not even when, as book dealer Jake

Zeitlin related, they were offered in 1932 for two dollars each. (During his lifetime, Weston's best-selling image was *Pepper No. 30* — but, according to his records, only twelve copies were sold.)

From 1923 to 1943 Weston kept journals he called daybooks. Edited by Nancy Newhall and published first in 1961, they come closer than any other document to conveying the creative and emotional life of a great photographer. In 1937 Weston received the first Guggenheim Fellowship ever awarded a photographer; it gave him the financial freedom to travel and photograph in California, Oregon, Washington, and the Southwest.

Fame came to Weston late in life. He was the subject of a film, *The Photographer* (1948), made by his friend and fellow member of Group f/64 Willard Van Dyke; and in 1946 Nancy Newhall mounted a major exhibition of Weston's photographs at the Museum of Modern Art in New York City. In his last years his cabin in the Carmel hills became a mecca for serious photographers and collectors.

Various women influenced Weston, including Margrethe Mather, whom he might have met as early as 1912. She collaborated with him (see illustration, page 215) and introduced him to a bohemian circle of writers and artists. Later, he lived and worked with Tina Modotti. In 1938 he married Charis Wilson, who is the nude in some of his most famous images; together they published two books, *The Cats of Wildcat Hill* and *California and the West.*

Of Weston's four sons by his first wife, Florence Chandler, three figure prominently in his art. Neil was often the model for Edward's male-nude studies. Brett, who became a highly regarded photographer himself (see preceding entry), worked with his father in the 1930s and 1940s. Stricken with crippling Parkinson's disease in the early forties, Edward came to depend on Brett to do his printing. Cole, the youngest son, became his father's assistant and took on his printing beginning in 1946. (He later reported that Edward remained a perfectionist while incapacitated, establishing a strict code of standards for each negative.) Working mainly in color, Cole also became a successful photographer in his own right. In accordance with his father's wishes and as executor of his estate, Cole Weston has continued to print Edward's negatives since the latter's death in 1958.

WORK   Chiefly (all in post-1922 sharp-focus style) nudes, studies of forms in nature (e.g., shells, vegetables, rock series at Point Lobos, Calif.), portraits, landscapes. Also includes early soft-focus pictorial work (e.g., portraits, still lifes). (See illustration, page 10.)

MEDIA   Chiefly silver prints, platinum prints. Also some color. Sizes range from 3×4 to 8×10. Weston made contact prints, often from 8×10 negatives.

SIGNATURE/OTHER IDENTIFICATION

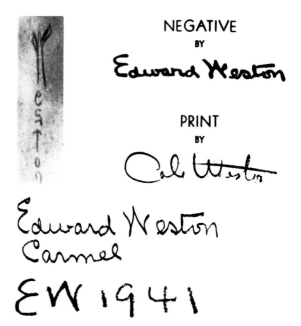

NEGATIVE
BY
Edward Weston

PRINT
BY
Cole Weston

*Edward Weston
Carmel*

EW 1941

AVAILABILITY AND PRICE   Through galleries and sometimes at auction.

Early platinum prints and most silver prints made by the photographer himself are rare; high to extremely high. Price is affected by condition and signature, which may appear in various ways or not at all. Early signed prints bear a stylized Weston signature; later ones carry his bold signature below the lower right corner of the image. In the 1930s Weston began to initial some prints and to write the full title and his name on the verso. There appears to be little consistency in this, however, and an

Edward Weston. *Margrethe Mather*, 1917. Platinum print. (Courtesy Target Collection, Museum of Fine Arts, Houston)

initialed vintage print has as much value as one fully signed. (In the mid-1930s Weston was persuaded for a short period to assign limited-edition numbers to some prints and mark them [e.g., "4/40"], but, in truth, the full editions were not completed, and he soon dropped the numbering entirely.)

Modern prints (from the original negatives) made by Cole Weston and identified by his signature on the verso are moderately high in price.

In 1955 Brett Weston was commissioned to make eight prints of each of 1,000 negatives Edward chose as his finest; about 800 negatives were printed before the project was abandoned. These so-called "project prints" have a warmer tone than other modern prints because of the paper used; often they are found unmounted. In 1975 the Weston estate mounted and identified the project prints remaining in its control, and Brett Weston signed them on the verso. Mounted and unmounted project prints are priced moderate to high.

The few prints made by the estate in the 1970s from 8×10 color transparencies that Edward Weston made during the last year he was able to photograph (ca. 1948) are moderate in price.

PORTFOLIOS *See* chapter 6 entry.

COLLECTIONS Amon Carter, Chicago, Illinois, IMP/GEH, MOMA, New Mexico, New Orleans, Oakland; Mexico City, RPS; most other major collections throughout the world.

SELECTED BIBLIOGRAPHY
Anita Brenner. *Idols behind Altars.* New York: Harcourt, Brace, 1929. Photographs by Weston and Modotti.
The Art of Edward Weston. Ed. and designed by Merle Armitage. New York: E. Weyhe, 1932.
Seeing California with Edward Weston. Westways: Automobile Club of Southern California, 1939.
Charis Wilson. *California and the West.* New York: Duell, Sloan & Pearce, 1940. Rev. ed., Millerton, N.Y.: Aperture, 1978. Also deluxe ed. with 1 print.
Walt Whitman. *Leaves of Grass.* New York: Limited Editions Club, 1942. Reprint, intro. by Richard Erlich. New York: Paddington, 1972.
Nancy Newhall. *The Photographs of Edward Weston.* New York: MOMA, 1946.
Charis Wilson Weston. *The Cats of Wildcat Hill.* New York: Duell, Sloan & Pearce, 1947.
Fifty Photographs: Edward Weston. Ed. and designed by Merle Armitage. New York: Duell, Sloan & Pearce, 1947.
My Camera on Point Lobos. Ed. by Ansel Adams. Yosemite National Park, Calif.: Virginia Adams, and Boston: Houghton Mifflin, 1950. Reprint, New York: Da Capo, 1968.
The Daybooks. Vol. 1: *Mexico.* Intro. By Beaumont Newhall. Foreword and technical note by Nancy Newhall. Rochester, N.Y.: GEH, 1961. Vol. 2: *California 1927–1934.* Intro. by Nancy Newhall. New York: Horizon Press, and Rochester, N.Y.: GEH, 1966. Reprint (both vols.), Millerton, N.Y.: Aperture, 1971.
The Flame of Recognition. Millerton, N.Y.: Aperture, 1965. Expanded ed., *Edward Weston: The Flame of Recognition,* 1971.
Ben Maddow. *Edward Weston: Fifty Years.* Millerton, N.Y.: Aperture, 1973. Bibliography. Another ed., Boston: New York Graphic Society, 1978.
Edward Weston: Nudes. Remembrance by Charis Wilson. Millerton, N.Y.: Aperture, 1977. Also deluxe ed. with 1 print.
Bernard Freemesser. "Edward Weston: A Chronological Bibliography." *Exposure* 15 (Feb. 1977): 29–32.
See also Life Library, *Great Photographers, Themes, Year 1976;* Szarkowski, *Looking;* chapter 7 catalogues.

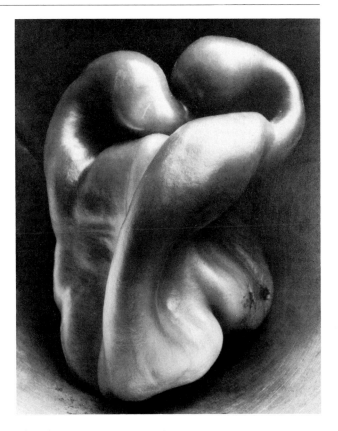

Edward Weston. *Pepper No. 30,* 1930. Silver print. (Courtesy The Witkin Gallery and The Edward Weston Estate)

White, Clarence H.
United States 1871–1925

Clarence Hudson White began to photograph in 1894 when he had free time from his position as a bookkeeper. He soon became noted as a pictorial photographer, and in 1898 his work came to the attention of Alfred Stieglitz, who later published it in *Camera Work.* In 1907 he began teaching photography at Teachers College of Columbia University, and in 1914 he founded the Clarence H. White School of Photography in New York City. A number of subsequently well-known photographers — Margaret Bourke-White, Laura Gilpin, Dorothea Lange, and Paul Outerbridge among them — were trained by White. He was a founding member of the Photo-Secession (1902) and was the first president of the Pictorial Photographers of America (1916), which he founded with others partly in reaction against the "straight" photography that Stieglitz had begun to advocate over pictorialism.

Like other members of the Photo-Secession, White was influenced by the paintings of James McNeill Whistler, with their softening of detail and abstraction of design as in Japanese prints. White's photographs are carefully controlled compositions marked by skillful manipulation of lighting effects. Peter C. Bunnell wrote: "He created a style, which at its inception was unique in photography. He showed that photography relied on contemplation and

Clarence H. White. *Spring,* 1898. Platinum triptych. (Courtesy The Metropolitan Museum of Art, The Alfred Stieglitz Collection, 1933)

planning, and that through the continued use of picture subjects that did not vary greatly, he could come to a deeper understanding of their intrinsic emotion ("Clarence H. White" [1972]).

WORK Includes genre scenes (particularly of women and children in intimate, quiet moments), nudes, portraits, still lifes, urban and pastoral landscapes. White also collaborated with Stieglitz on a series of figure studies (ca. 1909). (See illustration, page 105.)

MEDIA Platinum prints, palladium prints, gum-bichromate prints. In his early work, White often used pencil and white ink to alter the design and tones (he considered this the photographer's prerogative). He at times used a pinhole camera to achieve soft focus. His works are often signed and dated in pencil on the print or mount. Later work often bears the monogram "CHW" in red ink.

AVAILABILITY AND PRICE Through galleries and at auction. Most of White's estate material was donated to museum collections. Vintage pictorial photographs infrequently available; moderately high to high. Professional portrait work more commonly found; moderate to moderately high. *Camera Work* reproductions low to moderate.

SIGNATURE/OTHER IDENTIFICATION

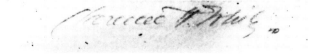

COLLECTIONS The Princeton (N.J.) University Art Museum holds the largest body of the photographer's work: the Clarence H. White Family Collection. Also Cleveland, IMP/GEH, Kansas, LOC, MMA, MOMA; RPS.

SELECTED BIBLIOGRAPHY
Jerald C. Maddox. *Photographs of Clarence H. White.* Lincoln: University of Nebraska Art Galleries, 1968.
Clarence H. White. Intro. by Maynard P. White, Jr. Millerton, N.Y.: Aperture, 1977. Bibliography.
Symbolism of Light: The Photographs of Clarence H. White. Ed. by William Innes Homer. Text by Maynard P. White, Jr. Wilmington: Delaware Art Museum, 1977. Bibliography.
Peter C. Bunnell and Clarence H. White, Jr. "The Art of Clarence Hudson White." *Ohio University Review* 7 (1965): 40–65. Bibliography.
Peter C. Bunnell. "Clarence H. White." *Camera*, Nov. 1972, pp. 23–40.
Camera Work: Reproductions (gravures, colored halftone) in nos. 3, 9, 23, 27, 32.
See also Green, *Camera Work*; Lawton and Know, *Knights*; Life Library, *Great Photographers, Print*; Naef, *Collection.*

White, Minor
United States 1908–1976

As an influential photographer, theoretician, critic, and teacher, White followed an independent path regardless of the changing styles in the photographic world. He had an early interest in photography and was encouraged by a grandfather who was an enthusiastic amateur. White studied botany and English in college and for several years supported himself at odd jobs while writing poetry. In the late 1930s he renewed his interest in photography; among his early influences he cited the photographs of Berenice Abbott, Ansel Adams, and Edward Weston, and the concepts in the book *America and Alfred Stieglitz.* In 1938/39 he served as a "creative photographer" for the federal Works Progress Administration, completing projects on iron-front buildings and the waterfront of Portland, Oregon. By 1942 his work had been exhibited nationally, published, and purchased by the Museum of Modern Art in New York City.

In 1946 White met Stieglitz, whose concept of equivalence became central to White's art. Stieglitz had postulated that the photograph can be an equivalent — a metaphor for an internal state — and White extended this concept, applying it to a mode of personal photography and teaching in which photography was conceived of as a spiritual discipline both for the photographer and the active viewer (see page 301, *Photograph as Metaphor*). White's interests in philosophies and psychologies such as Zen, Gurdjieff, and Gestalt were also incorporated into his work and teaching. He referred to "The Way through Camera Work," and, paraphrasing an old Zen saying, once wrote: "At the beginning of a photographer's life a photograph of a tree is a tree, a photograph of a mountain is a mountain, a photograph of a pepper is a pepper, but as he begins to be aware of a way of camera work, of equivalents, of photographs for contemplation, a photograph of a tree is no longer a tree but what-else-it-is; a photograph of a rock is no longer a rock but an expression of his soul. Then still later after due growth has come to pass, once again a photograph of a tree is a tree, a photograph of a spurting wave is a wave and one knows the taste of pure water" (*Aperture*, vol. 7, no. 2 [1959]).

Another approach that White began to develop in the 1940s was that of sequencing photographs — arranging them in series so that individual prints borrow significance from each other and make a unified statement. Among the subjects around which he built sequences was his explication of a Zen koan: "You know the sound of two hands clapping. What is the sound of one hand clapping?"

White taught for many years — at the Calfornia School of Fine Arts (now the San Francisco Art Institute), at the Rochester (New York) Institute of Technology, and at the Massachusetts Institute of Technology, as well as at many public and private workshops. One of the founders, in 1952, of the influential photographic publication *Aperture*, he served as publisher-editor until 1975. White produced a large body of writing, both published and unpublished. His photographs were unmanipulated and often realistic — what they signified was always as important to him as their formal composition. In exhibitions and publications he freely used his work and that of others in a lifelong journey of self-exploration.

WORK   Chiefly images functioning as metaphors (equivalents), including landscapes, portraits, close-ups of nature, human environments, manufactured objects; photographic sequences, some with words (e.g., *Sound of One Hand, Song without Words, Everything Gets in the Way*). Also includes cityscapes and portraiture in Portland, Ore. (late 1930s–early 1940s); interpretive theatrical photographs (1949–1953; e.g., from *Dear Judas*). (See illustration, page 298.)

MEDIUM   Silver prints.

AVAILABILITY AND PRICE   Through galleries; moderately high to high.

SIGNATURE/OTHER IDENTIFICATION

PORTFOLIOS   *See* chapter 6 entry.

COLLECTIONS   The Princeton (N.J.) University Art Museum preserves the White archive: negatives, prints, correspondence, and manuscripts. Also Chicago, Harvard (Carpenter, Fogg), IMP/GEH, Kalamazoo, LOC, Louisville, New Mexico, New Orleans, Norton Simon, NYPL (Picture), Oakland, Oregon, Oregon Historical, Philadelphia, Ringling, San Francisco, UCLA; NGC.

SELECTED BIBLIOGRAPHY
Zone System Manual. Dobbs Ferry, N.Y.: Morgan & Morgan, 1961.
Mirrors Messages Manifestations. Millerton, N.Y.: Aperture, 1969. Bibliography.
John Upton. *Minor White, Robert Heinecken, Robert Cumming.* Long Beach: California State University Fine Arts Gallery, 1973.
The New Zone System Manual. With Richard Zakia and Peter Lorenz. Dobbs Ferry, N.Y.: Morgan & Morgan, 1976.
Minor White: Rites & Passages. Text by James Baker Hall. Millerton, N.Y.: Aperture, 1978.
Aperture. Published and edited by White, 1952–75.
Camera, Aug. 1959.
Exposure 14, no. 3 (1976): 7–12. Reprints of 4 essays by White: "When Is Photography" (1943), "What Is Photography" (1948), "Call for Critics" (1960), "The Workshop Idea in Photography" (1961).
See also "Silence of Seeing" in Coke, *100 Years;* Danziger and Conrad, *Interviews;* Hume, *The Great West;* Lyons, *Photographers;* Life Library, *Art, Great Photographers, Themes, Year 1977;* chapter 7 catalogues, especially four exhibitions conceived by White (pages 301–302).

Minor White. *Two Barns, Dansville, New York,* 1955. Silver print. (Courtesy The Minor White Archive–Princeton University, and Light Gallery)

Winningham, Geoff
United States 1943–

A Houston resident who teaches at Rice University, Winningham blends humor with sophisticated awareness of visual incongruities, whether photographing professional wrestler Johnny Valentine's flying foot-stomp, Miss Appaloosa Queen 1972 in her spotted pantsuit, or couples dancing at the local high-school prom.

He reflected: "One thing about photography that is, to me, extraordinarily wonderful and utterly unique to the medium [is] that you can photograph almost without a thought. It's so easy to do, particularly the way I work, with a light, fast camera. Some photographs, curiously enough a lot of the best of my own work, are a complete surprise to me on the contact sheet because I can hardly remember even taking them. I respond to something and later I've got an image. I look at the image and my first response is a question: 'I made that?' When that kind of thing begins to happen successfully, it just astonishes me in its quick and very lyrical way. A simple response to a subject, and a whole picture results, full of all sorts of things, richer and more complex than anyone's imagination" (*Geoff Winningham: Photographs*, p. 16).

Geoff Winningham. *Miss Appaloosa Queen, Houston Livestock Show*, 1972. Silver print. (Courtesy The Witkin Gallery)

WORK   Includes extensive studies of professional wrestlers; scenes from the Houston Livestock Show and Rodeo; events at the Houston Astrodome; couples at dances.

MEDIA   Silver prints, color. (Size about 16×20.)

AVAILABILITY AND PRICE   Through galleries; moderate.

SIGNATURE/OTHER IDENTIFICATION

PORTFOLIO   *See* chapter 6 entry.

COLLECTIONS   Harvard (Carpenter), Houston, MOMA.

SELECTED BIBLIOGRAPHY
Friday Night in the Coliseum. Houston: Allison Press, 1971.
Going Texan: The Days of the Houston Livestock Show and Rodeo. Houston: Mavis Kelsey, 1972.
Geoff Winningham: Photographs. Interview by E. A. Carmean, Jr. Houston: Museum of Fine Arts, 1974.
35mm Annual 1968, and 1973.
See also Hume, *The Great West*; Life Library, *Year 1973*; Szarkowski, *Mirrors*; chapter 7 catalogues.

Winograd, Garry
United States 1928–

Winogrand is a photographer of the U.S. social landscape who records the flow of mores and milieux with an interested and somewhat impolite eye. He began photo-graphing while in the Air Force during World War II and later studied painting at City College of New York and Columbia University. In 1951 he enrolled in Alexey Brodovitch's class in photojournalism at the New School for Social Research (New York City). Beginning in 1953 he did free-lance advertising photography and since 1973 has taught at the University of Texas (Austin).

Many of Winogrand's photographs are humorous, at least at first glance. Some are enigmas — apparently rational narratives that, in fact, may or may not be true; they may also be little stories that exist only because the camera recorded a chance combination of personae. His images often tilt, with horizon lines askew; he once said he likes to see how far he can push things before the image comes apart. A much-quoted Winogrand remark: "I photograph to find out what something will look like photographed" (*Peculiar to Photography* catalogue, listed in chapter 7).

Henri Man Barendse wrote: "Winogrand's pictures demonstrate, with their ambiguous and uncertain relationships between people, things and events, that what the camera catches in the briefest of moments has little bearing on our jaded assumptions about the flow of natural time. His rude, irrational pictures deny us the comfort of our everyday rationale. We are reminded once again of Daumier's observation that photographs describe everything and explain nothing" (ibid.).

WORK   Chiefly images of contemporary U.S. life (e.g., people and animals at the zoo, people on the street, public events). Also advertising and magazine work.

MEDIUM   Silver prints.

AVAILABILITY AND PRICE   Through galleries; moderate to moderately high.

SIGNATURE/OTHER IDENTIFICATION

PORTFOLIO   *See* chapter 6 entry.

COLLECTIONS   IMP/GEH, MOMA.

SELECTED BIBLIOGRAPHY
The Animals. Text by John Szarkowski. New York: MOMA, 1969.
Women Are Beautiful. New York: Farrar, Straus & Giroux, 1975.
Public Relations. Texts by Tod Papageorge and John Szarkowski. New York: MOMA, 1977.
"Monkeys Make the Problem More Difficult: A Collective Interview with Garry Winogrand." *Image* 15 (July 1972): 1–4.
See also Hume, *The Great West*; Life Library, *Documentary, Year 1974*; Szarkowski, *Mirrors*; chapter 7 catalogues.

Wolcott, Marion Post
United States 1910–

Wolcott is known for the documentary work she did for the Farm Security Administration (FSA) during the 1930s Depression. She studied at New York University, the New School for Social Research (New York City), and the University of Vienna. She first began to photograph while in Vienna and bought herself a camera, but still thought of photography as only a pleasant pastime. Later, influenced by the work of Paul Strand and particularly by the direction of Ralph Steiner, she decided to make photography her profession. She free-lanced in New York City, then went to work in 1936 for the Philadelphia *Evening Bulletin*, doing fashion and feature work.

When Wolcott became dissatisfied with stories that confined her work too often to the society page, Steiner referred her to Roy Stryker of the U.S. Resettlement Administration. In 1938 Stryker hired her for the FSA at a time when he was expanding the agency's photographic coverage to include productive and prosperous aspects of farm life as well as rural problems. Wolcott had always been a city person and perhaps because of this many of her images show a romantic view of rural areas, emphasizing the beauty, lushness, and tranquility; others, however, demonstrate her compassionate view of poverty.

After the FSA period, Wolcott traveled widely, lived abroad, and continued to photograph, mainly in 35mm color, for her own pleasure.

WORK Best known for FSA images (some color). (See illustration, page 137.)

MEDIA Silver prints, color.

AVAILABILITY AND PRICE Signed vintage FSA silver prints from Wolcott's personal collection are available through galleries and at auction; moderately high. Modern prints made and signed by the photographer available through galleries; moderate. Modern FSA prints (black and white only) from the Library of Congress extremely low. Wolcott is arranging to make some of her recent 35mm color work available.

SIGNATURE/OTHER IDENTIFICATION

COLLECTIONS LOC (FSA work), Minnesota, MMA, San Francisco.

SELECTED BIBLIOGRAPHY
See bibliography in FSA entry.

A sampling of photographers' portfolios (identified from left to right). TOP ROW: Manuel Alvarez Bravo, *Fifteen Photographs.* SECOND ROW: Elliott Erwitt, untitled; Piet Zwart, *12 Fotografien;* Jacques Henri Lartigue, untitled; Ralph Eugene Meatyard, *Portfolio Three.* THIRD ROW: Judy Dater, *Ten Photographs;* Steve Salmieri, untitled; George A. Tice, *Portfolio V; Edward Weston Portfolio;* William Clift, *New Mexico.* FOURTH ROW: Duane Michals, untitled; George Krause, *Saints and Martyrs;* Rhode Island School of Design, *Portfolio 1973.* BOTTOM ROW: Walker Evans, untitled; Berenice Abbott, *Ten Photographs; A Portfolio of Ten Photographs by Brassaï.* (Photo by Keith Knight)

6

Limited-Edition Portfolios

The tradition of original photographic portfolios began in the mid-nineteenth century. In Europe in the 1840s, '50s, and '60s, albums on architecture, railroads, and similar topics were compiled by photographers such as Edouard-Denis Baldus, Charles Marville, the Bisson *frères,* Henri Le Secq, and Roger Fenton. In the United States, beginning in the 1860s, photographers of the American West such as William Henry Jackson, Timothy H. O'Sullivan, and A. J. Russell prepared portfolios commissioned by the railroad companies or sponsored by the U.S. government; their purpose was to acquaint citizens of the East with the natural wonders of the unsettled West and to attract pioneers to the frontier.

Nineteenth-century portfolios and albums were not considered works of art, as portfolios currently are, so unfortunately most were issued erratically and without careful records that would aid today's historians and collectors. Consequently, it is difficult to find such vintage issuances, much less afford them. There is, however, no lack of contemporary ones for you to consider: photographers and publishers offer many handsome limited-edition portfolios at reasonable prices. The marked increase in popularity of this particular form of presentation can be traced from the early 1970s, concurrent with the rising general interest in collecting photographic works.

Usually presented in a box and accompanied by a foreword, introduction, or similar text, a portfolio generally offers collectors a mini-retrospective of a photographer's career or a selection of images on a theme for which the individual is well known. In addition, several schools and workshops offer group portfolios featuring the selected work of teachers and students (see page 292). Since a portfolio can be personally published by the photographer, many young and lesser-known artists issue their work in this form.

Most portfolios are initially sold at a price lower than the sum total of the individual prints if they were to be purchased separately. This saving, plus the attractiveness of a "package," makes portfolios appealing to many collectors. Once purchased, portfolios can be split up for display, for single-print sales, or for the sake of joint owners.

There may or may not be restrictions on continued printing of the individual images in a portfolio. *The portfolios themselves, however, are limited in number.* Edition size ranges from as few as five to as many as 250. Some photographers and publishers, as in the case of the later Ansel Adams portfolios, promise that no further prints will be made from the negatives. Others restrict printing again from the negatives for several years. Because printing the quantity involved can be arduous, a photographer often makes portfolio prints with an assistant or hires someone to print them under his or her supervision, although some sturdy souls still make all their prints themselves. (When Brassaï undertook to print his 1973 portfolio for Witkin-Berley, Ltd., he required prolonged use of his apartment's small kitchen/darkroom; according to his wife, they had to dine out for months.)

Most portfolios state whether or not the prints are made by the photographer, and if not, who made them. As with individual prints, portfolio prints made by the photographer are usually more desirable from the collector's viewpoint. But portfolio prices do not seem to be as affected when the prints are made by another person as do single-print prices. As a collector, you should remember that galleries buy at wholesale price, usually 40 to 50 percent of the asking price, so if you wish to sell a portfolio you own, you will not receive the full retail value unless you sell to another collector. As you will see from the marked increases between prices at issuance and current values, many portfolios have been extremely good buys through the years — though such increases have occurred over a period of time, not overnight.

The following selection of portfolios, although by no means all-inclusive, is the most extensive available survey of contemporary portfolio publishing. The portfolios, listed alphabetically by the photographer or issuer, all contain original photographic prints, not gravure or other reproductions. Portfolios such as *The Mexican Portfolio* by Paul Strand, the *Stieglitz Memorial Portfolio,* and several portfolios

by Lucien Clergue are excluded here for this reason and are listed instead in the photographer's entry in chapter 5. Additional biographical data about most photographers listed in this chapter can be found by consulting appendix B and the index.

The information in this chapter was drawn from a variety of sources: personal inspection of many portfolios, gallery or publisher announcements, specifics supplied by the photographer, and so forth. In a few cases exact data was unobtainable. Information regarding introduction, foreword, or other text reflects title terminology used in the individual portfolio and is provided whenever possible. The format of the portfolio presentation-case, box, or folder is the determining factor for the listed order of image and mount dimensions: height precedes width; dimensions are in inches. Prints may be assumed to be silver prints if not otherwise noted, and they are believed made by the photographer if no other attribution is given. Data about the numbering of editions and about signatures, stamps, and other identification is also listed when known. "Current value" reflects market value as of spring 1979, based on dealer prices, auction prices, and the estimate of the authors.

Abbott, Berenice

Ten Photographs. Selected major images. Roslyn Heights, N.Y.: Witkin-Berley, 1976. Foreword by the photographer; introduction by Hilton Kramer. To 14×11 on 20×16 mounts, each signed. Edition: 50, plus 5 artist's proofs. Price at issuance: $2,750. Current value: $3,500.

Berenice Abbott's New York. New York: Parasol Press, 1978. 12 prints, to 14×11 on 18×14 mounts, each signed and numbered. Edition: 60. Price at issuance: $3,500. Current value: $3,500.

See also Atget, Eugène.

Adál (Adál Maldonado)

Evidence of Things Not Seen. Portraits of Duane Michals, André Kertész, Ralph Gibson, and other photographers. New York: published by the photographer, 1975. Introduction by Victor Hernandez Cruz. 10 prints, to 7½×6½ on 13½×10½ mounts, each signed. Edition: 10. Price at issuance: $750. Current value: $1,000.

Adams, Ansel

Parmelian Prints of the High Sierras. San Francisco: Jean Chambers Moore, 1927; text pages printed by Grabhorn Press. (The word *parmelian* was created by the publisher, who was wary of the salability of a portfolio of "photographic" prints.) 18 prints, about 6×8 on 10×12 Kodak Opaline paper, unmounted, each signed "A. E. Adams" (at that time the photographer used his middle name, Easton). Edition: 150 projected (never completed; number released unknown). Price at issuance: $50. Current value: up to $10,000.

Portfolio I. Landscapes, natural objects, and a portrait of Alfred Stieglitz, to whom the portfolio is dedicated. San Francisco: published by the photographer and Grabhorn Press, 1948. Foreword by the photographer. 12 prints, to 10×8 on 18×14 mounts, each signed. Edition: 75 (including 10 issued for E. Weyhe, New York City). Price at issuance: $100. Current value: up to $10,000.

Portfolio II. Landscapes from national parks and monuments; made on Guggenheim Fellowship grant. San Francisco: published by the photographer and Grabhorn Press, 1950. Foreword by the photographer. 15 prints, to 10×8 on 18×14 mounts, each signed. Edition: 100, plus 5 presentation copies. Price at issuance: $100. Current value: up to $10,000.

Portfolio III: Yosemite Valley. San Francisco: Sierra Club, 1960; text pages printed by Grabhorn Press. Foreword by the photographer. 16 prints, to 14×11 on 18×14 mounts, each signed. Edition: 250, plus 8 presentation copies. Price at issuance: $150. Current value: up to $10,000.

Portfolio IV: What Majestic Word. Nature studies. In memory of Russell Varian, 1898–1959; sponsored by the Varian Foundation, Palo Alto, Calif. San Francisco: Sierra Club, 1963. 15 prints, to 10×8 on 18×14 mounts, each signed. Edition: 100, plus 10 presentation copies. Price at issuance: $150. Current value: up to $10,000.

Portfolio V. Selected images. New York: Parasol Press, 1971. Foreword by Nancy Newhall. 10 prints, to 20×16 on 29×23 mounts, each signed. Edition: 100, plus 10 presentation copies lettered A-J. Price at issuance: $1,200. Current value: $12,000 and up.

Portfolio VI. Selected images. New York: Parasol Press, 1974. Foreword by Beaumont Newhall and Nancy Newhall. 10 prints, 20×16 on 29×23 mounts, each signed. Edition: 100, plus 10 presentation copies lettered A-J. Price at issuance: $3,500. Current value: $12,000 and up.

Portfolio VII. Selected images. New York: Parasol Press, 1976. Foreword by the photographer. 10 20×16 prints and 1 24×20 print, all on 29×23 mounts, each signed, plus 1 original 3½×4½ signed Polaroid print unique to each portfolio. Edition: 100, plus 15 presentation copies lettered A-O. Price at issuance: $10,000. Current value: $12,000 and up.

Alvarez Bravo, Manuel

Fifteen Photographs. Images of Mexico. New York: Double Elephant Press, 1975. Introduction by André Breton, translated by Richard Seaver. To 7½×9½ on 15×20 mounts, each signed. Edition: 75, plus 15 artist's proofs. Price at issuance: $2,500. Current value: $5,000.

Untitled. Images of Mexico. London: Acorn Editions, 1977. 15 prints, to 7½×9½ hinged and overmatted on 14×17 archival board, each signed on verso. Edition: 100. Price at issuance: $5,000. Current value: $5,000.

Andrews, Weston

Untitled. Fantasy poses of women in Victorian costume. New York: Neikrug Portfolios, 1977. 10 one-of-a-kind sepia-toned Polaroid prints, 5×4 in 10½×8 overmats. Edition: 10. Price at issuance: $1,600. Current value: $1,600.

Apeiron Workshops, Inc.

See Schools and workshops.

Arbus, Diane

Portfolio. A selection of her best-known images, 1962–1970. New York: published by the photographer, 1971; completed by her estate. Of the projected edition of 50, only a few were printed and signed by Arbus before her death in 1971. Subsequent prints were made by Neil Selkirk and signed by Doon Arbus (the photographer's daughter). 10 prints, to 14×14 on 20×16 photographic paper, unmounted, issued in a Lucite box of the same dimensions. Price at issuance: $1,500. Current value: $5,000.

Art Institute of Chicago, School of the

See Schools and workshops.

Atget, Eugène

Untitled. Selected images from the photographer's 30-year study of Paris and environs. New York: Berenice Abbott, 1956. Printed posthumously from the original plates by Berenice Abbott. 20 prints, 10×8 on 13×10 mounts; printed number on verso of each mount corresponds with title-sheet number. Edition: 100 (about 50 completed in 1956, the remainder in the early 1970s). Price at issuance: $150. Current value: up to $6,000.

Avedon, Richard

Avedon. Portraits of famous people; issued in conjunction with the 1970 Avedon exhibition at the Minneapolis Institute of Arts. New York: published by the photographer, 1970. 11 prints, 24×20, unmounted, each numbered and signed. Edition: 35. Price at issuance: $1,500. Current value: $20,000.

Avedon. Selected images of women and fashion in Paris, late 1940s and 1950s. New York: published by the photographer, 1978. Printed from the original negatives, under the photographer's supervision. 11 prints, 18×14, unmounted, each numbered and signed on the verso. Edition: 75, plus 10 artist's proofs. Price at issuance: $5,000. Current value: not established.

Baer, Morley

Portfolio I: Andalu. Images of Spain's southernmost province, 1957–1959. Monterey, Calif.: published by the photographer, 1976. 12 prints, 10×8 on 16×14 mounts, each signed. Edition: 50. Price at issuance: $1,500. Current value: $1,500.

Portfolio II: Garapata Rock. Images of the Monterey coast. Monterey, Calif.: published by the photographer, 1976. 15 prints, 10×8 on 16×14 mounts, each signed. Edition: 50. Price at issuance: $1,250. Current value: $1,250.

Baltz, Lewis

Tract Houses. Sausalito, Calif.: published by the photographer, 1972. 25 prints, 6×9 on 11×11 mounts, each signed on verso. Edition: 12. Price at issuance: $1,000. Current value: $3,000.

The New Industrial Parks near Irvine, California. Sausalito, Calif.: published by the photographer, 1974. 51 6×9 prints, each signed on verso; in 2 portfolios on 11×11 mounts, unmounted in the remainder. Edition: 21. Price at issuance: $2,500. Current value: $5,000.

Nevada. Landscapes, images of buildings and objects near Reno. New York: Castelli Graphics, 1978. 15 prints, 6⅛×9 in overmats to 15×18, each signed, numbered, and dated. Edition: 40, plus 6 artist's proofs and 2 exhibition sets. Price at issuance: first 5, $1,500; next 5, $2,000; next 10, $2,500; remainder undetermined.

Bayard, Hippolyte

Untitled. Selected images, 1840–1850. Paris: Société Française de Photographie, 1965. Printed posthumously by Claudine Sudre from the original waxed-paper negatives. 30 calotype prints, each signed on verso by Sudre and bearing the stamp of the Société Française de Photographie. Edition: not available. Price at issuance: $1,200. Current value: not available.

Bayer, Herbert

10 Fotomontagen, 1929–1936. Selected surrealistic montages. Munich: Galerie Klihm, 1969. Printed in U.S. under the photographer's supervision. To 16×10, unmounted, each signed, numbered, and dated. Edition: 40. Price at issuance: not available. Current value: $4,500.

10 Fotoplastiken, 1932–1936. Selected surreal images. Munich: Galerie Klihm, 1969. Printed in U.S. under the photographer's supervision. To 16×10, unmounted, each signed, numbered, and dated. Edition: 40. Price at issuance: not available. Current value: $4,500.

Becher, Bernhard
Becher, Hilla

Industrial Buildings. Munich: Schirmer Mosel, 1975; distributed by Sonnabend Gallery. 14 prints, 7⅔×10¼ on 10¼×12¾ mounts, each printed and signed by the photographers, with the publisher's stamp on each mount. Edition: 50, plus 5 artist's proofs. Price at issuance: $1,200. Current value: $1,500.

Benedict-Jones, Linda

Time Release. Self-portraits and interiors. Amsterdam: Galerie Fiolet, 1976. 15 prints, 9×6½ on 15¾×11¾

mounts and overmats, each signed. Edition: 10. Price at issuance: $900. Current value: $900.

Bernhard, Ruth

The Eternal Body, 1948–1970. Studies of women, mostly nudes. San Francisco: published by the photographer, 1976. Introduction by Wynn Bullock. 10 prints, 10×8 on 17×14 mounts, each signed. Edition: 15. Price at issuance: $1,500. Current value: $3,000.

The Gift of the Commonplace, 1935–1970. Images of ordinary objects. San Francisco: published by the photographer, 1976. Introduction by Wynn Bullock; essay by the photographer. 10 prints, 10×8 on 17×14 mounts, each signed. Edition: 15. Price at issuance: $1,500. Current value: $3,000.

Ruth Bernhard. *Luminous Body.* From *The Eternal Body, 1948–1970.* Silver print. (Courtesy the artist)

Blossfeldt, Karl

12 Fotografien. Plant forms. Cologne: Galerie Wilde, 1975. Introduction by Volker Kahmen. Printed posthumously for this edition from the original plates. 10×8 on 17×13 mounts. Edition: 50. Price at issuance: $1,500. Current value: $1,500.

Brady, Mathew B.

Mathew Brady's Great Americans. Portraits of Abraham Lincoln, Mary Todd Lincoln, Oliver Wendell Holmes, Nathaniel Hawthorne, and others. New York: Time-Life Books, 1975. Printed posthumously by the Time-Life Books Photography Laboratory from the original plates. 10 prints, to 3¼×2½ on 10¾×8¾ mounts, each numbered within the blind-stamped logo of the Meserve Collection. Edition: 2,500. Price at issuance: $150. Current value: $150.

The World of Phineas T. Barnum. Portraits of nineteenth-century circus celebrities. New York: Time-Life Books, 1976. Printed posthumously by the Time-Life Books Photography Laboratory from the original plates. 8 prints, to 3½×2¾ on 13½×10½ mounts, each numbered; each mount blind-stamped with the logo of the Meserve Collection. Edition: 5,000. Price at issuance: $250. Current value: $250.

Brassaï

Transmutations. Clichés-verres. Lacoste (Vaucluse), France: Galerie Les Contards, 1967. 12 prints, to 10×8 on 20×15 mounts, each signed. Edition: 100 (many badly discolored because of poor mounting material). Price at issuance: $100. Current value: $3,000.

A Portfolio of Ten Photographs by Brassaï. A selection of his best-known images, including *Bijou, Matisse and His Model, Picasso.* Roslyn Heights, N.Y.: Witkin-Berley, 1973. Introduction by A. D. Coleman; foreword by the photographer. To 14×11 on 20×16 mounts, signed only on title sheets. Edition: 50, plus 5 artist's proofs. Price at issuance: $950. Current value: $4,500.

Breitenbach, Josef

Seven Portraits. Washington, D.C.: Graphics International, 1976. Introduction by A. Hyatt Mayor. To 14×11 on 20×16 mounts, each signed. Edition: 25, plus 3 artist's proofs. Price at issuance: $1,200. Current value: $1,200.

Bruguière, Francis

Untitled. Cut-paper abstractions, surreal montages, multiple exposures, and still lifes, 1920s–1930s. New York: Witkin Gallery, 1977. Introduction by James L. Enyeart; foreword by Rosalinde Fuller. Printed posthumously by George A. Tice from the original negatives.

Karl Blossfeldt. *Papaver orientale,* ca. 1900–1928. Silver print. (Courtesy Galerie Wilde)

10 prints, 10×8 on 17×14 mounts. Edition: 15, plus 4 artist's proofs. Price at issuance: $1,500. Current value: $1,500.

Buechel, Eugene

Rosebud and Pine Ridge Photographs, 1922–1942. Images of the South Dakota Sioux Reservation. St. Francis, S. Dak.: Buechel Memorial Dakota Museum, 1975. Printed posthumously by David Wing from the original

Eugene Buechel. *Group of Six Girls,* November 1926. Silver print. (Courtesy David Wing)

negatives. 41 prints, to 6½×11 on 11×14 Brovira paper, unmounted. Edition: 12. Price at issuance: $2,000. Current value: $2,000.

Bullock, Wynn
Photographs, 1951-1973. Selected images. Monterey, Calif.: published by the photographer, 1973. Introduction by Ansel Adams. 12 prints, to 10×8 on 15×13¼ mounts, each signed and numbered. Edition: 25, plus 6 artist's proofs. Price at issuance: $1,500. Current value: $7,000.

Callahan, Harry
Landscapes, 1941-1971. New York: Light Gallery, 1972. 10 prints, 10×8 on 20×16 mounts, each signed. Edition: 25. Price at issuance: $200. Current value: $3,000.

See also Schools and workshops: Rhode Island School of Design.

Caponigro, Paul
Portfolio I. Landscapes and nature images. Redding, Conn.: published by the photographer, 1960. 12 prints, 10×8 on 17×14 mounts, each signed. Edition: 50. Price at issuance: $200. Current value: $3,000.

Portfolio II. Landscapes, 1957-1970. Redding, Conn.: published by the photographer, 1973. 8 prints, 9×7 to 12×10 on 18×15 mounts, each signed. Edition: 100. Price at issuance: $800 (50 offered pre-issuance at $300). Current value: $2,800.

Portfolio III: Stonehenge. Santa Fe, N.Mex.: published by the photographer, 1977. Introduction by the photographer. 12 prints, 14×11 on 21×17 mounts, each signed. Edition: 60, plus 7 artist's proofs. Price at issuance: $3,000. Current value: $4,500.

See also Schools and workshops: Apeiron Workshops, Inc.

Center for Photographic Studies (Louisville, Ky.)
See Schools and workshops.

Clark, Larry
Teen Lust. Images of teenagers engaged in sexual activity. Tulsa: published by the photographer, 1974. Introduction by the photographer. 7 prints, to 9¼×6¼ on 14×11 photographic paper, each signed. Edition: 5. Price at issuance: $1,000. Current value: $1,000.

Tulsa. Images from the book of the same name. New York: Lustrum Press, 1975. Introductory statement by the photographer. 10 prints, to 8⅜×5½ on 19½×14½

mounts, each signed. Edition: 50. Price at issuance: $1,500. Current value: $1,500.

Clift, William
Old City Hall, Boston. Boston: published by the photographer, 1971. Introduction by Sinclair Hitchings. 108 prints, 4×5 on 12×14 photographic paper, unmounted. Edition: 12. Price at issuance: $500. Current value: $1,000.

New Mexico. Santa Fe, N.Mex.: published by the photographer, 1977. Introduction by Eliot Porter. 8 prints, to 9×12 on 15×18 mounts, each signed and numbered. Edition: 100. Price at issuance: $285. Current value: $600.

Coburn, Alvin Langdon
A Limited Edition Portfolio. Selected images. Rochester, N.Y.: Light Impressions and International Museum of Photography at George Eastman House, 1977. Introduction by William Jenkins. 10 prints, to 12×10 in 17×14 overmats. Printed posthumously by Michaela Murphy from the original negatives. Edition: 200. Price at issuance: $250. Current value: $250.

Cornfield, Jim
Fat Tuesday. Images of costumed New Orleans residents and visitors to Mardi Gras, 1975. Los Angeles: William Dailey, 1976. 12 prints, to 10×7 on 14×11 mounts, each signed. Edition: 25. Price at issuance: $250. Current value: $250.

Dater, Judy
Ten Photographs. Portraits of women. Roslyn Heights, N.Y.: Witkin-Berley, 1973. Introduction by Jack Welpott. To 9×7 on 20×16 mounts, each signed. Edition: 25, plus 7 artist's proofs. Price at issuance: $950. Current value: $1,200.

Davenport, Alma
Totems. Selected composite and collaged images. Providence, R.I.: published by the photographer, 1978. Introduction by the photographer. Polaroid color prints, 10×8 in 17×14 overmats, each signed. Portfolios numbered 1-49, 21 prints each; 50-100, 6 prints each. Edition: 100. Price at issuance: $950 (portfolios 1-49); $375 (portfolios 50-100). Current value: $950, $375, respectively.

Davis, Philip
The Dexter Portfolio. Images of Dexter, Mich., a small farming community. Dexter: published by the photographer, 1972. Signed introductory statement by the photographer. 10 prints, 9×7 on 15½×14 mounts. Edition: 50. Price at issuance: $200. Current value: $300.

DeCarava, Roy

Untitled. Images, 1940s–1960s, of New York City, Harlem, blacks. New York: published by the photographer, 1977. 12 prints, to 14×11 on 20×16 mounts, each signed. Edition: 25. Price at issuance: $3,000. Current value: $3,000.

de Lory, Peter

Landscapes One, 1971–1976. Views of Massachusetts and the West. Sun Valley, Idaho: published by the photographer, 1978. Introduction by Alex Sweetman. 10 prints, including 1 split-toned and 1 hand-colored, to 10×14½ in 16×20 overmats, each signed, dated, titled, and numbered. Edition: 15, plus 1 artist's proof. Price at issuance: $500. Current value: $750.

de Meyer, Adolf (Gayne)

L'Après-midi d'un faune. Images of Nijinsky's first choreographed masterpiece, 1912. New York: Eakins Press Foundation, and London: Dance Books, 1978. Commentaries by Sergei Diaghilev, Auguste Rodin, and Jacques-Emile Blanche. Printed posthumously by Richard Benson from copy negatives. 33 palladium prints, to 10×8 mounted in 18×14 folders, each signed and numbered by Benson. Edition: 250. Price at issuance: $750. Current value: $950.

Diniz, Pepe

Untitled. Portraits of Brassaï, Paul Strand, Tennessee Williams, and others. New York: Neikrug Portfolios, 1977. Introduction by Jacob Deschin. 15 prints, to 10×8 on 14×11 mounts, each signed. Edition: 25, plus 3 artist's proofs. Price at issuance: $575. Current value: $575.

Disfarmer, Mike

The Heber Springs Portraits. Little Rock, Ark.: Peter A. Miller, 1977. Printed posthumously by Peter A. Miller from the original negatives. 10 prints, 10×7 in 18×14 overmats, each signed and numbered by Miller. Edition: 50, plus 5 artist's proofs. Price at issuance: $500. Current value: $500.

Drtikol, Frantisek

Untitled. Selected images. Rochester, N.Y.: International Museum of Photography at George Eastman House, 1975. Printed posthumously by Gerry Dartt from the original negatives. 9 prints, 10⅞×8½ in 14⅝×17⅞ overmats. Edition: 100. Price at issuance: $175. Current value: $175.

Edgerton, Harold

Seeing the Unseen. Strobe-lit stopped-action images of high-speed motion. Cambridge, Mass.: published by the photographer, 1977. Introduction by Geoffrey W. Holt. Black-and-white prints by Gus Kayafas; dye transfer color prints by Boris Color Lab, Boston, under supervision of the photographer. 7 black and whites and 5 dye transfers, all 14×11 on 20×16 mounts, signed, dated, and numbered by the photographer. Edition: 60, plus 7 artist's proofs. Price at issuance: $1,950. Current value: $2,400.

Eggleston, William

14 Pictures. Selected images. Published privately, 1974; distributed by Graphics International, Washington, D.C. Dye transfer color prints by K&S Color Lab, Chicago. To 13×19 on 16×20 photographic paper, unmounted, each signed, stamped, and numbered by the photographer. Edition: 15, plus 1 *hors commerce.* Price at issuance: $2,000. Current value: not established.

Election Eve. New York: Caldecot Chubb, 1977. Preface by Lloyd Fonveille. Printed by Dimension Color Lab, New York City. 100 Type C color prints, to 10×15 on 16×22 photographic paper, unmounted, bound in two volumes, each volume signed by the photographer. Edition: 5, plus 2 artist's proofs. Price at issuance: $15,000. Current value: $15,000. (See color plate 5.)

Erwitt, Elliott

Untitled. Selected best-known images, 1948–1968. Roslyn Heights, N.Y.: Witkin-Berley, 1974. Introduction by Peter C. Bunnell. 10 prints, to 13×9 on 20×16 mounts, each signed. Edition: 25, plus 5 artist's proofs. Price at issuance: $1,150. Current value: $2,000.

15 Photographs. Selected images. Geneva: Acorn Editions, 1977. To 8×10 in 14×17 overmats, each signed and numbered. Edition: 100. Price at issuance: $3,750. Current value: $3,750.

Evans, Frederick H.

F. H. Evans, 1853–1943: Ten Photographs. Landscapes and images of cathedrals. New York: Witkin Gallery, 1971. Preface by George A. Tice; introduction by Evan Evans (the photographer's son); both signed by Tice and Evans, respectively. Printed by Tice from the original glass slides (he made negatives from these positives in order to print the edition). To 9¼×6½ on 18×14 mounts; in portfolios numbered 1–10 on platinum paper, in portfolios 11–60 on silver paper; special label designed in the style of F. H. Evans's period bookplate affixed to the back of each mount lists print number and portfolio number. Edition: 60, plus 5 artist's proofs (platinum). Case stamped in gold on the platinum portfolios, in silver on the silver ones. Price at issuance: $1,200 (platinum); $600 (silver). Current value: $2,500, $1,200, respectively.

Evans, Walker

Untitled. Selected images. New Haven, Conn.: Ives-Sillman, 1971. Introduction by Robert Penn Warren; essay by Walker Evans. Printed by Thomas A. Brown from the original negatives, under the photographer's supervision. 14 prints, to 9½ × 7½ on 18 × 14¾ mounts, each signed. Edition: 100. Price at issuance: $1,200. Current value: $7,000.

Selected Photographs. New York: Double Elephant Press, 1974. Introduction by Lionel Trilling. Printed by Richard Benson, John Deeks, and Lee Friedlander from the original negatives, under the photographer's supervision. 15 prints, to 15½ × 12 on 19¾ × 15 mounts, each signed. Edition: 75, plus 15 artist's proofs. Price at issuance: $3,500. Current value: $6,000.

I. Selected images, 1929–1971 (the first of three projected portfolios). New Haven, Conn.: published by the photographer's estate, with Washington, D.C.: Graphics International, 1977. Printed posthumously by Thomas A. Brown and Baldwin Lee. 15 prints, to 10 × 8 on 20 × 16 mounts; each print embossed in the margin with the estate's seal. Edition: 75, plus 15 *hors commerce.* Price at issuance: $4,500. Current value: $4,500.

Feininger, Andreas

Shells/Forms of Nature/Trees/New York. 4 portfolios, each published by the photographer, with New York: International Center of Photography, 1976. Each portfolio has the same introduction by Bhupendra Karia. Each printed by Raffi Atamian from the original negatives, under the photographer's supervision. 12 prints each, to 12½ × 9½ on 17 × 14 mounts, each signed. Edition: 100 of each. Price at issuance: $1,500 each. Current value: $1,750 each.

Freund, Gisèle

Untitled. Portraits of André Gide, Virginia Woolf, Colette, Joyce, Malraux, and others. Washington, D.C.: Graphics International, 1977. 10 dye transfer color prints, to 9½ × 6½ on 20 × 16 mounts, each signed. Edition: 30, plus 6 *hors commerce.* Price at issuance: $4,000. Current value: $4,000.

Friedlander, Lee

Photographs and Etchings. London: Petersburg Press, 1969. 16 loose sheets, 18 × 30, each containing a print by the photographer, to 7 × 10½ on 18 × 30 mounts, side by side with an etching by Jim Dine, each sheet numbered and signed by both artists. Edition: 75, plus 15 artist's proofs. Price at issuance: $2,000. Current value: $4,500.

Fifteen Photographs. Street scenes, 1962–1972. New York: Double Elephant Press, 1973. Introduction by Walker Evans. To 7¼ × 11 on 15½ × 20 mounts, each signed. Edition: 75, plus 15 artist's proofs. Price at issuance: $1,875. Current value: $4,000.

Photographs of Flowers. Tampa: Graphicstudio of the University of South Florida, and New City, N.Y.: Haywire Press, 1975. 15 prints, to 8½ × 13 on 16 × 20 mounts, each signed. Edition: 70, plus 20 (for the patrons of the project) numbered I–XX, and 10 artist's proofs. Price at issuance: $2,000. Current value: $4,000.

Friedman, Benno

White Sands. Landscapes of White Sands, N.Mex. New York: Light Gallery, 1976. 10 monoprints, 16 × 20, unmounted, each signed. Edition: 10, plus 3 artist's proofs. Price at issuance: $2,500. Current value: $3,000.

Lee Friedlander and Jim Dine. Untitled, 1969. From *Photographs and Etchings.* Silver print; etching. (Courtesy Petersburg Press)

Gibson, Ralph

Days at Sea. New York: Lustrum Press, 1975. Introductory statement by the photographer. 10 prints, 8¾×5½ on 19½×14 mounts, each signed. Edition: 50. Price at issuance: $1,000. Current value: $1,750.

See also Schools and workshops: Apeiron Workshops, Inc.

Giles, William B.

Mother of Pearls. Landscapes and nature studies. Santa Cruz, Calif.: published by the photographer, 1977. Introduction by Paul Caponigro. 18 contact prints, 5×4 in 14×11 overmats, each signed and numbered. Edition: 100, plus 2 artist's proofs. Price at issuance: $750. Current value: $1,250.

Gossage, John R.

Gardens. Washington, D.C.: Hollow Press and Castelli Graphics, 1978. Introductory text (quotations) selected by Walter Hopps. 24 prints, to 7⅜×10¾ on 13½×16½ photographic paper, bound as a book, last page signed and numbered. Edition: 25, plus 3 artist's proofs and 6 exhibition sets. Price at issuance: $2,900. Current value: $2,900.

Grosz, George

Erste Landung, New York, 1932. First impressions of New York City. New York: Kimmel/Cohn Gallery, 1977. Title page with poem by the photographer. Printed posthumously by Igor Bakht from the original negatives. 10 prints, 5⅛×7⅜ on 14×17 mounts, each numbered within the Grosz estate blind stamp, and stamped on verso with the Grosz estate signature facsimile. Edition: 75. Price at issuance: $1,200. Current value: $1,500.

George Grosz. *Over the Rail,* 1932. Silver print. (Courtesy Kimmel/Cohn Photography Arts)

Hare, David

Pueblo Indians of New Mexico as They Are Today. Selected portraits. New York: published by the photographer, with the Museum of Natural History, 1941. Introduction by Clark Wissler. 20 dye transfer color prints, to 12×9½ on 17½×13⅜ mounts. Edition: 30. Price at issuance: $300. Current value: $3,000.

Hausmann, Raoul

Untitled. Selected images, primarily from the early 1930s. Nice, France: Roger Vulliez, 1978. Introduction by the photographer. Printed posthumously by Vulliez from the original negatives. 12 prints, to 10×8 on 20×16 mounts, each numbered. Edition: 60. Price at issuance: $1,500. Current value: $1,500.

Henri, Florence

Portfolio mit 12 Fotografien. Still-life compositions and portraits, 1928–1932. Cologne: Galerie Wilde, 1974. In-

Florence Henri. *Portrait,* 1928. Silver print. (Courtesy Galerie Wilde)

troduction by Klaus-Jürgen Sembach. 10×7 on 17×13 mounts, each signed. Edition: 50, plus 8 numbered I–VIII. Price at issuance: $760. Current value: $1,900.

Hine, Lewis Wickes

Two untitled portfolios. Images of Ellis Island immigrants. Each marked "Lewis Hine 1874-1940." New York: Photo League, 1942. Introduction by Marynn Older. Printed posthumously by the Lewis Hine Memorial Collection Committee from the original negatives. 4 prints each, to 4½×6½ on 12×10 mounts. Edition: 30 of each. Price at issuance: $25 each. Current value: $500 each.

Portfolio 1. Selected images. Rochester, N.Y.: International Museum of Photography at the George Eastman House, 1974. Printed posthumously by Gerry Dartt from the original negatives. 10 prints, 10×8 in 14×11 overmats. Edition: 50. Price at issuance: $140. Current value: $200.

Hockney, David

Twenty Photographic Pictures. Selected images. New York and Paris: Sonnabend Editions, 1976. Printed by Lucien Treillard. Type C color prints, 9¼×7 on 15½×14½ mounts, each signed. Edition: 80, plus 20 numbered I–XX. Price at issuance: $2,000. Current value: $3,000.

David Hockney. *Pink Hose,* 1976. Type C color print. (Courtesy Sonnabend Gallery)

Hyde, Philip

Northern Yosemite and the Ritter Country. San Francisco: published by the photographer, 1951. Introduction by the photographer. 10 prints, 7×5 and 10×8 on 17×14 mounts. Edition: 25. Price at issuance: $65. Current value: $500.

Ionesco, Irina

Nocturnes. New York: Lustrum Press, 1975. Introductory statement by the photographer. 10 prints, 11¾×8¼ on 19½×14½ mounts, each signed. Edition: 25. Price at issuance: $1,250. Current value: $1,250.

Jacobi, Lotte

Portfolio I. Portraits, 1920–1930s. Deering, N.H.: published by the photographer, 1978. Introduction by Otto Steinert. Printed by Carlos Richardson under the photographer's supervision. 10 prints, to 10×8 on 17×14 mounts, each signed and numbered. Edition: 25, plus 5 artist's proofs. Price at issuance: $1,500. Current value: $2,000.

Josephson, Kenneth

Untitled. Selected images. Louisville, Ky.: Center for Photographic Studies, 1975. Foreword by Alex Sweetman. 10 prints, to 5¾×9 on 11×14 mounts, each signed. Edition: 25, plus 6 artist's proofs. Price at issuance: $400. Current value: $500.

See also Schools and workshops: Art Institute of Chicago, School of the.

Marcia Keegan. *Florence Ashton Holmes.* From *The Vaudevillians,* 1975. Silver print. (Courtesy Houghton Management)

Keegan, Marcia

The Vaudevillians. Studies of old vaudevillians living in the Times Square area. New York: Houghton Management, 1975. Introduction by the photographer. 12 prints, to 9½×6½ on 17×14 mounts, each signed. Edition: 35. Price at issuance: $450. Current value: $450.

Kepes, Gyorgy

Untitled. Photograms, and abstract compositions and portraits. Boston: Vision Gallery and Mary and Tom House, 1977. Introduction by Philip Hofer. Printed by Chris Enos from the original negatives, under the photographer's supervision. 12 prints, to 10×8 on 17×14 mounts, each signed and numbered by the photographer. Edition: 20, plus 5 artist's proofs. Price at issuance: $2,000. Current value: $2,000.

Kertész, André

Volume I. Selected images, 1913–1929. (See *Volume II* data.)

Volume II. Selected images, 1930–1972. Both portfolios New York: Light Gallery, 1973. 10 prints each, 10×8 on 18×14 mounts, each signed. Edition: 50 of each. Price at issuance: $1,800 each, $3,000 for both. Current value: $5,000 each, $9,000 for both.

See also Women's Campaign Fund.

Killip, Chris

Isle of Man. Portraits and landscapes of the Irish Sea island. Roslyn Heights, N.Y.: Witkin-Berley, 1973. Introduction by Nigel Kneale. 12 prints, to 7½×6 on 14×11 mounts, each signed. Edition: 25, plus 5 artist's proofs. Price at issuance: $350. Current value: $750.

Chris Killip. *St. Luke's Church, Baldwin,* 1973. Silver print. (Courtesy Witkin-Berley, Ltd.)

Klein, William

New York 54/55. Selected images from the book *New York.* Paris: Atelier J. M. Bustamante / Bernard Saint-Genès, 1978. Introduction by Alain Jouffroy. 12 prints, to 10×12 on 16×20 mounts, each signed and numbered. Printed by J. M. Bustamante from the original negatives, under the photographer's supervision. Edition: 50, plus 10 artist's proofs. Price at issuance: $2,400. Current value: $2,400.

Krause, George

Saints and Martyrs. Images of church statues. Philadelphia: Photopia, 1976. Introduction by Carole Kismaric. 10 prints, to 7×5 on 14×11 mounts, each signed. Edition: 30. Price at issuance: $1,100. Current value: $1,500.

Krims, Leslie

The Only Photographs in the World Ever to Cause a Kidnapping Portfolio. Female nudes. New York: Light Gallery, 1971. Includes 5 facsimile pages of actual newspaper accounts explaining the facts behind the title. 6 prints, 7×5 on 18×14 mounts, each signed. Edition: 25. Price at issuance: $800. Current value: $1,000.

Kumler, Kipton

A Portfolio of Plants. Lexington, Mass.: published by the photographer, 1977. Introduction by Hilton Kramer. 10 platinum and palladium prints, 14×11 on 22×17 artist's drawing paper, bound. Edition: 50, plus 5 *hors commerce.* Price at issuance: $2,000. Current value: $2,000.

Lartigue, Jacques Henri

Untitled. Selected images, 1905–1929, including the famous *Cousin "Bichonade" in Flight* and *Zissou in His Tire Boat.* Roslyn Heights, N.Y.: Witkin-Berley, 1972. Foreword by the photographer. Introduction by Anaïs Nin. Printed by Jean Yves du Barre from the original negatives, under the photographer's supervision. 10 sepia-toned prints, to 9½×6 on 15×13 mounts. Portfolios numbered 1–10, each print signed; 11–50, title sheet only signed. Edition: 50, plus 5 artist's proofs. Price at issuance: $950. Current value: $4,000.

The Jacques-Henri Lartigue Portfolio. Selected images, 1903–1916. New York: Time-Life Books, 1977. Printed by Time-Life Books Photography Laboratory from the original negatives, under the photographer's supervision. 10 prints, to 8½×7½ mounted in 16×13 folders, each numbered, plus one color gravure from an autochrome; title page signed by the photographer. Edition: 7,500. Price at issuance: $500. Current value: $500.

Lav, Brian

Portfolio One. Selected images. Garwood, N.J.: published by the photographer, 1978. Introduction by George A. Tice. 8 prints, to 11½×13½ on 15×18 mounts, each signed and numbered. Edition: 35, plus 4 artist's proofs. Price at issuance: $525. Current value: $650.

Lennard, Erica

Desirée. New York: Lustrum Press, 1975. Introductory statement by the photographer. 10 prints, to 8⅜×5⅝ on 19½×14½ mounts, each signed. Edition: 50. Price at issuance: $1,000. Current value: $1,000.

Liebling, Jerome

Untitled. Selected images, 1949–1974, from the photographer's photographic essays, including slaughterhouse scenes and Georgia Governor George Wallace. Amherst, Mass.: published by the photographer, 1976. Introduction by Alan Trachtenberg. 10 prints, to 12×9 on 16×10 mounts, each signed. Edition: 25. Price at issuance: $950. Current value: $1,950.

Los Angeles Center for Photographic Studies

See Schools and workshops.

Magritte, René

La Fidelité des Images. Images of the artist and his friends (some of which were studies for his surrealist paintings). Brussels and Hamburg: Sonnabend Editions and Lebeer Hossmann, 1976. Printed posthumously from the original negatives. 16 prints, to 4½×3¼ on 15×12¼ mounts, each print signed, numbered, and authenticated by Georgette Magritte (the photographer's widow). Edition: 100, plus 10 *hors commerce* numbered I–X. Price at issuance: $1,800. Current value: $1,800.

René Magritte. *La Descente de la Courtille,* 1928. Silver print. (Courtesy Sonnabend Gallery)

Maldonado, Adál

See Adál.

Marsh, Reginald

Photographs of New York. Washington, D.C.: Middendorf Gallery and Jem Hom, with the estate of the photographer, 1977. Introduction by Norman Sasowsky. Printed posthumously by Ron Stark from the original negatives. 50 prints, to 7¼×5¹/₁₆ on 10×8 Portralure paper, each bearing the estate stamp. Edition: 25, plus 4 artist's proofs. Price at issuance: $6,500. Current value: $6,500.

Mather, Margrethe

See chapter 5 entry.

Meatyard, Ralph Eugene

Portfolio Three. Louisville, Ky.: Center for Photographic Studies, 1974 (third in the series published by the center). Introduction by Van Deren Coke; comment by Conrad J. Pressma. Printed posthumously at the workshop from the original negatives, under the supervision of Madelyn Meatyard (the photographer's widow). 10 prints, to 7×6½ on 15×12 mounts, each stamped with a description on verso of mount. Edition: 100, plus 30 artist's proofs. Price at issuance: $125. Current value: $500.

See also Schools and workshops: Center for Photographic Studies.

Méndez Caratini, Héctor M.

Petroglifos De Boriguen. Images of prehistoric rock engravings throughout Puerto Rico. San Juan: published by the photographer, 1978. Introduction by the photographer. 20 prints, to 7½×9 on 18×14 mounts, each signed, numbered, and dated. Edition: 20. Price at issuance: $600. Current value: $600.

Meyerowitz, Joel

The Cape. Images of Cape Cod, Mass. New York: published by the photographer, 1977. Introductory text excerpted from Henry James's *American Notes.* 15 color contact prints, to 10×8 on 15×13 mounts, each signed. Edition: 25, plus 10 artist's proofs. Price at issuance: $1,500. Current value: $2,200.

Michals, Duane

Untitled. In the words of the photographer:

These will be unique because they will be one-of-a-kind documents. Each one will be put together with a different selection of photographs and the text will vary as my observations change. No two will be alike. These are not portfolios in any sense. Portfolios always seem to me like loaves of bread. I've always been troubled by all those similar, impersonal, perfect prints. I longed for the artist's thumbprint.

New York: published by the photographer, 1972–. Printed by the photographer with a private printer. Each 15×12 album, designed so that individual prints may be removed for framing and easily returned without damage, contains a single sequence of 6 or 8 prints. All notes are handwritten by the photographer. Edition: 25 projected (10 completed as of 1978). Price at issuance: $1,000. Current value: $3,000.

10 Fotografien. Portraits of Tennessee Williams, Andy Warhol, René Magritte, and others. Cologne: Galerie Wilde, 1975. Introduction by Wulf Herzogenrath. To 7×4½ on 10×8 photographic paper in 17×12 overmats, each signed. Edition: 30, plus 5 artist's proofs. Price at issuance: $1,800. Current value: $1,800.

See also Schools and workshops: Apeiron Workshops, Inc.; Women's Campaign Fund.

Minick, Roger

Delta Portfolio. Selected images from the book *Delta West: The Land and People of the Sacramento–San Joaquin Delta.* Albany, Calif.: published by the photographer, 1976. 12 prints, to 10×8 on 16×13 mounts, each signed. Edition: 100. Price at issuance: $750. Current value: $1,000.

The Ozark Portfolio. Regional studies of people and landscapes. Albany, Calif.: published by the photographer, 1976. 12 prints, to 10×8 on 16×13 mounts, each signed. Edition: 100. Price at issuance: $750. Current value: $1,000.

Model, Lisette

Twelve Photographs. Selected images, including *Singer at Metropole Cafe, Woman at Coney Island, Famous Gambler.* Washington, D.C.: Graphics International, 1977. Introduction by Berenice Abbott. Printed by Richard Benson and Gerd Sander from the original negatives, under the photographer's supervision. 19¼×14⅞, unmounted, each numbered and signed by the photographer on verso. Edition: 75, plus 15 artist's proofs numbered I–XV. Price at issuance: $2,400. Current value: $3,000.

Morath, Inge

Untitled. Selected images, including portraits. New York: Neikrug Portfolios, 1977. Introduction by Arthur Miller. 15 prints, to 14×11 in 16×20 overmats, each signed. Edition: 50, plus 3 artist's proofs. Price at issuance: $850. Current value: $850.

See also Women's Campaign Fund.

Morgan, Barbara

Dance Portfolio. Images of Martha Graham, Doris Humphrey, José Limón, and others. Scarsdale, N.Y.:

published by the photographer, 1977. Essays by Clive Barnes, Peter C. Bunnell, and the photographer. 10 prints, to 14×11 on 20×16 mounts, each signed and numbered. Edition: 50, plus 10 artist's proofs. Price at issuance: $1,800. Current value: $3,000.

See also Women's Campaign Fund.

Mucha, Alphonse Marie

Settings and Models: A Suite of Ten Photographs. London: Academy Editions, and Washington, D.C.: Graphics International, 1975. Selected and introduced by Graham Ovenden. Printed posthumously by Howard Gray and Richard Benson from the original plates. To 7⅛×5⅛ on 15×12½ mounts, each numbered and bearing the estate stamp on mount. Edition: 75 numbered 1–75; 75 numbered I–LXXV, plus 25 *hors commerce.* Price at issuance: $2,000. Current value: $2,000. (Illustrated on next page.)

Muray, Nickolas

Untitled. Selected portraits. Rochester, N.Y.: International Museum of Photography at George Eastman House, and New York: Prakapas Gallery, 1978. Introduction by Robert Sobieszek. Printed posthumously by Michaela Murphy from the original negatives. 12 prints,

Lisette Model. *Blind Man, Paris,* 1937. Silver print. (Courtesy Graphics International, Ltd. Copyright by Lisette Model)

to 10×8 in 17×14 overmats, each initialed by Murphy. Edition: 100. Price at issuance: $375. Current value: $375.

Alphonse Marie Mucha. Untitled. From *Settings and Models,* 1975. Silver print. (Courtesy Graphics International, Ltd.)

Muybridge, Eadweard

Yosemite Photographs, 1872. Chicago: Chicago Albumen Works, and Yosemite National Park, Calif.: Yosemite Natural History Association, 1977. Introductory essay by Robert Bartlett Haas; "A Personal, Historical and Technical Note on Albumen Printing" by Joel Snyder. Printed posthumously by Doug Munson and Charles B. Reynolds from copy negatives. 10 gold-toned albumen prints, to 17×21½ on 24½×29½ mounts, each embossed in lower right corner with title, number, the photographer's name, and the copublishers' names. Edition: 300, plus 4 *hors commerce.* Price at issuance: $1,250. Current value: $1,250.

Nadar

Portfolio No. 1. Portraits, 1854–1860. Lacoste: Claudine Sudre, 1978. Introduction by Philippe Neagu. Preface by André Jammes. Printed posthumously by Claudine Sudre from the original collodion negatives. 10 silver prints, on 20×16 mounts. Edition: 50. Price at issuance: $4,000. Current value: $4,000.

Narahara, Ikko

Seven From Ikko. Selected images from the book *Where Time Has Vanished.* Tokyo: UNAC TOKYO, 1977. Introduction by Shuzo Takiguchi. 7 prints, to 11½×15½ sandwiched in 14½×19½ paper, each signed; 1 print, to 2½×3¾, repeated on the cover (this image done as a daguerreotype in deluxe portfolios). Edition: 30 regular, 7 deluxe, plus 5 artist's proofs. Price at issuance: $1,200 (regular). Current value: $1,200 (regular).

Nash, Paul

A Private World. Landscapes, nature studies, other selected images. London: Fischer Fine Art, with Paul Nash Trustees and Tate Gallery Publications Department, 1978. Introduction by John Piper; notes by Clare Colvin. Printed posthumously by David Lambert from the original negatives. 25 prints, to 8¾×11⁹/₁₆ on 16¾×14⅛ mounts, each blind-stamped with the mark of the Paul Nash Trustees and the Tate Gallery Archives Department. Edition: 45, plus 6 artist's proofs. Price at issuance: $500. Current value: $500.

Newman, Arnold

Ten Portraits. Including George Grosz, Max Ernst, Mondrian, Braque, and Picasso. New York: Light Gallery, 1972. To 14×11 on 18×14 mounts, each signed. Edition: 25. Price at issuance: $1,250. Current value: $3,000.

Owens, Bill

Untitled. Selected images from his books *Suburbia, Our Kind of People,* and *Working: I Do It for the Money.* San Francisco: Bill Owens and John Berggruen Gallery, 1977. Introduction, technical page, and captioned interleaves by the photographer. 8 prints, to 6½×8½ on 11×14 mounts. Edition: 25. Price at issuance: $750. Current value: $750.

Parker, Olivia

Ephemera. Split-toned still lifes. Boston: published by the photographer, 1977. Introduction by Gyorgy Kepes. 10 prints, to 7×5 on 15½×12 mounts. Edition: 25, plus 3 artist's proofs. Price at issuance: $600. Current value: $600.

Pearson, James

Signs. City scenes of frayed posters and billboards. New York: published by the photographer, 1975. Introduction by George A. Tice. 10 prints, to 6½×4½ on 14×11 mounts, signed on the introductory page. Edition: 50. Price at issuance: $150. Current value: $150.

Peterhans, Walter

Walter Peterhans: Photographs. Still-life compositions. Washington, D.C.: Sander Gallery. Introduction by Klaus-Jürgen Sembach. Printed by Gerd Sander from the original negatives. 10 prints, to 15×12 in 22×18 over-mats, each stamped, dated, and numbered on verso. Edition: 35, plus 10 artist's proofs. Price at issuance: $1,250. Current value: $2,000.

Pietrodangelo, Donato

The Maine Series. Landscapes and interiors along coastal Maine. Tallahassee, Fla.: published by the photographer, 1978. Introductory statement by the photographer. 6 Type C color prints, to 11×11 on 20×16 photographic paper, each signed. Edition: 25, plus 2 artist's proofs. Price at issuance: $400. Current value: $425

Pildas, Ave

Bijou. Images of movie-theater box offices. Los Angeles: published by the photographer, 1975. 12 prints, to 6⅛×4⅛ on 10×8 photographic paper, unmounted, each signed. Edition: 24, plus 2 artist's proofs. Price at issuance: $50. Current value: $400.

Porter, Eliot

Portfolio I: The Seasons. Nature studies. San Francisco: Sierra Club, 1964. Introduction by the photographer. 12 dye transfer color prints, 10×8 on 20×15 mounts, signed on the colophon only. Edition: 105. Price at issuance: $225. Current value: $1,600.

Portfolio II: Iceland. Santa Fe, N.Mex.: published by the photographer, 1975. Introduction by the photographer. 12 dye transfer color prints, 10×8 on 20×15 mounts, signed on the colophon only. Edition: 100, plus 10 artist's proofs. Price at issuance: $1,000. Current value: $1,000.

Ray-Jones, Tony

Untitled. Scenes of English life. London: Photographic Collections, 1975. Introduction by Peter Turner. Printed posthumously from the original negatives, under Turner's supervision. 15 prints, to 8×5¼ on 18×14 mounts. Edition: 125, plus 12 artist's proofs. Price at issuance: $1,500. Current value: $1,500.

See also Schools and workshops: Apeiron Workshops, Inc.

Raymond, Lilo

Still Life. New York: Helios Gallery, 1976. Introduction by Cecil Beaton. 6 prints, to 14×11 on 20×16 mounts, each signed. Edition: 15. Price at issuance: $550. Current value: $750.

Renger-Patzsch, Albert

Untitled. Images of glass objects, 1930s. Cologne: Galerie Wilde, 1977. Printed posthumously from the original negatives. 10 prints, 8×10 on 12¾×17 mounts, numbered, dated, and stamped "Galerie Wilde, Köln" on verso. Edition: 30. Price at issuance: $1,110. Current value: $1,110.

Renner, Eric

Untitled. Selected pinhole-camera images. New York: Carl Solway Gallery, 1975. 12 prints, to 9×28½ on 32×40 mounts, each signed. Edition: 12. Price at issuance: $600. Current value: $600.

Rhode Island School of Design (RISD)

See Schools and workshops.

Riss, Murray

Untitled. Selected images. Louisville, Ky.: Center for Photographic Studies, 1975 (fourth in the series published by the center). Introduction by William E. Parker. 10 prints, to 8¼×6½ on 15×12 mounts, each signed. Edition: 35, plus 6 artist's proofs. Price at issuance: $300. Current value: $375.

Robinson, Henry Peach

Henry Peach Robinson, 1830–1901. Selected composite images, plus 9 single images from negatives used to make the composites. London: Photographic Collections, with the Royal Photographic Society, 1976. Introduction and notes by Margaret Harker; essay by Ian Jeffrey. Printed posthumously by Howard Grey from the original plates. 13 prints, to 40×15 on 46×30 mounts, plus 1 collotype from a pencil sketch by the photographer. Edition: 45, plus 6 artist's proofs. Price at issuance: $3,000. Current value: $6,000.

Lilo Raymond. *Onion Flower,* 1974. Silver print. (Courtesy the artist and Helios Gallery)

Rochester Institute of Technology (RIT)
See Schools and workshops.

Rohde, Werner
Untitled. Female portraits, images of mannequins, and a self-portrait. Cologne: Galerie Wilde, 1977. Biographical text and citation by Paul Citroën. 12 prints; in regular portfolios to 11×8 on 16¾×12½ mounts, in deluxe portfolios to 15×11 on 21×17½ mounts; each signed and numbered. Edition: 40 regular, 10 deluxe. Price at issuance: $850 (regular). Current value: $1,050 (regular).

Rothstein, Arthur
Untitled. Selected images, 1935–1939, from the photographer's Farm Security Administration work. New York: published by the photographer, 1976. Includes a 4-page booklet with statement by Rothstein, a biography, and quotes from Cecil Beaton, William Saroyan, Gene Thornton. 8 prints, to 12×9¾ on 20×16 mounts, each signed. Edition: 25. Price at issuance: $1,000. Current value: $1,000.

Rubinstein, Eva
Untitled. Interiors, portraits, nude studies. New York: Neikrug Portfolios, 1975. Introduction by John Vachon. 12 prints, to 10×8 on 11×14 mounts, each signed. Edition: 35, plus 3 artist's proofs. Price at issuance: $575. Current value: $750.

See also Women's Campaign Fund.

Salmieri, Steve
Untitled. Selected images, 1966–1976. New York: published by the photographer, 1976. 12 prints, to 17¾×14 on 20×16 Agfa paper, plus a 12×9½ self-portrait mounted on the case. Edition: 50. Price at issuance: $1,000. Current value: $1,000.

Sander, August
Rheinlandschaften. Rhine landscapes. New York: Parasol Press, 1974. 12 prints, to 9×11 on 17¼×21½ mounts, each signed, dated, and numbered by Gunther Sander (the photographer's son) and embossed with the August Sander seal. Edition: 75, plus 6 artist's proofs. (At the completion of the edition the negatives were retired.) Price at issuance: $2,000. Current value: $2,000.

Bildende Kunstler. Portraits of the "Cologne Progressives." 12 prints, published and prepared as *Rheinlandschaften.* Edition: 75, plus 6 artist's proofs. Price at issuance: $2,000. Current value: $2,000.

San Francisco State University Photography Dept.
See Schools and workshops.

Schaefer, John P.
BAC: Where the Waters Gather. Images of a Spanish mission. Tucson, Ariz.: published by the photographer, 1978. 14 prints, to 7¼×5½ on 14×11 mounts, each signed. Edition: 25. Price at issuance: $500. Current value: $500.

Schools and workshops
Several schools and workshops issue limited-edition portfolios of selected prints by students and teachers at the end of each year or session. The size of these editions varies, running up to 100. They are usually offered at modest prices in the range of $75–$150. Among those issuing portfolios for the longest time and most consistently are: Apeiron Workshops, Inc.; School of the Art Institute of Chicago; Center for Photographic Studies (no longer in operation); Rhode Island School of Design; Rochester Institute of Technology.

APEIRON WORKSHOPS, INC., Millerton, N.Y.
The First Portfolio, 1975. Images by visiting instructors Paul Caponigro, Linda Connor, Ralph Gibson, Mark Goodman, Emmet Gowin, Charles Harbutt, Danny Lyon, Elaine Mayes, Duane Michals, Ron Morris, Enrico Natali, Bea Nettles, Peter Schlessinger, Aaron Siskind, Bill Staffeld, George A. Tice, Jerry N. Uelsmann, and Minor White. 18 prints, to 12½×8½ on 17×14 mounts. Edition: 40. Price at issuance: $1,050. Current value: $2,000.

Steve Salmieri. *Parade,* 1966. Silver print. (Courtesy the artist)

Triptych: The Second Apeiron Portfolio, 1978. Three images each by Linda Connor (printing-out paper and Azo paper, gold-toned), Ralph Gibson (Type C color), Mark Goodman (resin-coated), Charles Harbutt (silver), Robert Heinecken (photo-lithographs, each with a unique Polaroid SX-70 print mounted on it), Burk Uzzle (silver), each signed; and Tony Ray-Jones (silver prints made posthumously by Lawrence McFarland from the original negatives, under the supervision of the photographer's widow, imprinted with the Tony Ray-Jones estate stamp). Introductory text by Peter Schlessinger. 21 prints, to 16×16, unmounted, or in 16×16 overmats. Edition: 50, plus 10 artist's proofs. Price at issuance: $1,500. Current value: $2,000.

ART INSTITUTE OF CHICAGO, SCHOOL OF THE.
Various faculty and graduate-student portfolios. First issued in 1969, annually since 1974, including work of Harold Allen, Ken Josephson, Joyce Neimanas, Todd Walker. Print sizes vary but all are on 14×11 mounts. Editions: 40 or more. Prices vary.

Underware, 1977. Images by faculty and visiting artists, including Linda Connor, Robert Heinecken, Joseph Jachna, William Larson, Aaron Siskind, Keith Smith. Introduction by Robert Loescher; afterword by Nathan Lyons. 18 prints, to 16×20, each signed and dated. Edition: 50. Price at issuance: $400. Current value: $800.

CENTER FOR PHOTOGRAPHIC STUDIES, Louisville, Ky.
Invitational Portfolio #1, 1973 (first in the series published by the center). Images by 28 photographers, including Arnold Gassan, Ralph Eugene Meatyard, Henry Holmes Smith, Minor White. Introduction by Conrad J. Pressma. 28 prints, 5×7 and 7½×7½, all on 14×11 mounts. Edition: 100 for sale, plus 28 (one each) for the photographers. Price at issuance: $28. Current value: $1,000.

See also Meatyard, Ralph Eugene; Riss, Murray; Smith, Henry Holmes.

LOS ANGELES CENTER FOR PHOTOGRAPHIC STUDIES.
Silver See, 1977. Images by Los Angeles–area photographers, including Jo Ann Callis, Eileen Cowin, Darryl Curran, Robert W. Fichter, Robbert Flick, Judith Golden, Robert Heinecken, Claire Henze, Steve Kahn, Robert Ketchum, Victor Landweber, Jerry McMillan, Philip Melnick, Marion Palfi, Sheila Pinkel, Leland Rice, Kay Shuper, Arthur Taussig, Edmund Teske, Robert Von Sternberg, Max Yavno. Introduction by Victor Landweber. 21 prints (silver, Type C color, cyanotype, photo-silkscreen, and other mixed media), to 20×16, each signed and dated. Edition: 45. Price at issuance: $500. Current value: $2,500.

RHODE ISLAND SCHOOL OF DESIGN (RISD), Providence.
Portfolios issued annually since 1968. Early ones contain prints by Harry Callahan, later ones by Chester Michalik, Aaron Siskind. Print sizes vary but all are mounted on 14×11 mounts. Editions: vary. Prices at issuance: $50–250. Current values: vary, although marked increases are to be expected.

ROCHESTER INSTITUTE OF TECHNOLOGY (RIT).
Portfolios issued annually since 1973. Include work by Charles Arnold, Betty Hahn, John Pfahl. Print sizes vary but all are mounted on 14×11 mounts. Editions: vary. Prices at issuance: $50–250. Current values: vary, although marked increases are to be expected.

SAN FRANCISCO STATE UNIVERSITY PHOTOGRAPHY DEPARTMENT.
Out of State, 1978. Images by teachers, students, and alumni, including Robert Barry, Ann Bogazianos, Lawrie Brown, Greg DeLory, John Gutmann, Harvey Himelfarb, William Kane, Dale Kistemaker, Gregory MacGregor, Ted Orland, Leland D. Rice, Catherine Wagner, John Spence Weir, Jack Welpott, Neal White, Don Worth. Essay by Henry Holmes Smith. 14 black-and-white and 2 Ektacolor RC prints, to 17×14 on 20×16 mounts, each signed. Edition: 11, plus 18 artist's proofs. Price at issuance: $960. Current value: $1,200.

Seidenstücker, Friedrich

Untitled. Street scenes of Berlin, 1925–1940. Cologne: Galerie Wilde, 1977. 10 prints, 6¼×8¾ on 12¾×17 mounts, and each numbered, dated, and stamped "Galerie Wilde, Köln" on verso. Edition: 50. Price at issuance: $885. Current value: $885.

Seuphor, Michel

10 Fotografien. Selected images, 1929–1930, including portraits of Mondrian and Léger. Cologne: Galerie Wilde, 1976. Introduction by Jürgen Wilde. Printed under the photographer's supervision. 8×10 on 13×17 mounts, each signed and numbered. Edition: 50. Price at issuance: $1,100. Current value: $1,100.

Shore, Stephen

Twelve Photographs. Street scenes of various parts of the United States. New York: Metropolitan Museum of Art, 1976. Witter Bynner quotation from the introduction to *The Jade Mountain.* Printed by Marie Dick and Stanley Silverman of Berkey K&L, under the photographer's supervision. 10×8 Ektacolor prints on 20×16 mounts, each signed by the photographer. Edition: 50, plus 6 artist's proofs. Price at issuance: $1,500. Current value: $1,500.

Siskind, Aaron

Terrors and Pleasures of Levitation. The human figure suspended in air — jumping, diving, etc. New York: Light Gallery, 1972. 10 prints, to 10×9½ on 20×16 mounts, each signed. Edition: 15. Price at issuance: $800. Current value: $2,000.

See also Schools and workshops: Apeiron Workshops, Inc.; Art Institute of Chicago, School of the; Rhode Island School of Design.

Smith, Henry Holmes

Untitled. Selected abstract images. Louisville, Ky.: Center for Photographic Studies, 1973 (second in the series published by the center). Introduction by Frederick Sommer. 10 prints, 11×9 on 20×16 mounts, each signed. Edition: 100. Price at issuance: $125. Current value: $500.

See also Schools and workshops: Center for Photographic Studies.

Smith, W. Eugene

Ten Photographs. Selected images from major essays: "A Man of Mercy" (Albert Schweitzer), "Nurse Midwife," "Minamata." Roslyn Heights, N.Y.: Witkin-Berley, 1977. Foreword by the photographer. To 14×11 on 20×16 mounts, each signed. Edition: 25, plus 5 artist's proofs. Price at issuance: $4,500. Current value: $12,000.

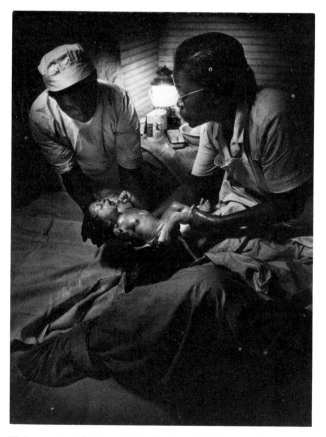

W. Eugene Smith. *Nurse Midwife Maude Callen, North Carolina,* 1951. Silver print. (Courtesy Witkin-Berley, Ltd.)

Steiner, Ralph

Untitled. Selected images, 1920s–1930s. Thetford, Vt.: published by the photographer, 1978. Introduction by Willard Van Dyke; preface by the photographer. 10 prints, 10×8 on 17×14 mounts, plus 1 5×7 print affixed to cover. Edition: 25. Price: $1,500 throughout 1978; thereafter, $2,000.

Lou Stoumen. *12 Midnight, Times Square, N.Y.C.,* 1940. Silver print. The accompanying "soundtrack" reads: "12 Midnight. Let's. Please. My ship sails tomorrow. Always. I do, yes I do. You're beautiful, that's why. I always will. You could tell your mom you stayed with your girlfriend. Of course I do. Of course I'll write. But don't you want me to be able to remember you in the dearest way? . . ." (Courtesy the artist)

Stoumen, Lou

Times Square, 1940. Los Angeles: Hand Press, with New York: Witkin Gallery, and Los Angeles: G. Ray Hawkins Gallery, 1976. Text ("Soundtrack") by the photographer. 18 prints, to 12×9 on 13⅞×10⅞ mounts, each signed and titled on verso. Edition: 25, plus 3 artist's proofs. Price at issuance: $900. Current value: $1,600.

Strand, Paul

Portfolio I: On My Doorstep, 1914–1973. Still lifes, landscapes, portraits. Millerton, N.Y.: Aperture/Michael Hoffman, 1976. Foreword by the photographer. Printed by Richard Benson under the photographer's supervision. 11 prints, to 10×13 on 16×20 mounts, each stamped and numbered. Edition: 50, plus 8 artist's proofs. Price at issuance: $10,000. Current value: $10,000.

Portfolio II: The Garden, 1957–1967. 6 prints, published and prepared as *Portfolio I.* Edition: 50, plus 8 artist's proofs. Price at issuance: $6,000. Current value: $10,000.

Struss, Karl F.

A Portfolio. Selected images of New York City and California, 1909–1930. Ann Arbor, Mich.: Photofolio of Ann Arbor, 1978. Introduction by John and Susan Harvith. Printed by Philip Davis from the original negatives and plates, under the photographer's supervision. 15 platinum prints, to 4½×3¾ on 12×9 mounts, each numbered, and signed by the photographer. Edition: 75, plus 15 artist's proofs. Price at issuance: $3,000. Current value: $3,000.

Karl Struss. *Vanishing Point II: Brooklyn Bridge from New York Side,* 1912. Platinum print. (Courtesy the artist and Photofolio of Ann Arbor. Copyright © by Karl Struss)

Sudek, Josef

See chapter 5 entry.

Sussman, Leonard

Subways. Photographs and etchings of New York. New York City: published by the photographer, 1977. 10 photographs, to 7×9 on 20×15 mounts, each signed; 5 etchings, to 9×14 on 20×15 paper, each signed. Edition: 30, plus 5 artist's proofs. Price at issuance: $850. Current value: $850.

Leonard Sussman. *Token Booth, Wall Street, IRT, Lexington Ave.,* 1977. Silver print. (Courtesy the artist)

Szabo, Steve

The Eastern Shore. Washington, D.C.: Quindacqua, 1976. Introduction by the photographer. 10 platinum prints, 10×8 in 16×14 overmats, each signed and numbered. Edition: 25, plus 10 artist's proofs. Price at issuance: $1,800. Current value: $1,800.

Talbot, William Henry Fox

W. H. F. Talbot: A Weekend of Events at Lacock Abbey to Mark the Centenary of his Death, One Hundred Years Ago/17–18th September, 1977. Anonymous modern replicas of the photographer's images, produced according to the chemistry set down in his patents. Lacock, England: Monmouth Calotype, 1978. 9 calotypes, to 6×8 in 11×14 paper folders, each numbered and blind-stamped with the seal of Monmouth Calotype; colophon dated and numbered, signed by Cristel Amiss and Michael Gray. Edition: 25. Price at issuance: $550. Current value: $550.

Tice, George A.

The first four portfolios were published in Colonia, N.J., by the photographer. Each: 12 prints, to 6½×4½ on 14×11 mounts, unsigned; title page signed by the photographer and each mount embossed with his monogram.

Amish Portfolio, 1968. Landscapes, portraits of the Amish people. Introduction by Jacob Deschin. Edition: 50. Price at issuance: $75. Current value: $750.

George A. Tice. *Two Amish Boys, Lancaster, Pa.,* 1962. From *Amish Portfolio.* Silver print. (Courtesy the artist)

Trees, 1969. Introduction by the photographer. Edition: 50. Price at issuance: $75. Current value: $600.

Bodie, 1971. Images of the California ghost town. Introduction by Lee D. Witkin. Edition: 50, plus 5 artist's proofs. Price at issuance: $150. Current value: $600.

Peekamoose, 1973. Landscapes of the Catskill Mountain region. Introduction by James L. Enyeart. Edition: 50. Price at issuance: $150. Current value: $600.

Portfolio V. Selected images, 1967–1976. Carteret, N.J.: published by the photographer. Individual images printed in silver, platinum, or palladium (photographic process used for each negative will never be repeated). 10 prints, 8×10 to 11×14 on 16×20 mounts, each mount signed on verso and embossed with the photographer's monogram. Edition: 100, plus 10 artist's proofs. Price at issuance: $1,500. Current value: $2,000.

See also Schools and workshops: Apeiron Workshops, Inc.

Tress, Arthur

The Dream Collection. Images re-creating children's dreams. New York: published by the photographer, 1976. Introductory statement by Duane Michals. 12

prints, to 10¾×10¾ on 18×14 mounts, each signed. Edition: 50. Price at issuance: $625. Current value: $625.

Uelsmann, Jerry N.

Portfolio. Selected well-known images. Roslyn Heights, N.Y.: Witkin-Berley, 1972. Introduction by Robert Fichter; foreword by the photographer. 10 prints, including one on aluminum, to 13×10 on 20×16 mounts, each signed. Edition: 25, plus 7 artist's proofs. Price at issuance: $695. Current value: $3,000.

See also Schools and workshops: Apeiron Workshops, Inc.

Van Der Zee, James

Eighteen Photographs. Selected images, including Harlem portraits. Washington, D.C.: Graphics International, with New York: James Van Der Zee Institute, 1974. Introduction and chronology by Regenia A. Perry. Printed by Richard Benson from the original negatives, under the photographer's supervision. Edition: 75, plus 15 presentation copies numbered I–XV. (At the completion of the edition the negatives were retired.) Price at issuance: $2,000. Current value: $2,000.

See also Women's Campaign Fund.

Van Dyke, Willard

Ten Photographs. Selected images. New York: Van Productions, 1977. Introduction by Beaumont Newhall. Printed by the photographer and Guy Jaconelli. 10×8 on 17×14 mounts, each signed. Edition: 25, plus 5 artist's proofs. Price at issuance: $1,500. Current value: $1,500.

Vignes, Michel

Concierges des Paris, 1870–75. San Francisco: published by the photographer, 1978. Introduction by the photographer. 10 prints, to 11¾×8 on 14×11 photographic paper, each signed and dated. Edition: 15. Price at issuance: $1,000. Current value: $1,000.

Vink, John

Untitled. Cologne: Galerie Wilde, 1975. Introduction by Ralph Gibson. 12 prints, to 5×7 in 12¾×16¾ overmats, each signed and numbered by the photographer. Edition: 25, plus 5 numbered I–V. Price at issuance: $680. Current value: $930.

Vishniac, Roman

The Vanished World. Images of Jewish ghettos, Eastern Europe, mid-1930s. Roslyn Heights, N.Y.: Witkin-Berley, 1977. Introduction by the photographer. 12 prints, in portfolios numbered 1–25 to 14×11 on 20×16 mounts, in portfolios 26–50 to 20×16 on 28×22 mounts, each signed. Edition: 50, plus 5 artist's proofs. Price at issuance: $2,500 (portfolios 1–25); $3,000 (portfolios 26–50). Current value: $4,000, $4,500 respectively.

Weston, Brett

The following portfolios were all published in Carmel, Calif., by the photographer. The prints, all made and signed by him, are boxed in a variety of folios and cases.

San Francisco, 1938. 12 prints, 10×8 on 18×16 mounts. Edition: 25. Price at issuance: $50. Current value: $3,500.

White Sands, 1949. Landscapes of White Sands, N.Mex. Foreword by Nancy Newhall. 10 prints, 10×8 on 14×12 mounts. Edition: 75. Price at issuance: $75. Current value: $3,500.

New York, 1951. Selected images of the city, 1940s. Foreword by Beaumont Newhall. 12 prints, 10×8 on 16×14 mounts. Edition: 50. Price at issuance: $75. Current value: $3,500.

Brett Weston. *Skylight, Midtown,* 1947. From *New York.* Silver print. (Courtesy the artist)

Ten Photographs, 1958. Mostly nature details. Contact printed from 14×11 negatives on 18×14 mounts. Edition: 50. Price at issuance: $100. Current value: $3,500.

Baja California, 1967. 15 prints, 10×8 on 15×13¼ mounts. Edition: 50. Price at issuance: $100. Current value: $3,000.

Japan, 1970. 15 prints, 8×10 on 13¼×15 mounts. Edition: 50. Price at issuance: $200. Current value: $2,000.

Europe, 1973. Foreword by Gerald Robinson. 12 prints, to 14×11 on 18×15 mounts. Edition: 100. Price at issuance: $200. Current value: $2,500.

Oregon, 1975. Foreword by Bernard Freemesser. 15 prints, 14×11 on 18×13¼ mounts. Edition: 50. Price at issuance: $1,200. Current value: $1,500.

Portraits of My Father, 1976. Photographs, 1929–1942, of Edward Weston. Introduction by Ansel Adams. 10 prints, 10×8 on 15×13¼ mounts. Edition: 100. Price at issuance: $1,850. Current value: $2,500.

Twenty Photographs, 1970–1977, 1977. Foreword by Rosario Mazzeo. To 11×14 on 15×18 mounts, each signed and numbered. Edition: 100. Price at issuance: $3,500. Current value: $3,500.

Weston, Edward

50th Anniversary Portfolio. Selected images from his life's work. Carmel, Calif.: published by the photographer, 1952. Foreword by the photographer. Printed by Brett Weston from the original negatives, under the photographer's supervision. 12 prints, 10×8 on 15×13 mounts, each initialed by Edward Weston. Edition: 100. Price at issuance: $100. Current value: $10,000.

Edward Weston Portfolio. Selected images. Roslyn Heights, N.Y.: Witkin-Berley, 1971. Introduction by Wynn Bullock; foreword by Cole Weston. Printed by Cole Weston. 10 prints, including one from a color transparency, to 10×8 on 20×16 mounts; verso of each mount includes handwritten title, negative number, and signature by Cole Weston on stamp reading "Negative by Edward Weston [facsimile signature]. Print by Cole Weston [signature]" (see illustration, page 270), plus label stating number of print and edition. Edition: 50, plus 5 artist's proofs. Price at issuance: $600. Current value: $2,000.

Desnudos. Female nudes, 1920–1945. Carmel, Calif.: Cole Weston, 1972. Introduction by Charis Wilson. Printed by Cole Weston from the original negatives. 11 prints, 10×8 on 16×14 mounts, plus a 3½×4½ print mounted on the cover of the case; verso of each mount prepared as in *Edward Weston Portfolio.* Edition: 100 projected (30 completed as of 1978). Price at issuance: $700. Current value: $2,000.

Six Nudes of Neil, 1925. Classic studies of an eight-year-old boy. New York: Witkin Gallery, 1977. Introduction by Neil Weston; comment by George A. Tice. Printed by Tice from the original negatives. 6 brown-toned palladium prints, to 4½×3½ on 14×11 mounts, each with a label signed by Tice and Neil Weston. Edition: 25, plus 5 artist's proofs. Price at issuance: $1,200. Current value: $1,500.

White, Minor

Sequence 6. A series of images based on city subjects and ocean forms. San Francisco: published by the photographer, 1951. Foreword by the photographer. 14 prints, 5×10 to 8×10 on 14×17 mounts, each signed. Edition: 25. Price at issuance: $125. Current value: $4,000.

Minor White. *Nude Foot, San Francisco,* 1947. From *Jupiter Portfolio.* Silver print. (Courtesy Light Gallery)

Jupiter Portfolio. Selected images from his life's work. New York: Light Gallery, 1975. Fable by Peter Rasun Gould in the colophon. 12 prints, 11×14 on 16×20 mounts, each signed. Edition: 100. Price at issuance: $1,200. Current value: $5,000.

See also Schools and workshops: Apeiron Workshops, Inc.; Center for Photographic Studies.

Winningham, Geoff

A Texas Dozen. Selected images from the books *Going Texan* and *Friday Night in the Coliseum.* Houston: Cronin Gallery, 1976. Introduction by Robert Adams.

15 prints, 16×20 on 20×24 mounts, each signed. Edition: 15, plus 2 artist's proofs. Price at issuance: $2,000. Current value: $2,000.

Winogrand, Garry

Fifteen Photographs. New York: Double Elephant Press, 1974. Essay by the photographer. To 8½×13 on 15×20 mounts, each signed. Edition: 75. Price at issuance: $2,000. Current value: $3,000.

Women's Campaign Fund

Ten Photographers. Individual images by Eve Arnold, Jill Freedman, Ernst Haas, André Kertész, Duane Michals, Inge Morath, Barbara Morgan, Eva Rubinstein, Neal Slavin, and James Van Der Zee. Washington, D.C.: Women's Campaign Fund, 1978. 10 prints, to 11¾×7⅜ in 20×16 overmats, each signed. Edition: 75. Price at issuance: $1,750. Current value: $2,000.

Piet Zwart. *Waschschüssel,* 1930. Silver print. (Courtesy Galerie Wilde)

Yavno, Max

Portfolio One: Image as Poem. Scenes of San Francisco and other places. Los Angeles: G. Ray Hawkins Gallery, 1977. Introduction by Ben Maddow. 14 prints, 11×14 on 16×20 mounts, each signed. Edition: 50, plus 3 artist's proofs. Price at issuance: $1,200. Current value: $1,600.

See also Schools and workshops: Los Angeles Center for Photographic Studies.

Zwart, Piet

12 Fotografien. Selected images. Cologne: Galerie Wilde, 1974. Introduction by Kees Broos. Printed under the photographer's supervision. 10×8 on 17×13 mounts, each signed. Edition: 25, plus 5 artist's proofs. Price at issuance: $1,600. Current value: $1,600.

Max Yavno. *Garage Doors, San Francisco,* 1947. Silver print. (Courtesy G. Ray Hawkins Gallery)

View of the exhibition titled Photograph as Metaphor/Photograph as Object/Photograph as Document of Concept, held in 1973 in the Art Museum and Galleries of California State University, Long Beach. Installation by Robert Heinecken. (Courtesy California State University, Long Beach)

7

Contemporary Group Exhibitions and Catalogues

This chapter lists some of the many shows of contemporary photography mounted in recent years. The purpose is not to give an all-inclusive list of exhibitions — that would be a book in itself — but to provide some information on many contemporary photographers who do not have individual entries in chapter 5.

The shows are divided into five general and sometimes overlapping categories:

PHOTOGRAPH AS METAPHOR Images with symbolic meaning for the photographer or viewer.

EXPANDED IMAGERY Photography plus handwork; three dimensionality; new media such as laser photography; or the like.

SOCIAL LANDSCAPE Images of "people and people things," as Lee Friedlander put it.

NEW DOCUMENTARY Images that describe without interpreting.

GENERAL A collection of shows that include work in a variety of styles.

Within each category, the shows are listed chronologically and numbered, followed by an alphabetical list of the exhibitors; numbers following the photographers' names correspond to the shows in which their work appeared. Unless otherwise noted, an exhibition catalogue was published for each show, and names generally are listed as they appear in the catalogues. *Italicized* photographers have entries in chapter 5; others are listed in appendix B.

Photograph as Metaphor

The shows in this category were all assembled and arranged by Minor White, who was the leading contemporary exponent of the photograph as an equivalent — that is, a metaphor for internal feelings. Many of the photographers in these shows thought of their photographs as equivalents, while others did not view their own work this way. White used their images to create his own statements and to entice viewers to create and explore their own personal reactions.

For one show he gave photographs exponential rankings ranging from Light¹ to Light⁷: "Images which lead us to our Creator can be called Light⁷.

This function, however, only flares up when we have dropped many, if not all of the masks by which we hide from ourselves. All of us walk in miracle constantly, but live isolated in apathy and unawareness. If we stumble over a pebble and are illuminated, we keep our eyes on the ground looking ever after — for more pebbles — or more Light⁷ images. We need to recall that Light⁷ images themselves are but a sign post on the Way" (*Light⁷*).

1 *Light⁷*. Ed. and text by Minor White. Millerton, N.Y.: Aperture, and Cambridge: Massachusetts Institute of Technology Hayden Gallery, 1968.

2 *Be-ing Without Clothes.* Exhibition and catalogue conceived and developed by Minor White. Millerton, N.Y.: Aperture, and Cambridge: Massachusetts Institute of Technology Hayden Gallery, 1970.

3 *Octave of Prayer.* Compiled and text by Minor White. Millerton, N.Y.: Aperture, and Cambridge: Massachusetts Institute of Technology Hayden Gallery, 1972.

4 *Celebrations.* Selection and text by Minor White and Jonathan Green. Preface by Gyorgy Kepes. Millerton, New York: Aperture, and Cambridge: Massachusetts Institute of Technology Hayden Gallery, 1974.

Expanded Imagery

The photographers in the following group of shows create combined images, mix photographic and handwork, use new materials such as vacuum-molded plastics, or employ old processes such as gum-bichromate printing. They may start with images they make themselves or use those found in the mass media.

"In the 60's the painters and sculptors broke down the two media barriers between painting and sculpture so that they became one. This and the re-discovery of photo silkscreen, paint-on emulsions, plastics, and numerous other materials, unleash[ed] the artist to work where he may, with whatever imagery he chooses. Now, in the 70's, it is not surprising to find photographic imagery pervading painting, sculpture, printmaking, and drawing" — Tom Muir Wilson (*Into the 70's*).

1 *Contemporary Photographers: The Persistence of Vision.* Ed. and text by Nathan Lyons. New York: Horizon, and Rochester, N.Y.: GEH, 1967.
2 *Into the 70's: Photographic Images by Sixteen Artists/Photographers.* Text by Tom Muir Wilson, Orrel E. Thompson, and Robert M. Doty. Akron: Akron Art Institute, 1970.
3 *Photographic Synthesis.* California College of Arts and Crafts (Oakland), 1970. No catalogue.
4 *Photography into Sculpture.* Museum of Modern Art (New York City), 1970. No catalogue.
5 *Graphic/Photographic.* Fullerton: California State College, 1971. For this show, photographers only are listed below.
6 *Photo/Graphics.* Text by Van Deren Coke. Rochester, N.Y.: GEH, 1971.
7 *Photo Media: Elements and Technics of Photography Experienced as an Artistic Medium.* New York: Museum of Contemporary Crafts, 1971.
8 *Photography into Art.* London: Arts Council of Great Britain, 1972.
9 *Light and Lens: Methods of Photography.* Ed. by Donald L. Werner. Text by Werner and Dennis Longwell. Dobbs Ferry, N.Y.: Morgan & Morgan, and Yonkers, N.Y.: Hudson River Museum, 1973.
10 *New Art from Photosensitized Materials.* Text by Neal Spitzer. Poughkeepsie, N.Y.: Vassar College Art Gallery, 1973.
11 *3M Color.* Ed. by Cheryl Douglas. Text by Cheryl Douglas, Sonia Sheridan, Darryl Curran, Douglas H. Dybvig, Thomas J. Evensen, and John W. Ulseth. Carmel, Calif.: Friends of Photography, 1973.
12 *Photography Unlimited.* Cambridge, Mass.: Fogg Art Museum, 1974.
13 *Synthetic Color.* Carbondale: Southern Illinois University, University Galleries, 1974.
14 *Photographic Process as Medium.* Text by Rosanne T. Livingston. New Brunswick, N.J.: Rutgers University Art Gallery, 1975.
15 *New Blues.* Tempe: Arizona State University Memorial Union Art Gallery, 1976.

Social Landscape

The shows that follow delineated an area of major concern to photographers in the 1960s and the 1970s — the social landscape: people and the often unlikely environments they create. The photographer records them not with any intention of social reform but rather to point out the odd reality of it all. Many of the photographs are of evanescent events that are as minor in importance as they are fleeting in time. They are antinews, or at least non-news: things as they are rather than things as they should be, could be, or are thought to be.

Photographers of the social landscape, as Thomas H. Garver observed in *12 Photographers*, "are less concerned with explicit messages than with implicit commentary, though to call them 'cool' for their seemingly noncommittal approach is inadequate. Their photographs are not visual 'no-comments' but rather records of real events offered to an audience who may not always believe the events are that way."

1 *Contemporary Photographers: Toward a Social Landscape.* Ed. and text by Nathan Lyons. New York: Horizon, and Rochester, N.Y.: GEH, 1966.
2 *New Documents.* Text by John Szarkowski. New York: MOMA, 1967.
3 *12 Photographers of the American Social Landscape.* Text by Thomas H. Garver. Waltham, Mass.: Brandeis University, 1967.

New Documentary

In this category, related to the social landscape, are a number of shows that also present photographs of the environment, but photographs that are executed in a spare, dry style that does not introduce emotion, personal bias, or even irony. Many of the photographers represented are interested in conceptual or minimal art, and their intention is to produce documents: camera-made descriptions of what is in front of the lens rather than images that convey how they feel about their subject matter.

A rigorous lack of overtly intentional style is, paradoxically, the essence of these photographers' styles. Photographer Nicholas Nixon wrote in *New Topographics:* "The world is infinitely more interesting than any of my opinions concerning it. This is not a description of a style or an artistic posture, but my profound conviction."

1 *The Crowded Vacancy.* Davis: University of California Memorial Union Art Gallery, 1971.

2 *14 American Photographers.* Text by Renato Danese. Baltimore: Baltimore Museum of Art, 1974.

3 *The Extended Document: An Investigation of Information and Evidence in Photographs.* Text by William Jenkins. Rochester, N.Y.: IMP/GEH, 1975.

4 *New Topographics: Photographs of a Man-altered Landscape.* Text by William Jenkins. Rochester, N.Y.: IMP/GEH, 1975.

5 *Peculiar to Photography.* Albuquerque: University of New Mexico Art Museum, 1976.

General

The shows in this largest group do not fit neatly into any of the preceding categories. Some of the following exhibitions were invitational in nature: specific photographers were asked to submit work. Other shows were selected from photographs submitted in response to a general call for work. The photographers listed here are a sampling of those who have actively exhibited their work in recent years.

1 *American Photography: The Sixties.* Lincoln: University of Nebraska Sheldon Memorial Art Gallery, 1966.

2 *Photograph, U.S.A.* Lincoln, Mass.: De Cordova Museum, 1967.

3 *Photography 1968.* Lexington, Ky.: Lexington Camera Club, 1968.

4 *Young Photographers.* Text by Van Deren Coke. Albuquerque: University of New Mexico Art Museum, 1968.

5 *Young Photographers '68.* Lafayette, Ind.: Purdue University, 1968.

6 *Vision and Expression.* Ed. by Nathan Lyons. New York: Horizon, and Rochester, N.Y.: GEH, 1969.

7 *California Photographers 1970.* Davis: University of California Memorial Union Art Gallery, 1969.

8 *Photography Invitational 1971.* Little Rock: Arkansas Arts Center, 1971.

9 *60's Continuum.* Text by Van Deren Coke. Rochester, N.Y.: GEH, 1972 (*Image* 15, Mar. 1972).

10 *Photographers Midwest Invitational.* Minneapolis: Walker Art Center, 1973.

11 *Light & Substance.* Albuquerque: University of New Mexico Art Museum, 1974.

12 *New Images in Photography: Object and Illusion.* Miami: University of Miami Lowe Art Museum, 1974.

13 *Nine Photographers.* Akron: Akron Art Institute, 1975.

14 *The Photographers' Choice.* Ed. by Kelly Wise. Danbury, N.H.: Addison House, 1975.

15 *(photo) (photo)² ... (photo)ⁿ: Sequenced Photographs.* Text by David Bourdon. College Park: University of Maryland Art Gallery, 1975.

16 *Aspects of American Photography, 1976.* St. Louis: University of Missouri, 1976.

17 *Emerging Los Angeles Photographers.* Carmel, Calif.: Friends of Photography, 1976 (*Untitled 11,* 1976).

18 *The Less Than Sharp Show.* Chicago: Chicago Photographic Gallery of Columbia College, 1977.

Beckley, Bill: 15
Becotte, Michael: 6, 11
Beitzell, Neil: 6
Bellak, David J.: 7
Beltran, George: 4
Benbenuato, John: 5
Bennett, Gordon: 2, 6, 7
Benson, John: 14
Benton, Stephen / Casdin-
   Silver, Harriet: 11
Berchen, William P.: 2
Berger, Paul: 7
Berglund, Magnus: 7
Berinsky, Burton: 2
Berko, Ferenc: 2
Bernhard, Ruth: 2
Bishop, Michael: 6, 7, 9
Bisilliat, Maureen: 6
Blanchard, Stanley: 6
Blankfort, Jeffrey A.: 2
Blondeau, Barbara: 6
Blumberg, Donald: 2, 6
Borodác, Ladislaus: 6
Bourdeau, Robert: 14
Brenner, Susan: 7
Bridgeman, Bill: 7
Brink, Bertil: 7
Brook, John: 1, 2
Brooks, Ellen: 7, 11
Brooks, Robert: 5
Brown, Dean: 6
Brown, Robert E.: 4, 5,
   6, 11
Brown, Robert / Pennuto,
   James: 7
Bullaty, Sonja: 2
Bullock, Wynn: 1, 2, 14
Burchard, Jerry: 7
Burgess, James L.: 4
Burlison, Barry: 6
Burns, Gary: 17
Butler, Owen: 18
Cabanban, Orlando: 5
Cahan, Andrew: 13
Callahan, Harry: 1, 12, 14
Callis, Jo Ann: 17
Calman, Wendy: 14
Caponigro, Paul: 1, 16
Carrey, Bobbi: 14
Carroll, Wendell: 4
Casdin-Silver, Harriet /
   Benton, Stephen: 11
Chapman, Nancy Jean: 4
Chappell, Walter: 14
Cheek, Vernon: 10
Cheng, Carl: 4, 6
Chiarenza, Carl: 1, 2
Ciccone, Stan: 7

Cinnamond, Roger: 7
Cohen, Lynne: 10, 14
Cohen, Mark: 6, 9, 12
Coke, Van Deren: 1, 2, 3
Coleman, Barbara Jean: 4
Colley, David: 4, 5, 6
Colwell, Larry: 6
Compère, Charles: 6
Connor, Linda S.: 6, 7, 8,
   11, 18
Converse, Gordon N.: 2
Cook, John: 2, 13
Cordier, Pierre: 6
Cosindas, Marie: 1
Coslow, Gail: 7
Cowans, Adger: 2
Cowin, Eileen: 11, 17
Crane, Barbara: 5
Crouch, Jerry: 3
Cugini, Thomas: 6
Cumming, Robert: 14, 15
Cunningham, Imogen: 1, 2
Curran, Darryl J.: 5, 6, 7, 11
Current, William R.: 1
Currie, David: 5
Curry, Phillip W.: 4
Daehn, Marcia: 5
D'Agostino, Peter: 4
D'Alessandro, Robert: 6, 9
Dater, Judy: 2, 6, 7, 9, 12,
   14
Davidson, Bruce: 1
Davies, Bevan: 5
Davis, Phil: 10
Deal, Joseph: 14
Dean, Nicholas: 2
Dearstyne, John: 4
De Cock, Liliane: 2
Deeks, Jon: 7
Diamond, Paul: 9, 14
Dibbets, Jan: 15
Di Biase, Michael: 2
Dickinson, Donald: 6
Di Giulio, Lou Brown: 17
Dilley, Clyde H.: 6, 13
Divola, John M.: 17
Doherty, William: 4, 5, 9
Donaldson, Jamie: 3
Douglas, Edward: 7
Dow, James: 8
Drisch, Russell: 9
Edelstein, Victor: 2
Eggleston, William: 16
Epstein, Ellen: *see* Ellen
   Land-Weber
Erben, Kurt W.: 6
Erceg, Donald J.: 6
Ermi, Jiří: 6

Erwitt, Elliott: 1
Estabrook, Gwen Wid-
   mer: 10
Estabrook, Reed: 8
Faller, Richard L.: 2, 5
Fallon, James: 6
Feininger, Andreas: 2
Feldstein, Peter: 4, 10
Fernandez, Antonio A.: 6
Fernandez, Benedict J.: 6
Fichter, Robert W.: 3, 5,
   7, 9, 12
Fielder, Sheila White: 2
Fitch, Steve: 11
Fleischhauer, Carl: 6
Flick, Robbert: 7, 14
Foss, Jack: 5
Foster, Steven D.: 6
Frank, Robert: 1
Freedman, Jill: 6
Fridenmaker, Charles: 5, 6
Friedlander, Lee: 16
Friedman, Benno: 9, 16
Friedman, James: 13
Gagliani, Oliver: 6, 11
Gardener, George: 5
Gassan, Arnold: 1
Gates, Jeff: 17
Gates, Richard: 6
Gedney, William: 6
Gerdes, Ingeborg: 7
Gersh, Stephen: 5
Gibson, Ralph: 12
Gierlach, Z. S.: 3
Giles, William: 5
Gilpin, Laura: 16
Glover, William: 7
Gohlke, Frank: 9, 10, 11
Golden, Judith: 17
Gordon, Elly: 6
Gowin, Emmet: 5, 6, 8, 9,
   12, 16
Graham, Renni: 7
Groover, Jan: 14, 15
Grossi, Emilio: 1
Haas, Ernst: 1
Hahn, Betty: 6, 8, 9, 11,
   12, 16
Haiko, Robert F.: 6
Halámek, Zdenek: 6
Halberstadt, Milton: 1
Hall, James Baker: 3
Hallman, Gary L: 4, 9,
   10, 18
Hamilton, W. Brooks: 3
Hampton, Raymond E.: 3
Harbutt, Charles: 1
Hare, Chauncey: 6

Harris-McLeod, Pamela: 6
Harrison, Glenn Roy: 7
Häusser, Robert: 6
Hayes, Eugene: 4, 6
Heath, David: 1
Hein, Max: 7, 9
Heinecken, Robert F.: 1, 6,
   7, 8, 11, 12, 14, 16
Hernandez, Anthony: 7
Heron, Reginald: 3, 6, 10
Heyman, Ken: 1
Hill, Warren: 5, 6
Himelfarb, Harvey: 7, 9, 11,
   12
Hindson, Bradley: 6
Hirsch, Walter: 6
Hlobeczy, Nicholas Carl: 1
Hoare, Tyler James: 7
Hofmanis, Helena: 7
Holler, Gordon: 7
House, Suda: 17
Hudetz, Larry: 5
Hutchison, James: 17
Hyde, Scott: 8
Imai, Hisae: 6
Jachna, Joseph D.: 1, 10
Jacobs, Brian M.: 6
Johansson, Håkan: 6
Johnson, Thos: 7
Johnston, Helen: 7
Jones, Harold: 3, 4, 5, 6, 8,
   9, 11, 12
Josephson, Kenneth: 1, 8,
   10, 14
Kaczmarek, Janis: 7
Kahn, Steve: 11, 17
Kalisher, Simpson: 1
Kasper, Jo Diane: 6
Kasten, Barbara: 7, 8
Katsiff, Bruce: 6
Kawada, Kikuji: 6
Kessler, Chester: 5
Ketchum, Cavalliere: 3, 4,
   5, 10
Kievets, Dennis C.: 6
Kimball, Rosalind S.: 6
Klein, Irwin B.: 6
Klipper, Stuart: 10
Koral, Barry: 4
Kraft, James: 3, 4, 5, 6, 9
Kramer, Arthur: 6
Krims, Leslie: 6, 8, 9, 12,
   14, 15
Kronengold, Eric: 4
Krot, Paul: 6
Kunié: 6
Kurihara, Tatsuo: 6

Color plate 1
Alfred Stieglitz. *Marie Rapp-Boursault, 291 Gallery, New York City, 1915.* Modern dye transfer print made from the original autochrome. (Courtesy The Witkin Gallery)

Color plate 2
Dean Brown. *Ice Wings, Glacier Bay, Alaska,* June 1971. Dye transfer print. (Courtesy Carol Brown)

COLOR PLATE 3
Eliot Porter. *Sculptured Rock, Marble Canyon, Arizona,* June 1967. Dye transfer print. (Courtesy the artist)

COLOR PLATE 6
Bea Nettles. *Elizabeth, Landscape and Three Figures,* 1976. Kwik-Print. (Courtesy The Witkin Gallery)

COLOR PLATE 7
Lucas Samaras. *Photo-Transformation, 7/27/76.* Polaroid SX-70 print. (Courtesy The Pace Gallery, New York City)

COLOR PLATE 8
Joel Meyerowitz. *New York City,* 1976. Dye transfer print. (Courtesy the artist)

APPENDIXES

GENERAL BIBLIOGRAPHY

INDEX

A

Daguerreotypists

The following list of some one thousand names aims to include as many known daguerreotypists (and firms) as possible. Many of the names were taken directly from daguerreotype cases, others were drawn from reliable written histories or from city directories of the period, and still others were furnished by major collectors. Because of space limitations, only basic information, when known, about place and date of activity has been included. (All data refers to *daguerrean* activity, as opposed to work using later photographic processes that the daguerreotypist may have also employed.) Fuller information about key figures may be found in specialized sources or in the histories and surveys listed in the general bibliography. Not much more than a name and a location survives for many daguerreotypists, however, and in many instances records are nonexistent, incomplete, or contradictory.

Life dates, when known, are given here immediately after the names, followed by places of known activity. (When known to be different, the daguerreotypist's native country is included in parentheses, although in many instances this information is simply not available.) Other dates indicate known activity; readers can assume that daguerreotypists included without dates worked during the peak period of daguerrean activity, 1840-1855.

Many daguerreotypists worked in partnerships as well as independently (for instance, E. W. Baker may have been a principal in the listed firm Baker and Armington). For the most part, no attempt has been made here to link firms with separately listed individuals who might have been affiliated with them.

Italicized daguerreotypists have separate entries in chapter 5. Others listed who are known to have used later photographic media in addition to the daguerreotype appear in appendix B and in other parts of this book (consult the index).

Abel, Henry. Boston, 1842
Adams, Charles. Boston, 1850–52
Adams, Dan. Nashville, ca. 1845
Adams, George. Worcester, Mass.,
  1849–53
Adams, J. S. Boston, ca. 1846
Adams, Samuel. Hallowell, Maine,
  ca. 1849
Adam-Salomon, Antoine Samuel.
  1811–81. France
Alabern, Dom Ramon. Spain
Allen, A. M. Pottsville, Pa.
Allen, C. Keene, N.H., ca. 1849
Allen, C. V. Boston, ca. 1855–56

Allen, William. New York City, ca.
  1851
Allevy. Paris, 1850s
Alschuler, S. D. Chicago
Amadio, Josh. London
Amsden, Freeman. Boston, ca.
  1859
Anděl, Bedřich. Prague, 1850s
Anderson, D. H. Richmond
Andrews, J. D. Worcester, Mass.,
  ca. 1853
Anson, Rufus. New York City,
  1851–67
Anthony, Edward

Anthony, Henry T. 1814–84. New
  York City
Anthony, J. B. Poplar Grove, S.C.
Apor, (Baron) Károly. 1815–92.
  Hungary
Appleby, R. B. Rochester, N.Y.
Arago, François Jean Dominique.
  1786–1853. France
Armstrong, Agnes. Peekskill, N.Y.
Atkins, Joseph. Brooklyn, ca. 1848–
  49
Atwood, N. C. Keene, N.H., ca.
  1849
Auguste. France

Babbitt, Platt D. Niagara Falls, 1854–ca. 1870

Bailey, Morris. Lowell, Mass., 1853

Bailey, Thomas. Columbia, S.C.

Baker, E. H. Providence, 1844

Baker, E. W. Providence, 1843–50

Baker, F. S. Baltimore

Baker, Isaac W. California, 1853–60

Baker and Armington. Providence, ca. 1848

Balch, H. A. Joliet, Ill.

Ball, James P. Cincinnati, 1853–59

Banda, Josef. Crete

Barbarry. France

Barber, Alfred. 1809–84. Nottingham, England, 1841–42

Barboni, J., and Son. Brussels

Bardwell, Jex. Detroit

Barker. Leavenworth, Kans., ca. 1859–60

Barnard, E. A. Alabama

Barnard, George N.

Barnes, C. Mobile, Ala., ca. 1850–60

Barnes, J. T. New York City, ca. 1851

Barnes, Marcelia. Salem Crossroads, N.Y.

Barns, C. Toronto, ca. 1843

Barrows, James. Boston, ca. 1849

Bart, Godefried. Romania (itinerant)

Bartholomew (Prof.)

Bartlett, H. H. Hartford

Bartlett, W. H. C. West Point, N.Y., ca. 1854

Bartlett and Evans. Boston, ca. 1859

Bartlett and Fuller. Hartford, ca. 1849

Batchelder, B. P. Boston, ca. 1858

Batchelder, Nathaniel. Danvers, Mass.

Batchelder, Perez M. California, ca. 1852–55

Battersby, Joseph. Chicago

Bayard, Hippolyte

Beals, A. J. (or A. T.). New York City, ca. 1851–54

Beals, Henry. New York City, ca. 1851

Bear, John W. U.S.

Beard, Richard. England, ca. 1840

Beck, Vilmos. Szombathely, Hungary, mid-1840s

Beckers, Alexander. (Germany.) New York City, 1843–58

Beckers and Piard. New York City, ca. 1851

Beckmann (Mme.). New York City

Beech, W. P. Homer, N.Y.

Beekman and Brothers. New York City

Beers, C. F. Boston, ca. 1858

Bell, J. R. Boston, ca. 1858–59

Bemis, Samuel. 1789–1881. Boston

Benedict, P. H. Syracuse, N.Y.

Bennett, John A. Mobile, Ala., ca. 1844; South America (under name Juan A. Bennett), ca. 1845–52

Bennett, N. S. Washington, D.C.

Bennett and Daboll. Providence, ca. 1843

Benson (Mr.). Hawaii, ca. 1856

Benson, W. Boonville, Mo.

Bent, Isabel. Boston, ca. 1859

Berkowski and Busch. Königsberg, Germany

Bernard. London

Bernard (Mr.). Glasgow

Bernoud. France

Bertrand, A. France

Bestuzhev, Nikolai Aleksandrovich. Russia, 1850s

Betts, Charles J. (U.S.) Matamoros, Mexico (with U.S. troops), 1846

Bianchi, Barthélmy-Urbain. Toulouse, France, 1840s

Biow, Hermann. 1810–1850. Hamburg, Germany

Bisbee, A. Dayton, ca. 1853–54

Bisson, Auguste-Rosalie / Bisson, Louis-Auguste

Black, James Wallace. 1825–96. Boston

Blakely, Alexander. *See* Bleakley, Alexander

Blanchard, (Mrs.) E. H. Providence, ca. 1844

Blanchard, Thomas, Jr. Iowa City, Iowa, ca. 1854

Bleakley (Blakely), Alexander. Toronto, 1851–61

Bliss, T. G. New Bedford, Mass., ca. 1853

Blondelis. Vilnius, Lithuania, ca. 1854

Bliss, T. G. New Bedford, Mass., ca. 1853

Bogardus, Abraham. 1822–1908. New York City, 1846–87

Bogert, William. New York City, ca. 1851

Boisseau, Alfred. b. 1823. (France.) New Orleans, New York City, Cleveland, 1845–ca. 1859

Boles. Lawrence, Kans., ca. 1859–60

Bolles, Jessie H. Charlestown, S.C., ca. 1857–59

Bonijol, L. Geneva

Booker, Richard Young. 1804–76. Nottingham, England, 1849–51

Booth, H. C. Low Harrogate, England

Borchardt, Karl Wilhelm Friedrich. b. 1816. (Germany.) Estonia

Bosch, Johann. Zagreb, ca. 1841

Bothwick and Stanley. Scotland, ca. 1846

Bowdoin, D. W. Boston and Salem, Mass., ca. 1846–48

Bowdoin and Litch. Boston, ca. 1856

Bowen, N. O. Norwich, Conn.

Bowers, P. New York City, ca. 1851

Bowes. Providence, ca. 1849

Bradbury, C. Lowell, Mass., ca. 1853

Bradlee, J. E. Boston

Bradley, Henry W. San Francisco

Bradley and Rulofson (Henry W. Bradley; William Henry Rulofson [1826–78]). San Francisco, 1863 and after

Brady, Mathew B.

Brand, Edwin L. Chicago

Brand Brothers. Brussels

Braun, Adolphe

Brayton. Providence, ca. 1849

Bridge, Erastus. Lawrence, Mass., ca. 1853

Briggs, Jesse. Boston, ca. 1858–59

Brightley (Prof.).

Brinckerhoff, J. Dewitt. New York City

Britt, Peter. 1819–1905. (b. Switzerland.) New York City; Oregon; 1844–54

Broadbent, Samuel. Philadelphia

Broadbent and Phillips. Philadelphia, 1850s

Bronk, Edwin. New York City; St. Louis; Winchester and Columbus, Ohio

Brown, Eliphalet, Jr. 1816–86. (U.S.) China Seas and Japan (with U.S. Navy expedition), 1852–54

Brown, F. A. Manchester, N.H., ca. 1849

Brown, H. S. Milwaukee

Brown, James A. b. 1819. New York City, 1843–54

Brown, Nicholas. St. Louis, 1857–60

Brown, S. A. Boston, 1850–56

Bruderer. Geneva

Bryant, Henry. 1812–81. Virginia, 1844–46

Bubeník, J. J. Bratislava, Slovakia, 1840s
Buchtel, Joseph. U.S., ca. 1853
Buda, Elek. ca. 1812–90. (Hungary.) Transylvania
Budai, Károly. Hungary
Buell, E. W. Pittsfield, Mass., ca. 1849–53
Buell, L. W. Keokuk, Iowa, ca. 1853–55
Burdick, O. L. Davenport, Iowa
Burgess, Nathan G. New York City, 1844–59
Burritt, E. Toronto, ca. 1846
Buschmann, Joseph Ernest. 1814–53. Antwerp
Bussell, J. P. Boston, ca. 1850–51
Buswell, Luther. New York state, ca. 1851
Butler, George. Boston, ca. 1855
Butler, William H. New York City, 1847–53
Byerly, Jacob. Frederick, Md.

Cable, Rufus E. New Mexico; Denver; Kansas City, Mo.
Cady, James. New York City
Cahill, M. S. Boston, ca. 1852–59
Cajander, Henrick. 1804–48. Turku, Finland
Campbell, B. F. Boston, 1848–59
Campbell, John. Jersey City and Union City, N.J., ca. 1854–60
Campbell and Davis. Boston, ca. 1846
Caneva, Giacomo. Rome, 1850s
Canfield (Dr.). Philadelphia
Canfield, H. D. St. Louis, ca. 1851–53
Cannon, J. Boston, ca. 1846–49
Cannon, M. Boston, ca. 1850
Cannon, Marsena. 1812–1900. Salt Lake City, 1850–61
Cannon and Chaffin. Salt Lake City
Carden and Co. (later Carden and Norton). New York City, ca. 1853–54
Carey, P. M. Savannah
Carleton. Toronto, ca. 1848
Carlton, G. C. Amesbury, Mass., ca. 1849
Carlton, S. L. Portland, Maine, ca. 1849
Carvalho, Solomon N. 1815–99. Baltimore, New York City, Rocky Mountains
Cathan, Lucius H. 1817–ca. 1890.

Active Townshend, Vt.; Boston; ca. 1843–51 and after
Catherwood, George. Central America, 1841
Chamberlain, William G. (U.S.) Peru and Chicago, 1855–59
Chamberlin, F. Boston, ca. 1859
Chamberlin, Philo. Brunswick, Maine, ca. 1849
Champney, L. C. Massachusetts, Vermont, 1842–44
Chandler, Martin. Marshfield, Mass., ca. 1853
Channing, William Francis. 1820–1901. Boston, 1840s
Chapin, Moses Sanford. Worcester, Mass., 1850–ca. 1865
Charter, (Miss) S. R. Boston, 1845–49
Chase, Lorenzo G. Boston, 1844–55
Chauffourier, Gustavo Eugenio. 1907. (Italy.) Balkans (itinerant)
Cherbuin, L. *See* Falkeisen, J. J.
Chevalier, Charles. 1804–59. France
Chevalier, Vincent. b. 1770. France
Chilton, Howard. New York City, 1843
Chilton, James R. 1810–63. New York City, 1839–ca. 1843
Choloniewski, Hipolit. (Poland.) Lvov, Ukraine, ca. 1843
Church, Edwin. St. Louis, New York City, Memphis, ca. 1851
Churchhill, R. E. Albany, N.Y.
Clafflin (or Clafin), C. R. B. Worcester, Mass., ca. 1853
Clark, Anson. 1783–1847. West Stockbridge, Mass., 1841–44
Clark, D. G. Boston, 1850–54
Clark, David. New Brunswick, N.J., ca. 1853–54
Clark, F. J. Utica, N.Y.
Clark, George, Jr. Boston, 1854–59
Clark, H. H.
Clark, J. M. (U.S.) South America, New York City, ca. 1846–51
Clark, J. R. New York City, ca. 1846–47
Clark and Holmes
Clark Brothers. Utica and Syracuse, N.Y.; Boston
Claudet, Antoine François Jean
Clausel, Alexandre-Jean-Pierre. 1802–84. Troyes, France
Clifford, R. A. Milwaukee, 1850s
Coale, George B. Baltimore
Cobb, Luther. Providence, 1850–55
Cobb and Co. Providence, ca. 1849

Cobin, C. S. Providence, ca. 1849
Cocke, Archibald Lewis. England
Coffin, A. K. Boston, 1855–56
Collagan, C. H. Boston, ca. 1858
Collard. Poitiers, France
Collins, T. P. Westfield and Springfield, Mass., ca. 1853
Collins, Thomas P. and D. C. Philadelphia, ca. 1848
Compte, Louis. (France.) South America
Comsett, M. W. Boston, ca. 1858–59
Cone, D. D. Fisherville, N.H., ca. 1849
Connelly, A. H. Boston, ca. 1853
Constable, William. Brighton, England, 1841–51
Cook, George Smith. 1819–1902. New Orleans; New York City; Charleston, S.C.
Cook, Jane. New York City, ca. 1846
Cook and Walter. Iowa (itinerant), ca. 1845
Cooke, Josiah. Boston
Cooley, Otis H. Springfield, Mass., 1849–53
Cooley, S. A. Hartford, ca. 1849
Coombs, Fred. St. Louis, San Francisco, Chicago, 1846–50
Cooper, F. London
Cooper, J. T. England
Cornelius, Robert. 1809–93. Philadelphia, ca. 1839–42
Cortelyou, J. H. U.S., ca. 1850
Cresson, Charles. Philadelphia
Cressy and Emerson. Dover, N.H., ca. 1849
Cridland, T. W. Lexington, Ky.
Crockett, E. East Thomaston, Maine, ca. 1849
Crosby, Robert R. Boston, 1847–57
Crowe, Levi. Westchester, Pa., ca. 1850
Cundall, Joseph. 1818–95. England, ca. 1852
Currie, William. Philadelphia
Cutting, James Ambrose. 1814–67. Boston, ca. 1853–54
Cutting and Turner. Boston, ca. 1858–59

Daguerre, Louis Jacques Mandé
Daice, Adolf. Bucharest, ca. 1851
Dalee, A. G. d. 1879. Lawrence, Kans., ca. 1858
Dancer, John Benjamin. 1812–87. Liverpool, England

Darling. Boston, ca. 1841-42

D'Aubigny, Blanc. France

Dauthendey, Carl. (Germany.) Leipzig; Dessau; St. Petersburg, Russia

Davidson, Thomas. Scotland, ca. 1841

Davie, Daniel T. b. 1819. Utica and Syracuse, N.Y., ca. 1848-52

Davignon. St. Petersburg, Russia

Davis, Ari. Boston and Lowell, Mass., ca. 1841

Davis, Daniel, Jr. 1813-87. Boston

Davis, J. J. P. Boston, 1849-54

Davis, John Frederick. Nottingham, England, 1851-61

Davis and Co. Boston, 1857-59

Davos, W. P. Union Springs, N.Y.

Debevoise and Brother. New York City, ca. 1851

Dehme, G., and Jamrath, F. Berlin

Delemotte and Alary. Algeria, ca. 1850

della Rovere, (Pater) Vittorio. b. 1811. Italy, ca. 1845

Demarest, Abraham G. New York City, ca. 1851

Denny, C. B. Rochester, N.Y.

Dereimer, C. B. Auburn, N.Y.

Derussy. Paris, 1840s-50s

Desarnod, Auguste Joseph. 1812-49. Porvoo, Finland

Dessauer, L. W. (b. Germany.) Toronto, ca. 1843

Disbrow, Charles. New Haven, Conn., ca. 1849

Disdéri, André Adolphe-Eugène

Disdéri (Mme.). France

Doane, Thomas C. Montreal, 1847-68

Dobyns, T. C. Vicksburg, Va.; Louisville, Ky.; New Orleans; Nashville; St. Louis; Memphis; New York City, 1850-53 and after

Dobyns and Spaulding. St. Louis

Dodge, C. W. Boston, ca. 1857-59

Dodge, Edward Samuel. 1816-82. Augusta, Ga., ca. 1850-52; Poughkeepsie, N.Y.

Doe, R. W. Haverhill, Mass., ca. 1853

Dondez. France

Donné, Alfred. 1801-78. France

Donovan, M. B. Boston, ca. 1856

Dörffel, Theodor. Berlin

Dowd and Cornwall. New York City, ca. 1851

Drake, J. L. C. Effingham, N.H., ca. 1849

Draper, (Dr.) John William. 1811-82. New York City, ca. 1839

Drew, Clement. Boston, 1841-60

Drew, George H. Boston, ca. 1857

Dubosq-Soleil (Louis Jules Dubosq [1817-86]; Jean-Baptiste-François Soleil [1798-1878]). Paris

Duchochois, P. C. New York City

Dunning, V. Utica, N.Y.

Dunshee, E. S. Fall River, Mass., 1853; Bristol, R.I., 1855

Durang, W. A. New York City, ca. 1851

Durheim, Carl. 1810-90. (Switzerland.) Germany, 1845-49

Easterly, Thomas M. 1809-82. St. Louis and Liberty, Mo., 1846-82

Eastman, W. B. Boston, 1851-59

Edouart, Alexander. 1818-92. San Francisco, after 1852

Edwards (Mr.). Glasgow

Edwards, Jonas M. New York City, 1843-45; Washington, D.C., late 1840s

Edwards, William S. Boston, ca. 1855

Egerton, John. England

Ehrman, Charles. Philadelphia

Elliott, E. Chester, S.C.

Ellis, (Dr.) Alexander John. 1814-90. (England.) Rome, 1840-41

Ellis, Lemuel. Boston, ca. 1854

Ellis and Burnham. Bangor, Maine

Emery, George A. Boston, ca. 1856-57

Emmerson, J. H. Keokuk, Iowa, 1853-55

Ennis, T. L. Philadelphia

Ernst. Paris

Ettinghausen, (Prof.) von. Austria

Evans, G. Philadelphia

Evans, G. Utica, N.Y.

Evans, O. B. Buffalo, ca. 1850-55

Evans and Harrison. Buffalo, 1850s

Everett, Lorenzo C. Fitzwilliam, N.H., ca. 1849

Everett, R., Jr. Utica, N.Y.

Eynard, Jean Gabriel. (Switzerland.) Geneva and Paris

Fahrenburg, Albert. Louisville, Ky., ca. 1859

Fales, Charles. New Bedford, Mass., ca. 1849-53

Falkeisen, J. J., and Cherbuin, L. Milan, 1840s

Fanconier. St. Petersburg, Russia

Fanshaw (Mr.). Burlington, Iowa, ca. 1848

Faris, Thomas. Cincinnati, 1841-52; New York City, 1858-64

Fassett, Samuel Montague. Chicago, 1856-60

Fassett and Cook. Chicago, 1857-60

Feilner, T. C. Bremen, Germany

Felton, George W., Jr. Salem, Mass., ca. 1853

Fessenden, Benjamin. Boston, 1851-59

Field, Erastus Salisbury. 1805-1900. New York City, 1840s

Fields, William. Burlington, Iowa, ca. 1853

Finley, A. C. Jerseyville, Ill.

Finley, M. Canandaigua, N.Y.

Fish, A. A. Boston, 1844-61

Fish and Co. Boston, ca. 1855

Fish and Heywood. Boston, ca. 1856

Fisher, J. T., and Co. Toronto, ca. 1850

Fitz, Henry. 1808-63. New York City, Baltimore, 1839-42

Fitzgibbon, John H. ca. 1816-82. St. Louis

Fizeau, Hippolyte. 1819-96. France

Fletcher, S. Boston, ca. 1850

Flint, A. Montpelier, Vt.

Foard, James F. Liverpool, England

Fogg, C. W. Waltham, Mass., ca. 1853

Folger and Co. Boston, ca. 1857

Fontayne, Charles H. 1814-58. Baltimore, Cincinnati

Ford, J. M. San Francisco and Sacramento, Calif., ca. 1854-56

Foss, Plummer. Boston, 1847-49

Foster, B. Portland, Maine, ca. 1843

Foster, Lucian. New York City, 1843-46

Foucoult, Jean Bernard Léon 1819-68. France

Fowler, William H. New York City, ca. 1851

Fox, H. J. St. Louis

Franc, Bedřich. Slovakia, ca. 1840

Frazer, John. Philadelphia

Frazier, John. Jefferson City, Mo., ca. 1850-51

Fredricks, Charles (Carlos) DeForest. 1823-94. (U.S.) South America, 1843-ca. 1852; New York City, 1855 and after

French, Benjamin. Boston

Frink and Co.   Maine, ca. 1849
Frost, D. V.   Augusta, Pa.
Fuller, George.   England
Fuller, George.   1822-84. Boston, 1840-47
Fuller, John S.   Madison, Wis.
Fuller, N.   Richmond, ca. 1845

Gage, Franklin B.   1824-74. St. Johnsbury, Vt., 1851 and after
Gaige, J. G.   d. 1869. Arizona and New Mexico (itinerant), ca. 1862-69
Galpin, S. S.   New Haven, Conn., ca. 1849
Gardner, Cordelia A.   New York City, 1851
Garlick, Theodatus.   1805-84. Cleveland, ca. 1841
Garnier, J.   Avignon, France
Gatewood, E. H.   Boonville, Mo.
Gaudin, Marc Antoine.   France
Gauthier, Théophile.   1811-72. France
Gavit, Daniel E.   1819-75. New York City and Albany, N.Y., ca. 1850-52
Gay, C. H.   New London, Conn.; Providence; ca. 1845
Geer and Benedict.   Syracuse, N.Y.
Germon, Washington L.   Philadelphia, ca. 1850
Gervien, Theodor.   Tartu, Estonia
Gibson, George W.   Fall River, Mass., 1844
Gilchrist, George C.   Lowell, Mass., ca. 1849-53
Gilchrist and Currier.   Lowell, Mass.
Girault de Prangey, Joseph-Philibert.   1804-92. (France.) Italy, Greece, Egypt, Near East, 1841-43
Giroux (Mme.).   France
Gleisner, Jan.   (Poland.) Lvov, Ukraine, ca. 1839
Goddard, Emerson.   Cumberland and Woonsocket, R.I., ca. 1849-55
Goddard, John Frederick.   1795-1866. England
Goddard, M. J.   Lyons, N.Y.
Godquin.   France
Gola, Adám.   Buda, Hungary, ca. 1845
Gollob, Ludwig.   Austria-Hungary
Goodwin, (Mrs.) O. E.   Minneapolis, ca. 1859
Gorgas, John M.   Pittsburgh; Madison, Ind.; Ohio and Mississippi rivers; ca. 1847-56

Gouin, A.   France
Goupil-Fesquet, Frédéric.   (France.) Egypt, 1839
Gouraud, François.   d. 1848. (b. France.) New York City, Boston, Providence, Buffalo, 1839-42
Graves, E. R.   Lockport, N.Y., ca. 1853
Gray, L.   Oswego, N.Y.
Gregg.   Leavenworth, Kans., ca. 1859-60
Grekov, Aleksei.   Russia
Griswold, Victor M.   1819-ca. 1872. Tiffin, Ohio; Lancaster, Pa.; 1850-52
Gros, (Baron) Jean-Baptiste-Louis.   1793-1870. France
Guilford, E. R.   Amesbury, Mass., ca. 1853
Gurney, Jeremiah.   New York City, 1840 and after

Haas, Philip.   New York City; Washington, D.C.; 1844-57
Hacker, Theodore S.
Hadley, S. D.   Boston, ca. 1854
Hadley and Eastman.   Boston, ca. 1850
Haines, C. E., and Brother.   New Bedford, Mass., 1849-53
Hale, C.   Boston, ca. 1842-45
Hale, Luther Holman.   1821-85. Boston, Mass, 1846-59
Hall, Alfred.   Lawrence, Mass., ca. 1853
Hall, W. H.   Rouses Point, N.Y.
Halsey and Sadd.   Quebec City, Oct. 1840
Ham, Francis W.   Portsmouth, N.H., ca. 1849
Hamilton, George.   Boston, 1852-59
Hanson, Peter.   1821-87. New York City, ca. 1849
Harley and Metcalf
Harpy, Jason.   Lawrence, Mass., ca. 1853
Harrington, Lewis L.   New York City, ca. 1851
Harrison, Charles C.   d. 1864. New York City, ca. 1851
Harrison, Gabriel.   ca. 1818-1902. New York City, Brooklyn, 1844 and after
Harrison, J. T.   Wisconsin
Harrison and Hill.   Brooklyn
Hart, James.   St. Paul, ca. 1858
Hartman, Henry G.   Rochester, N.Y.

Hartshorn, W. S.   Providence, 1848-50
Hartsook, James.   Iowa City, Iowa, ca. 1854
Haskell, M.   Jersey City, N.J.
Haskins, F. W.   Fitchburg, Mass., ca. 1853
Haskins, Fred.   Boston, ca. 1859
Hastings, S. H.   Lowell, Mass., ca. 1849
Hathaway, William.   New Bedford, Mass., ca. 1853
Hatstat, A. J.   Boston, ca. 1857-58
Hawes, Josiah Johnson
Hawes (Howes), Samuel P.   Lowell, Mass., ca. 1849-53
Hawkes, B. F.   Boston, ca. 1852-53
Hawkins, Ezekiel C.   Cincinnati, 1844-60
Hawkins and Faris.   U.S. 1844-49
Hayden, Hiram Washington.   Waterbury, Conn., ca. 1851
Hayden, L. P.   New York City
Hayes and Co.   New York City, ca. 1851
Hayward, G. W.   Boston, ca. 1849-59
Hazleton, B. C.   Boston, ca. 1859
Heard, John A.   Boston, ca. 1851-52
Heller, Jozsef.   d. 1861. Buda, Hungary
Helmes, John C.   New York City, ca. 1851
Helsby, Tomas C.   (b. U.S.) Mexico; Buenos Aires, 1846; Valparaiso, Chile, after 1846
Hendee, D. H.   U.S., ca. 1853
Henderson, J.   New York City, ca. 1851
Henderson, James.   London
Hesler, Alexander.   1823-95. Madison, Wis.; Galena, Ill.
Hewitt, John M.   Louisville, Ky., ca. 1848
Heywood, J. B. (or J. D.).   Boston, ca. 1857-58
Higgins, B. L.   Syracuse, N.Y.
Higgins, O. T.   Boston, ca. 1854-59
Hill, Levi L.   1816-65. Westkill and Saugerties, N.Y.
Hill, R. H.   Kingston, N.Y.
Hills.   Brooklyn, ca. 1853 and after
Hillyer, Hamilton Briscoe.   ca. 1833-1903. Austin, Tex.
Hirst, J. W.   Pittsfield, Mass., ca. 1853
Hogg, Jabez.   1817-99. England
Hogg, (Mr.) R.   London
Holcomb, J. G.   Augusta, Maine

Holcomb, Sarah. Massachusetts and New Hampshire (itinerant), ca. 1846

Holmes, A. Boston, ca. 1849

Holmes, S. C. (or S. A.). New York City, ca. 1851–55

Holt, G. M. A. New York City

Holyroyd (Mr.). High Harrogate, England

Hopes, Caroline. St. Louis, ca. 1846

Horgan, Stephen H. U.S., 1870s

Horn, Vilem. 1809–91. Prague, 1841–65

Horton, H. W. Boston, ca. 1858–59

Hossauer, J. G. Bremen, Berlin

Hough, Eugenio K. Petersburg, Va., ca. 1858

Hough and Anthony. Providence, ca. 1847; Pittsburgh

Housekeeper, Cheney H. Philadelphia, ca. 1850

Hovey, Douglas. 1828–86. Philadelphia; Rochester, N.Y.

How, Willard. Boston, ca. 1856

Howard, David. Boston, ca. 1853

Howard, L. Norman. New York City, ca. 1851

Howe, Elias. 1819–67. Cambridgeport, Mass., ca. 1841 and after

Howe, George M. Portland, Maine, ca. 1853–54

Howell, E. M. New York City

Howell, W. B. Lexington, Mo.

Howes, Samuel P. See Hawes, Samuel P.

Howie (Mr.). Edinburgh

Hoyt, Mary S. Syracuse, N.Y.

Hoyt, Samuel. Lowell, Mass., ca. 1849

Hubert. France

Huddleston, J. S. F. Boston, ca. 1841

Hudson, E. A. Syracuse, N.Y.

Huet, H. J. Brussels

Hughes, Cornelius Jabez. 1819–84. (England.) Glasgow, London

Hull, H. B. Parkersburg, W.Va., 1850s

Humnicky, J. H. Bern, Switzerland, 1840s

Humphrey, Samuel Dwight. New York City and Canandaigua, N.Y.; ca. 1849 and after

Hunt, Caleb. Cleveland, ca. 1854

Hunt, John W. New York City, ca. 1851

Hunter, John. Chicago

Hunting, J. M. Boston, ca. 1853–57

Huntley, P. C. Paris, N.Y.

Hutchinson

Hyde, F. W. Fairfield, Vt., ca. 1849

Ingersoll, William. Boston, ca. 1859

Insley, H. E. (U.S.) Toronto (itinerant), ca. 1844; New York City, ca. 1851

Isenring, Johan Baptist. 1796–1860. Switzerland

Isings. Philadelphia

Ives, Ezra. Norwich, Conn., ca. 1849

Ives, Ira A. New York City, ca. 1851

Ives, Loyal Moss. Boston, 1844–56

Jacobs, Emil. New Orleans, 1851–65

Jacquard, Charles Le Maire. France

James, D. E., and Co. Boston, 1856–58

Jamrath, F. See Dehme, G.

Jaquith, Nathaniel. New York City, ca. 1851

Jarvis, (Dr.) William. b. 1822. St. Paul, ca. 1859

Jaschke, František. Prague, 1850s

Jedlik, Anyos. 1800–95. Hungary

Jenney, James. Middleborough, Mass., ca. 1853

Jennings, Oliver. Oregon, 1850s

Jerome and Co. Bangor, Maine, ca. 1849

Jobard, M. Belgium

Johnson, C. N. Batavia, N.Y.

Johnson, Charles E. Cleveland, ca. 1850–51

Johnson, George. California

Johnson, John. England

Johnson, John. New York City, ca. 1839

Johnson, W. S. Providence, ca. 1850

Johnson, Walter R. d. 1852. Philadelphia, ca. 1839–40

Johnson, William S. England

Johnston, D. B. Utica, N.Y.

Joly de Lotbinière, Pierre Gustave. (Canada.) Mideast, 1839 and after

Jones, J. (John). Baltimore, ca. 1848

Jones, J. Wesley. California, west of Rockies, the Plains, 1850–51

Jones, William B. Boston, ca. 1849–50

Jordan and Merrill. Bangor, Maine, ca. 1849

Jordon, William N. Boston, ca. 1854

Jube, T. S. New York City

Kaehnlein. Austria-Hungary

Kaim, E. Nottingham, England, 1847–49

Kallain. Austria-Hungary

Kawalky. Pest, Hungary, ca. 1844–61

Keith, (Dr.) George Skene. Scotland, 1844–48

Kelly, J. H. St. Anthony, Minn., ca. 1855

Kelsey, C. C. Chicago, ca. 1853–54

Kelsey, John. Philadelphia; Rochester, N.Y.; ca. 1853–55

Kenney. U.S.

Kent, W. H. London

Kenyon, H. P. Westerly, R.I., ca. 1855

Kern, Edward Meyer. 1823–63. (U.S.) China Seas and Bering Strait (survey), 1853–54

Kertson. New York City, ca. 1853–54

Khogler. Pest, Hungary, ca. 1843

Kilburn, William Edward. England, 1846–62

Kimball, J. A. New York City, ca. 1853–54

Kimball, William Hazen. 1817–92. Concord, N.H., 1844–ca. 1849

King, H. B. Boston, 1849–50; Taunton, Mass., 1850–59

King and Brother. New York City, ca. 1851

Klemens, Josef B. Prague, 1840s

Knapp, A. H. Boston, ca. 1855

Knapp, William R. New York City, ca. 1851

Knight, William. Racine, Wis.

Knoch, C. (Russia.) Estonia

Kobell, Franz von. 1803–75. Germany

Kornis, (Count) Zsigmond. 1827–55. (Hungary.) Transylvania

Kozič, Eduard. Slovakia, ca. 1850s

Kratochwilla, Franz. Austria

Krebs, A. R. U.S.

Krohne, Alexander. New York City

Krtička. Prague, after 1847

Kuczynski, Stefan Ludwik. Cracow, Poland, ca. 1840

Lacey, Z. Great Barrington, Mass., ca. 1853

Lancey, Samuel F. Roxbury, Mass., ca. 1853

Landry

Landy, James M. 1838–87. New York City

Lane, W. N. Nashua, N.H., ca. 1849

Lang, L. Portland, Maine, ca. 1849

Langdell, John. Nashua, N.H., ca. 1849

Langenheim, Frederick / Langenheim, William

Lawrence, Martin M. b. 1808. New York City, 1842–ca. 1854

Lay and Heywood. Boston, ca. 1858

Lazarus, Charles L. New York City, ca. 1851

Le Bleu, F. Hawaii, ca. 1846–47

Legendre. France

Leinback, T. Salem, N.C.

Le Lieure, Henri. Turin, Italy, 1850s

Lemercier. Belgium

Lerebours, Noël-Marie Paymal. 1807–73. France

Lerow, Jacob H. Boston, ca. 1850

Lerow and Co. Boston, ca. 1847–49

Lesbros. Rouen, France

Levitskii, Sergei L'vovich. 1819–98. (Russia.) St. Petersburg, Paris

Lewis, W. and W. H. New York City

L'Homidieu, Charles. Charleston, S.C.

Lilienthal, Theodore. New Orleans

Lincoln, Ambrose. Boston, ca. 1859

Lindhberg, Pehr. 1785–1868. Finland, Sweden

Lion (Lyons), Jules. New Orleans

Lipowitz, Aleksander. Poznan, Poland, 1842–55

Lipschütz, Beno. Finland, ca. 1843

Litch, Albert. Boston, ca. 1844 and after

Litch, Whipple and Co. Boston, ca. 1845

Litch and Graviss. Waterbury, Conn.

Lloyd, John R. Tallahassee, Fla.

Lloyd, S. H. U.S., ca. 1850–51

Lobethal. Prague, 1840s

Long Brothers (Enoch Long [b. 1823]; H. H. Long). Augusta, Ga.; St. Louis, 1846–65

Long, Enoch. b. 1823. Alton, Quincy, and Galena, Ill.

Louchet. France

Lounsberry, P. Burlington, Vt., ca. 1850–52

Lovering, R. F. Boston, ca. 1849–51

Lovering and Davis. Boston, ca. 1847

Lowe, R. Cheltenham, England

Lowell, John L. Ware, Mass., ca. 1853

Lucas, Stephen. Plymouth, Mass., ca. 1851

Ludlow, Frank G. Carson City, Nev., ca. 1862

Lullin, Jean Gabriel Bynard. Geneva

Lyons, J. L. New London, Conn., ca. 1849

Lyons, Jules. *See* Lion, Jules

Macaire, Cyrus. (b. France.) Southern U.S., 1840–41

Macaire, Hippolyte. France, 1851–60s

McBride, H. Albany, N.Y.

McBriggs, D. B. and J. U.S.

McClees, James E. Philadelphia

McClees and Germon. Philadelphia

McDonald, A., D., and R. Buffalo, N.Y.

McDonnell, Donald and Co. Buffalo and Toronto, ca. 1850

McGuire, James. New Orleans

McIntosh, H. P. Newburyport, Mass.

McIntyre, S. C. Tallahassee, Fla.; San Francisco; ca. 1845–50

McKeen, John G. New York state, ca. 1851

McKeney, E. H. Biddeford, Maine

Maguire, George. New York state, ca. 1851

Maitland, Rebecca. New York City, ca. 1851

Majocchi, G. A. Milan, Italy

Makko, Ludvik. Russia (itinerant); Tartu, Estonia; 1851–54

Manchester, Henry N. Providence, 1848–60

Manchester, Edwin H. Providence, 1848–60

Manchester and Chapin. Providence, ca. 1853

Manchester and Co. Providence, ca. 1847

Manicke, C. U.S., 1850s

Mann and Blodgett. Boston, ca. 1854–56

Marastoni, Jakab. 1804–1860. Pest, Hungary, ca. 1841–48

Marcus, J. B. Chenango, N.Y.

Marks, H. R. Baltimore

Marsters. Baltimore

Marston. Carson City, Nev.; San Francisco

Martens, Friedrich von. 1809–75. (Germany.) France

Martin, Anton. Vienna

Martin, J. E. Detroit

Martin, Jane P. Patterson, N.J.

Mascher, John F. Philadelphia, ca. 1852–57

Mason, L. Taunton, Mass., ca. 1849

Mason, William G. Philadelphia, ca. 1839

Masury, Samuel. Salem, Mass., 1849; Providence, 1845–50; Boston, until 1860

Masury and Hartshorn. Providence, ca. 1848

Masury and Silsbee. Boston, ca. 1852–55. Also Masury, Silsbee and Co. Boston, ca. 1855–57

Maszák, Hugó Szegedi. 1831–1916. (Hungary.) Transylvania

Mauch, C. H. Cologne, 1850s

Maxham, Benjamin D. Worcester, Mass., ca. 1856

Mayall, John Jabez. 1810–1901. (England.) Philadelphia, 1840–46; London and Brighton, England, 1846 and after

Mayer, Frank Blackwell. 1827–99

Mayer, John S. New York City, ca. 1851

Mayer and Pierson. France, 1850s

Mayer Brothers. France

Mayow, H. C. U.S., ca. 1860

Mayr, Christian. ca. 1805–51. New York City

Mazek, Ignacy. (Poland.) Cracow, Paris, early 1840s–after 1857

Meade, Charles Richard. d. 1858. New York City and Albany, N.Y., 1842 and after

Meade, Henry. d. 1865. New York City and Albany, N.Y., 1842 and after

Merrick, (Dr.) G. W. Adrian, Mich.

Metcalf, W. New York City

Mezey, Lajos. 1820–80. (Hungary.) Transylvania

Miko, (Count) Imre. (Hungary.) Transylvania

Miles, Charles T. Fayette, Mo.

Miller, R. A. Lowell, Mass., ca. 1853

Miller, W. A. Boston, ca. 1848

Millet, A. Paris

Millet, D. France

Minis. Petersburg, Va., ca. 1857

Mitchell, P. R. Dexter, Maine, ca. 1849

Moissenet, Dobyns, Richardson and Co. New Orleans, ca. 1853–54

Moissenet, F. New Orleans

Möllinger, Franziska. 1817–80. (Switzerland.) Germany

Monell, J. W. St. Anthony, Minn., ca. 1854–60

Moore, Henry. Lowell, Mass., ca. 1843

Moore, J. B. Boston, ca. 1850–53

Moore and Co. Boston, ca. 1849

Moore and Walter. Philadelphia

Moore and Ward. St. Louis

Moore and Weed. Boston, ca. 1859

Morand, Augustus. (U.S.) South America, southern U.S., New York City; ca. 1840–56

Morand, G. H. and A., and Co. New York City, 1842–45

Morelli, Achille. Rome, ca. 1840–41

Morrill and Smith. South Newburyport, Mass., ca. 1849

Morrison, J. W. C. Bath, Maine, ca. 1849

Morse, Samuel Finley Breese. 1791–1872. New York City, 1839–40

Moses, Morris. Trenton, N.J., 1850–65

Moulthrop, M. New Haven, Conn., ca. 1849

Moulton, J. C. Fitchburg, Mass., ca. 1853

Moulton, J. W. Salem, Mass., ca. 1853

Mozart, J. M. C. Boston, ca. 1851

Muller, C. J. New York City

Myers, J. S. Poughkeepsie, N.Y.

Nahl, Hugo Wilhelm Arthur. ca. 1820–89. California, mid-1850s

Naramore, William. Bridgeport, Conn., ca. 1849

Natterer, Johan and Joseph. Austria

Naumann, W. Germany

Navakovic, N. Zagreb

Naya, Carlo. 1816–82. (Italy.) Prague, 1844

Needles. Leavenworth, Kans., ca. 1857

Neff, Peter, Jr., and William. ca. 1856

Nègre, Charles

Negretti and Zambra. England

Neupert, Carl. Finland, Norway, Russia

Newcomer's Gallery. Philadelphia

Nichols, C. Boston, ca. 1856

Nichols, John P. Boston, ca. 1849–51

Nichols, Sheldon K. Hartford, Conn.; San Francisco

Nicholson, John. 1825–93. Columbus and Franklin, Ind., 1850–60

Nicklin, Richard. d. 1854. England

Nicols, A. C. Fulton, N.Y.

Ninet, A. L. P. Belgium (itinerant)

North, Enrique. (U.S.) Buenos Aires, ca. 1848

North, William C. Cleveland and Dayton, Ohio; ca. 1853–54

North, William C. Boston, ca. 1849

Notman, William

Nye, A. G. Weymouth, Mass., ca. 1853

Ohr, M. L. Indianapolis, 1850s

Orbeton, William S. Boston, ca. 1850

Ormsbee, A. Saco, Maine, ca. 1849

Ormsbee, Marcus. Boston, ca. 1852–60

Ormsbee and Silsbee. Portland, Maine, ca. 1849; Boston, ca. 1852

Osborn, James M. New York City, ca. 1851

Outley, J. J. St. Louis

Page, Charles G. Washington, D.C., ca. 1843

Page, J. Boston, ca. 1848

Page and Chessman. U.S.

Paige, Blanchard P. Washington, D.C., 1850–65

Paine, George P. St. Louis

Palmer (Mr.). (U.S.) New Orleans; Mexico

Palmer, Eli J. Toronto, 1849–70

Pardee (Parde), Phineas, Jr. New Haven, Conn., ca. 1842–45

Parker, T. M. Burlington, Vt., ca. 1849

Parkhurst, Otis J. Milford, Mass., ca. 1853

Parsons, George F. Hartford, Conn., ca. 1849

Parsons, L. V. Auburn, N.Y.

Partridge, A. C. Wheeling, W.Va.

Partridge, H. E. Boston, ca. 1850

Pattinson, H. L. (England.) U.S.

Pearsall, Alva. d. 1898. Brooklyn, until 1879

Pearson and Grove. Lowell, Mass., ca. 1849

Peck, Samuel. New Haven, Conn., ca. 1847–ca. 1860

Pennell, Joseph. New York City; Cabotsville (now Chicopee) and

Boston, Mass.; Waterbury, Conn.; ca. 1840–48

Perkins, Elijah R. Topsfield, Mass., ca. 1853

Perkins, J. S., Jr. Newburyport, Mass., ca. 1853

Perraud. (France.) Rome, 1845–46

Perry, Edward (E. C.). New York City and Lancaster, N.Y.; Danville, Vt.; Chicago; ca. 1846–57

Perry and Co.

Peters, M. B. Pittsfield, Mass., ca. 1849

Petitpierre, Edouard. 1789–1862. (Switzerland.) Berlin

Pettee, Joseph. Boston, ca. 1848–49

Petters, Christoph Heinrich Hermann. 1806–75. Germany

Pettigrew, Samuel. Lexington, Va., 1857

Philips, A. B. St. Louis

Piard, Victor. New York City

Pickering (Mr.). Glasgow

Picot, J. England

Pierson (also Pierson Frères). Paris, 1850s

Pike and Arbuckle. Northampton, Mass., ca. 1849

Plitt, Angus. St. Louis

Plumbe, John, Jr. 1809–57. (Wales.) Lexington, Ky.; Washington, D.C.; Boston; Baltimore; New York City; Philadelphia

Plumbe, Richard. Boston, ca. 1848–50

Plumier, Alphonse. Brussels, Liège, Antwerp

Plumier, Victor. Paris, 1850s

Pohlmann, I. Bucharest, ca. 1845

Pollack. Baltimore

Popkins, Benjamin F. Greenfield, Mass., ca. 1853

Popowitz (Poppawitz), G. Edinburgh; Nottingham, England, 1846

Porges, J. Prague and Carlsbad, Bohemia, 1850s

Porter, Martin. West Cornwall, Conn., ca. 1849

Porter, William Southgate. 1822–89. Philadelphia, Cincinnati

Post, Jacob A. New York City, ca. 1851

Powelson and Co. New York City, ca. 1851

Powelson and Mendham. New York City

Powers, E. M. Richmond, ca. 1855–56

Pratt, E. W.   New York City, ca. 1854

Pratt, William A.   b. 1818. (England.) Richmond, ca. 1846–56

Pratt and Bowes.   Providence, ca. 1848

Prevost, Victor.   New York City

Price's Gallery.   Baltimore

Priz, Wilhelmina.   Bucharest, ca. 1842

Proctor, Alfred.   Boston, 1853–59

Prosch, George W.   (U.S.) Newark, N.J.; New York City; Canada; 1840–55

Pruden, Henry.   Lockport, N.Y., area, ca. 1853

Prud'homme, John Francis Eugene.   1800–92. New York City, ca. 1851

Pumphrey, William.   England

Quith, J. A.   New York City

Radwanski, Jedrzej.   1800–60. Poland, ca. 1839

Ragg, G. S.   (U.S.) Denmark, New York state

Rahmann, Ferdinand.   Austria-Hungary

Rankin.   Leavenworth, Kans., ca. 1855

Rath, Pavel.   Slovakia, ca. 1850s

Read, George.   Philadelphia, ca. 1842

Reed, G. M.   New York City, ca. 1854

Reese and Co.   New York City, ca. 1853–54

Reeves.   London, ca. 1850

Reeves, Nelson B.   New York City, ca. 1851

Rehn, Isaac A.   Philadelphia, ca. 1849–59

Rehnstrom, Fredrik.   1819–57. Finland, 1844–51

Rehula, Antonín.   Prague, 1850s

Reiser, Carl.   Austria

Relph, John.   Liverpool, England

Rendu, Abel.   France

Rice, J. L.   Boston

Rice, L. C.   Boston, ca. 1850

Rice, Samuel.   New York City, ca. 1851

Rice and Heard.   Boston, ca. 1849

Rice and Parks.   Boston, ca. 1848

Richards, F. De Bourg.   Philadelphia, 1848–66

Richebourg.   France

Rickard, P.   Fitchburg, Mass., ca. 1853

Rider, G. W.   Providence, ca. 1855; Boston, ca. 1859

Ritten, E. D.   Danbury, Conn.

Roberts, Thomas.   Derby, England, 1840s

Robinson, Charles.   Minneapolis, ca. 1859

Robinson, E. P.   Boston, ca. 1847

Robinson, Joseph C.   New York City, Cincinnati, ca. 1848–51

Rockwood, George.   New York City

Rogers, C. T.   St. Louis, ca. 1854

Rood and Comsett.   Boston, ca. 1856–57

Rood and Edwards.   Boston, ca. 1855

Root, Marcus A.   1808–88. Mobile, Ala.; New Orleans; St. Louis; Philadelphia; New York City

Root, Samuel.   1819–89. Dubuque, Iowa; Philadelphia; New York City

Ross and Thompson.   Edinburgh

Rulofson, William Henry.   1826–78. (Canada.) St. John, New Brunswick, before 1846–after 1849; California, 1849 and after

Rulofson and Cameron.   Sonora, Calif., 1848–57

Ryder, James F.   U.S. (itinerant), 1847; Cleveland, 1850–58

Sabatier-Blot, Jean-Baptiste.   1801–81. France

Saben, P.   Boston, ca. 1847

Sabine, James E.   Santa Fe, N.Mex.; Colorado; ca. 1855–57

Sachse, Louis.   Berlin

St. Croix, de.   France

Saint-Victor, Niepce de.   France

Saladin.   Moulins, France

Salen, P. T.   Boston, ca. 1850

Sampson, J. S.   Augusta, Maine, ca. 1849

Sawyer, John.   Boston

Saxton, Joseph.   Philadelphia, ca. 1839

Schall, Johann Carl.   1805–85. Berlin

Schnelle, Friederich.   Germany

Scholtz, Maurycy.   Warsaw, after 1839

Schoonmaker.   Troy, N.Y.

Schuh, Karl.   d. 1865. Vienna

Schutz, Thomas.   Bremen, Germany

Scotchler, J.   Boston, 1855–58

Scott, W. P.   (U.S.) Hawaii, ca. 1850

Seager, D. W.   (England?) New York City, ca. 1839–40

Seaver, C.   Boston, ca. 1857–58

Seaver and Butler.   Boston, ca. 1854–56

Seely, Charles.   New York City

Seligman, Siegmund (Sigismund).   1830–76. Santa Fe, N.Mex., ca. 1854–56

Selkirk, James H. and J.   Matagorda, Tex., ca. 1851–60

Selleck, S.   New York City

Shamp, Moses.   Fairfield, Iowa

Shannon, Julia.   U.S.

Sharp, Philip Thomas.   Boston, 1852–62

Sharp, Thomas.   Somerset County, England

Shaw, F. G.   Maine, ca. 1849

Shaw, G. B.   (b. England.) New Zealand, 1855

Shaw, George.   Birmingham, England

Shaw, S. L.

Shepard, N. H.

Shepherd, Nicholas H.   Springfield, Ill., 1845–48

Shew, Jacob.   Baltimore, Philadelphia, San Francisco, 1841–62

Shew, Myron.   Philadelphia, 1841–51 or after

Shew, Truman.   Philadelphia, 1841–48

Shew, William.   1820–1903. Boston, ca. 1848–50; San Francisco

Shorb, J. R.   Winsboro, S.C.

Shumway, E. G.   Amherst, Mass., ca. 1853

Sidell.   New York City, ca. 1851

Siko, Miklos.   (Hungary.) Transylvania

Silsbee, Case and Co.   Boston, ca. 1859

Silsbee, George M.   Boston, ca. 1852–57

Simmons, J. F.   Milford, Mass., ca. 1853

Simons, Montgomery P.   Philadelphia, Richmond, ca. 1848

Simpson, A. J.   Lowell, Mass., ca. 1849–53 or after

Sims, Thomas.   Weston-super-Mare, England

Sissons, N. E.   Albany, N.Y.

Skoff, Primus.   (b. Venice.) Nový Jičín, Czechoslovakia, ca. 1843

Smith, David.   Enfield, Mass., ca. 1853

Smith, E. A. Boston, ca. 1842

Smith, Hamilton L. Cleveland, ca. 1840; Gambier, Ohio

Smith, Hannibal L.

Smith, L. C. Sharon, Vt., ca. 1843

Smith, Matt K. Oregon, 1850s

Smith, Morris. New Bedford, Mass., ca. 1849-53

Snell, William. Salem, Mass., ca. 1853

Snelling, Henry Hunt. b. 1817. New York City, 1850s

Somerby. Boston, before 1844

Southworth, Albert Sands / Hawes, Josiah Johnson

Spieler, William F. Philadelphia, 1844-60

Stack, Charles. Marienbad, Zagreb

Stahl, I. Cracow, Poland, and elsewhere, early 1840s

Stamm and Upman. Milwaukee

Stancliff, J. W. Hartford, Conn., ca. 1849 and after

Stangenwald, (Dr.) Hugo. 1829-99. Hawaii, ca. 1850-65

Stangenwald and Goodfellow. California

Stanley, J. H. S. b. 1800. Houston, Tex., 1850-70

Stanley, John Mix. 1814-72. Washington, D.C., ca. 1842; survey for transcontinental railroad, 1853

Stansbury, B. New York City

Starkweather, J. B. Boston, ca. 1854-57

Stauffer, Jacob. Richmond (now Mt. Joy), Pa., 1839-58

Steinheil, Carl August von. 1801-70. Germany

Stelzner, Carl Ferdinand. 1805-94. Hamburg.

Stephens, John Lloyd. Central America, 1841

Stevens, Ephraim. Manchester, N.H., ca. 1849

Stevens, J. W. Craftsbury, Vt., ca. 1849

Stevenson, John G. Washington, D.C.

Stiba, Julius. Germany

Still, John. Philadelphia

Stimson, John. Boston, ca. 1853-55

Stock, Joseph Whiting. 1815-55. Springfield, Mass.

Stone, G. W. Boston, ca. 1850

Stone, J. Boston, ca. 1851-55

Stonehouse (Mr.). Whitby, England

Strasz, Maksymilian. Poland, ca. 1840

Strohberger, Josip. Zagreb

Strong, Walter. New York City, ca. 1851

Stroud, William. Norristown, Pa.

Stuhr. (Germany.) Pest, Hungary, ca. 1844

Stull, John. Philadelphia

Suscipi (Suscipj), Lorenzo. Rome, early 1840s

Susse, Frères. France

Sutton and Brothers. Chicago

Swallow, A. L. Burlington, Iowa

Swasey and Chapin. Chicopee, Mass., ca. 1849

Swift, Charles. Boston, ca. 1853-57

Swift, H. B. Philadelphia

Swift, R. R. Chicopee, Mass., ca. 1849-53

Szàthmari, Carol Popp (de). Bucharest, 1843-44

Szczepanski, K. (Poland.) Prague, Cracow, early 1840s

Szczodrowski, Karol. Warsaw, 1840s

Talbot, J. W. Petersborough, N.H.

Tarsch, Ferenc. Pest, Hungary, ca. 1842

Taylor, George F. Boston, ca. 1850

Telfer, William. England

Tensi, Baptist. Scandinavia, ca. 1843

Thacher, L. P. Middleborough, Mass., ca. 1853

Thayer, Charles. Charlestown, Mass., ca. 1849-53

Theyer, Martin. Austria

Thiérry, I. Lyons, France

Thiésson, E. France

Thomas (M.). Paris

Thompson, Frederick. Toronto, ca. 1853

Thompson, John. Boston, ca. 1854-56

Thompson, Josiah W. New York, ca. 1851

Thompson, L. Norwich, Conn., ca. 1849

Thompson, S. N. Roxbury, Mass., ca. 1853

Thompson, Warren. (U.S.) Philadelphia, 1840-46; Paris, 1847-59

Thomson and Davis

Tilley, J. H. Newport, R.I., ca. 1855

Tomlinson, William Agur. 1819-ca. 1862. New Haven, Conn.; New York City, Poughkeepsie, and Troy, N.Y.; ca. 1846-62

Townshend, S., Jr. Providence, ca. 1845

Treffray (Mr.). Glasgow

Troendle, Joseph F. Louisville, Ky., ca. 1859

Trufant, A. F. Boston, ca. 1855-56

Turner. Geelong, Australia

Turner, Austin A. Boston, New York City

Tuttle, Moses C. St. Paul and St. Anthony, Minn., 1853-ca. 1873

Tyler and Co. Boston, ca. 1855

Upton

Ussing, Johan Ludwig. Germany

Vail, J. H. New Brunswick, N.J.

Vaillat, E. Paris, Lyons

Vállas, Antal. 1809-69. Austria-Hungary

Van Alstin, Andrew Wemple. 1811-57. Worcester, Mass., 1843-57

Vance, Robert H. d. 1876. San Francisco, Sacramento, and Marysville, Calif.; ca. 1851-61

Van Loan, Samuel. Philadelphia, 1844-54

Vannerson, Julian. Washington, D.C., ca. 1853-54

Venino, Francis. New York City, 1850s

Vernet, Horace. 1789-1863. France

Vogel, William. St. Louis.

Voigtländer, Evans and Co. London

Von Schneidau, John Frederick Polycarpus. 1812-59. (Sweden.) New York City, Chicago; 1849-55

Vrba, Jan. Brno, Slovakia, ca. 1841

Wagner, Krisztián. Sopron, Hungary, mid-1840s

Wakefield (Mr.). Portland, Ore.

Walker, G. G. and Co. Providence, ca. 1850-55

Walker, S. L. Poughkeepsie and Albany, N.Y.

Walker, Sheldon H. Holyoke, Mass., ca. 1853

Walsh, Thomas. New York City, ca. 1851

Walters, Charles J. B. New York City, ca. 1858-60

Walzl, Richard. Baltimore

Ward, C. Springfield, Mass., ca. 1853

B

Additional Photographers

Often a collector comes across an old photograph by a photographer whose name is unfamiliar or about whom information is not readily available. One might also purchase a relatively recent photograph but still find it hard to locate data about the person who made it; many photographers, especially young ones, have yet to be recognized in print. For the collector in such a predicament, the following list of thousands of photographers may help by providing a little biographical information — or at least the reassurance that some documentation exists.

The list, which also includes many well-known photographers, was compiled from a wide variety of sources: photographs, reliable written histories, directories issued by photographic organizations, exhibition and auction catalogues, magazines, newspapers, annuals, and so forth. Because of space limitations, only basic information, when known, about place and dates of activity has been included. In many instances the available facts are incomplete or contradictory (variant transliterations and similar inconsistencies sometimes occur). Fuller information about many of the photographers may be found in specialized sources or in the histories and surveys cited in the general bibliography (for stereographers, see the two books by William Culp Darrah; no attempt has been made here to incorporate these lists).

The names are generally listed exactly as in the original source — that is, with abbreviated first names, with initials only, with unusual spellings or diacritics, and so forth — although an effort has been made to verify them when possible. Honorifics and titles — such as "Cav." (*cavaliere* = sir),

"Dott." (*dottore* = doctor), or "Ing." (*ingegnere* = engineer) — are usually included if given in the source.

When known, the country of main activity immediately follows the name. (If known to be different, the photographer's native country is given in parenthesis, although in many instances this information is not available.) The country has usually been omitted for brevity's sake when a specific region, state, city, or other locality is mentioned.

Unless otherwise indicated, the years given here are life dates. In their absence, a period of activity is included when known. For this century, the phrases "Active 20th c." and "Contemporary" are both used; the latter term, somewhat more specific, suggests that most activity occurred after about 1950.

Many photographers worked in partnerships or firms as well as independently (for instance, Humphrey Lloyd Hime may have been a principal in the listed firm Armstrong, Beere, and Hime). For the most part, no attempt has been made here to link firms with separately listed individuals who might have been affiliated with them.

This appendix does not include photographers featured in chapter 5 as main entries or in group entries (all such individuals can be found in the index). Daguerreotypists in appendix A, unless known to have used later photographic media in addition to the daguerreotype, are also excluded. Most other photographers mentioned in *The Photograph Collector's Guide* do appear here, with supplemental data whenever possible. Photographers whose names are preceded by an asterisk (*) are also listed in chapter 7, which may be consulted for a bit of additional information.

Despite extensive research, inadvertent omissions and errors are inevitable in an endeavor of this scope. The authors would appreciate receiving corrections, in care of New York Graphic Society, 41 Mt. Vernon Street, Boston, Massachusetts 02106.

Aaron, G. U.S. Active 20th c.
*Aarons, Jules. U.S. 1921–
Aarons, Leo. U.S. Contemporary
Abbati, Giuseppe
Abbe, Ernst. Germany. 1840–1905
Abbe, Kathryn. U.S. Contemporary
Abbenseth, William H. U.S. 1892–1972
*Abell, Raymond. U.S. 1940–
Abell, Sam. Contemporary
Aberhard, Laurence. New Zealand. 1949–
*Abernathy, Billy. U.S. 1938–
Abin Martin, José Gerardo. Mexico. Contemporary
Abney (Capt.). Active London, 19th c.
Abney, (Sir) William de Wiveleslie. England. 1843–1920
*Abrahams, Ivor. Contemporary
Abrahamson, Inger. Active 20th c.
Abramovice, Aurel. Active Bucharest, 20th c.
Abramson, Michael. U.S. 1944–
Abreu, Luis. Brazil. Contemporary
Acconci, Vito. U.S. 1940–
*Ace Possible (Susan Hiller). Contemporary
Acevedo Mendoza, Jorge. Mexico. Contemporary
Adál (Adál Maldonado). U.S. (b. Puerto Rico). 1948–
Adam, Monique. Belgium. 1949–
Adam, Pierre. Active Paris, 20th c.
Adams, Charles J. Active Worcester, Mass., 20th c.
Adams, Eddie. U.S. Contemporary
Adams, George. U.S. Active 20th c.
Adams, Gilbert. England. Active 20th c.
Adams, John. Peru. Active 1851–54
*Adams, John P. U.S. 1932–
Adams, Marcus. Active London, 20th c.
Adams, Mark Bentley. New Zealand. 1949–
Adams, S. F. Active Oak Bluffs and New Bedford, Mass., ca. 1860–80
Adams, Washington Irving Lincoln. U.S. Active late 19th c.

Adam-Salomon, Antoine Samuel. France. 1811–81
Adamson, Edwin S. Australia and New Zealand. Active 20th c.
Adamson, John
Addison, N. U.S. Active 19th c.
Adèle (studio). Active Vienna, ca. 1865–75
Adelman, Robert. U.S. 1930–
Adelskold, C. A. Sweden. 1824–1907
Adkin, George Leslie. New Zealand. 1888–1963
Adolph, Heinrich G. Active Copenhagen, 20th c.
Adriaan, John. U.S. (b. South Africa). Active 20th c.
Aegerter, Chr. Active Bern, Switzerland, 20th c.
Aerts, Louis. Belgium. Active 20th c.
Agha, M. F. U.S. Active 20th c.
Agnew, Thomas. 1794–1891
Aguado (Count) Olympe. France. 1827–94
Aguilar Aguirre, Raúl. Mexico. Contemporary
Aguilera Hernández, Carlos. Mexico. Contemporary
Aguinaco Llano, Jorge Pablo de. Mexico. Contemporary
Ahern, R. F. U.S. Active 20th c.
*Ahlsted, David. U.S. 1943–
Ahumada Salaiz, Alicia. Mexico. Contemporary
*Aiken, Roger. U.S. Contemporary
Aimard. France
Aiton, William Townsend. 1766–1849
Ajtay-Heim, (Dr.) Jeno. Active Budapest, 20th c.
Akcock, William. Active 20th c.
*Akiba, David. Contemporary
Akiyama, Ryoji. Japan. 1942–
Akkerman, J. Netherlands. Active 20th c.
Alario, Joseph. Italy. Active 20th c.
Albeem, Wayne. Active Seattle, 20th c.
Albert, F. Germany. Active ca. 1865
Albert, Josef. 1825–86. Active Munich

Albert, Paul. U.S. Contemporary
Albert, Prince. Great Britain (b. Germany). 1819–61
*Albertine, Richard. Contemporary
Alberts, Andrea. U.S. 1946–
Albin-Guillot, Laure. France. Contemporary
*Albrecht, Jim. U.S. Contemporary
Albright, H. Oliver. Active San Francisco, ca. 1903
Albuquerque Ruegger, Maria Beatriz de. Brazil. Contemporary
Alcock, William A. Active New York City, 20th c.
Alda, Arlene. U.S. Contemporary
Aldana Espinosa, Guillermo. Mexico. Contemporary
Aldapa, Ignacio. Mexico. Contemporary
Aldis
Alenius, Hans. Sweden. 1937–
Alexander, Michael. U.S. Active 20th c.
Alinari, Romualdo. d. 1890. Active Florence
Allan Brothers. England. Active late 19th c.
Alland, Alexander. U.S. (b. Sebastopol, Crimea). 1902–
Allen, Albert Arthur. Active 20th c.
Allen, Charles and Gabriel. U.S. Active 20th c.
Allen, Charles Smith. Active Wales, ca. 1890
Allen, Edward L. Active Boston, ca. 1860–80
Allen, Frances and Mary. Active Deerfield, Mass., 1890s
Allen, Harold. U.S. Contemporary
Allen, Joseph W. New Zealand. Active ca. 1867–85
Allen, Leslie. U.S. 1954–
Allen and Rowell. U.S. Active 19th c.
Alley, E. H. Active Toledo, Ohio, 19th c.
Allilouyev, S. Ivanov. Active Moscow, 20th c.
Alloend Bessand, H. France. Active 20th c.
Almasy, Paul. France (b. Austria-Hungary). 1906–

Almeida, Helena. Portugal. Contemporary

Almeida Herrera, Luis. Mexico. Contemporary

Alophe, Marie-Alexandre. France. 1811–83

Alpern, Leon. Active Warsaw, 20th c.

Alpert, Max. Russia. 1899–

Alter, Fritz. Germany. Active 20th c.

Altobelli, Gioacchino. Active Rome, 1860s–70s

Altschul, M. Active Copenhagen, 20th c.

*Alvarez, Richard. U.S. Contemporary

Alvarez Fuentes, Jorge. Mexico. Contemporary

Alves Neto, Abelardo Bernardino. Brazil. Contemporary

Alves Santos, Rosa Maria. Brazil. Contemporary

Alviña, Luis. Peru. Active 19th c.

Ambler, Maurice. England. Active 20th c.

Amenya. U.S. Active 20th c.

Amero, Emilio. b. 1857

Amic-Gazán. Peru. Active 19th c.

Amson, Marcel. France. Active 20th c.

Amurski, I. G. U.S.S.R. Active 20th c.

Anchier, E. France. b. 1860

Andà, Héctor de. Mexico. Contemporary

Anda, Juan Manuel. Peru. Active 19th c.

Andel, Jaroslaw. Czechoslovakia. 1949–

Andermatt, Jürg. Switzerland. 1941–

Anderson, Domenico. 1854–1938. Active Rome

*Anderson, Donald R. U.S. Contemporary

Anderson, Erica. U.S. 1914–

*Anderson, Hollis. U.S. 1944–

Anderson, J. W. Active late 19th c.

Anderson, John A. U.S. (b. Sweden). 1869–1948

Anderson, John H. England. Active early 20th c.

Anderson, Katherine M. Active Ohio, 20th c.

*Anderson, Lawrence. U.S. Contemporary

Anderson, Marge. U.S. 1950–

Anderson, Marilyn. U.S. Contemporary

Anderson, P. D. Active San Francisco, 20th c.

Anderson, Paul L. Active New Jersey, 20th c.

Anderson, Peter. U.S. ca. 1918–

Anderson, Robert W. Active Toronto, 1860s

Andersson, Andrey. Active 20th c.

Andersson, Gosta. Sweden. Contemporary

Andrade, Yolanda. Mexico. Contemporary

André, Jacques. Active 20th c.

André, Rogi. France. Active 20th c.

Andreae-Held, Barbara. Colombia. Contemporary

Andrée, Salomon August. Sweden. 1854–97. Also active the Arctic

Andreola, Salvatore. Italy. Active 20th c.

*Andrews, Alice. *See* Wells, Alice

Andrews, Mary Ellen. U.S. Contemporary

*Andrews, Michael. U.S. 1945–

Andrews, Weston. U.S. Contemporary

Andriesse, Emmy. Netherlands. 1914–53

Andujar, Claudia. Brazil. 1931–

Angel Juarez, Adrien del. Mexico. Contemporary

Angelo. Active Budapest, 20th c.

Angenendt, Erich. Germany. Active 20th c.

Angenendt, Rudi. Germany. Active 20th c.

Angerer, Ludwig. Romania. 1827–79. Active Bucharest and Vienna

Angerer, Viktor (Victor). 1839–94

Angerer, Wilhelm. Austria. Active 20th c.

*Angier, Roswell. U.S. 1940–

Anginot, Dominique. France. 1949–

Anglonnes, (Prince) Giron des

Angulo, Anibal. Mexico. Contemporary

Angulo, Chappie. Mexico. Contemporary

Angyalfi, Andor. Active Sopron, Hungary, 20th c.

Anikeyev, Sybil. U.S. 1896–

Anschütz, Ottomar. Germany. 1846–1907

Ansdell, Richard. England. Active 19th c.

Ansiglioni, Giuliano. Active Rome, 1860s

Anson-Herrick. U.S. Active 20th c.

Anthony, Eugene. Active 20th c.

Anthony, Gordon. England. Active 20th c.

Anthony, Henry T. 1814–84. Active New York City

Anthony, John. Active Jerusalem, 1860s

Antmann, Fran. U.S. Contemporary

Antoine, Franz. Austria. 1815–86

Antonini, Marko. Active Zagreb, ca. 1876

Aonzo, (Cav.) Enrico. Active Genoa, Italy, 20th c.

Apers, P. Active Paris, 20th c.

Appert, E. Active Paris, 1870s

Arago, François Jean Dominique. France. 1786–1853

*Arakawa, Shusaku. Contemporary

Arakelyan, S. Active Boston, early 20th c.

Aral. Active 20th c.

Arana Cedeño, Marcos. Mexico. Contemporary

Araujo, Dulce. Brazil. Contemporary

Araujo, Odilón. Brazil. Contemporary

Arauz, Juan Víctor. Mexico. Contemporary

Arbuthnot, Malcolm. England. 1874–1968

Arce, Enrique. Mexico. Contemporary

Archer, Charles K. Active Pittsburgh, 20th c.

Archer, Frederick Scott. England. 1813–57

Archer, Fred R. U.S. Active 20th c.

*Arena, John P. U.S. 1916–

Arenas Sánchez, Lucio. Mexico. Contemporary

Arentz, Dick

Argall, Frederick. Active Truro, Mass., 1870s

Armstrong, Beere, and Hime. Active Toronto, 19th c.

Armstrong, Christa. U.S. Contemporary

Armstrong-Jones, Antony. *See* Snowdon

Arnault, Daniel. France. Contemporary

*Arndt, Thomas. U.S. 1944–

Arnfeld, Julius. Active 20th c.

*Arnold, Bill. U.S. 1941–

Arnold, Charles. U.S. Contemporary

Arnold, Eve. England (b. U.S.). 1913–

Arnoux, H. Active Port Said, Egypt, 1860s

Arnoux and Zangaki (Langaki). Egypt. Active 1880s.

Arrowsmith, Clive. England. Active 20th c.

Arruda Hermano, Odessa. Brazil. Contemporary

Arthaud, Claude. France. Active 20th c.

Arthaud, Marcel. France. Active 20th c.

Arthur, James. England. Active late 19th c.

Artus, Otto Michael. Germany. 1917–

Asch, David. Active 20th c.

Aschauer, Julius. Active Vienna, 20th c.

Ascher, Daisy. Mexico. Contemporary

Aschkenas, David. U.S. Contemporary

Ashjian, Lucy. Active New York City, 20th c.

Ashton, F. G. Canada. 1888–1967

Askenas, Ulf. Sweden. Active 20th c.

Asser, E. J.

Assman, George Mickey. U.S. Active 20th c.

Astman, Barbara. Canada. Contemporary

Aston, W. Smedley. Active late 19th c.

*Asturias, Esther. U.S. Contemporary

Aszmann, Ferencz. Hungary. Active 20th c.

Atkeson, Ray. U.S. Active 20th c.

Atkins, Anna. England. Active 19th c.

Atkins. Ollie. U.S. Active 20th c.

Atkinson, E. England. Active late 19th c.

Attie, David. U.S. Contemporary

Aubert, L. Active Chartres, France, 20th c.

Aubry, Charles. France. Active 1860s and after

Auerbach, Erich. England. Active 20th c.

Aufsberg, Lala. Germany. Active 20th c.

Aughiltree, Jas. W. Active Plainfield, N.J., 20th c.

Auhamescu, George. Active Bucharest, 20th c.

Auquier, Yves. Belgium. 1934–

Auradon, Jean-Marie. France. 1887–1958

Austen, Alice. U.S. 1866–1952

Austin, Terence V. New Zealand (b. England). 1945–

Autry, Max Mun. U.S. Active 20th c.

Auvillain. France. Active 20th c.

Avilés, Alfredo Apey. Chile. Active 20th c.

Avilés, Hipócrates. Mexico. Contemporary

Avison, David. U.S. 1937–

Aylett, Charles. Active Toronto, 20th c.

Ayres, Thomas. England. Active 1880s

Ayscough, Anthony. England (b. Scotland). 1910–39

Azhderian, Reuben B. Active Newark, N.J., 20th c.

B. K. (publisher). Active Paris, 1860s

Baader, Johannes. Germany. Contemporary

Baasch, Kurt W. U.S. (b. Venezuela). 1891–1964

Babbage, Charles. England. 1792–1871

*Baber, Jack. U.S. 1931–

Bacard *fils*. France. Active ca. 1870

*Bach, Lawrence. U.S. Contemporary

Bachmann, Christine. Germany. Contemporary

Bachrach, Bradford. U.S. 1910–

Bachrach, David, Jr. U.S. (b. Germany). 1848–1921. Active Baltimore and Washington, D.C., 1868 and after

Bachrach, Fabian. U.S. 1917–

Bachrach, Louis Fabian, Sr. U.S. 1881–1961

Bäckström, Helmer. Sweden. 1891–1964

Bacon, Francis. England. 1909–

Bacon, Franklin W. U.S. 1819–1901

Bacon and Taylor. Active Rochester, N.Y., 1865

Baden-Powell, (Baron) Robert Stephenson Smyth. 1857–1941

Badger, Gerry. England. Contemporary

Badura, Michael. Germany. 1938–

Baer, Morley. U.S. Contemporary

Baich, Paul. Canada (b. Yugoslavia). Contemporary

Baigent, Gary. New Zealand. 1941–

Bailey, G. S., and Co. Active Vancouver, 19th c.

Bailey, H. England. Active ca. 1869

Bailey, J. Edward. Contemporary

Bailey, James. U.S. Contemporary

Bailey, Marsha. U.S. Contemporary

*Bailey, Oscar. U.S. 1925–

Bailey, W. Active Leicester, England, 20th c.

Baillieu d'Avricourt. France. Active mid-19th c.

Baillou, (Baron) Leo. Austria. Active ca. 1900

Baird, John. Active Glasgow, 20th c.

Bairstow, Herbert. Active Halifax, Canada, 20th c.

Baker, F. W. England. Active 20th c.

Baker, Mikal. U.S. 1946–

Baker, Ray Stannard. U.S. 1870–1946

Baker, W. India (b. England). Active 1870s

Baker and Burke. Active 19th c.

Baker and Record. Active Saratoga Springs, N.Y., 1870s

Baldev. Contemporary

Baldi and Wurthle. Active Salzburg, Austria, 1860s

*Baldinger, Richard. U.S. Contemporary

Baldry, W. F. England. Active ca. 1900

*Bales, Carol. Contemporary

Balish, Leonard. U.S. Contemporary

Ball, B. L. Active New England, late 19th c.

Balla, Demeter. Hungary. Active 20th c.

Balla, Giacomo. Italy. 1871–1958

Ballaine, Jerry. U.S. Contemporary

Balley, Emanuel. Active Pilsen, Czechoslovakia, 20th c.

Balmer, Ruth. U.S. Active 20th c.

Balogh, Rudolf (Rudolph). Active Budapest, 20th c.

Balterman, Lee. Contemporary.

Baltermans. U.S.S.R. Contemporary

Balzer, Richard. U.S. Contemporary

Bamberger, J. Germany. Active ca. 1870

Bancroft, Duncan. Canada. Active 20th c.

Bandholts, F. J. Active Iowa, ca. 1900

Bang, N. Chr. Active Copenhagen, 20th c.

*Banish, Roslyn. U.S. 1942–

*Banks, David F. U.S. 1943–

Baquijano. Peru. Active 19th c.

Baraban, Joe. U.S. 1945–

Barabás, Miklós. 1810–98. Active Pest, Hungary, 1862–64

Bar-Am, Micha. Israel. Contemporary

Baratti (Col.).

Barbarosa Arguelles, Arturo. Mexico. Contemporary

Barbarosa da Silva, Sebastiano. Brazil. Contemporary

Barbey, Bruno. France (b. Switzerland). 1941–

Barbieri, Placido. Italy. Active 20th c.

Barbour, John. U.S. Active 20th c.

Barboza, Anthony. U.S. 1946–

Barcalow. Active New York City, 19th c.

Barclay. Active Rome (b. England), ca. 1860

Barda, Clive. England. Contemporary

Bardoff, Eme. Germany. Active early 20th c.

Bardon, Marcel. U.S. Active 20th c.

Bardu, Luigi. Italy. Active mid-19th c.

Barenne, Charles. Active Paris, 1860s

Barford, Murry. Active Luton, England, 20th c.

Barhydt, J., and Gregg, S. Active Rochester, N.Y., 1870s

Barker, (Dr.) Alfred Charles. New Zealand (b. England). 1819–73

Barker, William. Active Keighley, England, ca. 1900

Barlow, Roger. U.S. Active 20th c.

Barnack, Oscar. Germany. 1879–1936

Barnard and Gibson. U.S. Active mid-19th c.

Barnbaum, Bruce. U.S. 1943–

*Barnes, James A. U.S. 1938–

Barnes, O. C. Active Stowe, Vt., 19th c.

Barnett, Walter H. Australia. 1862–1934

Barney, Danford

Baron (Baron Stirling Henry Nahum). Active London, 20th c.

Baron, Paul L. Contemporary

Baronio, Joyce. U.S. Contemporary

Barraud, William. England. Active 1880s–90s

Barraza, Alberto. Peru. Active late 19th c.

Barraza Fuentes, F. Peru. Active 19th c.

Barreswil, Louis Charles. 1817–70

Barrett, Arthur

Barrett, Mary Louise. U.S. Active 20th c.

Barreuther, H. U.S. Active early 20th c.

Barrie, N. Active Isle of Wight

Barros, Geraldo de. Brazil. Contemporary

Barrows, Robert A. Active Philadelphia, 20th c.

Barry, Robert W. U.S. Contemporary

Barszczewski, Leon. Poland, 1849–1910

Bartas, Franz. New Zealand. Active 20th c.

Bartels, Karl Otto. Germany. Active 20th c.

Bartik, A. Austria. Active ca. 1900

*Bartlett, Dick. U.S. Contemporary

Bartlett, George O. Active Reading, Pa., 19th c.

Bartlett, Linda. U.S. Contemporary

Bartlett, R. H. New Zealand. Active 1880s

Bartoli, Giovanni. Italy. Contemporary

Barton, (Mrs.) G. A. England. Active late 19th c.

Barton, Paul. Contemporary

Barton, W. Harvey. Active Bristol, England, 19th c.

*Baruch, Ruth-Marion. U.S. (b. Germany). 1922–

Bary, Herbert de. Germany. 1905–

Barzykowskii, Th. Active Warsaw, 20th c.

Basch, Peter. U.S. Contemporary

Baskerville, Harry, Jr. U.S. Active 20th c.

Bass, (Dr.) Edward A.

Bassano, Alexander. Active London, 1860s

Bassano, Oscar. England. Active 19th c.

Basset, C. Active Rouen, France, 1860s

Basset, René. France. Contemporary

Bastide, Alain G. France. Contemporary

Bastin, Christine. Belgium. 1947–

*Batchelder, David. U.S. 1939–

*Bates, Herbert E. U.S. 1940–

Bath, Phil. Active 20th c.

Batham, Teré. New Zealand. 1943–

Batho, Claude. France. 1935–

Batho, John. France. 1939–

Battelle, W. Active Taunton, Mass., 19th c.

Batut, Arthur. Belgium. Active 19th c.

Baubion-Mackler, Jeannie. U.S. (b. France). Contemporary

Bauer, F. Bulgaria (b. Germany). Active 19th c.

Bauer, Francis. 1758–1840

Bauer, Frank. Active 20th c.

Bauer, Friedrich. Germany. Active 20th c.

Bauer, Karlheinz. Germany. Contemporary

Bauer, Leopold. Active Strasbourg, France, 20th c.

Baum, Yngve. Sweden. 1945–

Bauman, Frank. U.S. Active 20th c.

Baumann, Ernst. Germany. Active 20th c.

Baumann, Horst. Germany. Contemporary

Baumeister, Willi. Germany. 1889–1955

*Baumgarten, Lothar. Germany. 1944–

Baumgartl, Monika. Germany (b. Czechoslovakia). 1942–

Baur, Harry. U.S. Active 20th c.

Bavagnoli, Carlo. Italy. Contemporary

Baxter, W. Raleigh

Bay, Didier. France. 1944–

Bayer, K. Poland. Active 19th c.

Bayes, Derek W. Contemporary

Bayley, R. Child. 1869–1934

Bayliss, Charles. Australia. 1850–97

Bazeille, G. Active Saintes, France, 20th c.

Bazin. France. Active 19th c.

Bazire, Gustave. Active Cherbourg, France, 20th c.

Beach. H. M. U.S. Active early 20th c.

Beal, David. Contemporary

Beal, Joshua H. Active New York City, 19th c.

Beals, Jessie Tarbox. U.S. 1871–1942

Beal's Art Gallery. Active Minneapolis, 19th c.

Beard, Peter Hill. U.S. 1938–

Bearden, Alan. Active 20th c.

Beattie, Francis S.

Beattie, W. B. (Bill), Jr. New Zealand. 1902–

Beaudequin, Jean-Louis. France. 1954–

Beausacq, Ingeborg de. Active New York City (b. Germany), 20th c.

Béchard, E. Active Cairo, 1870s

Beck, Martin. England. Active 20th c.

Beck, Maurice. England. 1886–1960

*Beck, Thomas. U.S. Contemporary

Beckel Brothers. Active Lockport, La., 19th c.

Becker, Caroline. Finland. 1832–81

Becker, Murray. U.S. Active 20th c.

Becker and Maass. Germany. Active early 20th c.

Beckett, Robert. England. Active 19th c.

*Becotte, Michael. U.S. 1945–

Becquerel, Edmond. 1820–91

Beer, A. Germany. Active 19th c.

Beers, A. E. Active Rushville, N.Y., 1860s

Beers Brothers. U.S. Active 19th c.

Behles, Edmondo. 1841–1921. Active Rome (b. Germany)

Behrens-Rogasen, Friedrich. Germany. Active early 20th c.

Bein, Renate. Germany. Contemporary

*Beitzell, Neil. U.S. 1939–

Belcher, Ray. U.S. 1944–

Bélin, Edouard. France. 1876–1963

Bell, Charles M. Active Washington, D.C., late 19th c.

*Bellak, David J. U.S. Contemporary

Bellanca, Joseph. U.S. 1930–

Bellander, Sven Didrik. Sweden. 1921–

Bellet, Edmond. Active Amiens, France, 20th c.

Belli, Filippo. 1836–1927. Active Rome

*Beltran, George. U.S. 1934–

Belzeaux, Pierre. France. Contemporary

Benatovich, Deanna. U.S. Contemporary

*Benbenuato, John. U.S. Contemporary

Benck Vargas, Antonio Luiz. Brazil. Contemporary

Benda, Arthur. Active Vienna, 20th c.

Bendov. Palestine (b. Russia). Active early 20th c.

Bendowski, Kazimierz. Poland. 1948–

Benecke, R. Active St. Louis, 19th c.

Benedict-Jones, Linda. Contemporary

Bengston, Jim. Norway (b. U.S.). 1942–

Benjamin. Active Paris, Florence, ca. 1900

Benndorf, Daura. Active 20th c.

Bennett, Charles Harper. England. 1840–1927

Bennett, Derek

*Bennett, Gordon. U.S. 1933–

Bennett, Walter. Active 20th c.

*Benning, Kurt. Germany. 1945–

Bennoch. U.S. Active 1860s

Benor-Kalter, J. Active Jerusalem, 20th c.

Benque, M. M., and *Cie*. Active Paris, Milan, 19th c.

Benson, Harry. U.S. Contemporary

*Benson, John. U.S. 1927–

Benson, Richard. U.S. 1943–

Bente, Herman. Active Copenhagen, 20th c.

Bentley, B. W. England. Active ca. 1876

*Benton, Stephen. U.S. 1941–

Benton-Harris, John. England. Contemporary

Beny, Roloff. Canada. 1924–

Ben-Yusuf, Zaida. U.S. Active ca. 1896–1915

Benzur, Gabriel. U.S. Active 20th c.

Berbieri, Leonardo. Peru. Active ca. 1863

*Berchen, William P. U.S. (b. Germany). 1920–

Berekmeri, Zoltan. U.S. Contemporary

Bérenger, (Marquis) de. France. Active mid-19th c.

Berens. Stephen L. U.S. 1952–

Beresford, G. C. England. Active ca. 1902

Berg, Bengt. Sweden. 1885–1967

Berger, Anthony. U.S. Active mid-19th c.

Berger, Charles. U.S. Contemporary

*Berger, Eileen K. U.S. Contemporary

Berger, Frederick W. England. Active 19th c.

Berger, Isadore. U.S. Active 20th c.

Berger, J. Austria. Active ca. 1870

*Berger, Paul E. U.S. 1948–

Berger, Robert. U.S. 1954–

Bergerson, Phil. Canada. Active 20th c.

Berggren, G.

Bergheim, P. Active Middle East, 1880s

Bergler, Marianne. Active Vienna, 20th c.

*Berglund, Magnus. U.S. Contemporary

*Berinsky, Burton. U.S. Contemporary

Berka, L. E. Czechoslovakia. Active 20th c.

*Berko, Ferenc. U.S. (b. Austria-Hungary). 1916–

Berman, Mieczyslaw. Poland. 1893–1975

Bermeo y Emiloc, Hermógenes. Peru. Active 19th c.

Bernard, Jean

Bernatzik, Hugo Adolf. Austria. 1897–1953

Bernheim *jeune*. Active Paris, 1860s

Bernoud, Alphonse. Active Naples and Florence, 19th c.

Bernstein, Dan. U.S. Contemporary

Berres, Joseph. 1796–1844

Berretty, Dom. Active 20th c.

Berry, G. R. Active Liverpool, 19th c.

Berry, Ian. England. 1934–

Berry, Miles

Berssenbrugge, Hans (Henri). ca. 1873–1959. Active Rotterdam

Bertall. Active Paris, 1860s

Berthaud, M. France. Active 1860s

Bertillon, Alphonse

Bertoglio (Ing. Cav.). Active Turin, Italy, 20th c.

Bertrand, A. Active Rome (b. France), ca. 1860

Bertsch, Adolphe. France. Active mid-19th c.

Besnyö, Eva. Netherlands. Active 20th c.

Beszédes, Sándor. Active Esztergom, Hungary, ca. 1868

Bethers, Ray. Active San Francisco, 20th c.

Bethout. Active Paris, 20th c.

Betti, Giulio. Active Rome, 1860s

Bettridge, George. Contemporary

Betzel, Manfred. Germany. Contemporary

Betzler, Hannes. Active 20th c.

Beuret, Patric. France

Bevan, Dennys. England. Contemporary

Beville, Henry. Active 20th c.

Bey Saudic. Active 1880s

Beydler, Gary. U.S. 1944–

Beyer, Charles. Active Paris, 19th c.

Beyer, Günther. Germany. Active 20th c.

Beyer, Karol. Poland. 1818–77

Bezzola, Leonardo. Switzerland. 1929–

Bhalerao, T. L. Active Hyderabad, India, 20th c.

Bhatt, Shreedam. India. Active 20th c.

Biasi, Mario di. Italy. Contemporary

Bibet, V. Peru. Active 19th c.

Bidermanas, Izis. *See* Izis

Biefeld, Otto. Active Pilsen, Bohemia, and Stuttgart, Germany; 1860s

Bieri, Rudolf. Contemporary

Biermann, Aenne. Germany. 1898-1933

Bierstadt, Edward. Active New Bedford, Mass., 1859-65

Bierstadt Brothers. Active New Bedford, Mass., 19th c.

Bignon, P. France. Active 20th c.

Bijlstra, K. G. Netherlands. Active 20th c.

Biliman and Co. Active Oxford, England, early 20th c.

Bill, Charles K. Active New York City, 1860s-70s

Billard, A. France. Active ca. 1865

Biloreaux, Adolphe. Active Paris, 1850s-60s

Binde, Gunar. Contemporary

Binder, Alexander. Germany. Active 20th c.

Bing, Joseph M. Active New York City, 20th c.

Bingham, Frederick V. Canada. Active 1880s

Bingham, Howard. Contemporary

Bingham, Robert. d. 1870. Active Paris, 1855-62

Bingler, Manfred. Switzerland. 1928-

Binns, Frederick Charles. New Zealand (b. England). 1853-1915

Biot, Jean-Baptiste. France. 1774-1862

Biow, Hermann. Germany. 1810-50

Birn, Samuel. Active Brno, Czechoslovakia, 20th c.

Birnbaum, Enrico. Active Rome, 1855-65; Civitavecchia, Italy, 1869 and after

Birns, Jack. U.S. Active 20th c.

Birtles, J. England. Active late 19th c.

Bischofberger, Josef. Switzerland. 1931-

Bischoff. Peru. Active 19th c.

Bishop, E. Active 20th c.

Bishop, Robert C. U.S. 1921-

*Bisilliat, Maureen. U.S. 1931-

Bittner, Hans. Germany. Active 20th c.

Bittner, Heinz. Germany. Contemporary

Bitzan, Heinz. Austria. Active 20th c.

Bizanski, Stanislaw. Poland. Active 1870s

Black, Alexander. U.S. 1859-1940

Black, James Wallace. 1825-96. Active New Hampshire and Boston

Black, Stuart G. England. Active 20th c.

Black and Case. Active Boston (1865) and Newport, R.I.

Blackman, (Dr.) J. Gary. New Zealand. 1929-

Blackwell, Ben. U.S. 1944-

Blackwell, Fred. U.S. Contemporary

Blahut, John. Canada. Contemporary

Blair, G. L. A. Great Britain. Active 20th c.

Blaise, Gabriel. Active Tours, France, 1870s

Blakemore, John. England. 1936-

*Blanchard, Stanley. U.S. 1943-

Blanchard, Valentine. England. 1831-1901

*Blankfort, Jeffrey A. U.S. 1934-

Blazer, Carel. Netherlands. Contemporary

Blenck, Helmut and Erna. Germany. Active 20th c.

Blickensderfer, Clark. Active Denver, 20th c.

Bliss, W. P. Active New Mexico, 1878-79

Bloch, A. Active Copenhagen, 20th c.

Bloch, Ernest. Switzerland. 1880-1959

Block, Lou. U.S. Active 20th c.

Bloem, F. Netherlands. Active 20th c.

*Blondeau, Barbara. U.S. 1938-74

Bloom, Suzanne. U.S. 1943-. *See also* Manual

Blossfeldt, Karl. Germany. 1865-1932

Blücher, Friedrich Adolf von. Germany. Active 20th c.

Blue, Patt. U.S. Contemporary

Bluestone, Henry. U.S. Active 20th c.

Blum, Kurt. Switzerland. 1922-

*Blumberg, Donald. U.S. 1923-

Blüme, Jochen. Germany. Contemporary

Bobak, Chr. Active Bergen, Norway, 20th c.

Bobir, Nikolai. Ukraine. Active late 19th c.

Boch, Monika von. Germany. Contemporary

Bock, Tony. Canada (b. England). 1948-

Bode, Allie. b. 1869

Bode, Frances N. Active New York City, 20th c.

Bodine, A. Aubrey. U.S. 1906-70

Bodmer, C. France. Active 1860s-90s

Boehl and Koenig. Active St. Louis, 19th c.

Boer, Ben. New Zealand (b. Netherlands). 1927-

Boestert, J. H. den. Netherlands. Active 20th c.

Bogardus, Abraham. 1822-1908. Active New York City, 1846-87

Bogazianos, Ann. U.S. Contemporary

Boger, Bert. Germany. Active 20th c.

Bog-Jensen, O. Active Odense, Denmark, 20th c.

Böhm, Franz Josef. Austria. Active ca. 1870-1910

Böhmer (Oberl.). Germany. d. 1908

Bois-Prévost, Serge. France. Contemporary

Boissonnas, Edmond-Edouard. Switzerland. 1891-1924

Boitouzet, J. Active Paris, 1850s

Boittier, Albert. France. Active 20th c.

Boje, (Dr.) Walter

Bokhonov, I. A. Active Moscow, 20th c.

Bolas, Thomas. England. Active early 20th c.

Bolberltz, H. Austria-Hungary. Active 19th c.

Boldyrev, Ivan Vasil'evich. Russia. Active 19th c.

Bollaert. France. Active 20th c.

Bolles, G. E. Active Brooklyn, 1890s

Bologna, Achille. Italy, Spain. Active 20th c.

Bologna, Emiglia. Active Venice, 1870s

*Boltanski, Christian. France. 1944-

Boltin, Lee. U.S. Contemporary

Bolton, Gambier. England. Active 1860s-70s

Bolton, Julia. Active Massachusetts, ca. 1900

Bolton, W. B. England. 1848-99

Bonaparte, (Prince) Roland Napoléon. France. 1858-1924. Active 1880s

Bonath, John Paul. U.S. 1951-

Bond, Howard

Bonebakker, As. Netherlands. Active 20th c.

Bonetti, Luca. Switzerland. 1947-

Bongé, Lyle. U.S. 1929-

*Boni, Robert. Contemporary

Bonin, Volker. Sweden. Active 20th c.

Bonnard, Pierre. France. 1867–1947

Bonnay, Charles. U.S. Contemporary

Bonnet, Jules. Switzerland. 1840–1928

Bonney, A. D. U.S. Active Portland, Maine, ca. 1880s

Bonney, Thérèse. France. 1897–1978

Bononno, Robert. U.S. Contemporary

Bons, J. Russell. England. Active early 20th c.

Bonsall, I. H. Active Arkansas City, Kansas, 1860s

Bony, Oscar. Argentina. 1941–

Boogaerts, Piere. Belgium. 1946–

Bookbinder, Lester. U.S. Contemporary

Boole, A. and J. Active London, 1870s

Boon, Thomas. Peru. Active ca. 1853

Boorne and May. Active Calgary, Northwest Territory, Canada, 1890s

Booth, Arturo W., and *Cia.* Active Buenos Aires, 1890s

Booth, Weston. U.S. Active 20th c.

Borchards, R. Active Latvia (b. Germany), 19th c.

Borchardt, Carl Amandus. Estonia. 1834–1912.

Borchardt, Charles. Finland. 1834–92

Borchardt, Robert. Active Derpt (Tartu), Estonia, ca. 1850s

Bordnick, Barbara. U.S. Contemporary

Boretti, Toefil. Active Warsaw, 19th c.

Borgoyne. Active Birmingham, England, 1860s

Borntraeger, Carl. Germany. Active 19th c.

*Borodác, Ladislaus. U.S. (b. Czechoslovakia). 1933–

Borrenbergen, J. Emile. Active Antwerp, 20th c.

Borsos, Jozsef. 1821–83. Active Budapest

Borthwick and Stanley

Bortnyik, Alexander. Hungary. Active 20th c.

Borup, Charles. Active London, 20th c.

Bosch, Carlos. Argentina. 1945–

Boscheron, M. P. Active Paris, 20th c.

Boshier, Derek. England. 1937–

Boskman, Ij. Netherlands. Active 20th c.

Bösnjak, Kamilo. Croatia. Active 19th c.

Bossu, Gaston. France. Active 20th c.

Bostock, C. W. Active Australia, New Zealand, 20th c.

Bosworth, Rhondda. New Zealand. 1944–

Bothamley, Arthur Thomas. ca. 1836–1938. Active Wellington, New Zealand, 1860s–70s

Böttcher, Georg. Active Munich, 19th c.

Bouchard, Thomas. U.S. Active 20th c.

Boulat, Pierre. Contemporary

*Bourdeau, Robert. Canada. 1931–

Bourgeois, Ulrich. Active New England, late 19th c.

Bourges, Fernand. Active 20th c.

Boutan, Louis. France. Active 19th c.

Bouton, Charles-Marie. France. 1781–1853

Bouvier. Peru. Active ca. 1860

Bouvier, Nicolas. Switzerland. 1929–

Bovi, M. Germany. Active ca. 1900

Bow, Adolf. England. Active 1860s

*Bowen, Nicolas N. U.S. Contemporary

Bowen and Son. England. Active late 19th c.

Bowers, Harry. U.S. 1938–

Bowie's Stereoscopic Views. Active Corry, Pa., 19th c.

Bowman. Active Glasgow, early 20th c.

Bowman, Stanley. U.S. Contemporary

Bowman, W. E. Active Ottawa, Ill., 1880s

Bowser, Floyd. U.S. Contemporary

Boyd, Robert. U.S. Active 20th c.

Boyesen, Peter Thyge (Pietro). 1819–1882. Active Rome (b. Denmark)

Boys, (Sir) Charles Vernon. England. 1855–1944

Brack, Dennis. Contemporary

Bracklow, Robert. Active New York City, ca. 1900

Bradford, Anne. U.S. Contemporary

Bradley, George. Active Connecticut, late 19th c.

Bradley and Rulofson (Henry W. Bradley; William Henry Rulofson [b. Canada; 1826–78]). Active San Francisco, 1863–78

Bradna, Franz. Active Vienna, 19th c.

Brady, G. S.

Bragaglia, Antonio Giulio. Italy. 1889–1963

Braggaar, H. Netherlands. Active 20th c.

Bragge, James. New Zealand (b. England). 1833–1908

Brainerd, J. M.

Brainos, Hilda. Active New York City, 20th c.

Brake, Brian. b. New Zealand. 1927–

Branc, Janko. Yugoslavia. Active 20th c.

Brancusi, Constantin. France (b. Romania). 1876–1957

Brand, Edwin L. Active Chicago, 1858–70

Brandejs, Adolf. 1818–72. Active Prague

Brandel, Konrad. Poland. 1838–1920

Brandl, St. Germany. Active 20th c.

Brandseph, Fr. Active Stuttgart, Germany, ca. 1863–70

Brandt, Bert. Contemporary

Brandt, Friedrich Christian. 1823–91

*Brannen, Robert. U.S. Contemporary

Branzi, Piergiorgio. Italy. Active 20th c.

Braquehais, B. France. Active ca. 1854–75

Brasch, C. Active Leipzig, Germany, 19th c.

Bratter, Maurice. U.S. 1905–

Braun, Gaston. France. Active 19th c.

Bravo, Nacho. U.S. Active 20th c.

*Breakwell, Ian. Great Britain. 1943–

Breese, Charles. d. 1875. Active Birmingham, England

Brehm, Frederick W. U.S. 1871–1950

Brehm, Hugo. Mexico. Active 20th c.

*Breil, Ruth. U.S. Contemporary

Breitenbach, Josef. U.S. (b. Germany). 1896–

Breitner, Georg Hendrik. Netherlands. 1857–1923

Bremard, Maurice. Active early 20th c.

Bremer, Caj. Finland. Contemporary

Brenes, José Manuel Holgado. Spain. Contemporary

Brenneis, John Martin. U.S. Active 20th c.

*Brenner, Susan. U.S. Contemporary

Bretzman, C. F. U.S. Active early 20th c.

Breuer-Courth, Carl. Germany. Active 20th c.

Breuning, Wilhelm. Germany. Active 19th c.

Breuninger, Mugg. Germany. Active 20th c.

Brewer, T. M. Canada. Active 20th c.

Brewster, (Sir) David. Scotland. 1781–1868

Breyer, Karl. Germany. Contemporary

Breyer, Lavoslav. Active Zagreb, 19th c.

Bricarelli, Stefano. Active Turin, Italy, 20th c.

Bride, Ella E. M. Active 20th c.

Bridge, Lionel. U.S. (b. Australia). ca. 1900–70

Bridge (Rev). b. England. Active Italy, Malta, Sicily, Egypt, Palestine, 19th c.

*Bridgeman, Bill. U.S. Contemporary

Bridges, Bill. U.S. Contemporary

Bridges, Robert. Active Athens, ca. 1847

Bridson, J. Active 1880s

Briggs, (Dr.) Daniel H. Active 19th c.

Briggs, Jesse. Active Boston, mid-19th c.

Bright, Emmett. Contemporary

*Brihat, Denis. France. 1928–

Brill, Fritz. 1904–

Brill, Julius. Active New York City, 1860s

Brimacombe, Jerry. Contemporary

Brinckerhoff, J. Dewitt. Active New York City, 19th c.

Brinckmann-Schroeder, Hilda. Active Braunschweig, Germany, 20th c.

Brindst, Henriette. Switzerland. Contemporary

*Brink, Bertil. U.S. Active 20th c.

Briquet, A. France. Active ca. 1860–95

Bristol, Horace. Active San Francisco, 20th c.

Brittin, Peter. U.S. Contemporary

Broadbent and Phillips. Active Philadelphia, 1860s–70s

Broadbent and Taylor. Active Philadelphia, 1880s

Brock, J. A. Canada. Active 1880s

Brockmann, F. and O. Switzerland. Active 1860s

Brockner, A. Estonia. Active 19th c.

Brodovitch, Alexey. U.S. 1898–1971

Brodsky, Michel. Active Paris, 20th c.

Broffman, Martin. U.S. Contemporary

Brogi, Carlo. Italy. Active ca. 1860–80

Brogi, Giacomo. 1822–81. Active Florence

Bronson, T. S. Active New England, late 19th c.

Bronstein, Ted. U.S. Contemporary

*Brook, John. U.S. 1924–

Brooks, Linda. U.S. Contemporary

Brooks, Reva. Mexico (b. Canada). 1913–

*Brooks, Robert. U.S. Contemporary

Broom, Mrs. Albert. England. 1863–1939

Broomer, Edwin. England. Active 20th c.

Browell, Anthony. Australia. Contemporary

Brown, Barnes, and Bell. Active Liverpool, 19th c.

Brown, Charles H. Active California, 20th c.

Brown, E. H. Active Dallas, 20th c.

Brown, Gillian. U.S. Contemporary

Brown, Hugh Patrick. U.S. Contemporary

*Brown, Jim. Scotland. 1947–

Brown, Josiah. Active Mauch Chunk, Pa., 19th c.

Brown, Ken. U.S. 1944–

Brown, Lawrie. U.S. 1949–

*Brown, Robert E. U.S. 1937–

Brown, Robin J. Contemporary

Brown, T. U.S. Active mid-19th c.

Brown, W. Cal. Active New Mexico, 1882–89

Brown Brothers. Active New York City, ca. 1900

Browne, J. C. Active Philadelphia, 19th c.

Browne, Victor Carlyle. New Zealand. Contemporary

Brownell, Rowena P. U.S. Active 20th c.

Browning, Benjamin. England. Active 19th c.

*Brownton, Cheri. U.S. Contemporary

Brucherseifer, Katharine. Active New York City, 20th c.

Bruchet, Patrick. France. Contemporary

Brück and Sohn. Active Meissen, Germany, 19th c.

Bruell, Johannes. Switzerland. 1938–

Brugger, Albrecht. Germany. Active 20th c.

Brumfield, John. U.S. Contemporary

Brunet, Annik. U.S. (b. Senegal). 1950–

Bruning, Walter P. Active Euclid, Ohio, 20th c.

*Brunner, Edy. Switzerland. Contemporary

Brus, Johannes. Germany. 1942–

Bryce, David. England. Active 1860s

*Brylc, Dennis. Contemporary

Bryley, Edward William. 1802–70

Bryson, John. U.S. Active 20th c.

Brzozowsky, J. Lithuania. Active 19th c.

Bucher, Louis F. Active Newark, N.J., 20th c.

Buckland, David. England. Contemporary

Buckle, Samuel. England. Active 19th c.

Buckley, William. U.S. 1931–

Buckman, C. H. Active Dover, England, 19th c.

Bucko, Jan. Contemporary

Buclers, Martin. Latvia. b. 1860

Bucliu, Jorge. Peru. Active ca. 1864

Bucovich, Mario von. U.S. (b. Germany). Active 20th c.

Budan, Viktor. Contemporary

Buechel, Eugene, S. J. 1874–1954. Active South Dakota (b. Germany)

Bugeja, Vincent. Active Paris, 20th c.

Buis, Simon. New Zealand (b. Netherlands). 1927–

Bujak, Adam. Poland

Bülch, Agost. Active Székesfehérvár, Hungary, 19th c.

Bulhak, Jan. 1876–1950. Active Wilno, Poland

Bull, Clarence Sinclair. U.S. d. 1979

Bulla, K. K. Active St. Petersburg and Chertkov, Russia, early 20th c.

*Bullaty, Sonja. U.S. (b. Czechoslovakia). 1923–

*Bullis, Larry. U.S. Contemporary

Bullock, Calvin. U.S. Active early 20th c.

Bullock, John G. U.S. 1854–1939

Bullock, T.

Bulté, Michel

Bundt, L. van de. Netherlands. Active 20th c.

Bundy, J. K. Active Middletown, Conn., 1870s

Bundy and Williams. Active New Haven, Conn., 19th c.

Bunge A. A. Active Russian Arctic, 19th c.

Bunker, (Rev.) A. Burma (b. U.S.). Active 1880s

Bunnell, Peter C. U.S. 1937–

Bunnell, S. L. Active California, early 20th c.

*Bunnen, Lucinda. U.S. 1930–

Bunsen, Robert Wilhelm. Germany. 1811–99

Bunyan, Curtis A. U.S. Contemporary

Bunz, Agathe. Germany. Contemporary

Bunzl, George. England (b. Austria). Active 20th c.

*Burchard, Jerry. U.S. 1947–

Burchartz, Max. Germany. 1887–1961

Burchfield, Jerry. U.S. 1947–

Burckhardt, Rudolph. U.S. Active 20th c.

Burden, Shirley. U.S. 1908–

Bureau, F. Active 19th c.

Bureš, Joseph. Active Sofia, Bulgaria, 1880s

*Burford, Byron. U.S. Active 20th c.

Burger, I. France. Active ca. 1890

Burgess, E.

*Burgess, James L. U.S. 1942–

Burgess, John. England. Active 19th c.

*Burke, Gay. U.S. 1946–

Burke, James. U.S. Active 20th c. (deceased)

Burke, James E. U.S. Active mid-19th c.

Burkert, Heribert. Germany. 1953–

*Burkert, Robert. U.S. 1930–

Burkhard, Balthasar. Switzerland. 1944–

Burks, Ed. U.S. Contemporary

Burleigh, G. N. Active Taylorville, Ill., 1870s

*Burlison, Barry. U.S. 1941–

Burnett, C. J. Active Edinburgh, 19th c.

Burnett, David. U.S. Contemporary

Burnham, T. R. U.S. Active 19th c.

Burnite and Wheldon. Active Harrisburg, Pa., 1864 and after

Burns, Archibald. Active Edinburgh, 1860s–70s

*Burns, Gary. U.S. 1949–

*Burns, Jody. U.S. Contemporary

Burns, Marsha Hardy. U.S. 1945–

Burns, Michael. U.S. 1942–

*Burrell, Fred. U.S. Contemporary

Burri, René. Switzerland. 1933–

Burriel, Oscar. Argentina. 1943–

*Burrows, Roger. England. 1945–

Burt, Gordon H. New Zealand. Active 20th c.

Burton, Alfred Henry. New Zealand (b. England). 1834–1914

Burton, Herman. Active Brussels, 20th c.

Burton, L. Easton. Active California, 20th c.

*Burton, Richard. U.S. Contemporary

Burton, Walter John. New Zealand (b. England). 1836–80

Burton Brothers. Active Dunedin, New Zealand, 1868–98

Busch, Glenn. New Zealand. 1948–

Buschmann, Joseph Ernest. 1814–53. Active Antwerp

Büse, Gisela. Germany. Active 20th c.

Busey, Norval H. Active Baltimore, 1880s

Busgers, G. E. Netherlands. Active 20th c.

Bushby and Hart. Active Lynn, Mass., ca. 1870

*Bushman, Naomi. U.S. Contemporary

Bushnell (Dr.)

Butchart, D. C. Active Ontario Provinces and Toronto, ca. 1859–63

Butcher, Solomon Devore. Active Nebraska, 19th c.

*Butler, Owen. Contemporary

Butler, Samuel. England. 1835–1902

Butler, T. H. Active Decatur, Ill., ca. 1870

Buttfield, Helen. U.S. Contemporary

Butyrin, Vitaly. U.S.S.R. Active 20th c.

Buvat, Patrice. France. 1950–

Byerly. Active Frederick, Md., 1860s

Byers, Abraham. U.S. Active mid-19th c.

Byers, Bill. U.S. 1936–

Byk, Suse. Active Berlin, 20th c.

Byrne and Co. England. Active late 1880s

Byron, Joseph. U.S. (b. England). 1846–1922

Byron, Percy Claude. U.S. 1879–1959

Byron Studio. Active New York City, late 19th c.

C. G. France. Active 19th c.

*Cabanban, Orlando. U.S. Contemporary

Cadars, Paul. Active Paris, 20th c.

Caffin, Charles H. U.S. 1854–1918

*Cahan, Andrew. U.S. 1949–

Caillaud, Louis. Active Paris, 20th c.

Caillon, François. France. 1954–

Caire, N. J. Active Victoria, Australia, 1870s–80s

Caldesi and Montecchi. Active London (both b. Italy), 1850s

Caldwell, B. W. Active 20th c.

Caldwell, John W. Active Honolulu, 20th c.

Calfee, H. B. U.S. Active 19th c.

California Panorama Co. U.S. Active early 20th c.

Callaghan, Lewis. U.S. 1906–

Callaghan, Mary E. Active New York City, 20th c.

Callahan, Dennis. Active Arkansas, ca. 1863

Calland, Eustace G. England. Active ca. 1900

*Callaway, Nicholas. Contemporary

*Callis, Jo Ann. U.S. 1940–

*Calman, Wendy. U.S. 1947–

Camacho, Toti. Spain. Contemporary

Camarsac, Lafon de. France. 1821–1905. Active 1860s

Cameron, Dennis. Contemporary

Cameron, Henry Herschel Hay. England. Active 1885–1905

Camisa, Alfredo. Italy. Active 20th c.

Cammick, Murray. New Zealand. 1953–

*Camp, Peter. Contemporary

Campbell, Alfred S. Active New Jersey, ca. 1896

Campbell, Bryn. Wales. 1933–

Campbell, Carolee. U.S. 1936–

Campbell, G. Active Edinburgh, 19th c.

Campbell, Helen. Active Southampton, England, 20th c.

Campbell, J. F.

Chaplin, Gillian. New Zealand (b. South Africa). 1948–

*Chapman, Nancy Jean. U.S. 1945–

Chapman-Taylor, James Walter. New Zealand. 1878–1958

*Chappell, Walter. U.S. 1925–

Charbonnier, Jean-Pierre. France. 1921–

Chardon, H. France. Active 20th c.

Chargesheimer. Germany. Contemporary

Charles, Lalie. England. Active ca. 1900

Charnaux, F. Active Geneva, 19th c.

Chase, William M. Active Baltimore, ca. 1865–80

Chauffourier, Gustavo Eugenio. d. 1907. Active Rome and Palermo, Italy, 1872 and after

Chauvel, Théophile-Narcisse. France. 1831–1909

Chaux. Active Paris, 20th c.

Chávas, Ricardo. Brazil. Contemporary

Chaves de Leone, Ricardo. Brazil. Contemporary

Chávez Mayol, Humberto. Mexico. Contemporary

*Cheek, Vernon. U.S. Contemporary

Cheney, C. H. Active London, 1850s

Cheney, Edward. England. Active 19th c.

Cheney, F. H. England. Active 1850s

*Cheng, Carl. U.S. 1942–

Chen Zie-huang. China. Contemporary

Cheong, Hung. Active Yokohama, 19th c.

Cherney, Lawrence. U.S. Active 20th c.

Chesley, Paul. U.S. 1946–

Chessex, Luc. Switzerland. 1936–

Chester, K. U.S. Active 20th c.

Cheung Yu-chiu. Active Hong Kong, 20th c.

Chevalier, Charles. France. 1804–59

Chevalier, Vincent. France. b. 1770

Chevojon, A. Active Paris, late 19th c.

Chevreul, Michel-Eugène. France. 1786–1889

*Chiarenza, Carl. U.S. 1935–

Chiewitz-Magnusson, Euphrosyne. Finland. Active 19th c.

Child, Frank. Active New England, ca. 1900

Child, W. Active Leeds, England, 19th c.

Childe, A. M. England. Active 1860s

Childe, Thomas. China. Active 1870s

Chillingworth, John. England. Active 20th c.

Chin, Benjamin

Chin, Manly. China. Contemporary

Chintamon, Hurrichand. India. Active 19th c.

Chit, F. Active Bangkok, 19th c.

Choccano, Ricardo. Peru. Active ca. 1896

Chodzkiewiez. France. Active 1850s

Chojnaka, Anna. Poland. Active 20th c.

Cholten, S. Active St. Louis, 19th c.

Choplin, Leo. U.S. Active 20th c.

Choynowsky, Mieczyslaw. Mexico. Contemporary

Chrétien, André. France. Active 20th c.

*Christenberry, William. U.S. 1936–

Christians, George. U.S. 1923–

Christins *Frères*. Active Tallinn, Estonia, late 19th c.

Christman, S. P. Active Berlin, 19th c.

Christofferson, Per. Norway. Contemporary

Church, Albert Cook. Active New England, late 19th c.

Church, Fred. U.S. Active late 19th c.

Churchill, Bob. U.S. Active 20th c.

Churchill and Denison. U.S. Active ca. 1867

Ciavolino, Michael. U.S. 1924–

*Ciccone, Stan. U.S. Contempoary

*Cieslewicz, Roman. Contemporary

Cifra, Jan. Contemporary

Čikoš-Sesija, Bela. Active Zagreb, 19th c.

Cimetta, G. Active Venice, mid-19th c.

Cinencio, Francisco. Mexico. Contemporary

*Cinnamond, Roger. U.S. Active 20th c.

Cioni, Vello. Italy. Contemporary

Claass, Arnaud

Clafin (or Clafflin), C. R. B. Active Worcester, Mass., 1861–83

Claine, Guillaume. 1811–69. Active Brussels

Clair-Guyot, Jean. France. Active 20th c.

Claridge, John. England

Clark, David. Active New Brunswick, N.J., 1860s–70s

*Clark, David K. Contemporary

Clark, Ed. U.S. Active 20th c.

Clark, Fiona. New Zealand. 1954–

Clark, Joe. U.S. Contemporary

Clark, L. Wilson. Active Washington Territory, 1870s

Clark, Lionel. England. Active late 19th c.

Clark, Neal. U.S. Active 20th c.

Clark, Timothy. Canada. Active 20th c.

Clarke, George W. Active Boston, ca. 1870

Clarot, Johan Baptist. 1795–1854. Active Pest, Hungary (b. Austria)

Clary. Active Hot Springs, Ark., ca. 1868–78

Claudet, Frank George. England. b. ca. 1837. Also active France, British Columbia, 1850s–60s

Clausel, Alexandre-Jean-Pierre. 1802–84. Active Troyes, France

Clausen, Rosemarie. Germany. Contemporary

Clausing, Heiner. Germany. Active 20th c.

Clavijo, C. Peru. Active ca. 1860–80

Clayton, Brian C. England. Active 20th c.

Clech, Bertrand. France.

Clemens, Jean. U.S. Active early 20th c.

Clemente, Max. Mexico. Contemporary

Clement-Van Loenhoud, B. Netherlands. Active 20th c.

Clerk Maxwell, (Sir) James. *See* Maxwell, (Sir) James Clerk

Clermont, Raymond. France. Contemporary

Cleveland, Les. New Zealand. Contemporary

*Cleveland, Walter. U.S. 1940–

Clift, William. U.S. 1944–

Clifton, Alan. England. Contemporary

Clin, Serge. France. Contemporary

Clonbrock (Baron). Ireland. Active 1860s

Clonbrock, (Lady) Augusta Crofton. Ireland. Active 1850s–60s

Clough, A. F. Active New England, 1870s

Cloutier, James. U.S. Contemporary

Clyde, Thomas. Germany. 1916–

Cobb, Elijah. U.S. 1950–

Cobb, William Henry. U.S. 1860–1909

Cochrane, Archibald. England. Active 1899–1922

Cocke, Archibald Lewis

Cocking, Edward

Cockrel, Loren. U.S. Active 20th c.

Coe and Sons. Active New York City, early 20th c.

Coen, Giuseppe. Italy. 1812–56

Coffey, Pat. U.S. Active 20th c.

Coghill, (Sir) J. England. Active 1850s

Cohen, John. U.S. 1932–

Cohen, Joyce Tenneson. U.S. Contemporary

*Cohen, Lynne. U.S. 1944–

Cohen, Santiago. Mexico. Contemporary

Cohn, Fritz. Israel. Contemporary

Colamedici, Giovanni Battista. Active Rome, ca. 1860

Cole. Active Peoria, Ill., 1860s

*Coleman, Barbara Jean. U.S. 1942–

Coles. Active Pekin, Ill., 1860s–70s

*Colescott, Warrington. U.S. 1921–

Colin, Maurice. Active Paris, 20th c.

Collard. Active Poitiers, France, 19th c.

Collen, Henry. 1800–75. Active St. Albans, England, 1841–63

*Colley, David. U.S. 1940–

Collie, Keith

*Collier, Bonnie Baldwin. U.S. Contemporary

Collier, Compton. England. Active 20th c.

Collina, Giovanni. Italy. Active 20th c.

Collingburn, John B. England. Active 20th c.

Collinge, J. Walter. Active California, 20th c.

Collins, Jack. Active Paris (b. U.S.), ca. 1914–18

*Collins, Myron. Contemporary

Collins, Richard. New Zealand. 1941–

Collins, Tudor W. New Zealand. 1898–1970

Collot (Staff Surgeon). England. Active ca. 1893

Colmenares, E. R. Peru. Active 1876–96

*Colwell, Larry. U.S. Contemporary

Comesaña, Eduardo. Argentina. 1940–

*Compère, Charles. U.S. 1935–

Conant, Howell. U.S. Active 20th c.

Cones, Nancy Ford. 1870–1962. Active Loveland, Ohio

Conklin, Paul. U.S. Contemporary

*Connor, Linda S. U.S. 1944–

Conroy, James. U.S. Contemporary

Consilvia, Thomas. U.S. Contemporary

Constant, A., and Moses, L. Active New Orleans, 1860s

Constant, Eugène. Active Rome (b. France), 19th c.

Constantine, D. Active Athens, ca. 1860

Conta, Beatrix van

Continent Stereoscope Co. U.S. Active 1860s

Contreras de Oteyza, Carlos. Mexico. Contemporary

*Converse, Gordon N. U.S. 1920–

Cook, Gene. U.S. Active 20th c.

Cook, George F. U.S. Active mid-19th c.

Cook, George Smith. U.S. 1819–1902

Cook, Jerry. U.S. Active 20th c.

*Cook, John. U.S. 1940–

Cook, L. W. Active Boston and Weymouth Landing, Mass., ca. 1870s

Cook, Susan. U.S. Contemporary

Cook, Ted. U.S. Active 20th c.

Cooke, Josiah Parsons. U.S. 1827–94

Cookson, J. H. England. Active 20th c.

Cooley, Sam A. U.S. Active Hilton Head Island, S.C.; Jacksonville, Fla.; 19th c.

Coolidge, Baldwin. Active Boston, ca. 1890–1910

Cools, Philippe. Active Antwerp, 20th c.

Coonley, J. F. Active ca. 1880

Coonley and Wolfersberger. Active Philadelphia, 19th c.

Cooper, J. T.

Cooper, N. B. Active Bombay, 20th c.

Cooper, Ron. U.S. Contemporary

Cooper, W. A. Active late 19th c.

Coplan, Maxwell Frederic. Active New York City, 20th c.

Coppens, Martien. Active Eindhoven, Netherlands, 20th c.

Coppola, Horacio. Brazil. Also active Buenos Aires, 20th c.

Corbett, J. New Zealand. Active 19th c.

*Cordier, Pierre. Belgium. 1933–

Cordiglia. Peru. Active ca. 1887

Cordiglia, Adrien. Active Barcelona, 19th c.

Cordoni, David. U.S. 1943–

Cordova, Cesar. Mexico. Contemporary

Corinaldi, (Dott.) Giulio. Active Milan, 20th c.

Cornelius, Peter. Germany. 1913–70

*Cornell, Joseph. U.S. 1903–72

Cornfield, Jim. U.S. Contemporary

Corot, Jean Baptiste Camille. France. 1796–1875

Corpron, Carlotta M. U.S. 1901–

Corral Varela (Corrales), Raúl. Cuba. Contemporary

Cortright, Steve. U.S. Contemporary

*Coslow, Gail. U.S. Contemporary

*Cosloy, Jeffrey. Contemporary

*Cosmos. U.S. 1941–

Costa, Ana Regina. Brazil. Contemporary

Costa, Tony. U.S. Contemporary

Costa Junior, Manuel Antonio da. Brazil. Contemporary

Costain, Harold Haliday. U.S. Active 20th c.

Coster, Gordon. U.S. Active 20th c.

Coster, Howard. 1885–1959. Active South Africa, England.

Coster, Roger. U.S. Active 20th c.

Cotton, T. A. England. Active ca. 1895

Coupier, Jules. France. Active 19th c.

Courcy, Michael de. Canada. 1944–

Courret, Aquiles. Peru. Active 1863–73

Courret, Eugenio. Peru. Active ca. 1863

Courret, Hermanos. Active Lima, ca. 1865

Coutinho, A. Brazil. Active mid-19th c.

Coutinho, Maria Aparecida. Brazil. Contemporary

Coutu, Gilles. Canada. Contemporary

Covarrubias, Mito. Mexico. Contemporary

Covarrubias Alvarez, Felipe. Mexico. Contemporary

*Cowans, Adger. U.S. 1936–

Cowherd, Barney. U.S. Contemporary

*Cowin, Eileen. U.S. 1947–

Cowrie, Christa. Mexico. Contemporary

*Cox, Gary. Contemporary

Cox and Carmichael

Coxhead, F. A. New Zealand. Active 19th c.

Coyne, James. U.S. Active 20th c.

Craddock. India. Active 19th c.

Craft. Peru. Active ca. 1854

Craig, David and Eleanor. Active Pittsburgh, 20th c.

*Craig, John D. U.S. 1947–

Craik, J. England. Active ca. 1889

Cramer, C. L. Active San Francisco, 1880s

Cramer, James

Cramer, Konrad. 1888–1963. Active New York state (b. Germany)

*Crampton, Nancy. U.S. Contemporary

Crandall, Robert. U.S. Active 20th c.

Crane, Arnold H. U.S. Contemporary

*Crane, Barbara Bachmann. U.S. Contemporary

Crane, F. M. Active Ogdensburg, New York, 1880s

Crane, Ralph. U.S. Contemporary

Cranham, Gerry. England. 1929–

Crary, Clare J. Active Warren, Pa., 20th c.

Cratsley, David Bruce. U.S. 1944–

Cravens, Don. U.S. Contemporary

Crawford, J. H. Active Dixon, Ill., ca. 1863

Crawford, Ralston. Canada. 1906–

Crawford, William

Crawford, Winnifrid E. England. Active 20th c.

Creifeld. Active Cologne, 19th c.

Cremer, George. Active Philadelphia, ca. 1876

Cremer, Harry R. Active New Jersey, 20th c.

Cremer, James. Active Pennsylvania, ca. 1876

Cresley, (Maj.) F. England. Active ca. 1860s

Crickmay, Anthony. England. Contemporary

Crissman, J. Active Yellowstone, Wyo., 1880s

Cristeto, Armando. Mexico. Contemporary

Critcherson, G. P. Active Worcester, Mass., 1870s

Critcherson and Storer. Active Newport, R.I., 19th c.

Crocker, Merriam Nathan. 1827–1927. Active New York state

Crockwell, J. H. . Active Salt Lake City, 19th c.

Croft, James Page. England. Active late 19th c.

Crolard, A. France. Active ca. 1850s

Crombie, J. N. ca. 1831–78. Active Nelson, Auckland, and Napier, New Zealand (b. England)

Cronquist, Gustaf W. Sweden. 1878–1967

Crookes, (Sir) William. England. 1832–1919

Cros, Charles. France. 1842–88

*Cross, Lloyd. U.S. Contemporary

Crossley, F. H. England. Active 20th c.

*Crouch, Jerry. U.S. 1928–

Crouch, Steve. U.S. Contemporary

Crowe, A. Active Stirling, Scotland, 19th c.

Croy, Otto. Germany. 1902–

Cruickshank, Allan D. U.S. Active 20th c.

Crupi. Italy. Active 1860s

Cruz, Candido. Brazil. Contemporary

Csik, Ferenc. Active Sopron, Hungary, 20th c.

Csorgeo, (Dr.) Tibor. Active Budapest, 20th c.

Cuccioni, Tommaso. d. 1864. Active Rome

Cuellar, Rogelio. Mexico. Contemporary

*Cugini, Thomas. Switzerland. 1938–

Cognoni, Ignazio. 1822–1903. Active Rome

Culot, Jacques. Belgium. Contemporary

Culp, Rusty. U.S. 1946–

Culver, Joyce. Contemporary

Cummings, H. K. Active New England, late 19th c.

*Curran, Darryl J. U.S. 1935–

*Current, William R. U.S. Contemporary

*Currie, David. U.S. Contemporary

Currier, Charles H. 1851–1938. Active Boston

Curry, F. C. Active mid-19th c.

*Curry, Phillip W. U.S. 1940–

Curry, W. England. Active ca. 1870

Curtin, Dennis P. U.S. Contemporary

Curtin, Walter. England. Contemporary

Curtis, Betty Jean. U.S. Contemporary

Curtis, George E. U.S. Active 19th c.

Curton, Walter A. Canada. Active 20th c.

Curwood, Colin. England. 1951–

Cury, Antonio José. Brazil. Contemporary

Cushing, George M. U.S. Active 20th c.

Cushing, William. Active St. Augustine and Palatka, Fla., ca. 1868–98

Cutting, James Ambrose. 1814–67. Active Boston

Cuvelier, Adalbert. France. Active 1850s

Cymorek, Dorothea. Germany. Active 20th c.

Cyprian, (Dr.) Tadeusz. Poland. Active 20th c.

Cyzas, Edvardus. Lithuania. Active 19th c.

Cyzas, Henrikas. Lithuania. Active 19th c.

Cyzas, Vaclovas. Lithuania. Active 19th c.

Czerny, Edward. Poland. Active 20th c.

Dabac, Toso. Active Zagreb, 20th c.

Dabrzanski, Lukasz. Poland. b. . 1864

Dady Burjor, Homi K. Active Bombay, 20th c.

*Daehn, Marcia. U.S. Contemporary

*D'Agostino, Peter. U.S. 1940–

Dagron, Prudent. France. 1819–1900. Active 1860s–70s

Dahinden, Josef. Switzerland. 1863–1931

*Dailey, Alma Davenport. *See* Davenport, Alma

Dain, Martin. U.S. Active 20th c.

Dajee, (Dr.) Narayen. India. Active 1850s

Dalain, Yvan. Switzerland. Active 20th c.

Dalal, (Miss) R. J. Active Bombay, 20th c.

*Dale, Jack. Canada. 1928–

Dalefield, Bryony. New Zealand. 1951–

D'Alessandri, Antonio. 1818–1895. Active Rome

D'Alessandri Brothers. Italy. Active 19th c.

*D'Alessandro, Robert. U.S. 1942–

Daley, John Stewart. New Zealand. 1946–

Dallemagne, Alexandre. France. Active 19th c.

Dallmeyer, John Henry. England (b. Germany). 1830–83

Dallmeyer, Thomas Ross. 1859–1906

Dally, Frederick. Canada (b. England). b. 1838. Active 1863 and after

Dalmas (Comte de). Active Paris, 20th c.

d'Almeida, Joseph-Charles. 1822–80

Da Miano, André. U.S. Active 20th c.

D'Amore, Richard. U.S. Contemporary

Dance, Lynn. U.S. 1949–

Dancer, John Benjamin. England. 1812–87

Danchov, Georgi. 1846–1908. Active Chirpan and Plovdiv, Bulgaria, 1866 and after

Dandridge, Frank. U.S. Contemporary

Danesi, Michele. 1809–87. Active Rome, 1839 and after

Daniell, George. U.S. 1911–

Daniels, John T. U.S. Active early 20th c.

*Danko, Steve. U.S. Contemporary

Dankowski, Joseph. U.S. 1932–

Dannenberg, J. C. A. India. Active ca. 1870s

Danti, Maximiliano. Peru. Active ca. 1842

Dantzic, Jerry. U.S. 1925–

Danuser, Hans. Contemporary

Daran, Walter. U.S. Contemporary

Darbois, Dominique. France. Active 20th c.

Darby, Eileen. U.S. Active 20th c.

*D'Arcangelo, Allan. U.S. 1930–

Darley, H. J., and Co. U.S. Active early 20th c.

Darling, Dennis Carlyle. U.S. 1947–

D'Asaro, Ronald. U.S. Active 20th c.

Dauman, Henri. U.S. (b. France). Contemporary

Daumantas, V. Active Vilnius, Lithuania, 19th c.

Davalos Orozco, Eduardo. Mexico. Contemporary

Davanne, Louis Alphonse. France. 1824–1912

Davay, Shankerlal. Active 20th c.

Davenport, Alma (Alma Davenport Dailey). U.S. Contemporary

Davenport, Elizabeth. New Zealand. 1951–

Davenport, Linda. U.S. Contemporary

Davey. Peru. Active ca. 1879

David, Albert. Active Versailles, 20th c.

Davidson, W. B. Active New England, ca. 1887–92

Davie, W. Galsworthy. England. Active ca. 1900

*Davies, Bevan. U.S. Contemporary

Davies, George Christopher. England. Active 1880s

Daviette, Philogone. Peru. Active ca. 1844–45

Davillá, D. F. Peru.

Davis. Peru. Active ca. 1854

Davis, Dwight A. U.S. Active late 19th c.

Davis, Lynn. U.S. Contemporary

Davis, Margo. U.S. Contemporary

Davis, Myron. U.S. Active 20th c.

*Davis, Philip. U.S. 1933–

Davis, S. U.S. Active 19th c.

Davis, Saul. Canada. Active 1850s–60s

Davis and Co. Active Boston, 1850s–60s

Dawson, Fielding. U.S. Contemporary

Daziero, J. Active Moscow and St. Petersburg, Russia, ca. 1880

*Deahl, David. Contemporary

*Deal, Joseph. U.S. 1947–

Dean, Loomis. Active 20th c.

*Dean, Nicholas. U.S. 1933–

Dearstyne, Howard. U.S. 1903–

*Dearstyne, John. U.S. 1943–

Debabov, D. Russia. Active 20th c.

DeBelardini, Luigi. Active Rome, ca. 1870

Deberny-Peignot (studio). Active Paris, 20th c.

Debitte and Hervé. Active Rouen, France, 19th c.

Debitzka. Croatia. Active 19th c.

De Boer, Eddy Posthuma. Netherlands. Contemporary

Debraines, Yves. Switzerland. Contemporary

Debschitz-Kunowski, Wanda von. Active Berlin and Munich, early 20th c.

Dechy, Mor. 1851–1917. Active the Himalayas (b. Hungary)

Deckel, Friedrich. 1871–1948

Decken, Ernst v. d. Germany. Active 20th c.

Decker, E. Active Cleveland, 1870s

DeClerq, Louis. France. Active 1850s–60s

*De Cock, Liliane. U.S. (b. Belgium). 1939–

*de Courcy, Michael. Canada. Contemporary

Dederko, Marian. Poland. 1880–1965

*Dee, James. U.S. 1945–

*Deeks, Jon. U.S. Contemporary

Defraoui, Chérif. Switzerland. 1932–

Degand, E. Active Nice, France, 1860s–70s

Degoix, C. Active Genoa, Italy, ca. 1860

Deiner, Christian. East Germany. 1937–

Dejmo, Kurt. Sweden. Active 20th c.

DeJongh, Auguste. Switzerland. 1866–1948

De Keyser, Gilbert. Belgium. 1925–

Dekkers, Ger. Netherlands. 1929–

Delaborde, Michel. France. 1935–

Delacre, Henri. Active Paris, 20th c.

Delacroix, Eugene. U.S. 1892–1967

DeLamater, R. S. Active near Hartford, ca. 1868–78

Delamet and Durandelle. Active Paris, 1860s–70s

De La Rue, Warren. England. 1815–89

Delbert, Christian. France. 1944–

Delessert, Benjamin. France. d. 1868

Delessert, Pierre-M.

Delgado, Alejandro. Mexico. Contemporary

Delgado Qualthrough, Luis. Mexico. Contemporary

Délié, Hippolyte. Active Cairo, 1870s

Dell'Acqua, Arturo. U.S. Contemporary

Delluc, Michel. France. Contemporary

Delmaet and Durandelle. Active Paris, 1860s–70s

Delome, A. Peru. Active ca. 1866

DeLory, Greg. U.S. Contemporary

*de Lory, Peter. U.S. 1948–

Del Re, Marco. Italy. 1950–

Delton, Jean. Active Paris, 1860s–80s

Delvert, Ray. France. Active 20th c.

*DeMaio, Joe. U.S. Contemporary

Demarest, F. M. U.S. Active 20th c.

De Maus, David Alexander. Active Port Chalmers, New Zealand, ca. 1875–99

Dement'ev, Pavel. Russia. Active 1890s

Demeter de Semeria, Charles. Active Paris, 20th c.

de Morgoli, Nicholas. France. Active 20th c.

*Dena. U.S. Contemporary

Denier, Andrei Ivanovich. Russia. 1820–92

Denise, Amédée

Denkeler, Friedhelm. Germany. Contemporary

Denkstein, Jeno. Active Budapest, 20th c.

De Nooijer, Paul. Netherlands. Contemporary

Denso, Paul. Germany. Active 20th c.

Denton, Frank J. b. 1869. Active Wanganui, New Zealand, 1899 and after

De Palma, Victor. U.S. Active 20th c.

Dermer, Charles. Active 20th c.

Dermer, Irwin

Dermid, Jack. U.S. Active 20th c.

Deroche, Matthieu

Desai, M. Active Bombay, 20th c.

Desai, R. L. Active Gwalior, India, ca. 1920

Desarzens, Isabelle. Contemporary

Desavary, Charles Paul Etienne. France. Active 1850s–70s

Deschamps, Bernard. France. Contemporary

Deschanel, Emile. France. Active ca. 1855

Desire, E. Egypt. Active 19th c.

Désjardins, M. France. Active 20th c.

Desmaisons, E. Active Paris, 1860s

Desmarets, Paul. France. Active 19th c.

Desmond, Anna, and Co. Active Los Angeles, early 20th c.

Desplanques, E. Active Brussels, 1850s

Dessaur, Fernando. Active New York City, ca. 1870s

Detlor and Waddell. Active Bradford, Pa., ca. 1878–98

Detroit Publishing Co. U.S. Active 1898 and after

*Dettling, Walter. Contemporary

Deubel, Cindy. U.S. Active 20th c.

De Van, Frederick Douglas. U.S. Contemporary

Deveril, Herbert. Active Wellington, New Zealand, 1873 and after

Deverney, Luc

de Visser, John. Canada. Active 20th c.

De Vos, Leon. U.S. Active 20th c.

DeWolfe, George. U.S. 1945–

D'Hoy, Charles. Belgium. 1823–92

Diamond, Hugh Welch. England. 1809–86

*Dian, Russell. U.S. Contemporary

Díaz González, Raúl. Mexico. Contemporary

Díaz Infante, Juan José. Mexico. Contemporary

Díaz Rivera, Juan Jorge. Mexico. Contemporary

*Di Biase, Michael. U.S. 1925–

Dice and McClymonds. U.S. Active early 20th c.

Dick, Henry Wright. England. Active ca. 1900

Dickensen, Arthur. Australia, New Zealand. Active 20th c.

Dickins, C. S. S. Active Rome (b. England), ca. 1852

*Dickinson, Donald A. Canada. 1941–

Diebold, Karl. Active Sopron, Hungary, 20th c.

Diedrich, Bernard. Contemporary

Diener, Christian. Germany. 1937–

Diennes, André de. France. Active 20th c.

Dietrich, Rudolf W. U.S. Contemporary

Dietrich, Siegfried. Germany. Active 20th c.

Dietz, Donald. U.S. 1945–

Dietz, G. Estonia. Active 19th c.

Dieuzaide, Jean. France. Contemporary

Diez-Dührkoop, Minya. Germany. 1873–1929

Digo, Nikolai Dmitrievich. Russia. Active 1880s

Dijkstra, J. T. Netherlands. Active 20th c.

Dijon, Maurice. France. Active 20th c.

Dikeakos, Christos. Canada. Active 20th c.

Dillard, Tom. U.S. Active 20th c.

Dille, Litz. Canada. 1922–

*Dilley, Clyde H. U.S. Contemporary

Dillon. Active Washington, D.C., mid-1870s

Din Dayal, Lala. India. b. 1844

Dinion, Samuel. U.S. Active 20th c.

Diniz, Pepe. U.S. (b. Morocco). 1945–

Dinturff, Edward C. Active Onondaga County, N.Y., late 19th c.

Dinwiddie, William. U.S. Active late 19th c.

DiPerna, Frank. U.S. 1947–

Disdéri (Mme.). France. Active 1850s–60s

Disfarmer, Mike. U.S. 1884–1959

*Disney, Wes. U.S. Contemporary

Disraeli, Robert. U.S. Active 20th c.

Distler, Carl C. U.S. Active Newport, Ky., 20th c.

Dítě, Emanuel. 1819–72. Active Prague

Dittmer, Harry. Sweden. 1910–

Diváld, Károly. Czechoslovakia, Hungary. 1830–97.

*Divola, John M. U.S. 1949–

Dixon, Daniel. U.S. Active 20th c.

Dixon, Henry. England. Active 1860s–80s

Diyal, Deen. India. Active 19th c.

Dmitriev, Maksim Petrovich. 1858–1948

Doane, H. R. Active Delavan, Wis., 1860s

Dobo, Michael. U.S. Contemporary

Dobrzanski, Lukasz. Poland. 1864–1909

Doctor, Albert. 1818–83. Active Budapest

Dodd, Ian. Australia. Contemporary

Dodero, Louis. France. Active 19th c.

Doerr and Jacobson. U.S. Active 19th c.

Doeser, J. Netherlands. Active 20th c.

*Doherty, William. U.S. 1940–72

Dohrn, Enrique. Peru. Active ca. 1870

Dolan, Dwight E. Canada. Active 20th c.

*Dolan, Edwin. Contemporary

Dolique, Patrick. France. 1949–

Doll, Don. U.S. 1937–

Doloy, Roger. France. Active 20th c.

Dombrowski, Herbert. Germany. Contemporary

Dominic, Zoë. Contemporary

Dominis, John. U.S. Active 20th c.

Dominquez Rodríguez, Juan Manuel. Mexico. Contemporary

Domon, Ken. Japan. 1909–

Donaghy, Don. U.S. 1936–

Donaldson. Active Adrian, Mich., 1870s

*Donaldson, Jamie. U.S. 1944–

Dondero, Mario. Italy. Contemporary

Doniz, Rafael. Mexico. Contemporary

Donkin, W. F.

*Donoho, David. Contemporary

*Donohue, Bonnie. U.S. Contemporary

Donovan, Duncan. Canada. 1857–1933

Donovan, Terence. England. Contemporary

Dontenville, E. France. Active 1860s

Doolittle, James N. Active Los Angeles, 20th c.

Doone, Val. England. Active 20th c.

*Doray, Audrey. Canada. Contemporary

Dorea Falcao, Juraci. Brazil. Contemporary

*Doren, Arnold. U.S. Contemporary

Döring, Wolf Henry. Germany. Active 20th c.

Dornac. France. Active ca. 1900

Doroshow, Helen. U.S. 1928–

Dorr, Nell. U.S. 1895–

Dorsey, Paul. U.S. Active 20th c.

Dorys, Benedykt. Poland. b. 1901

Dosal, Herminia. Mexico. Contemporary

Dosekin. Active Kharkov, Russia, 19th c.

Dospevski, Ivan. Active Samokov, Bulgaria, 1840–89

Dossenbach, Hans. Switzerland. 1936–

Doudna, Fred M. Active Detroit, 20th c.

Dougall, William. Active Invercargill, New Zealand, mid-1880s

Doughty, John G. Active Winsted, Conn., 1885–86

Doughty, T. M. V. d. 1911. Active Winsted, Conn., ca. 1860–90

*Douglas, Edward. U.S. Contemporary

Douglas, H. Active London, 20th c.

Douglass, E. M. Active Brooklyn, 1860s

Dovizielli, Pietro. Active Rome, 1850s–60s

*Dow, James. U.S. 1942–

Dow, Jas. M. Active Ogdensburg, N.Y., 1860s–70s

Dow and Wilson. Active Ogdensburg, N.Y., 1860s–70s

Dowe, L. Active San Francisco, 1880s

Downey, W. and D. England. Active 1880s–90s

Dow's Studios. Active Ogdensburg, N.Y., 1860s–70s

Draffin, J. England. Active 1860s

Draper, Louis. U.S. Active 20th c.

Draper and Husted. Active Philadelphia, 1860s

Drašković, (Count) G. Croatia. Active 1855–56

Drexler-Gauch, Aug. Active St. Gall, Switzerland, 20th c.

Driemann, J. Canada

Driffield, Vero Charles. 1848–1915

*Drisch, Russell. U.S. Contemporary

*Drobeck, Carol. U.S. Contemporary

Drtikol, Frantisek. Czechoslovakia. 1878–1961

Drucker, Walter R. U.S. 1950–

Druet, E. France. Active ca. 1900

Druks, Michael. Israel. 1940–

Drury, A. K. Active Le Roy, N.Y., 1860s–70s

*Dryden, Ian. England. 1944–

Dubin, Nancy. U.S. Contemporary

*DuBois, Alan B. U.S. Contemporary

Duboscq, Louis Jules. France. 1817–86

Dubosq and Soleil. France. Active 19th c.

Dubreuil, Pierre. France, Belgium. Active ca. 1900

Düby-Müller, Gertrud. Switzerland. Active early 20th c.

Duca, N. Al. Active Bucharest, 20th c.

*Duchamp, Marcel. France. 1887–1968

Duchenne, Guillaume Benjamin Amand. France. 1806–75

Duchochois, P. C. Active New York City, 19th c.

Duckert, D. Belgium. Active 20th c.

Ducom, Jacques. France. Active 19th c.

Ducos du Hauron, Louis. France. 1837–1920

Ducrot, Jérôme. France. Contemporary

Dudinski. Romania, Bulgaria. Active 1890s

Duitz, Murray. U.S. Contemporary

Duivepart, Julien. Active Antwerp, 20th c.

Dujardin, P. Active Paris, ca. 1875

Dujmović, Stanko. Croatia. Active ca. 1885

Dulovits, Jenö. Hungary. Active 20th c.

Dumas, Nora

Dumas-Vorzet, Maurice. France. Active 20th c.

Dumont, John E. Active late 19th c.

Duncan, Kenn. U.S. Contemporary

Duncan McCulloch, J. R. Active Maryland, 20th c.

Dundas, (Lady) E. England. Active 1850s

Dunklee and Freeman. U.S. Active 19th c.

*Dunkley, Ken. U.S. Contemporary

Dunmore (J. L.) and Critcherson. Active Boston, 1865–75

Dunning, E. G. Active Stamford, Conn., 20th c.

Dunshee. Active Providence, 1860s–70s

Dunshee, C. E. Active Rochester, N.Y., 1870s–80s

Dunshee, E. P. Active Boston, 1870s

Dunshee, E. S. Active Rochester, N.Y., 1865–75

Dunshee, H. S. Active Rochester, N.Y., 1865–75

Dunshee, S. E. Active Rochester, N.Y., 1865–75

Dunshee Brothers. Active Rochester, N.Y., 1870s–80s

Dunsmore, Donald. Contemporary

Dupain, Max. Australia, New Zealand. Active 20th c.

Dupius, (Dr.) J. France. Active 20th c.

Dupont, Aimé. Active Paris (b. France), 1865–70; New York City, 1870–80

Durat, Pierre. Active Paris, 1870s

Duren, Lista. U.S. 1949–

Durgan, Frank. Active Sacramento, Calif., 1865–70

Durieu, Eugène. Active Paris, 1850s–60s

Duroni, A. Active Milan, 19th c.

Duroni and Murer. Active Paris, 1860s

Durrell, James E. U.S. Active 20th c.

Duryea, Drix. U.S. Active 20th c.

Dusen, Juan Van. Mexico. Contemporary

Duthis, Andrew. Active Glasgow, 19th c.

Dutkiewicz, Melecjusz (Meletius). 1836–1897. Active Warsaw, 19th c.

Dutoit, Marjolaine. Switzerland. 1948–

Dutoit, Ulysse. Switzerland. 1944–

*Dutton, Allen. U.S. 1922–

Dutton, J. and J. Active Bath, England, 19th c.

Dutton and Michaels. China. Active ca. 1863

Duval, C. A., and Co. England. Active 19th c.

Duval, Remy. France. Active 20th c.

Dyubyuk, Vladimir Aleksandrovich. Russia. 1842–92

Dzimski. Bohemia. Active ca. 1860

Earl, Andy. England. 1955–

Eastlake. (Sir) Charles Lock. England. 1793–1865

Eastlake, (Lady) Elizabeth Rigby. England. 1809–93

Eastman, George. U.S. 1854–1932

Eastmead, J. J. Active Rochester, England, ca. 1877

Eaton, A. B. Active Lowell, Mass., 1860s

Eaton, C. K. Active Pasadena, Calif., 20th c.

Eaton, Edric L. b. 1835. Active Nebraska and elsewhere, 1860s and after

Eaton, John. Australia, New Zealand. Active 20th c.

Eaton, Robert. England. 1819–71. Also active Rome, ca. 1855

Eberhardt, A. Germany. Active 20th c.

Ebert, Bob. U.S. Active 20th c.

Ecclesia, (Cav.) Ottaviano. Active Turin, Italy, 20th c.

Echagüe, José Ortiz. Spain. b. 1886

Eckener, Lotte. Germany. Active 20th c.

Eckert, Jindřich. 1833–1905. Active Prague, 1870s

Eckstein, Berry Morton. Contemporary

Eckstrom, Tom. Contemporary

Ecobichow, Phillippa. Contemporary

*Edelstein, Victor. U.S. 1924–

Eder, Josef Maria. 1855–1944. Active Vienna

Eder, Susan. U.S. Contemporary

Ederheimer, Guy, Jr. U.S. Active 20th c.

Edis, Olive. England. Active ca. 1907

Edison, Thomas Alva. U.S. 1947–1931

Edminston. Active London, 20th c.

Edouart. Active San Francisco, 1860s

Edouart and Cobb. Active San Francisco, 1860s

Edwards, Ernest. 1837–1903. Active Bernese Alps (b. England)

Edwards, J. D., and Son. Active Atlanta, 1880s

Edwards, Mark. England. 1947–

Edwards, Mary Jeannette. U.S. Active 20th c.

Edwards, N. P. Peru

Edwards and McPherson. Active New Orleans, 19th c.

Egel, Aaron. U.S. Active 20th c.

Eginton, Robert. U.S. Contemporary

Eglington, Judith. Canada. Contemporary

Ehlert, Max. Germany. Active 20th c.

Ehrenberg, Myron. U.S. Active 20th c.

Ehret, Frank A. Active U.S. West, 1880s

Ehrmann, Alfred. Active 19th c.

Ehrmann, Gilles. France. Contemporary

Eickemeyer, Rudolf, Jr. U.S. 1862–1932

Eide, Waldemar. Active Stavanger, Norway, 20th c.

Eidenbenz, Willi. Switzerland. 1909–

Eilers, Bern F. Netherlands. Active 20th c.

Eilmes, Wolfgang. Germany. Contemporary

Einzig, Richard. England. Active 20th c.

Eisen, F. C. Active Cologne, 1860s

Eisenmann, Charles. Active New York City, 1870s

Eisner, Regina. U.S. Active 20th c.

Eke, Michael. Active Budapest, 20th c.

Eleta, Sandra. Panama. Contemporary

Elfont, Charles. Contemporary

Elgort, Arthur. Contemporary

Eliasson, Lief. Sweden. Active 20th c.

Eliasz-Radzikowski, Walery. Poland. Active 19th c.

Elite (studio). Active Brisbane, Australia, late 19th c.

Elk, Ger van. Netherlands. 1941–

Elkind, Ricardo. Brazil. Contemporary

Ellenby, Maggie. England. Contemporary

Ellinwood, J. G. Active Manchester, N.H., 1860–75

Ellinwood and McClary. Active Manchester, N.H., 1860s

Elliott, James J. England. 1835–1903

Elliott and Fry. England. Active 1880s–90s

Ellis, (Dr.) Alexander John. England. 1814–90

Ellis, Alfred. Active London, 1890s

Ellis, Harry C. Active Paris (b. U.S.), 1890s–1925

Ellis, Rennie. Australia. Contemporary

Ellis and Wallery. England. Active 1880s–90s

Ellison, William. Active Quebec, 19th c.

Ellison and Co. Canada. Active ca.1852–65

Elrod Brothers. Active Lexington, Ky., 1860s

Elsken, Ed. van der. Netherlands. 1925–

Elston, Stephen R. U.S. 1948–

Emden, Hermann. Germany. Active 19th c.

Emerson, Edwin. Active Troy, N.Y., 1850s–60s

Emery, A. G. Active Marquette, Mich., 1860s

Emilia. Active Bologna, Italy, 19th c.

Emmermann, Curt. Germany. Active 20th c.

Emmons, Chansonetta Stanley. U.S. 1858–1937

*Endsley, Fred S., III. U.S. Contemporary

Engelberg, Morton R. U.S. Contemporary

Engelskirchen, Hein. Germany. Contemporary

England, Thomas. U.S. Contemporary

Engle, Horace. U.S. Active 1880s

Engler, H. Germany. Active ca. 1880

English, Pat. Active 20th c.

Engman, Anders. Sweden. 1933–

Enkelmann, Siegfried. Germany. Active 20th c.

*Enos, Chris. U.S. 1944–

Enyeart, James L. U.S. 1943–

Eppridge, William. U.S. Contemporary

*Epstein, Ellen. See Land-Weber, Ellen

*Erben, Kurt W. Austria. 1946–

*Erceg, Donald J. U.S. 1939–

*Erceg, Joseph. U.S. Contemporary

Eremine, G. Active Moscow, 20th c.

Erhard, Otto. Germany. b. 1869

Ericson, A. W. 1848–1927. Active California (b. Sweden)

Ermakov, D. d. 1914. Active Tiflis, Russia, 1870s

*Ermi, Jiří. Czechoslovakia. 1945–

Ervin, William F. Active Denver, 20th c.

Erwin *Frères*. Active Paris, ca. 1870

Escamilla, Elsa. Mexico. Contemporary

Eschen, Fritz. Active Berlin, 20th c.

Escher, Charles. Hungary. Active 20th c.

Eseler, Theo. Germany. Active 20th c.

Eson, Thure. Sweden. Active 20th c.

Espinosa, B. Peru. Active ca. 1868

Espinosa Carbrera, Mario Antonio. Brazil. Contemporary

Esplugas, A. Spain. Active 19th c.

Esson, James. Active Preston, Ontario, 1875–98

*Estabrook, Gwen Widmer. Contemporary

*Estabrook, Reed. U.S. 1944–

Estabrooke, Edward M. Active mid-19th c.

Esten, Jack. England. Active 20th c.

Esterházy, (Count) D. Austria-Hungary. Active 19th c.

Estrada de Monterrubio, María Elena. Mexico. Contemporary

Estrin, Mary Lloyd. U.S. 1944–

Ettling, John, and Co. Active New York City, 19th c.

Eurenius, W. A. Sweden. Active ca. 1870

Eutrope, S. W. Australia, New Zealand. Active 20th c.

Evans, F. Jas. Active York, Pa., 1860s

Evans, Horace. Active Los Angeles, ca. 1915–21

Evans, Louella. U.S. Active ca. 1865

Evans, O. B. Active Buffalo, ca. 1850–55

Evans, Philip. Great Britain. 1943–

Evans, Terry. U.S. 1944–

Evans and Prince. Active York, Pa., 1860s

*Evergon (Albert Lunt). Canada. 1946–

Evrard, Jacques. Belgium. 1943–

Ewald, Inés. Mexico. Contemporary

Ewing, R. D. Active Peterborough, Ontario, 19th c.

Export, Valie. Austria. 1940–

Eyerman, C. U.S. Active 20th c.

Eyerman, J. R. U.S. Active 20th c.

Ezzio, Deborah. Contemporary

F. G. O. S. Great Britain. Active 1880s

Fabry, Joseph. Venezuela. Contemporary

Facio, Sara. Argentina. Contemporary

Fage, André. France. Contemporary

Fagersteen, G. Active Yosemite Valley, 1870s

Faitless and Becforth. Active London, 19th c.

Fajans, Maksymilian. 1827–90. Active Warsaw

Falco, Louis. Contemporary

Falk. Active Sydney, Australia, ca. 1891

Falk, Benjamin J. U.S. 1853–1925

Falk, Sam. U.S. Active 20th c.

Falla. Peru

Faller, Marion. U.S. Contemporary

*Faller, Richard L. U.S. 1941–

Faller, Will. U.S. 1940–

*Fallon, James. U.S. 1946–

Fallon, William J. U.S. Active 20th c.

Famin, C. France. Active 1860s–70s

Faraday, Michael. England. 1791–1867

Farber, Daniel. U.S. 1906–

Farber, Edward R. U.S. 1915–

Farbman, N. R. U.S. Active 20th c.

Farbman, Patricia. U.S. Active 20th c.

Fardel, H. Active Paris, 20th c.

Fardon, George Robinson. 1806–86. Active San Francisco and Victoria, British Columbia (b. England); ca. 1849–62

Farini, Lulu. Active Bridgeport, Conn., 1880s

Farkas, Shelly. U.S. Contemporary

Farrar, A. B. Active Bangor, Maine, 1870s

Farrougia, A. Turkey. Active 1870s

Farsari, A., and Co. Active Yokohama, ca. 1900

Faruffini, Federico. 1831–69. Active Rome, 1867–69

Fassett, Samuel Montague. Active Chicago, 1861–64

Faul, Henry. Active Denver and Central City, Colo., 1861–64

Faulkner, Douglas. U.S. Active 20th c.

Faulkner, M. M. Active Niles, Mich., 1850s–60s

Faulkner, Robert. Active London, 19th c.

Faurer, Louis. U.S. 1916–

Fauvarque-Omez, Alfred. France. Active 20th c.

Fay, C. R. Active Malone, N.Y., 1860–78

Fay, E. B. Active New York City, 1865–75

Fay, Irene. U.S. (b. Switzerland). 1914–

Feather, Rachel. New Zealand. 1954–

*Featherstone, David. U.S. Contemporary

Fechner, Wilhelm. Active Berlin, ca. 1868–1900

*Feder, Jack. U.S. Contemporary

Fegel, Joh. F. Netherlands. Active 20th c.

Fehl, Fred. U.S. Contemporary

Fehr, Gertrude. Switzerland. b. 1898

Feijo, Bete. Brazil. Contemporary

Feiler, Franz. Active Munich, 20th c.

Fein, Philip. U.S. Active 20th c.

Feininger, T. Lux. U.S. (b. Germany). 1910–

Feinstein, Harold. U.S. Contemporary

Feldman, Hans-Peter. Germany. 1941–

*Feldstein, Peter. U.S. 1942–

Felegyhazy, (Dr.) Ladislaus. Active Budapest, 20th c.

Felici, Giuseppe. Active Rome, 1863 and after

Felixzon, A. W. Finland. Active 19th c.

Felizardo, Luiz Carlos. Brazil. Contemporary

Fell, S. B. Active Morrisburg, Ontario, 1870s

Fellman, Sandi. U.S. 1952–

Fels, Florent. France. 1891–1977

Felsen, Theo. Active Cologne, 20th c.

Felt, Louis W. Active Chicago, 1870–1900

Felt, Peter A. Active Chicago, 1874–79

Felt, S. W. Active Chicago, 1870s

Felton, Herbert. England. Active 20th c.

Fematt Enríquez, Miguel. Mexico. Contemporary

Fenzl, Fritz. Germany. Contemporary

Fergus, John. Scotland. Active 1862–85

Ferguson, E. Lee

Ferguson, Larry S. U.S. 1954–

Ferguson, Robert. Active Cheshire, England, 20th c.

Ferguson, W. Active Keswick, England, 1860s

*Fernandez, Antonio A. U.S. 1941–

*Fernandez, Benedict J.   U.S. 1935–

Fernández, Manuel.   Peru. Active ca. 1863

Fernandez Ackermann, Luis.   Venezuela. Contemporary

Fernández Nogueras, Ernesto.   Cuba. Contemporary

Fernley, W. R.   Active ca. 1910

Ferrar (Ferrez), Marc.   Brazil. Active ca. 1870s–90s

Ferrer Mortimor, Mario.   Cuba. Contemporary

Ferrero, (Dott. Ing.) Federico.   Active Turin, Italy, 20th c.

Ferri, Stanislao.   Contemporary

Ferrier and Lecadre.   Active Paris, 19th c.

Ferrier (*Père, Fils*) and Soulier.   Active Paris, 1850s

Fescourt, F.   France. Active 1860s–70s

Feurer, Hans.   Switzerland. 1940–

Feyfar, Zdenko.   Contemporary

Ficke, Arthur Davison.   U.S. 1883–1945

Fickert, Hermann.   Croatia. Active 19th c.

Fidler, Hynek.   1836–70. Active Prague

Fidon, Alain.   France

Fiedler, Franz.   Germany. 1885–1956

Fiedler, Julio.   Active Zagreb, 19th c.

Fieger, Erwin.   Germany. 1928–

*Fielder, Sheila White.   U.S. 1938–

Fielding, Malcolm.   England. Contemporary

Fields, John J.   Australia, New Zealand (b. U.S.) 1938–

Fierlants, Edward.   Belgium. 1819–69

Fietta, Edouard.   Active Strasbourg, France, 19th c.

Fifield, H. S.   Active Lincoln, N.H., 19th c.

Figari, Armida T. de.   Peru. Contemporary

Figueroa, Alberto.   Cuba. Contemporary

Figueroa, Salvador.   Mexico. Contemporary

Filan, Frank.   U.S. 1905–52

Filipowski, Stefan.   Contemporary

Filley, Myron T.   Active New England, late 19th c.

Filmer, (Lady) Mary.   England. Active ca. 1840–1903

Finck, Heinz-Dieter.   Switzerland. 1942–

Fink, Larry.   U.S. Contemporary

Fink, Peter.   U.S. 1917–

Finkle, Harvey.   U.S. Contemporary

Finlay, Clare L.   d. 1936

Finlay, Ian.   Ireland. Contemporary

Finlayson, Graham.   England. Active 20th c.

Finley, H. Marshall.   d. 1900. Active Canandaigua, N.Y., 1841–80

Finley, Halleck.   U.S. Active 20th c.

Finsler, Hans.   Switzerland. 1891–1972

*Fiorelli, Thomas P.   Contemporary

Fiorenza, Vito.   Italy

Fiorillo, I.   Italy. Active 1860s

Fiorucci, Vittorio.   Canada. 1932–

Firth, Edgar M.   Active Worcester, England, 20th c.

Fisbein, Jorge.   Argentina. 1945–

Fischer, G.   Germany. Active 19th c.

Fischer, Hal.   U.S. Contemporary

Fischer, Niels

Fischer, Rudolf.   1881–1957

Fischer, (Dr.) Walter.   Active Berlin, 20th c.

Fischer and Brothers.   Active Baltimore, 1850s–60s

Fischerwer, Gertruda.   Czechoslovakia. Active 20th c.

Fishbeck, Frank.   Contemporary

Fisher.   Active Moscow, early 20th c.

*Fisher, Elaine.   U.S. Contemporary

Fisher, Frank.   U.S. Active 20th c.

Fisher, Lydia.   Venezuela. Contemporary

Fisher, S. R.   Active Norristown, Pa., 19th c.

*Fisher, Shirley.   Contemporary

Fisher, Van.   U.S. Active 20th c.

Fison, Frederick W.   England. Active 1890s–1900

*Fitch, Steve.   U.S. 1949–

Fitz, Grancel.   U.S. Active 20th c.

Fitz, J. J.   Australia. Active ca. 1870

Fitzgibbon, John H.   1816–82. Active St. Louis (b. England), 1846–82

Fitzgibbon-Clark, Maria Louisa.   Active St. Louis, 1869–1906

Fitzsimmons, Joan.   U.S. Contemporary

Fizeau, Hippolyte.   France. 1819–96

Flachéron, (Comte) F.   Active Rome (b. France), 1850–52

Flaglor, Amasa P. and Durose.   Active San Francisco, 1870s–90s

Flaherty, Frances.   U.S. Active 20th c.

Flaherty, Robert Joseph.   U.S. 1884–1951

Flakelar, Barrie.   Canada. Active 20th c.

Flamant, E.   France

Flannery, Henry.   U.S. Active 20th c.

Fleckenstein, Louis.   U.S. 1866–1943

*Fleischhauer, Carl.   U.S. 1940–

Fleischman, Trude.   U.S. (b. Austria). Active 20th c.

Fleischmann, Susan.   U.S. Contemporary

Fleris, Stanislovas.   Lithuania. 1858–1915

Fletcher, Christine.   Active San Francisco, 20th c.

Fletcher, Dave.   U.S. Active 20th c.

Fleury-Husson, Jules.   *See* Champfleury

*Flick, Robbert.   U.S. (b. Canada). 1939–

Flodin, Ferdinand.   1863–1935. Active Worcester, Mass (b. Sweden), 1887–99; Sweden, 1900 and after

Florea, Johnny.   U.S. Active 20th c.

Flores Estrada, Florencio.   Mexico. Contemporary

Floret, Evelyn.   U.S. Contemporary

Flory, Louis Paul.   Active New York City, 20th c.

Flöter, Hubs.   Germany. 1910–77

Flowers, Adrian.   England.

Floyd and Co.   Active Hong Kong, 1860s–70s

Flüschow, Gugliemo

Fly, Camillus S.   Active Tombstone, Ariz., 1880s

Foley, E. F.   Active New York City, 20th c.

Foley, Florence.   Active Bisbee, Ariz., 20th c.

Foley, Jane Tuckerman.   U.S. 1941–

*Foley, Jean.   U.S. Contemporary

Folkmann, Jul.   Active Copenhagen, 20th c.

Folsom, A. H.   U.S. Active 19th c.

Folsom, E. S.   Active Katonah, N.Y., 1870s

Folsom, Karl.   Contemporary

Fondiller, Harvey V.   U.S. Contemporary

Fonsagrives, Fernand.   France. Active 20th c.

Fontaine, G.   Active Paris, 1855–88

Fontana, Franco.   Italy. 1933–

Fontana Albrozzi, Roberto Dario.   Venezuela. Contemporary

Fontcuberta, Joan.   Spain. Contemporary

Fonteyne, Karel.   Belgium

Foons, A. B.   U.S. Active mid-19th c.

Foote, David A.   Active Wolcott, N.Y., 1870s

Föppel, Heinz.   Germany. Active 20th c.

*Forbes, Conrad.   Contemporary

Forcella and Funch.   Active Florence, 19th c.

Ford, Arthur.   Australia. Active 20th c.

Ford, Charles Henri.   U.S. Active 20th c.

Ford, Sue.   Australia. Contemporary

Formiguera, Pere.   Spain. 1952–

Forney, Ralph.   U.S. Active 20th c.

Forrest, Brian.   U.S. Contemporary

Forrest and Lozo.   Active Toronto and Belleville, Ontario, 1860s–70s

Forrester, (Baron) Joseph James.   Portugal (b. England). 1809–61

Forsell, Gunnar.   Sweden. 1904–

Forshew, Frank.   U.S. Active New York state, 19th c.

Forsyth, N. H.   Active Butte, Mont., 1890s

Forth, Robert F.   U.S. Contemporary

*Foss, Jack.   U.S. Contemporary

Foster, Ken.   New Zealand (b. England). 1934–

Foster, Peter Le Neve.   England. 1809–79

*Foster, Steven D.   U.S. 1945–

Fotografia Imperatori.   Active northern Italy, 1865

Foulsham and Banfield.   Active London, ca. 1900

Fouret, E.   Active Cherbourg, France, 20th c.

Fowler, S. J.   Active Auburn, N.Y., 1860s

Fox, Andrew J.   1826–1919. Active St. Louis, 1854–95

Fox, Charles J.   Active Toronto (b. England), ca. 1855

Fox, Edward.   Active Brighton, England, 1880s

Fox, Flo.   U.S. Contemporary

Fox, (Dr.) George Henry.   U.S. Active late 19th c.

Fox, J. Marsden, and Gates, Menzo E.   Active Rochester, N.Y., 1860s–70s

Foy, Joseph Michael.   b. 1847. Active Thames, New Zealand (b. England)

Foy Brothers.   Active Thames, New Zealand, 1870s

Fradelle.   Active 1880s

*Frajndlich, Abe.   U.S. Contemporary

Franchi de Alfaro, III, Luciano.   Brazil. Contemporary

Francisco.   Peru. Active ca. 1848

Franck (François de Villecholles).   Active Paris, 1857–82

*Franck, Kurt.   Contemporary

Franck, Martine.   France. Contemporary

*Francken, Ruth.   France (b. Czechoslovakia). 1924–

Franco, Fernell.   Columbia. Contemporary

Frank, Dick.   U.S. Contemporary

Frank, JoAnn.   U.S. 1947–

Frankenhauser, Fritz.   Germany. Active 20th c.

Franklin, Charly.   U.S. Contemporary

Franklin. W. H.   Active Deal, England, 20th c.

Franzel, Tomáš.   b. 1822. Active Prague

Fraprie, Frank Roy.   U.S. 1874–1951

Frausto Flores, Gloria.   Mexico. Contemporary

Frear, Bettie.   Active Chicago, 20th c.

Freddie, Jørn.   Denmark. Contemporary

*Fredericks, Michael, Jr.   Contemporary

Frederiksen, Carl.   Denmark. Active late 19th c.

Fredricks, Charles (Carlos) DeForest.   U.S. 1823–94

*Freed, Arthur.   U.S. Contemporary

*Freed, David.   U.S. 1936–

*Freed, Leonard.   U.S. 1929–

*Freedman, Jill.   U.S. 1939–

Freeman, Emma B.   1880–1928. Active California, 1911–27

Freeman, F. A.   Active Boston, 1860s

Freeman, G. W.   Active Charlestown, Mass., 1860s

Freeman, J.   Active Nantucket, Mass., 1868–78

Freeman, R. S.   Active London, 1860s

Freeman, Robert.   England. Contemporary

Freeman, Tina.   U.S. 1951–

*Freeman, Vida.   U.S. Contemporary

Freemesser, Bernard.   U.S. 1926–77

Freese, David.   U.S. Contemporary

Freid, Joel.   Contemporary

Freire Enciso, René.   Mexico. Contemporary

Freitag, Wolfgang.   Germany. Contemporary

Freni, Al.   U.S. Contemporary

Frese Marquez, Reinaldo.   Mexico. Contemporary

Freson, Robert.   Contemporary

Freulich, Roman.   U.S. Active 20th c.

Freund, Carl.   Germany. Active ca. 1900

Freund, David.   U.S. 1937–

Freundl, Eduard.   Active Vienna, 20th c.

Frey, Theo.   Switzerland. 1908–

Freyria, Luis Antonio.   Mexico. Contemporary

Freytag, Heinrich.   Germany. Active 20th c.

Frick, R. N.   Active Los Angeles, 1880s

Fricke, (Dr.) George.   Active Braunschweig, Germany, 20th c.

*Fridenmaker, Charles.   U.S. Contemporary

Fridrich, Frantisek Josef Arnost (1829–92), and Preuss, K.   Active Prague, 1860s–70s

Friedel, Michael.   Germany. Contemporary

Friedkin, Anthony Enton.   U.S. 1949–

Friedlaender, S., and Horowitz.   Active New York City, 1860s–70s

Friedlander, Marti.   New Zealand (b. England). 1928–

Friedli, Werner.   Switzerland. 1910–

*Friedman, Benno.   U.S. 1945–

*Friedman, James.   U.S. 1950–

Friend, Herve.   Active California, 19th c.

Friese-Greene, Willam.   1855–1921

Friis, S.   Denmark. Active 20th c.

Fripp, Paul.   Active Bath, England, 20th c.

Frisch, A.   Brazil. Active ca. 1865

Frisch, J.   Active Weimer and Erfurt, Germany, ca. 1870

Frisch, Jürgen.   Germany. Contemporary

Frisse, Jane Courtney.   U.S. Contemporary

Fristrom, Edward.   Active Brisbane, Australia (b. Sweden), late 19th c.

Fristrom, Oscar.   Active Brisbane, Australia (b. Sweden), late 19th c.

Fritsche, Yu. F.   Russia. Active 1840s

Froidevaux, Dominique

Froissard (Froissart).   Active Lyons, France, 1850s

Frond, Victor.   Brazil (b. France). Active 1857–65

Frost, E. S., and Son. Active Pasadena, Calif., 1880s

*Fry, George B., III. Contemporary

Fry, Peter Wickens. England. d. 1860

Fuchs, August J. Active Vienna, 20th c.

Fuchs, Leo. U.S.

Fuentes, Arturo. Mexico. Contemporary

Fuentes, Juan. Peru. Active ca. 1856-62

Fuguet, Dallett. 1868-1933. Active New York City, 1885-1910

Fuhrmann, Ernst. Germany. Active 20th c.

Fujii, Hideki. Contemporary

Fukase, Masahisa. Japan. 1934-

Fukuhara, Shinzo. Japan. 1883-1948

Fukumuro, Eitaro. Japan. Active 20th c.

Fulton, Hamish. England. Active 20th c.

Fumo, Marty. U.S. Contemporary

Funke, Jaromir. Czechoslovakia. 1896-1945

Furlong, James N., and Crispell, T. Active Las Vegas, Nev., and New Mexico, 1850-90

Furman, Robert Henry. U.S. 1840-1905

Furne *Fils*. France. Active 19th c.

Furness, Alfred. Active 20th c.

Furnier. Peru. Active ca. 1846

Fürst, A. Croatia (itinerant). Active 19th c.

Furukawa, Shuji. Japan. Active 20th c.

Fusco, Paul. U.S. Contemporary

Fuse, Tanio. Japan. Contemporary

Futcher, Gilbert N. England. Active early 20th c.

Fyfe, Andrew. 1792-1861

Gabain, Edward. Germany. Active 20th c.

Gabler, A. Active Interlaken, Switzerland, 1860s-90s

Gabriel, (Dr.) Charles Louis. Australia. 1857-1927

Gaede, Marc. U.S. Contemporary

Gaedicke, Johannes. Germany. 1853-1916

Gaensly, G. W. Brazil. Active mid-19th c.

Gagern, Verene von. Germany

Gagnon, Charles. Canada. 1934-

Gaillard, Paul. France. Active 1850s

Gale, Joseph. England. d. 1906

Galella, Ron. U.S. Contemporary

*Galen, William. U.S. Contemporary

Galimberti, Giulio. Active Milan, 20th c.

Gallagher, Barrett. U.S. Active 20th c.

Gallatin, Albert Eugene. U.S. 1881-1952

Gallot, Charles. France. Active 1870s

Galloway, Ewing. U.S. Active 20th c.

Gambier, M. Active New York City, 1880s

Gamboa, Harry. U.S. Contemporary

Ganz, J. Active Zurich (b. Switzerland) and Brussels, 1860s-80s

Garanin, Antoli. Russia. 1912-

Garavito, José. Peru. Active ca. 1863

Garban, André. Active Paris, 20th c.

García, Adrián Francisco. Mexico. Contemporary

Garcia, Hector. U.S. Contemporary

García, Jordi. Spain. 1958-

García, José. Peru. Active ca. 1863

García Favela, Jorge. Mexico. Contemporary

García Filho, Januário. Brazil. Contemporary

García Luna Mondragon, Francisco. Mexico. Contemporary

García N. de Almeida, Lourdes. Mexico. Contemporary

García Noriega, Francisco Javier. Mexico. Contemporary

Garcin, A. Active Geneva, 1870s

Gard, Emery R. Active Chicago, 1863-66

Gardel, Bernard

*Gardener, George. U.S. Contemporary

Gardin, Gianni Berengo. Italy. 1930-

Gardner, A. B. Active Utica, N.Y., 1859-78

Gardner, B. L. Active New York City, 20th c.

Gardner, James. U.S. Active mid-19th c.

Gardner, M. M. and W. H. Active Atlanta, 1865-75

Gardner, W. B. Active Sherborn and Somerset, Mass., 1868-78

Gardner and Frey. Active Utica, N.Y., 1850s-60s

Garnet, Tony. U.S. Active 20th c.

Garnett and Sproat. England. Active 1860s

Garnier, J. Active Avignon, France, 1850s-60s

Garo, John H. 1870-1939. Active Boston

Garreaud, Emilio. Peru. Active 1855-59

Garreaud, Fernand. Peru. Active 19th c.

Garrett, M. U.S. Active 20th c.

Garrigues, J. Tunisia. Active 1860s

Garrison, Eleanor. Active Brookline, Mass., 20th c.

Garrity, Mary. Active Chicago, 1885-95

Garrod, Richard M. U.S. 1924-

Garzón. Spain. Active 1880s

Gasche, Willi. Switzerland. Active 20th c.

Gasperini, Paolo. Venezuela. Active 20th c.

*Gassan, Arnold. U.S. 1930-

Gastal. Active Paris, 1855-65

Gaston, F., and Mathieu. Active Paris, 1850s-60s

Gaston, Paul. U.S. Active early 20th c.

Gates, G. F. Active Watkins, N.Y., 1861-76

*Gates, Jeff. U.S. 1949-

*Gates, Richard. England. 1943-

*Gatewood, Charles. U.S. 1942-

Gatszegi, Tibor. Canada. 1928-

Gaubatz, Douglas. U.S. 1950-

Gaudard, Pierre. Canada. Active 20th c.

Gaudin, Sylvie

Gauditano, Rosa Jandira. Brazil. Contemporary

Gaul, Otto John. Active Buffalo, 20th c.

Gaumy, Jean. France. Contemporary

Gaupman, R. Germany. Active 19th c.

Gauthier, Lucien. France. Active 20th c.

Gautrand, Jean-Claude. France. Contemporary

Gay-Lussac, Joseph-Louis. 1778-1850

Gaynor, Robert. Canada. Active 20th c.

Gaze, Henry Edward. New Zealand. b. 1888. Active until 1948

Geake, Thomas, Jr. Active Sherborne, England, 19th c.

Gedda, Hans. Sweden. 1942-

*Gedney, William. U.S. 1932-

Geering, Edmund. Active Aberdeen, Scotland, 19th c.

Gehr, Herbert. U.S. Active 20th c.

Gehring. Active Chicago, late 19th c.

Geibert, Ron.   U.S. 1952–

Geiges, Leif.   Germany. Active 20th c.

Geiser, Karl.   Switzerland. 1898–1957

Gell, R.   South Africa. Active ca. 1900

Gelpi, Rene.   U.S. Contemporary

Gelpke, André.   Spain. 1947–

Gengler, David W.   U.S. 1946–

Gentile, Charles.   Active Chicago, 1874–85

Gentili, Giovanni.   Italy. Active 19th c.

George, Christopher.   U.S. Contemporary

George, H. B.   Active Bernese Alps (b. England), 1860s

Georgiev, Stoyan.   Bulgaria. Active late 19th c.

Geotzman.   Active Yukon Territory, ca. 1900

Gerard, Charles.   France. Active 1850s–80s

Gerber, Friedrich.   Switzerland. 1797–1872

*Gerdes, Ingeborg.   U.S. (b. Germany). 1938–

Gerdts, Joern.   U.S. Active 20th c.

Gerhard, K.   Germany. Active 20th c.

Gerlach, Arthur.   1898–

Gerlach, Monte H.   U.S. 1950–

Germano, Thomas.   U.S. Contemporary

Gerneshausen, Kenneth J.   U.S. Active 20th c.

Gernsheim, Alison.   Switzerland. 1911–69

Gernsheim, Helmut.   Switzerland (b. Germany). 1913–

Gerschel *Frères*.   Active Strasbourg, France, 1870s

*Gersh, Stephen.   U.S. 1942–

Gershwin, Charles.   U.S. Contemporary

Gerstenberg.   Germany. Active 20th c.

Gerster, Georg.   Switzerland. 1928–

Gerstmann.   South America. Active early 20th c.

Gertinger, Julius.   Austria. Active ca. 1875

Geruzet, M.   Active Brussels, 19th c.

Gervais-Courtellemont.   France. Active 1890s

Gerz, Jochen.   Germany. 1940–

Gesinger, Michael.

Gessner, Helmuth.   Active Graz, Austria, 20th c.

Getman and Bowdish.   Active Richfield Springs, N.Y., 1864–66

Ghemar *Frères*.   Active Brussels, 1860s

Ghirri, Luigi

Giacobetti, Francis.   Contemporary

Giacomelli, Mario.   Italy. 1925–

Giaha, Ben.   U.S. Active 20th c.

Gibson, James F.   U.S. Active 19th c.

Gibson, Tom.   Canada (b. Scotland). 1930–

Gibson and Sons.   Active Penzance, England, 20th c.

Gicquel, Clément.   Active Limoges, France, 20th c.

Giegel, Philipp.   Switzerland. 1927–

*Gierlach, Z. S.   U.S. 1915–

Gigli, Ormand.   U.S. Active 20th c.

Gihon, John Lawrence.   1839–78. Active Philadelphia (b. U.S.); also Argentina and Venezuela, 1869–76

Gilbert, Gerry.   Canada. Active 20th c.

Gilbert, Paul.   New Zealand. 1954–

Gilbert, R. A.   Active Concord, Mass., ca. 1900

Gilbert and Bacon.   Active Philadelphia, 1870s–90s

Gilbertson, George.   Active Toronto, 1864–67

*Gilbreath, Ford.   U.S. Contemporary

Giles, Herbert.   U.S. Active 20th c.

*Giles, William B.   U.S. 1934–

*Gill, Charles.   Contemporary

Gill, Jock.   U.S. 1945–

Gill, Leslie.   U.S. Active 20th c.

Gill, William L.   Active Lancaster, Pa., 19th c.

Gillespie, S. M.   Active Butler and New Castle, Pa., 1860s–90s

Gillette, Guy.   U.S. Active 20th c.

Gillo, R.   Active London, 1860s

Giloux, Marc.   France. 1952–

Gilpin, Henry.   U.S. 1922–

Gilson, François.   France. 1951–

Gilula, Stan.   U.S. 1947–

Gimenez Cacho, Julieta.   Mexico. Contemporary

Gimpaya, Frank.   U.S. Contemporary

Ginsberg, Paul.   Contemporary

Giovanelli, (Dott.) Enrico.   Active Milan, 20th c.

Giovannini, Francesco.   Italy. Contemporary

Girard, F.   Active Utica, N.Y., 1880s–90s

Girault de Prangey, Joseph-Philibert.   France. 1804–92

Giroux, André.   France. 1801–79

*Gittleman, Len.   U.S. 1932–

Giulio, Cesare.   Italy. Active 20th c.

Giwartowski, Jozef.   Active Warsaw, 19th c.

Glaisher, James.   England. 1809–1903

Glaserfeld, (Dott.) Leopoldo von.   Active Merano, Italy, 20th c.

Glass, Douglas.   England. 1901–

Glassner, Helga.   Active Berlin, 20th c.

Glastra, Geri.   Netherlands. Contemporary

Glatzel, Heidrun.   Germany. 1946–

Gleason, Herbert W.   1855–1937. Active Boston

Glinn, Burt.   U.S. 1925–

Gloaguen, Hervé.   France. 1937–

Globus, Rick, Ronald, and Stephen.   U.S. Contemporary

Gloeden, (Baron) Wilhelm von.   1856–1931. Active Italy, Sicily (b. Germany), 1890s–1920s

Gloster, Dorothy.   U.S. Contemporary

*Glover, William.   U.S. Contemporary

Gluck, Barbara.   U.S. Contemporary

Godard, Adolphe.   Active Genoa, Italy, 19th c.

Goddard, John Frederick.   England. 1795–1866

Godefroy.   France. Active 1870s–90s

Godfrey, (Rev.) E.   India. Active ca. 1870

Godfrey, George W.   1818–88. Active Rochester, N.Y.

Godfrey, Mark.   U.S. Contemporary

Godfrey, William M.   Active Los Angeles, 1854–73

Godinez, E.   Active Seville, Spain, 1860s

Godwin, Fay.   England. Contemporary

Goehr, Laelia.   England. Contemporary

Goell, Jonathan.   U.S. Contemporary

Goelst, K. L. F.   Netherlands. Active 20th c.

Goertz, Josef.   Germany. 1949–

Goerz, Carl Paul.   1854–1923

Goes, José A. C.   Brazil. Contemporary

Goetz, Emil.   Switzerland. 1869–1958

Goetz, Louis A.   Active San Francisco, 20th c.

Gogala, Ivo.   Yugoslavia. Active 20th c.

*Gohlke, Frank William. U.S. 1942–
Gold, L. Fornasieri. U.S. Contemporary
Goldbeck, E. O. U.S. b. 1892
Goldberg, Beryl. U.S. Contemporary
*Golden, Judith. U.S. 1934–
Goldensky, Elias. Active early 20th c.
Golder and Robinson. Active New York City, 1860s–70s
Goldes, David. Contemporary
Goldsmith, C. England. Active 1890s
Göllner, Max. Germany. Active 20th c.
Golsh, A. C. Active Los Angeles, 1880s–90s
Gomel, Robert. U.S. Contemporary
Gómez. Peru. Active 19th c.
Gómez, Manuel. Central America. Active 20th c.
González, Raúl. Guatemala. Contemporary
González Arriaga, José Antonio. Mexico. Contemporary
González Chávez, Rubén. Mexico. Contemporary
González Marquez, Joaquín. Mexico. Contemporary
González Ruiz, Alejandro. Mexico. Contemporary
González Salazar, Efrain. Mexico. Contemporary
Good, Frank Mason. Active London (b. England) and Near East, 1860–90
Goode, H. New Zealand. Active 19th c.
*Goode, Joe. U.S. 1944–
Goodman, Mark. U.S. Contemporary
Goodwin. Active Providence, 1885–95
Goodwin, Hannibal Williston. U.S. 1822–1900
Goodwin, Henry Buergel. Sweden. 1878–1931
Goossens, Philippe. Belgium. 1939–
*Gordon, Elly. U.S. 1943–
Gordon, H. Active Aberdeen, Scotland, 1860s
Gordon, Richard. Contemporary
Gorham and Co. Active Providence, 1860s
Görlich, Ulrich. Germany. Contemporary
*Gormley, Tom. U.S. 1937–
Gorny, Hein. Germany. 1904–67
Goro, Herb. U.S. Contemporary
Gorska, L. U.S. Active 20th c.

Gorsky, Arthur. Active Bucharest, 20th c.
*Gossage, John R. U.S. 1946–
Gothard, Jenö. Hungary. 1857–1909
Gothe, L. Active Frankfurt, 1870s
Götlin, Curt. Sweden. b. 1900
Gottdiener Estrada, Elena. Mexico. Contemporary
Gottheil, Phil. U.S. Active 20th c.
Gottscho, Samuel. 1875–1971
Gouanier de Launay, M. E. L. France. Active 1870s
Gould, Fletcher O. Active Pasadena, Calif., 20th c.
Goupil and *Cie*. Active Paris, ca. 1855
Goustin, Herman. U.S. Contemporary
Gowland, Peter. U.S. Contemporary
Goya Narganes, Luis Fernando. Mexico. Contemporary
Goyzueta, Diego. Peru. Active ca. 1896
Gozzano, Renato. Italy. Contemporary
Grabill, John C. H. Active Dakota Territory, 1888–91
Grabner, (Dr.) Alfred. Active Vienna, 20th c.
Grace, Arthur. U.S. Contemporary
Gräff, Werner. Germany. b. 1901
*Graham, Anthony. Contemporary
Graham, F. S. 1863–1914. Active North Dakota
Graham, R. B. Burma. Active 1880s
*Graham, Renni. U.S. Contemporary
Granach, Stephen. U.S. 1952–
Granado Mauri Tadeu, Gregorio. Brazil. Contemporary
Grandmaître. Active Paris, 20th c.
Grant, Allan. U.S. Contemporary
Gras, Janie. France. 1938–
Grasshoff, Johannes. 1835–71. Active Berlin, 1868–71
*Gravenhorst, Hine. Contemporary
Graves, C. H. Active Philadelphia, 1890–1910
Graves, Kenneth. U.S. 1942–
Gravning, Wayne. U.S. 1935–
Gray. Active Boston, 1870s
Gray, Eric. England. Active 20th c.
Gray, Howard
Gray, R. D. Active New York City, 1890s
Gray, W. Active New York City, 1890s
Gray Brothers. South Africa. Active 1880s
Grazda, Edward. U.S. Contemporary

Graziadei, (Conte Cav.) Ernest. Active Venice, 20th c.
Grcevic, Mladen. Yugoslavia. Contemporary
Grecco, Gilberto. Brazil. Contemporary
Greco, Eugenio. Italy. Contemporary
*Green, Jonathan. U.S. Contemporary
Green, Ruth. U.S. 1949–
Green, Ruzzie. Active New York City, 20th c.
Greene, J. Bulkley. France (b. England). Active mid-19th c.
Greene, John B. Egypt. Active 1850s
Greene, Matt. U.S. Active 20th c.
Greene, Milton H. U.S. Contemporary
Greene, Plymon B. Active Chicago, 1861–92
Greenly, Colin. U.S. Contemporary
Greenwood and Hartley. England. Active 19th c.
Gregg, Sherman. 1836–91. Active Rochester, N.Y.
Gregoire, Normand. Canada. Active 20th c.
Gregor, Carola. U.S. Active 20th c.
Gregor, Miro. Contemporary
Grehan, Farrell. U.S. Contemporary
Greig, R. Michael. Canada (b. Switzerland). 1946–
Greim, Michal. Poland. 1828–1911
Grekov, Fedorovich. Russia. 1800–ca. 1855
Gremmler, Karl Theodor. Germany. Active 20th c.
Grendene, Gabriel. Switzerland. 1950–
Grenier, J., *Fils*. Active Alsace, 1860s
Gresley, (Maj.) F. England. Active 1860s
Grey and Hall. Active Brighton, England, 1850s
Gribovsky, Antonin. Contemporary
Grier, Robert. U.S. 1946–
Griesche, Frank. Germany. Contemporary
Grieshaber, Fritz. Germany. Active 20th c.
Griffin, A. U.S. Active 20th c.
Griffin, Brian. England. 1948–
Griffin, L. V. Active Rochester, N.Y., 1860s
Griffith, F. R. India, Far East. Active ca. 1863
Griffith, George W. Active Philadelphia, 1898–1910

Griffith and Griffith.   Active 1890s

Griffiths, Ken.   England. Contemporary

Grindat, Henriette.   Switzerland. 1923–

Grisar, Erich.   Germany. Active 20th c.

Griswold, M. M.   Active Ohio, 1850–80

Griswold, Victor M.   U.S. 1819–ca. 1872

Grob, Ulric.   Active mid-19th c.

Grobet, Lourdes.   Mexico. Contemporary

Groebli, René.   Switzerland. 1927–

Grom, Srecko.   Yugoslavia. Active 20th c.

Gronefeld, G.   Germany. Active 20th c.

Grooteclaes, Hubert.   Belgium. 1927–

Gros, H. F.   Active Transvaal, South Africa, 1880s

Gros, (Baron) Jean-Baptiste-Louis. 1793–1870 (b. France). Active Bogotá, Colombia, 1842; Greece, 1843 and after

*Grossi, Emilio.   U.S. 1924–

Grossman, Henry.   U.S. Contemporary

Grotecloss, John H.   Active New York City, 19th c.

Grotz, Paul.   U.S. Active 20th c.

Grove, W. H.   England. Active ca. 1900

Grove, (Sir) William Robert.   England (b. Wales). 1811–96

Groves, Bill.   U.S. Contemporary

Grozkinsky, Henry.   U.S. Contemporary

Gruber, Bettina.   Germany. 1947–

Gruber, Ferencz.   Active Budapest, 20th c.

Gruber, L. Fritz.   Germany. Active 20th c.

Grumbkow, G. von.   Peru. Active ca. 1876

Grunbaum, Dorien.   U.S. Contemporary

Grunberg, A. D.   Active Moscow, 20th c.

Grundy (Mr.).   Active Sutton Coldfield, England, ca. 1861

Grundy, William Morris.   England. 1806–59

Gruyaert, Harry.   Belgium. 1941–

*Grylls, Vaughan.   Contemporary

Gualina, Alain

Gualle, J. A.   Peru. Active 19th c.

Gübelin, Daniela.   Switzerland. 1947–

*Guéniot, Claudine.   France. 1946–

Guerard, Henri.   Active Paris, 1860s–70s

Guerin, Fritz W.   1845–1903. Active St. Louis (b. Ireland)

Guerrero, Raul.   U.S. Contemporary

Gueuvin, A.   Active Paris, 1860s

Guggenbühl, Heinz.   Switzerland. 1905–

Guibert, Maurice.   France. Active 1890s–1920s

Guijosa Aguirre, Vicente.   Mexico. Contemporary

Guilbert, Henry D.   Active 20th c.

Guild, W. H.   Active New York City, 1860s

Guillot, Laura Albin.   France. Active 20th c.

Guillot, Yves.   France. 1951–

Guillot-Saguez.   France. Active ca. 1846

Guindon, George F.   U.S.

Guler, Ara.   Turkey. 1928–

Gullers, Karl Werner.   Sweden. 1916–

Gulliver, Neil.   England. 1944–

Gulmez *Frères*.   Active Istanbul, ca. 1880

Güngerich, Werner.   Germany. Contemporary

Gunn, André.   Netherlands. Active 20th c.

Gunnison, Floyd W.   1882–1943. Active Canandaigua, N.Y.

Gunter, Charlton.   U.S. Contemporary

Gunterman, Mattie.   British Columbia. Active 1898–1912

Gunthart, Willi.   Switzerland. Active 20th c.

Günther, Hermann.   Active Berlin, ca. 1865–80

Gurenius, W. A., and Quist, P. E. Active Stockholm, 1870s

Gurley and Harris.   Active Utica, N.Y., 1878–84

Gurney, Jeremiah.   Active New York City, 1840–70

Gurovitz, Judy.   U.S. Contemporary

Gurrola, Juan José.   Mexico. Contemporary

Gusew, M.   Lithuania. Active 19th c.

Gushiken, José.   Peru. Contemporary

Gutch, J. W. G.   Scotland. Active 1850s

Gutekunst, Frederick.   1832–1917. Active Philadelphia

Gutiérrez Báez, Sergio.   Mexico. Contemporary

Gutmann, John.   U.S. (b. Germany). 1905–

Gutša, Vladimir.   Croatia. Active 19th c.

Gutschow, Arvid.   Germany. b. 1900

Guzman, Juan.   Mexico. Active 20th c.

Gwinner, Jacob.   Switzerland. 1797–1875

Haab, Armin.   Switzerland. Contemporary

Haack, C.   Active Vienna, 1870s

Haag, Michel.   France. 1950–

Haar, Ferencz.   Active Budapest, 20th c.

Haas, Robert.   U.S. (b. Austria). Active 20th c.

Haas, Rudi.   Canada. 1935–

Haas and Peale.   Active South Carolina, 1862–64

Haase, L.   Active Berlin, ca. 1862–1890

Haase, L., and Co.   Active Berlin, 1860s

Haberkorn, Ernst Erwin.   Active 20th c.

Habib, Charles-André.   Switzerland. 1949–

Hadcock, Henry L.   Active New England, ca. 1900

Haeberlin, Peter W.   Switzerland. 1912–53

Haenchen, Karl Ludwig.   Germany. Active 20th c.

Haes, Frank.   England. 1832–1916

Hagel, Otto.   U.S. Active 20th c. (deceased)

Hagemeyer, Johan.   U.S. (b. Netherlands). 1884–1962

Hageny, Jack W.   U.S. Active 20th c.

Haglon.   France. Active 1870s.

Hahn, Helmut.   Germany. Contemporary

Hahn, Hugo.   Austria. Active ca. 1905

Hahn, Hust.   Germany. 1906–

Hahn, Joh. E.   Austria. Active ca. 1900.

Hahne, Kurt.   Germany. Active ca. 1910

*Haiko, Robert F.   U.S. 1942–

Haile, Roger C.   U.S. Contemporary

Hailey, Jason.   U.S. 1925–

Haist, Grant.   U.S. Contemporary

*Hajek-Halke, Heinz. Contemporary

*Hajicek, James. U.S. 1947–

Hak, Miroslav. Czechoslovakia. 1911–

*Halámek, Zdenek. U.S. 1943–

Halbe, L. W. U.S. Active ca. 1900

Halberstadt, Ernst. U.S. 1910–

*Halberstadt, Milton. U.S. 1919–

Hale, B. F. Active Rochester, N.Y., 1860s–70s

Halevi, Marcus. U.S. 1945–

Halik, Antonio. Mexico. Contemporary

Haling, George. Contemporary

Halip, J. Russia. Active 20th c.

Halkier, V. Active Copenhagen, 20th c.

Hall. Active Chicago, 1870s

Hall, Basil. 1788–1844

Hall, Bennett. U.S. 1954–

Hall, Chadwick. U.S.

Hall, D. W. Active California, early 20th c.

Hall, Henry. Active Arlington, N.J., 20th c.

*Hall, James Baker. U.S. 1935–

Hallberg, Gyula. Active Budapest, 20th c.

Halle, Rita. Peru. Contemporary

Hallen, Ernest. Active Canal Zone, 1910–20

Hallensleben, Ruth. Germany. 1898–1977

Haller, F. G. Hungary. Active 20th c.

*Haller, Susan. U.S. 1949–

Halleur, Herman. d. 1867

Halliday, Frank A. Active Calgary, Alberta, 20th c.

Halling, Jorgen. Canada. 20th c.

Halmi, Robert. Contemporary

Halpern, David. U.S. 1936–

*Halus, Siegfried. U.S. Contemporary

*Haluska, André. U.S. 1947–

Hamasaki, Mark. U.S. 1955–

Hamaya, Hiroshi. Japan. 1915–

Hamberg, Johan Peter. Finland. 1817–98

Hamburg, Harry. U.S. 1928–

Hamelaine. Active Rouen, France, 1860s

Hamilton, David. England. 1933–

*Hamilton, Herbert. Contemporary

Hamilton, Jeanne. U.S. Contemporary

*Hamilton, Richard. England. 1922–

Hamilton, Virginia. U.S. Contemporary

*Hamilton, W. Brooks. U.S. Contemporary

Hamlin, Elizabeth. U.S. Contemporary

Hammarskiöld, Caroline. Sweden. 1930–

Hammarskiöld, Hans. Sweden. 1925–

Hammerbeck, Wanda. U.S. 1945–

Hammerschmidt, W. Active Berlin (b. Germany), 1860s; active Egypt, 1870s

Hammett, N. D. Active Nova Scotia, 1880s

Hammond, Byron. 1876–1942. Active Canadian Rockies (b. U.S.)

*Hammond, Richard. U.S. Contemporary

Hammond, Walden. Active Leamington, England, 20th c.

*Hampton, Raymond E. U.S. 1934–

Hanaya, Kanbei. Japan. Active 20th c.

Hanffstengel, Renta Von. Mexico. Contemporary

Hanfstaengl, Franz. 1804–77. Active Munich

Hanfstaengl, Hanns. Active Dresden, 1860s

Hankimo, Eino. Finland. Contemporary

Hanna, Forman. Active Globe, Ariz., 20th c.

Hansen, Georg. Active Copenhagen, 19th c.

Hansen, Marie. U.S. Active 20th c.

Hansen, Steve. U.S. Contemporary

*Hanson, Bill. U.S. 1928–

*Hanson, Bob. U.S. Contemporary

Hanson, David. U.S. 1941–

Harand. Active Paris, 20th c.

Hardh, Carl Adolph. Finland. 1935–75

Harding, G. H. S. U.S. Active Berkeley, Calif., 20th c.

*Harding, Goodwin. U.S. Contemporary

Harding, William James. 1827–99. Active Wanganui, New Zealand (b. England)

Hardman, E. Chambre. Active Liverpool, 20th c.

Hardwick, T. Frederich. England. 1829–90

Hardy, A. N. Active Boston, 1870s

Hardy, Bert. England. 1913–

Hardy, Rex, Jr. U.S. Active 20th c.

Hardy and Van Arnam. Active Troy, N.Y., 1890s

*Hare, Chauncey. U.S. 1934–

Hare, David. U.S. Active 20th c.

Hare, William Clyde. U.S. Active 20th c.

Harings, Jan. Netherlands. Contemporary

Harissiadis, Dmitrios. Greece. Active 20th c.

*Harper, Mark. U.S. 1947–

Harriman, Edward Henry. 1848–1909. Active Alaska, 1899

Harrington, Diane. U.S. Contemporary

Harris, Alex. U.S. 1949–

Harris, Chris. U.S. Contemporary

Harris, Clayton Stone. Active Philadelphia, 1890s

Harris, George. U.S. Active 20th c.

Harris, George J., and Sons. Active New York City, 1890s

Harris, Martin. U.S. Active 20th c.

Harris, Michael. U.S. 1933–

Harris, Ned. U.S. Contemporary

Harris, Pamela. U.S. Contemporary

Harris, R. South Africa. Active 1880s

Harris, Richard. Australia. Contemporary

*Harris, Ross. U.S. 1938–

Harris, W. U.S. Active 19th c.

Harris and Green. Active Utica, N.Y., 1870–80s

*Harris-McLeod, Pamela. Canada (b. U.S.). 1942–

Harrison, Gabriel. ca. 1818–1902. Active New York City, Brooklyn, 1844 and after

*Harrison, Glenn Roy. U.S. Contemporary

Harrison, W. H. 1841–97

Hart, A. P. Active Elmira, N.Y., 1860s

Hart, Charles S. Active Watertown, N.Y., 1868–78

Hart, E. H. U.S. Active late 19th c.

Hart, William Patterson. Active Queenstown, New Zealand, ca. 1880–99

Harting, G. W. Active New York City, 20th c.

Hartland, Harford. England. Active 20th c.

Hartley. 1847–87. Active Chicago, 1873–87

*Hartman, Erich. U.S. 1922–

Hartman, Harry. U.S. Active 20th c.

Hartman, Jesse. U.S. Active 20th c.

Hartsook. U.S. Active 20th c.

Hartt, Richard. U.S. Active 20th c.

Hartung, Edward. 1909–

Hartwig, Edward. Poland. 1909–

Hartz, Jacques. Germany. Contemporary

*Harvey, David Alan. Contemporary

Harvey, W. J. U.S. Active 20th c.

Harwood, G. W. Active 19th c.

Harz, Hermann. 1906– ca. 1975. Germany

Hase, E. Germany. Active 20th c.

Hase, Eduard, and Sulce, V. Croatia. Active 19th c.

Haskins, Sam. South Africa. 1926–

Hass, Hans. Austria. 1919–

Hassner, Rune. Sweden. Active 20th c.

Hastings. Active Boston, 1890s

Hatami, Shahrohk. Iran. Contemporary

Hattersley, Ralph. U.S. Contemporary

Hauert, Roger. France. Active 20th c.

Haufs, Friedrich. Germany. Active 20th c.

Haug, Werner. Switzerland. 1951–

Haun, Declan. U.S. Contemporary

Hausammann, Suzanne. Switzerland. Active 20th c.

Hauser, Heinrich. Germany. 1901–55

Hausheer, Rosmarie. Switzerland. 1943–

*Häusser, Robert. Germany. Active 20th c.

Haut, Wolfgang. Germany. Contemporary

Hautecoeur, A. Active Paris, 19th c.

Hautmann, A. Active Florence, 19th c.

Havell, John F. 1782–1857

Havemann, Victor. U.S. Active 20th c.

Havens, O. Pierre. Active Savannah, Ga.; Ossining, N.Y.; 1868–78

Havindon, John. England. Active 20th c.

Hawarden, (Lady) Clementine. England. 1822–65

Hawkes, E. B. Australia, New Zealand. Active 20th c.

Hawkins, G. L. Active Oxford, England, 20th c.

Haxton, David. Contemporary

Hayasaki, Osamu. Japan. 1933–

Hayashi, Hosoki. Contemporary

Hayashi, Shiniro. Japan. Active 20th c.

Hayd, Viktor. Germany. Active 20th c.

Hayek-Halke, Hein. b. 1898

Hayes, Dannielle B. U.S. Contemporary

*Hayes, Eugene. U.S. 1936–

Haynes, J. E. U.S. Active 20th c.

Hayward, E. J. Active Santa Barbara, Calif., 1868–78

Hayward, Judson. Active Hackensack, N.J., 20th c.

Haz, Nicholas. b. 1883. Active New York City (b. Hungary)

Hazeltine, Martin M. Active Stockton, Calif., 1870s

Hearn, Dennis. U.S. Contemporary

*Hearsum, T. R. Contemporary

*Heath, David. Canada (b. U.S.). 1931–

Heath, Vernon. England. 1819–95

Hebeisen, Heinz. Switzerland. 1951–

Heberger, J. N. Active Rochester, N.Y., 1880s

Heckel, Vilém. Czechoslovakia. Contemporary

Hedderly, James. Active London, 1870s

Hedgecoe, John. England. Contemporary

Hedin, Svante. Sweden. 1928–

Hedley. Active Medina and Rochester, N.Y., 1890s

Hedwig, Murray. New Zealand. 1949–

*Heemskerk, Kees. Contemporary

Heering, Walther. Germany. 1902–77

Hege, Fritz. Germany. Active 20th c.

Hege, Walter. Germany. 1893–1955

Hegg, E. A. Active the Klondike

Heggeman, Dieter. Germany. Contemporary

Heidersberger, Heinrich. Germany. 1906–

Heidt, Hanns. Germany. Active 20th c.

Heijne, J. C. Netherlands. Active 20th c.

Heilborn, Emil. Sweden. 1900–

Heilbron, Kenneth. U.S. Active 20th c.

Heimburg, J. von. Germany. Active 20th c.

*Hein, Max. U.S. 1943–

Heinemann, Jürgen. Germany. Contemporary

Heiniger, Ernst A. Switzerland. 1909–

Heinrich, Anne-Marie. Argentina. Contemporary

Heins, Greg. Contemporary

Heismann, Paul. U.S. Active 20th c.

Heizer, Michael. U.S. 1944–

Held, Louis. Germany. Active late 19th c.

Helders, Johan. Active Ottawa, 20th c.

Heldt, Carlos. Peru. Active ca. 1870

Helfritz, Hans. Germany. Active 20th c.

Heller, Louis Herman. U.S. (b. Germany). 1839–1928. Active Yreka, Calif., 1870s

Heller, Ursula. Switzerland. 1949–

Hellmund, Georg. Active Munster, Germany, 20th c.

Hellmuth, Charles A. Active New York City, 20th c.

Helmer-Peterson, K. Denmark. Active 20th c.

Helprin, Benson R. U.S. 1935–

Hempen, Hans. Germany. Contemporary

Hemphill, W. England. Active 1860s

*Hendel, James. Contemporary

*Henderson, Arnold. U.S. Contemporary

Henderson, Bruce. Central America. Contemporary

Henderson, H. Active Kingston, Ontario, 1860s

Henderson, James. Active London, 19th c.

Hendricks, W. Active Stamford, Conn., 1870s

Hendrickson, Horatio. Active Yonkers, N.Y., 1900–37

*Henkel, James. U.S. 1947–

Henn, Franz. Switzerland. 1879–1963

Hennah and Kent. Active 1860s

Henneman, Nikolaas. England (b. Netherlands). 1813– ca. 1875

Henri, Florence. U.S. (b. Germany). 1895–

Henriques, Bob. U.S. Active 20th c.

Henriquez, Ana Cristina. Venezuela. Contemporary

Henry, Diana Mara. U.S. Contemporary

Henry, Eugene P. Active Brooklyn, 20th c.

Henry, Richard. U.S. Contemporary

Hens, J. J. Netherlands. Active 20th c.

Henschel and Benque. Active Rio de Janeiro, 1870s

Hensel, Loudolph. Active Pike County, Pa., 1868–78

Henze, Carlos. Mexico. Contemporary

Henze, Claire. U.S. 1945–

Hepworth, T. C. England. 1834–1905

Herbert, John Rogers. England. Active 19th c.

Herbert, Walker. England. Active 1850s

Herbig, Udo. Germany. Active 20th c.

Herdeg, Hugo. Switzerland. 1909–53

Herlick, George. U.S. Active 20th c.

Hermagis, J. Hyacinthe. d. 1868

Herman, Andrew. U.S. Active 20th c.

Herman, Larry. England. Contemporary

Hermann, Ottó. Hungary. Active 19th c.

*Hernandez, Anthony. U.S. 1947–

Hernández Arestegui, Ana Luisa. Mexico. Contemporary

Hernes, Jaime. Mexico. Contemporary

*Heron, Reginald. U.S. 1932–

Herrera Martínez Negrete, Germán. Mexico. Contemporary

Herrick, Anson. Active San Francisco, 20th c.

Herrick, H. J. Active Vicksburg, Miss., 1860s

Herrick, Josephine Ursula. Active Cleveland, 20th c.

Hers, François. France. Contemporary

Herschel, Alexander Stewart. England. 1836–1907

Herschel, (Sir) John Frederick William. England. 1792–1871

Herschtritt, Léon

Hershorn, Shel. U.S. Contemporary

Hertel, C. Active Mainz, Germany, 1865–75

Hertel, Frederich. Active Weimar, Germany, 1880s

Hertwig, Aura. Active Berlin, ca. 1900–15

Hertzberg, Benjamin. U.S. Active 20th c.

Hertzberg, John. Sweden. 1871–1935

Hervey, Antoinette B. Active New York City, 20th c.

Herz, Adolf. Active Lucerne, Switzerland, 20th c.

Herzog, L. Germany. Active 1870s

Herzog, Rudi. Germany. Contemporary

Hess, Fridolin. Hungary. Active ca. 1865

Hess, Lilo. U.S. Active 20th c.

Hess, Nina and Carry. Active Frankfurt, Germany, 20th c.

Hesser, E. Bower. U.S. Active 20th c.

Hesson, Barry. New Zealand. Contemporary

Hester, Wilhelm (William). Active Seattle and Tacoma, Wash., 1893–ca. 1920

Heuvel, H. J. J. van den. Netherlands. Active 20th c.

Heuzé, Jean-Jacques. France. 1948–

Hewitt, Charles. England. Active 20th c.

Hewitt, George W. U.S. 1841–1917

Hewson, Paul. New Zealand. 1948–

Heyman, Abigail. U.S. 1942–

*Heyman, Ken. U.S. 1930–

Heyn. U.S. Active early 20th c.

Heyne, Renate. Germany. 1947–

Heywood. Active Boston, 1861–78

Heywood, J. B. (or J. D.). Active Boston, 19th c.

Hicke, Augusto. Active 19th c.

Hickling, Dorothy. Active London, 20th c.

Hidalgo, Franzisco

Hielscher, Kurt. Germany. 1881–1948

Higgins (Dr.). England. Active 19th c.

Higgins, Chester, Jr. U.S. Contemporary

Higgins, J. J., and Co. Active Boston, 1880s

High, George Henry. d. 1945. Active Chicago, 1916–45

Highton, W. Lincoln. U.S. Active 20th c.

Hilborn, Ormison O. Active Ionia, Mich., 20th c.

Hilbrandt, James. U.S. 1934–

Hill, Bernard. New Zealand. Active 20th c.

Hill, Edward. U.S. 1935–. *See also* Manual

*Hill, Fred. U.S. Contemporary

Hill, H. H. Active Hamilton, N.Y., 1880s

Hill, John T. U.S.

Hill, Leon. U.S. Active 20th c.

Hill, Paul. U.S. 1941–

*Hill, Tony. England. 1946–

*Hill, Warren. U.S. 1928–

Hiller, Karol. Poland. 1891–1939

*Hiller, Susan (Ace Possible). Contemporary

Hilliard, John. England. 1945–

Hillman, L. Active Watkins, N.Y., 1870s

Hills, E. R. Active Brookline, Mass., 1868–78

Hills and Saunders. Active Oxford, England, 1860s

Hime, Humphrey Lloyd. Active Toronto, 1840s

*Himelfarb, Harvey. U.S. 1941–

Himes, Charles. U.S. Active 19th c.

Himmel, Paul. Active 20th c.

Hindle, Thos. Active late 19th c.

Hindley, John. U.S. Active 20th c.

Hinds, A. L. Active Benton, Maine, 1868–78

*Hindson, Bradley. U.S. 1935–

Hinkle, D. H. Active Germantown, Pa., 1860s–90s

Hinshaw, T. E. Active Illinois (itinerant), late 19th c.

Hinton, John Henry. China. Active early 20th c.

Hirano, S. Active Seattle, 20th c.

Hiriarte y Valencia, Pedro. Mexico. Contemporary

Hirl, Hans. Active Vienna, 20th c.

Hirsch, H. Germany. Active ca. 1870

Hirsch, Hardmuth. Contemporary

*Hirsch, Walter. Sweden. 1935–

Hirsh, Hy. U.S. Active 20th c.

*Hiser, Cheri. U.S. 1935–

Hissong, George W. Active Lagrange, Ind., 1880s

Histed, E. Walter. U.S. Active early 19th c.

Hitrov, Thoma. 1840–1906. Active Sophia, Bulgaria; Bucharest, Ploesti, and Braila, Romania

Hitrova, Boika. Austria, U.S. (b. Bulgaria). Active early 20th c.

Hitrova, Ivanka. Active Berlin (b. Bulgaria), early 20th c.

*Hlobeczy, Nicholas Carl. U.S. 1927–

Hoag, James M. Active Adrian, Mich., ca. 1879

Hoag and Quicks. Active Cincinnati, 1860s

Hoard and Tenney. Active Winona, Minn., 1870s

*Hoare, Tyler James. U.S. Contemporary

Hoban, Tana. U.S.

*Hochhausen, Sandy. Contemporary

Hockenberry, B. E. U.S. Active early 20th c.

Hodgson, James

Hodler, Ferdinand. Switzerland. 1853–1918

Hoegh, Emil von. 1865–1915

Hoehn, George. U.S. 1935–

*Hoenich, Paul Konrad. Austria. 1907–

Hoepffner, Marta

Hoeven, J. v. d. Netherlands. Active 20th c.

Hoffer, Eugen. Finland. Active 19th c.

Hoffers, Carl Eugen. Finland. 1832–93

Hoffert, W. Active Berlin, 1890s

Höfflinger, C. Active Frankfurt, Germany, 1860s

Hoffman, Bernard. Active New York City, 20th c.

Hoffman, Julia E. U.S. 1856–1934

Hoffman, W. Active Dresden, 1865–75

Hoffmann, Heinrich. Germany. 1885–1957

Hoffmann Assis, Valdir. Brazil. Contemporary

Höflinger, Jakob. Switzerland. Active mid-19th c.

Höflinger, Louis. Active Derpt (Tartu), Estonia, 1857–76

*Hofmanis, Helena. U.S. Contemporary

Hogarth, J. England. Active 1850s

Hogg, S. Active early 20th c.

Hogstraten, A. Active The Hague, 1890s

*Hohn, Hubert. Canada. Contemporary

Hoinkis, Ewald. Germany. 1897–1960

Holbrook, David. U.S. Contemporary

Holcombe, James W. Active Venice (b. England), 1890s

Holden, (Rev.) J. England. Active 1850s

Holder, Preston. U.S. 1907–

Holdt, H. Active Munich, 20th c.

Hollan, Lewis. Active Budapest, 20th c.

Holland, Bernard C. U.S. Contemporary

*Holler, Gordon. U.S. Contemporary

Hollyman, Thomas. U.S. Active 20th c.

Holmes, Burton. U.S. 1870–1958

Holmes, Martha. U.S. Active 20th c.

Holmes, Oliver Wendell. U.S. 1809–94

Holmes, R. B. Active 19th c.

Holmes, Silas A. d. 1886. Active New York City

Holmes, William B. Active New York City, 19th c.

*Holmgren, Robert. Contemporary

Holt and Gray. Active New York City, ca. 1861–68

Holt and Madsen. Active Copenhagen, 20th c.

Holtermann, Bernhard Otto. Australia (b. Germany). 1838–85

Holzhauser, Karl-Martin. Germany. 1944–

Holzl, Gyula. Active Budapest, 20th c.

Høm, Jesper. Denmark. Contemporary

Hommel, Paul. Germany. Active 20th c.

Homolka, Florence. U.S. Active 20th c.

Honoré, Tony. Active Paris, 20th c.

Honty, Tibor. U.S.S.R. Contemporary

Hood, P. H. Active 19th c.

Hook, W. E. Active Colorado, 1880s; New Mexico, 1890s

Hooper, W. W. India. Active ca. 1876–77

Hoops, Millie. Active Los Angeles, 20th c.

Hooyer-Dubois, (Mme.) E. Netherlands. Active 20th c.

Hope. Active New York City and Goshen, N.Y., 1860s

Hope, J. O. U.S. Active Watkins, N.Y., 1868–78

Hopker, Thomas. Germany. Contemporary

Hopkins, A. C. Active Palmyra, N.Y., 1880s–90s

Hopkins, Thurston. England. Active 20th c.

Hoppenot, Helen. Active 20th c.

Hopps, W. G. Active Rush City, Minn., ca. 1895

Horcasitas, Javier. Mexico. Contemporary

Horch, Frank. U.S. Active 20th c.

Horenstein, Henry. U.S. 1947–

Horgan, Stephen Henry. U.S. 1854–1941

Horne, Fallon. d. 1858

Hornickel, Ernst. Germany. Active 20th c.

Horowitz, Bruce. U.S. 1949–

*Horowitz, Ryszard. Poland. Contemporary

Horsburgh, J. Active Edinburgh, 1860s

Horsey, H. G. England. Active 1880s

Horton, N. S. Active St. Lambert, Quebec, 20th c.

Horton, P. David. U.S. Contemporary

Horton, W. H. Active New England, ca. 1900

Horvat, Frank. France. Contemporary

Horwich Bros. Active ca. 1900

Hosking, Eric. England. 1909–

Hotze, Gertrud. Germany. Active 20th c.

Houck, William, Jr. U.S. Active 20th c.

Houdlette, A. B. Active New England, ca. 1900

Hough Bros. Active Rochester, N.Y., 1890s

Houghton (Major). India. Active ca. 1870

*House, Suda. U.S. 1951–

Houseworth, Thomas. U.S. 1829–1915

Hovey, E. P. and J. S. Active Rochester and Rome, N.Y., 1880s–90s

Howard, Chantal. U.S.

Howard, Eric. Contemporary.

Howard, W. H. England. Active 1860s

Howard and Co. Active Plattsburg, N.Y., 1870s

Howarth, Anthony. England. Active 20th c.

Howe, F. L. Active New York City and Atlanta, 1890s

Howe, Graham. U.S. 1950–

*Howe, Jane. U.S. Contemporary

Howell, William R. Active New York City, 1870s

Howes, Alvah and George (Howes Brothers). Active Massachusetts, ca. 1890s

Howieson, William. Active Australia, New Zealand, 20th c.

Howitt, William and Mary. England. Active 1860s

Howland, S. S. Active 1870s

Howlett, Robert. England. 1830–58

Hoyt, Herman. Active Colorado, San Francisco, early 20th c.

*Hrbek, Charles J. U.S. Contemporary

Hruska, Martin. Czechoslovakia. Contemporary

Huard. Russia. Active ca. 1862

Hubbard, W. P. Active Buffalo, 20th c.

Huber, Timo. Austria. 1944–

Hubin, Marcel. Active Paris, 20th c.

Hübinette, Gosta. Active Stockholm, 20th c.

Hübl, (Baron) Arthur von. Austria. b. 1852

Hubmann, Franz. Austria. Contemporary

Hubmann, Hanns. Germany. 1910–

*Hudetz, Larry. U.S. Contemporary

Hudson. Ireland. Active 1860s

Huebler, Douglas. U.S. 1924–

Huested, E. Active Albany, N.Y., 1870s

Hughes, Alice. England. d. 1920

Hughes, Cornelius Jabez. 1819–84. Active London (b. England), Glasgow, and Isle of Wight

Hughes, Jim. U.S. Contemporary

Hugnet, Georges. France. Active 20th c.

Hugo, Charles Victor. France. 1826–71

Hugo, François Victor. France. 1828–73

Hugo, Leopold. Active 20th c.

Hugo, Victor Marie. France. 1802–85

Hühn, Julius. Croatia. Active 19th c.

Huizinga, Menno. Netherlands. Active 20th c.

Hull, Arundel C. Active Laramie, Wyo., 1868

Humbert, Marcel H. Active Geneva, 20th c.

*Hume, Richard P. (Sandy). U.S. 1946–

Hümmer, W. Germany. Active ca. 1900

Humphrey, (Dr.) Orman B. Active Bangor, Maine, 20th c.

*Hunt, Adrian Phipps. Contemporary

Hunt, Robert. England. 1807–87

Hunter, Debora. U.S. 1950–

Hupka, Robert. U.S. Active 20th c.

Hüppi, Adolf. Switzerland. Active 20th c.

Hurd, L. F. Active Greenwich, N.Y., ca. 1868–78

Hurd, W. P., and Smith, William O. Active North Adams, Mass., ca. 1871

Hurley, (Capt.) Frank. Antarctica (b. Australia). 1885–1962

Hurley, Joseph. 1885–1962

Hürlimann, Martin. Switzerland. b. 1897

Hurn, David. England (b. Wales). 1934–

Hurrell, George. U.S. Active 20th c.

Hurter, Ferdinand. England (b. Switzerland). 1844–98

Husband, Florence. U.S. 1904–

Husband, Herman. Peru. Active ca. 1847

Husnik, Jacob. 1837–1916

*Husom, David. U.S. Contemporary

Hutchins, Robert B. New Zealand (b. Australia). 1922–

Hutchins, Tom. Australia. Active 20th c.

Hutchinson, E. T. B. Active Brisbane, Australia, late 19th c.

Hutchinson, Eugene. Active New York City, 20th c.

Hutchinson, H. S., and Co. Active New Bedford, Mass., ca. 1900

Hutchinson, Peter. U.S. Contemporary

*Hutchison, James. U.S. 1946–

*Hyde, Philip. U.S. 1921–

Hyman, Martin. U.S. Active 20th c.

Ibarra Chavarria, Enrique. Mexico. Contemporary

Ibbetson, Boscawen. Switzerland (b. England)

Ichac, Pierre. France. Active 20th c.

Ichimura, Tetsuya. Japan. 1930–

Ickovic, Paul. U.S. (b. England). 1944–

Idzumi, Yasowo. Active Seattle, 20th c.

Iffland, Heinrich. Germany. Active 20th c.

Iger, Martin. U.S. Active 20th c.

Iglesias Gotes, Enrique. Mexico. Contemporary

Ignatius, Ernst. Estonia. Active ca. 1854

Ihrt, Fred. Germany. Contemporary

Ikam, Catherine. France. Contemporary

*Ikeda, M. Japan. 1934–

Ikko. Japan. 1931–

Illidge, Ralph. Australia, New Zealand. Active 20th c.

*Imai, Hisae. Japan. Contemporary

Impey, (Capt.) E. C. India (b. England). Active 1860s

Imsand, Marcel

Ina, Nobuo. 1898–

Incandela, Gerald. U.S. (b. Tunisia). 1952–

Inch, Dennis. U.S. Contemporary

Inchiostri, Dragan. Active Zagreb, 19th c.

Inés, Antonio de. Spain

Ingalls. Active Rome, N.Y., 1890s

Ingersoll, T. W. Active St. Paul, 1878–1907

Ingersoll, W. B. Active New York City, 19th c.

Ingham, John. 1841–1915. Active Ashton-upon-Mersey, England

Inglis, James. 1835–1904. Active Montreal (b. Scotland), ca. 1867

Inha, I. K. Finland. 1865–1930

Inverarity, D. G. U.S. Active ca. 1900

Ionesco, Irina. 1946–

Iooss, Walter, Jr. U.S. Contemporary

Irion, Christopher. U.S. 1949–

Irons, Raymond. England. Contemporary

*Isabelle, B. G. Contemporary

Iscovici, Bernard. Active Bucharest, 20th c.

Isert, Gerhard. Germany. Active 20th c.

Ishimoto, Yasuhiro. U.S. 1921–

Israel and Co. Active Baltimore, 1865–75

Ittenbach, Max. Germany. Contemporary

Iturbide, Graciela. Mexico. Contemporary

Ivanitskii, A. Active Tiflis, Russia, mid-19th c.

Ivanov, Panayot. Active Tryavna and Gabrovo, Bulgaria, 1860s–70s

Iversen, Earl. U.S. 1943–

Ives, Frederick Eugene. U.S. 1856–1937

Ives, Herbert Eugene. 1882–1953. Active Philadelphia

Iwamiya, Takeji. Japan. 1920–

Iwasaki, Carl. U.S. Contemporary

Iwasaki, Yozan T. Active Seattle, 20th c.

Izis (Izis Bidermanas). France (b. Lithuania). 1911–

*Jachna, Joseph D. U.S. 1935–

*Jackson, Richard

*Jacobs, Brian M. U.S. 1943–

Jacobs, Fenno. U.S. Active 20th c.

*Jacobs, Judy. U.S. 1951–

Jacobs, Lou, Jr. U.S. Contemporary

Jacobs, Raymond. U.S. Active 20th c.

Jacobsen, Birger. Active Copenhagen, 20th c.

Jacobsen, Nancy. U.S. Contemporary

Jacobshagen, Keith. U.S. 1941–

Jacoby, Max. Germany. Contemporary

Jacoby, W. H. Active Minneapolis, 1880s

Jacot, Monique. Switzerland. 1934–

Jacquard, Charles Le Maire. Active Sedan, France, 1840s–60s

Jaeckin, Just. Contemporary

Jaeger, (Dr.) Charles H. Active New York City, 20th c.

Jaffe, Morris H. U.S. Contemporary

Jager, A. Active Amsterdam, ca. 1884

Jäger, Gottfried. Germany. 1937–

Jägermann. Austria. Active 19th c.

Jago, H. U.S. Active early 20th c.

Jahan, Pierre. France. Contemporary

Jahudka, Josef. Austria. Active ca. 1900

James, C. H. Active Philadelphia, 1868–78

James, Christopher. U.S. 1947–

James, (Sir) Henry. England. 1803–77

Jandira Gauditano, Rosa. Brazil. Contemporary

Jankovich, G. Active Venice, 1880s

Jansen, Bernd. Germany. Active 20th c.

*Jansen, Catherine. U.S. 1945–

Janssen, Pierre Jules César. France. 1824–1907

*Janu, Rudolph. U.S. 1934–

Jaquish, Richard. U.S. Contemporary

Jarche, A. Louis. U.S. Active 20th c.

Jarger, H. Active New Jersey, ca. 1885

Jaring, Cor. Netherlands. Contemporary

Jårlås, Sven. Sweden. 1913–70

Jarsche, James. England, France. Active 20th c.

Jarvis, Lucius F. 1865–1943. Active California, 1880s

Jarvis Studio. Active Ottawa, 1880s

Jasinka, (Mme.) Halina. Poland. Active 20th c.

Jaskari, P. K. Finland. Active 20th c.

Jaunsudrabinš, J. Latvia. Active 19th c.

Jay, Bill. U.S. 1940–

Jeanmoigin, Yves. France. Contemporary

Jeanrenaud, A. France. d. 1855

Jeffs, Howard. England. Contemporary

Jefry, J. A. Australia, New Zealand. Active 20th c.

Jekyll, Gertrude. England. 1843–1932

Jenicek, Jiři. Active 20th c.

Jenkins, Harry. Active Evanston, Ill., 20th c.

Jenney, J. A. Active Detroit, 1865–75

Jensen, Julie. U.S. Contemporary

Jensen, Maurice. U.S. Active 20th c.

Jenshel, Leonard. U.S. Contemporary

Jerome, Henri. Active Paris, 20th c.

Jesse, Nico. France. Active 20th c.

Jeudy, Maurice. France. Active 20th c.

*Jevne, James. Contemporary

Jicinsy, Karel. Czechoslovakia. Contemporary

Jiménez, Agustin. Mexico. Active 20th c.

*Jimenez, Orlando E. U.S. Contemporary

Jiménez, Ramón. Mexico. Contemporary

Jiménez Romero, Humberdo Miguel. Mexico. Contemporary

Jiru, Vaclav. Contemporary

Joaillier. Active Greece, Turkey, 1880s

Job, Charles. England. Active 20th c.

Jobso, Jakob. Estonia, Latvia. 1830–1902

Jocelyn, (Lady) Fanny. England. Active 19th c.

Joel, Charlotte. Active Berlin, early 20th c.

Joel, Yale. U.S. Contemporary

Johannes, B. Active Bavaria, 1878–82

Johansen, A. Denmark. Active 20th c.

*Johansson, Håkan. Germany (b. Sweden). 1939–

Johansson, Sven-Gosta. Sweden. Active 20th c.

John, L. R. U.S. 1951–

John, Paul Willy. Germany. Active 20th c.

Johns, John H. G. New Zealand (b. England)

Johns, Richard. U.S. Active 20th c.

Johns, W. E. Active Lexington, Ky., 1880s–90s

Johnson. Active Sioux City, Iowa, 1870s

Johnson, Belle. Active Monroe, Miss.

Johnson, C. W. J. Active California, ca. 1880

Johnson, Clifton. 1865–1940. Active Massachusetts

Johnson, Clinton. Active Los Angeles, early 20th c.

Johnson, Ellen Foscue. U.S. Contemporary

Johnson, J. W. New Zealand. 1876–1954

Johnson, Laura Adelaide. 1843–1907. Active Rochester, N.Y., 1887–1903

Johnson, Lee. U.S. Contemporary

Johnson, Marguerite. U.S. Active 20th c.

Johnson, N. G. Active Washington, D.C., 1880s

Johnson, Robert H. U.S. Active 20th c.

Johnson, Thor. Sweden. Contemporary.

*Johnson, Thos. U.S. Contemporary

Johnson, Williams and Co. Active New York City, 1865–75

Johnston, Alfred Cheney. U.S. Active 20th c.

Johnston, C. M. Active Ottawa, 20th c.

Johnston, Carl Truman. U.S. Active 20th c.

*Johnston, Helen. U.S. Contemporary

Johnston, J. B. Active Edinburgh, 1840s–50s

Johnston, J. Dudley. 1868–1955. Active London

Johnston, J. S. Active New York City, late 19th c.

Johnston Brothers. U.S. Active New York City, 1860s

Joly, Charles Jasper. 1864–1906

Joly, John. Ireland. 1857–1933

Joly de Lotbinière, Pierre-Gustave. France. 1798–1865

Jonas, Calvert. Active 19th c.

Jonas, Jonathan. Contemporary

Jones, A. H. Active Honolulu, 20th c.

*Jones, Allen. England. 1937–

Jones, Baynham. England. Active 1860s

Jones, (Rev.) Calvert. (b. England.) Active Naples; Malta; Rome, 1845–55

Jones, Fred. Active London, 1860s

Jones, Gerald E. 1881–1963. Active Auckland, New Zealand

Jones, H., and Co. Active Baltimore, 1860s

*Jones, Harold. U.S. 1940–

Jones, Harold N. Australia, New Zealand. Active 20th c.

Jones, John F. Active Toledo, Ohio, 20th c.

*Jones, Pirkle. U.S. 1915–

Jones, Ray. U.S. Active 20th c.

Jones, Richmond. U.S. (b. Canada). Contemporary

Jones, Stedman. Active Paris, 20th c.

Jones, W. H. Active Missouri, early 20th c.

Jones-Griffiths, Philip. England. Contemporary

Jongh, Edouard de. Switzerland. 1859–1926

Jongh, Francis de. Switzerland. 1864–1928

Jongh, de, *Frères*. Russia. Active 19th c.

Joniaux, Georges. France. Active 20th c.

Jonsson, Rune. Sweden. 1932–

Jordan and Co. Active New York City, 1860s

Jordan Brothers. Active Utica, N.Y., 1860s

*Jorden, Bill. U.S. 1936–

Jorgensen, Carl. Denmark. Active 20th c.

Jorgensen, Louis. Denmark. Active 20th c.

Jorgensen, Orloff. Active Copenhagen, 20th c.

Jorgensen, Victor. U.S. Active 20th c.

Jory, Samuel C. Active Toronto, mid-19th c.

Josefsberg, Steven Kent. U.S. 1946–

Joseph, Roz. U.S. Contemporary

Jouan, C. Active Paris, ca. 1860

Jourdrin, Jean-Philippe. France. 1954–

Jousson, Pierre. France. Contemporary

Jovanović, Anastas. Serbia. Active ca. 1850s

Joyce, Paul. England. 1941–

Judd, M. E. Active Syracuse, N.Y., 1868–78

Judge, Fred. Active Hastings, England, 20th c.

Judice, Edward. U.S. 1936–

Judkins. Active Seattle, 1880s–90s

Juhl, Ernest W. Germany. 1850–1915

Julia, E. Active Madrid, 1860s

Julien, J. Active Geneva, 1870s

Jullia, Julio. Peru. Active ca. 1863

Jumisco, Phil. U.S. Contemporary

Jumonji, Bishin. Japan. Contemporary

Jung, C. Active Paris, ca. 1871

Jung, Reinhold. Germany. Contemporary

Junker, Aage. Active Copenhagen, 20th c.

Junker, Henk. Netherlands. Active 20th c.

Jurkowski, Stanislaw. Russia (b. Poland).

Kabrt, Josef. Czechoslovakia. Active 20th c.

*Kaczmarek, Janis. U.S. Contemporary

Kahan, Robert. U.S. Contemporary

Kahlenberg, Rolf. Contemporary

*Kahn, Richard. Contemporary

*Kahn, Steve. U.S. 1943–

Kalb, Leticia. Mexico. Contemporary

Kalcenavs, Indrikis. Latvia. Active 19th c.

Kaleya, Tana. France. Contemporary

*Kalisher, Simpson. U.S. 1926–

Kaminski, Edward. U.S. Active 20th c.

Kammer, H. Germany. Active 20th c.

Kammerer, Viktor. Active Vienna, 20th c.

Kanberg, J. J. Active Chicago, 1890s

Kane, William. U.S. Contemporary

Kanne, K. Germany. Active 20th c.

Kannepa, A. Russia. Active 20th c.

Kanzelbach, Wolfgang. Germany. Contemporary

*Kaplan, Alan. Contemporary

Kaplan, Fred. U.S. Contemporary

Kar, Ida. England (b. Russia). 1908 (or 1917)–

Karales, James H. U.S. Contemporary

*Karant, Barbara. U.S. 1952–

Karastoyanov, Anastas. 1822–80. Active Sofia, Bulgaria; Belgrade, after 1858

Karastoyanov, Dimiter. Bulgaria. Active late 19th c.

Karastoyanov, Ivan. Bulgaria. Active late 19th c.

Karelin, Andrei Osipovich. Russia. 1837–1906

Karfeld, Kurt Peter. Germany. Active 20th c.

Karger, George. U.S. d. 1973

Kargopoula, B. Active Constantinople, 1860s

Karlsson, Sig. T. Sweden. Contemporary

Karnitschnigg, (Gen.-Major) Maximilian. Active Graz, Austria, 20th c.

Karoleev, Stoyan. Bulgaria. d. 1893

Karrick, V. A. Active St. Petersburg, Russia (b. Scotland), 19th c.

Kasparik, Karel. Czechoslovakia. Active 20th c.

*Kasper, Jo Diane. U.S. 1945–

*Kasper-Murawski, Darlyne. U.S. Contemporary

Kassin, E. U.S.S.R. Contemporary

*Kasuba, Aleksandra. U.S. Contemporary

Katan, Hans. Netherlands. Contemporary

Kater, Edward. England. Active 1840s–50s

Katschner, (Ing.) Emil. Czechoslovakia. Active 20th c.

*Katsiff, Bruce. U.S. 1945–

*Katz, Brian M. Contemporary

Katz, Paul. U.S. 1942–

Katz, Shelly. U.S. Contemporary

Katzenberger, George. U.S. 1951–

Kauffman, Mark. U.S. Contemporary

Kaufman, Elliot. U.S. Contemporary

Kaufman, Irving J. U.S. Contemporary

*Kaufman, Michael. Contemporary

Kaufman, Pettus. U.S. Active 20th c.

*Kawada, Kikuji. Japan. 1933–

Kawakami, Rokuo. Japan. Contemporary

*Kay, Kristine. U.S. 1945–

*Kayafas, Gus. U.S. Contemporary

Kaye, (Sir) John William. England. 1814–76

Kayser, Alex. Switzerland. 1949–

Keapek, H. Active Zagreb, 19th c.

Kearton, Cherry. England. 1873–1940

Kearton, Richard. England. 1862–1928

Keegan, Marcia. U.S. 1942–

Keely. Active Philadelphia, 1860s

Keen, James N. U.S. Active 20th c.

Keetman, Peter. U.S. Active 20th c.

Keighley, Larry P. U.S. Active 20th c.

Keith. Active Liverpool, 19th c.

Kelham, Augustus. England. Active ca. 1870

Kelley, E. W. Active Chicago, 1868–1908

Kelley, Robert. U.S. Active 20th c.

Kelley and Chadwick. Active Chicago, 19th c.

Kellogg Brothers. Active Hartford, 1868–78

Kells, Harold H. Canada. Active early 20th c.

*Kelly, Charles. Contemporary

Kemmerich, Alfons. Germany. Contemporary

Kempe. Active Rochester, N.Y., 1860s

Kempe, Fritz. Germany. 1909–

Kempe and Gates. Active Rochester, N.Y., 1860s

Kempen, Wink van. Netherlands. 1948–

Kempf, Michel

Kempin, Lely. Germany. Active 20th c.

Ken, A. Active Paris, 1860s

Kennedy, Clarence. U.S. 1892–1972

Kennedy, J. F. Active Hot Springs, Ark., 1868–98

Kennerly, David Hume. U.S. Contemporary

Kennet, Richard. 1817–96

Kenny-Levick (Mrs.). Active Hyderabad, India (b. England), late 19th c.

Kensett, J. W. England. Active 1850s

Kent, J. H. Active Rochester, N.Y., 1870s

Kent, Thelma R. 1899–1946. Active Christchurch, New Zealand

Kenton, Erle C. b. 1896. Active Los Angeles

Kepler, Franz. Germany. Active 20th c.

Kerff, Gerhard. Germany. Active 20th c.

Kergel, Helmut. Germany. Contemporary

Kerlee, Charles E. Active Los Angeles, 20th c.

Kernan, Sean. U.S. 1942–

*Kerr, Pamela. South Africa. 1927–

Kerry. Active Sydney, Australia, late 19th c.

Ker-Seymour, Barbara. England. Contemporary

Kershaw, Morris. New Zealand. Active 20th c.

*Kerslake, Kenneth. U.S. 1930–

Kertson. Active New York City, 1850s–60s

Kertson and Thompson. Active New York City, 1850s–60s

Kesley, Max. U.S. Active 20th c.

*Kessler, Chester. U.S. Contemporary

Kesting, Edmund. Germany. 1892–1970

*Ketchum, Cavalliere. U.S. 1937–

Ketchum, Robert. U.S. 1947–

Kettel, Max. Active Geneva, 20th c.

Kew, George A. U.S. Active 20th c.

Keyes, Murray K. U.S. Active 20th c.

Keyes and Osborn. Active Dixon, Ill., 1868–78

*Kezar, Lucy. Contemporary

Kezys, Algimantas. U.S. Contemporary

Khambatta, S. J. Active Bombay, 20th c.

Khan, Ahmud Ali. Active Lucknow, India, 19th c.

Khandalavala, K. J. Active Bombay, 20th c.

Kharegat, Sorab J. Active Bombay, 20th c.

Khlamov, V. Active Tiflis, Russia, 19th c.

Kiem, John H. Active East Orange, N.J., 20th c.

Kientzle, A. Active Philadelphia, 1860s

Kientzle, Fr. Germany. Active ca. 1900

*Kievets, Dennis C. U.S. 1937–

Kikuyi, Hawada. Japan. 1933–

Kilgore, Andrew. U.S. 1940–

Kiljan, G. Netherlands. Active 20th c.

Killie, C. A. China. Active 1880–1900

Killip, Chris. 1946–. Active Isle of Man

Kilmer, (Dr.) Theron. 1872–1946

Kimball, Howard A. Active Concord, N.H., ca. 1860s–80

Kimball, M. H. Active New York City, 1860s

*Kimball, Rosalind S. *See* *Moulton, Rosalind Kimball

Kimball, W. G. C. Active Concord, N.H., 1868–78

Kimball and Cooper. Active New York City, 1860s

Kimber, K. Active Yokohama, ca. 1900.

Kimelman, Don. U.S. Contemporary

Kimmel, Ed. France. Active 20th c.

Kimura, Ihei. 1901–

Kinch, Bruce. U.S. 1944–

Kinder, (Rev.) John. New Zealand (b. England). 1819–1903. Active 1860s–70s

*Kindermann, Helmmo. U.S. 1947–

Kindl, Oldrich. Czechoslovakia. Active 20th c.

*King, B. A. U.S. 1934–

King, Henry. Active Sydney, Australia, 1880s

King, Horatio Nelson. 1830–95. Active Bath, England

King, M. F. Active Portland, Maine, 1868–78

King, Tony. Contemporary

Kingsley, Charles. England. 1819–75

Kinsky, Imre. Active Budapest, 20th c.

Kipperman, Barry. U.S. 1943–

Kira, Hiromu. U.S. Active 20th c.

Kirchner, Ernst Ludwig. Germany. 1880–1938

Kirkland, Wallace W. U.S. Active 20th c.

Kirkton, Kent. U.S. Contemporary

Kirlian, Semyon and Valentina. U.S.S.R. Active 20th c.

Kirstein, Erich. Germany. Active 20th c.

*Kirstel, Richard. U.S. Contemporary

Kiser Photo Co. Active Portland, Ore., early 20th c.

Kistemaker, Dale. U.S. 1948–

*Kitaj, R. D. U.S. 1932–

*Kitching Group (Kees Heemskerk, Rolet, Walter Dettling). Contemporary

Kitrosser, I. France. Active 20th c.

Kiyooka, Roy K. Canada. Active 20th c.

Klages, Jürg. Switzerland. 1924–

Klagsbrunn, Kurt D. Brazil. Active 20th c.

Klasson, Eva. Sweden. Contemporary

Klauber, E. Active Louisville, Ky., 1890s

Klauer, Enrique. Peru. Active 19th c.

Klauke, Jürgen. Germany. 1943–

Klee, Hermann. Austria. Active ca. 1860 70

Klein, Aart. Netherlands. Active 20th c.

Klein, Alex. Mexico. Contemporary

Klein, George J. Active Chicago, 1870s

Klein, H. S. U.S. Active 19th c.

*Klein, Irwin B. U.S. 1933–74

*Klein, Rodger Hudson. U.S. 1945–

Klein, Sardi. U.S. Contemporary

Kleinburg Zelenetz, Pedro. Mexico. Contemporary

Kleinod, Urda. Germany. Contemporary

Klemenz, Hans-Peter. Austria. Contemporary.

Klempfner, M. Active Prague, 1870s

Klepikoff, P. W. Active Moscow, 20th c.

Klett, Mark. Contemporary

Kletz, Jaroly. Hungary. Active 20th c.

Klier, P. Active Rangoon and Mandalay, Burma, ca. 1900

*Kliks, Michael. Contemporary

*Klipper, Stuart. Contemporary

Kloch, Ferdynand. Active Warsaw, 19th c.

Klösz, György. Active Budapest, 1860s

Kluetmeier, Heinz. U.S. Contemporary

Klumb, R. H. Active Rio de Janeiro and Petrópolis, Brazil, 1855–80

Klute, Jeannette. U.S. 1918–

Knapp, August. Australia, New Zealand. Active 20th c.

Knapp, Peter. Switzerland. 1931–

Knapp, Steven. Contemporary

Knébel, Ferenc. Active Szombathely, Hungary, 1860s–70s

Knecht, Sylvain. France. Contemporary

Knee, Ernie. U.S. 1907–

Kneib, Hans. Active Vienna, 20th c.

Kniesche, R. F. U.S. Active 20th c.

Knight, Charles. Active Isle of Wight, 19th c.

Knight, John Prescott. England. 1803–81

Knight, Keith. U.S. 1952–

Knight, Philip B. U.S. d. 1953

Knight, W. M. Active Buffalo, 1860s

Knight and Eales. Active Batavia, N.Y., 1860s

Knittel, Wilhelm. Austria. Active 20th c.

Knobel, (Capt.) Harry Edward. England. Active early 20th c.

Knoche, Paul. Germany. Active 20th c.

Knop, Beate. Belgium (b. Germany). 1943–

Knopf, Hans. U.S. Active 20th c.

Knottenbelt, Marianna. Canada. 1948–

Knowlton Brothers. Active Northampton, Mass., 1868–78

Knox, David. U.S. Active mid-19th c.

Knudsen, K. Norway. Active 19th c.

Kobayashi, T. U.S. Active 20th c.

*Kobb, Seth. Contemporary

Kobell, Franz von. Germany. 1803–82

Kobi, Hans. Contemporary

Kobler, Cyril

Kobza, Jano. Contemporary

Koch, Carl-August. Switzerland. 1845–97

Koch, Christian. Germany. Active 20th c.

Koch, Pitt. Germany. Contemporary

Koch and Wilz. Active Paris, 1860s

Kocjanic, Peter. Yugoslavia. Active 20th c.

Koenigswald, R. von. Germany. Active 20th c.

Koga, Mary. U.S. 1920–

*Kohl, Paul. U.S. 1942–

*Kohlhöfer, Christof. Germany. 1942–

Kohn, Samuel. 1837–1910. Active Prague

Koike, (Dr.) K. Active Seattle, 20th c.

Kolb Brothers. U.S. Active early 20th c.

Kolbrenner, Bob. U.S. Active 20th c.

Kollath, Kenneth. U.S. Contemporary

Koller, Károly. Hungary. 1838–89. Active 1861–89

Komers, Jean. Czechoslovakia. Active 20th c.

Koner, Marvin. U.S. Active 20th c.

Konig, Christian. Active Nuremburg, 19th c.

König, Ernst. 1869–1924

Koparkar, S. K. Active Poona, India, 20th c.

Kopelaw, Gerry. Canada. 1949–

Koplik, Jaroslav. Czechoslovakia. Active 20th c.

Koppel, Rolf. U.S. 1937–

Koppitz, Rudolf. Germany. d. 1936

Koppman, G., and Co. Active Hamburg, 1860s

*Koral, Barry. Contemporary

Korda, Alberto. Cuba. Contemporary

Kordysz, Josef. Active Kiev, Russia (b. Poland), 19th c.

Korling, Torkel. U.S. Active 20th c.

Korn, Alfred. 1870–1945

Kornic, Ante. Yugoslavia. Active 20th c.

Korody, Tony. U.S. Contemporary

Korolov, Yuri. U.S.S.R. Contemporary

Korth, Fred G. Active Chicago, 20th c.

Korzunas, Abdonas. Active Vilnius, Lithuania, 19th c.

Kosel, Hermann. Active Vienna, 1880–1915

Koshida, Jyo. Contemporary

Kosmer, John. U.S. Contemporary

Kostiuk, Michael. U.S. Contemporary

Köstler, B. Active Munich, ca. 1872

Kowalinski, Aleksander. Active Warsaw, 19th c.

Kowall, Earl. Canada. 1948-

Kozacek, Ivan. Contemporary

Kozlowski, Justyn. Active Suez Canal (b. Poland), 1860s

Kózmata, Ferenc. 1856-1902. Active Pest, Hungary, 1870s

*Kraft, James. U.S. 1938-

Kraft, Kurt. Germany. Active 20th c.

Krainin, Ewing. U.S. Active 20th c.

*Kramer, Arnold. Contemporary

*Kramer, Arthur. U.S. 1924-

Kramer, Oscar. Active Vienna, 1867-69

Kramer, Rudolf. Germany. Active 20th c.

Kramer, Vojtech. 1805-78. Active Domazlice, Bohemia

Kramolin, Alajos. Hungary. 1812-92. Active 1840s

Kramskoi, I. N. Russia. Active 1870s

Krasner, M. M. U.S. Active 20th c.

Krasovec, Franc. Yugoslavia. Active 20th c.

*Krastof, Mark. U.S. 1942-

Krause, Gregor. Active ca. early 20th c.

Krause, Peter H. Germany. Active 20th c.

Krause, Robin. Contemporary

Krause, Waltraud. Germany. Contemporary

Krause-Skaisgirren, Erich. Germany. Active 20th c.

Krauss, F. E. Germany. Active 20th c.

Krauss-Vonow, K. Contemporary

Krausz, Sigmund. Active Chicago, late 19th c.

Kraysler, Joseph. Active New York City, 20th c.

Krebs, Hans. Switzerland. 1938-

Krementz, Jill. U.S. 1940-

Kremer, Vladimír. b. 1839. Active Prague

Kressmann, Friedrich. Switzerland. 1886-1972

Krewaldt, Robert. Germany. Active ca. 1890

Krieger, Ignacy. Active Cracow, Poland, mid-19th c.

Kriger, Jeffrey. U.S. Contemporary

Kristin, Hans. Estonia. Active 1899-1912

Křiž, Martin. Moravia. Active ca. 1863

Křiž, Vilem. U.S. (b. Czechoslovakia). 1921-

Kroehle, Ch. Peru. Active ca. 1890s

Kroehnke, Louise. U.S. 1951-

Kroh, Carl. Austria. Active ca. 1870

*Kroll, Eric. U.S. Contemporary

Krone, Hermann. Germany. 1827-1916

*Kronengold, Eric. Contemporary

*Krot, Paul. U.S. 1939-

Kroth, Eva. Germany. Contemporary

Kruckenhauser, Stephan. Austria. Active 20th c.

Krueger, Katherine. U.S. Active 20th c.

*Krule, Bernard. Contemporary

Krull, Germaine. Germany, Holland, France (b. Poland). 1897-

Krupka, (Ing.) Jaroslav. Active Prague, 20th c.

Krupsaw, Warren. U.S. 1943-

Krupy, Alex. Active Chicago (b. Russia), 20th c.

Krüse, Olney. Brazil. Contemporary

Kruss, A. Active Hamburg, 19th c.

Krysztofik, M. R. Poland. Active 20th c.

Krziwanek, K. Active Vienna, ca. 1885

*Krzyzanowski, Michel Szulc. Netherlands. 1949-

Kubota, Hiroji. Japan. Contemporary

Kucharski, Marian. Contemporary

Kudojarov, Boris. U.S.S.R. 1903-73

Kuelner. Peru. Active 19th c.

Kuhfal, A. Germany. Active early 20th c.

Kuhn, J. Active Paris, 19th c.

Kühn and Bauer. Germany. Active ca. 1875

Kujawa, G. von. Germany. Active 20th c.

Kuklik, Karel. Contemporary

Kuligowski, Eddie. France. Contemporary

Kulley, (Dr.) Gabriel A. Active Innsbruck, Austria, 20th c.

Kumler, Kipton. U.S. 1940-

Kunchev, Hristo Popdimitrov. Active Tryavna and Turnovo, Bulgaria, 19th c.

*Kunié. Japan. 1942-

Kunishige, F. A. Active Seattle, 20th c.

Kunszt, (Dr.) Janos. Hungary. Active 20th c.

Kunz, Albrecht Leo. Switzerland. Active 20th c.

Kuoni, Charles F. Active Chicago, 20th c.

Kuppel, Edmund. Germany. 1947-

Kurata, S. Japan. Contemporary

*Kurihara, Tatsuo. Japan. 1937-

Kuron, Victor. Germany. Active 20th c.

Kurtkranz. Germany. Contemporary

Kurtz, Karl E. U.S. 1942-

Kurtz, William. 1834-1904. Active New York City (b. Germany)

Kurzweil. Austria. Active ca. 1900

Kutschbach, W. L. Active Sherburne, N.Y., 20th c.

Kuwahara, Kineo. Japan

Kuzmanoff, Leon. U.S. Contemporary

Labelle, Ronald. Canada. 1942-

Laborde, Charles. 1808-83

Laboye, Roland. France. 1944-

*Labrot, Syl. U.S. 1929-77

Lacan, Ernst. 1829-79

Lacheroy, H. France. Active 20th c.

Lachmann. Active Prague, 1860s

Lachowicz, Andrzej. Poland. 1939-

*Lacin, Kent. U.S. Contemporary

Lackenbach, Bob. U.S. Active 20th c.

Lacks, George. U.S. Active 20th c.

Lacroix. France. Active 1895-1914

Laffeaty (Corp.). England. Active 19th c.

Lafosse, M. Active Manchester, England, 19th c.

Lafranchini, H. von. Croatia. Active 19th c.

Lafron, L. Active Paris, 1870s

Lagocki, Zbigniew. Poland. 1927-

Lagrange, (Comte) de. India (b. France). Active mid-19th c.

Laguarde, Céline. France. Active 1903-08

*Laing, Gerald. England. 1936-

Laing, Janet E. England. Active 1907-13

Lais, Bernard. Active Tallinn, Estonia, late 19th c.

Lais, Stefano. 1832-92. Active Rome, 1860-70

Laizerovitz, Daniel. Uruguay. Contemporary

*Lake, Jerry Lee. U.S. 1941–

Lake-Price, William. England. Active 19th c.

Lakin. Active Montgomery, Ala., 19th c.

Lamarca, José. Argentina. 1938–

Lamarre, René. Active Amiens, France, 20th c.

Lamater, R. S. Active Hartford, 1860s

Lambert, Bonnie. U.S. Contemporary

Lambert, Herbert. ca. 1881–1936. Active London and Bath, England

Lambeth, Michel. Canada. 1923–77

Lamothe Silva, Carlos. Mexico. Contemporary

Lamson, J. H. Active Portland, Maine, 1860s

Lamy, E. France. Active 1860s–70s

Lancaster, W. J. 1845–1925

Land, Edwin Herbert. U.S. 1909–

Land, William. U.S. Active 20th c.

Landau, (Mlle.) Ergy. Active Paris, 20th c.

Landesman, Geoffrey. U.S. Active 20th c.

Landry, Bob. U.S. Active 20th c. (deceased)

Landsman, Beatrice. U.S. Active 20th c.

*Land-Weber, Ellen (Ellen Epstein). U.S. 1943–

*Landweber, Victor. U.S. 1943–

Landy, James M. U.S. 1838–87

Lane, Walter B. U.S. Active 20th c.

*Lang, Candid. Switzerland. 1930–

*Lang, Gerald. U.S. 1939–

Lang, R. Active Brooklyn, 1880s–90s

Langaki. *See* Zangaki

Langdon, William. U.S. Active 20th c.

Langdon and Tallman. Active Batavia, N.Y., 1860s

Langdon-Davies, F. H. Active Cambridge, England, ca. 1900

Lange, O. V. Active San Francisco, 1860s

Lange, Vidie. U.S. Contemporary

Langer and Pommerrenig. Active Prague, 1860s

Langerock. Active Paris, 1860s–70s

Langhans, J. F. 1851–1919. Active Marienbad; Prague, after 1876

Lang-Kurz, Ursula. Germany. Active 20th c.

Lannoy, Richard. England. Active 20th c.

Lansky, Ida. U.S. Contemporary

*Lanyon, Andrew. Great Britain. 1947–

Lanzano, Louis. U.S. 1947–

Lapow, Harry S. U.S. Contemporary

Laquan, I. Active New York City, 20th c.

Larios Chávez, Gilberto. Mexico. Contemporary

Larka, Karel. Sweden. Active 20th c.

Larkin, J. E. Active Elmira, N.Y., 1860s–70s

*La Rocca, Ketty. Italy. Contemporary

La Roche, Frank. Active Seattle, late 19th c.

Laroche, Martin. England. Active mid-19th c.

Laroche, Silvester. 1809–86. Active London (b. Canada)

Larondelle, Georges. Belgium. 1950–

Larrañaga. Peru. Active ca. 1896

Larrañaga Pérez, Juvencio. Mexico. Contemporary

Larsen, Lisa. U.S. d. 1959

*Larson, William G. U.S. 1942–

Larsson, Ake V. Sweden. Active 20th c.

Larsson, Bernard. Sweden, Germany. Active 20th c.

*LaRue, William. U.S. 1928–

Lasarte, Enrique. Peru. Active 19th c.

Lassaigne, Jean-Louis. 1800–59

Lasserre, Juliette. Active Paris, 20th c.

Latchford, Joan. Canada. 1926–

Lategan, Barry. Contemporary

Latere, Charles. U.S. Active 20th c.

Latham, John. Active London, 19th c.

Latimer, H. A. Active Boston, ca. 1890–1920

Lattre, A. de. Peru. Active 1845–46

Läubli, Walter. Switzerland. 1902–

Lauffer, Sophie Louise. Active Brooklyn, 20th c.

Laughead, Jim. U.S. Active 20th c.

Launey and Goebel. Active Savannah, 1870s–80s

Launois, John. U.S. Contemporary

*Lauré, Jason

Laurence, George R. U.S. Active early 20th c.

Laurent, J. Active Paris (b. France), Madrid, 1860s–70s

Lauschmann, (Dr.) Jan. 1901–. Active Prague

Laussedat, (Col.) Aimé. France. 1819–1907

Lav, Brian. U.S. Contemporary

La Valle, F. Peru. Active ca. 1887

Lavenson, Alma R. U.S. 1897–

Lavergne. France. Active 20th c.

Lawrence, C. A. Active Nashua, N.H., 1860s–70s

Lawrence, Frank. Active Worcester, Mass., 1860s–70s

Lawrence, Macy. U.S. Contemporary

*Lawrence, Nick. U.S. 1940–

Lawrence, Peter. Australia, New Zealand. Active 20th c.

Lawrence, Richard Hoe. U.S. Active 1880s

Lawrence, William Mervyn. Ireland. 1840–1931

Lawrie, G. W., and Co. India. Active 19th c.

Laws, P. Maitland. Active Newcastle, England, 19th c.

Lay, F. L. Active Boston, 1850s

*Laytin, Peter. U.S. Contemporary

*Layton, Peter. England (b. Czechoslovakia). 1937–

*LaZar, Arthur. U.S. 1940–

Lazarnick, Nathan. U.S. d. 1955

Lazarus, Marvin. U.S. Contemporary

Lazergues and Dallemagne. France. Active 1860 and after

Lazi, Adolf. Germany. 1884–1955

*Lazorik, Wayne R. U.S. 1939–

Leach, Donald M. U.S. Active 1890s

Leaf, Earl. U.S. Active 20th c.

Leano, Nicolás. Peru. Active ca. 1863

Leatherby, Alan. New Zealand. 1949–

*Leavitt, Carl. Contemporary

Le Bas. Japan (b. France). Active ca. 1865

*Lebeck, Robert. Germany. 1929–

Lebleux, Fernando. Peru. Active ca. 1845

LeBlondel, A. Active Lille, France, 1860s

*Lebowitz, Richard. U.S. 1937–

Le Campion, Hubert. France. Contemporary

Lecca, Ignacio. Peru. Active ca. 1869

Lecchi, S. Active Rome, 1844 and after

LeClerc, Carlos. Spain. Active ca. 1900

Leclerc, Martin. Canada. Active 20th c.

Lecouturier, Jacky. Belgium. 1948–

Lecram. France. Active 20th c.

Lecuyer, Raymond. France. Active early 20th c.

Lederer, Helmut. Germany. Active 20th c.

Lederle, Charles. Active Cleveland, 20th c.

Ledezma, Silvia Yolanda. Mexico. Contemporary

Ledger, Henry. England. Active 1860s

Ledot. Active Paris, 19th c.

Lee, A. A. Active Batavia, N.Y., 19th c.

Lee, Edmund. U.S. Active 20th c.

Lee, W. J. Active New York state, 1860s–70s

Lee, Washington

Leemput, J. van

Leen, Nina. U.S. (b. Russia). Contemporary

Lees, David. Italy (b. U.S.). Contemporary

Leeser, Paulus. Contemporary

Leeston-Smith, Cyril. England. Active 20th c.

Leet, Frank F. Active New York state, 20th c.

Lefebure, P. Active Paris, 20th c.

Le Folzalvez, (Commandant) H. Active Paris, 20th c.

Le Gall, Jean-Louis. France. 1940–

Lege, G. M. Active Paris, 1870s

Leger, Jules. India, Mauritius (b. France). Active mid-19th c.

Legrady, George. 1950–

Le Guay, L. Australia. Active 20th c.

Lehmann, Egon. Germany. Contemporary

Lehmann, Minnette. U.S. Contemporary

Lehnkering, A. L. Active Rochester, N.Y., 1880s

Leibovitz, Annie. U.S. Contemporary

Leigh, Dorien. England. Active 20th c.

Leigh-Hunt, Jocelyn. Africa. Active 20th c.

Leighton, J. Harold. Active Bradford, England, 20th c.

Leighton, John. 1823–1912

*Leighton, Ron. U.S. 1944–

Leirens, Charles. Belgium. 1888–1964

Leisgen, Barbara. Belgium (b. Germany). 1940–

Leisgen, Michael. Belgium (b. Austria). 1944–

Lekegian, G., and Co. Egypt. Active ca. 1890

Leland, E. J. Active Worcester, Mass., 19th c.

Le Lieure, Henri. Active Rome, 1871 and after

Lemaître, Augustin-François. France. 1790–1870

LeMer, Le Rue. Active Harrisburg, Pa., 1860s

Lemercier and Co. Active Paris, 1870s

*Lemkin, James. U.S. 1946–

Lemoine, René. Active Paris, ca. 1900

Lemon, E. R. U.S. Active 1890s

Lemus, Louis. U.S. Active 20th c.

Lenare. Contemporary

Lenart, Branko. Austria. Contemporary

Lenbach, Franz von. Germany. 1836–1904

Lendvai-Dircksen, Erna. Germany. b. 1883

Lenhart, Otakar. Czechoslovakia. Active 20th c.

Lennard, Elizabeth. U. S. 1953–

Lennard, Erica. U.S. 1951–

*Lennebacker, Wayne R. U.S. 1941–

Lent, Max. U.S. Contemporary

Lent, Tina. U.S. Contemporary

Lentsch. Croatia. Active 19th c.

Leon, Encarnacion. Spain. Contemporary

*Leonard, Cheryl N. U.S. Contemporary

*Leonard, Joanne. U.S. 1940–

Leonardi, Cesare. Italy. 1935–

Leong Hong-peng. Contemporary

Leonian, Phillip. U.S. 1927–

Leoussi, Helen. Contemporary

Le-Plongeon, Augusto. Peru. Active ca. 1862

Le Prat, Thérèse. France. 1895–1966

Le Prince, Louis-Aimé. 1842–90

Le Querrec, Guy. France. Contemporary

Lerebours, Noël-Marie Paymal. France. 1807–73

Lerma Uzeta, Víctor. Mexico. Contemporary

Lerner, Frank. U.S. Contemporary

Lerner, Nathan. U.S. 1915–

*Lerner, Norman. U.S. 1927–

Lerski, Helmar (Swiss, b. France). 1871–1957. Active U.S., 1911–15; Berlin, 1915–29; Palestine, 1931–48; Zurich

LeSage. Ireland. Active 1860s–70s

Lessing, Alma. Germany. Active late 19th c.

Letzer. Active Vienna, 20th c.

Leutzinger, G. Active Rio de Janeiro, 1860s–70s

Leventon, Alex. Active Rochester, N.Y., 20th c.

Levi, Hans. U.S. 1935–

Levin, C. Handy. U.S. Active 1860s

*Levin, Robert Louis. U.S. Contemporary

*Levine, Michael Grayson. U.S. Contemporary

Levinson, Joel D. U.S. Contemporary

Levinstein, Leon. U.S. Active 20th c.

Levinthal, Hermann. Active Berlin, ca. 1868–86

Leviton, Jay. U.S. Contemporary

Levitskii, Sergei L'vovich. 1819–98 (b. Russia). Active St. Petersburg, Paris

Lévy, Léon and J. France. Active ca. 1870s

Levy, Louis Edward. U.S. (b. Bohemia). 1846–1919

Levy, Max. U.S. 1857–1926

*Levy, Richard. Contemporary

Levy and Cohen. U.S. Active 19th c.

Lévy and Neurdein. France. Active 1890s

Lewczynski, Jerzy. Poland. 1924–

Lewicki, Jan. Poland. Active 19th c.

Lewis, Earl V. U.S. Active 20th c.

Lewis, F. Andre. U.S. Contemporary

Lewis, Glen. Canada. Active 20th c.

Lewis, R. A. Active New York City, 1860s

Lewis, Thomas. Active Waltham, Mass., 1870s

Lewitsky, C. L. Active St. Petersburg, Russia (b. Germany), ca. 1855–85

Lex-Nerlinger, Alice. Germany. 1893–

Li, Meiner. Germany. Active early 20th c.

Libby, Minnie. Active Norway, Maine, 1886–1940s

Liberman, Alexander. U.S. (b. Russia). 1912–

Lichfield, Patrick. England. Contemporary

Lichtenstein, (Prince) H. Austria-Hungary. Active 19th c.

Lichtner, Marvin. U.S. Contemporary

Lichtwark, Alfred. Germany. 1852–1914

Lieb, Leo. U.S. Active 20th c.

Lieberman, Harry. Canada. Active 20th c.

Liébert, Alphonse J. France. 1827–1914

Liebert, Petter Christoffer. Finland. 1818–66

*Liebman, Steven. U.S. 1942–

Liesgang, Paul Eduard. 1836–96

Lifson, Ben. U.S. 1941–

Liftin, Joan. U.S. Contemporary

Ligey, Pierre. Active Paris, 20th c.

Liias, Raimo. U.S. 1950–

Lilienthal, Theo. Active New Orleans, 1860s–70s

Linares. Spain. Active 19th c.

Linck, Anthony. U.S. Active 20th c.

Lincoln, Edwin Hale. Active Massachusetts, ca. 1880–1940

Lindahl, Alex. Active Stockholm, 19th c.

Lindblom, Norman. U.S. Active 20th c.

Linde, E. Active Berlin, 1870s

Lindegaard, Jens. Denmark. Active 20th c.

Lindeke, Caroline Saunders. U.S. 1949–

Linden, Hal (Harry Lindsay). Active London, 20th c.

Lindenmann, Robert P., Jr. U.S. 1946–

Lindey, Alexander. U.S. Active 20th c.

Lindquist, John. U. S. Contemporary

*Lindquist, Therold S. U.S. Contemporary

Lindroos, Björn. Switzerland. 1918–

*Lindroth, Linda. U.S. Contemporary

Lindsay, Harry. *See* Linden, Hal

*Lindstrom, John. Contemporary

Link, Eberhard. Germany. 1952–

Link, Ernst. Switzerland. 1874–1963

Link, Johann. Switzerland. 1819–1900

Link, Philipp. Switzerland. 1862–1918

Link, Richard. U.S. Contemporary

Linn, J. Birney. Active Tennessee, 1860s–70s

Linn, Judy. U.S. 1947–

*Lintault, M. Joan. Contemporary

Lipnitski. Active Paris, early 20th c.

Lippman, Irving. U.S. Active 20th c.

Lippmann, Gabriel. France. 1845–1921

*Lissack, Selwyn Leonardo. South Africa. 1942–

Lissitzky, Lazar (El). Russia. 1890–1941

List, Herbert. Germany. 1903–75

*Little, Don and Michel. U.S. Contemporary

Litton, Martin. U.S. Contemporary

*Litwack, Georgia. U.S. 1922–

Liveright, Pat. Active Newark, N.J., 20th c.

Livick, Stephen. Canada. 1945–

*Livingston, Jacqueline Louise Barrett. U.S. 1943–

Ljungdahl, Goesta P. U.S. Active 20th c.

Ljungstedt, C. A. Finland. Active 19th c.

Llewelyn, Dillwyn. England. 1810–82

Llewelyn, J. D. Active 1850s

Lloyd, Harvey. 1925–

Lloyd, John. Great Britain. Active ca. 1861

Lloyd, Susan. U.S. Contemporary

Loayza, Jorge and Victoria. Peru. Contemporary

Lobatón. Peru. Active ca. 1899

Lobdell, Martin. U.S. Active 20th c.

Lobovikov, Sergei Aleksandrovich. Russia. 1870–1941

Löcherer, Aloïs. Germany. 1815–62

Lock and Whitfield. England. Active 1870s

Lockett. Active London, 1860s

Lockman, Marshall. U.S. Active 20th c.

Locks, Norman. U.S. Contemporary

Lockwood, Lee. U.S. Contemporary

Loczy, Lajós. Hungary. Active 19th c.

*Lodise, Rocco M. U.S. 1941–

Loeffler, J. U.S. Active 19th c.

Loescher and Petsch. Germany. Active late 19th c.

Lofman, J. Germany. Active 20th c.

Lohmann, Helen. Active New York City, early 20th c.

Lohse, Bernd. Germany. 1911–

Lohse, Remie. Active New York City, 20th c.

Lombardi, P. Italy. Active 19th c.

*Lomeo, Angelo. U.S. 1921–

Longquist, Harald. Sweden. Active 20th c.

Lookanoff, Victor. Active 20th c.

Loop, H. W. India. Active ca. 1880

*Loori, John. Contemporary

Lopes Crispino, Luis. Brazil. Contemporary

*Lopez, Andre A. U.S. 1942–

*Lopez, José. U.S. 1941–

López, Soledad. Venezuela. Contemporary

López Castillo, Maritza. Mexico. Contemporary

López Marin, Rogelio. Cuba. Contemporary

Lorca, Germán. Brazil. Contemporary

Lorelle, Lucien. France. Active 20th c.

Lorent, (Dr.) August Jakob. Germany. 1813–84

Lotar, Eli. France. 1905–ca. 1970

Lotschniker, Anton. Active Zagreb, 19th c.

Lötvös, (Baron) Loránd. Hungary. 1848–1919

Lotze, Maurizio. 1809–90. Active Verona, Italy (b. Germany)

*Loufek, Robert. Contemporary

Louis, Christian. France.

Louise, Ruth Harriet. U.S. Active 20th c.

Louviot, A. France. Active ca. 1859

Love, Jeffrey. U.S. 1952–

Lovell, J. L. Active Amherst, Mass., 19th c.

Lovins, Amory B. England (b. U.S.). 1947–

*Lowe, Walter. U.S. 1933–

Lowell, Percival. Korea (b. U.S.). Active 1880s

Lown, Lynn. U.S. 1947–

Löwry, J. Active Vienna, ca. 1870

Lubianitsky, Leonid. U.S. (b. U.S.S.R.). 1938–

Luboshez, Nahum. Russia. 1869–1925

Lubśchez, Ben J. Active New York City, 20th c.

Lucas, Joseph George. U.S. 1952–

Lucas, R. C. England. Active 19th c.

Luce, William Blake. Active Massachusetts, ca. 1898

Luckardt, Fritz. Active Vienna, ca. 1870

Luckhaus, Arthur. U.S. Active early 20th c.

Ludin, Emil. Active Zurich, 20th c.

Ludwig, Allan. U.S. Contemporary

Luke, Monte. Australia, New Zealand. Active 20th c.

Lullin, Théodore. Active 19th c.

Lumière, Auguste Marie Louis Nicolas. France. 1862–1954

Lumière, Louis Jean. France. 1864–1948

Luna Pedroza, Renato de. Brazil. Contemporary

Luna Ponce, Guillermo. Mexico. Contemporary

Lund, Chris. Canada. 1923–

*Lunt, Albert (Evergon). Canada. 1946–

Lupercio. Active 20th c.

Luskačová, Marketa. Czechoslovakia. 1944–

Luswergh, Angelo. 1793–1858. Active Rome

Luswergh, Giacomo. 1819–91. Active Rome

Luswergh, Tommaso. 1823–1907. Active Rome

Lüthi, Urs. Switzerland. 1947–

Luynes, Duc de (Honoré Théodoric Paul Joseph d'Albert). France. 1802–67

Luzuriaga Arias, Camilo. Ecuador. Contemporary

Lynn, Jennifer. U.S. Contemporary

Lynne, Jill. U.S. 1944–

Lyon, Fred. U.S. Contemporary

Lyon, William A. Active Toronto, 1860s

*Lyons, Joan. U.S. 1937–

Lyte, Farnham Maxwell. 1828–1906

Lytle, A. D. Active Baton Rouge, La., 19th c.

M. R. and *Ca.* Peru. Active 19th c.

Maar, Dora. France, Germany (b. England). 1909–

McAllister, James. Active Christchurch, Wellington, Hawera, and Stratford, New Zealand (b. Scotland), late 19th c.

*McArthur, Peter. U.S. Contemporary

MacAskill, Wallace R. 1890–1956. Active Halifax, Nova Scotia

McBean, Angus. England. 1904–

McBride, Will. U.S. Active 20th c.

*McCall, Anthony. England. Contemporary

McCarter, Graham. Australia. Contemporary

McCarthy, Joseph. U.S. Active 20th c.

McCarthy, Tom. U.S. Contemporary

McCartney, Linda Eastman. U.S. Contemporary

*McCaughey, Sam. U.S. Contemporary

McClintock, Walter. U.S. Active ca. 1900

McClure, C. L. U.S. Active early 20th c.

McCook, Philip. Active Hartford, 1890s

*McCormack, Dan. Contemporary

McCormick, L. M. Active late 19th c.

McCosh, John. India (b. England). Active late 1840s

McCoy, Dan. U.S. Contemporary

McCullum and Butterworth. Active Boston, 19th c.

McDarrah, Fred William. U.S. 1926–

Macdomnic, Godfrey. England. Active 20th c.

McDonald, Allan. New Zealand. 1952–

McDonald, D. Active North Melbourne, Australia, ca. 1866

McDonald, (Capt.) H. C. India. Active ca. 1870

MacDonald, Ian. New Zealand. Contemporary

McDonald, (Sgt.) J. Active Sinai Peninsula (b. England), 19th c.

McDonald, James. New Zealand. 1865–1935

MacDonald, Pirie. 1867–1942. Active New York City and Albany, N.Y.

MacEachern, Ian. Canada. 1942–

McFarland, Lawrence. U.S. 1942–

McGarrigle, John. Active Auckland, New Zealand, ca. 1869–76

McGaskell. Canada. Active 20th c.

M'Ghie, J. Active Lanarkshire, Scotland, ca. 1860s

McGill, Peter. U.S. 1952–

McGlashon, A. Scotland. Active ca. 1860

McGowan, Kenneth. U.S. Active 20th c.

McGraw, B. F. U.S. Active 20th c.

MacGregor, Gregory. U.S. 1941–

MacGregor, Helen. England. Active 20th c.

McGuirk, Paul. U.S. Contemporary

Mach, Ernst. Czechoslovakia. 1838–1916

Mächler, René. Switzerland. 1936–

Macia y Pichardo, Enrique. Mexico. Contemporary

Macijauskas, Alexander. Lithuania. 1938–

Mack, Ulrich. Germany. 1934–

McKenna, Rollie. U.S. Active 20th c.

McKeown, Joseph. U.S. Contemporary

MacKichen, Margaret. U.S. 1948–

McKittrick, Margaret. U.S. Active 20th c.

MacLaughlin, Patricia. U.S. 1944–

McLaughlin-Gill, Frances. U.S. Contemporary

Maclay, David. U.S. Contemporary

McLean, Amelia H. Active Kennebunkport, Maine, 20th c.

*McLoughlin, Michael D. U.S. 1936–

McManigal, J. W. U.S. b. 1892

McMurtry, Edward. Active Pasadena, Calif., 20th c.

MacNaughtan, W. E. Active New York City, 20th c.

McNeely, Burton. U.S. Active 20th c.

*MacNeil, Ronald L. U.S. 1941–

*MacNeil, Wendy Snyder. U.S. 1943–

McNeill, Crombie. Canada. 1941–

McPhail, Edward I. Active Buffalo, 20th c.

*McPherson, Larry. U.S. 1943–

McQuaid, James. U.S. Contemporary

*Macrae, J. Denis. U.S. Contemporary

MacRae, Wendall. U.S. 1900–

Macurdy, J. C. Active Oil City, Pa., 19th c.

*McWilliams, John, IV. U.S. 1941–

Madden, Ross. U.S. Active 20th c.

Maddick-Lownds, Mead. U.S. Active 20th c.

*Maddox, Conroy. England. Contemporary

*Maddox, Jerald C. U.S. 1933–

Maddox, Richard Leach. England. 1816–1902

Mädler, Johann Heinrich von. Germany. 1794–1874

Madon, S. R. Active Bombay, 20th c.

*Maenza, Dave. U.S. Contemporary

Magalhaes, Ayrton de. Brazil. Contemporary

Maggs, Arnaud. Canada. 1926–

Mahan, Jim. U.S. Contemporary

Mahr, Mari. England (b. Chile). Contemporary

Maillard, Ella. Switzerland. 1901–

Maine, Tony. U.S. Contemporary

Maisel, Jay. U.S. 1931–

Maitland, G. F. U.S. Active 19th c.

Makanna, Philip. U.S. 1940–

Malamoud, Jean-F. France

Malave, George. U.S. Contemporary

Maldonado, Adál. *See* Adál

Maldonado, Fernando. Mexico. Contemporary

Mallard, Henri. Australia, New Zealand. Active 20th c.

Malmberg, Hans. Sweden. 1927–

Maloch, Jan. 1825–1911. Active Prague

Malone, Thomas A. England. Active 1840s

Maloney, Joe. U.S. 1949–

Manakia, I. and M. Romania. Active 19th c.

Manchee, Doug. U.S. Contemporary

Manchester, Ellen. U.S. 1945–

Mancini, Salvatore. U.S. Contemporary

Mancova-Steckova, Margita. Contemporary

Mandel, David. U.S. 1947–

Mandel, Julien. Active Paris, 20th c.

Mandel, Mike. U.S. Contemporary

*Mandel, Rose. U.S. Contemporary

Mandelbaum, Ann. U.S. Contemporary

Mandelbaum, Lyn. U.S. 1950–

Mang, Michele. Active Rome (b. Germany?), 1860s

Manganelli, Ange. France. Contemporary

Manly, Thomas. England. Active early 20th c.

Mann, Hans. Argentina. Active 20th c.

*Mann, Margery. U.S. 1919–77

Mann, Sally. U.S. 1951–

Manos, Constantine. U.S. Contemporary

Mansuy, A. Active Paris, 1860s

Mante, Louis-Amedée. France. 1826–1913

Mantz, Werner. Germany. 1901–

Manual (Edward Hill [1935–]; Suzanne Bloom [1943–]). U.S.

Manuel, Henri. France. Active early 20th c.

Manzini Paolini, Ameris. Brazil. Contemporary

Mapplethorpe, Robert. U.S. 1946–

Maraini, Fosco. Italy. Contemporary

Maravalhas, Haroton César. Brazil. Contemporary

*Marchael, James. U.S. 1935–

Marckwardt, Salome E. Active New York City, 20th c.

Marconi, Guglielmo. England (b. Italy). 1874–1937. Active Paris

Marcus, Peter. U.S. Active 20th c.

Mardelli Malta, Ricardo. Brazil. Contemporary

Mareines, Sulamita. Brazil. Contemporary

Marek, Antonin. Active Prague, 1860s

Mares, F. H. Ireland. Active 1860s–70s

Marey, Etienne Jules. France. 1830–1904

Margaritis, Ph. Active Athens, Ga., 19th c.

Margio, Luiz Claudio. Brazil. Contemporary

Margolis, Richard. U.S. Contemporary

Marguery, A. France. Active 20th c.

Mariannecci, Antonio. Active Rome, mid–19th c.

Mariluz, Pedro Pablo. Peru. Active ca. 1858–66

Mariño, E. Peru. Active 19th c.

Mariot, Emil. Germany. Active 1860s

Marklund, Hans. U.S. Active 20th c.

Markolesku, Honori. Active Turnov, Bohemia, 19th c.

Markova, Nadine. Mexico. Contemporary

*Marks, Lewis, Jr. U.S. Contemporary

Marnitz, Frigyes. Active Budapest, 20th c.

Marosovich, Girolamo de. Active Skradin, Croatia, ca. 1890

Marquez, Miguel B. Spain. 1950–

Marquis, Jean. France. Contemporary

Marsadie, C. Active Bordeaux, 20th c.

Marsden, Simon. England. 1948–

Marsh, W. P. Active Bognor Regis, England, ca. 1900

Marshall, Barbara M. U.S. Contemporary

Martin, A. Active Colorado, 1880s–90s

Martin, Adolphe Alexandre. France. 1824–96

Martin, André. France. 1928–

*Martin, Anthony Dirk. U.S. Contemporary

Martin, Anton. 1812–82

Martin, Ira W. 1886–1960. Active New York City

Martin, Josiah. New Zealand. 1843–1916

Martin, Peter. U.S. Active 20th c.

Martin, Rita. Active London, early 20th c.

Martin, Robert. U.S. Active 20th c.

Martincek, Martin. Czechoslovakia. 1913–

Martinet. Active Paris, 19th c.

Martínez González, Rosa Lilia. Mexico. Contemporary

Martínez Grandal, Ramón. Cuba. Contemporary

Martins Laurencio, Delfim. Brazil. Contemporary

Martins Pereira, Luis Humberto. Brazil. Contemporary

Martone, Michael. U.S. Contemporary

Marucha. Cuba. Contemporary

Marumo, Shin-Ichi. Active Tokyo, 20th c.

Maryland, William. U.S. Active 19th c.

Maschhaupt, I. W. Netherlands. Active 20th c.

Masciuch, Taras. Canada. Active 20th c.

Masclet, Daniel. France. 1892–1969

Maskell, Alfred. England. Active late 19th c.

Mason, Samuel J. Active Niagara Falls, N.Y., ca. 1875

Mason, W. T. Peru. Active 19th c.

Mason and Co. Active London, 19th c.

Masri Dabbah, Isaac. Mexico. Contemporary

Massak. Austria. Active 1870

Massar, Ivan. U.S. Active 20th c.

Massar, Phyllis. U.S. Contemporary

Masselis, Lucien. France. Active 20th c.

Masson. Active Seville, Spain, 19th c.

Mastyukov, M. P. Russia. Active 19th c.

Masui, Adrien. Belgium

Maté, Olga. Hungary. Active 20th c.

Mather, John A. Active Titusville, Pa., 19th c.

Mathews, Grayson. Contemporary

Mathewson, Thomas. Active Brisbane and elsewhere in Australia, 1864 and after

Matsushima, Shimpei. Japan. Active 20th c.

Matthews, Kate. U.S. 1870–1956

Matthies-Masuren, Fritz. 1873–1938

Matthys, Max Eugen. Switzerland. 1933–

Matus, Barry. U.S. Contemporary

Matzdorff, A. Germany. Active 20th c.

Matzkows, Joachim. Germany. Contemporary

Mau (Dr.). Active Altona, Germany, late 19th c.

Mauche, Edouard. Active Rome, 1850–55

Maudry, Othmar. Germany. Active 20th c.

Maul, Alfred. Germany. Active early 20th c.

Maumann, Manuel. Switzerland. 1947–

Maund, William J., Jr. U.S. Contemporary

Mauney, Michael. U.S. Contemporary

Maunier, V. G. France. Active 1850s

Maunoury, Eugenio. Peru. Active 1861–65

Maupin, Clifton and Terrence. Active Pomona, Calif., 20th c.

Maurer, Jean-Pierre. Switzerland. 1942–

Maurer, Oscar. Active early 20th c.

Mauss, Peter. U.S. Contemporary

Mautner, Robert. U.S. 1949–

Max. France. Active 1870s

Max, John. Canada. 1936–

Maxson, Holly. U.S. Contemporary

Maxwell, (Sir) James Clerk. England (b. Scotland). 1831–79

*May, Dora R. U.S. 1915–

*May, Robert C. U.S. 1935–

Mayall, John Jabez. England. 1810–1901

May and Widmater. Active Munich, 19th c.

Mayer, Fred. Switzerland. 1933–

Mayer, György. b. 1817. Active Budapest (b. Hungary), Graz, Belgrade, Zagreb

Mayer, Marshall. U.S. 1952–

Mayer and Pierson. Active Paris, 1860–70

Mayes, Elaine. U.S. 1938–

Mayfield, Jim. U.S. Contemporary

Mayhew, Henry. England. 1812–87

Maynard, John Parker. 1816–98

Mayne, Roger. England. Contemporary

Mayo, Herbert. 1796–1852

Mayor, A. Hyatt. U.S. 1901–

Maza Pérez, José Luis. Mexico. Contemporary

Mazawa, Shigeto. Active 20th c.

Maziarz, Carol. U. S. Contemporary.

Mazzer, Bob. England. Contemporary

Meagher, Thomas Francis. U.S. (b. Ireland). 1823–67

*Meatyard, Christopher. U.S. 1955–

Mebius, Friedrich Günther. Active St. Petersburg, Russia (b. Germany); Finland; Tallinn, Estonia; 1850s

*Medina, Luis. U.S. 1943–

Medina Ramos, Fabrián. Mexico. Contemporary

Medley, J. V. and Ishulman. U.S. Active early 20th c.

Mednick, Sol. U.S. 1916–

Medrano, Bárbara. Guatemala

Meek, Richard. U.S. Contemporary

Meerkämpfer, E. Germany. Active 20th c.

Meeussen, Victor. Netherlands. Active 20th c.

Meier, Annemarie. Switzerland. 1943–68

Meijer, Reiner J. Netherlands. Active 20th c.

Meiner, Johannes. Switzerland. 1867–1941

Meinerth, Carl. Active Newburyport, Mass., 19th c.

Meinholtz, A. Germany. Active 20th c.

Meisel, Ulric E. U.S. Active 20th c.

Meisenbach, Georg. 1841–1912

Meissonier, Jean-Louis-Ernest. France. 1815–91

Meitner-Graf, Lotte. England (b. Austria). d. 1973

Mejía, Julia Elvira. Colombia. Contemporary

Mélandri. France. Active 1860s–70s

Melby, David. U.S. 1942–

Meldner, Katharina. Germany. 1943–

Mele, Pietro Francesco. U.S. Active 20th c.

Melhuish, Arthur James. d. 1895

Melley, Edouard. Peru. Active 1890s

Mellor, Doug. U.S. Contemporary

*Melnick, Philip. U.S. 1935–

Melo Viana, Alberto. Brazil. Contemporary

Meluish, William. 1823–88. Active Dunedin, New Zealand, 1856 and after

Melzer, Otto. Austria. Active ca. 1900

Menapace, John. U.S. 1927–

Mendelsohn, Eric. Germany, England, U.S. 1887–1953

Mendez, Frank Xsavior. U.S. Contemporary

Méndez, Oscar. Mexico. Contemporary

Méndez Caratini, Héctor M. Puerto Rico. Contemporary

Méndez Defosse, Jorge. Mexico. Contemporary

Méndez Hernández, Pablo. Mexico. Contemporary

Mendoza, Felipe. Mexico. Contemporary

Mendoza Hartmann, Jorge Eduardo. Mexico. Contemporary

Meneguzzo, Pier Antonio. Italy. Contemporary

Menéndez. Peru. Active 1890s

Menezes Negri, José Roberto. Brazil. Contemporary

Menke, H. William. Active early 20th c.

Mennie, Donald. China. Active early 20th c.

Menschenfreund, Joan. U.S. Contemporary

Merille. Peru. Active ca. 1860s

Merisio, Pepe

Merkel Frank, Ricardo. Mexico. Contemporary

Merlo, Lorenzo. Italy

Merrick and Co. Active Brighton, England, 19th c.

*Merritt, Richard D. U.S. 1921–

Merritt, Vernon. U.S. Contemporary

Mersel, H., Jr. Netherlands. Active 20th c.

Mertens, (Dr.) E., and *Cie.* Active Berlin, ca. 1893

Mertens, Robert. U.S. 1950–

Merwanjee Bomanjee and Co. Active Bombay, 1850s

*Mesaros, Ronald. U.S. 1942–

Mesens, Edouard L. T. Belgium. Contemporary

Mesney, Doug. U.S. 1945–

Messager, Annette. France. 1943–

Messer, William. U.S. Contemporary

Messerli, Niggi. Contemporary

Métayer, Nicole. France. 1934–

Metenkov, V. L. Active Ural Mountains (b. Russia), 19th c.

Metnick, Alan D. Contemporary

Mettee, Holmes I. Active Baltimore, 20th c.

*Metz, Gary. U.S. 1941–

Metzger, Jack. Switzerland. 1918–

Metzner, Sheila. U.S. 1939–

Meulendijk, P. Netherlands. Active 20th c.

Meurisse. France. Active early 20th c.

Meyer, Carlos. Peru. Active ca. 1893

Meyer, Fred R. Active Buffalo, early 20th c.

Meyer, Hoppner. Active Toronto, 1855 and after

Meyer, K. Robert. Estonia. Active 19th c.

*Meyer, Pedro. Mexico. 1935–

Meyer, Veden Hans. 1931–

Meyere, Ian de. Active Stockholm, 20th c.

Meyer-Pfundt, H. Germany. Active 20th c.

*Michaelson, Ronald. U.S. Contemporary

*Michalik, Chester J. U.S. 1935–

Michaud, Julio. Mexico. Active 1860s–70s

Michelsen, H. W. Active Copenhagen, 20th c.

Michetti, Francesco Paolo. Italy. Active 19th c.

Middendorp, G. Netherlands. Active late 19th c.

Middleton, Ken. Australia. Contemporary

Midorikawa, Yohichi. 1915–

Midwinter, W. H. Active Bristol, England, 19th c.

Mieckowski, Jan. 1830–89. Active Warsaw

Mielert, Fritz. Active Dortmund, Germany, 1910–25

Mieth, Hansel. U.S. Active 20th c.

Miethe, Adolf. Germany. 1862–1927

Miethke and Wawra. Active Vienna, ca. 1860–75

Migdoll, Herbert. U.S. Contemporary

Migiurski, Karol Joseph. Active Odessa, Russia (b. Poland), 1870s

Miki, Jun. Japan. 1919–

Mikolasch, Henryk. Poland. 1872–1931

Mikoolina, Elizabeth. Russia. Active 20th c.

Miley, Michael. U.S. Active 19th c.

Millais, (Sir) John Everett. England. 1829–96

*Millan, Peter. U.S. 1935–

Millan Maria, Salvador. Mexico. Contemporary

Millar, Charles Howard. Canada. 1856–1939

Millen, Jack G. U.S. Active 20th c.

*Miller, Allan. U.S. Contemporary

Miller, Ardean. U.S. Active 20th c.

Miller, Brian Charles. U.S. 1947–

Miller, Francis. U.S. Active 20th c. (deceased)

Miller, Hugh. Scotland. 1802–56

Miller, John. New Zealand. 1950–

Miller, Judith. U.S. Contemporary

Miller, Laurance W. U.S. 1942–

Miller, Laurence G. U.S. 1948–

Miller, M. China. Active 1860s

Miller, Malcolm (Mac). New Zealand. 1950–

*Miller, Wes. Contemporary

Millet, Jean-François. France. 1814–75

Mills, F. W. England. Active early 20th c.

Mills, Herbert. Active Bolton, England, 20th c.

*Mills, John. U.S. Active 20th c.

Milne, R. Canada. Active mid-19th c.

*Milow, Keith. England. Contemporary

*Milton, Peter. U.S. 1930–

Minassian, Jacques. France. 1946–

*Mindel, Stephen. U.S. 1938–

*Mindline, David. England. 1915–

Mines, Diana. U.S. Contemporary

Minguet, A. France. Active 20th c.

Minick, Roger. U.S. 1944–

Minkkinen, Arno Rafael. U.S. (b. Finland). 1945–

Minotti, Josef. Croatia. Active 19th c.

Miranda. Active Cognac, France, 19th c.

Miranda Miranda, Antonio. Peru. Contemporary

Miranda Salgado, Juan Antonio. Mexico. Contemporary

*Mirano, Virgil Marcus. U.S. 1937–

Miré, G. de. Active Paris, 20th c.

Miserachs, Xavier. Contemporary

Misonne, Joseph. Belgium. Active 20th c.

Misrach, Richard. U.S. 1949–

Misrach, Roger. U.S. Contemporary

Misuraca, William N. Active Brooklyn, 20th c.

Mitchell, C. L. Active Philadelphia, ca. 1900

Mitchell, Michael. Canada. 1943–

Mitchell, Mike. U.S. 1945–

*Mitchell, Suzanne. U.S. 1948–

Mittelholzer, Walter. Switzerland. 1894–1937

Miyake, Katsumi. 1874–1954

*Miyasaki, George. U.S. 1935–

Miyatake, Toyo. b. 1895. Active Los Angeles (b. Japan)

Moberley, Connie. U.S. Contemporary

Modavis, Howard B. U.S. Active 20th c.

Model, Lisette. U.S. (b. Austria). 1906–

Moeller, J. R. U.S. Active 19th c.

Moffat, Curtis. U.S. 1887–1949

Moffat, John. Active Edinburgh, 1870s

Moffitt, W. H. Australia, New Zealand. Active 20th c.

Moholy, Lucia. Germany, Switzerland (b. Bohemia). ca. 1900–

Mohr, Jean. Switzerland. 1925–

Moigno, Abbé. 1804–84

Molard, Humbert de. France. d. 1874

Molina Flores, Diego. Guatemala. Contemporary

Molinard, Patrice. France. Active 20th c.

Molind, A. U.S. Active 20th c.

Molins, Pompeo. b. 1827. Active Rome, 1860s–93

Molkenboer, K. Netherlands. Active 20th c.

Moller (Dr.). Active Copenhagen, 20th c.

Moller, Amandus. Peru. Active 19th c.

Möllinger, Franziska. Germany (b. Switzerland). 1817–80

Monaghan, Kevin. U.S. 1948–

Moncalvo, Riccardo. Active Turin, Italy, 20th c.

Monchart, Léon. France. Active 20th c.

Monckhoven, Désiré Charles van. 1834–82

Monet, Claude. France. 1840–1926

Monkewitz, Nicolas. Switzerland. 1948–

*Monner, Alfred A. U.S. 1909–

Monoco. Italy. Active ca. 1880

*Monory, Jacques. France. 1934–

Monroe, Robert. U.S. 1923–

Monsivais, Daniel. Mexico. Contemporary

Monson, Peter David Tyler. U.S. 1945–

Monteith, (Dr.) George Dalrymple. 1807–62. Active Wellington, New Zealand, late 1850s and after

Montenegro, Milton. Brazil. Contemporary

Montenegro Chávez Fernández, Carlos. Peru. Contemporary

Monterrubio Pérez, Mauricio. Mexico. Contemporary

Montes, Tey. Mexico. Contemporary

Montes de Oca, Alejandro. Mexico. Contemporary

Monti, Paolo. Italy. Active 20th c.

Montizon, (Count) de. Active London, 1850s

Montmorency, (Lt.) R. H. de. Active India, ca. 1870

Montobio, J. F. Peru. Active ca. 1854

Montserrat, Tomás. Spain. 1873–1944

Montufar Avila, Carlos. Panama. Contemporary

Monvel. France. Active mid-19th c.

Moodie, George. ca. 1865–1947. Active Dunedin, New Zealand, late 1890s–1916

Moon, Karl. U.S. 1878–1948

Moore, Charles. U.S. Contemporary

Moore, R. A. and Nelson Augustus. U.S. Active 19th c.

Moore, Raymond. England. 1920–

Moore, Truman. U.S. Contemporary

Moorehouse, Lee. U.S. b. ca. 1900

Moosbrugger, Bernhard. Switzerland. 1925–

Mora, José Maria. U.S. Active New York City, 19th c.

Moragrega, Miguel. Mexico. Contemporary

Morais, Silvio

Moraites, P. Greece. Active 1860s and 1870s

Moral, Jean. U.S. Active 20th c.

Moral, Manuel. Peru. Active 19th c.

Morales, Angel. Mexico. Contemporary

Morath, Inge. U.S. Contemporary

Morehouse, Marion. U.S. Active 20th c.

Morell, Abe, Jr. U.S. 1948–

Moreno, Sergio. Mexico. Contemporary

Moreno Pesqueira, Luis. Mexico. Contemporary

Moreschi, Ernesto. Active Milan, 20th c.

Morgan, Rodney McKay. U.S. Active 20th c.

Morgan, Willard D. U.S. 1900–67

*Morimoto, Hiromitsu. U.S. (b. Japan). 1942–

Morinaga, G. Active Seattle, 20th c.

Moriyama, Daidoh. Japan. 1938–

Moriyama, Hiromichi. Japan. 1938–

*Moriyasu, Hiro. U.S. Contemporary

*Morocco, Joan K. U.S. Contemporary

Morris, George J. U.S. Active 20th c.

Morris, Michael. Canada. Active 20th c.

Morris, Nelson. U.S. Active 20th c.

Morris, Ron. U.S. Contemporary

Morrison, Robin. Australia. 1944–

Morrow, Stanley J. U.S. Active 19th c.

Morse, Jonathan. U.S. 1948–

Morse, Ralph. U.S. Active 20th c.

Morteira, Humberto. Italy. Active 20th c.

Mortimer, Francis James. England. 1874–1944

Mortimer-Lamb, H. Canada. 1872–1970

Mosbacher, Aenne. Active 20th c.

Moscioni, Romualdo. Active Rome, from 1868

Moser, Ludwig Ferdinand. 1805–80. Active Berlin

Moses, Stefan. Germany. 1928–

Mosinger, Franjo. Active Zagreb, 19th c.

Mostyn, (Lady) Augusta. England. Active 19th c.

Mottar, Robert. U.S. Active 20th c.

Mott-Smith, John. U.S. 1930–

*Moty, Eleanor. U.S. 1945–

Moulin. France. Active 19th c.

Moulin, Gabriel. U.S. Active 20th c.

Moulton, Henry deWitt. Peru (b. U.S.). Active 1859–63

Moulton, J. W. and J. S. Active Salem, Mass., 19th c.

*Moulton, Rosalind Kimball (*Rosalind S. Kimball). U.S. 1941–

Moulu, Edmond. Active Brussels, 20th c.

*Moy, David S. U.S. 1948–

*Mozingo, James. U.S. Contemporary

Mudd, James. Active Manchester, England, 1854–70

Mudford, Grant Leighton. Australia. 1944–

Muehlen, Bernis von zur. U.S. Contemporary

Mueller, Lynn. U.S. 1947–

Muench, David. U.S. Active 20th c.

Muench, Josef. U.S. Active 20th c.

Mugnier, George François. U.S. 1857–1938

Mühlbauer, A. Active Zagreb, 19th c.

Muhr, Adolf F. Active Seattle, late 19th c.

Muir and Moodie. Active Dunedin, New Zealand, late 1890s–1916

Mukherjii, P. C. India. Active 19th c.

Mulas, Ugo. Italy. Active 20th c.

*Mulcare, K. C. Contemporary

Mulder, (Dr.) Denis. Active 20th c.

Mulheran, J. India. Active 1870s

*Mullen, Rodney. U.S. 1943–

Müller, H. W. Germany. 1859–1933

Müller, Johannes. Germany. Active ca. 1900

Muller, John. U.S. Active New York City, 20th c.

Muller, Leopold Karl. Active Middle East, 1880s

Muller, (Dr.) M. Active Budapest, 20th c.

Muller, (Dr.) Robert. Active Graz, Austria, 20th c.

Müller-Brunke, Heinz. Germany. Active 20th c.

Mullis, Edwin. Kenya. Active 20th c.

Müllritter, Peter. Germany. Active 20th c.

Mulnier, Ferdinand. Active Paris, ca. 1870

Mulvany, John. U.S. 1937–

Mundert. France. Active 19th c.

Mundy, Daniel Louis. Active Christchurch, New Zealand, 1860s–70s

Muñiz, Félix. Peru. Active 19th c.

Muñiz, Hermanos. Peru. Active 19th c.

Muñiz, Paulo. Brazil. Contemporary

Muñoz Castillo, Javier. Mexico. Contemporary

Munroe, Joseph. U.S. Active 20th c.

Munzig, Horst. 1934–

Muray, Arthur. Active New York City, 20th c.

Murdoch, (Miss) H. M. Active Boston, 20th c.

Muro, Juan. Spain (b. Argentina). 1948–

*Murray, Joan. U.S. Contemporary

Murray, John. England. Contemporary

Murray, Louis R. Active Ogdensburg, N.Y., 20th c.

Murray, R. Egypt. Active 19th c.

Murray, Samuel. U.S. Active 19th c.

Murray, (Capt.) W. G. England. Active 1870s.

Mustchin, Jill. England. 1939–

Muzet and Joquet. Active Lyons, France, 19th c.

Mydtskov, H. J. Denmark. Active 20th c.

Myer, Don. U.S. Contemporary

Myers, Eveleen. England. Active late 19th c.

Myers, Joan. U.S. Contemporary

*Myers, Stephen S. U.S. 1942–

Myers, Stowe. U.S. Active 20th c.

Mylius, Carl Friedrich. Germany. 1827–1916

Myren, John. Norway. Active 20th c.

*Myrvaagnes, Eric R. U.S. 1939–

Mysse, G. Active Sevastopol, U.S.S.R., 20th c.

Nadar, Paul (Paul Tournachon). France. 1856–1939

Nadeau, Luis

Nadir, Mark. U.S. Active 20th c.

Nagano, Shigeichi. 1926–

Nahum, (Baron) Stirling Henry. *See* Baron

Naitoh, Masatoshi. Japan. 1938–

Nakagawa, Masaaki. Japan. Active 20th c.

Nakagawa, Susumu. Active Los Angeles (b. Japan), 20th c.

Nakamura, K. U.S. Active 20th c.

Nakamura, Masaya. Japan. 1926–

Nakayama, I. Laguan. Active New York City, 20th c.

Nakayama, Iwata. 1895–1949

Nalawalla, N. J. Active Bombay, 20th c.

Namuth, Hans. Active 20th c.

Nan, George. U.S. Contemporary

Nano, Ed. U.S. Active 20th c.

Nappelbaum, Ida. Active Leningrad, 20th c.

Narahara, Ikko. Japan. 1931–

Narayen, Shivashanker. India. Active 19th c.

Nardelli Malta, Ricardo. Brazil. Contemporary

Nasmyth, James. England. 1808–90

*Natali, Enrico. U.S. Contemporary

Natori, Yohnosuke. Japan. 1910–62

Natzmer, Gert von. Germany. Active 20th c.

Nauman, Bruce. U.S. 1941–

Naumann, T. S. Germany. Active ca. 1865

Navarro, Martínez. Peru. Active 19th c.

Navarro, Rafael. Spain. 1940–

Naylor, Henry. Active Leeds, England, 1850s

*Neal, Don. U.S. 1948–

Neame, S. Edwin. England. Active early 20th c.

Neeland Brothers. Canada. Active late 19th c.

*Neevel, Paul. U.S. Contemporary

Negretti, Henry. 1818–79

Negretti, José. Peru. Active 19th c.

*Neiman, Yehuda. Poland. 1931–

*Neimanas, Joyce. U.S. 1944–

*Nellis, Edward. U.S. 1948–

Nelson, Charles. U.S. Active 20th c.

Nelson, Janet Wagner. U.S. 1930–

Nelson, Lusha. U.S. Active 20th c.

*Nemser, Bob. U.S. Contemporary

Nerlinger, Oscar. Germany. 1893–1969

Nessi. Italy. Active 1880s

*Nestor, Helen. U.S. Contemporary

Netto, F. S. W. b. 1783

Neubauer, Hartmut. Germany. 1947–

Neuman, Jan A. Poland. 1900–41

*Neustein, Joshua. Poland. 1940–

*Neusüss, Floris Michael. Germany. 1937–

Nevill, (Lady) Caroline. England. Active 19th c.

Nevitt, Bryan. Canada. Active 20th c.

*Newberry, James. U.S. 1937–

Newell, Eva. 1845–1919. Active Southington, Conn.

Newhall, Beaumont. U.S. 1908–

Newhall, Nancy Wynne. U.S. 1908–74

Newland, J. W. Peru. Active 1846–47

*Newman, Alan. Contemporary

Newman, Juan. Peru. Active 1846

*Newman, Teddy. U.S. 1943–

Newnes, F. R. and E. Active Oxford, England, early 20th c.

Newnham-Davis, Henry. England. Active 1850s

*Newstead, Eddie. England. 1943–

Newton, Henry Jotham. U.S. 1823–95

Newton, (Sir) William J. England. 1785–1869

Neyra Torres, Elsa Lucia. Mexico. Contemporary

Niccolai, Giulia. Italy. Active 20th c.

Niccolini, Dianora. U.S. (b. Italy). 1936–

Nicholls, Horace W. 1867–1941. Active South Africa (b. England), ca. 1899

Nichols, Toni. U.S. Active 20th c.

Nickel, Richard. U.S. 1928–72

Nicklin, Richard. England. d. 1854. Also active the Crimea

Nickoliay, N. Active Vilnius, Lithuania, 19th c.

*Nicolas, Françoise. Contemporary

Niederland, Margot. U.S. 1946–
Niedling, Charles. Germany. Active late 19th c.
Nielsen, E. Fogh. Active Copenhagen, 20th c.
Niemeyer, J. Otto. Brazil. Active mid-19th c.
Niepce, Claude. France. 1763–1828
Niepce, Isadore. France. 1805–68
Niepce, Janine. France
Niepce de Saint-Victor, Claude Félix Abel. France. 1805–70
Nikitin, Alekseevich. Active Tiflis, Russia, 1870s
Niklitschek, Alexander. Active Vienna, 20th c.
Nilsen, (Dr.) Arthur. Active New York City, 20th c.
Nilsen, Florence Z. Active New York City, 20th c.
Nilson, Severin. Sweden. 1846–1918
Nilsson, Artur. Sweden. 1900–
Nilsson, Karl-Hakan. Sweden. Active 20th c.
Nilsson, Lennart. U.S. 1922–
Nilsson, Ole. Netherlands. Active 20th c.
Ninci, Giuseppe. 1823–90. Active Rome, 1860s–70s
Nitsche, Erik. U.S. Active 20th c.
Nivison, Frank R. Active Fall River, Mass., 20th c.
*Nixon, Nicholas. U.S. 1947–
Noah, Barbara. U.S. Contemporary
*Nobile, Anthony. U.S. 1938–
Noble, Anne. New Zealand. 1954–
Nocella, Sam. U.S. Active 20th c.
Nodler, P. U.S. Active 20th c.
*Noggle, Anne. U.S. 1922–
Noguera, José Pérez. Active Barcelona, 20th c.
Nojima, Kozo. 1889–1964
Noordhoek, Wim. Netherlands. 1916–
Norden, H. Austria. Active ca. 1865
Nordhoff, Hans. Active Munich, 20th c.
Noriega, M. Carlos. Mexico. Contemporary
*Norlin, Kurt. Contemporary
Norman, Carl and Co. England. Active 19th c.
*Norman, Dorothy. U.S. 1905–
Normand, Alfred-Nicholas. France. 1822–1909
*Normark, Don. U.S. 1928–
Norris, Richard Hill. 1831–1916

North, Kenda. U.S. Contemporary
Northampton (Marquis of). England. 1790–1851
Northrop, W. B. England. Active early 20th c.
Norton, Tom. U.S. Contemporary
Nosiglia, Agustín. Peru. Active 19th c.
Nostits (Count). Russia. 19th c.
Nothelfer, Gabriele (1945–) and Helmut (1945–). Germany.
Nottage, George Swan. 1823–85
Novak, Karel. Germany. Contemporary
Novák, Karl. Czechoslovakia. Active 20th c.
Noval, Liborio. Cuba. Contemporary
Noverre, J. H. Active Toronto, 1860s
Novitskii, Petr. Russia. 1885–1942
Novlan, Patricia. U.S. Active 20th c.
Novotny, Milon. Contemporary
*Nowack, Stanley A., Jr. U.S. Contemporary
*Nowak, Waclaw. Poland. 1924–
Nowinski, Ira. Contemporary
Nunes, Henrique. Spain. Also active Lisbon, ca. 1870s
*Nunez, Anne Morgan. Contemporary
Nuñez Cabrera, Alberto. Mexico. Contemporary
Nutting, Wallace. U.S. 1861–1941
Nyblin, Daniel. Finland (b. Norway). 1856–1923
Nyfeler, Albert. Switzerland. 1883–1969

Oakes (Capt.). India. Active 19th c.
Obernetter, Johann Baptist. Bavaria. 1840–87.
Obregon, Eduardo. Mexico. Contemporary
*Obremski, George. U.S. Contemporary
Ochoa Altamirano, Luis Manuel. Mexico. Contemporary
Ochsner, (Dr.) B. J. Active Durango, Colo., 20th c.
*O'Connell, Ed. Contemporary
Oda, Will Hiroshi. U.S. 1943–
Oddner, George. Contemporary
Oddo, L. Peru. Active 19th c.
Odier, James. France. Active mid-19th c.
Odiorne, William. France. Also active England, 20th c.

Ödman, Per. Sweden. Contemporary
Oertel, C. Active Berlin, 20th c.
Oettli, Max. New Zealand. 1947–
Offenberg, Peter A. Norway. Active 20th c.
Offner, Mortimer. Active New York City, 20th c.
Ogasawara, F. Y. Active Portland, Ore., 20th c.
Ogawa, K. China (b. Japan). Active early 20th c.
*Ogawa, Takayuki. Japan. 1936–
Ohara, Ken. Japan. 1942–
Ohlsson, Olivia. Estonia (b. Sweden). Active mid-19th c.
Okamoto, Hisao. Active Kobe, Japan, 20th c.
Okamoto, Yoichi. Contemporary
Okamura, Akihiko. Contemporary
*Okenga, Starr. U.S. Contemporary
Okninski, Ryszard. Poland. b. 1848
Oksanen, Mikke. Contemporary
*Okuhara, Tetsu. U.S. 1942–
Okun, Jenny. England (b. U.S.). 1953–
*Oldenburg, Claes. U.S. 1929–
O'Leary, John C. Mexico. Contemporary
Olivares, Eduardo. Mexico. Contemporary
Olivares Larraguibel, Javier. Mexico. Contemporary
Olivares Larraguibel, Jorge. Mexico. Contemporary
Olivares Larraguibel, Ladislao. Mexico. Contemporary
Oliver. U.S. Active mid-19th c.
Oliver, Richard. U.S. Active 20th c.
Oliverius, (Ing.) Fr. Active Prague, 20th c.
*Olivotto, Germano. Italy. Contemporary
Ollman, Arthur. U.S. 1947–
Olphert, Derek. New Zealand. 1931–
*Olson, Irving J. U.S. 1913–
Olson, John. U.S. Contemporary
Olson, Lennart. Sweden. Active 20th c.
Olszynski, Marcin. Active Warsaw, 19th c.
Oneglio, Piero. Active Turin, Italy, 20th c.
O'Neil, Elaine. U.S. 1946–
*O'Neill, Patrick. U.S. 1939–
Ongania, Ferdinand. Italy. Active mid-19th c.

Onishi, H. Active Seattle, 20th c.

Oom, G. Netherlands. Active 20th c.

Oorthuys, Cas. Netherlands. 1908–

Oosterlynck, Léopold. Belgium. 1946–

*Oosterwold, Brandie. Netherlands. 1943–

Oppenheim, A. F. Germany. Active 19th c.

Oppenheimer, Gerard. U.S. Active 20th c.

Opton, Suzanne. U.S. 1945–

Orland, Ted. U.S. Contemporary

Ornitz, Don. U.S. Contemporary

Ortega Pérez, José Luis. Brazil. Contemporary

Ortega Ramos, Beatriz. Mexico. Contemporary

Ortega Rivera, Julio. Mexico. Contemporary

Ortega Rodríguez, Ricardo. Mexico. Contemporary

Orth, Herbert. U.S. Contemporary

Ortiz, Monasterio Pablo. Mexico. Contemporary

Ortiz Echangue, J. Spain. Active 20th c.

Ortiz Peralta, Víctor. Mexico. Contemporary

Ortiz Ponton, Pablo. Mexico. Contemporary

*Osman, Colin. England. Contemporary

Osoha, Laszlo. Active Budapest, 20th c.

Osorio, Carlos. Spain. 1951–

Ost, Adolf. Active Vienna, 19th c.

Osterloff, E. Poland. Active 20th c.

Ostroróg, Stanislaw. See Walery

Ottenheim. Active Versailles, 20th c.

Otthofer, G. Active Paris, 20th c.

Otto. France (b. Austria). Active early 20th c.

Owen, A. Y. U.S. Active 20th c.

Owen, (Sir) Hugh. Wales. 1804–81

Ozievsky, M. Russia. Active 20th c.

Pabel, Hillman. b. 1910

Pach Brothers. U.S. Active 19th c.

Pacheco, Joaquim. Active Rio de Janeiro, 1854–90

Pacheco Mejía, Roberto. Mexico. Contemporary

*Paden, Donald. U.S. 1943–

*Page, Allen. Contemporary

Page, Homer Gordon. U.S. 1918–

Page, Tim. Contemporary

Pagenhardt, Eduard von. Germany. Active 20th c.

Paine, Wingate. U.S. 1915–

Paiva, Rolano. Argentina. 1942–

Pajunen, Timo Tauno. U.S. 1945–

Palmer, J. A. Active Aiken, S.C., 19th c.

*Palmer, Phil. U.S. 1911–

Palomer, P. Spain. 1945–

Palomino, Juan de la C. Peru. Active 19th c.

Pam, Max. Australia. Contemporary

Panades, Juan Ramón. Spain. Contemporary

Pancoast, C. R. Active late 19th c.

*Panda, Robin. U.S. 1937–

Pandian, (Dr.) A. J. Active Tanjore, India, 20th c.

*Pannucci, Cynthia. U.S. 1947–

Panov, M. Active Moscow, 19th c.

Paolini, Ameris M. Brazil. Contemporary

Paolini, Giulio. Italy. 1940–

*Paolozzi, Eduardo. England. 1924–

*Papageorge, Tod. U.S. 1940–

Paradise. Active New York City, 19th c.

Parčić, Dragutin. Active Zadar, Croatia, mid-19th c.

Pardee, John. U.S. Active 20th c.

Pardoe (Dr.). Active Bound Brook, N.J., 20th c.

Parish, F. E. Active Birmingham, England, 20th c.

Park, Bertram. Active London, 20th c

*Parker, Anne. Contemporary

Parker, F. Active El Paso, Tex., late 19th c.

*Parker, Fred. U.S. 1938–

Parker, Olivia. U.S. 1941–

Parkes, Alexander. England. 1813–90

Parks, Gordon, Jr. (Gordon Rogers). U.S. d. 1979

Parks, J. G. Active Montreal, 19th c.

Parr, Martin. England. 1952–

Parr, Th. India. Active ca. 1901

Parris, Edmund Thomas. 1793–1873

Parry, Linda. U.S. Contemporary

Parry, Roger. France. 1905–

Parry, William S. Active Newcastle, England, mid-19th c.

*Parsons, David. England. 1943–

Parsons, (Rev.) Harry. China. Active 20th c.

Parsons, William (Earl of Rosse). England. 1800–67

Partington, J. A., Jr. Active New York City, 20th c.

Partridge. Active Boston and Alaska, 19th c.

Partridge, Rondal. U.S. 1917–

Paschkoff, B. Active Paris, London, 20th c.

Pascoe, John Dobree. New Zealand. 1908–72

*Paternite, Stephen. U.S. 1952–

Pateson, Robert. England. Active 1860s

Patillo Studio. New Zealand. Active 19th c.

Patrick, Ian. France. Contemporary

Patrick, J. Active Edinburgh, 19th c.

Pattellani, Federico. Italy. Active 20th c.

Patterson, Bruce. U.S. 1950–

*Patterson, Donald Wright, Jr. U.S. 1937–

Patterson, Freeman. Canada. Active 20th c.

*Patterson, Marion Louise. U.S. 1933–

Pauels, Máximo. Peru. Active ca. 1895

Paul, Robert William. Great Britain. 1869–1943

Payne. Active London, 19th c.

Payne, Chris F. Canada. Active 20th c.

Pazon, Joe. U.S. Active 20th c.

Peabody, Charles and Jeanette. Active Cambridge, Mass., ca. 1900

Peacock, Peggy. Canada. 1949–

Pearson, André. Active Bristol, England, 20th c.

Pearson, James. U.S. 1951–

Pearson, Maria. Active 20th c.

Pease, Benjamin Franklin. Peru. Active 1853–80

Pec. France. Active mid-19th c.

Pechmann, (Baron) v. Active Altona, Germany, 20th c.

Pechotsch, Rudolf. Active Vienna, 20th c.

Peck, Henry S. U.S. Active 1864–70

Pecsi, Jozsef. Active Budapest, 20th c.

Pector. France. Active mid-19th c.

Pedersen, Thomas. Denmark. Active 20th c.

Pedevilla, Jacinto. Peru. Active 1846-53

Pedroli, Gino. Switzerland. b. 1898

Pekar, Frant. Active Prague, 20th c.

Peldan, Lars Johan. Finland. 1827-73

Pelech, Josef. Active Prague, 20th c.

Pelham, Lynn. U.S. Contemporary

Pellegineschi, Paolo. Italy. Active 20th c.

Pellegrini, Guido. Active Milan, 20th c.

*Pelletier, Brian. U.S. 1941-

Peltier, J. G. Active Nantes, France, 20th c.

Peñafiel, Manuel. Mexico. Contemporary

Penard, Jacques. Active Paris, 20th c.

Penati, Gianni. U.S. (b. Italy). 1930-

Penley, Aaron. England. Active mid-19th c.

Pennebaker, John Paul. U.S. Active 20th c.

Pennington, Harry. U.S. Active 20th c.

*Pennuto, James. Contemporary

Penone, Giuseppe. Italy. 1947-

Penrice, (Miss) K. Active Bournemouth, England, 20th c.

Peppel, Chr. van der. Netherlands. Active 20th c.

Pepper, J. U.S. Active 20th c.

Perckhammer, Heinz von. Germany. Active 20th c.

Percy, John. Peru (b. England). 1817-89

Perea Cordoba, José Luis. Guatemala. Contemporary

Pereire, (Baron) Gustave. France. Active ca. 1900

Peress, Gilles. France. 1946-

Peretti-Griva, D. Riccardo. Active Turin, Italy, 20th c.

Peretti-Griva, Domenico. Italy. Active 20th c.

Pérez, Mazda. Brazil. Contemporary

Pérez Olagaray, Maria Elena. Mexico. Contemporary

Pergon, Alberto. Mexico. Contemporary

Périer, Paul. France. Active 1850s and after

Perini, A. Italy. Active 20th c.

*Perkis, Philip. U.S. 1935-

*Perlmutter, Abigail. U.S. Contemporary

*Perlmutter, Jack. U.S. 1920-

Peroche and Heyland. Italy. Active 19th c.

Perpigna, de. Active ca. 1899

Perquin, Co. Netherlands. Active 20th c.

Perrault, Jean-Claude. France. Contemporary

Perry, Frederic. Active New England, ca. 1900

Perry, Joseph. Active Dunedin, New Zealand, ca. 1865

Persico, Antonio. Italy. Active 20th c.

Perutz, Otto. Germany. 1847-1922

Peryer, Peter. New Zealand. 1941-

Pesak, K. F. Czechoslovakia. Active 20th c.

Peskin, Hy. U.S. Contemporary

Pesme and Varin. France. Active 1850s

Petagna, Michele. Active Florence, before 1863; Rome, 1865 and after

Peteani, O. von. Germany. Active ca. 1900

Peter, Richard. Germany. Active 20th c.

Peterhans, Walter. Germany, U.S. (b. Germany). 1897-1960

Peters, James. Canada. Active 19th c.

Peters, Paul. Canada. Active 20th c.

*Petersen, Anders. Sweden. 1944-

Peterson, Robert. U.S. Contemporary

Petit, Pierre. France. b. 1832

Petit, Thomas J. U.S. 1942-

Petrescu, Stelian. Romania. Active late 19th c.

*Petricone, Paul. U.S. 1923-

*Petrillo, Thomas. U.S. 1949-

Petrocelli, Joseph. Active New York City, 20th c.

Petrov, I. Lithuania. Active 19th c.

Petrov, Nikolai Aleksandrovich. Russia. 1876-1940

Petrov, S. Active Vilnius, Lithuania, mid-19th c.

Petschler, H., and Co. Active Manchester, England, 19th c.

Petschow, Robert. Germany. Active 20th c.

Petters, Christoph Heinrich Hermann. Germany. 1806-75

Petzval, Josef Max. 1807-91

Pexa, Edward. Active Vienna, 20th c.

*Pfahl, John. U.S. 1939-

Pfeffer, Barbara. U.S. Contemporary

Pfeifer, Marijan. Yugoslavia. Active 20th c.

Pfuhl, Joachim. Germany. Contemporary

Phelps Company. England. Active 19th c.

Philippi. Contemporary

Philipsen, Emil. Denmark, Finland. Active 19th c.

Phillips, Charles. U.S. Contemporary

Phillips, Robert. U.S. Contemporary

*Phillips, Walter. Contemporary

Philo, T. L. Active Batavia, N.Y., 19th c.

Philpot, J. B. Active Florence, 19th c.

*Piaskowski, Nata. U.S. Active 20th c.

Picasso, Pablo. France (b. Spain). 1881-1973

Piccard, August. Switzerland. b. 1884

Picker, Fred. U.S. Contemporary

Pickering, Edward Charles. 1846-1919. Active Cambridge, Mass.

Pickering, William Henry. 1858-1938. Active Cambridge, Mass.

Piel, Gerald. U.S. 1928-

Pieniowski, Hakân. Sweden. 1948-

Pierce, Bill. U.S. Contemporary

Pierpont, J. L. G. U.S. Active 19th c.

Pierre, Lucien. Active Paris, 20th c.

Pierscinski, Pawel. Poland. 1934-

Pierson, Louis. France. Active mid-19th c.

Pietrodangelo, Donato. Italy. Contemporary

Pietrusov, G. G. Russia. Active 20th c.

Pietzch, P. M. Spain, Italy. Active 20th c.

Pietzner, C. Austria. Active ca. 1900.

Piffard, Henry G. U.S. Active late 19th c.

Pike, Laurence. England. Active late 19th c.

Pike and Sons. Active New York City, 19th c.

Pikous, Jan

*Pilbrow, David. U.S. 1940-

Pildas, Ave. U.S. 1939–

Pine Brothers. Active New Jersey, 19th c.

Pineda Velazquez, Sergio. Mexico. Contemporary

Pinelo, Juan. Mexico. Contemporary

Pinkel, Sheila. U.S. 1941–

Pinnell, Paige. U.S. 1944–

Pinner, Erna. Active 20th c.

Piper, C. Welbourne. England. Active early 20th c.

*Piper, John. England. 1903–

*Pirone, Joe. Contemporary

Pirou, Eugène. France. Active ca. 1860–90

*Pistoletto, Michelangelo. Italy. Active 20th c.

Pitcairn-Knowles, Andrew. England. 1871–1956

Pitkänen, Matti. Finland. Active 20th c.

Pivoriunas, Atanas. Contemporary

Pizon, (Dr.) Pierre. France. Contemporary

Pizzighelli, Giuseppe. Austria. 1849–1912

Plachy, Sylvia. U.S. (b. Hungary). 1943–

Plateau, Joseph-Antoine-Ferdinand. Belgium. 1801–83.

Plauszewski, P. France. Active late 19th c.

Pleterski, Roland. U.S. Active 20th c.

Plevinski, Wojtech. Poland. 1929–

Plicka, Karel. Czechoslovakia. b. 1894

Pliny, Bartlett. Active Boston, 19th c.

Plossu, Bernard. France, U.S. (b. Vietnam). 1945–

Pohl, Joseph Johann. 1825–1900

Pointer, H. Active Brighton, England, late 19th c.

*Poirier, Ann (1942–) and Patrick (1942–). France

Poitevin, Alphonse-Louis. France. 1819–82

*Poitier, Jacqueline. Contemporary

*Poliak, Leslie. U.S. 1949–

Pollack, Charles. U.S. Active 19th c.

Pollitt, John Smith. England. Active mid-19th c.

Pollock, Charles. Active Boston, 19th c.

Pollock, Henry. U.S. 1826–89

Pollock, (Sir) Jonathan Frederick. England. 1783–1870

Polo, Miguel Angel Yañez. Spain. 1940–

Poltoratskaya, L. K. Russia. Active 19th c.

*Polumbaum, Theodore. U.S. 1924–

Pommer, Franjo. Active Zagreb, 19th c.

Pond, C. L. Active Buffalo, 19th c.

Ponte Vivares, Yves del. Mexico. Contemporary

Ponthuis, Marie. France. Contemporary

Ponting, Herbert. 1871–1935. Active the South Pole

Ponton, Mungo. Scotland. 1802–80

Ponton d'Amécourt (Vicomte de). France. Active ca. 1893

*Poon, Irene. U.S. Contemporary

Pope, Kenneth. U.S. Active 20th c.

Popper, Grete. Active Prague, 20th c.

Popper, Paul. Active 20th c.

*Porett, Thomas. U.S. 1942–

Porte (Dr.). France. Active 20th c.

*Porter, Liliana. Argentina. 1941–

Porter, Timothy. Canada. Active 20th c.

Posas, Florencia. Mexico. Contemporary

Potonniée, Georges. 1862–1949

Pottier, Philippe. France. Active 20th c.

Potts, Charles. U.S. Active 20th c.

Potts, David. Australia, England. Active 20th c.

Poulsen, Alex. Active Copenhagen, 20th c.

Poulsen, Paul C. Active Brisbane, Australia, late 19th c.

Poulton. England. Active ca. 1880s

Pouncy, John. ca. 1820–94. Active Dorchester, England

Poundstone, Jesse. Active late 19th c.

Powderly, Terence Vincent. U.S. 1849–1924

Powel, Peter. Active 20th c.

*Powell, James. Contemporary

Power, Mark. U.S. 1937–

Powers, Hiram. 1805–73. Active Florence (b. U.S.), 1860s

Powers, L. Active Florence, 1860s

*Pozzi, Lucio. Italy. Contemporary

Prado Salazar, Alberto. Peru. Contemporary

Prager, Marcia A. U.S. Contemporary

Prasse, Alvin W. U.S. Active 20th c.

Prather, Winter. U.S. Active 20th c.

Pratsch, Charles Robert. U.S. Active ca. 1885–1920

Pratt, Charles. U.S. 1926–76

Pratt, Ernest M. Active Los Angeles, 20th c.

Pravenec, J. Active Prague, 20th c.

Prearo, Penna. Brazil. Contemporary

Preisig, Dölf. Switzerland. 1940–

Presser, Beat. Contemporary

Presser, Gustav. Active Vienna, 20th c.

Presser, Sem. Netherlands. Active 20th c.

Pressma, Conrad J. U.S. Contemporary

Preston, Hart. U.S. Active 20th c.

Preston, J. H. Active Brisbane, Australia, late 19th c.

Pretsch, Paul. Austria. 1803–73

Preuss, K. Czechoslovakia. Active 19th c.

Prevost, Victor. 1820–81. Active Rome (b. France), 1843; New York City, 1849 and after

Pribék, Antal. Active Székesfehérvár, Hungary, 19th c.

Price, J. Active South Ramsgate, England, 19th c.

*Price, Kenneth. U.S. 1935–

Price, William Lake. England. ca. 1810–96

Primoli, (Count) Giuseppe. 1852–1927. Active Rome, 1885–1905

Pringle, Barry. U.S. Contemporary

Prini, Emilio. Italy. Active 19th c.

Prosek, Josef. Contemporary

Proust, Frédéric. France. Contemporary

Prümm, Theodor. Active Berlin, 19th c.

Prusakov, Boris. Active 20th c.

Pucher, Johan August. b. 1814

Puhlmann, Rico. Contemporary

Puhn, Alfred. U.S. Active 20th c.

Puig, Alfredo Guito. Active 20th c.

Pulman. U.S. Active 1870s

Pulman, G. and E. Active Auckland, New Zealand, 1860s

Pumphrey, William. England. Active 19th c.

Purcell, Rosamond Wolff. U.S. 1942–

Purvis, Alston. U.S. 1943–

*Putzar, Edward. Contemporary

Pye, John. England. 1782–1874

Pywell, William R.   U.S. Active mid-19th c.

Quarella, Doris.   Switzerland. 1944–
*Quarterman, Dale.   U.S. Contemporary
Queiros Mattoso, Adriana de.   Brazil. Contemporary
Quennoy, Louis.   Active Bordeaux, 20th c.
Quentin, J.   Active 19th c.
Quetier, E.   Active Paris, 1870s
Quick, Herb.   U.S. 1925–
Quigley, Edward.   U.S. Active 20th c.
Quinby and Co.   Active Charleston, S.C., 19th c.
Quinet, Achille.   France. Active mid-19th c.
Quintana, Maria de Guadalupe E. de.   Mexico. Contemporary
Quirarte, Xavier.   Mexico. Contemporary
Quirk, Philip.   Australia. Contemporary

Rabending, Emil.   Austria. 1823–86
Rabending and Monckhoven.   Active Vienna, 19th c.
*Rabetz, Walter.   U.S. 1940–
Rabinovitch, Ben Magid.   U.S. 1884–1964
Rabinovitch, Mendel.   Brazil. Contemporary
Radaelli, Rita.   Brazil. Contemporary
*Radin, Michael.   Contemporary
Radochonska, Lucia
Radowski, F. H.   U.S. Active 20th c.
Radwanski, Jedrzej.   Poland. 1800–60
Radzikowski, Eliasz.   Poland. 1840–1905
Rae, A., and Son.   Active 1860s
*Ragazzini, Vincenzo.   Italy. 1934–
*Raginsky, Nina.   U.S. 1941–
Raimond-Dityvon, C.   France. Contemporary
Rainer, Arnulf.   Austria. 1929–
*Rainone, Mike.   U.S. Contemporary
Ramchundra, Muccoond.   India. Active 19th c.
Ramhab, Gyula.   Active Budapest, 20th c.
Ramírez, Eduardo.   Mexico. Contemporary

Ramírez, Teodoro.   Peru. Active 19th c.
Ramírez Bautista, José de Jesús.   Mexico. Contemporary
Ramos, Ramón Zabalza.   Spain. 1938–
Ramrakha, Priya.   d. 1968
Ramskou, Markus.   Denmark. Active 20th c.
Ranalli, Daniel.   U.S. Contemporary
Rankin, Nancy.   U.S. 1944–
Ranney, Edward.   U.S. 1942–
Ransom, Robert.   U.S. Contemporary
Rantoul, Neal T.   U.S. Contemporary
*Rantzman, Karen S.   Contemporary
Raota, Pedro Luis
Rapoport, I. C.   U.S. Contemporary
Rapos, Lubomir.   Contemporary
Rashov, Hrissan.   Bulgaria. Active 1860s–70s
Rasmussen, Knud.   Active Copenhagen, 20th c.
Rathenau, Ernest.   Active 20th c.
Ratnagar, F. R.   Active Bombay, 20th c.
Rau, William H.   Active Philadelphia, 19th c.
Rauh, W.   Germany. Active 20th c.
*Rauschenberg, Christopher.   U.S. 1951–
Rautert, Timm.   Germany. 1941–
Ravanesi, Bill.   U.S. Contemporary
Ravid, Joyce.   U.S. Contemporary
Ray, William R.   U.S. Contemporary
Rayleigh, John William Strutt.   England. 1842–1919
*Raymo, James.   U.S. Contemporary
Raymond, Lilo.   U.S. (b. Germany). 1922–
Raymond, Mary E.   Active Cleveland, 20th c.
*Read, David D.   U.S. 1939–
Read, Frank H.   England. Active 1900–11
Reade, Joseph Bancroft.   1801–70
Reader, John.   England. Contemporary
Rebolledo Arango, Santiago.   Colombia. Contemporary
Redfield, Robert S.   U.S. Active early 20th c.
Redl, Harry.   U.S. Contemporary
Reed, Rixon.   U.S. 1951–
Reed, Roland.   Active Montana, early 20th c.
Reed, S.   England. Active 19th c.

*Reed, Terry.   Contemporary
Reed, Werner.   U.S. Contemporary
Reekie, John.   U.S. Active mid-19th c.
*Reep, Richard B.   U.S. Contemporary
Reeve, Lovell.   Active London, mid-19th c.
Reeves, Ian.   Canada. 1950–
Reeves, John.   U.S. 1938–
Regan, Ken.   U.S. Contemporary
Regis.   Germany. Active ca. 1870
Regnault, Henri-Victor.   France. 1810–78
Rehbinder, Wladimir.   Active Paris, 20th c.
Rehn, Isaac A.   Active Philadelphia, mid-19th c.
Reiber, Philip B.   U.S. Active 20th c.
Reichman, Michael.   Canada. Active 20th c.
Reichmann, Vilem.   Contemporary
Reiger, G.   Active Rome, mid-19th c.
Reinberg, Johan Jakob.   Finland. 1823–96
Reisner, George Andrew.   b. U.S. 1867–1942
Reiss, Tjark.   U.S. Active 20th c.
Reiszmann, Mariann.   Active Budapest, 20th c.
Reiter, O. C.   Active Pittsburgh, 20th c.
Rejda, Roger.   U.S. 1944–
*Remesar, Luis.   Cuba. Contemporary
Remfeldt, Aage.   Denmark. Active 20th c.
Remorino, Félix.   Peru. Active 19th c.
Renai, Denes.   Active Budapest, 20th c.
René, Gilbert.   France. Active 20th c.
René-Jacques.   France. Active 20th c.
Renes, D.   Netherlands. Active 20th c.
*Renfro, Donald.   U.S. Contemporary
*Renfrow, Charles
Renner, Eric.   U.S. 1941–
Rentmeester, Co.   U.S. (b. Netherlands). 1936–
*Resnick, Marcia.   U.S. 1950–
Retzlaff, Erich.   Germany. Active 20th c.
Revelle, Barbara Jo.   U.S. 1946–

*Rexroth, Nancy. U.S. 1946–
Reynaud, Emile. 1844–1918
Reynolds, Bert. U.S. Contemporary
Reynolds, Charles. U.S. Contemporary
Ribera, Fermin and Abad. Active Barcelona, 20th c.
Ricciardi, Mirella. b. Kenya. 1933–
Rice, (Sgt.) George W. Active the Arctic, 1881–84
Rice, (Maj.) H. J. Active Poona, India, 20th c.
Rich, Hang. Contemporary
*Rich, Linda. Contemporary
Richard, Franz. Active Heidelberg, 19th c.
*Richards, Dick. U.S. 1929–
*Richards, Eugene. U.S. 1944–
Richards, J. Cruwys. Active late 19th c.
Richards, Mrs. Wynn. Active Chicago, 20th c.
Richardson, Benjamin. U.S. 1834–1925
Richardson, Villroy L. Peru. Active 1859–71
Riche, Fran. U.S. Contemporary
Richez, Jacques. Belgium. Contemporary
Richie, Robert Yarnell. U.S. Active 20th c.
Richter, Alfred W. U.S. Active 20th c.
Richter, (Rev.) G. India. Active ca. 1870
Richter, Jos. Austria. Active ca. 1865
Rickerby, Arthur. U.S. d. 1972
Ridas-Prous, J. M. Contemporary
Rider-Rider, William. England. Active early 20th c.
Ridzenieks, Vilas. Latvia. Active 19th c.
Riebesehl, Heinrich. 1938–
Riebicke, G. Germany. Active 20th c.
Riecke, Friedrich. Germany. Active 20th c.
Riedel, August. Brazil (b. Germany). Active ca. 1868
Riefenstahl, Leni. U.S. (b. Germany). 1902–
Rieks, Arthur. Active 20th c.
Rieksts, Janis. Latvia. b. 1887
Rietmann, Otto. Switzerland. 1856–1942
Rigby, Ranald. Active Lancashire, England, 20th c.
Riger, Robert. U.S. 1924–

Riggins, Marie. Active Cleveland, 20th c.
Riis, Charles Conrad. Finland (b. Denmark) 1837–1915
Rijmes, Joanne. U.S. Contemporary
Rinehart, Frank A. U.S. 1861–1928
Ringger, Art. Switzerland. 1946–
*Rinke, Klaus. Germany. 1939–
*Risager, Robert. Denmark. 1922–
*Riss, Murray. U.S. Contemporary
Risse, Edmund. Germany. Active late 19th c.
Ritchie, Cranston. U.S. Contemporary
Rittase, William M. U.S. b. 1894
Ritter, Molkenteller, and Co. Active Bombay and Poona, India, 19th c.
Ritter, Wolfgang. Germany. Contemporary
Ritterbusch, Klaus. Germany. 1947–
Rittlinger, Herbert. Germany. Active 20th c.
Rivas, Humberto. Argentina. 1937–
Rive, Roberto. Active Naples and Rome, 1860s
Rivera Conde, Sergio. Mexico. Contemporary
Rivero, Maria del Carmen. Mexico. Contemporary
Rivers, Jean. U.S. Active 20th c.
*Rivers, Larry. U.S. 1923–
Riwkin, Anna. Sweden (b. Russia). d. 1970
Rizzo, John. U.S. 1948–
Robakowski, Josef. Poland. 1939–
Robbins, Frank. U.S. Active 19th c.
Robbins, Kenneth. U.S. Contemporary
Robert, Jeanne. France. Active 20th c.
Robert, Louis. France. 1811–82
Roberts, Bruce. U.S. Active 20th c.
Roberts, W. Germany. Active 20th c.
Roberts, W. J. Active Luton, England, 20th c.
Robertson, David. England. Active ca. 1860
Robertson, G. Active Somme, France, 20th c.
Robertson, Grace. England. Active 20th c.
Robinson, Abby. U.S. Contemporary
Robinson, Benjamin W. Active Pittsburgh, 20th c.
Robinson, Bonnell. Contemporary

Robinson, Cervin. U.S. 1927–
Robinson, David. U.S. Contemporary
*Robinson, Gerald H. U.S. 1927–
Robinson, Jerome. U.S. Active 20th c.
Robinson, Karl Davis. Active New York City, 20th c.
Robinson, Ralph P. England. Active late 19th c.
*Robinson, Sue Carol. U.S. Contemporary
Robinson, William F. U.S. 1946–
Robuchon, Jules. France. Active ca. 1875
Rocca de Chandal, Geri della
Roche, Denis. France. 1937–
Roche, John P. U.S. Active 20th c.
Roche, T. C. Active New York City, mid-19th c.
Rocher. France. Contemporary
Rock, Joseph F. China. Active early 20th c.
Rockwood. Active New York City, 19th c.
Rockwood and Co. U.S. Active 1870s
Rodan, Don. U.S. 1950–
Rodger, Thomas. England. Active mid-19th c.
Rodgers, H. J. Active Hartford, ca. 1850s–80s
Rodrigo, E. Carlos. Peru. Active ca. 1880s
Rodríguez, Alberto. Peru. Active ca. 1890s
Roentgen Wilhelm Conrad. Germany. 1845–1923
Rogers, Bob. U.S. Contemporary
Rogers, Gordon. See Parks, Gordon, Jr.
Rogers, John. Active New York City, 19th c.
Rogi, André. Active Paris, 20th c.
*Rogovin, Milton. U.S. Contemporary
Rohde, Rudi. Germany. Contemporary
Rohde, Werner. Germany. 1906–
Roinashvili, Aleksandr. 1846–98. Active Georgia, Russia
Roiter, Fulvio. Italy. 1926–
*Roitz, Charles. U.S. 1935–
*Rolet. Contemporary
Rollman, Wilhelm. 1821–1909
Rombaut, Emile. Active Antwerp, 20th c.
Rome, Stuart A. Contemporary

*Romeike, Carla M. U.S. Active 20th c.

Romer, Witold. Active Lvov, Poland, 20th c.

Romero, José P. U.S. Contemporary

Rommles and Jonas. Germany. Active late 19th c.

Rona, (Dr.) Eugen. Romania. Active 20th c.

Ronay, D. Active Budapest, 20th c.

Rondin, Hector. Contemporary

Ronis, Willy. Active 20th c.

Ronninger, Herman. Sweden. 1895–1976

Röntgen, Wilhelm Conrad. *See* Roentgen

Rood and Emerson. Active New York City, 19th c.

*Root, Nile. U.S. 1926–

Rosa Fernández, Reginaldo. Brazil. Contemporary

Rosales Ramírez, Arturo. Mexico. Contemporary

Roscoe, (Sir) Henry Enfield. England. 1833–1915

Rose, A. Peru. Active ca. 1868

Rose, Ben. U.S. Contemporary

Rose, Uli. Contemporary

*Rosenbaum, Alvin. U.S. 1945–

Rosenberg, Carl Gustaf. Sweden (b. France). 1883–1957

Rosenfeld, Doris. Switzerland. Active 20th c.

*Rosenquist, James. U.S. 1933–

*Rosenstock, Ronald. U.S. 1944–

Rosher, Cyril. Active Victoria, British Columbia, 20th c.

Rosling, Alfred. England. Active ca. 1860s

Ross, Alan. U.S. 1948–

Ross, Andrew. 1798–1859

*Ross, Donald. U.S. 1912–

*Ross, Elliot. U.S. 1947–

Ross, Kip. U.S. 1903–

*Ross, Merg. U.S. 1941–

Rosse, Earl of. *See* Parsons, William

Rossetti, Dante Gabriel. England. 1828–82

Rössler, Jaroslav. Czechoslovakia. b. 1902

Rosty, Pál. Hungary. 1830–79

Rotan, Thurman. U.S. b. 1905

Roth, H. P. Switzerland. Active 20th c.

Roth, Ruth Jacobi. U.S. Active 20th c.

Roth, Sanford. U.S. 1906–62

Rothe, Emil Fr. Germany. Active ca. 1870

*Rothenstein, Michael. England. 1908–

Rothkegel, Max. Germany. Active 20th c.

Rotorua. New Zealand. Active early 20th c.

Rottmayer and Zintl. Active Graz and Trieste, Austria, ca. 1880

Rouget, Bernard. French Morocco. Active 20th c.

Rougier, Michael. U.S. Active 20th c.

Roullé, Ladevéze A. France. Active 1880s–90s

Rousset, Ildefonse. France. Active 1850s–60s

Routh, Robert D. U.S. Contemporary

Rowan, Roy. Contemporary

Rowell, Frank. Active Boston, ca. 1860–80

Rowinski, David. U.S. Active 20th c.

Roye. England. Active 20th c.

Royle, Ralph. U.S. Active 20th c.

Rozaffy, Ruth Staudinger. U.S. Active 20th c.

Rozycki, Andrzej. Poland. 1942–

Ruat, Dominique. Contemporary

Rübelt, Lothar. Germany. b. 1901

Ruben Díaz, Miguel Angel. Mexico. Contemporary

*Rubenstein, Meridel. U.S. 1948–

Rubenstein, Raeanne. U.S. Contemporary

Rubin, Len S. U.S. 1916–

Rubin, Mark. U.S. 1946–

Rubinger, David. Israel. Contemporary

Rubini, Gail. U.S. Contemporary

*Ruble, Gary. U.S. Contemporary

Rubow, Carl. Germany. Active 20th c.

Rudaux, Lucien. France. Active 20th c.

Rude, Ernest. Active Oslo, 20th c.

Rudinger, Hugo. Active Vienna, 20th c.

Rudolph, Paul. 1858–1935

Rueda, Angel de la. Mexico. Contemporary

Rueda, Jorge. Spain. 1943–

Rueda Ramírez, Emma. Mexico. Contemporary

*Ruether, David. U.S. 1942–

*Rugolo, Lawrence. Contemporary

Ruiz, José. Peru. Active 19th c.

Ruiz Camino, Martha. Mexico. Contemporary

Ruiz Granados, Marcos. Mexico. Contemporary

Ruiz Ramos, Cecilia. Mexico. Contemporary

Rulofson, William Henry. *See* Bradley and Rulofson

Runeberg, Kristian. Finland. Active 20th c.

Ruohomaa, Kosti. U.S. 1914–61

Rupp, August. Germany. Active 20th c.

Rupp, Vilem (1821–93), and Beckel, Josef. Active Prague

Rupprecht, Mihály. Hungary. Active ca. 1863

Ruse, John. Active Oslo, 20th c.

*Rusk, Grant. U.S. 1949–

Ruskin, John. England. 1819–1900

Russell, (Capt.) A. T. U.S. Active 19th c.

Russell, Charles. 1820–87

Russell, Guy. U.S. Contemporary

Russell, Rae. U.S. Active 20th c.

Russell, Russ. U.S. Contemporary

Russell, Ted. U.S. Contemporary

Russell, (Sir) William Howard. Great Britain. 1820–1907. Also active elsewhere

Russell and Sons. Active Worthing, England, 19th c.

Russoniello, Alexander. U.S. 1947–

Russov, (Dr.) E. Active Yuryev (Tartu), Estonia, late 19th c.

Rust, Carola. Active New York City, 20th c.

Rust, Ulrich. Germany. Contemporary

Rustin, Arnold. U.S. Contemporary

Rutberg, Alan. U.S. 1948–

Rutherfurd, Lewis Morris. U.S. 1816–92

Rutten, Henzy. Active Brussels, 20th c.

Ruzicka, (Dr.) D. J. Active Jackson Heights, N.Y., 20th c.

Ruzicka, Drahomir Joseph. U.S. 1870–1960

Ryan, John Julius. Active Chicago, 20th c.

Rzewuski, Walery. 1837–88. Active Cracow, Poland

Saab Hassen, Akram. Mexico. Contemporary

Saad, Georges. France. Active 20th c.

Saavedra, Juan de la Mata. Peru. Active ca. 1857

Sabatier-Blot, Jean-Baptiste. 1801–81. France.

Sacchi, Luigi (also E. Sacchi). Active Milan and Rome, ca. 1839 and after

Saché (John?). Active India, 1860–80

Sachker, Reinhold. 1844–1919. Active Yuryev (Tartu), Estonia

Sackett, Joel. Contemporary

Sadik, Ahmen. Egypt. Active 20th c.

*Sadler, Richard. England. 1927–

Sadovy, John. England. Active 20th c.

Saebens, Hans. Germany. b. 1895

Saeboe, Per. Active Voss, Norway, 20th c.

Saenger, B. Russia. Active late 19th c.

*Sage, Linn. U.S. 1937–

*Sahlstrand, James M. U.S. 1936–

Saichet, Arkadi. U.S.S.R. 1898–1959

Saidman, Rueben. England. Active 20th c.

St. Aubyn, John G. Active Purley, England, 20th c.

St. Croix (Mother). ca. 1860–1940. Active New Orleans

St. George, Andrew. U.S., Cuba. Active 20th c.

*Saint-Jean, Michel. Canada. 1937–

Saint-Mémin, Charles Balthazar Julien Fevret de. U.S. (b. France). 1770–1852

Saintot, René. Active Paris, 20th c.

Saito, Satoshi. Japan. 1936–

Saitz, Hans. Austria. Active ca. 1900

Salas, Osvaldo. Cuba. Contemporary

Salas, Roberto. Cuba. Contemporary

Salaün, Philippe. France. 1943–

Salazar, Félix. Peru. Active ca. 1856–90

*Salbitani, Roberto. Italy. 1945–

Salman, William J. U.S. Contemporary

Salmieri, Steve. U.S. 1945–

*Salmo, Frank. U.S. 1942–

Saltzmann, Jeffrey. U.S. Contemporary

Salviati, P. Active Venice, ca. 1870

Salwen, Ellen. U.S. Contemporary

Salzmann, Laurence. U.S. Contemporary

Samberg, Rouben. U.S. 1918–

Samore, Sam. U.S. Contemporary

Sampaio Neto, Vivente. Brazil. Contemporary

*Sample, Tricia. U.S. 1949–

Sampson, Alden. U.S. Active 1890s

Sampson Mitrani, Luis. Mexico. Contemporary

Sánchez, Enrique. Active Canary Islands, 20th c.

Sánchez, Simón. Peru. Active ca. 1853

Sánchez Uribe, Jesús. Mexico. Contemporary

Sandberg, Tom. Norway. 1953–

Sandels, Karl. Sweden. 1906–

Sanders. U.S. Active late 19th c.

*Sanders, Charles. U.S. 1921–

Sanders, Norman. U.S. 1927–

Sanders, Walter. U.S. Active 20th c.

Sanderson, E. L. U.S. Active ca. 1900

Sandhage, Douglas E. U.S. Contemporary

Sanger, Shepherd Edward. 1869–1927

Sanglau, Achille. Active Rome, 1863 and after

Sanguinetti, Ricardo. Argentina. Contemporary

Sankova, Galina. U.S.S.R. 1904–

Sannes, Sanne. Netherlands. Contemporary (deceased)

Santeul, C. de. Active Paris, 20th c.

Saporiti, Pietro. Spain. Active 20th c.

Sarabie, Manuel. Peru. Active 19th c.

Sargent, Nickola M. U.S. Contemporary

Sargent, S. C. Active Taylors Falls, Minn., ca. 1892

Sarkangalvis, K. Active Valmiera, Latvia, 19th c.

Sarkany, Jeno. Active Sopron, Hungary, 20th c.

Sarolides, G. Greece(?). Active 1880s

Sarony, Oliver François Xavier. 1820–79. Active Scarborough, England (b. Canada)

Sarra, Valentino. U.S. Active 20th c.

Sarramon, Christian. France. 1942–

Sarsini, Enrico. Italy. 1939–

Sasgen, Peter. U.S. Contemporary

Sasha. Active 20th c.

Sato, Akira. 1930–

Satyan, T. S. India. Active 20th c.

Saulitis, A. Active Riga, Latvia, 19th c.

Saunders, J. Active Alfred Center and Friendship, N.Y., 19th c.

Saunders, Richard. U.S. Active 20th c.

Saunders, Sylvia. U.S. Active 20th c.

Saunderson, Alex. England. Contemporary

Savage and Ottinger. U.S. Active 1860s and after

Savolainen, Mikko. Contemporary

Savrasov, S. I. Russia. Active late 19th c.

Sawyer, J. R. Active Norwich, England, 19th c.

*Sawyers, Arthur. U.S. Contemporary

Sayce, B. J. 1837–95

Sayre, Nora. Active Cambridge, Mass., 20th c.

Sazo, Serge de. France. Active 20th c.

Scavullo, Francesco. U.S. 1929–

Schaarwächter, J. C. Active Berlin, ca. 1872–1900

Schaefer, John P. U.S. 1934–

*Schaeffer, Richard W. U.S. 1949–

Schaepman, C. J. J. Netherlands. Active 20th c.

Schalkwijk, Bob. Mexico. Contemporary

Schall, Johann Carl. Germany. 1805–85

Schall, Roger. France. Active 20th c.

Schamberg, Morton L. U.S. 1881–1918

Schapiro, Constantin. Active St. Petersburg, Russia, ca. 1870–85

Schapiro, Steve. U.S. Contemporary

Schardin, Hubert. 1902–66

Scharf, Otto. Germany. d. 1916

Scharfman, Herb. U.S. Contemporary

Schatz, Arthur. U.S. Contemporary

Schätz, Joseph Julius. Germany. Active 20th c.

*Scheer, Sherie. U.S. 1940–

Scheichenbauer, Franco. Contemporary

Scheidegger, Ernst. Switzerland. 1923–

Scheimpflug, Theodor. Austria. 1865–1911

Scheiner, Julius. Germany. 1858–1913

Scheler, Max. Germany. Active 20th c.

Schell, Sherril. 1877–1964. Active London (b. U.S.)

Schemboche, Michele. (b. France). Active Rome and Turin, Italy, 1871 and after

Schenk, Gustav. Germany. Active 20th c.

Schensky, Franz. 1871–1957

*Scherbatskoy, Serge A. Contemporary

Scherer, M. Germany. Active ca. 1880

Scherman, David. U.S. Active 20th c.

Scherman, Rowland. U.S. Contemporary

Schermerhorn, E. J. G. Java. Active 20th c.

Scherschel, Frank. U.S. Active 20th c.

Scherschel, Joe. U.S. Active 20th c.

Scheuerle, Joe. U.S. Active early 20th c.

Schiaparelli, Cesare. Italy. Active late 19th c.

Schieanul, Costache Sturdza. Romania. Active ca. 1852

Schieren, H. V. Active Montclair, N.J., 20th c.

*Schietinger, James. U.S. 1946–

Schild, Ewald. Austria. Active 20th c.

Schiller, Larry. U.S. Contemporary

Schiller, Robert M. U.S. Active 20th c.

*Schilling, Alfonse. U.S. Contemporary

Schirner, Max. Germany. 1891–1952

Schläpfer, Hans R. Switzerland. 1929–

Schlapper, Fee. Germany. Contemporary

Schlater, George Friedrich. 1804–70. Active Derpt (Tartu), Estonia

Schleinitz, Egon G. Germany. Active 20th c.

*Schlessinger, Peter. U.S. 1946–

Schlumberger, Ernst. Germany. Active 20th c.

Schmid, Carl. Active Basel, Switzerland, 20th c.

Schmid, Claus. Germany. Active 20th c.

Schmid, Hans Peter

Schmidt, C. Active Nuremberg, 19th c.

Schmidt, C. L. Germany. Active 20th c.

Schmidt, Ferdinand. Germany. Active ca. 1860–70

Schmidt, Henry A. 1861–1944

Schmidt, Michael. Germany. Contemporary

Schmückler, Oren. Germany. 1954–

Schnall, Ben. U.S. Active 20th c.

Schnebele, Walter. Germany. Active 20th c.

Schneeberger, Ad. Active Prague, 20th c.

Schneeberger, H. Active Paris, 20th c.

Schneeman, Carolee. U.S. Contemporary

Schneider, Elfe. Active 20th c.

Schneider, Jan O. 1814–62. Active Prague

Schneider, Martin. U.S. Active 20th c.

*Schneider, Robert. U.S. 1945–

Schneider, Roland. Switzerland. 1939–

*Schneider, Ted R., Jr. U.S. 1945–

Schneider, Ursula. U.S. (b. Germany). 1906–77

Schneiders, Toni. Germany. 1920–

Schnell, Fred. U.S. Contemporary

Schnitzer, Klaus. U.S. 1944–

Schoenfeld, Diana. U.S. 1949–

Schoepf, Hermann. Germany. Active 20th c.

Schoffers, Irm

Schokine, L. W. Russia. Active 20th c.

*Scholtz, Max. U.S. Contemporary

Schomer, Alberto. Spain. Contemporary

Schönbein, Christian Friedrich. Germany. 1799–1868

Schonewolf, H. W. Active Buffalo, 20th c.

*Schott, John. U.S. 1944–

Schrager, Victor. U.S. 1950–

Schraudenbach, Kurt. Germany. Active 20th c.

Schreiber, George Francis. 1803–92. Active Philadelphia (b. Germany)

Schreiber, George Francis, and Sons. Active Philadelphia, until 1920s

*Schreier, Michael. Canada (b. Austria). 1949–

*Schroeter, Rolf. Switzerland. 1932–

Schudel, Peter. Switzerland. 1942–

Schueter, F. J. Active Texas, early 20th c.

Schuh, Gotthard. Switzerland. 1898–1969

Schuh, Karl. d. 1865. Active Vienna

Schuitema, Hans. Netherlands. Active 20th c.

Schuitema, Paul. Netherlands. b. 1897

Schulerud, Gunnar. Active Trondheim, Norway, 20th c.

Schulke, Flip. U.S. Contemporary

*Schulman, Joseph M. U.S. Contemporary

Schultheis, Emil. Switzerland. 1913–

Schultz, Bruno. Active Berlin, 20th c.

Schultze, George. Active New York City, ca. 1885

Schulz, Carl. Active Derpt (Tartu), Estonia, 19th c.

Schulze, Alfred Otto-Wolfgang. *See* Wols

*Schulze, John. U.S. 1915–

Schumacher, Iwan. Switzerland. 1947–

Schumann and Sohn. Germany. Active ca. 1890

Schürmann, Walter. Active Winterthur, Switzerland, 20th c.

Schürmann, Wilhelm. Germany. 1946–

Schuster, Václav. Active Prague, 20th c.

Schutzer, Paul. U.S. Active 20th c. (deceased)

Schwachman, Irene. U.S. 1915–

Schwaebe. Active 20th c.

Schwarm, Larry. U.S. 1944–

Schwartz, Bern. U.S., England. d. 1978

Schwartz, C. Active Berlin, 19th c.

*Schwartz, Elliot. 1949–

Schwarz, Patricia. U.S. Contemporary

*Schweet, Shirley. U.S. 1920–

Schweikardt, Eric. Contemporary

Schweizer, Helmut. Germany. 1946–

Schwennicke, Fritz. Germany. Active 20th c.

Schwoiser, Ludwig. Active Zagreb, 19th c.

Scolik, S. Charles. 1854–1928

Scott, Dixon. England. Active 20th c.

Scott, Montague. Active Auckland, New Zealand, 1850s

Scott-Stewart, Dick. England. Contemporary

Scowen and Co. Ceylon. Active 1860s

Scurlock, Addison. 1883-1964. Active Washington, D.C.

Sealy, Edwin Percy. New Zealand (b. England). 1839-1903

Sealy, H. B. Active Wellington, New Zealand, ca. 1848

Seamans, Laurie. U.S. 1922-

Sears. Active California, ca. 1880

Sedgfield, Russell W. England. d. 1902. Active ca. 1842-72

Seeberger, Jean. France. Active early 20th c.

Seed, Brian. England. Contemporary

Seed, Suzanne Liddell. U.S. 1940-

Seeff, Norman. U.S. Contemporary

Seehausen, Gilbert. Active Chicago, 20th c.

*Seeley, J. U.S. Contemporary

Seeley, William Frederick. U.S. Contemporary

Seewald, Hannah. Germany. Active 20th c.

Seggern, Heinrich von. Germany. Active early 20th c.

Seghers, Carroll. U.S. Active 20th c.

Séguier, (Baron) Pierre-Armand. 1803-76

Segura, Víctor. Mexico. Contemporary

Seid, Eva. U.S. Contemporary

Seiden, Gustav. Active Budapest, 20th c.

Seidenberg, Jean. U.S. Contemporary

Seidenstücker, Friedrich. Germany. 1882-1966

Seidling, Clifford

Seiler, Herbert. Germany. Active 20th c.

Seitz, Sepp. U.S. 1946-

Sekaer, Peter. U.S. Active 20th c.

Seler-Sachs, Cäcilie. Germany. Active 20th c.

Sella, Vittorio. Italy. 1859-1943

Sellman, Ture. Sweden. 1888-1969

Selmer, H. Active Bergen, Norway, ca. 1870

Seltzer, Kathleen. U.S. Contemporary

*Semak, Michael. Canada. 1934-

Semond, Carl. Germany. Active 20th c.

Sempolinski, Leonard. Poland, b. 1902

Senn, Paul. Switzerland. 1901-53

Sennett, Tomas. U.S. 1941-

Sereny, Eva. Contemporary

*Sesto, Cameron. Contemporary

Sesto, Carl. U.S. 1945-

Seton, Charles. U.S. 1953-

Seuphor, Michel (F. L. Berckelaers). France. 1901-

*Seventy, Sylvia. U.S. 1947-

Sever, Jiři. Czechoslovakia. 1904-68

Severin, Kurt. U.S. Active 20th c.

Severn, Merlyn. England. Active 20th c.

Seymour, Barbara Kerr. England. Active 20th c.

Seymour, Maurice. Active Chicago, 20th c.

Shabacon, Charles. Canada. Active 20th c.

Shadbolt, Cecil Victor. England. 1859-92

Shadbolt, George. 1830-1901. England

Shaikhet, A. Russia. Active 20th c.

Shames, Stephen. U.S. 1947-

Shapiro, Konstantin. Active St. Petersburg, Russia, 19th c.

*Shapiro, Nancy. U.S. 1939-

Sharp, Joseph Henry. U.S. 1859-1953

Sharp, Vincent. Canada. 1937-

*Sharpe, Geraldine. U.S. 1929-

Shaw, Lauren. U.S. 1946-

Shaw, Mark. U.S. Contemporary (deceased)

Shaw, R. M. Active Paris, 20th c.

*Shaw, Robert. Contemporary

Shay, Arthur. U.S. Contemporary

Shea, Mike. U.S. Active 20th c.

Shearer, John. U.S. Contemporary

Sheeres, John W. Active Oceanport, N.J., 20th c.

Shepherd, Charles. India (b. England). 19th c.

Shere, Sam. U.S. 1905-

*Sheridan, Sonia Landy. U.S. 1925-

Sherman, Bob. U.S. Contemporary

Sherman, William Flagg. Active New York City, 20th c.

Sherring, R. V. West Indies. Active 1876-86

Shields, William Gordon. Active New York City, 20th c.

Shietinger, Jim. U.S. 1946-

Shimada, Kinsude. Japan. Active 20th c.

Shimotsusa, M. Active Tokyo, 20th c.

Shindo, T. K. Active Los Angeles, 20th c.

Shinoyama, Kishin. Japan. 1940-

*Shipman, Dru. U.S. 1942-

Shiraoka, Jun. Japan. 1944-

Shishkin, I. I. Russia. Active ca. 1870s

Shomabhai Artist. Active Bombay, 20th c.

Shook, Melissa. U.S. 1939-

Shore, Stephen. Active London, 20th c.

Shorey, William F. Active Baltimore, 19th c.

Shrader, R. Owen. Active Pasadena, Calif., 20th c.

Shrout, William C. U.S. Active 20th c.

Shterenberg, A. P. U.S.S.R. Active 20th c.

Shuman, (Dr.) Harry B. Active Boston, 20th c.

*Shuper, Kay. U.S. 1947-

*Shustak, Lawrence N. New Zealand (b. U.S.). 1926-

*Shuster, Edward. U.S. Contemporary

Shwachman, Irene. U.S. 1915-

Sibert, Serge. France. 1953-

Sidman (firm). U.S. Active 19th c.

Sidoli, Francesco. Active Rome and Piacenza, Italy

Siede, Michael. U.S. Contemporary

*Siegel, Stephen. Contemporary

Siembab, Carl. U.S. Contemporary

*Sievers, Edwin. U.S. 1932-

*Sikkema, Brent. U.S. 1948-

Silber, Mark. U.S. Contemporary

*Silberman, Bruce. U.S. 1953-

Silberstein, Maurice. Mexico. Contemporary

Silistrarianu, Corneliu. Active Bucharest, 20th c.

Silva, Meinel. Peru. Contemporary

Silva D'Avila, Antonio Carlos. Brazil. Contemporary

Silver, Walter. U.S. Contemporary

Silverstone, Marilyn. U.S. Contemporary

Silverthorne, Jeffrey. U.S. 1946-

Silvester, Hans. France. Contemporary

Silvestre, Louis. France. Active 20th c.

Simacourbe, Georges

Simart, Pierre-Charles. France. 1806–57

Simelli, Carlo Baldassare. Active Rome, 1850s–60s

Simenov, Simeon. Active Tryavna, Bulgaria, 1870s

Simmons, John Scott. Australia, New Zealand. Active 20th c.

Simon, Elizabeth Youngblood. U.S. Active 20th c.

*Simon, Lawrence. U.S. 1943–

*Simon, Michael. U.S. (b. Hungary). 1936–

*Simon, Peter. U.S. 1936–

Simon, Stella. b. 1878

Simonetti, Vera. Brazil. Contemporary

Simonyi, Antal. 1821–92. Active Pest, Hungary, ca. 1855

Simpson, (Dr.) B. India. Active ca. 1870

Simpson, George Wharton. 1825–80

Simpson, R. V. Australia, New Zealand. Active 20th c.

Simpson, William. 1823–99

Simqu, M. K. U.S. Contemporary

Sims, Thomas. Active Weston-super-Mare, England, 19th c.

Sinats, Andrejs. 1943–

Singleton, T. Channel Islands. Active 19th c.

Singley, B. L. U.S. Active late 19th c.

*Sinick, Gary. Contemporary

Sinigaglia. Active Padua, Venice, 19th c.

Sinkinson, Bertram. Active Stafford, England, 20th c.

*Sinsabaugh, Art. U.S. 1924–

Sipple, K. R. Active Buffalo, 20th c.

Sipprell, Clara. U.S. (b. Canada). ca. 1880–1975

Sirkis, Nancy. U.S. Contemporary

Sjöberg, Axel. Sweden. b. 1866

Sjöstedt, Ulf. Sweden. 1935–

Skadding, George. U.S. Active 20th c.

Skaife, Thomas. England. Active 19th c.

Skara, John. U.S. Active 20th c.

Skladanek, Clement (Klemens). Active Warsaw, 20th c.

*Skoff, Gail. U.S. 1949–

*Skoogfors, Leif. U.S. 1940–

Skoorikhin, A. V. U.S.S.R. Active 20th c.

Skowraneck. Poland. Active early 20th c.

Skutta, C. Active Vienna, 19th c.

Slade, Paul Stewart. U.S. d. 1979

Slawny, Wladyslaw. Poland. Active 20th c.

Slingsby, Robert. Active Lincoln, England, 19th c.

Sloan, J. D. U.S. Contemporary

*Slosberg, Ken. U.S. 1944–

*Smalley, Gayle. U.S. Contemporary

Smart, John. U.S. Contemporary

Smiley, Karen. U.S. Contemporary

Smillie, T. W. Active Washington, D.C., 19th c.

Smirkarov, Xenophont. Active Samokov, Bulgaria, 1871–81

Smit, K. H. Netherlands. Active 20th c.

Smith, A. G. Dew. England. Active late 19th c.

Smith, Bradley. U.S. Active 20th c.

Smith, C. Leeston. England. Active 20th c.

Smith, Edwin. England. 1912–71

Smith, Eleanor. Active San Diego, Calif., 20th c.

Smith, Erwin E. U.S. Active 20th c.

Smith, G. A. England. Active 20th c.

Smith, G. E. Kidder. U.S. Active 20th c.

Smith, Graham. England. 1947–

*Smith, Gregory. U.S. 1907–

Smith, Hamilton L. U.S. Active 19th c.

Smith, Ian. England. Active 20th c.

Smith, (Dr.) Julian. Active Melbourne, Australia, 20th c.

*Smith, June Marie. U.S. Contemporary

Smith, Kenneth Dudley. Active Staten Island, N.Y., 20th c.

Smith, Marian. Active New England, ca. 1900

*Smith, Mason Philip. U.S. 1933–

Smith, Michael A. U.S. 1942–

Smith, Ming. U.S. Contemporary

*Smith, Philip. U.S. 1939–

Smith, Ray. U.S. Contemporary

Smith, Samuel. England. Active 19th c.

*Smith, Stephen. U.S. Contemporary

Smith, (Rev.) Theophilus. Active Sheffield, England, ca. 1865

Smith, W. Morris. U.S. Active mid-19th c.

Smithson, Robert. U.S. 1938–

Smyth, Charles Piazzi. Great Britain. 1819–1900

Snelson, Kenneth. U.S. 1927–

Snitzer, Jim. U.S. 1951–

Snowdon (Antony Charles Robert Armstrong-Jones). England. 1930–

Snowden, John. U.S. Active 20th c.

*Snyder, John MacDonald. Contemporary

*Snyder, Leslie. Contemporary

Sochurek, Howard. U.S. Active 20th c.

Sokolsky, Melvin. Contemporary

Solar Calleja, Alejandro. Mexico. Contemporary

Soleil, Jean-Baptiste-François. France. 1798–1878

Sollet. France. Active late 19th c.

Solomon, Rosalind. U.S. 1930–

Solowinski, John Raymond. U.S. Active 20th c.

*Soluri, Tony. Contemporary

Sommer (Lord). England. Active ca. 1868

Sommer and Behles. Active Rome and Naples, 19th c.

Sommerer, Karl. Canada. Active 20th c.

*Sommese, Lanny. U.S. Contemporary

*Sonneman, Eve. U.S. 1946–

*Sonnier, Keith. U.S. 1941–

Sonrel, A. Active Boston, 1870s

Sorce, Wayne. U.S. 1946–

Sorgato. Active Bologna, 19th c.

Sosa, David. Mexico. Contemporary

Sougez, Emmanuel. France. 1889–1972

Sourbeer, Wayne. U.S. 1927–

Source, Wayne. U.S. 1946–

Southwell (firm). Active London, 19th c.

Souza, Al. U.S.

*Soverns, Wayne. Contemporary

Spahn, Boris. Germany. Active 20th c.

Sparks, Jack. U.S. Active 20th c.

*Sparks, Paul J. U.S. Contemporary

Sparling, Marcus. England. d. 1860

Speekhout, G. J. Netherlands. Active 20th c.

Speiser, Jean. U.S. Active 20th c.

Spelterini, Eduard. Switzerland. 1852–1931

Spence, John. U.S. 1943–

Spencer. Peru. Active 19th c.

Spencer, Charles S. Active Tauranga, New Zealand, 1880s
*Spencer, Ken. Contemporary
*Spencer, Michael. Canada. 1948–
Spencer, Terence. South Africa, England. Contemporary
Spiller, John. 1833–1921
Spiller, Willy. Switzerland. 1947–
*Spinski, Victor. U.S. Contemporary
Spithover, Joe. Active Rome, 1860s
*Spitzer, Neal. U.S. Contemporary
Spitzmuller. Active Paris, 20th c.
Sponner, Karl. Active Vienna, 20th c.
Spooner, F. Ed. Active New York City, early 20th c.
Sprague, Edward. U.S. Active ca. 1900
Springs, Alice. France (b. Austria). Contemporary
Spronz, Karoly. Active Budapest, 20th c.
*Sprout, Randy J. U.S. Contemporary
Spühler, Emil. Switzerland. 1910–
*Spuris, Egons. U.S.S.R. 1931–
Spurny, Miloslav. Contemporary
Spurr, Melbourne. U.S. Active 20th c.
Squier, P. F. Active East Pittsburgh, Pa., 20th c.
Squire, G. E. Peru. Active 19th c.
Sreznevskii, V. I. Active Moscow, 19th c.
Staal, J. G. Netherlands. Active 20th c.
Stacey, George. Active New York City, 19th c.
Stack, Richard. U.S. Contemporary
Stackelberg, Ebba. Active Tallinn, Estonia, late 19th c.
Staffeld, Bill. U.S. Contemporary
Stahl, Augusto. Brazil. Active ca. 1853
Ståhlberg, Karl Emil. Finland. 1862–1919
Staller, Eric. U.S. 1947–
*Stamm, Paul. U.S. Contemporary
Stampfer, Simon von. 1792–1864
Standl, Ivan. Active Zagreb, 19th c.
Stankowski, Anton. Germany. b. 1906
Stanton, H. B. T. Active London, 20th c.
Staples, Howard. U.S. Active 20th c.
Staples, John. England. Active 19th c.

Starbuck, Fletcher. Canada. Contemporary
Starck, Robert. U.S. 1945–
*Stark, Larry. U.S. 1940–
*Stark, Robert Voy. U.S. 1939–
Starr, Nina Howell. U.S. 1903–
*Starr, Ron. Contemporary
*Starr, Steve. Contemporary
Starzik, Albert. Active Zagreb, 20th c.
Stasov, S. I. Russia. Active early 20th c.
Staub, Christian. Switzerland. 1918–
Staub, Hans. Switzerland. b. 1894
Stauder, Hermann. Switzerland. 1887–1949
Steadry, Rick. U.S. Contemporary
Stebbins, Nathaniel L. 1874–1922. Active Boston
Steele, Thomas Sedgwick. b. 1845. Active Hartford
Steen, Ricardo van. Brazil. Contemporary
*Steenerson, Mark. U.S. 1941–
Stefani, Bruno. Active Milan, 20th c.
Steffen, Don Carl. U.S. Contemporary
*Steffen, Fred W. U.S. 1931–
Steigenberger, J. Germany. Active 1870s
Steiger, Carla. Contemporary
*Stein, Bernard M. U.S. 1929–
*Stein, Harvey. U.S. Contemporary
Stein, Jacob. Peru. Active ca. 1852
Stein, Sally Ann. U.S. Contemporary
Steinberg, Robert J. U.S. 1948–
Steinberg, Ron. U.S. Contemporary
Steinberg, Saul. U.S. 1914–
Steiner, Albert. Switzerland. 1877–1965
Steinert, Otto. Germany. 1915–78
*Steinhauser, Judith H. U.S. Contemporary
Steinheil, Carl August von. Germany. 1801–70
Steinheimer, Charles. U.S. Active 20th c.
Steinhoff, Ilse. Germany. Active 20th c.
Steinmetz. U.S. Active 20th c.
Steinmetz, Richard A. U.S. 1947–
Stellman, Louis J. U.S. Active 20th c.
Steltser, Ulli. Germany. 1923–
Stenger, Erich. Germany. 1878–1957

Stepan, Bohumil. Czechoslovakia. Contemporary
Stephanian, Charles T. Contemporary
Stephany, Jaromir. U.S. Contemporary
Stephens, Nicholas M. U.S. Active 20th c.
Stephenson, J. W. Active Oregon, 20th c.
*Sterling, Joseph. U.S. Contemporary
Stern, Ed. U.S. Contemporary
*Stern, Irvin, Jr. U.S. 1923–
Stern, Marilyn. U.S. Contemporary
Stern, Phil. U.S. Active 20th c.
Sternberg, Robert von. 1939–
Sternberger, Marcel. U.S. Active 20th c.
*Stevens, Jon Ellis. U.S. 1944–
Stevens, Joseph Earle. Active ca. 1890s
Stevens, Roy. U.S. Active 20th c.
Stevenson, Lionel. Canada. Active 20th c.
Stevenson, W. England. Active ca. 1866
*Stewart, Doug. U.S. Contemporary
Stewart, John. Active Pau, France, 1850s
Stewart, John. England. 1919–
Stiasni, Anton. Croatia. Active 19th c.
Stick, John C. Active Los Angeles, 20th c.
*Stiebel, Manfred. Germany. 1935–
*Stieglitz, Mary. Contemporary
Stieneker, J. W. Netherlands. Active 20th c.
Stillfried and Anderson. Japan. Active 1870s–80s
Stillman, William James. U.S. 1828–1901. Also active Europe
*Stiltz, Thomas Charles. U.S. Contemporary
Stirling, Edmund. U.S. Active early 20th c.
Stirling-Maxwell, (Sir) William. Scotland. 1818–78
*Stock, Dennis. U.S. 1928–
Stoddard, John T. Active Northampton, Mass., ca. 1887
Stoddard, Senecca Roy. Active Glens Falls, N.Y., 1870–1915
Stokes, J. Active Ipswich, England, 1850s
Stokes, Telfer. U.S. Contemporary
Stoklas, Franjo, and Stockmann, Nikola. Active Vienna and Zagreb, 19th c.

Stoller, Ezra. U.S. 1915–

Stone, Clive. New Zealand. 1950–

Stone, Erika. U.S. Contemporary

*Stone, Jim. U.S. 1947–

*Stone, Michael. U.S. 1945–

Stone, Sasha. Active Brussels (b. Germany), 20th c.

Stout, Ernie. U.S. Active 20th c.

Stoy, Werner. U.S. Contemporary

Strache, Wolf. Germany. 1910–

Strahl, Marion. U.S. Active 20th c.

*Straka, Ron. U.S. 1935–

Strandberg, Wilhelm. Finland. 1829–97

Strasser, Alex. Germany. Active 20th c.

Strasz, Maksymilian. Poland. Active 19th c.

*Strauss, Irene. Contemporary

Straussas, A. 1834–96. Active Vilnius, Lithuania

Strecker, Ignac. Hungary. Active 19th c.

*Streetman, Evon. U.S. 1932–

Strelechi, Jean de. Active Paris, early 20th c.

Streliaev, Leonid. Brazil. Contemporary

Strelisky, Lipót. Active Pest, Hungary, 19th c.

Strelow, Liselotte. Germany. Active 20th c.

Strempel, Karl. Austria. Active ca. 1900

Strock, George. U.S. Active 20th c.

Strohmeyer and Weyman. U.S. Active late 19th c.

Stromberg, Bruce. U.S. 1944–

*Stromsten, Amy. U.S. Contemporary

Stuart, J. Active Inverness, Scotland, 19th c.

Stuart, Maryland. U.S. Active 20th c.

Stuart-Wortley, A. H. P. 1832–90

Stubenrauch, Bob. U.S. Active 20th c.

Stubna, Anton. Contemporary

Stuck, Franz von. Germany. 1863–1928

*Stuler, Jack. U.S. 1932–

Stupa, György. Hungary. Active ca. 1850

Sturdevant, E. K. Active San Antonio, Tex., 1880s

*Sturr, Edward R. U.S. 1937–

Sturtevant, Roger. U.S. b. 1903

*Stussy, Jan. U.S. 1921–

Styles, A. F. Active Burlington, Vt., ca. 1860s–70s

Styrsky, Jindrich. Czechoslovakia. 1899–1942

Suchy, Karl. Active Vienna, 20th c.

*Sudre, Jean-Pierre. France. 1921–

Sugimoto, Hiroshi. U.S. Contemporary

Sulcs, C. Latvia (b. Germany). Active 19th c.

Sulke, Rudolf. Active Vienna, 20th c.

Sulla, Drahotin

Sullivan, Mark. U.S. Contemporary

*Sultan, Larry. U.S. Contemporary

Sumits, William J. U.S. (b. England). Active 20th c.

Sunami, Soichi. 1885–1971

*Sundance, Erik. Contemporary

Sundgren, Gunnar. Sweden. b. 1901

Surdam and White. Active New York City, 19th c.

Suris, Sherry. U.S. 1944–

Suschitzky, W. England. Active 20th c.

Suscipi (Suscipj), Lorenzo. Active Rome, 1850s

Sussman, Leonard. U.S. 1947–

Sutu, Jon. Romania. Active 20th c.

Suzukawa, George. U.S. Contemporary

Suzuki, Laquan S. Active New York City, 20th c.

Svendsen, Karina E. Norway. 1939–

Svoboda, A. Active Asia. 19th c.

Swain, George P. Active East Orange, N.J., 20th c.

Swan, Boris de. Mexico. Contemporary

Swan, George Henry. New Zealand (b. England). 1833–1913. Active 1863–70

Swan, (Sir) Joseph Wilson. 1828–1914. Active Newcastle, England

Swank, Luke. U.S. b. ca. 1890

Swanson, Richard. U.S. Contemporary

*Swartz, Joel. U.S. 1944–

Swatko, Juliana. U.S. Contemporary

*Swedlund, Charles. U.S. Contemporary

Sweetman, Alex. U.S. Contemporary

Sweikowskis, Albertas. Active Vilnius, Lithuania, 19th c.

Swistcheff-Paola, N. J. Active Moscow, 20th c.

Switkowski, Jan. Poland. 1876–1942

Switzer, (Dr.) B. W. India. Active ca. 1870

Swope, John. U.S. d. 1979

Swope, Martha. U.S. Contemporary

Syed, Asad K. Active Palanpur, India, 20th c.

Sykes, Homer. England. 1949–

Symes, Christopher and John. England. Active 20th c.

Symonds, C. P. Active Lisbon, 19th c.

Synge, John Millington. Ireland. 1871–1909.

Syrosahl, Will. U.S. Active 20th c.

Syrus, Napoleon. Active London (b. France), 19th c.

Szabo, Lajos. Active Budapest, 20th c.

Szabo, Steve. U.S. 1940–

Szacinski, Ludwik. Norway. 1844–94.

Szarkowski, John. U.S. 1925–

Szasz, Suzanne. U.S. Contemporary

Szàthmari, Carol Popp (de). Romania (also the Crimea). Active 19th c.

Szczuka, Mieczyslaw. Poland. 1898–1927

Szekely, (Dr.) György. Active Vienna and Budapest, 20th c.

Szilasi, Gabor. Canada. Contemporary

Szollosy, Kalman. Active Bucharest and Budapest, ca. 1900

Szubert, Awit. Poland. b. 1837

Szweycer, Michal. Poland. 1809–71

Tabard, Maurice. France. b. 1897. Also active U.S.

Taber, Isaiah West. U.S. 1830–1912

Taconis, Kryn. Netherlands. Contemporary

Taeschler, Johann-Baptiste. Switzerland. 1805–66

Taeschler, Josef-Ludwig. Switzerland. 1846–1924

*Taft, Wes. Contemporary

*Tagliaferro, Aldo B. Italy. 1936–

Tairraz and *Cie.* Active Chamonix, France. 19th c.

Tajiri, Shinkichi. U.S. 1923–

Takamatsu, Jiro. Japan. 1936–

Takanashi, Yutaka. Japan. 1935–

Talbot. Active ca. 1900

Tames, George. U.S. Active 20th c.

Tamms, Friedrich. Germany. Active 20th c.

Tamura, Shigeru. Japan

Tanaka, Chotoku. Contemporary

Tane, Vito Domburi-Bar. U.S. Contemporary

Tanner, (Capt.) H. C. B. Active India, ca. 1870

Tanner, Robert C. U.S. Contemporary

Tanqueray, Paul. England. Active 20th c.

Tanuma, Takeyoshi. U.S. Contemporary

Tappe, Horst. Switzerland. Contemporary

Tarango, Harvey. U.S. Contemporary

Tardy, Georges. Active Nevers, France, 20th c.

Tas, Filip. Belgium (b. England). 1918–

*Tatlock, Hugh. U.S. 1912–

Tatsugi, S. Japan. Active 20th c.

Taunt, Henry. 1842–1922. Active Oxford, England

Taupenot, J. M. France. 1824–56

Taupin and Co. France. Active ca. 1860s–70s

Tauran, Paul. Netherlands. Contemporary

*Taussig, H. Arthur. U.S. 1941–

*Tavenner, Pat. U.S. Active 20th c.

Taylor, A. and G. England. Active 19th c.

Taylor, A. S., Jr. Active New York City, 19th c.

Taylor, (Capt.) C. C. Active India, ca. 1870

Taylor, Mrs. Cecil. Active New York City, 20th c.

Taylor, Harold Dennis. 1862–1943

Taylor, Jeremy. Canada. 1938–

Taylor, John C. U.S. Active late 19th c.

Taylor, John Wilson. U.S. d. 1918

*Taylor, Randy. Contemporary

Taylor, Will F. England. Active 20th c.

Taylor and Lamson. Active New York City, 19th c.

Tchan Fon-li. Contemporary

Teisseire, Louis. Active Bordeaux, 20th c.

Teixeira, Evandro. Brazil. Contemporary

Telberg, Val. Switzerland. Contemporary

*Téllez, Eugenio. Chile. 1939–

Téllez-Girón López, Roberto. Mexico. Contemporary

Téllez Sánchez, David. Mexico. Contemporary

Temmler, Heinz. Germany. Active 20th c.

Tenney, Gordon. U.S. Active 20th c.

Terayama, Shuji. Japan. Contemporary

Terekhov, I. A. Russia. Active 19th c.

*Teres, Michael Jerome. U.S. 1940–

Terreros. Active Peru, 19th c.

Terry, Arturo. Peru. Active 1848–52

*Terry, John. Contemporary

Tessié du Motay, Charles-Marie. France. d. 1880

Testa, A. Active Genoa, Italy, 20th c.

*Testa, Ron. U.S. 1942–

Testonji, R. D. Active Bombay, 20th c.

Teynard, Félix. 1817–92. Active Egypt (b. France), 1851–52

*Thatcher, Richard. U.S. 1946–

Thayer, Bert Clark. U.S. Active 20th c.

Thege, Miklós Konkoly. Hungary. 1842–1916

Théret, Hélène. France. Contemporary

Thiel, Charles. U.S. Active 20th c.

Thiele, Rheinhold. England, Germany. Active ca. 1900

Thielemann, Anton. Germany. Active 20th c.

*Thomas, George. Contemporary

Thomas, Gwenn. U.S. Contemporary

Thomas, Lew. U.S. 1932–

Thomas, Peter. Canada. Active 20th c.

Thompson, A. R. England. Active 20th c.

Thompson, C. Thurston. d. 1867

Thompson, F. F. Active Canandaigua, N.Y., 19th c.

*Thompson, Jerry. U.S. 1945–

Thompson, Octavius. b. 1864. Active Toronto

Thompson, Peter Hunt. U.S. Contemporary

Thompson, Ted. U.S. 1948–

Thompson, William. England. Active 19th c.

Thompson, William H. Active Hartford, early 20th c.

Thoms, William John. England. 1803–85

Thöne, A. A. Netherlands. Active 20th c.

Thorbecke, Ellen. China (b. Netherlands). Active 20th c.

Thorek, Max. U.S. Active 20th c.

Thorlichen, Gustav. Argentina. Active 20th c.

*Thorne, Edwin, Jr. Contemporary

Thorne, G. W. Active New York City, 19th c.

Thurston, Jacqueline. U.S. 1939–

Thwing, Walter E. U.S. Active 20th c.

Tibaut, Raymond. Active Brussels, 20th c.

*Tichy, Frank. U.S. 1924–

*Tichy, Rose. U.S. 1924–

Tiedge, Janos. Hungary. Active ca. 1853

Tiefbruner, Sandor. Active Sopron, Hungary, 1862–75

Tiemann, H. N. U.S. Active 20th c.

Tiidermann, Heinrich. Estonia. 1863–1904

*Tilson, Joe. England. 1928–

Timberman, Elizabeth. U.S. Active 20th c.

Timiryazev, Kliment Arkad'evich. Russia. 1843–1920

Tingley, George E. 1864–1958. Active Connecticut

Tinnib, Carlos. Peru. Active 19th c.

Tipton, W. H. U.S. Active mid-19th c.

Tissandier, Gaston. France. 1843–99

Title, Robert. Canada. Active 20th c.

Toan, Do Van. New Zealand. 1946–

Tohmatsu, Shohmei. Japan. 1930–

Tolmer, Claude. France. Active 20th c.

Tomescu, (Ing.) N. N. Romania. Active 20th c.

*Tomiyama, Haruo. Japan. 1936–

Tomkins, Judy. U.S. Contemporary

Tömöry, Francois. Croatia. Active 19th c.

Tomzak, Anne. U.S. Contemporary

Tönnies, Heinrich. Active Aalborg, Denmark, ca. 1864–1902

Tooming, Peter. Czechoslovakia. Contemporary

Topley. Active Ottawa, late 19th c.

Torbert, Stephanie B. Contemporary

Torre, Iginio. Active Genoa, 20th c.
Torvbraten, Steiner
Toscani, Oliviero. 1942–
*Toth, Carl. U.S. 1947–
Tott, Heinrich. Active Zurich, 20th c.
Tournachon, Adrien. France. b. 1825
Tournachon, Paul. *See* Nadar, Paul
Tournay, J. Monaco. Active 20th c.
Tournier, H. France. Active 19th c.
Tourtin, Emile. France. Active mid-19th c.
Toutain, Pierre. Contemporary
Towers, Bob. U.S. Contemporary
Towler, John. 1811–89. Active Geneva, N.Y.
Trachman, Michail. U.S.S.R. 1918–
Traeger, Ronald. U.S. 1937–68
*Tranter, Carol. Contemporary
Trasmallo, César. Mexico. Contemporary
Trasov, Vincent. Canada. Active 20th c.
*Traub, Charles H. U.S. 1945–
*Traube, Alex. U.S. 1946–
Traube, Arthur. 1878–1948
Trauzettel, Helmut. Germany. Active 20th c.
Travers, William Thomas Locke. 1819–1903. Active New Zealand (b. Ireland), 1850–1903
Travnik, Juan. Argentina. Contemporary
Trebitsch, Rudolf. Germany. Active ca. 1900
Trejo Zúñiga, Víctor Manuel. Mexico. Contemporary
Tremaux, Pierre. Active Sudan, ca. 1855
Trepte, E. Germany. Active 20th c.
Tress, Dawn Mitchell. U.S. Contemporary
Tretick, Stanley. U.S. Contemporary
Treufeldt, Aadu. Estonia. 1874–1956
Trevor, Paul. England. 1952–
*Trimble, Michael. U.S. 1945–
Triolo, Tony. U.S. Contemporary
Tripp, T. Harvey. U.S. Active 20th c.
Tristram, H. B. England. Active ca. 1880s
Tritschler, Alfred. Germany. Active 20th c.
Troch, Bernhard. Germany. Active ca. 1900

Troth, H. Active 19th c.
Troup, Henry. U.S. Contemporary
Trow, Susan. Canada. 1946–
*Truax, Karen. U.S. 1946–
Trudeau, Harold. U.S. Active 20th c.
Truelsen, William. Active Copenhagen, 20th c.
Trueman and Caple. Canada. Active ca. 1880–1900
Trustrum, Noel. New Zealand. 1950–
Tsuchida, Hiromi. Japan. 1939–
Tsukahara, Takuya. Contemporary
Tsukane, T. K. U.S. Active 20th c.
Tubbs, G. L. Active Geneva, N.Y., 19th c.
Tucker, Clarence W. Active California, 20th c.
Tucker, (Mrs.) H. A. England. Active 1840s
Tuckerman, Jane. *See* Foley, Jane Tuckerman
Tuck Tai. China. Active ca. 1885
Tuggener, Jacob. Switzerland. 1904–
Tulinov, M. Active Moscow, 19th c.
Tumanov, S. B. Russia. Active Transbaikalia, 19th c.
Tuminello, Ludovico. 1824–1907. Active Rome, 1842–49 and after 1869; Turin, 1849–69
Tunney. Active Edinburgh, 1870s
Turnbull, R. F. Active New York City, late 19th c.
Turner, Austin A. U.S. Active 19th c.
Turner, Benjamin Bracknell. England. 1815–94
Turner, John B. New Zealand. 1943–
Turner, Judith. U.S. Contemporary
Turner, Pete. U.S. 1934–
Turner, Peter. England. 1947–
*Turnquist, Trudy. U.S. 1946–
Turpin, Earle. Active South Carolina, 19th c.
Turpin, Gilles. France. 1948–
Turqueti, Roger
Twardzicki, Walery. Active Warsaw, 19th c.
Tweedie, Merlyn. New Zealand. 1953–
*Tweedy-Holmes, Karen. U.S. 1942–
Tyree, Frederick. b. 1867. Active Nelson and Takaka, New Zealand (b. England), 1880s–1906

Tyree, William. Active Nelson, New Zealand (b. Australia), late 19th c.
Tyson, C. J. Active Gettysburg, Pa., 19th c.
Tyson, Elizabeth R. Active Boston, ca. 1900

Ubac, Raoul. Belgium. 1910–
Uchatius, (Baron) Franz von. Austria-Hungary. 1811–81
Udo, Mils. Germany. 1937–
Ueda, Shoji. 1913–
Uematsu, Keiki. Japan. Contemporary
Ufer, Oswald. Active Rome (b. Germany), 1860s–70s
Ugarte, F. Peru. Active 19th c.
Uhle, Max. Peru. Active 19th c.
Uhrboom, Odd. Sweden. 1941–
Uhrbrock, Donald C. U.S. Contemporary
Ulitine, W. J. Active Moscow, 20th c.
*Ulrich, David A. U.S. 1950–
Ulyatt, Trevor. New Zealand. 1947–
Underwood, William Lyman. b. U.S. Active New England; New Orleans; Florida Keys; the Bahamas; ca. 1900
*Unger, Sam. Contemporary
Ungern-Sternberg, (Baron) Theodor. Estonia. Active late 19th c.
Unpiao, Khu. Philippine Islands. Active 20th c.
Unsworth, Colin J. Active Manchester, England, 20th c.
Unterberger, Fr. Austria. Active ca. 1870
Unwalla, J. N. Active Bombay, 20th c.
Unwin, Herbert John. Canada. Active early 20th c.
*Upton, John D. U.S. 1932–
Urban, Aristeau Joâo. Brazil. Contemporary
Urbina. Peru. Active ca. 1896
Urie. Active Glasgow, 19th c.
Ustinov, Alexander. U.S.S.R. 1909–

Vaccaro, Tony. Italy. Active 20th c.
*Vácha, Pavel. Czechoslovakia. 1940–
Vacquerie, Auguste. France. 1819–95

Vadas, Erno. Active Budapest, 20th c.

Vail, Floyd. Active New York City, 20th c.

*Vail, Roger. U.S. Contemporary

*Valastro, S. C. U.S. 1922–

Valdés, Hermanos. Peru. Active 19th c.

Valent, Ferdinand. Contemporary

Valenta, Cenek. Czechoslovakia. Active 20th c.

Valente, Alfred. Active 20th c.

Valenziani, Enrico. 1842–1906. Active Rome, 1870s–80s

Vales, Roman. Active Maribor, Yugoslavia, 20th c.

Vallarino, Vincent. U.S. 1953–

Valle, Angel del. U.S. Contemporary

Valle, Arturo. Italy. Active 20th c.

Vallestro, S. C. U.S. Contemporary

Vallou de Villeneuve, Julien. France. 1795–1866

Vålme, Rein. Sweden. 1936–

Van Anda, George H. U.S. Active 20th c.

Van Blarcum, Artie. U.S. 1925–

Van Borselen, W. J. Netherlands. Active 20th c.

Vandamm, Florence. U.S. Active early 20th c.

Van Degryse, Claude. 1940–

*Vanderbilt, Paul. U.S. 1905–

Vanderpant, John. 1884–1939. Active Vancouver, 1919–39

Van der Veen, Eddie. France. Contemporary

*Van Der Vegt, R. L. U.S. Contemporary

Van Der Weyde, Henry. Active London, 1890s

*Van Dyke, Peter. U.S. 1944–

Van Elk, Ger. Contemporary

*Van Heydenreich, Richard. U.S. Contemporary

Van Lint, J. E. Active Pisa, Florence, 1860s–80s

Van Moerkerken, E. Netherlands. Active 20th c.

Vanneste, Leon. Contemporary

Van Oosten, H. A. Canada (b. Netherlands). 1948–

Van Pelt, Richard. Contemporary

Van Sickle, Kenneth R. U.S. Contemporary

Van Sprang, Alfred. Active the Far East, 20th c.

Van Uffel, Francis. Belgium. 1949–

Van Vechten, Carl. U.S. 1880–1964

Van Zel, Oscar. Active 19th c.

Varga, Gjuro. Active Zagreb, 19th c.

Vargas, David. Peru. Active 19th c.

Vargas, Max T. Peru. Active 19th c.

Vargas Basánez, Rubén. Mexico. Contemporary

Vasari, Cesare. b. 1847. Active Rome

Vaslot, Edmond. Active Cherbourg, France, 20th c.

Vásquez, Pedro. Contemporary

Vassos, John. U.S. 1898–

Vater, Regina. Brazil. Contemporary

*Vaughan, Caroline. U.S. Contemporary

Vaughn. Peru. Active 19th c.

Vavrek, Vladimir. Contemporary

Vázquez, Ignacio. Mexico. Contemporary

Vázquez Báeza, Eduardo. Mexico. Contemporary

Vázquez Enríquez, Augusto. Mexico. Contemporary

Vázquez Orozco, Gustavo. U.S. Contemporary

Vecsenyi, Istvan. Active Budapest, 20th c.

Velarde, Bartolomé. Peru. Active ca. 1860

Velhu, Luiz Carlos. Brazil. Contemporary

Vencill, Truman. U.S. Active 20th c.

Venkatesh. India. Active 20th c.

Ventosa, (Comte) de la. Active Madrid, 20th c.

Venturini. Active Rome, 20th c.

Vera, Francisco. Argentina. Active 20th c.

Verboom, P. Netherlands. Active 20th c.

Verburg, Joann. U.S. Contemporary

Vercheval, Georges. Belgium. 1934–

Veress, Ferenc. 1832–1916. Active Cluj, Hungary, 1860–80

Verger, Pierre. Contemporary

Vermeylen, Edmond. France. Active 20th c.

Vermosen, Gaston. Netherlands. 1942–

Verne, Jules. France. 1828–1905

Vernet, Horace. France. 1789–1863

Vernon. Active London, 20th c.

Vernouille, Leopold S. Active Vienna, 20th c.

Veronesi, Luigi. Italy. 1908–

Verzaschi, Enrico. Active Rome, 19th c.

Vesteli, E. Active Tiflis, Russia, 1880s

Vetter, Leo. Active Zagreb, 19th c.

Viancini Asta, Mario. Mexico. Contemporary

Victoire. Active Lyons, France, late 19th c.

*Victoria, Theodosius. U.S. 1944–

Vidal, Léon. France. ca. 1833–1906

Vidyavrata. India. Active 20th c.

Vieira, Valerio. Brazil. 1862–1941

Vigier (Vicomte). France. Active 19th c.

Vigneau, André. France. 1892–1965

Vignes, (Lt.) L. Active the Red Sea (b. France), 1860s

Vignes, Michel. Contemporary

Vignoles, Charles. England. 1793–1875

Vilanger, Ica. Germany

Vilet, Jacques. France. Contemporary

Villalba, Ricardo. Peru. Active 19th c.

Villalobos, A. G. Peru. Active 19th c.

Villecholles, François de. See Franck

Villers, André. France. 1930–

Villet, Grey. U.S. Active 20th c.

Viñas, Julio. Peru. Active 19th c.

Vinet, Pierre. Canada. 1940–

Vink, John. Belgium. 1948–

Viollet, Roger. France. Active 20th c.

Virzikovskis, L. Latvia (b. Poland). Active 19th c.

Visinskis, P. Lithuania. Active 19th c.

*Viskupic, Gary A. U.S. 1944–

Vittet, Daniel. Switzerland. 1943–

Vivian, Graham. England. Active 1850s–60s

Vogel, Hermann Wilhelm. Germany. 1834–98

Vogt, Christian. Switzerland. 1946–

Voigtländer, Peter Friedrich. Germany. 1812–78

Vollum, E. P. Active California, ca. 1859

*Von dem Bussche, Wolfe. U.S. (b. Germany). 1934–

*Von Sternberg, Robert. 1939–

Von Wichert, Tom. Germany. Active 20th c.

Vorisek, (Ing.) Jos. Active Prague, 20th c.

Vorobeichic, M. Active 20th c.

Vos, Martin. Active 20th c.

Vosta, Cenek. Czechoslovakia. Active 20th c.

Voutta, Klaus-Peter. Germany. Contemporary

Vroom, Richard. Canada. Contemporary

Vuillard, Jean Edouard. France. 1868–1940

*Wade, Bob. U.S. 1943–

Wadia, D. R. D. Active Bombay, 20th c.

Wagenaar, G. A. W. Netherlands. Active 20th c.

Wagner, Catherine. U.S. Contemporary

Wahlberg, Arne. Sweden. 1905–

Waite, C. B. Mexico (b. U.S.). Active 1900–10

Wakae, Kanjii. Japan. 1944–

Wakefield, Hy. U.S. Active 20th c.

Wakely, Edwin Nelson. Active Connecticut, 1885–1915

Wakely, George D. Active the Rocky Mountains, 1860s

Walburn, Arthur. Active Devon, England, 20th c.

Waldack, Charles. Active Cincinnati, 19th c.

Waldmüller and Muche. Active Bolzano, Austria, ca. 1910

Waldorf, Joe. England. Active 20th c.

Waldvogel, Fred. Switzerland. 1922–

Walery (Stanislaw Ostroróg). Active Paris (b. Poland), 19th c.

Walker, H. G. U.S. Active 20th c.

Walker, Melanie. U.S. Contemporary

Walker, Ron. U.S. (b. England). 1947–

Walker, Samuel A. Active London, 19th c.

Walker, W., and Sons. Active London, 19th c.

Walker, William. Active London, ca. 1865

Wall, E. J. England. Active early 20th c.

Wall, Herman V. U.S. Active 20th c.

Wallace, Bob. U.S. Active 20th c.

Wallace, J. Laurie. U.S. (b. Ireland). 1864–1934

*Wallace, Larry L. Contemporary

*Wallis, Helen. U.S. Contemporary

Walsh, John. Australia. Contemporary

Walters, Day. U.S. Contemporary

Walther, Hedda. Germany. Active 20th c.

Walusinski

Walzl, Richard. Active Baltimore, 19th c.

Wanamaker, Lewis Rodman. U.S. 1863–1928

Wane, Marshall. Active Edinburgh, 19th c.

*Wang, Sam. U.S. Contemporary

*Wang, Wayne. U.S. Contemporary

Wangenheim, Wolfgang von. Germany. Contemporary

Wanski, Tadeusz. Active Poznan, Poland, 20th c.

Ward, Fred. U.S. Contemporary

Ward, Patrick. England. Contemporary

*Ward, Richard. U.S. 1943–

Ward, William. U.S. Active 20th c.

Wardak, Jerzy. Contemporary

Ward and *Ca*. Peru. Active 1847–48

Wardenaer, Thorleif. Active Oslo, 20th c.

Warnecke, William. U.S. 1881–1939

Warner, W. Harding, and Co. Active Bristol, England, late 19th c.

Warnerke, Leon. 1837–1900

Warnod. France. Active 19th c.

Warren, F. L. England. Active 1850s

Warren, G. K. Active Boston, 1860s

Warren, H. F. U.S. Active ca. 1865

Warren, John. Active 19th c.

Warren, William. U.S. Contemporary

*Warrington, Ann. *See* *Wills, Ann Warrington

Washburn, Bradford. U.S. 1910–

Wasser, Julien. U.S. Contemporary

*Wasserman, Cary. U.S. 1939–

Watabe, Yukichi. Japan. Active 20th c.

Watanabe, Yoshio. Japan. 1907–

Waterhouse, James John. 1842–1922

Waters, R. J. Active California, 19th c.

Wathen, Ted. Contemporary

Watkins, Charles. England. Active ca. 1860

Watkins, Herbert. Active London, ca. 1860

Watkins, John. England. Active 1850s

Watkins, Margaret. Active New York City, 20th c.

Watson, A. Active Philadelphia, 19th c.

*Watts, Robert. Contemporary

Wayman, Stan. U.S. Contemporary (deceased)

Weaver, Peter S. Active Hanover, Pa., 19th c.

Webb, Alex. U.S. Contemporary

Webb, G., and Son. England. Active 19th c.

Webb, John. England. 1950–

Webb, Todd. U.S. 1905–

Weber, Al. U.S. 1930–

Weber, Alfons. U.S. Active Chicago, 20th c.

Weber, Harvey A. U.S. Active 20th c.

Weber, Wilson. Brazil. Contemporary

Weckel, Virginia Field. U.S. Active 20th c.

Weddell, Ralph R. Active Shelton, Conn., 20th c.

Wedge, James. England

*Weege, William. U.S. 1935–

Weeks, Daniel K. U.S. 1952–

Weil, Emanuel M. U.S. Active 20th c.

Weil, Mathilde. U.S. Active early 20th c.

Weil, Susan. U.S. Contemporary

Weinberg, A. S. Active Groningen, Netherlands, 20th c.

Weiner, Dan. U.S. 1919–59

*Weir, John Spence. U.S. 1930–

*Weir, Thomas

Weisbrot, Michael. U.S. Contemporary

Weismann, Lawrence. Canada. Active 20th c.

Weiss, Eva. U.S. Contemporary

*Weiss, John. U.S. Contemporary

Weiss, William, and Co. Bermuda. Active early 20th c.

Weissman, Lawrence. Canada. Active 20th c.

Welbland, Sean. England.

Weld, George F. U.S. Active 20th c.

Welinder, Edvard. Sweden. 1901–59

Weller, Peter. Germany. Active 20th c.

Weller, Sam. Active London, 20th c.

*Wells, Alice (Alisa Wells; Alice Andrews). U.S. 1929–

Welsch, Ulrike. U.S. (b. Germany). 1940–

Welzel, Otto. Germany. Active 20th c.

Wendler, Rudolph. Active Graz, Austria, 20th c.

Wenger, Jane. U.S. Contemporary

Wenner, L. France. Active 20th c.

Wentworth, Bertrand H. U.S. Active ca. 1900

*Wenzel, Ann. Contemporary

Werner, A. Active late 19th c.

Werner, Karolina. Active Budapest, ca. 1858

Werner, Louis, Jr. Active New York City, 20th c.

*Wernick, Sam. U.S. Contemporary

Wertoff, Dsiga. Active 20th c.

Wesner, H. B. Active California, early 20th c.

Wesney, Len. New Zealand. 1946–

Westendarp Galofre, Jorge. Mexico. Contemporary

Westerlund, Jan Olav. Sweden. Contemporary

Westerveld, H. F. P. Netherlands. Active 20th c.

Westman, Tony. Canada (b. U.S.). 1946–

Weston, Bruce. Canada. Active 20th c.

Weston, Chandler. U.S. Active 20th c.

Weston, Delight. Active Blue Hill, Maine, 20th c.

Weston, Theodore. 1911–

Westra, Ans. New Zealand (b. Netherlands). 1936–

*Wexler, Joan. Contemporary

Wey, Francis. 1812–82

Weyermann, Hans. Switzerland. 1941–

*Wheatley, Duncan. U.S. Contemporary

Wheatstone, (Sir) Charles. England. 1802–75

Wheeler, Edmund. 1800–77. Active Christchurch, New Zealand, 1863 and after

Wheeler, Robert. U.S. Active 20th c.

Wheeler and Barton. Active Boston, 19th c.

Wheeler and Son. New Zealand. Active 19th c.

Whipple, George Mathews. U.S. 1842–93

Whipple, John Adams. U.S. 1822–91

Whistler, John. England. 1830–97

White, Frank. U.S. Contemporary

White, Franklin. Active Lancaster, N.H., ca. 1858–68

White, H. C. Active China, 19th c.

White, Henry. England. 1819–1903

White, Linda Szabo. U.S. Contemporary

*White, Neal. U.S. 1947–

White and *Ca*. Peru. Active 1847–49

Whitehead, John M. England. Active 20th c.

Whitfield, G. C. Active London, 19th c.

Whitlock, H. J. Active Birmingham, England, 1850s

Whitmore, James. U.S., Italy. Active 20th c. (deceased)

Whitney, Morgan. U.S. 1869–1913

Whitney and Paradise. Active New York City, 19th c.

*Whybrow, Gerry. England. 1937–

Wicpalek, (Dr.) H. Czechoslovakia. Active 20th c.

*Widmer, Gwen. U.S. Contemporary

Wieczorek, Antoni. Poland. 1898–1940

Wiener, Leigh. U.S. Contemporary

Wierum, Paul. Active Chicago, 20th c.

*Wigger, Paul J. U.S. 1942–

Wiggleworth and Binns. Active Wellington, Christchurch, and Dunedin, New Zealand, 1874–ca.1900

Wiggli, Oscar. Switzerland. 1927–

Wigh, Leif. Sweden. 1938–

Wiklund, Per. Contemporary

Wilczek, (Count) H. Austria-Hungary. Active 19th c.

Wild, Hans Oswald. England. Active 20th c.

*Wild, Terry. U.S. 1947–

Wilde, Friedrich. 1824–1911

Wilding, Dorothy. Active London, 20th c.

Wiley, J. S. Active Brisbane, Australia, 1890s

*Wilgus, Jack F. U.S. 1943–

Wilhelm, Henry. U.S. Contemporary

Wilhelmy, Liselott. Peru. Active 20th c.

Wilkes, G. Active ca. 1900

Wilkes, Jack. U.S. Active 20th c.

Wilkinson, C. S. Australia. Active 19th c.

*Wilkinson, David. Contemporary

William of Ballarat. Australia. Active 19th c.

Williams, J. A. Active Newport, R.I., 19th c.

Williams, James Leon. England. b. 1852

Williams, John. Australia. Contemporary

Williams, Larry E. U.S. 1950–

Williams, Mary. Active New York City, 20th c.

Williams, Roger. England. 1946–

Williams, Shedrich. U.S. Contemporary

Williams, Stephen Guion. U.S. Contemporary

Williams, T. R. England. 1825–71

Willinger. Active Hollywood, Calif., 20th c.

Willinger, M. Germany. Active 20th c.

Willis, David P. U.S. Contemporary

Willis, William. England. 1841–1923

Willmann, Manfred. Contemporary

Willoughby, Bob. U.S. Active 20th c.

*Wills, Ann Warrington (Ann Warrington). U.S. 1944–

Wilp, Charles. Germany. 1937–

Wilse, A. B. Active Oslo, 20th c.

*Wilson, B. U.S. Contemporary

Wilson, Charles A. England. 1865–1958

Wilson, E. H. China. Active ca. 1900

*Wilson, Fred J. U.S. 1945–

*Wilson, Harry. U.S. 1943–

Wilson, Helena Chapellin. U.S. (b Venezuela). Contemporary

Wilson, Leslie Hamilton. Scotland. 1883–1968

Wilson, Mildred Ruth. Active New York City, 20th c.

Wilson, (Sir) Thomas M. England. Active 19th c.

*Wilson, Tom Muir. U.S. 1930–

Wilson, Wallace. U.S. Contemporary

*Winans, William A. U.S. 1943–

Windeat, William. Active Toronto, 1860s

Window, F. R. Active London, 1860s

Window and Bridge. Active London, 1860s

Window and Grove. Active London, 19th c.

Windsor, David. U.S. Contemporary

Windstosser, Ludwig. Germany. 1921–

Winkelmann, Henry. New Zealand (b. England). 1860–1931

Winquist, Rolf. Sweden. b. 1910 (deceased)

Winter and Pond. Active Juneau, Alaska, late 19th c.

Winter Brothers. Active Vienna, 19th c.

Winther, Hans Thoger. Active Oslo (b. Denmark), 19th c.

Wirz, Paul. Active 20th c.

*Wise, Kelly. U.S. 1932–

Wiskovsky, Eugen. Czechoslovakia. 1888–1964

Witesell, Wood. U.S. 1875–1964

Witney, Dudley. Canada (b. England). Contemporary

Witteman Brothers. Active 19th c.

Wittner, Dale. U.S. Contemporary

Wohlauer, Ronald W. U.S. 1947–

Wohrl, Hans. Active Linz, Austria, 20th c.

Wolbarst, John. U.S. 1915–

Wolf, Carl

Wolf, Estelle. U.S. Active 20th c.

Wolf, Reinhart. Germany. 1930–

Wolfensberger, Andreas. Switzerland. 1942–

Wolff, Bernard Pierre. U.S. (b. France). 1930–

Wolff, G. Germany. Active 20th c.

Wolff, Paul. Germany. 1895–1951

Wolff, Werner. U.S. Active 20th c.

Wolfs, Roger. Belgium. 1932–

Wolgensinger, Michael. Switzerland. 1913–

Wolin, Jeffrey A. Contemporary

*Woller, Ellen E. U.S. 1943–

Wolman, Baron. 1942–

Wols (Alfred Otto-Wolfgang Schulze). France (b. Germany). 1913–51

Wood, B. U.S. Active late 19th c.

Wood, H., Jr. Active New York City, 19th c.

*Wood, John. U.S. 1922–

*Wood, Myron. U.S. 1921–

Wood, Richard Carver. U.S. Active 20th c.

Wood, Robertson. Canada. Active 20th c.

Wood, Roger. England. Active 20th c.

Woodall, Ronald. Canada. Contemporary

Wood and Gibson. U.S. Active 1862–65

Wood and Murray. Active Chicago, 19th c.

Woodburn, William L. Active Newark, N.J., 20th c.

Woodbury, D. B. U.S. Active mid-19th c.

*Woodman, Donald. Contemporary

Woods, Edward L. U.S. Active 1880s

Woods, Lucia. U.S. 1937–

Woodside, Henry. South Africa (b. Canada). Active 19th c.

*Woodward, Stephen S. U.S. 1943–

Worden, Willard E. Active San Francisco, 20th c.

Worsinger, K. J. U.S. Active 20th c.

*Worth, Don. U.S. 1924–

Worth, Peter J. England. 1917–

Wortley, (Col.) A. H. P. England. 1832–90

Wothly, Jakob. d. 1873

Wrigglesworth, James Dacey. 1836–1906. Active Christchurch and Wellington, New Zealand, 1863–late 19th c.

Wright, Hamilton, Jr. U.S. Active 20th c.

Wright, James. U.S. Active mid-19th c.

Wright, John J. U.S. Active ca. 1900

Wrigley, Kevin. U.S. 1951–

Wundshammer, Benno. Germany. Active 20th c.

Würthle. Austria. Active ca. 1890

Wurts, Richard. U.S. Active 20th c.

Wüst, Ursula. Germany. Contemporary

Wyatt, Thomas. 1799–1859

Wyer, Henry S. Active Nantucket, Mass., ca. 1885–1905

Wyman, Ida. U.S. Active 20th c.

Wyndham, Olivia. Active 20th c.

Wynfield, David Wilkie. England. 1837–87

*Wynn, Richard. Contemporary

Wyns, Gaston. Active Brussels, 20th c.

Wyss, Kurt. Switzerland. 1936–

Wyss, Max A. Switzerland. 1908–

Yamada, Koji. Japan. Active 20th c.

Yampolsky Urbach, Marianne. Mexico. Contemporary

Yasui, Nakaji. Japan. 1901–42

*Yates, Jack. England. 1923–

Yates, Steve. U.S. 1949–

Yato, Tomatsu. Japan. Contemporary

Yegi, M. Active late 19th c.

Yeremin, George. Russia. Active 20th c.

*Yetton, Terry. England. 1944–

Yevonde (Mme.) Active London, 20th c.

Ygnatovitch, Boris V. U.S.S.R. b. 1899

York, Frederick. Active London, 1848–90

Yotova, Elena. Bulgaria. Active late 19th c.

Yould, Philip. U.S. Active 20th c.

Young, Andrew. Scotland. Active 19th c.

Young, Becky. U.S. Contemporary

Youssef, Mohamed. Egypt. Active 20th c.

Yu. China. Active early 20th c.

Yulsman, Jerry. U.S. Active 20th c.

Yurkovskii, Sigizmund. Poland. Active 19th c.

Yvon, Albert. France. Active 20th c.

Zabe, Michel. Mexico. Contemporary

Zabinski, Roman. U.S. Active 20th c.

Zagarino, Frank. U.S. Contemporary

Zahner, M. H. Active Niagara Falls, N.Y., 19th c.

Zajky, (Dr.) Zolten. Active Budapest, 20th c.

Zambelli, Torquato. Italy. Active 20th c.

Zane, Arnold. U.S. Contemporary

Zanetta, Alo. Switzerland. 1945–

Zangaki (Langaki). Egypt (b. Cyprus or Turkey). Active 1860s. *See also* Arnoux and Zangaki

Zapryanov, Todor. b. 1836. Active Braila, Romania (b. Bulgaria)

Zarak, Martha. Mexico. Contemporary

Zaugg, Klaus. Italy

Zavala Medellin, Andrés. Mexico. Contemporary

Zaza, Michele. Italy. 1948–

Zdenek, Halamek. Czechoslovakia. 1943–

Zeiss, Carl. Germany. 1816–88

Zelaya, Elena. Mexico. Contemporary

Zelensky. Active Pecs, Hungary, 19th c.

Zeller, Adolf. Austria. Active ca. 1860

Zelm, Robert. U.S. 1944–

Zelma, Georgi. U.S.S.R. 1906–

Zelun, George. U.S.S.R. Active 20th c.

Zeman, Hilde. Germany. Active 20th c.

Zeman, Viktor. Germany. Active 20th c.

Zerbe, Jerome. U.S. Active 20th c.

Zerr, Ernst. Germany. Active ca. 1890

Zetterstrom, Tom. U.S. Contemporary

Zeyk, Miklos. Transylvania. 1780–1850

Zieff, Howard. U.S. 1927–

Zieg, W. W. Active Pittsburgh, 20th c.

Ziegler, Franz. Active The Hague, 20th c.

Zielke, Willy. Germany. 1902–

Zille, Heinrich. Germany. 1858–1929

Zimmerman, C. T. Active Minnesota, 1870s

Zimmerman, John. U.S. Contemporary

*Zimmerman, Tom. U.S. 1938–

Zingher, Maurice. Active 20th c.

Zoetmuller, Steef. Active The Hague, 20th c.

Zographov, Ivan Stoyanov. 1835–1900. Active Panagyurishte, Bulgaria

Zola, Emile. France. 1840–1902

Zomer, Nico. Netherlands. Active 20th c.

Zuber, René. Active Paris, 20th c.

Zucconi, George. U.S. Contemporary

Zugaj, Zbigniew. Contemporary

Zulpo-Dane, Bill. U.S. 1938–

Zuzunaga, Mariano. Peru. 1953–

Zwart, Piet. Germany. b. 1885

Zych, Alois. Active Prague, 20th c.

C

Museums, Galleries, Auction Houses, Exhibition Spaces

The following addresses form a list of selected locations, worldwide, for the viewing, study, or purchase of photographic works. The locations fall into four categories: museums, galleries, auction houses, and exhibition spaces. Addresses in the United States are listed first, grouped by category and subdivided by state and city. Addresses outside the United States follow, grouped by country and subdivided by category (auction houses appear under England and Germany only).

The category *museums* — which includes museums, libraries, archives, historical societies, and other collections open to the public or to qualified researchers — lists some three hundred locations that preserve photographic material. Among these, twenty-seven major collections are summarized, based on information supplied by their curators. Because museums are continually expanding and cataloguing their photographic holdings, not every known collection is reflected in the list.

The *galleries* category lists commercial outlets that consistently exhibit and sell photographic work such as daguerreotypes, prints, portfolios, posters, and books (but not photographic apparatus such as cameras). In addition to the material on display, most of them carry inventory that can usually be viewed on request. Some galleries act as exclusive agents for certain photographers. Many furnish catalogues and price lists at no charge or for a small fee. (Another commercial source of photographic work, not listed here, is private dealers — individuals or firms that sell by appointment or by mail order. They generally do not mount exhibitions, but usually provide catalogues and price lists of their stock, as galleries do. Their names may easily be found in telephone directories or advertisements in photographic periodicals, by inquiring at local museums, et cetera.)

The *auction houses* listed are firms that regularly sell photographic works at auction. Catalogues are available before every auction, describing the items and the conditions of sale; post-sale lists of prices realized are also issued. Such publications may be purchased individually or through annual subscription. (Collectible photographs also often turn up at household and estate auctions, which are announced in antique-collector's publications and in newspapers.)

The category *exhibition spaces* includes noncommercial facilities that mount changing displays of photographs (which may or may not be offered for sale); they are often located on the premises of schools, public buildings, or similar institutions. Exhibition spaces in the United States are listed here separately from museums and galleries, most of which also mount displays of photographs; in the listings of locations outside the United States, however, the categories for museums, galleries, and exhibition spaces have been combined when specific information for making the distinction was not available.

Addresses in addition to those listed here can be found in various regularly published directories that list museums, libraries, picture collections, or photo agencies.

A key to the abbreviations used in chapter 5 for citing collection locations is included at the end of this appendix.

United States

Museums and Other Public Collections

ALABAMA

Birmingham
Birmingham Museum of Art
2000 Eighth Ave. N. 35203

Tuscaloosa
University Art Gallery
University of Alabama 35486

ARIZONA

Phoenix
Phoenix Art Museum
1625 N. Central Ave. 85004

Tempe
Arizona State University Art Collections
85281

Tucson
Center for Creative Photography
University of Arizona
843 E. University Blvd. 85721
James L. Enyeart, Director

Established in 1975, the Center for Creative Photography is a leading center for photographic research. Central to the collection are the photographs and personal archives of Edward Weston, Paul Strand, Ansel Adams, Harry Callahan, Wynn Bullock, Aaron Siskind, Frederick Sommer, and Dean Brown, as well as the Edward Weston-Johan Hagemeyer correspondence.

There are also: large collections of work by Imogen Cunningham, Jerry Uelsmann, and Weegee (Arthur H. Fellig); a holding of portfolios by a wide range of photographers; a collection of rare books, with specific emphasis on the period 1850–1880; and a rapidly growing research library of more than 1,300 books and 400 bound periodicals. Special collections include Ansel Adams's donation of his personal collection of work by other photographers; the Nancy Newhall manuscript archives and Ansel Adams correspondence; and (on loan) the Sonya Noskowiak collection of her work and that of Edward Weston.

Public exhibition space features changing displays of material from the collection, and there is a program of traveling exhibitions, workshops, and lecture series. A pilot SELGEM program to computerize the archival data has been started, and a growing collection of videotaped oral histories of photographers is an additional feature.

University of Arizona Museum of Art
Olive and Speedway 85721

ARKANSAS

Little Rock
Arkansas Arts Center
MacArthur Park 72203

CALIFORNIA

Berkeley
The Bancroft Library
University of California 94720

Carmel
Friends of Photography
Sunset Center
San Carlos and Ninth 93921

Claremont
Pomona College Art Gallery
Montgomery Art Center 91711

Davis
Memorial Union Art Gallery
University of California 95616

Fresno
Fresno Arts Center
3033 E. Yale Ave. 93703

Laguna Beach
Laguna Beach Museum of Art
307 Cliff Dr. 92651

La Jolla
La Jolla Museum of Contemporary Art
700 Prospect St. 92037

Los Angeles
Los Angeles County Museum of Art/
Natural History
5905 Wilshire Blvd. 90036

Southwest Museum
Highland Park 90042

UCLA University Research Library
Department of Special Collections
Boni Collection on the History of Photography
405 Hilgard Ave. 90024
Hilda Bohem, Curator

In the early 1950s a purchase by J. Gregg Layne provided this repository with many early California photographs. In 1965 Albert Boni donated his collection of books and early images concerning the history of photography.

There are about 500,000 prints and negatives, primarily from the nineteenth and early twentieth centuries, as well as albums of calotypes and several thousand cartes de visite and theatrical cabinet prints. There is a strong emphasis on California history, typified by Carleton E. Watkins's photographs of Yosemite and the missions. Other photographers represented are: William Henry Fox Talbot, Julia Margaret Cameron, William Henry Jackson, Timothy H. O'Sullivan, Eadweard Muybridge, Edward Weston, Imogen Cunningham, and Ansel Adams.

The materials are available for scholarly research. Access to primary source materials is very restricted.

Oakland
The Oakland Museum
1000 Oak St. 94607
Therese Heyman, Senior Curator, Prints and Photographs

Until the mid-1960s this collection was historically oriented to images by early California photographers. Since that time, a representative collection of contemporary Californian work has been added, as well as images by George Fiske, Eadweard Muybridge, and Edward Weston.

A major, unparalleled collection of 50,000 prints and negatives by Dorothea Lange, her personal papers, and the Lange library of photography books are a major asset of the collection.

Some items are on public exhibition. The study collection, Lange collection, and library are open by appointment. Unless the applicant is a local resident, an appointment should be made by letter.

Pasadena
Norton Simon Museum of Art
(formerly Pasadena Museum of Modern Art)
Colorado and Orange Grove Blvds. 91105

Pasadena Public Library
285 E. Walnut St. 91101

Riverside
California Museum of Photography
University of California 92502

Sacramento
California State Library
Ninth and N Sts. 95809

San Francisco
California Historical Society
2090 Jackson St. 94109

California Palace of the Legion of Honor
Lincoln Park 94121

M. H. de Young Memorial Museum
Golden Gate Park 94118

San Francisco Museum of Modern Art
(formerly San Francisco Museum of Art)
McAllister St. and Van Ness Ave. 94102

San Marino
Henry E. Huntington Library and Art Gallery
1151 Oxford Rd. 91108

Santa Barbara
Santa Barbara Museum of Art
1130 State St. 93101

Santa Clara
de Saisset Art Gallery and Museum
University of Santa Clara 95053

Stanford
Stanford University
94305

  Albert M. Bender Rare Book Room
  University Library

  Stanford University Museum
  Museum Way and Lomita

COLORADO

Boulder
Western Historical Collections
University of Colorado
Fine Arts Building 80302

Denver
Colorado State Museum
State Historical Society of Colorado
200 Fourteenth Ave. 80203

Denver Public Library
1357 Broadway 80203

Grand Junction
Historical Museum and Institute of Western Colorado
Fourth and Ute Sts. 81501

CONNECTICUT

Hartford
Wadsworth Atheneum
600 Main St. 06103

Middletown
Davison Art Center
Wesleyan University
301 High St. 06457

New Haven
New Haven Colony Historical Society
Whitney Ave. 06510

Yale University
06520

  Beinecke Rare Book and Manuscript Library
  1603A Yale Station
  Archibald Hanna, Curator, Western Americana Collection
  Donald Gallup, Curator, American Literature Collection

There is no photographic collection in the traditional sense at Yale: photographs are scattered throughout the library and university community in various collections.

The Western Americana Collection includes The Walter McClintock Collection — photographs taken of the Blackfoot Indians by McClintock at the turn of the century. This material includes 250 hand-colored enlarged prints, lantern slides, and about 1,100 negatives. William Henry Jackson's photographs are also well represented.

The American Literature Collection has about 200 prints by Alfred Stieglitz, given by Georgia O'Keeffe, plus a large number of his papers. There are also prints by Carl Van Vechten and Danford Barney. Photographs of many renowned writers taken by various celebrated photographers are included, such as a Gertrude Stein portrait by Man Ray, Mr. and Mrs. Eugene O'Neill by Edward Steichen, and groups of photographs of Mark Twain and Walt Whitman.

Some of the material is accessible to the public. Visitors should write in advance for an appointment.

Yale University Art Gallery
1111 Chapel St.
2006 Yale Station 06520

DELAWARE

Wilmington
Delaware Art Museum
2301 Kentmere Pkwy. 19806

Eleutherian Mills Historical Library
Hagley Museum
Barley Mill Rd. and Brandywine Creek 19807

DISTRICT OF COLUMBIA
(WASHINGTON, D.C.)

Corcoran Gallery of Art
Seventeenth St. and New York Ave., N.W. 20006

Georgetown University
Special Collections Division
Thirty-seventh and O Sts., N.W. 20007

Joseph H. Hirshhorn Museum and Sculpture Garden
Eighth St. and Independence Ave., S.W. 20560

Library of Congress
Prints and Photographs Division
10 First St., S.E. 20545
Jerald C. Maddox, Curator

The Prints and Photographs Division was founded in 1897 to house the growing pictorial collection of the Library of Congress, but did not encompass photography formally until the 1940s. There are now more than eight million images in the 800 different collections.

The Master Photographs Collection consists of photographs that document and illustrate significant aspects from throughout the history of photography — for example, calotypes by William Henry Fox Talbot and daguerreotypes by Mathew Brady, a wide representation of Photo-Secession work, and twentieth-century photographs by Ansel Adams, Brett Weston, and George Krause.

For a description of the Farm Security Administration holdings and illustrated examples, see pages 136–138.

The collection is catalogued by photographer. An appointment is not necessary unless special research consultation is required.

National Archives and Record Service
General Services Administration
Pennsylvania Ave. and Eighth St., N.W. 20408

National Collection of Fine Arts
Eighth and G St., N.W. 20560

National Gallery of Art
Constitution Ave. and Sixth St., N.W. 20565

National Portrait Gallery
Eighth St. and F St., N.W. 20560

The Phillips Collection
1600 Twenty-first St., N.W. 20009

Smithsonian Institution

National Air and Space Museum
Independence Ave. and Seventh St., S.W. 20560

National Museum of History and Technology
Constitution Ave. between Twelfth and Fourteenth Sts., N.W. 20560

National Museum of Natural History
Constitution Ave. and Tenth St., N.W. 20560

The above Smithsonian Institution photographic collections extend to approximately 800,000 images. There are vast reserves of daguerreotypes, stereographs, and cartes de visite, plus several hundred thousand glass-plate negatives, primarily from the Underwood and Underwood Picture Agency. Also included is a sizable collection of William Henry Fox Talbot's work and other items of major historical interest.

The Smithsonian Institution is continually acquiring both modern and vintage work (for example, several hundred of John Draper's photomicrographic daguerreotypes were recently acquired). There is a permanent exhibition on the history of photography.

The National Museum of Natural History includes material in the National Anthropological Archives, formerly the Bureau of American Ethnology.

See also the following divisions of the Smithsonian Institution: District of Columbia — Joseph H. Hirshhorn Museum and Sculpture Garden, National Collection of Fine Arts, National Gallery of Art, and National Portrait Gallery; Manhattan — Archives of American Art.

United States Department of the Interior
C St. between Eighteenth and Nineteenth Sts., N.W. 20240

FLORIDA

Gainesville
University Gallery
University of Florida 32601

Lakeland
Polk Public Museum
800 Palmetto 33801

St. Petersburg
Museum of Fine Arts
255 Beach Dr. N. 33701

Sarasota
John and Mable Ringling Museum of Art
Box 1838
33578

Tampa
Florida Center for the Arts
University of South Florida
4202 E. Fowler Ave. 33620

GEORGIA

Atlanta
High Museum of Art
1280 Peachtree St., N.E. 30309

Columbus
Columbus Museum of Arts and Crafts, Inc.
1251 Wynnton Rd. 31906

ILLINOIS

Carbondale
University Museum
Southern Illinois University 62901

Chicago
Art Institute of Chicago
Michigan Ave. and Adams St. 60603
David Travis, Assistant Curator of Photography

In 1949 the photographic collection received its initial gift, The Alfred Stieglitz Collection, from Georgia O'Keeffe. Since that time the institute has been actively collecting photographs. There is no permanent public display, but exhibitions of photography have been mounted from time to time since 1900.

The collection has a wide range of work by contemporary photographers as well as by major figures in the history of photography. There are over fifty images each by Eugène Atget, Francis Bedford, Maxime Du Camp, Francis Frith, Arnold Genthe, Johan Hagemeyer, Gertrude Käsebier, Richard Nickel, and Edward Weston.

The material may be viewed by appointment.

Exchange National Bank
LaSalle and Adams St. 60690
Joel Snyder, Curator, Permanent Collection of Photography

This collection is an outgrowth of the personal collection of Samuel William Sax, chairman of the board and chief executive officer of the Exchange National Bank. In 1967 Sax invited Beaumont Newhall to establish a broadly based photographic collection for display in the bank. By the end of 1968, the collection comprised nearly 500 prints by 60 photographers; it was published as *A Collection of Photographs* (Millerton, N.Y.: Aperture, 1969). The collection presently has over 2,000 prints, representing the work of 250 photographers. In addition, there are a number of anonymous daguerreotypes, tintypes, and paper prints.

The collection is strongest in representing the period 1839–1920. There are a significant number of prints by William Henry Fox Talbot, Charles Nègre, Roger Fenton, Alexander Gardner, Timothy H. O'Sullivan, Julia Margaret Cameron, John Thomson, Peter Henry Emerson, Alfred Stieglitz, Alvin Langdon Coburn, Edward Steichen, Frank Eugene, and Alphonse Mucha, among others. In the more contemporary period, the bank has in-depth collections of the work of Paul Strand, Edward Weston, Walker Evans, Henri Cartier-Bresson, Brassaï, Manuel Alvarez Bravo, and Robert Capa, as well as a solid collection of work by young photographers.

About one quarter of the collection is on permanent display and the remainder can be viewed by appointment.

Museum of Contemporary Art
237 E. Ohio St. 60611

University of Chicago
Goodspeed Hall
5845 S. Ellis 60637

Urbana
Krannert Art Museum
University of Illinois
500 Peabody Dr. 61820

INDIANA

Bloomington
Indiana University Art Museum
47401

Institute for Sex Research
416 Morrison Hall
Indiana University 47401

Notre Dame
Art Gallery
University of Notre Dame 46556

KANSAS

Lawrence
Museum of Art
University of Kansas 66045

Topeka
Kansas State Historical Society
120 W. Tenth 66612

KENTUCKY

Berea
Berea College 40403

Louisville
Photographic Archives
University Library
University of Louisville-Belknap Campus 40208
James C. Anderson, Curator

The Photographic Archives includes the work of approximately 30 twentieth-century photographers. The largest collection is the 17,000 negatives and an equal number of prints by Clarence John Laughlin. The archive also houses portions of Roy Stryker's photodocumentation proj-

ects, including Farm Security Administration work.

LOUISIANA

New Orleans
New Orleans Museum of Art
Box 19123
Lelong Ave. 70179
Tina Freeman, Curator of Photography

In 1973 the museum established a substantial fund for the specific purchase of photographs. The collection, although comparatively small thus far, covers a spectrum of the history of photography and includes work by Timothy H. O'Sullivan, Gertrude Käsebier, Eugène Atget, Man Ray, Clarence John Laughlin, Edward Weston, Minor White, and Diane Arbus. A permanent photography exhibition opened in 1978.

MAINE

Brunswick
Bowdoin College Museum of Art
Walker Art Building 04011

Orono
University of Maine Art Gallery
Carnegie Hall 04473

Portland
Portland Museum of Art
111 High St. 04101

Waterville
Colby College Art Museum
04901

MARYLAND

Baltimore
Baltimore Museum of Art
Art Museum Dr.
Wyman Park 21218

University of Maryland
Baltimore County Library
5401 Wilkens Ave. 21228

MASSACHUSETTS

Andover
Addison Gallery of American Art
Phillips Academy 01810

Boston
Boston Athenaeum
10½ Beacon St. 02108

Boston Public Library
Print Department
666 Boylston St. 02117

Museum of Fine Arts
465 Huntington Ave. 02115

Museum of Science
Science Park 02114

Cambridge
Harvard University
02138

   Carpenter Center for the Visual Arts
   19 Prescott St.

   Fogg Art Museum
   32 Quincy St.
   Davis Pratt, Curator of Prints and
      Drawings

The collection is essentially a small teaching library that emphasizes twentieth-century U.S. photographers. There are a few examples by each of a range of contemporary photographers, and the museum continues to add work by new artists. Ben Shahn is represented by 3,000 vintage prints. There are also a number of images by Timothy H. O'Sullivan and a few by Mathew Brady.

   Access to the collection is limited, but public exhibitions are mounted periodically.

   Houghton Library
   Harvard Yard

   Semitic Museum
   6 Divinity Ave.

   Widener Memorial Library
   Harvard Yard

Massachusetts Institute of Technology
02139

   Hayden Gallery
   Room 7-145

   MIT Historical Collections
   Room N52-260

Northampton
Smith College Museum of Art
01060

Norwood
Norwood Historical Society
93 Day St. 02062

Salem
Peabody Museum of Salem
161 Essex St. 01970

Waltham
Brandeis University
02154

Wellesley
Wellesley College Museum
Jewett Arts Center 02181

Worcester
American Antiquarian Society
Salisbury St. and Park Ave. 01609

Worcester Art Museum
55 Salisbury St. 01608

MICHIGAN

Ann Arbor
Michigan Historical Collection
Bentley Historical Library
1150 Beal 48105

University of Michigan
48104

    Alumni Memorial Hall
    State St. and S. University

Detroit
Detroit Institute of Arts
5200 Woodward Ave. 48202

Flint
Flint Institute of Arts
1120 E. Kearsley St. 48503

Kalamazoo
Kalamazoo Institute of Arts
314 S. Park St. 49006

MINNESOTA

Minneapolis
Minneapolis Institute of Arts
201 E. Twenty-fourth St. 55404

University of Minnesota
55455

    Social Welfare History Archives
    Meredith Wilson Library

University Gallery
316 Northrop Memorial Auditorium

Walker Art Center
Vineland Place 55403

Moorhead
Plains Art Museum
521 Main Ave. 56560

MISSOURI

Kansas City
William Rockhill Nelson Gallery of Art/
    Atkins Museum of Fine Arts
4525 Oak St. 64111

St. Louis
Missouri Historical Society
Lindell and De Baliviere 63112

St. Louis Art Museum
Forest Park 63110

Washington University
Gallery of Art 63130

Springfield
Springfield Art Museum
1111 E. Brookside Dr. 65807

NEBRASKA

Aurora
Plainsman Museum
68818

Lincoln
Sheldon Memorial Art Gallery
University of Nebraska 68508

Omaha
Joslyn Art Museum
2218 Dodge St. 68102

NEW HAMPSHIRE

Hanover
Hopkins Center Art Galleries
Dartmouth College 03755

NEW JERSEY

Newark
Newark Museum
49 Washington St. 07101

Princeton
Princeton University
08540
Peter C. Bunnell, McAlpin Professor of
    the History of Photography and Mod-
    ern Art

Art Museum

Firestone Library

Marquand Art and Archaeology Library

Princeton's collection is located primarily
in two centers at the university: the Art
Museum and the Firestone Library. The
Art Museum began its collection in 1970
with various purchases from the David H.
McAlpin Fund, and later was the recipient
of McAlpin's private collection of some
500 prints. The Firestone Library houses
and collects original photographs in its
various divisions: Western Americana,
Rare Books and Manuscripts, and Graphic
Arts Collection. The Firestone and Marquand libraries combined have about
5,000 photography books.

Photographs were collected at Princeton
as early as the mid-nineteenth century,
but cataloguing of all holdings was not
begun until 1973. Some of the photographers well represented at Princeton are:
Mathew Brady, Alexander Gardner, Lewis
W. Hine, William Henry Jackson, Gertrude Käsebier, Eadweard Muybridge,
Timothy H. O'Sullivan, Charles Sheeler,
and William Henry Fox Talbot. There are
also albums of the work of Lewis Carroll
(in the M. L. Parrish Collection of Victorian Novelists), Francis Frith, and Edward
S. Curtis.

The collection is open to the public.
There are no set hours, but appointments
are accepted. A published catalogue of the
university collection of photographs is in
preparation.

Trenton
New Jersey State Museum
205 W. State St. 08625

NEW MEXICO

Albuquerque
University of New Mexico
University Art Museum 87131

Van Deren Coke, Director, University
Art Museum

The photographic print collection began
with the opening of the museum in 1964.
It contains over 3,000 items covering the
entire history of the medium and is one of
the most comprehensive university-art-
museum photographic collections in the
country.

All major processes are represented.
About two-thirds of the collection is nineteenth-century material. The collection is
designed primarily as a teaching aid but is
open to qualified researchers by written
appointment.

Santa Fe
Museum of New Mexico
Photographic Archives
Box 2087
87501

NEW YORK

Brooklyn
Brooklyn Museum
Eastern Pkwy. and Washington Ave.
11238

Long Island University
Brooklyn Center
385 Flatbush Ave. Ext. 11201

Buffalo
Albright-Knox Art Gallery
1285 Elmwood Ave. 14222

Hempstead
Emily Lowe Gallery
Hofstra University Museum 11550

Ithaca
Johnson Museum of Art
Cornell University 14850

Manhattan
American Geographical Society
Broadway and 156th St. 10032

American Museum of Natural History
Central Park West and Seventy-ninth St.
10024

Archives of American Art
41 E. Sixty-fifth St. 10021

Avery Architectural Library
Columbia University 10027

Fashion Institute of Technology Library
227 W. Twenty-seventh St. 10001

International Center of Photography
1130 Fifth Ave. 10028
Cornell Capa, Director

The creation of archival facilities and the
gathering and cataloguing of a permanent
collection for the ICP Archives is in progress. The print collection presently comprises approximately 1,500 examples by
over 100 twentieth-century photographers, including prints by Robert Capa,
Weegee (Arthur H. Fellig), Dan Weiner,
and David Seymour ("Chim").

The ICP Archives will be open by appointment; its inauguration is expected in
1980.

Jewish Museum
1109 Fifth Ave. 10028

LIFE Picture Collection
Time Inc.
Time and Life Building
1271 Avenue of the Americas 10020

Metropolitan Museum of Art
Department of Prints and Photographs
Fifth Ave. and Eighty-second St. 10028
Weston J. Naef, Curator

The museum first acquired photographs in
1928 and the collection has grown contin-
uously since then. Most of the significant
figures in the history of photography are
represented.

In 1933 Alfred Stieglitz donated his personal collection of 350 Photo-Secession
photographs. The majority of the collection is nineteenth-century material, including items such as the Southworth and
Hawes Collection of daguerreotypes and
a sizable number of books with original
photographs.

The Print Room is open to the public by
appointment made two weeks in advance.

Museum of the City of New York
1220 Fifth Ave. 10029
Albert K. Baragwanath, Curator, Portraits
and Prints

In 1942 Percy C. Byron presented to the
Museum of the City of New York a collection of about 10,000 photographic
prints and negatives from the files of Byron and Company, a five-generation firm
of photographers. (The New York studio
of the firm was established in 1888, and in
the years that followed the signature "By-

ron" appeared on countless photographs
documenting life in New York City.)

Also significant in the collection are 350
exhibition prints and negatives ("Changing New York") taken by Berenice Abbott
in the mid-1930s, and 400 glass-plate negatives by Jacob Riis. The museum also has
some material by other twentieth-century
photographers.

The collection is open to the public by
appointment.

Museum of Modern Art
Department of Photography
11 W. Fifty-third St. 10019
John Szarkowski, Curator

The museum's photography collections
include approximately 15,000 prints. The
Department of Photography was officially
established as an independent curatorial
function in 1940, but photographs have
been collected since 1930 on the basis of
their aesthetic and technical excellence.
The collections, which are conceived as a
tool that might contribute to a fuller understanding of the medium's achievements and potential, cover the entire history of the medium, although greater
emphasis has been placed on twentieth-
century works. The collections are catalogued by photographer rather than by
subject. The museum's twentieth-century
holdings are strong in works by the following photographers: Ansel Adams, Diane
Arbus, Eugène Atget, Bill Brandt, Brassaï;
Harry Callahan, Henri Cartier-Bresson,
Walker Evans, Lee Friedlander, Gertrude
Käsebier, Dorothea Lange, Man Ray, Tina
Modotti, László Moholy-Nagy, Alexander
Rodchenko, Frederick Sommer, Edward
Steichen, Alfred Stieglitz, Jerry Uelsmann,
Edward Weston, and Clarence H. White.

The department also maintains a library
of 2,000 photographic books, supplemented by a biographical clipping file, articles by and about photographers, exhibition announcements, and other miscellaneous data that come to the attention
of the department. This supplemental material is generally filed by photographer.

In 1968 the museum acquired the largest single collection of the work of Atget,
which had been preserved by Berenice Abbott since Atget's death in 1927. The museum has undertaken to organize, preserve, and catalogue for the first time this
collection of approximately 4,000 prints.
The department has also collected and
preserved supplementary archival material bearing on Atget's life and work.

The Edward Steichen Archive was formally established in July 1968; it was designed to collect, preserve, catalogue, and

supervise the use of original materials, other than artworks, relevant to the study of Steichen's contribution to modern photography and to modern art in general. The archive's materials include exhibition catalogues, correspondence, notebooks, taped and written interviews, magazine and newspaper articles, and other documentary materials by and about Steichen, spanning five decades.

The Department of Photography collection is available for use by scholars of serious and specific intention. Due to very limited staff and space, such use is restricted and must be scheduled in advance.

New-York Historical Society
Print Room
170 Central Park West 10024
Wendy J. Shadwell, Curator of Prints

The photographic archives of this museum and library of American history were enhanced in 1906 with a gift (from its president, Samuel V. Hoffman) of 42 waxpaper negatives — apparently the oldest remaining photographic views of New York City — made by the French photographer Victor Prevost in 1853/54.

At present the holdings, almost exclusively nineteenth-century images, number over 100,000 items, of which more than 50,000 are negatives. In most instances the photographers are not identifiable. The largest part of the collection comprises portrait files and street files. There are also stereographs of streets and buildings, daguerreotypes, and cartes de visite.

Among the twentieth-century materials are some 4,000 photographs by Arnold Genthe, 760 by Jacob Riis and Robert Bracklow, and 500 by H. N. Tiemann, as well as many architectural street scenes.

A selection of photographs from the Society's collection was published in *Old New York in Early Photographs, 1853–1901* (New York: Dover, 1973). The Print Room is open regularly for research; there is an admission charge for nonmembers.

New York Public Library

Fifth Ave. and Forty-second St. 10018
  Local History and Genealogy
    Division
  Photography Archive
  Picture Collection
  Rare Book Division

111 Amsterdam Ave. (Lincoln Center)
  10023
  Library and Museum of the
    Performing Arts

Pierpont Morgan Library
29 E. Thirty-sixth St. 10016

Whitney Museum of American Art
945 Madison Ave. 10021

Poughkeepsie
Vassar College Art Gallery
Taylor Hall 12601

Rochester
International Museum of Photography at
  George Eastman House
900 East Ave. 14607
Robert J. Doherty, Director

The IMP/GEH Archives constitute a major resource center: over 400,000 original photographs, a library of approximately 30,000 volumes, and a large collection of nineteenth-century material, including daguerreotypes, tintypes, and stereographs. The Equipment Archive of over 4,000 cameras, plus lenses and other equipment, is presumed the largest in the world. The archives have subject information files on photographers, processes, galleries, collections, and related subjects. Acquisition of the 3M/Sipley Collection in 1977 greatly strengthened the holdings of American historical photographic material.

The museum, regularly open to the public, has on permanent display a broad cross section of images tracing the prehistory and history of photography. Access to the archives is by appointment only, made well in advance.

The IMP/GEH Print Service offers materials in the collection for reproduction and study — including still photographs, original negatives, motion-picture stills, and photographs of cameras and apparatus. Copy prints of exhibition quality from original negatives by many photographers are also available (use has been restricted by donors in some cases); a schedule of fees is available from the Print Service.

Visual Studies Workshop
31 Prince St. 14607

Schenectady
Schenectady Museum
Nott Terrace Heights 12308

Staten Island
Staten Island Historical Society
302 Center St. 10306

Syracuse
Everson Museum of Art
401 Harrison St. 13202

Yonkers
Hudson River Museum
511 Warburton Ave.
Trevor-Park-on-Hudson 10701

NORTH CAROLINA

Chapel Hill
University of North Carolina
27514

Charlotte
Mint Museum of Art
501 Hempstead Pl. 28207

Durham
Duke University Art Museum
Box 6877 College Station 27708

OHIO

Akron
Akron Art Institute
69 E. Market St. 44308

Cincinnati
Cincinnati Art Museum
Eden Park 45202

Cleveland
Cleveland Museum of Art
11150 East Blvd. 44106

Columbus
Rinhart Collection
Ohio State University 43210

Dayton
Dayton Art Institute
Forest and Riverview Ave. 45405

Delaware
Ohio Wesleyan University
Humphries Art Hall 43015

Milford
The Antique Camera Museum
1065 Jer Les Dr. 45150

Oberlin
Allen Memorial Art Museum
Oberlin College 44704

OREGON

Eugene
University of Oregon
97403

Library

Museum of Art

Portland
Oregon Historical Society
1230 S.W. Park Ave. 97205

Portland Art Museum
1219 S.W. Park Ave. 97205

PENNSYLVANIA

Philadelphia
Academy of Natural Sciences of
Philadelphia
Nineteenth St. and Benjamin Franklin
Pkwy. 19103

Free Library of Philadelphia
Print and Picture Department
Logan Square 19103

Museum of the Philadelphia Civic
Center
Thirty-fourth St. and Civic Center Blvd.
19104

Philadelphia Museum of Art, Alfred
Stieglitz Center
Twenty-sixth St. and Benjamin Franklin
Pkwy. 19130
Kneeland McNulty, Curator of Prints,
Drawings, and Photographs

The Alfred Stieglitz Center, under the auspices of the Print Department, was established with a gift of photographic materials from the Stieglitz estate. Among
large bodies of work in the collection are
photographs by: Stieglitz, Paul Strand,
Minor White, Robert Frank, Jerry Uelsmann, Clarence John Laughlin, Edward S.
Curtis, Dorothy Norman, Frank M. Sutcliffe, Edward Weston, various nineteenth-
century French photographers, Ansel
Adams, and Eadweard Muybridge (collotypes), plus two complete sets of *Camera
Work* gravures.

The material may be viewed by appointment. A permanent exhibition space for
photographs was opened in 1978.

Temple University
Beech and Penrose Ave. 19126

Pittsburgh
Museum of Art
Carnegie Institute
4400 Forbes Ave. 15213

Titusville
Drake Well Museum
R.D. 3
16354

RHODE ISLAND

Providence
Museum of Art
Rhode Island School of Design
224 Benefit St. 02903

SOUTH CAROLINA

Charleston
Gibbes Art Gallery
135 Meeting St. 29401

TENNESSEE

Knoxville
The Tennessee Valley Authority
Graphics Dept.
400 Commerce Ave. 37902

University of Tennessee
37916

Memphis
Brooks Memorial Art Gallery
Overton Park 38112

Nashville
Carl Van Vechten Gallery of Fine Arts
Fisk University 37203

TEXAS

Austin
Humanities Research Center
Photography Collection
Box 7219
University of Texas at Austin 78712

This major collection was begun in 1964
with the acquisition of the Gernsheim
Collection, then the largest private photographic collection known. It contains

fine examples by many of the leading European photographers of the Victorian era.
At present the entire photography collection comprises 200,000 photographs, 7,000
books and journals, and 1,500 pieces of
apparatus.

There is a public display of some duplicate material. The public is not allowed
access to the stacks, but materials are
brought to the reading rooms on request.
No appointment is necessary.

Corpus Christi
Corpus Christi Museum
1919 N. Water St. 78401

Dallas
Dallas Museum of Fine Arts
Fair Park 75226

Forth Worth
Amon Carter Museum of Western Art
3501 Camp Bowie Blvd. 76101

Forth Worth Art Museum
1309 Montgomery St. 76107

Galveston
Rosenberg Library
2310 Sealy Ave. 77550

Houston
Menil Foundation, Inc.
3363 San Felipe Rd. 77019

Museum of Fine Arts
1001 Bissonnet St. 77005

San Antonio
Witte Memorial Museum
3801 Broadway 78209

UTAH

Salt Lake City
Utah State Historical Society
603 E. S. Temple 84102

VIRGINIA

Richmond
Valentine Museum
1015 E. Clay St. 23219

Virginia Museum of Fine Arts
Boulevard and Grove Ave. 23221

WASHINGTON

Seattle
Seattle Art Museum
Volunteer Park 98112

University of Washington Libraries
98195

Tacoma
Tacoma Art Museum
Twelfth and Pacific Ave. 98402

WASHINGTON, D.C.
See DISTRICT OF COLUMBIA

WISCONSIN

Madison
Madison Art Center
720 E. Gorham St. 53703

Galleries

CALIFORNIA

Carmel
Weston Gallery
Box 655
93921

Cupertino
Photo-Arts of Cupertino
10025 Mann Dr. 95014

Fullerton
309 Malden Gallery
309 Malden Ave. 92632

Los Angeles
Broxton Gallery
669 N. La Cienega Blvd. 90069

Dream
Pacific Design Center
8687 Melrose Ave, 90069

G. Ray Hawkins Gallery
9002 Melrose Ave. 90069

The Photo Album
835 N. La Cienega Blvd. 90069

Soho Cameraworks Gallery
8221 Santa Monica Blvd. 90046

Newport Beach
Susan Spiritus Gallery
3336 Via Lido 92663

San Francisco
Berggruen Gallery
228 Grant Ave. 94108

Camerawork
70 Twelfth St. 94103

Lawson de Celle Gallery
54 Kissling St. 94103

Focus Gallery
2146 Union St. 94123

Grapestake Gallery
2876 California St. 94115

Simon Lowinsky Gallery
228 Grant Ave. 94108

Secret City Gallery
306 Fourth Ave. 94118

Thackrey and Robertson
2266 Union St. 94123

Stephen Wirtz Gallery
228 Grant Ave. 94108

Saratoga
Camera Work Gallery
14501-B Big Basin Way 95070

Studio City
The Livingroom Gallery
13025 Ventura Blvd. 91604

Venice
Janus Gallery
21 Market St. 90291

Yosemite National Park
Ansel Adams Gallery
Box 455
95389

COLORADO

Denver
Colorado Photographic Arts Center
1301 Bannock St. 80204

CONNECTICUT

New Canaan
Photo Graphics Workshop
212 Elm St. 06840

New Haven
Archetype
159 Orange St. 06510

DISTRICT OF COLUMBIA
(WASHINGTON, D.C.)

Lunn Gallery/Graphics International, Ltd.
3243 P St., N.W. 20007

Sander Gallery
2604 Connecticut Ave., N.W. 20008

Street Corner Gallery, Ltd.
4932 Wisconsin Ave., N.W. 20016

Washington Gallery of Photography
216 Seventh St., S.E. 20003

FLORIDA

Tampa
Gulf Coast Photographic Gallery
3941 W. Kennedy Blvd. 33609

IDAHO

Sun Valley
The Shadow Catcher Gallery
83353

ILLINOIS

Chicago
The Darkroom
2424 N. Racine Ave. 60614

Allan Frumkin Gallery
620 N. Michigan Ave. 60611

The Gilbert Gallery
218 E. Ontario 60611

Douglas Kenyon Gallery
155 E. Ohio St. 60611

Pallas Photographica Gallery
315 W. Erie St. 60610

INDIANA

Fort Wayne
Gallery 614
614 W. Berry St. 46802

IOWA

Grinnell
East Street Gallery
723 State St. 50112

LOUISIANA

New Orleans
Images Gallery
8124 Oak St. 70118

MAINE

Addison
Cape Split Place, Inc.
04606

MARYLAND

Chevy Chase
A Street Corner Gallery
5502 Center St. 20015

MASSACHUSETTS

Boston
Boris Gallery
35 Lansdowne St. 02215

Harcus–Krakow Gallery
7 Newbury St. 02115

Kiva Gallery
231 Newbury St. 02115

Panopticon Gallery
69 Newbury St. 02115

Photoworks Gallery
755 Boylston St. 02161

Stephen T. Rose Gallery
216 Newbury St. 02116

Carl Siembab Gallery
162 Newbury St. 02116

Vision Gallery
216 Newbury St. 02116

Voices Gallery
220 North St. 02113

Stockbridge
Image Gallery
Main St. 01262

MICHIGAN

Ann Arbor
Arcade Gallery
229 Nickels Arcade 48104

Art World's Photo Gallery
213½ S. Main 48104

Union Gallery
530 State St. 48104

Birmingham
Halsted 831 Gallery
560 S. Woodward 48011

MINNESOTA

Minneapolis
Peter M. David Gallery, Inc.
920 Nicollet Mall 55402

J. Hunt Gallery
3011 E. Twenty-fifth St. 55406

Lightworks
25 University Ave. E. 55414

Oxman's Gallery
639 Second Ave. N. 55403

MISSOURI

Columbia
Columbia Gallery of Photography
1015 E. Broadway 65201

NEW JERSEY

Montclair
Silvermind Gallery
18 S. Fullerton Ave. 07042

Westwood
Hannibal Goodwin
186–190 Center Ave. 07675

NEW MEXICO

Albuquerque
Quivira Photograph Gallery
111 Cornell Dr., S.E. 87106

NEW YORK

Bronx
Focal Point Gallery
278 City Island Ave. 10464

Buffalo
Andromeda Gallery
493 Franklin St. 14203

CEPA Gallery and Workshop
30 Essex St. 14213

Ithaca
The Photography Gallery
104 N. Aurora St. 14850

Manhattan
Castelli Graphics
4 E. Seventy-seventh St. 10021

Crossroads Gallery
2639 Broadway 10025

Eleventh Street Photo Gallery
330 E. Eleventh St. 10003

Floating Foundation of Photography
Pier 40 South, West St. 10014

Focus II Gallery
163 W. Seventy-fourth St. 10023

Foto Gallery
492 Broome St. 10012

Fourth Street Gallery
Minority Photographers, Inc.
67 E. Fourth St. 10003

Robert Freidus Gallery
158 Lafayette St. 10013

Gombinski Gallery of Art
46 Walker St. 10013

O. K. Harris
383 W. Broadway 10012

Images Gallery
11 E. Fifty-seventh St. 10022

Sidney Janis
6 W. Fifty-seventh St. 10019

M. Knoedler and Co.
19–21 E. Seventieth St. 10021

Light Gallery
724 Fifth Ave. 10019

Marlborough Gallery
40 W. Fifty-seventh St. 10019

Multiples
55 E. Eightieth St. 10021

Neikrug Galleries, Inc.
224 E. Sixty-eighth St. 10021

Pace Gallery
32–34 E. Fifty-seventh St. 10022

Pfeiffer Gallery
825 Madison Ave. 10022

Prakapas Gallery
19 E. Seventy-first St. 10021

Robert Samuels Gallery
795 Broadway 10003

Robert Schoelkopf Gallery
825 Madison Ave. 10022

Sonnabend
420 W. Broadway 10012

The Space
154 W. Fifty-seventh St. 10019

The Witkin Gallery, Inc.
41 E. Fifty-seventh St. 10022

Daniel Wolfe Gallery
30 W. Fifty-seventh St. 10019

Rochester
Light Impressions Gallery
8 S. Washington St. 14614

The Workshop Gallery
Visual Studies Workshop
31 Prince St. 14607

Sea Cliff
Sea Cliff Photograph Co.
310 Sea Cliff Ave. 11579

Ohio

Cleveland Heights
Herbert Ascherman Gallery
1785 Coventry Rd. 44118

Columbus
Photogenesis Camera Shop and Gallery
4930 N. High St. 43214

East Palestine
Vista Gallery of Contemporary Photography
164 S. Market St. 44413

Oregon

Portland
Blue Sky Gallery
2315 N.W. Lovejoy 97210

The Shado Gallery
2910 S.E. Lambert St. 97202

Pennsylvania

Philadelphia
Hahn Gallery
8439 Germantown Ave. 19118

The Photography Place
132 S. Seventeenth St. 19103

Photopia
1728 Spruce St. 19103

South Carolina

Greenville
Silver Eye Studio
401 W. Croft St. 29609

Texas

Dallas
The Afterimage
The Quadrangle, No. 151
2800 Routh St. 75201

Houston
The Cronin Gallery
2424 Bissonnet 77005

Virginia

Richmond
Photoworks
204 N. Mulberry St. 23220

Washington

Seattle
Equivalents
1822 E. Broadway 98102

Phos Graphos
108 S. Jackson 98104

Photo Printworks
114 W. Elliott 98119

Silver Image Gallery
83 S. Washington 98104

Washington, D.C.
See District of Columbia

Wisconsin

Madison
Sunprint Gallery
638 State St. 53703

Milwaukee
Infinite Eye Gallery
2553 N. Downer Ave. 53211

Auction Houses

California

Los Angeles
Sotheby Parke Bernet, Inc.
7660 Beverly Blvd. 90036

San Francisco
California Book Auction Company
270 McAllister St. 94102

New York

Manhattan
Christie's East
219 E. Sixty-seventh St. 10021

Hastings Galleries, Inc.
121 E. Twenty-fourth St. 10016

Phillips
525 E. Seventy-second St. 10021

Sotheby Parke Bernet, Inc.
980 Madison Ave. 10021

Swann Galleries, Inc.
104 E. Twenty-fifth St. 10010

Exhibition Spaces

ARIZONA

Tempe
Memorial Union Art Gallery
Arizona State University 85281

CALIFORNIA

Berkeley
Darkroom Workshop/Gallery
2051 San Pablo Ave. 94702

University Art Museum and Photography
  Gallery
University of California
2223 Fulton St. 94720

Capitola
Photo Workshop
201-D Monterey 95010

Carmel
Friends of Photography
Sunset Center
San Carlos and Ninth 93921

Claremont
Galleries of the Claremont Colleges
Montgomery Art Center 91711

Lang Art Gallery
Scripps College
Ninth and Columbia 91711

Costa Mesa
Department of Photography
Orange Coast College
2701 Fairview Rd. 92626

Davis
Memorial Union Art Gallery
University of California 95616

El Cajon
Grossmont College Art Gallery
8800 Grossmont Dr. 92020

Fullerton
Muckenthaler Cultural Center
1201 W. Malvern 92633

Long Beach
The Art Galleries
California State University at Long Beach
1250 Bellflower Blvd. 90840

Los Angeles
Los Angeles Center for Photographic
  Studies
412 S. Parkview 90057

Municipal Art Gallery
Barnsdall Park
4804 Hollywood Blvd. 90027

Frederick S. Wight Art Galleries
University of California 90024

San Diego
Gallery of the Department of Art
Center for Photographic Arts
California State University at San Diego
  92115

San Francisco
San Francisco Art Institute
800 Chestnut St. 94133

San Rafael
Bull's Eye Gallery
153 Picnic Ave. 94901

Santa Cruz
The Neary Gallery / Center for
  Photography
1362 Pacific Garden Mall 95060

CONNECTICUT

Bridgeport
University of Bridgeport
285 Park Ave. 06602

DISTRICT OF COLUMBIA
(WASHINGTON, D.C.)

Explorers Hall
National Geographic Society
Seventeenth and M Sts., N.W. 20036

FLORIDA

Coral Gables
Lowe Art Museum
University of Miami
1301 Miller Dr. 33124

GEORGIA

Atlanta
Nexus
608 Forrest Rd., N.E. 30312

HAWAII

Volcano
Volcano Art Center
Box 318
96785

ILLINOIS

Carbondale
Mitchell Gallery
Southern Illinois University 62901

Chicago
Artemisia Gallery/Fund
9 W. Hubbard St. 60610

Chicago Center for Contemporary
  Photography
Columbia College
600 S. Michigan Ave. 60611

David and Alfred Smart Gallery
University of Chicago 60637

DeKalb
University Center Gallery
Northern Illinois University 60115

Evanston
Photography Gallery
Evanston Art Center
2603 Sheridan Rd. 60201

Normal
Center for the Visual Arts Gallery
Illinois State University 61761

IOWA

Cedar Falls
Photography Gallery
Art II Building
University of Northern Iowa 50613

Sioux City
Sioux City Art Center
513 Nebraska St. 51101

KENTUCKY

Berea
Berea College Art Museum
40403

MAINE

Rockport
Maine Photographic Workshop
04856

MARYLAND

Baltimore
Photo Gallery
Maryland Institute College of Art
1300 W. Mount Royal Ave. 21217

College Park
Art Gallery
University of Maryland 20742

MASSACHUSETTS

Amherst
Student Union Gallery
University of Massachusetts 01002

Boston
City Hall
1 City Hall Sq. 02201

Institute of Contemporary Art
955 Boylston St. 02115

Brockton
Brockton Art Center
Oak St. on Upper Porter's Pond 02401

Cambridge
Cambridge Photo Co-op
188 Prospect St. 02139

Clarence Kennedy Gallery
Polaroid Corporation
770 Main St. 02139

Massachusetts Institute of Technology
02139

    Compton Gallery

    Creative Photography Gallery

Project, Inc.
141 Huron Ave. 02138

Lincoln
De Cordova and Dana Museum and Park
Sandy Pond Rd. 01773

Pittsfield
Berkshire Museum
39 South St. 01201

Waltham
Brandeis University 02154

Williamstown
Williams College Museum of Art
Main St. 01267

MINNESOTA

Minneapolis
Minneapolis College of Art and Design
133 E. Twenty-fifth St. 55404

Pro Color Gallery
611 Fourth Ave. S. 55415

MONTANA

Billings
Yellowstone County Fine Arts Center
401 N. Twenty-seventh St. 59101

NEW JERSEY

Jersey City
Courtney Gallery
Jersey City State College
2039 Kennedy Blvd. 07305

Madison
University Center Gallery
Drew University 07940

Newark
City without Walls
41 Shipman St. 07102

New Brunswick
Department of Art Gallery
Douglass College
Rutgers University 08903

NEW YORK

Albany
University Art Gallery
State University of New York at Albany
1400 Washington Ave. 12203

Annandale-on-Hudson
Kline Commons Gallery
Bard College 12504

Brockport
Fine Arts Gallery
State University of New York at
    Brockport 14420

Brooklyn
Pratt Institute Gallery
215 Ryerson St. 11205

Flushing
Queens Museum
New York City Building
Flushing Meadow, Corona Park 11368

Manhattan
Camera Club of New York
37 E. Sixtieth St. 10022

Diana Gallery
Diana Custom Prints
21 W. Forty-sixth St. 10036

Discovery Galleries/Modernage
319 E. Forty-fourth St. 10017

Eastman Kodak Exhibit Center
1133 Ave. of the Americas 10036

French Cultural Services
972 Fifth Ave. 10021

Gallery Lounge
Pace College
Pace College Plaza 10038

Grey Art Gallery
New York University
100 Washington Sq. East 10003

Midtown Y Gallery
344 E. Fourteenth St. 10003

New Gallery of the Educational Alliance
197 E. Broadway 10002

Nikon House
Rockefeller Center 10022

Nugent Gallery
Marymount Manhattan College
221 E. Seventy-first St. 10021

Pop Photo Gallery
1 Park Ave. 10016

Portogallo and Galate
72 W. Forty-fifth St. 10036

School of Visual Arts
209 E. Twenty-third St. 10010

Soho Photo Gallery
34 W. Thirteenth St. 10011

Women's Interart Center
549 W. Fifty-second St. 10036

Port Washington
Port Washington Library
245 Main St. 11050

Rochester
MFA Gallery
School of Photographic Arts and Sciences
Rochester Institute of Technology
1 Lomb Memorial Dr. 14623

Syracuse
Light Work
316 Waverly Ave. 13210

Photovisions Cooperative Gallery
Hanover Sq.
130 E. Genesee St. 13202

NORTH CAROLINA

Charlotte
The Light Factory
1626 East Blvd. 28203

Kingston
Kingston Arts Council
108½ W. Caswell St. 28501

OHIO

Columbus
Silver Image Gallery
Ohio State University
156 W. Nineteenth Ave. 43210

Dayton
Creative Photography Gallery
University of Dayton 45409

Springfield
Springfield Art Center
107 Cliff Park Rd. 45501

Yellow Springs
Grey Gallery
Antioch College 45387

OKLAHOMA

Tulsa
Philbrook Art Center
Box 2099
74101

PENNSYLVANIA

Bethlehem
Haupert Union Building
Moravian College 18018

Philadelphia
Philadelphia Art Alliance
251 S. Eighteenth St. 19103

Tyler School of Art
Temple University
Beech and Penrose Aves. 19126

University Park
Arts Building, Room 212A
College of Arts and Architecture
Pennsylvania State University 16802

TENNESSEE

Murfreesboro
Photographic Gallery
Middle Tennessee State University 37130

TEXAS

Denton
College of Fine Arts Gallery
Texas Woman's University
Sawyer and Oakland St. 76204

Waco
Waco Creative Arts Center
414 Franklin 76701

UTAH

Salt Lake City
Edison Street Gallery
231 Edison St. 84111

VERMONT

Manchester
Southern Vermont Art Center
05254

Northfield
The Image Coop
N. Main St. 05663

VIRGINIA

Bristol
Photography Gallery
Virginia Intermont College 24201

WASHINGTON

Cheney
Grande Photography Room
Eastern Washington State College 99004

Seattle
Photo Print Works
114 W. Elliott Ave. 98119

WASHINGTON, D.C.
See DISTRICT OF COLUMBIA

WISCONSIN

Beloit
Gallery 38A
Beloit College 53511

Madison
Madison Art Center, Inc.
720 E. Gorham St. 53703

Milwaukee
Milwaukee Art Center
750 N. Lincoln Memorial Dr. 53202

Milwaukee Center for Photography
Marshall Building
207 E. Buffalo St. 53202

Outside the United States

AUSTRALIA

Museums and Other Public Collections

Australian Centre for Photography
76A Paddington St.
Paddington (Sydney), New South Wales 2021

Australian National Gallery
Canberra, New South Wales

Geelong Art Gallery
Geelong, Victoria

National Gallery of Victoria
180 St. Kilda Rd.
Melbourne, Victoria 3004

Galleries/Exhibition Spaces

Church Street Photographic Centre
384 Church St.
Richmond (Melbourne), Victoria 3121

Ewing Gallery
Melbourne University
Swanson St.
Parkville (Melbourne), Victoria

The Image Gallery
42 Gurner St.
Paddington (Sydney), New South Wales

Pentax-Brummels Gallery
95 Toorak Rd.
South Yarra (Melbourne), Victoria

Photographers' Gallery
Punt Rd.
South Yarra (Melbourne), Victoria

Realities Gallery
Orange Rd.
Toorak, Queensland

AUSTRIA

Museums

Graphische Lehr und Versuchsanstalt
25 Westbahnstrasse
Vienna

Osterreichisches Fotomuseum
Bad Ischl 4820

Galleries/Exhibition Spaces

Fotoforum
Technischen Universität
9 Getreidemarkt
Vienna 1060

Fotogalerie im Forum Stadtpark
1 Stadtpark
Graz 8010

Fotogalerie Schillerhof
Café Schillerhof
Schillerplatz
Graz

Galerie Die Brücke
5 Bäckerstrasse
Vienna 1010

Innsbrucker Fotoschau
Kongresshaus
Innsbruck 6020

Kodak Galerie
4 Albert Schweitzer-Gasse
Vienna 1148

Kulturhaus
Stadt Graz
Graz 8010

P. P. Galerie
Linz 4020

Salzburg College
56 Leopoldskronstrasse
Salzburg 5020

BELGIUM

Museums

International Cultureel Centrum
50 Meir
Antwerp 2000

Ministère de la Culture Française
158 Av. de Cortenbergh
Brussels 1040

Musée d'Art Moderne et Ministère de la Culture
rue des Hêtres
Linkebeek 1630

Provinciaal Museum voor Kunstambachten
Het Sterckshof
160 Hooftvunderlei
Deurne (Antwerp) 2100
J. Walgrave, Curator

A permanent section, Foto en Film, was opened in 1968. In 1973 the museum acquired the Auer Collection from Geneva, and the photography collection has grown rapidly ever since.

There are about 10,000 prints and 35,000 negatives, 125 daguerreotypes, 40 calotypes, 45 ambrotypes, and 200 stereographs. About one third of the collection is nineteenth-century material, with a broad cross section of European photography, including work by Eugène Atget, Werner Bischof, Brassaï, André Adolphe-Eugène Disdéri, Francis Frith, László Moholy-Nagy, Nadar, Man Ray, and Albert Renger-Patzsch. There is a special selection of Belgian photography (this material is available in *Photographic Art in Belgium 1839–1940*, published in Dutch, French, German, and English). Contemporary United States photography has been added recently and holdings include Berenice Abbott, Ansel Adams, Diane Arbus, Imogen Cunningham, Judy Dater, and Jerry Uelsmann, among others.

The museum also has about 5,000 pieces of photographic apparatus, some 4,000 photography books, and archives such as the Agfa-Gevaert historical material.

An appointment is advisable.

Société des Expositions
Palais des Beaux-Arts de Bruxelles
10 rue Royale
Brussels 1000

Galleries/Exhibition Spaces

Aspects
72 rue du Président
Brussels 1050

Foto Galerij Paule Pia
57 Kammenstraat
Antwerp 2000

Galerie 5.6
14 St. Michielsplein
Ghent 9000

Kreatief Camera Galerie
68 Nieuwstraat
Herentals 2410

BRAZIL

Museums

Museu de Arte Contemporânea da
    Universidade de São Paulo
Parque Ibirapuera
C.P. 8191
São Paulo

Museu de Arte Moderna
Avda. Beira-mar
Rio de Janeiro

Galleries/Exhibition Spaces

Sociedade Fluminense de Fotografia
C.P. 118
Niterói 24000

CANADA

ALBERTA

Museums/Galleries/Exhibition Spaces

Edmonton Art Gallery
2 Sir Winston Churchill Sq.
Edmonton T5J 2C1

Walter Phillips Gallery
The Banff Centre
Banff

Southern Alberta Art Gallery
601 Third Ave. S.
Lethbridge T1J 0H4

BRITISH COLUMBIA

Museums/Galleries/Exhibition Spaces

Gallery of Photography
3619 W. Broadway
Vancouver

Nova Gallery
1972 W. Fourth
Vancouver V6J 1M5

Photographic Art Dealers
4574 Langara Ave.
Vancouver

Secession Gallery of Photography
Open Space
510 Fort St.
Victoria

Vancouver Art Gallery
1145 W. Georgia St.
Vancouver

MANITOBA

Museums/Galleries/Exhibition Spaces

Winnipeg Art Gallery
300 Memorial Blvd.
Winnipeg

NOVA SCOTIA

Museums/Galleries/Exhibition Spaces

Nova Scotia College of Art and Design
6152 Coburg Rd.
Halifax

ONTARIO

Museums

National Gallery of Canada
Lorne Building
Elgin and Slater Sts.
Ottawa K1A 0M8
James Borcoman, Director of Photography

Established in 1967 as part of the regular acquisition policy of the Gallery, the photography collection holds over 6,000 works, covering the period from 1835 to the present. Major holdings include: William Henry Fox Talbot, Charles Nègre, D. O. Hill and Robert Adamson, Eugène Atget, Edward Weston, Aaron Siskind, and Roger Mertin. The work of Auguste Salzmann, Francis Frith, Francis Bedford, Peter Henry Emerson, Pierre Tremaux, and Jules Robuchon is also represented. The Gallery also has a large collection of Civil War photographs by George N. Barnard, Alexander Gardner, Timothy H. O'Sullivan, and Wood and Gibson. Contemporary U.S. and Canadian photographs and an extensive library are additional features. (An illustrated article on the collection was published in *Arts Canada*, December 1974.)

Temporary exhibitions are mounted several times a year. The study room is open by appointment.

Public Archives of Canada
395 Wellington St.
Ottawa K1A 0N3

Galleries/Exhibition Spaces

Art Gallery of Ontario
Grange Park
Toronto M5T 1G4

Canada Council–Visual Arts
255 Albert St.
Ottawa

Deja Vue Gallery
122 Scollard St.
Toronto M5R 1G2

Agnes Etherington Art Centre
Queen's University
Kingston

Gallery Graphics
521 Sussex Dr.
Ottawa K1N 6Z6

Isaacs Gallery
832 Yonge St.
Toronto M4W 2H1

David Mirvish Gallery
596 Markham St.
Toronto

A Moment in Time
398 King St. E.
Toronto M5A 1K9

National Film Board of Canada
Photo Gallery
150 Kent St.
Ottawa

Photo Artists Canada
398 King St. E.
Toronto M5A 1K9

Photo Image 33
33 Brock St.
Kingston

Photowork
239 Gerrard St. E.
Toronto

Saw Gallery
72 Rideau St.
Ottawa K1N 5W9

A Space Exhibition
352 Spadina Ave.
Toronto

Yarlow/Salzman Gallery
211 Avenue Rd.
Toronto

York University Art Gallery
4700 Keele St.
Downsview (Toronto) M3J 1P3

PRINCE EDWARD ISLAND

Museums/Galleries/Exhibition Spaces

Confederation Art Gallery and Museum
Confederation Centre of the Arts
Box 848
Charlottetown C1A 7L9

QUEBEC

Museums

McCord Museum
McGill University
690 Sherbrooke St. W.
Montreal H31 1E9

Montreal Museum of Fine Arts
1379 Sherbrooke St. W.
Montreal H3G 1K3

Musée d'Art Contemporain
Cité du Havre
Montreal H3C 3R4

Musée d'Art de Joliette
145 rue Wilfred-Corbeil
Joliette

Galleries/Exhibition Spaces

Art 45
2175 Crescent
Montreal

Saidye Bronfman Centre of the
  YM/YWCA
5170 Cote St.
Montreal

La Chambre Blanche
531 St. Jean
Quebec

Galerie Mira Godard
1490 Sherbrooke St. W.
Montreal

Galerie Optica
451 S. François-Xavier
Montreal

Gallery Notkin
1650 Sherbrooke St. W.
Montreal

Gallery Photo Progressio
1417 MacKay St.
Montreal

La Maison Sauvegard
160 Notre Dame E.
Montreal

Power House Gallery
3738 St. Dominique
Montreal

Vehicule Art
61 St. Catherine W.
Montreal

Sir George Williams University
1455 DeMaisonneuve Blvd.
Montreal H3G 1M8

Workshop
7308 Sherbrooke St. W.
Montreal

Yajima/Galerie
1434 Sherbrooke St. W.
Montreal

SASKATCHEWAN

Museums/Galleries/Exhibition Spaces

Mendel Art Gallery
Saskatoon Gallery and Conservatory
  Corp.
950 Spadina Crescent E.
Box 569
Saskatoon S7K 3L6

Photographers' Gallery
The Dowding Building
234 Second Ave. S.
Saskatoon

CZECHOSLOVAKIA

Museums

Museum of Decorative Arts
Prague

DENMARK

Museums

Royal Academy of Fine Arts Library
Charlottenborg
1 Kongens Nytorv
Copenhagen 2550

Royal Library
Department of Prints, Maps, and
  Photographs
8 Christians Brygge
Copenhagen 1219

Thorvaldsen Museum
Slotsholmen
Copenhagen

Galleries/Exhibition Spaces

Gallery Huset
14 Magstraede
Copenhagen 1204

Image
6 Mejlgarde
Arhus 8000

ENGLAND
See **GREAT BRITAIN**

FINLAND

Museums/Galleries/Exhibition Spaces

Finska Fotografiska Museet
2b Hogbersgatan, F-72
Helsinki 00140

Waino Aaltosen
Itainen Rantakatu
Turku

FRANCE

Museums

Académie des Beaux-Arts
Archives
Paris

Archives Photographiques
3 rue du Valois
Paris 75042 (Sedex 01)

Bibliothèque Historique de la Ville de
Paris
2 avenue Octave Créard
Paris

Bibliothèque Nationale
Departement des Estampes et de la
Photographie
58 rue de Richelieu
Paris 75084
Bernard Marbot, Curator

The Cabinet des Estampes (now the Departement des Estampes et de la Photographie) was founded in 1667 by Louis XIV.
All printers established their patents
through this bureau, and beginning in
1851 every French photographer was required by law to deposit a copy of every
print offered for sale. In reality, friendly
contact existed between the photographers and the curators of the Cabinet and
there has been a continuous flow of prints
given to the Bibliothèque Nationale from
within France and abroad.

The library, with the aim of maintaining
an important collection with an international balance, has purchased samples of
work by non-French photographers. Some
4,000–5,000 new photographs are added
annually. The collection is catalogued
both by subject and photographer. Excellent facilities for preservation and conservation are an integral part of the department.

Open by appointment for research.

Caisse Nationale des Monuments Historiques et des Sites
Archives Photographiques
1 rue Valois
Paris

Fondation Nationale de la Photographie
25 rue du Premier Film
Lyons 69372

La Galerie du Photo-Club de Paris
28ᵗᵉʳ rue Gassendi
Paris 75014

Kodak-Pathé
Bureau de Recherches
30 rue des Vignerons
Vincennes

Mulhouse Textile Museum
3 rue des Bonnes-Gens
Mulhouse

Musée des Arts Décoratifs
107–109 rue de Rivoli
Palais du Louvre
Paris

Musée du Conservatoire National des
Arts et Métiers
292 rue St.-Martin
Paris 75003

Musée Nicéphore Niepce
28 quai des Messageries
Chalon-sur-Saône 71100

Musée Réattu
rue du Grand-Prieuré de Malte
Arles

Pavillon de la Photographie
Hôtel des Sociétés Savantes
190 rue Beauvoisine
Rouen 76000

Pompidou Center
35 boulevard de Sebastopol
Paris 75004

Société Française de Photographie
9 rue Montalembert
Paris 75007
J. J. Trillat, President

The Société Française de Photographie
was founded in 1853; among the founding
members were Hippolyte Bayard, the Bisson *frères*, Louis-Désiré Blanquart-Evrard,
Gustave Le Gray, and Charles Nègre. In
1855 a museum was started and members
were invited to donate gifts of their work.
Because many of the members participated in the beginnings of photography,
their gifts constitute an outstanding collection. Nadar, C. Puyo, and Robert
Demachy are well represented.

The collections include over 15,000
prints, negatives, and daguerreotypes, plus
some 5,000 volumes on the history of photography. The archives document many
important discoveries and therefore have
become an important center for research
and teaching.

Exhibitions are mounted regularly. The
collections are accessible by written appointment.

Galleries

Centre International de Séjour de Paris
Club Photographique
6 avenue Maurice Ravel
Paris 75012

FNAC Montparnasse
136 rue de Rennes
Paris 75006

Galerie Agathe Gaillard
3 rue du Pont Louis-Philippe
Paris 75004

Galerie Amerin Vie
1 rue Grasset
Nantes 4400

Galerie Contrejours
19 rue de l'Ouest
Paris 75014

Galerie Gérard Levy
17 rue de Beaune
Paris 75014

Galerie Jean Dieuzaïde
4 place St.-Etienne
Toulouse

Galerie Nikon
1 rue Jacob
Paris 75006

Galerie Octant
8–10 rue du 29 juillet
Paris 75001

Galerie Upsilone
5 rue St. Michel
Rennes 35000

Galerie Zabriskie
29 rue Aubry-le-Boucher
Paris 75004

Odéon-Photo
110 boulevard St. Germain
Paris

La Photogalerie
2 rue Christine
Paris 75006

La Remise du Parc
2 Impasse des Bourdonnais
Paris 75001

Sonnabend
12 rue Mazarine
Paris

Vinci et Niepce
7 rue Martignac
Paris 75007

Voir
42 rue Pargaminières
Toulouse

Exhibition Spaces

Galerie Municipale du Château d'Eau
place Laganne
Toulouse

GERMANY

Museums

Agfa-Gevaert Foto-Historama
Leverkusen

Akademie der Künste der DDR
58/59 Hermann-Matern Strasse
East Berlin 104

Deutsches Museum von Meisterwerken
  der Naturwissenschaft und Technik
1 Museumsinsel
Munich 26

Münchner Stadtmuseum
1 St.-Jakobs-Platz
Munich 2

Museum der Photographie
14 Lewickistrasse
Dresden a21, East Germany

Museum Folkwang
64 Bismarkstrasse
Essen

Museum für Kunst und Gewerbe
1 Steintorplatz
Hamburg 2 1

Museum Ludwig
L. Fritz Gruber Collection
Cologne 5 1

Nationalgalerie
Staatliche Museen
West Berlin

Neue Sammlung
3 Prinregentenstrasse
Munich 8 22

Polytechnisches Museum Dresden
15 Friedrich-Engels Strasse
Dresden 806, East Germany

Rheinisches Landesmuseum
14–16 Colmanstrasse
Bonn 53 1

Schiller Nationalmuseum
Schillerhöhe
Marbach 7142

Staatliche Landesbildstelle Hamburg
171 Kielerstrasse
Hamburg 2000

Wallraf-Richartz Museum
An der Rechtschule
Cologne

Galleries/Exhibition Spaces

Camera Galerie
49 Bolkerstrasse
Düsseldorf 4

Fotoforum
Gesamthochschule Kassel
Kassel 350

Galerie Breiting
1 Sächsische Strasse
West Berlin 1015

Galerie im Reik
44 Ruhrstrasse
Essen 4307

Galerie Krebaum
8 Im Faudenbuhl
Heddesheim 6805

Galerie M
Haus Weitmar
Bochum 463

Galerie A. Nagel
42 Fasanenstrasse
West Berlin 1015

Galerie Schürmann und Kicken
13 Ronheiderwinkel
Aachen 51

Galerie Spectrum
6 Holzmarkt
Hannover 3000

Galerie Wilde
6 Auf dem Berlich
Cologne 5030

Galerie "Z"
30 Silberstrasse
Hannover 3 51

Kunsthaus
Bielefeld

Landesbildstelle Berlin (Photographic
  Center of The Free City of Berlin)
West Berlin

Photogalerie Lange-Irschl
54 Türkenstrasse
Munich 8040

PPS Gallery
1 Feldstrasse/Hochhaus
Hamburg 2000 4

Werkstatt für Photographie
210 Friedrichstrasse
West Berlin 1 61

Auction Houses

Petzold K.G.
36 Maximilianstrasse
and
3 Apothekergässchen
Augsburg 8900

GREAT BRITAIN

Eɴɢʟᴀɴᴅ

Museums

Arts Council of Great Britain
4 St. James's Sq.
London SW1

Birmingham Reference Library
Birmingham

British Council
10 Spring Gardens
London SW1

British Museum
Great Russell St.
London WC1B 3DG

Cambridge University
Cambridge

Colman and Rye Libraries of Local
  History
Norwich

Fox Talbot Museum
Lacock, Wiltshire SN15 2LG

House of Commons Library
London

Imperial War Museum
Lambeth Rd.
London SE1

India Office Library and Records
Foreign and Commonwealth Office
197 Blackfriars Rd.
London SE1 8NG

Ipswich Museum
Ipswich

Kingston-on-Thames Public Library
Kingston-on-Thames

Kodak Museum
Kodak, Ltd.
Headstone Dr.
Harrow, Middlesex

Liverpool City Libraries
Liverpool

Manchester City Libraries
Manchester

Mansell Collection
42 Linden Gardens
London W2 4ER

Midland Arts Centre
Cannon Hill Park
Birmingham 12

Municipal Art Gallery
Leeds

Museum of English Rural Life
Reading University
Reading

Museum of Modern Art
30 Pembroke St.
Oxford

National Army Museum
Royal Hospital Rd.
London SW3

National Portrait Gallery
2 St. Martin's Pl.
London WC2H 0HE
John Hayes, Director

The collection, devoted almost exclusively to portraits, is comprised of approximately 50,000 original photographs and 100,000 negatives dating from the earliest days of photography to the present.

There are outstanding collections of work by Julia Margaret Cameron, Lewis Carroll, Howard Coster, and Cecil Beaton. In addition, the National Portrait Gallery holds the *Daily Herald* Newspaper Library.

Access to the collection is presently restricted to serious scholars with specific research projects.

Radio Times Hulton Picture Library
35 Marylebone High St.
London W1M 4AA

Royal Geographical Society
1 Kensington Gore
London SW7 2AR

Royal Library
Windsor Castle
Windsor Park

Royal Photographic Society of Great
  Britain
14 S. Audley St.
London W1Y 5DP

Science Museum
Exhibition Rd.
London SW7 2DD

Stonyhurst College
Clitheroe

University of Exeter Library
Exeter

Victoria and Albert Museum
The Library, Photograph Collection
Cromwell Rd.
London, SW7 2RL
Mark Haworth-Booth, Keeper of
  Photographs

The collection contains more than 250,000 items, primarily nineteenth-century photographs. The archives include a wide range of subject matter, from British and non-British architecture and topography to portraits and family albums.

Major holdings include work by D. O. Hill and Robert Adamson, Julia Margaret Cameron, Roger Fenton, Francis Frith, Eadweard Muybridge, Roger Mertin, and Camille (de) Silvy. Photographs are indexed by photographers or subject matter.

The museum maintains a permanent public display. The collection itself may be viewed by appointment.

Whitby Literary and Philosophical
  Society
Whitby

Galleries/Exhibition Spaces

Aberbach Fine Art Gallery
17 Savile Row
London W1

Albert Street Workshop
8 Albert St.
Hebden Bridge HX7

Amolfini
Narrow Quay
Bristol BS1 4QA

Art Faculty Concourse
Kedleston Rd.
Derby

Asahi Pentax Gallery
6 Vigo St.
London W1X 1AH

Battersea Arts Centre
Lavender Hill
London SW11

P. and D. Colnaghi
14 Old Bond St.
London W1X 4JL

Creative Camera Gallery
19 Doughty St.
London WC1N 2PT

Ealing College of Higher Education
St. Mary's Rd.
London W5 5RF

Earlsfield Library
Magdalen Rd.
London

Gallery of Photography
112 Pricedale Rd.
London W11

The Grapes
90–92 Whitechapel
Liverpool L1 6EN

Grass Roots Photographic Gallery
1 Newton St.
Manchester M1 1HW

Half Moon
27 Alie St.
London E1

Harrow College of Art and Technology
London

Hayward Gallery
South Bank
London

I.C.A.
Nash House
12 Carlton House Terrace
London SW1

Impressions Gallery of Photography
17 Colliergate
York

Inner Gallery
St. Edmund's Art Trust
Salisbury

Kettering Gallery
Sheep St.
London

Kodak Photo Gallery
246 High Holborn
London WC1

Marlborough Fine Art of London
6 Albemarle St.
London W1X 3HF

Midland Group Gallery
24–32 Carlton St.
Nottingham

Open Eye Gallery
90–92 Whitechapel
Liverpool L1 6EN

The Photographers' Gallery
8 Great Newport St.
London WC2

The Photographic Gallery
The University
Southampton SO9 5NH

Robert Self Ltd. Gallery
48–50 Earlham St.
London WC2

Serpentine Gallery
Kensington Gardens
London W2

Side Gallery
9 Side
Newcastle-upon-Tyne NE1 3JE

Spectro Arts Workshop
Bells Court
Pilgrim St.
Newcastle-upon-Tyne NE1 6RH

The Sutcliffe Gallery
1 Flowergate
Whitby YO21 3BA

York Library
Wye St.
London

Auction Houses

Christie's South Kensington
85 Old Brompton Rd.
London SW7 3JS

Phillips
7 Blenheim St., New Bond St.
London W1Y 0AS

Sotheby's Belgravia
19 Motcomb St.
London SW1X 8LB

SCOTLAND

Museums

Edinburgh Photographic Society
Edinburgh

Edinburgh Public Library
Edinburgh

Mitchell Library
Glasgow

Royal Scottish Museum
Department of Technology
Chambers St.
Edinburgh EH1 1JF

Scottish United Service Museum
The Castle
Crown Sq.
Edinburgh EH1 2YT

Scottish National Portrait Gallery
Queen St.
Edinburgh

Galleries

Webster of Oban Gallery of Photography
15 Stafford St.
Oban

ISRAEL

Museums

Israel Museum
Hakirya St.
Jerusalem 9100

Galleries/Exhibition Spaces

The White Gallery Ltd.
4 Habima Sq.
Tel Aviv

ITALY

Museums

Museo del Cinema
2 piazza San Giovanni
Turin

Galleries/Exhibition Spaces

Lucio Amelio
58 piazza del Martiri
Naples

Antra Studio
8 via Fiori Chiari
Milan

Il Cupolone
12r via del Servi
Florence 50122

Il Diaframma/Canon
10 via Brera
Milan

Galleria dell'Immagine
4 piazza Vecchia
Bergamo 24100

Galleria Documenta
2 via Santa Maria
Turin

Galleria Fotografica Nadar
26 vicolo del Tidi
Pisa 56100

JAPAN

Museums

National Museum of Modern Art
3 Kitanomaru Koen
Chiyoda-ku, 102
Tokyo

Galleries/Exhibition Spaces

Asahi Pentax Gallery
21–20, 3-chome
Nishi-Azabu, Minato-ku
Tokyo

Canon Salon
9–9, 3-chome
Ginza, Chou-ku
Tokyo

Nikon Salon
5–6, 3-chome
Ginza, Chou-ku
Tokyo

MEXICO

Museums

Museo de Arte Moderno
Bosque de Chapultepec
Mexico City

Galleries/Exhibition Spaces

Galeria de Fotografia
Casa del Lago, U.N.A.M.
Bosque de Chapultepec
Mexico City

THE NETHERLANDS

Museums

Print Room
University of Leiden
65 Rapenburg
Leiden

Stedelijk Museum
13 Paulus Potterstraat
Amsterdam

Galleries/Exhibition Spaces

Canon Photo Gallery
19 Reestraat
Amsterdam

Galerie Fiolet
86 Herengracht
Amsterdam

NEW ZEALAND

Museums

Alexander Turnbull Library
Box 12–349
Wellington

Auckland City Art Gallery
E. Wellesley St.
Auckland 1

Auckland Institute and Museum
The Domain
Auckland 1

Dunedin Public Art Gallery
Box 566
Logan Park
Dunedin

The Hocken Library
University of Otago
Box 56
Dunedin

Manawatu Art Gallery
Grey and Carroll Sts.
Palmerston North

National Museum
Buckle St.
Wellington 1

Nelson Provincial Museum
Hardy St.
Nelson

Galleries/Exhibition Spaces

Snaps: A Photographer's Gallery
30 Airedale St.
Auckland 1

NORWAY

Museums

Preus Fotomuseum
82 Langgt.
Horten 3190

Galleries/Exhibition Spaces

Gallerie for Fri Fotografi
49 Pilestredet
Oslo

PERU

Galleries/Exhibition Spaces

Galeria Secuencia
1130 Conquistadores
Lima 27

POLAND

Museums

Museum Sztuki
36 ul. Wieckowskiego
Lodz 90–734

Galleries/Exhibition Spaces

Union of Polish Art Photographers
8 Plac Zamkowy
Warsaw 00–277

PORTUGAL

Museums

Museu Nacional de Arte Antiga
largo 9 de Abril
Lisbon

REPUBLIC OF SOUTH AFRICA

Museums

Bensusan Museum of Photography and
  Library
17 Empire Rd.
Parktown (Johannesburg) 2001

SCOTLAND
See GREAT BRITAIN

SPAIN

Galleries/Exhibition Spaces

Fotomania
26 Ganduxer
Barcelona 21

La Photo Galeria
(El Photo Centro)
2 Plaza de la Republica Argentina
Madrid 6

Galleria Spectrum/Canon
86 Balmes
Barcelona 8

SWEDEN

Museums

Fotografiska Museet
Moderna Museet
Skeppsholmen
Stockholm 11149

Tekniska Museet
Museivägen
7 Gen
Stockholm

Galleries/Exhibition Spaces

Camera Obscura
Hall and Cederquist AB
Strandvägen 5A
Stockholm 114 51

Malmo Konsthall
St. Johannesgatan
Malmo

SWITZERLAND

Museums

Kunstgewerbemuseum der Stadt Zürich
60 Ausstellungsstrasse
Zurich 5

Galleries/Exhibition Spaces

Canon Photo Galerie
3 rue Saint-Léger
Geneva 1205

Galerie Form
2 Predigerplatz
Zurich 8001

Galerie Media
29 rue des Moulins
Neuchâtel 2000

Galerie Rivolta
1 rue de la Mercerie
Lausanne 1003

Galerie 38
38 Kirchgasse
Zurich 8001

Galerie Tolgge im Cafe Drahtschmidli
17 Wasserwerkstrasse
Zurich 8006

Kunsthaus Zürich
1 Heimplatz
Zurich 8001

Nikon Foto-Galerie
3 Schoffelgasse
Zurich 8001

Photo Art Basel
10 St. Alban-Vorstadt
Basel 4059

St. Galler Fotogalerie
6 Webergasse
St. Gallen 9000

VENEZUELA

Museums

Museo de Bellas Artes
Parque Sucre
105 Los Caobos
Caracas

Galleries/Exhibition Spaces

Fototeca
929 Apartado
Caracas

YUGOSLAVIA

Galleries/Exhibition Spaces

Focus
Podhod Zvezda
Ljubljana 6100

Galerie Spot/Galerije grada Zagreba
2 Katerinin Trg.
Zagreb 4100

Collection Abbreviations

The following list is a key to the abbreviations used in citing collection locations in chapter 5. Full addresses are given elsewhere in appendix C.

AAA	Archives of American Art New York, N.Y.	AGS	American Geographical Society New York, N.Y.
Academy of Natural Sciences	Academy of Natural Sciences of Philadelphia Philadelphia, Pa.	Akademie der Künste	Akademie der Künste der DDR East Berlin, Germany
Addison	Addison Gallery of American Art Andover, Mass.	Akron	Akron Art Institute Akron, Ohio
Agfa-Gevaert	Agfa-Gevaert Foto-Historama Leverkusen, Germany	Albright-Knox	Albright-Knox Art Gallery Buffalo, N.Y.

AMNH	American Museum of Natural History New York, N.Y.	Bureau of Ethnology	*See* Smithsonian (Anthropological Archives)
Amon Carter	Amon Carter Museum of Western Art Fort Worth, Tex.	Caisse Nationale	Caisse Nationale des Monuments Historiques et des Sites Paris, France
Antiquarian Society	American Antiquarian Society Worcester, Mass.	California (Bancroft)	University of California Berkeley, Calif. Bancroft Library
Antwerp	Provinciaal Museum voor Kunstambachten Deurne (Antwerp), Belgium	California Palace of the Legion of Honor	California Palace of the Legion of Honor San Francisco, Calif.
Archives Beaux-Arts	Archives, Academie des Beaux-Arts Paris, France	California (Santa Cruz)	University of California Santa Cruz, Calif.
Archives Photographiques	Archives Photographiques Paris, France	Cambridge	Cambridge University Cambridge, England
Arizona	University of Arizona Museum of Art Tucson, Ariz.	Canberra	Australian National Gallery Canberra, Australia
Arizona State	Arizona State University Art Collections Tempe, Ariz.	Caracas Carnegie	Museo de Bellas Artes Caracas, Venezuela Carnegie Institute Pittsburgh, Pa.
Arles	Musée Réattu Arles, France	CCP	Center for Creative Photography Tucson, Ariz.
Arts Council	Arts Council of Great Britain London, England	Chicago	Art Institute of Chicago Chicago, Ill.
Baltimore	Baltimore Museum of Art Baltimore, Md.	CHS	California Historical Society San Francisco, Calif.
Berea	Berea College Berea, Ky.	Cincinnati	Cincinnati Art Museum Cincinnati, Ohio
BM	British Museum London, England	Cleveland	Cleveland Museum of Art Cleveland, Ohio
BMFA	Museum of Fine Arts Boston, Mass.	Colby	Colby College Art Museum Waterville, Maine
BN	Bibliothèque Nationale Paris, France	Colman and Rye	Colman and Rye Libraries of Local History Norwich, England
BPL	Boston Public Library Boston, Mass.	Cologne	Museum Ludwig Cologne, Germany
Brandeis	Brandeis University Waltham, Mass.	Colorado	Colorado State Museum Denver, Colo.
British Council	British Council London, England	Columbia	Avery Architectural Library Columbia University New York, N.Y.
Brooklyn	Brooklyn Museum Brooklyn, N.Y.		
Brooks	Brooks Memorial Art Gallery Memphis, Tenn.	Commons	House of Commons Library London, England

Conservatoire National	Musée du Conservatoire National des Arts et Métiers Paris, France
Corcoran	Corcoran Gallery of Art Washington, D.C.
Cornell	Johnson Museum of Art Cornell University Ithaca, N.Y.
CSL	California State Library Sacramento, Calif.
Dallas	Dallas Museum of Fine Arts Dallas, Texas
Dayton	Dayton Art Institute Dayton, Ohio
Delaware	Delaware Art Museum Wilmington, Del.
Denver	Denver Public Library Denver, Colo.
Detroit	Detroit Institute of Arts Detroit, Mich.
Everson	Everson Museum of Art Syracuse, N.Y.
Exeter	University of Exeter Library Exeter, England
FIT	Fashion Institute of Technology Library New York, N.Y.
Florida	Florida Center for the Arts Tampa, Fla.
Folkwang	Museum Folkwang Essen, Germany
FOP	Friends of Photography Carmel, Calif.
Fotografiska	Fotografiska Museet Stockholm, Sweden
Geelong	Geelong Art Gallery Geelong, Australia
Harvard	Harvard University Cambridge, Mass.
(Carpenter)	Carpenter Center for the Visual Arts
(Fogg)	Fogg Art Museum
(Houghton)	Houghton Library
(Semitic)	Semitic Museum
(Widener)	Widener Memorial Library
High	High Museum of Art Atlanta, Ga.
Hirshhorn	Hirshhorn Museum and Sculpture Garden Washington, D.C.
Houston	Museum of Fine Arts Houston, Tex.
Huntington	Henry E. Huntington Library and Art Gallery San Marino, Calif.
ICP	International Center of Photography New York, N.Y.
Illinois	Krannert Art Museum University of Illinois Urbana, Ill.
Imperial War Museum	Imperial War Museum London, England
IMP/GEH	International Museum of Photography at George Eastman House Rochester, N.Y.
Indiana	Indiana University Art Museum Bloomington, Ind.
India Records	India Office Library and Records London, England
Institute for Sex Research	Institute for Sex Research Bloomington, Ind.
Israel Museum	Israel Museum Jerusalem, Israel
Kalamazoo	Kalamazoo Institute of Arts Kalamazoo, Mich.
Kansas	University of Kansas Museum of Art Lawrence, Kans.
Kansas Historical	Kansas State Historical Society Topeka, Kans.
Kingston-on-Thames	Kingston-on-Thames Public Library Kingston-on-Thames, England
Kodak	Kodak Museum Harrow, England
La Jolla	La Jolla Museum of Contemporary Art La Jolla, Calif.
LIFE	LIFE Picture Collection (Time Inc.) New York, N.Y.

Lisbon	Museu Nacional de Arte Antiga Lisbon, Portugal	
Liverpool	Liverpool City Libraries Liverpool, England	
LOC	Library of Congress Prints and Photographs Division Washington, D.C.	
Los Angeles (Art)/ (Natural History)	Los Angeles County Museum of Art/Natural History Los Angeles, Calif.	
Louisville	Photographic Archives University of Louisville Louisville, Ky.	
McGill	McCord Museum McGill University Montreal, Quebec	
Madison	Madison Art Center Madison, Wis.	
Manchester	Manchester City Libraries Manchester, England	
Mansell	Mansell Collection London, England	
Maryland	University of Maryland Baltimore County Library Baltimore, Md.	
Menil	Menil Foundation Houston, Tex.	
Mexico City	Museo de Arte Moderno Mexico City, Mexico	
Michigan	University of Michigan Ann Arbor, Mich.	
Minneapolis	Minneapolis Institute of Arts Minneapolis, Minn.	
Minnesota	University of Minnesota Minneapolis, Minn.	
Minnesota Archives	University of Minnesota Social Welfare History Archives Minneapolis, Minn.	
Mint	Mint Museum of Art Charlotte, N.C.	
Missouri	Missouri Historical Society St. Louis, Mo.	
MIT	Massachusetts Institute of Technology Cambridge, Mass.	

(Hayden)	Hayden Gallery
(Historical Collections)	MIT Historical Collections
Mitchell Library	Mitchell Library Glasgow, Scotland
MMA	Metropolitan Museum of Art New York, N.Y.
MOMA	Museum of Modern Art New York, N.Y.
Morgan	Pierpont Morgan Library New York, N.Y.
Mulhouse	Mulhouse Textile Museum Mulhouse, France
Musée des Arts Décoratifs	Musée des Arts Décoratifs Paris, France
Musée Nicéphore Niepce	Musée Nicéphore Niepce Châlon-sur-Saône, France
Museum of New Mexico	Museum of New Mexico Santa Fe, N.Mex.
National Archives	National Archives and Record Service Washington, D.C.
National Army Museum	National Army Museum London, England
Nationalgalerie	Nationalgalerie Staatliche Museen West Berlin, Germany
NCFA	National Collection of Fine Arts Washington, D.C.
Nebraska	Sheldon Memorial Art Gallery University of Nebraska Lincoln, Nebr.
Newark	Newark Museum Newark, N.J.
New Jersey	New Jersey State Museum Trenton, N.J.
New Mexico	University Art Museum University of New Mexico Albuquerque, N.Mex.
New Orleans	New Orleans Museum of Art New Orleans, La.
New York	Museum of the City of New York New York, N.Y.
NGC	National Gallery of Canada Ottawa, Ontario

NGV	National Gallery of Victoria Melbourne, Australia	Phillips	Phillips Collection Washington, D.C.
North Carolina	University of North Carolina Chapel Hill, N.C.	Phoenix	Phoenix Art Museum Phoenix, Ariz.
Norton Simon	Norton Simon Museum of Art Pasadena, Calif.	Photo-Club de Paris	La Galerie du Photo-Club de Paris Paris, France
Norwood	Norwood Historical Society Norwood, Mass.	Plainsman	Plainsman Museum Aurora, Nebr.
NPG	National Portrait Gallery London, England	Pomona	Pomona College Art Gallery Claremont, Calif.
NPG (U.S.)	National Portrait Gallery Washington, D.C.	Pompidou	Pompidou Center Paris, France
NYHS	New-York Historical Society New York, N.Y.	Portland (Maine)	Portland Museum of Art Portland, Maine
NYPL	New York Public Library New York, N.Y.	Portland (Ore.)	Portland Art Museum Portland, Ore.
(Genealogy)	Local History and Genealogy Division	Prague	Museum of Decorative Arts Prague, Czechoslovakia
(Lincoln Center)	Library and Museum of the Performing Arts Lincoln Center	Princeton	Princeton University Princeton, N.J.
(Photography)	Photography Archive	(Art Museum)	Art Museum
(Picture)	Picture Collection	(Library)	Firestone Library
(Rare Book)	Rare Book Division		
Oakland	The Oakland Museum Oakland, Calif.	Radio Times	Radio Times Hulton Picture Library London, England
Oberlin	Allen Memorial Art Museum Oberlin College Oberlin, Ohio	RGS	Royal Geographical Society London, England
Ohio Wesleyan	Ohio Wesleyan University Delaware, Ohio	Ringling	John and Mable Ringling Museum of Art Sarasota, Fla.
Oregon	Museum of Art University of Oregon Eugene, Ore.	RISD	Rhode Island School of Design Museum of Art Providence, R.I.
Oregon Historical	Oregon Historical Society Portland, Ore.	Royal Library	Royal Library Windsor Park, England
Paris	Bibliothèque Historique de la Ville de Paris Paris, France	Royal Scottish Museum	Royal Scottish Museum Edinburgh, Scotland
Philadelphia	Philadelphia Museum of Art Philadelphia, Pa.	RPS	Royal Photographic Society of Great Britain London, England
Philadelphia Civic Center	Museum of the Philadelphia Civic Center Philadelphia, Pa.	St. Louis	St. Louis Art Museum St. Louis, Mo.
Philadelphia Library	Free Library of Philadelphia Philadelphia, Pa.	St. Petersburg	Museum of Fine Arts St. Petersburg, Fla.

San Antonio	Witte Memorial Museum San Antonio, Tex.	Temple	Temple University Philadelphia, Pa.
San Francisco	San Francisco Museum of Modern Art San Francisco, Calif.	Tennessee	University of Tennessee Knoxville, Tenn.
Santa Barbara	Santa Barbara Museum of Art Santa Barbara, Calif.	Texas	Humanities Research Center University of Texas Austin, Tex.
São Paulo	Museu de Arte Contemporânea da Universidade de São Paulo São Paulo, Brazil	(Gernsheim)	Gernsheim Collection
		Tokyo	National Museum of Modern Art Tokyo, Japan
Schiller	Schiller Nationalmuseum Marbach, Germany	TVA	Tennessee Valley Authority Knoxville, Tenn.
Science Museum	Science Museum London, England	UCLA	University of California Los Angeles, Calif.
Scottish Museum	Scottish United Service Museum Edinburgh, Scotland	U. of Chicago	University of Chicago Chicago, Ill.
Scottish NPG	Scottish National Portrait Gallery Edinburgh, Scotland	U. of Colorado	University of Colorado Boulder, Colo.
Seattle	Seattle Art Museum Seattle, Wash.	U. of Florida	University Gallery University of Florida Gainesville, Fla.
Smith	Smith College Museum of Art Northampton, Mass.	U.S. Dept. of Interior	United States Department of the Interior Washington, D.C.
Smithsonian	Smithsonian Institution Washington, D.C.		
(Anthropological Archives)	National Anthropological Archives (formerly Bureau of American Ethnology) National Museum of Natural History	Utah	Utah State Historical Society Salt Lake City, Utah
		VA	Victoria and Albert Museum London, England
Société Française	Société Française de Photographie Paris, France	Vassar	Vassar College Poughkeepsie, N.Y.
Southwest	Southwest Museum Los Angeles, Calif.	Virginia	Virginia Museum of Fine Arts Richmond, Va.
Springfield (Mo.)	Springfield Art Museum Springfield, Mo.	VSW	Visual Studies Workshop Rochester, N.Y.
Stanford	Stanford University Stanford, Calif.	Wadsworth	Wadsworth Atheneum Hartford, Conn.
Stedelijk	Stedelijk Museum Amsterdam, Netherlands	Wallraf-Richartz	Wallraf-Richartz Museum Cologne, Germany
Stonyhurst	Stonyhurst College Clitheroe, England	Washington	University of Washington Libraries Seattle, Wash.
Sutcliffe	The Sutcliffe Gallery Whitby, England	Washington U.	Washington University St. Louis, Mo.
Tacoma	Tacoma Art Museum Tacoma, Wash.	Wellesley	Wellesley College Museum Wellesley, Mass.

Wesleyan	Davison Art Center Wesleyan University Middletown, Conn.	Worcester	Worcester Art Museum Worcester, Mass.
Whitby	Whitby Literary and Philosophical Society Whitby, England	Yale	Yale University New Haven, Conn.
		(Art Gallery)	Art Gallery
Whitney	Whitney Museum of American Art New York, N.Y.	(Beinecke)	Beinecke Rare Book and Manuscript Library

General Bibliography

The following bibliography includes books and magazines used in compiling *The Photograph Collector's Guide,* as well as many other sources recommended for further reading. It is divided into three categories: Histories and Surveys, Color Photography, and Current Periodicals. Revised or other variant editions are included when known; unrevised reprints such as paperback editions are excluded.

Books published in international co-editions are cited either by originating publisher or by United States publisher. Additional references can be found elsewhere in this book: chapter 4 lists sources of information about photographic care and restoration (page 61); chapter 5 includes a selected bibliography for each entry; and chapter 7 cites catalogues for a number of contemporary exhibitions.

Histories and Surveys

Andrews, Ralph W. *Photographers of the Frontier West: Their Lives and Their Works, 1875 to 1915.* New York: Bonanza, 1965.

———. *Picture Gallery Pioneers, 1850 to 1875.* New York: Bonanza, 1964.

Arts Council of Great Britain. *'From Today Painting Is Dead': The Beginnings of Photography.* London, 1972.

———. *The Real Thing: An Anthology of British Photographs 1840–1850.* London, 1975.

Beaton, Cecil. *British Photographers.* London: Collins, 1944.

———, and Buckland, Gail. *The Magic Image: The Genius of Photography from 1839 to the Present Day.* Boston: Little, Brown, 1975.

Bensusan, A. D. *Silver Images: History of Photography in Africa.* Cape Town: Timmins, 1966.

Besson, George. *La Photographie française.* Paris: Braun, 1936.

Billeter, Erika. *Malerei und Photographie im Dialog von 1840 bis Heute.* Bern: Benteli, 1977.

Blanquart-Evrard, Louis-Désiré. *La Photographie: Ses origines, ses progrès, ses transformations.* Lille, France: L. Danel, 1869.

Bossert, Helmut Theodor, and Guttman, Heinrich. *Aus der Frühzeit der Photographie, 1840–1870.* Frankfurt am Main: Societäts-Verlag, 1930.

Braive, Michel F. *The Era of the Photograph: A Social History.* London: Thames & Hudson, 1966. U.S. ed., *The Photograph: A Social History.* New York: McGraw-Hill, 1966.

Brothers, Alfred. *Photography: Its History, Processes, Apparatus and Materials.* London: Charles Griffin, 1892.

Buckland, Gail. *Reality Recorded: Early Documentary Photography.* Boston: New York Graphic Society, 1974.

Bull, Deborah, and Lorimer, Donald. *Up the Nile: A Photographic Excursion. Egypt 1839–1898.* New York: Potter, 1979.

Camera Work: A Photographic Quarterly [1903–1917]. Facsimile reprint. 6 vols. Nendeln, Liechtenstein: Kraus Reprint, 1969.

Castle, Peter. *Collecting and Valuing Old Photographs.* London: Garnstone Press, 1973.

Christ, Yvan. *L'Age d'or de la photographie.* Paris: Vincent, Fréal, 1965.

Coe, Brian. *The Birth of Photography: The Story of the Formative Years, 1800–1900.* New York: Taplinger, 1977.

Coke, Van Deren, ed. *One Hundred Years of Photographic History: Essays in Honor of Beaumont Newhall.* Albuquerque: University of New Mexico Press, 1975.

————. *The Painter and the Photograph.* Albuquerque: University of New Mexico Press, 1964. Rev. ed., subtitled *From Delacroix to Warhol,* 1972.

Colnaghi, P. & D., & Co. *Photography: The First Eighty Years.* London, 1976. Text by Valerie Lloyd.

Daniels, Patrick. *Early Photography.* New York: St. Martin, 1978.

Danziger, James, and Conrad, Barnaby, III. *Interviews with Master Photographers.* New York: Paddington, 1977.

Darrah, William Culp. *Stereo Views: A History of Stereographs in America and Their Collection.* Gettysburg, Pa.: Times & News, 1964.

————. *The World of Stereographs.* Gettysburg, Pa.: W. C. Darrah, 1977.

Doty, Robert, ed. *Photography in America.* Intro. by Minor White. New York: Random House, 1974.

————. *Photo-Secession: Photography as a Fine Art.* Rochester, N.Y.: George Eastman House, 1960. Rev. ed., subtitled *Stieglitz and the Fine-Art Movement in Photography.* New York: Dover, 1978.

Eder, Josef Maria. *The History of Photography.* Translated by Edward Epstean. New York: Columbia University Press, 1945. Unillustrated translation of *Geschichte der Photographie.* Halle, Prussia: Knapp, 1932. Another ed., New York: Dover, 1978.

Edey, Maitland. *Great Photographic Essays from LIFE.* Boston: New York Graphic Society, 1978.

The Focal Encyclopedia of Photography. London and New York: Focal Press, 1971.

Freund, Gisèle. *La Photographie en France au dix-neuvième siècle: Essai de sociologie et d'esthétique.* Paris: Monnier, 1936.

————. *Photographie et société.* Paris: Seuil, 1974. U.S. ed., Boston: Godine, in preparation.

Gassan, Arnold. *A Chronology of Photography.* Athens, Ohio: Arnold Gassan Handbook Co., 1972.

Gernsheim, Helmut. *Creative Photography: Aesthetic Trends, 1839–1960.* London: Faber & Faber, 1962.

————, and Gernsheim, Alison. *A Concise History of Photography.* New York: Grosset & Dunlap, 1965.

————. *Creative Photography, 1826 to the Present: An Exhibition from the Gernsheim Collection.* Detroit: Wayne State University Press, 1963.

————. *The History of Photography: From the Earliest Use of the Camera Obscura in the Eleventh Century up to 1914.* New York: Oxford University Press, 1955. Rev. ed., New York: McGraw-Hill, 1969.

————. *Masterpieces of Victorian Photography.* London: Phaidon, 1951.

Goodrich, L. Carrington, and Cameron, Nigel. *The Face of China: Photographs 1860–1912.* Millerton, N.Y.: Aperture, 1978.

Green, Jonathan, ed. *Camera Work: A Critical Anthology.* Millerton, N.Y.: Aperture, 1973.

Greenhill, Ralph. *Early Photography in Canada.* Toronto: Oxford University Press, 1965.

Gregorova, Anna. *Fotograficka Tvorba.* Czechoslovakia: Vydavatel'stvo Osveta, 1977.

Harrison, Jerome. *A History of Photography.* New York: Scovill, 1887.

Helsted, Dyvere, et al. *Rome in Early Photographs: The Age of Pius IX. Photographs 1846–1878 from Roman and Danish Collections.* Copenhagen: Thorvaldsen Museum, 1977.

Hillier, Bevis. *Victorian Studio Photographs.* Boston: Godine, 1976.

Hodgson, Pat. *Early War Photographs: 50 Years of War Photographs from the Nineteenth Century.* Boston: New York Graphic Society, 1974.

Howarth-Loomes, B. E. C. *Victorian Photography: An Introduction for Collectors and Connoisseurs.* New York: St. Martin, 1974.

Hume, Sandy, et al., eds. *The Great West: Real/Ideal.* Boulder: University of Colorado, Department of Fine Arts, 1977.

An Inquiry into the Aesthetics of Photography. Toronto: Artscanada, 1975.

Jammes, André, and Sobieszek, Robert. *French Primitive Photography.* Millerton, N.Y.: Aperture, 1970.

Jammes, Marie-Thérèse, and Jammes, André. *The First Century of Photography: Niepce to Atget.* Chicago: Chicago Art Institute, 1977.

Japanese Photographers' Society. *The History of Japanese Photography, 1840–1945.* Tokyo: Heibonsha, 1971.

Jenkins, Reese V. *Image and Enterprise: Technology and the American Photographic Industry, 1839–1925.* Baltimore: Johns Hopkins University Press, 1976.

Jonquières, Henri. *La Vieille photographie depuis Daguerre jusqu'à 1870.* Paris: Henri Lefebvre, 1935.

Kahmen, Volker. *Art History of Photography.* New York: Viking, 1974.

Kelly, Jain, ed. *Darkroom 2.* New York: Lustrum, 1978.

Lacey, Peter, and LaRotonda, Anthony. *The History of the Nude in Photography.* New York: Bantam, 1964.

Lawton, Harry W., and Know, George, eds. *The Valiant Knights of Daguerre: Selected Critical Essays on Photography and Profiles of Photographic Pioneers by Sadakichi Hartmann.* Berkeley: University of California Press, 1978.

Lécuyer, Raymond. *Histoire de la photographie.* Paris: Baschet, 1945.

Lewis, Eleanor, ed. *Darkroom 1.* New York: Lustrum, 1976.

Library of Congress. *Guide to the Special Collections of Prints and Photographs in the Library of Congress.* Ed. by Paul Vanderbilt. Washington, D.C., 1955.

————. *Image of America: Early Photography 1839–1900.* Text by Beaumont Newhall. Washington, D.C., 1957.

————. *Pictorial Americana: A Select List of Photographic Negatives in the Prints and Photographs Division of the Library of Congress.* Washington, D.C., 1955.

Life Library of Photography: *The Art of Photography; The Camera; Caring for Photographs; Color; Documentary Photography; Frontiers of Photography; Great Photographers; The Great Themes; Light and Film; Photo-*

graphing Children; Photographing Nature; Photography as a Tool; Photojournalism; The Print; Special Problems; The Studio; Travel Photography; Photography Year 1973, 1974, 1975, 1976, 1977, 1978, 1979. New York: Time-Life Books, 1970-79.

Literature of Photography Series, The. Peter C. Bunnell and Robert A. Sobieszek, advisory eds. New York: Arno, 1973. 62 books reproducing out-of-print technical, historical, and aesthetic publications, such as the 1911 edition of *Cassell's Cyclopaedia of Photography.* (Dover Publications, New York; Morgan & Morgan, Dobbs Ferry, N.Y.; and other publishers have also reprinted early photographic books.)

Loetscher, Hugo, et al., eds. *Photography in Switzerland, 1840 to Today.* Teufen, Switzerland: Niggli, 1974.

Lucie-Smith, Edward. *The Invented Eye: Masterpieces of Photography, 1839-1914.* New York: Paddington, 1975.

Lyons, Nathan, ed. *Photographers on Photography.* Englewood Cliffs, N.J.: Prentice-Hall, and Rochester, N.Y.: George Eastman House, 1966.

———. *Photography in the Twentieth Century.* New York: Horizon, and Rochester, N.Y.: George Eastman House, 1967.

Maddow, Ben. *Faces: A Narrative History of the Portrait in Photography.* Boston: New York Graphic Society, 1977.

Mann, Margery, and Noggle, Ann, eds. *Women of Photography: An Historical Survey.* San Francisco: San Francisco Museum of Art, 1975.

Marbot, Bernard. *Une Invention du XIXe siècle: Expression et technique [de] la photographie.* Paris: Bibliothèque Nationale, 1976.

Mathews, Oliver. *Early Photographs and Early Photographers: A Survey in Dictionary Form.* New York: Pitman, 1973.

Mees, C. E. Kenneth. *From Dry Plates to Ektachrome Film: A Story of Photographic Research.* New York: Ziff-Davis, 1961.

Moholy-Nagy, Lucia. *A Hundred Years of Photography, 1839-1939.* Harmondsworth, England: Penguin, 1939.

Morosow, Sergej. *Die Russische Künstlerische Photographie 1839-1917.* Moscow, 1955.

Naef, Weston J. *The Collection of Alfred Stieglitz: Fifty Pioneers of Modern Photography.* New York: Metropolitan Museum of Art, 1978.

———, and Wood, James N. *Era of Exploration: The Rise of Landscape Photography in the American West, 1860-1885.* Buffalo: Albright-Knox Art Gallery, and New York: Metropolitan Museum of Art, 1975.

Newhall, Beaumont. *The Daguerreotype in America.* New York: Duell, Sloan & Pearce, 1961. Rev. ed., Greenwich, Conn.: New York Graphic Society, 1968.

———. *The History of Photography from 1839 to the Present Day.* New York: Museum of Modern Art, 1949. Rev. ed., 1964.

———. *Latent Image: The Discovery of Photography.* Garden City, N.Y.: Doubleday, 1967.

———. *Photography: A Short Critical History.* New York: Museum of Modern Art, 1938.

———, and Newhall, Nancy. *Masters of Photography.* New York: Abrams, 1969.

Ovenden, Graham. *Pre-Raphaelite Photography.* New York: St. Martin, 1972.

Pfister, Harold Francis. *Facing the Light: Historic American Portrait Daguerreotypes.* Washington, D.C.: Smithsonian Institution Press, 1978.

Phillips, David R. *The Taming of the West: A Photographic Perspective.* Chicago: Regnery, 1974.

Pollack, Peter. *The Picture History of Photography: From the Earliest Beginnings to the Present Day.* New York: Abrams, 1958. Rev. ed., 1969.

Potonniée, Georges. *History of the Discovery of Photography.* Trans. by Edward Epstean. New York: Tennant & Ward, 1936.

Rinhart, Floyd, and Rinhart, Marion. *American Daguerreian Art.* New York: Potter, 1967.

———. *American Miniature Case Art.* New York: Barnes, 1969.

Rudisill, Richard. *Mirror Image: The Influence of the Daguerreotype on American Society.* Albuquerque: University of New Mexico Press, 1971.

Scharf, Aaron. *Art and Photography.* Baltimore: Penguin, 1969. Rev. ed., 1969.

———. *Creative Photography:* London: Studio Vista, 1965.

———. *Pioneers of Photography.* New York: Abrams, 1976.

Schoener, Allon, ed. *Harlem On My Mind: Cultural Capital of Black America 1900-1968.* New York: Metropolitan Museum of Art, 1969.

Sipley, Louis Walton. *Collector's Guide to American Photography.* Philadelphia: American Museum of Photography, 1957.

———. *Photography's Great Inventors.* Philadelphia: American Museum of Photography, 1965.

Skopec, Rudolf. *Photographie im Wandel der Zeiten.* Prague: Artia, 1963.

Snyder, Norman, et al., eds. *The Photography Catalog: A Sourcebook of the Best Equipment, Materials, Techniques and Resources.* New York: Harper & Row, 1976.

Steichen, Edward, ed. *The Family of Man.* New York: Museum of Modern Art, 1955.

Stelzer, Otto. *Kunst und Photographie.* Munich: Piper, 1966.

Stenger, Erich. *The History of Photography: Its Relation to Civilization and Practice.* Trans. by Edward Epstean. Easton, Pa.: Mack Printing, 1939.

———. *The March of Photography.* London: Focal Press, 1958.

Stott, William. *Documentary Expression and Thirties America.* New York: Oxford University Press, 1973.

Strasser, Alex. *Victorian Photography.* London: Focal Press, 1942.

Szarkowski, John. *From the Picture Press.* New York: Museum of Modern Art, 1973.

———. *Looking at Photographs: 100 Pictures from the Collection of The Museum of Modern Art.* New York: Museum of Modern Art, 1973.

―――. *Mirrors and Windows: American Photography since 1960.* New York: Museum of Modern Art, 1978.

―――. *The Photographer's Eye.* New York: Museum of Modern Art, 1966.

―――, and Yamagishi, Shoji, eds. *New Japanese Photography.* New York: Museum of Modern Art, 1974.

Taft, Robert. *Photography and the American Scene: A Social History, 1839–1889.* New York: Macmillan, 1938.

Thomas, Alan. *Time in a Frame: Photography and the Nineteenth-Century Mind.* New York: Schocken, 1977.

Thomas, D. B. *The First Negatives.* London: Science Museum, 1964.

―――. *The Science Museum Photography Collection.* London: Her Majesty's Stationery Office, 1969.

Tissandier, Gaston. *A History and Handbook of Photography.* London: Sampson Low, Marston, Searle & Rivington, 1878.

Travis, David. *Photographs from the Julien Levy Collection, Starting with Atget.* Chicago: Chicago Art Institute, 1976.

Tucker, Anne, ed. *The Woman's Eye.* New York: Knopf, 1973.

Vigneau, André. *Une Brève Histoire de l'art de Niepce à nos jours.* Paris: Laffont, 1963.

Wall, John. *Directory of British Photographic Collections.* New York: Camera/Graphic Press, 1977.

Welling, William. *Collectors' Guide to 19th-Century Photographs.* New York: Collier, 1976.

―――. *Photography in America: The Formative Years, 1839–1900.* New York: Crowell, 1978.

Werge, John. *The Evolution of Photography.* London: Piper & Carter, 1890.

Wiesenfeld, Cheryl, et al., eds. *Women See Women.* New York: Crowell, 1976.

Wise, Kelly, ed. *The Photographers' Choice: A Book of Portfolios and Critical Opinion.* Danbury, N.H.: Addison House, 1975.

Witkin Gallery, Inc., The. *The Julien Levy Collection.* Includes interview by Gretchen Berg. New York, 1977.

Worswick, Clark, and Embree, Ainslee. *The Last Empire: Photography in British India, 1855–1911.* Millerton, N.Y.: Aperture, 1976.

Bibliographies

Boni, Albert, ed. Vol. 1: *Photographic Literature.* New York: Morgan & Morgan, 1962. Vol. 2: *Photographic Literature 1960–1970.* Hastings-on-Hudson, N.Y.: Morgan & Morgan, 1972.

Catalogue of the Epstean Collection on the History and Science of Photography and Its Applications Especially to the Graphic Arts. New York: Columbia University Press, 1937.

Catalogue of the Photographic Library of the Camera Club of New York. New York, 1902. Reprinted in vol. 6, no. 1 of *Camera Notes.*

Van Haaften, Julia. "'Original Sun Pictures.' A Check List of the New York Public Library's Holdings of Early Works Illustrated with Photographs, 1844–1900." *Bulletin of the New York Public Library* 80, no. 3 (Spring 1977): 355–415.

Color Photography

Barret, André, ed. *Lumière: Les Premières Photographies en couleurs.* Paris: André Barret, 1974.

Beausoleil, Jeanne, et al. *Autochromes 1906–1928.* Paris: André Barret, 1978.

Berget, Alphonse. *Photographie des couleurs par la méthode interférentielle de M. Lippmann.* Paris: Gauthier-Villars, 1891.

Bessy, Maurice, and Lo Duca. *Louis Lumière, Inventeur.* Paris: Prisma, 1948.

Camera, July 1977.

Coe, Brian. *Colour Photography: The First Hundred Years, 1840–1940.* London: Ash & Grant, 1978.

Colors. Intro. by Henry Holmes Smith. Tallahassee: Florida State University, 1975. 40 original color photo-offset lithographs. 300 copies. Includes 4 prints each by Eileen Cowin, John Craig, Darryl Curran, Betty Hahn, Robert Heinecken, James Henkel, Virgil Mirano, Bea Nettles, Henry Holmes Smith, and Todd Walker.

De Maré, Eric. *Colour Photography.* Harmondsworth, England: Penguin, 1968.

Dmitri, Ivan. *Kodachrome and How to Use It.* New York: Simon & Schuster, 1940.

Ducos du Hauron, Alcide. *La Photographie des couleurs et les découvertes de Louis Ducos du Hauron.* Paris: Guyot [ca. 1899].

―――. *La Triplice Photographique des couleurs et l'imprimerie: Systeme de photochromographie Louis Ducos de Hauron.* Paris: Gauthier-Villars, 1897.

Ducos du Hauron, Louis. *L'Héliochromie; découvertes, constatations et améliorations importantes.* Agen, France: P. Noubel, 1874.

Dumoulin, Eugène. *Les Couleurs reproduites en photographie: Historique, théorie et pratique.* Paris: Gauthier-Villars, 1876.

Eder, Josef Maria. *Des Actions chimiques de la lumière colorée et de la photographie en couleurs naturelles.* Ghent: C. Annoot-Braeckman, 1881.

Elisofon, Eliot. *Color Photography.* New York: Viking, 1961.

Feininger, Andreas. *Successful Color Photography.* New York: Prentice-Hall, 1954.

Friedman, Joseph S. *History of Color Photography.* Boston: American Photographic, 1944.

Hill, Levi L. *A Treatise on Heliochromy; or, The Produc-*

tion of Pictures by Means of Light, in Natural Colors. New York: Robinson & Caswell, 1856.

Holmes, Charles. *Colour Photography, and Other Recent Developments of the Art of the Camera.* London: Studio, 1908.

Hübl, Arthur Freiherr von. *Die Theorie und Praxis der Farbenphotographie mit Autochrom- und anderen Rasterfarbenplatten.* Halle, Prussia: Knapp, 1921.

————. *Three-Colour Photography: Three Colour Printing and the Production of Photographic Pigment Pictures in Natural Colour.* London: Penrose, 1904.

Ives, Frederick Eugene. *The Autobiography of an Amateur Inventor.* Philadelphia: privately printed, 1928.

————. *Polychrome Process Color Photography: A Two-Negative, Double Print Trichromatic Process.* Philadelphia: privately printed, 1934.

Liberman, Alexander, ed. *Art and Technique of Color Photography.* New York: Simon & Schuster, 1951.

Lumière, Auguste, and Lumière, Louis. *La Photographie des couleurs.* Paris: Doin [ca. 1900].

Martin, Louis Claude, ed. *Colour and Methods of Color Reproduction.* London: Blackie, 1923.

Outerbridge, Paul. *Photographing in Color.* New York: Random House, 1940.

Reg, O. *Byepaths of Colour Photography.* Ed. by William Gamble. London: Lund Humphries [ca. 1924].

Rothstein, Arthur. *Color Photography Now.* New York: Chilton, 1970.

Sipley, Lewis Walton. *Frederick E. Ives: Photo-Graphic-Arts Inventor.* Philadelphia: American Museum of Photography, 1956.

————. *A Half Century of Color.* New York: Macmillan, 1951.

Spencer, D. A. *Colour Photography in Practice.* London: Pitman, 1938.

Valenta, Eduard. *Die Photographie in Naturlichen Farben.* Halle, Prussia: Knapp, 1894.

Vidal, Léon. *Photographie des couleurs: Sélection photographiques des couleurs primaires, son application à l'exécution de clichés et de tirages propres à la production d'images polychromes à trois couleurs.* Paris: Gauthier-Villars, 1897.

————. *Traité pratique de polychromie.* Paris: Gauthiers, 1903.

Wall, Edward John. *The History of Three-Color Photography.* Boston: American Photographic, 1925.

————. *Practical Color Photography.* Boston: American Photographic, 1922.

Wolff, Paul. *My Experiences in Color Photography.* Frankfurt am Main: Unschau, and New York: Grayson, and Cinefot International [ca. 1950].

Bibliographies

Gamble, William Burt, ed. *Color Photography: A List of References in the New York Public Library.* Intro. by E. J. Wall. New York: New York Public Library, 1924. Reprinted from *The Bulletin of the New York Public Library* for June, July, Aug., and Sept. 1924.

Current Periodicals

Listed here is a selection of currently published periodicals devoted to photography. Magazines that have ceased publication, such as *Album* and *Infinity*, are not listed; nor are many others that include articles on photography but cover other subjects as well, such as *Art in America* and *Life*.

UNITED STATES

Afterimage
4 Elton St.
Rochester, N.Y. 14607

Published by the Visual Studies Workshop.

American Photographer
485 Fifth Ave.
New York, N.Y. 10017

Aperture
Elm St.
Millerton, N.Y. 12546

Camera 35
1 Park Ave.
New York, N.Y. 10016

Exposure
Box 1651, FDR Post Office
New York, N.Y. 10022

Published by the Society for Photographic Education.

Image
900 East Ave.
Rochester, N.Y. 14607

Published by the International Museum of Photography at George Eastman House.

Modern Photography
130 E. Fifty-ninth St.
New York, N.Y. 10022

Petersen's Photographic Magazine
8490 Sunset Blvd.
Los Angeles, Calif. 90069

The Philadelphia Photo Review
Box 70
Arcola, Pa. 19420

Photograph
210 Fifth Ave.
New York, N.Y. 10010

Picture Magazine
3818 Brunswick Ave.
Los Angeles, Calif. 90039

Popular Photography
1 Park Ave.
New York, N.Y. 10016

The Print Collector's Newsletter
205 E. Seventy-eighth St.
New York, N.Y. 10021

Untitled
Box 239
Carmel, Calif. 93921

Published by Friends of Photography.

OUTSIDE THE UNITED STATES

Amateur Photographer
Oakfield House
Perrymount Rd.
Haywards Heath
Sussex RH16 3DH, England

Arte Fotográfico
Don Ramon de la Cruz 53
Madrid 1
Spain

Asahi Camera
Asahi Shimbun
Yuraku-cho, Chiyoda-ku
Tokyo, Japan

The British Journal of Photography
24 Wellington St.
London WC2E 7DH, England

Camera
C. J. Bucher Ltd.
Lucerne, Switzerland

Camerart
Hinode Building, 11, 2-chome
Kyobashi, Chuo-ku
Tokyo, Japan

Camera Mainichi
The Mainichi Newspapers
Tokyo 100, Japan

Canadian Photography
481 University Ave.
Toronto, Ontario M5W 1A7, Canada

Créatis
19 rue du Départ
Paris 75014, France

Creative Camera
19 Doughty St.
London WC1N 2PT, England

Foto
Królewska 27
Warsaw 00-950, Poland

Foto
Box 3263
Stockholm 10365, Sweden

Fotografare Novità
via Lipari 8
Rome 00141, Italy

Fotografia Italiana
via degli Imbriana 15
Milan 20158, Italy

Fotografie
Karl-Heine Strasse 16
Leipzig 7031, DDR (East Germany)

Foto Magazin
Ortlerstrasse 8
Munich 8000, Germany

History of Photography
10-14 Macklin St.
London WC2B 5NF, England

Nueva Lente
Fernández Ardemans 64
Apartado 8.425
Madrid, Spain

Ovo/Photo
Box 1431, Station A
Montreal, Quebec H3C 2Z9, Canada

Photo
63 Champs-Elysées
Paris 75008, France

Photo-Forum
Box 10-163
Auckland 4, New Zealand

Printletter
Box 250
Zurich 8046, Switzerland

Progresso Fotografico
viale Piceno 14
Milan 20129, Italy

Revue Fotografie
Dlouhá třída 12
Prague 11589, Czechoslovakia

Svensk Fotografisk Tidskrift
Nytorgsgatan 17
Stockholm 11622, Sweden

Zoom
2 rue du Faubourg Poissonière
Paris 75010, France

Index

Edited by Robin Bledsoe and Michael Brandon
Designed by Janis Capone
Typeset in Trump Medieval (text) and Horizon Bold (display) by DEKR Corporation
Printed by The Murray Printing Company
Color separations by Offset Separations
Color plates printed by The Leether Press
Paper supplied by S. D. Warren Paper Company
Bound by A. Horowitz and Son